PENGUIN BOOKS

THE NEW PENGUIN BOOK

'Wonderful . . . perhaps the last great one-volume work of its kind'
Stephen Knight, *The Times Literary Supplement*

'A wonderfully intelligent, adventurous, rich anthology, essential for
confirmed and potential poetry addicts alike' Hermione Lee,
Guardian, Books of the Year

'Seems like the most interesting anthology of verse there has ever
been. The principles of organization and selection make so many
poems, and their provenance, newly startling. The book includes the
reader in such a way that one doesn't have to bother about what has
been left out' Adam Phillips, *Irish Times*, Books of the Year

'An extraordinarily fresh take on the whole sequence of English
poetry . . . a very well-chosen and generous anthology' David Sexton,
Evening Standard, Books of the Year

'Compendious, judicious and eclectic, this collection will galvanize
your appreciation of the canon again. Indeed, its choices are so
compellingly well made – that is, all the poems chosen are good –
that it almost creates a new canon by itself' Nicholas Lezard,
Guardian, Books of the Year

'Keegan gives the twentieth century more space than any other, and
his post-war selection – crammed with Celts – is eye-opening and
bold . . . He is exceptionally good at hearing the voices of women
down the centuries' Jim McCue, *Evening Standard*

'The generosity of its inclusions dilates the canon. Discarding
conventions, he serves the poetic tradition. It is as though accreted
varnish has been carefully removed and the picture has regained a
compelling luminosity . . . an editor who is also a scholar with
genuine literary tact' Michael Schmidt, *Independent*

'He has a quantity of poems by Irish authors born after as well as before 1922 . . . and includes a good selection of poems in Scots, with a glossary . . . Included for the first time in this anthology, and very properly included, is the category of poems translated into English . . . Keegan has an excellent eye and ear. He includes poems that have to be there, adds some good new ones, and has produced a genuinely new book. That is quite an achievement' Michael Alexander, *Catholic Herald*

'The decision to print poems chronologically was an inspired one, heightening a sense of progression through time. This is a present to give any aspiring young person, opening their eyes to a whole world with something to suit every taste' Sir Roy Strong, *Daily Mail*, Books of the Year

'Radical and entertaining . . . moving through the familiar territory of ancients, Anons, ballads, the famous dead and dead famous in a way that will take the most jaded curriculum-follower into unexpected corners and connections' *The Times Educational Supplement*

'Serious, wide-ranging, and sometimes surprising . . . it's a book you should buy' Anthony Thwaite, *Sunday Telegraph*

'Seven hundred years of language, distilled into its sharpest and brightest forms, are here to be discovered . . . Again and again, the reader comes across thoughtful, and thought-provoking juxtapositions of poems . . . *The New Penguin Book of English Verse* demonstrates that we have the good fortune to live in the English language, perhaps the richest, most supple, promising, sharp-tongued and rule-breaking playground for poetry' Helen Dunmore, *Observer*

ABOUT THE EDITOR

Paul Keegan was formerly editor of the Penguin Classics, and is now Poetry Editor at Faber & Faber.

The New Penguin Book of
ENGLISH VERSE

Edited by Paul Keegan

PENGUIN BOOKS

PENGUIN BOOKS

Published by the Penguin Group
Penguin Books Ltd, 80 Strand, London WC2R 0RL, England
Penguin Putnam Inc., 375 Hudson Street, New York, New York 10014, USA
Penguin Books Australia Ltd, 250 Camberwell Road, Camberwell, Victoria 3124, Australia
Penguin Books Canada Ltd, 10 Alcorn Avenue, Toronto, Ontario, Canada M4V 3B2
Penguin Books India (P) Ltd, 11 Community Centre, Panchsheel Park, New Delhi – 110 017, India
Penguin Books (NZ) Ltd, Cnr Rosedale and Airborne Roads, Albany, Auckland, New Zealand
Penguin Books (South Africa) (Pty) Ltd, 24 Sturdee Avenue, Rosebank 2196, South Africa

Penguin Books Ltd, Registered Offices: 80 Strand, London WC2R 0RL, England

www.penguin.com

First published by Allen Lane The Penguin Press 2000
Published in Penguin Books 2001

6

Collection and Preface copyright © Paul Keegan, 2000
The acknowledgements on pp. 1104–8 constitute an extension of this copyright page
All rights reserved

The moral right of the editor has been asserted

Printed in England by Clays Ltd, St Ives plc

Contents

Preface

Anthologies beg questions of structure as well as of inclusion. The former tend to be given and to receive less attention than the latter, because their procedures are taken for granted. Thus most modern anthologies – whether they cover a particular period or the entire span – are arranged historically, poet by poet, by dates of birth. Such has been the settled practice since Arthur Quiller Couch's inaugurative *Oxford Book of English Verse* (1900), and has acquired a time-honoured air not least because it appears to honour time.

This convention is tenacious, but of relatively recent date. In earlier periods anthologies were conceived more as miscellanies, grouping poems by kind and assuming the community of the poem rather than the autonomy of the poet. It is worth remembering that even Palgrave's *Golden Treasury* (1861) is a hybrid, refracting poems through a lens which is by turns chronological and thematic (the latter 'in gradations of feeling or subject'), but not primarily author-centred.

The New Penguin Book of English Verse is closer in spirit to such older instances. It is arranged by poem rather than by poet, with each poem entering the sequence according to the date of its first appearance – whether in volume form, or periodical form, or occasionally (for the poetry of earlier periods) the approximate date at which it is known to have been circulating in manuscript. In other words, poems are restored to the moment when they became known to the public for whom the poet wrote.

A quite different anthology might have been compiled according to dates of composition – a view from the workshop – but it is the publishing moment which has been attended to in these pages: the view from where the reader was standing. This story has not been reproduced with complete fidelity: *The New Penguin Book* is intended to pass along and in some sense celebrate the main thoroughfares in the history of English verse. The rhythm of entry is therefore volume publication, when a poet gathered and ordered his or her work for a wider audience, and which allows for groupings of poems by one poet to be read together. The alternative would have been too atomized to be instructive or pleasurable.

The resulting sequence is nonetheless more oriented to poems as individuals, living in contingency – where the poem survives, in W. H. Auden's words, 'in the valley of its saying' – than to individual poets in isolated succession. Thus poems by the same poet are often dispersed in these pages, and poems by different poets follow upon each other. They also face each other, and sometimes answer or act in disagreement with each other's forms of knowing and proceeding. Even when these juxtapositions are not active, poems which appear at the same time testify to the truths of propinquity.

In a sense, *The New Penguin Book* is a thematic anthology, and its theme is chronology. Anthologies do no more than tell stories about the past and are themselves fictions, ideas of order. The sequence in the following pages makes no claim to documentary authority, because it excludes so much, because it is constructed with hindsight. The poetic landscape in, say, 1819, looked very different from what is now redeemed as significant from that year and the years surrounding. But the choice of poems in *The New Penguin Book* has to some degree been determined by its overall structure, that of the anthology as chronicle: this kind of poem was being written at such a date; this particular poem might have been read alongside that particular poem in this year.

Put differently, *The New Penguin Book* asks what happens when chronology is *not* dislocated by the usual procedure of entering poets in author-shaped parcels by dates of birth. For the standard template does entail significant dislocation, not least in the case of poets with long careers. Samuel Johnson was born in 1709 and died in 1784, after which the reader is usually returned a notional seventy years to the next poet in succession, Thomas Gray (b. 1716). Even where an editor enters poets by the date of their earliest included poem, rather than by date of birth, chronology is puzzled: to place all of a poet's work on the site of his or her earliest appearance is to untether the later poems from *their* proper milieu. Thus Johnson's 'The Vanity of Human Wishes' was first published in 1749, and tends to be followed in anthologies by his other canonical poem, 'On the Death of *Dr. Robert Levet*', published over three decades later in 1783. After which we are usually returned in anthology-time to Thomas Gray's 'Elegy in a Country Church Yard' (1751), and then on – or further backwards – to William Collins's 'Ode to Evening' (1746).

In the case of posthumously published poets, or poets whose poems were read in manuscript long before they were printed, other misalignments occur. Many Renaissance authors, from Sir Thomas Wyatt down to John Donne and beyond, circulated their verse almost entirely in manuscript, which means that their careers often occurred somewhat earlier than is apparent from publication dates. Donne has come to be seen as a later poet than he in fact was: the early elegies and satires were being read in the 1590s, and the bulk of his poetry was in circulation by the 1620s, though it was only printed in 1633.

Sometimes chronology tells a more delayed story than the one we have been accustomed to hearing. In the case of Andrew Marvell, whose poems were printed in 1681, three years after his death, there is less evidence for manuscript circulation, even for the great '*Horatian* Ode upon *Cromwel's* Return from *Ireland*', written perhaps thirty years earlier. Here an actual

date of publication gains significance, and Marvell can be read now as he
was read then: a Restoration poet as much as a metaphysical lyricist.
Contemporaries are those who wrote at the same time – but also those who
were first read at the same time. Traditionally fixed as stars of the one poetic
school, Donne and Marvell are set adrift on the floes of chronology.

The notion of poetic periods with easy – and therefore strict – demar-
cations has tended to be reinforced by the activity of anthologies which
present poets in isolation, removed from stylistic conflict (and from contem-
porary realities to which such conflict responds and corresponds). The
poet-by-poet model presents an apostolic succession of major figures, with
brief interludes in which minor figures, one-poem poets and Anon are
temporarily lodged, as in the passageways between old masters in a gallery.

A chronicle-ordering complicates the texture of periods by making each
more anomalously populous, its edges more blurred; and restores to these
fixities the circulating energy of what Alexander Pope termed 'poetry's
mutual commerce'. Major poetry is reconnected to a milieu, and minor
figures become less marginal to a sequence whose unit is the individual
poem. It is moreover significantly easier to speak of minor poets than of
minor poems; one effect of a poem-by-poem ordering is to encourage a
frame of mind which judges the poet by the poem, rather than vice versa.

Two kinds of poem which have no particular place to go – popular ballads
and poems by Anon (by which is usually meant folk-poetry) – have further
tended to embarrass or be embarrassed by the strong lines of the poet-by-
poet anthology. Anon tends to be entered all together in one or two places,
and the ballads together in another, making each seem as if produced by a
single author. Because of the constraints upon the kinds of poem commonly
admitted to each category, the resulting sequences do seem to share a unity
of intention, as of a collective poet with a putative *floruit* in the deep past
of oral tradition. *The New Penguin Book* enters Anon in many different
places, to reflect print history, so that he or she is allowed to be many poets
without names. As to ballads, instead of viewing the ballad tradition as an
autonomous story of oral transmission, I have followed the literary history
of the popular ballad – its several points of entry into the print canon. The
result is that ballads appear rather later than is usual in such anthologies,
and take their place as an informing aspect of eighteenth-century and
Romantic reading and writing.

The intention of *The New Penguin Book* has been to restore poems to
their places in the history of reading. This has led to the decision not
to modernize spelling and punctuation. Poems are written and published
(though textually this often means quite different things) into a given state
of the language – which modernization elides, since it takes for granted that
current meanings can be mapped exactly on to the older shapes of words,
and it conceals rhymes or wordplay. The progress of an anthology which
retains these older forms allows the printed voice of the poetry (acoustic,

verbal and visual) to be seen and heard, and allows readers to follow the common enterprise of the language evolving over seven hundred years.

That enterprise is the subject of *The New Penguin Book*, whence its focus upon the poetry produced in the language common to these islands: English – in its regional and national forms – and their cognate, Scots. No attempt has been made to include anglophone poetry from beyond this archipelago – no American verse, no Commonwealth verse – for reasons of space, and to maintain the pressure upon a chronology defined in local rather than global ways. In the twentieth century there have been terminal pressures upon the idea of the local, only the echo of which can be heard in these pages. With the significant exception that Americans T. S. Eliot and Ezra Pound (the English Pound, before his departure for Paris in 1920) are tutelary presences, and that Sylvia Plath is also present. These poets are part of the story, and their work first entered that story before it altered the wider picture.

Some non-residents have been included: news from a foreign country, in the form of translations from classical and European languages. Ezra Pound was the first to restate the Elizabethan intuition that 'a great age of literature is perhaps always a great age of translations, or follows it'. Some verse translations – from the Bible notably – have used a form of prose as their medium, and the borders of poetry and prose are occasionally crossed elsewhere in these pages – whether in Thomas Traherne's biblical prose inspirations, or in the (few) attempts to harness the European precedent of the prose poem to vernacular ends.

The New Penguin Book retains the titling of its predecessor, edited by John Hayward: *The Penguin Book of English Verse*. Verse, not Poetry, since 'verse' may still be thought of as the more inclusive term (and not only because we speak of light verse and comic verse) – more various in its occasions, and with a hint of serving some of the poetries excluded by Poetry. Or as Auden said, addressing the Workers' Educational Association in 1936: 'Really, to appreciate archdeacons, you need to know some bar-maids, and vice versa. The same is true of poetry.'

John Hayward's *Penguin Book* appeared over forty years ago. Since then our sense of the past has itself been altered by an extension of our present. Hayward began with *Tottel's Miscellany* in the 1550s and ended in the 1930s. The present *Penguin Book* extends the frame on either side, beginning with the high medieval legacy. But it makes no claim inclusively to represent the latter decades of the Twentieth Century. Although ending with poems from the early 1990s, no poet born after the outset of the 1950s has been included – in the interests of giving adequate representation to poets of the mid century and after, rather than a thin coverage of the generation which followed, who contribute to a chronology still in the making.

A Note on the Texts

The spelling and punctuation of the texts is reproduced as it appears in the printed sources, but older typographical conventions, such as the alternative forms of *i* and *j*, *u* and *v* found in sixteenth- and seventeenth-century printing, have been regularized. Capitalization of titles has been standardized.

Poems usually enter the sequence by their date of earliest publication. Where this is not the case, the publication date is occasionally offered at the end of a poem (in brackets), so that a reader can place it mentally at a different point of entry, or at least be aware of complication. Where publication occurred significantly later than composition, I have given the date of composition (cited as 'written'). When a poem was first published posthumously, it is entered at its date of publication if the original audience was still intact (many poets' works – their 'Remaines' – were collected at or shortly after their deaths as an act of *pietas*). There are varieties of posthumousness, willing and unwilling – intermediate states between what Donne called the 'presse' on the one hand and the 'fire' on the other. Poems by Shelley, Clare, Gurney and others were withheld due to circumstances beyond their control, such as censorship or rejection. Where posthumousness was protracted, I have entered a poem in the company of other poems by the same poet, or by date of composition.

In the case of circulation prior to print publication, I have entered poems by approximate dates of appearance. In many cases, however, I have held to a print date, where information is uncertain or where appearance in print is a significant event (Shakespeare's *Sonnets*, 1609) – and because Gutenberg is the centre of gravity for this anthology. In the case of medieval verse, where publication often took place only centuries later, I have ordered poems as in a miscellany, by approximate dates between 1300 and 1400.

Excerpts. Some short long poems – Keats's 'The Eve of St. Agnes', or Burns's 'Tam o' Shanter' – appear in their entirety. But excerpts are inevitable for the leviathans of the language (such as Spenser's *The Faerie Queene*, Wordsworth's *The Prelude*), and for much else. I have sometimes excerpted the openings, for as Keats remarked of *Paradise Lost*, 'there is always a great charm in the openings of great Poems'; on occasion excerpts have been chosen with an eye to a specimen, in the chronicling spirit of the anthology as a whole, rather than seeking out essences. (William Hazlitt's rebuke to the anthologist as pearl-diver still stands: 'those parts of any author which are most liable to be stitched in worsted, and framed and glazed, are not by any means always the best'.)

Many long poems are processes with several publication dates, rather than products entering the language at a single juncture, and the two excerpts from 'The Faerie Queene, or from Coleridge's 'The Ancient Mariner', reflect this aspect. Many short poems are also processes in time, subject to revision. I have often chosen a later text of a poem than the version which appeared on first publication, but have indicated important cases by appending two publication dates (Coleridge's 'The Eolian Harp': 1796, 1817). In other words, the texts reproduced in these pages did not necessarily take this form on their first appearance, but the gains in offering a later text have sometimes outweighed the claim to offer earliest texts on the grounds of strict account-ability to the story of inception and reception. Poets are entitled to last thoughts, even if at times this has meant placing these on the site of first thoughts.

Where there is a group of poems by the same author from a particular collection (George Herbert's *The Temple* 1633) – or in cases where poems by different authors are taken from the same source (Tottel's *Songes and Sonettes* 1557) – the beginning and ending of the group has been indicated by the device of a printer's leaf (§).

Medieval verse has been glossed, and poems in Scots are glossed through-out; otherwise there is no annotation. Poem titles are authorial, though this is not always easy to determine. Until the early seventeenth century short poems were usually untitled, and such titles as they bore were often supplied by editors or booksellers, or by the owners of the manuscripts in which they appear. I have not reproduced such titles (or given first-line titles to poems without titles), though on occasion I have given a familiar or traditionally ascribed title in square brackets. Editorial titles for excerpts also appear in square brackets. Where the title of a poem does not indicate that it is a translation this information has been indicated editorially.

Songs from plays, and poems from novels and other prose works (Sir Walter Scott, Lewis Carroll) have been included, but often I have given a frame: an immediately preceding speech, a stage direction, the identity of a speaker – to indicate that the item is independent but incomplete, abstracted from a context which can only be gestured towards – as is the case all ways round with anthologies.

The New Penguin Book of

ENGLISH VERSE

ANONYMOUS

Ich am of Irlande
And of the holy lande
Of Irlande.

Gode sire, pray Ich thee
5 For of saynte charité
Come and daunce with me
    In Irlande.

ANONYMOUS

Maiden in the morë lay,
In the morë lay,
    Sevenightë fullë and a –
    Sevenightë fulle and a –
5 Maiden in the morë lay,
In the morë lay,
    Sevenightë fullë and a day.

Well was hirë mete,
What was hirë mete?
10   The primerole and the –
    The primerole and the –
Well was hirë mete,
What was hirë mete?
    The primerole and the violet.

1 *Ich am* I am; 5 'For the sake of holy charity'

1 *in the morë lay* dwelt in the moor; 3 *sevenightë fullë* seven full nights; 8 'good was her food'; 10 *primerole* primrose;

Well was hirë dring,
What was hirë dring?
   The coldë water of the –
   The coldë water of the –
Well was hirë dring,
20   What was hirë dring?
   The coldë water of the wellë-spring.

Well was hirë bour,
What was hirë bour?
   The redë rose and the –
25   The redë rose and the –
Well was hirë bour,
What was hirë bour?
   The redë rose and the lilie flour.

ANONYMOUS

Al night by the rosë, rosë,
Al night bi the rose I lay,
Dorst Ich nought the rosë stele,
And yet I bar the flour away.

                          (1907)

15 *dring* drink; 21 *wellë-spring* spring; 22 *bour* chamber

3 *dorst* dared; *stele* steal; 4 *bar* bore; *flour* flower

§ [Harley Lyrics]

ANONYMOUS

Bitwenë March and Averil
When spray biginneth to springe,
The litel foul hath hirë wil
On hyrë lede to synge.
5   Ich live in love-longinge
For semeliest of allë thynge,
She may me blissë bringe,
Ich am in hire baundoun.
    An hendy hap Ichave y-hent,
10   Ichot from hevene it is me sent,
    From allë wommen my love is lent
    And light on Alysoun.

On hew hire her is fair ynogh,
Hire browës broune, hire eyen blake,
15 With lufsom chere she on me logh,
With middel smal and wel y-make.
But she me wol to hirë take
For to ben hire owen make,
Longe to live Ichulle forsake
20 And feyë falle adoun.
    An hendy, etc.

1 *Averil* April; 2 *spray* twig; *springe* sprout; 3 *foul* bird; *hirë wil* her desire; 4 *on
hyrë lede* in her language; 6 *semeliest* fairest; *thynge* things, creatures; 8 *baundoun*
power; 9 'a fair good fortune I have received'; 10 *Ichot* I know; 11 *lent* gone;
12 *light* alighted; 13 *on hew* in hue, colour; *her* hair; 15 *lufsom chere* lovely
expression; *logh* smiled; 16 *middel smal* slender waist; *wel y-make* well made; 17 *but
she* unless she; 18 *to ben* to be; *make* companion; 19 *Ichulle forsake* I will refuse;
20 *feyë* doomed, dead;

Nightës when I wende and wake –
Forthy myn wongës waxen won –
Lady, al for thinë sake,
25   Longinge is y-lent me on.
In world nis non so wyter mon
That al hire bounté tellë con,
Hire swyre is whitter then the swon,
And fairest may in toune.
30   An hendy, etc.

Ich am for wowyng al forwake,
Wery so water in wore,
Lest any revë me my make
Ichave y-yernëd yore.
35   Beter is tholen whilë sore
Then mournen evermore.
Geynest under gore,
Herknë to my roun.
        An hendy, etc.

(1792)

ANONYMOUS

Erthë tok of erthe
        erthë wyth wogh;
Erthe other erthë
        to the erthë drogh;

22 *Nightës* at night; *wende* toss; 23 *Forthy* for which cause; *wongës* cheeks; *waxeth won* grow pale; 25 *is y-lent me on* has come upon me; 26 *so wyter* wiser; 27 *bounté* excellence; 28 *swyre* neck; *swon* swan; 29 *may in toune* maiden alive; 31 *wowyng* wooing; *forwake* worn out; 32 *so water in wore* as water in a troubled pool; 33 *revë me my make* rob me of my mate; 34 *y-yernëd yore* yearned for so long; 35 *tholen whilë sore* suffer pain for a time; 37 *geynest under gore* most gracious woman alive; 38 *roun* song

1 *Erthë* earth; *tok* took; 2 *wogh* sin; 4 *drogh* drew;

Erthë leyde erthe
    in erthënë throgh;
Tho hevëde erthe of erthe
    erthe ynogh.

          (1811)

§   §   §

§ [Grimestone Lyrics]   **1350–1400**

ANONYMOUS

Gold and al this worldës wyn
    Is nought but Cristës rode;
I wolde be clad in Cristës skyn,
    That ran so longe on blode,
And gon t'is herte and take myn in –
    Ther is a fulsum fode.
Than yeve I litel of kith or kyn,
    For ther is allë gode.

ANONYMOUS

Gloria mundi est:
Als a se flouwende
Als a skiye pasende
Als the sadwe in the undermel
And als the dore turnet on a quel.

5 *leyde* laid; 6 *in erthënë throgh* in an earthen pit, grave; 7 *tho* then; *hevëde* had;
8 *ynogh* enough (7–8 'then had "earth" enough "earth" from "earth" ')

1 *worldës wyn* world's joy; 2 'is nothing without Christ's cross'; 4 *blode* blood;
5 *t'is herte* to His heart; *myn in* my lodging; 6 *fulsum fode* abundant food; 7 *than
yeve I litel of* then would I give little for; 8 *ther* there [with Christ]

1 *Gloria mundi est* the glory of the world is; 2 *als* as, like; *flouwende* flowing;
3 *skiye* cloud; *pasende* passing; 4 *sadwe* shadow; *undermel* early afternoon;
5 *quel* wheel

ANONYMOUS

Love me broughte,
And love me wroughtë,
   Man, to be thi ferë;
Love me fedde,
And love me ledde,
5   And love me lettëd herë.

Love me slow,
And love me drow,
   And love me leyde on berë;
10 Love is my pes,
For love I ches
   Man to byen derë.

Ne dred thee nought,
I have thee sought
15   Bothen day and night;
To haven thee,
Wel is me,
   I have thee wonne in fight.

    §   §   §

ANONYMOUS [The Dragon Speaks]*

'I wille you allë swalewë withouten any bot;
But some wille I save, and some wille I not.'

*part of a description, in Latin, of Fortune's wheel

2 *wroughte* created; 3 *ferë* companion; 6 *me lettëd herë* kept me here; 7 *slow* slew;
8 *drow* drew; 9 *leyde on berë* laid on a bier; 10 *pes* peace; 11 *ches* chose; 12 *byen
derë* buy [redeem] at a cost; 15 *bothen* both; 18 *wonne* won

1 *bot* deliverance

GEOFFREY CHAUCER *from* The Parliament of Fowls

[Catalogue of the Birds]

Whan I was come ayeyn into the place
That I of spak, that was so sote and grene,
Forth welk I tho myselven to solace.
Tho was I war wher that ther sat a queene
5   That, as of lyght the somer sonne shene
Passeth the sterre, right so over mesure
She fayrer was than any creature.

And in a launde, upon an hil of floures,
Was set this noble goddesse Nature.
10   Of braunches were here halles and here boures
Iwrought after here cast and here mesure;
Ne there nas foul that cometh of engendrure
That they ne were prest in here presence,
To take hire dom and yeve hire audyence.

15   For this was on seynt Valentynes day,
Whan every foul cometh there to chese his make,
Of every kynde that men thynke may,
And that so huge a noyse gan they make
That erthe, and eyr, and tre, and every lake
20   So ful was, that unethe was there space
For me to stonde, so ful was al the place.

And right as Aleyn, in the Pleynt of Kynde,
Devyseth Nature of aray and face,
In swich aray men myghte hire there fynde.
25   This noble emperesse, ful of grace,
Bad every foul to take his owne place,
As they were woned alwey fro yer to yeere,
Seynt Valentynes day, to stonden theere.

---

2 *sote* sweet; 3 *welk* walked; 6 *sterre* stars; *over mesure* beyond measure;
8 *launde* glade; 10 *here* her; 11 *cast* design; 12 *foul* bird; *engendrure* procreation;
13 *prest* eagerly ready; 14 *take hire dom* receive her decision; *audyence* hearing;
16 *chese his make* choose its mate; 20 *unethe* hardly; 23 *Devyseth* describes;
27 *woned* accustomed;

That is to seyn, the foules of ravyne
Weere hyest set, and thanne the foules smale
That eten, as hem Nature wolde enclyne,
As worm or thyng of which I telle no tale;
And water-foul sat lowest in the dale;
But foul that lyveth by sed sat on the grene,
35 And that so fele that wonder was to sene.

There myghte men the royal egle fynde,
That with his sharpe lok perseth the sonne,
And othere egles of a lowere kynde,
Of whiche that clerkes wel devyse conne.
40 Ther was the tiraunt with his fetheres donne
And grey, I mene the goshauk, that doth pyne
To bryddes for his outrageous ravyne.

The gentyl faucoun, that with his feet distrayneth
The kynges hand; the hardy sperhauk eke,
45 The quayles foo; the merlioun, that payneth
Hymself ful ofte the larke for to seke;
There was the douve with hire yën meke;
The jelous swan, ayens his deth that syngeth;
The oule ek, that of deth the bode bryngeth;

50 The crane, the geaunt, with his trompes soun;
The thef, the chough; and ek the janglynge pye;
The skornynge jay; the eles fo, heroun;
The false lapwynge, ful of trecherye;
The stare, that the conseyl can bewrye;
55 The tame ruddok, and the coward kyte;
The kok, that orloge is of thorpes lyte;

29 *foules of ravyne* birds of prey; 34 *sed* seed; 35 *so fele* so many;
37 *perseth* pierces; 39 *clerkes* scholars; *devyse conne* know how to describe;
40 *tiraunt* tyrant; *donne* dun, dull-brown; 41 *doth pyne* causes suffering;
42 *ravyne* rapine; 43 *distrayneth* grasps; 44 *sperhauk* sparrow-hawk; 45 *quayles
foo* quail's foe; *merlioun* merlin (small falcon); 47 *yën meke* meek eyes; 48 *ayens* in
anticipation of; 49 *ek* also; *bode* omen; 50 *geaunt* giant; 51 *thef* thief; *chough* crow;
janglynge pye chattering magpie; 52 *eles fo* eel's foe; 54 *stare* starling; *bewrye*
betray; 55 *ruddok* robin redbreast; 56 *orloge* timepiece; *thorpes lyte* small villages;

The sparwe, Venus sone; the nyghtyngale,
That clepeth forth the grene leves newe;
The swalwe, mortherere of the foules smale
60 That maken hony of floures freshe of hewe;
The wedded turtil, with hire herte trewe;
The pekok, with his aungels fetheres bryghte;
The fesaunt, skornere of the cok by nyghte;

The waker goos; the cukkow ever unkynde;
65 The popynjay, ful of delicasye;
The drake, stroyere of his owene kynde;
The stork, the wrekere of avouterye;
The hote cormeraunt of glotenye;
The raven wys; the crowe with vois of care;
70 The throstil old; the frosty feldefare.

What shulde I seyn? Of foules every kynde
That in this world han fetheres and stature
Men myghten in that place assembled fynde
Byfore the noble goddesse of Nature,
75 And everich of hem dide his besy cure
Benygnely to chese or for to take,
By hire acord, his formel or his make.

[Roundel]

Now welcome, somer, with thy sonne softe,
That hast this wintres wedres overshake,
And driven away the longe nyghtes blake!

Saynt Valentyn, that art ful hy on-lofte,
5 Thus syngen smale foules for thy sake:
Now welcome, somer, with thy sonne softe,
That hast this wintres wedres overshake.

---

57 *Venus sone* son of Venus; 58 *clepeth* calls; 59 *swalwe* swallow; *mortherere of the foules smale* murderer of bees; 61 *turtil* turtledove; 63 *fesaunt* pheasant;
64 *waker* watchful; *unkynde* unnatural; 65 *popynjay* parrot; 66 *stroyere* destroyer;
67 *wrekere* punisher; *avouterye* adultery; 69 *wys* wise; 70 *throstil* thrush;
frosty white-chested; 75 *dide his besy cure* worked diligently; 76 *benygnely* graciously; *chese* choose; 77 *formel* female (bird); *make* mate

1 *sonne* sun; 2 *wedres overshake* storms shaken off; 4 *on-lofte* on high;

Wel han they cause for to gladen ofte,
Sich ech of hem recovered hath hys make,
Ful blissful mowe they synge when they wake:
Now welcome, somer, with thy sonne softe,
That hast thes wintres wedres overshake,
And driven away the longe nyghtes blake!

(1478)

GEOFFREY CHAUCER *from* The Boke of Troilus

[Envoi]

Go, litel boke, go, litel myn tragedye,
Ther God thi makere yet, er that he dye,
So sende myght to make in som comedye!
But litel book, no makyng thow n'envie,
But subgit be to alle poyesye,
And kis the steppes where as thow seest pace
Virgile, Ovide, Omer, Lucan, and Stace.

And for ther is so gret diversite
In Englissh and in writyng of oure tonge,
So prey I to God that non myswrite the,
Ne the mysmetre for defaute of tonge;
And red wherso thow be, or elles songe,
That thow be understonde, God I bisiche!
But yet to purpos of my rather speche.

The wrath, as I bigan yow for to seye,
Of Troilus the Grekis boughten deere,
For thousandes his hondes maden deye,
As he that was withouten any peere
Save Ector, in his tyme, as I kan heere.
But weilawey – save only Goddes wille –
Despitously hym slough the fierse Achille.

9 *recovered* got back; *make* mate; 10 *mowe* may

2 *Ther God* may God; 3 *make in* compose; 4 *n'envie* do not contend with; 5 *subgit be* humble yourself; 6 *pace* pass; 12 *red . . . or elles songe* read . . . or else recited; 13 *understonde* understood; 14 *rather* earlier; 21 *slough* slew;

And whan that he was slayn in this manere,
His lighte goost ful blisfully is went
Up to the holughnesse of the eighthe spere,
25   In convers letyng everich element;
And ther he saugh with ful avysement
The erratik sterres, herkenyng armonye
With sownes ful of hevenyssh melodie.

And down from thennes faste he gan avyse
30   This litel spot of erthe that with the se
Embraced is, and fully gan despise
This wrecched world, and held al vanite
To respect of the pleyn felicite
That is in hevene above; and at the laste,
35   Ther he was slayn his lokyng down he caste,

And in hymself he lough right at the wo
Of hem that wepten for his deth so faste,
And dampned al oure werk that foloweth so
The blynde lust, the which that may nat laste,
40   And sholden al oure herte on heven caste,
And forth he wente, shortly for to telle,
Ther as Mercurye sorted hym to dwelle.

Swich fyn hath, lo, this Troilus for love!
Swich fyn hath al his grete worthynesse,
45   Swich fyn hath his estat real above,
Swich fyn his lust, swich fyn hath his noblesse,
Swych fyn hath false worldes brotelnesse.
And thus bigan his lovyng of Criseyde,
As I have told, and in this wise he deyde.

50   O yonge, fresshe folkes, he or she,
In which that love up groweth with youre age,
Repeyreth hom fro worldly vanyte,
And of youre herte up casteth the visage

24 *holughnesse* concavity; 25 'leaving on the reverse side each planetary sphere';
26 *avysement* observation; 27 *erratik sterres* wandering planets; *herkenyng* listening
to; *armonye* the music of the spheres; 29 *gan avyse* contemplated; 33 *to respect of* in
respect of; 35 *Ther* where; 36 *lough* laughed; 38 *dampned* damned; 39 *lust* desire
for earthly pleasure; 42 *sorted* assigned; 43 *fyn* end; 45 *real* royal;
47 *brotelnesse* brittleness; 52 *repeyreth hom* return home (to heaven);

To thilke God that after his ymage
Yow made, and thynketh al nys but a faire
This world that passeth soone as floures faire.

And loveth hym the which that right for love
Upon a crois, oure soules for to beye,
First starf, and roos, and sit in hevene above;
60   For he nyl falsen no wight, dar I seye,
That wol his herte al holly on hym leye.
And syn he best to love is, and most meke,
What nedeth feynede loves for to seke?

Lo here, of payens corsed olde rites!
65   Lo here, what alle hire goddes may availle!
Lo here, thise wrecched worldes appetites!
Lo here, the fyn and guerdoun for travaille
Of Jove, Appollo, of Mars, of swich rascaille!
Lo here, the forme of olde clerkis speche
70   In poetrie, if ye hire bokes seche.

O moral Gower, this book I directe
To the, and to the, philosophical Strode,
To vouchen-sauf, ther nede is, to correcte,
Of youre benignites and zeles goode.
75   And to that sothfast Crist, that starf on rode,
With al myn herte of mercy evere I preye,
And to the Lord right thus I speke and seye:

Thow oon, and two, and thre, eterne on lyve,
That regnest ay in thre, and two, and oon,
80   Uncircumscript, and al maist circumscrive,
Us from visible and invisible foon
Defende, and to thy mercye, everichon,
So make us, Jesus, for thi mercy, digne,
For love of Mayde and Moder thyn benigne.
      Amen.

(1483)

55 *fair* fairground; 58 *crois* cross; *beye* redeem; 59 *starf* died; 60 *falsen* prove false
to; 61 *holly* wholly; 63 *feynede* counterfeit; 64 *payens* pagans'; 67 *guerdoun for
travaille* reward for effort; 68 *rascaille* worthless rabble; 75 *starf on rode* died on the
cross; 81 *foon* foes

When Adam dalf and Eve span
Who was tho a gentelman?

(1530)

WILLIAM LANGLAND *from* **The Vision of Piers Plowman**

[Prologue]

In a somur sesoun whan softe was the sonne
I shope me into shroudes as I a shep were –
In abite as an heremite unholy of werkes
Wente forth in the world wondres to here,
5   And say many sellies and selkouthe thynges.
Ac on a May mornyng on Malverne hulles
Me biful for to slepe, for werynesse of-walked;
And in a launde as I lay, lened I and slepte,
And merveylousliche me mette, as I may telle.
10   Al the welthe of the world and the wo bothe
Wynkyng, as hit were, witterliche I seigh hit;
Of treuthe and tricherye, tresoun and gyle,
Al I say slepynge, as I shal telle.
    Estward I beheld aftir the sonne
15   And say a tour – as I trowed, Treuthe was there-ynne;
    Westward I waytede in a while aftir
And seigh a depe dale – Deth, as I leue,
Woned in tho wones, and wikkede spirites.
A fair feld ful of folk fond I ther bytwene
20   Of alle manere men, the mene and the pore,
Worchyng and wandryng as this world asketh.
    Somme putte hem to the plogh, playde ful selde,
In settynge and in sowynge swonken ful harde

---

1 *dalf* dug; *span* spun; 2 *tho* then

2 *shope me* dressed; *shroudes* rough garments; *shep* shepherd; 3 'in the habit of a
hermit, but not one dedicated to holy works'; 4 *here* hear; 5 *say* saw; *sellies* marvels;
selkouthe extraordinary; 6 *hulles* hills; 7 *of-walked* of walking; 8 *launde* grassy
clearing; *lened* reclined; 9 *me mette* I dreamed; 11 *witterliche* truly; *seigh* saw;
14 *aftir* in the direction of; 16 *waytede* looked; 17 *leue* believe; 18 *woned* dwelt;
wones regions; 22 *ful selde* seldom; 23 *swonken* worked;

And wonne that this wastors with glotony destrueth.
And summe putte hem to pruyde and parayled hem ther-aftir
In continance of clothyng in many kyne gyse.
In preiers and penaunces putten hem mony,
Al for love of oure lord lyveden swythe harde
In hope to have a good ende and hevenriche blisse,

30   As ankeres and eremites that holdeth hem in here selles,
Coveyten noght in contreys to cayren aboute
For no likerous liflode here lycame to plese.

   And summe chesen chaffare – thei cheveth the bettre,
As it semeth to oure sighte that suche men ythruveth;

35   And summe murthes to make as mynstrels conneth,
Wolleth neyther swynke ne swete, bote sweren grete othes,
Fyndeth out foule fantasyes and foles hem maketh
And hath wytt at wille to worche yf thei wolde.
That Poule prechede of hem preve hit I myhte:

40   *Qui turpiloquium loquitur* is Luciferes knave.

   Bidders and beggers fast aboute yede
Til here bagge and here bely was bretful ycrammed,
Fayteden for here fode and foughten at the ale.
In glotonye tho gomes goth thei to bedde

45   And ryseth with rybaudrye tho Robardes knaves;
Slep and also slewthe sueth suche ever.

   Pilgrymes and palmers plighten hem togyderes
To seke seynt Jame and seyntes of Rome,
Wenten forth on here way with many wyse tales

50   And hadde leve to lye aftir, al here lyf-tyme.
Eremites on an hep with hokede staves
Wenten to Walsyngham, and here wenches aftir;
Grete lobies and longe that loth were to swynke
Clothed hem in copis to be knowe fram othere

55   And made hemself heremites, here ese to have.

---

24 *that* what; 25 *pruyde* pride; *parayled* dressed; 26 *continance of clothyng* outward
show; *kyne gyse* kinds of way; 27 *mony* many (other people); 30 *ankeres* anchorites;
selles cells; 31 *cayren* wander; 32 *likerous liflode* dainty living; *lykame* bodies;
33 *chaffare* trade; *cheveth* succeeded; 35 *murthes* entertainments; *conneth* know how
to; 36 *swynke* labour; *swete* sweat; *othes* oaths; 37 *foles hem maketh* behave like
fools; 39 *Poule* Saint Paul; 40 'he who speaks filth . . .'; 41 *yede* went;
42 *bretful* brimful; 43 *fayteden* begged falsely; 44 *gomes* men; 45 *Robardes knaves*
robbers; 46 *slep* sleep; *slewthe* sloth; *sueth* follows; 47 *plighten* bound;
49 *tales* speeches; 50 *leve* leave; *lye* tell lies; 51 *on an hep* in a crowd;
hokede crooked; 53 *lobies* lubbers; *longe* tall; *swynke* labour; 54 *copis* long gowns;
to be knowe to be distinguished (as different);

I fonde ther of freris alle the foure ordres,
Prechyng the peple for profyt of the wombe,
And glosede the gospel as hem good likede;
For coveytise of copis contraryed somme doctours.
60 Mony of thise maistres of mendenant freres
Here moneye and marchandise marchen togyderes.
Ac sith charite hath be chapman and chief to shryve lordes
Mony ferlyes han falle in a fewe yeres,
And but holi chirche and charite choppe adoun suche shryvars
65 The moste meschief on molde mounteth up faste.

[Gluttony in the Ale-house]

Now bygynneth Glotoun for to go to shryfte
And kayres hym to kyrke-ward, his conpte to shewe.
Fastyng on a Friday forth gan he wende
By Betene hous the brewestere, that bad hym good morwen,
5 And whodeward he wolde the breuh-wyf hym askede.
    'To holy churche,' quod he, 'for to here masse,
And sennes sitte and be shryve and synege no more.'
    'I have good ale, gossip Glotoun, woltow assaye?'
    'Hastow,' quod he, 'eny hote spyces?'
10 'I have pepur and pyonie and a pound of garlek,
A ferthyng-worth fenkelsedes, for fastyng-dayes I bouhte hit.'
    Thenne goth Glotoun in and Grete Othes aftur.
Sesse the souteres sat on the benche,
Watte the wernare and his wyf dronke,
15 Tymme the tynekare and tweyne of his knaves,
Hicke the hackenayman and Hewe the nedlare,
Claryce of Cockes-lane and the clerc of the churche,
Syre Peres of Prydie and Purnele of Flaundres,
An hayward, an heremyte, the hangeman of Tybourne,

---

57 *wombe* belly; 58 *glosede* expounded; *as hem good likede* at will; 59 *doctours* doctors of theology; 60 *maistres* masters; 61 *marchen* go hand in hand; 62 *chapman* merchant; *shryve* shrive, confess; 63 *ferlyes* strange events; 64 *and but* unless; 65 *moste meschief* greatest misfortune; *molde* earth

1 *shryfte* confession; 2 *kayres hym* goes; *to kyrke-ward* to church; *conpte* reckoning (of sin); 4 *Betene* Betty's; *brewestere* ale-wife; 5 *whodeward* whither; 7 *sennes* then; *shryve* confessed; *synege* sin; 8 *assaye* have a taste; 10 *pyonie* peony (-seeds); 11 *fenkelsedes* fennel-seeds; 12 *Othes* oaths; 13 *Sesse the souteres* Sissy the shoemaker; 14 *Watte the wernare* Walt the warren-keeper; 16 *nedlare* needle-seller; 18 *Purnele* Prunella; 19 *hayward* hedge-warden;

Dawe the dikere, with a doseyne harlotes
Of portours and of pikeporses and of pilede toth-draweres,
A rybibour and a ratoner, a rakeare and his knave,
A ropere and a redyng-kynge and Rose the disshere,
Godefray the garlek-monger and Gryffyth the Walshe,

25   And of uphalderes an heep, herly by the morwe
Geven Glotoun with glad chere good ale to hansull.
    Clement the coblere cast of his cloke
And to the newe fayre nempnede hit forth to sull.
Hicke the hackenayman hit his hod aftur

30   And bade Bitte the bochere ben on his syde.
There were chapmen ychose this chaffare to preyse,
That ho-so hadde the hood sholde nat have the cloke,
And that the bettere thyng, be arbitreres, bote sholde the worse.
Tho rysen up rapliche and rouned togyderes

35   And preisede this peniworths apart by hemsulve,
And there were othes an heep, for on sholde have the worse.
They couthe nat by here conscience acorden for treuthe
Til Robyn the ropere aryse they bisouhte
And nempned hym for a noumper, that no debat were.

40   Hicke the hostiler hadde the cloke,
In covenaunt that Clement sholde the coppe fulle,
And have Hickes hood the hostiler and holde hym yserved;
And ho-so repentede hym rathest sholde aryse aftur
And grete syre Glotoun with a galon of ale.

45   There was leyhing and louryng and 'lat go the coppe!'
Bargaynes and bevereges bygan tho to awake,
And seten so til evensong, and songen umbywhile,
Til Glotoun hadde yglobbed a galoun and a gylle.
His gottes gan to gothly as two grydy sowes;

50   He pissede a potel in a pater-noster whyle,

---

20 *Dawe the dikere* Davy the ditch-digger; 21 *pilede* bald-headed;
22 *rybibour* fiddler; *ratoner* rat-catcher; *rakeare* street-sweeper; 23 *redyng-kynge*
master reed-thatcher; *disshere* dish-seller; 24 *Walshe* Welshman; 25 *uphalderes*
old-clothes dealers; *herly* early; 26 *to hanselle* as a treat; 28 *the newe fayre* (a game
of exchanges); *nempnede hit forth to sull* put it up for barter; 29 *hit* threw in;
30 *bade* asked; 31 *preyse* appraise; 33 *arbitreres* arbitrators; *bote* compensate;
34 *raplich* quickly; *rouned* whispered; 35 *preisede* valued; *peniworths* bargains;
36 *othes* oaths; 37 *acorden* agree; 38 *bisouhte* begged to get up; 39 'and nominated
him umpire, so that no dispute should occur'; 40 *hostiler* ostler;
42 *yserved* satisfied; 43 *ho-so repentede hym* whoever had regrets; *rathest* soonest;
45 *leyhing and louring* laughing and scowling; 47 *umbywhile* from time to time;
48 *yglobbed* gulped down; 49 *gothly* rumble; 50 *potel* potful;

He blew his rownd ruet at his rygebones ende,

That alle that herde the horne helde here nose aftur

And wesched hit hadde be wasche with a weps of breres.

He myhte nother steppe ne stande til he a staf hadde,

55 And thenne gan he go lyke a glemans byche,

Sum tyme asyde and sum tyme arere,

As ho-so layth lynes for to lacche foules.

    And when he drow to the dore, thenne dymmede his yes,

And thromblede at the thresfold and threw to the erthe,

60 And Clement the coblere cauhte hym by the myddel

And for to lyfte hym aloft leyde hym on his knees.

Ac Gloton was a greet cherl and greved in the luftynge

And cowed up a caudel in Clementis lappe;

Ys none so hungry hound in Hertfordshyre

65 Durste lape of that lyvynge, so unlovely hit smauhte.

    With alle the wo of this world his wyf and his wenche

Baren hym to his bed and brouhten hym ther-ynne,

And aftur al this exces he hadde an accidie aftur;

He sleep Saturday and Sonenday til the sonne yede to reste.

70 Then gan he wake wel wanne and wolde have ydronke;

The furste word that he spake was 'Who halt the bolle?'

His wif and his inwit edwitede hym of his synne;

He wax ashamed, that shrewe, and shrofe hym as swythe

To Repentaunce ryht thus: 'Have reuthe on me,' he saide,

75 'Thow lord that aloft art and alle lyves shope!

    'To the, God, I, Glotoun, gulty I me yelde

Of that I have trespased with tonge, I can nat telle how ofte,

Sworn "Godes soule and his sides!" and "So helpe me, God

        almyhty!"

There no nede ne was, many sythe falsly;

80 And over-sopped at my soper and som tyme at nones

More then my kynde myhte deffye,

And as an hound that eet gras so gan I to brake

And spilde that I aspele myhte – I kan nat speke for shame

The vilony of my foule mouthe and of my foule mawe –

85 And fastyng-dayes bifore none fedde me with ale

---

51 *ruet* trumpet; *rygebones* backbone's; 53 *wesched* wished; *weps of breres* sprig of
briars; 55 *glemans byche* minstrel's bitch; 56 *arere* backwards; 57 *layth* lays; *lacche
foules* catch birds; 58 *yes* eyes; 59 *thromblede* stumbled; 62 *ac* but; *greved in the
luftynge* gave trouble in lifting; 63 *cowed* coughed; *caudel* mess; 65 *lape of* lap up;
lyvynge leaving; *smauhte* smelt; 68 *accidie* fit of sloth; 71 *bolle* bowl;
72 *inwit* conscience; *edwitede* reproached; 75 *shope* created; 79 *sythe* a time;
80 *nones* noon; 81 *deffye* digest; 82 *brake* retch; 83 *that I aspele myhte* what I
might have kept in;

Out of resoun, among rybaudes, here rybaudrye to here.
   'Herof, gode God, graunte me foryevenesse
Of all my luyther lyf in al my lyf-tyme
For I vowe to verray God, for eny hungur or furste,

90 Shal nevere fysch in the Fryday defyen in my wombe
Til Abstinence myn aunte have yeve me leve –
And yut have I hated here al my lyf-tyme.'

(1550)

GEOFFREY CHAUCER *from* The Canterbury Tales

from The General Prologue

Whan that Aprill with his shoures soote
The droghte of March hath perced to the roote,
And bathed every veyne in swich licour
Of which vertu engendred is the flour;

5 Whan Zephirus eek with his sweete breeth
Inspired hath in every holt and heeth
The tendre croppes, and the yonge sonne
Hath in the Ram his half cours yronne,
And smale foweles maken melodye,

10 That slepen al the nyght with open ye
(So priketh hem nature in hir corages),
Thanne longen folk to goon on pilgrimages,
And palmeres for to seken straunge strondes,
To ferne halwes, kowthe in sondry londes;

15 And specially from every shires ende
Of Engelond to Caunterbury they wende,
The hooly blisful martir for to seke,
That hem hath holpen whan that they were seeke.

---

86 *rybaudes* ribalds; 88 *luyther* wicked; 90 *defyen* digest; 91 *yeve me leve* given me permission

---

1 *shoures soote* sweet showers; 2 *droghte* dryness; *perced* pierced; 3 *veyne* vein (of sap); *swich licour* such liquid; 4 *flour* flower; 5 *eek* also; 6 *holt* grove; 11 'so much does Nature prick them in their hearts'; 12 *longen folk to goon* people long to go; 13 *palmeres* pilgrims; *straunge strondes* foreign shores; 14 *ferne halwes* distant shrines; *kowthe* known; 16 *wende* make their way; 17 *seke* seek; 18 *hem hath holpen* helped them; *seeke* sick

Ther was also a Nonne, a Prioresse,
That of hir smylyng was ful symple and coy;
Hire gretteste ooth was but by Seinte Loy;
And she was cleped madame Eglentyne.
5   Ful weel she soong the service dyvyne,
Entuned in hir nose ful semely;
And Frenssh she spak ful faire and fetisly,
After the scole of Stratford atte Bowe,
For Frenssh of Parys was to hire unknowe.
10 At mete wel ytaught was she with alle;
She leet no morsel from hir lippes falle,
Ne wette hir fyngres in hir sauce depe;
Wel koude she carie a morsel and wel kepe
That no drope ne fille upon hire brest.
15 In curteisie was set ful muchel hir lest.
Hir over-lippe wyped she so clene
That in hir coppe ther was no ferthyng sene
Of grece, whan she dronken hadde hir draughte.
Ful semely after hir mete she raughte.
20 And sikerly she was of greet desport,
And ful plesaunt, and amyable of port,
And peyned hire to countrefete cheere
Of court, and to been estatlich of manere,
And to ben holden digne of reverence.
25 But for to speken of hire conscience,
She was so charitable and so pitous
She wolde wepe, if that she saugh a mous
Kaught in a trappe, if it were deed or bledde.
Of smale houndes hadde she that she fedde
30 With rosted flessh, or milk and wastel-breed.
But soore wepte she if oon of hem were deed,
Or if men smoot it with a yerde smerte;
And al was conscience and tendre herte.

2 *symple* unaffected; *coy* shy; 3 *ooth* oath; *but* only; 4 *cleped* called;
7 *fetisly* gracefully; 8 *after the scole of* in the manner of; 9 *unknowe* unknown;
10 *at mete* at table; *with alle* indeed; 13 *koude* knew how to; 15 'she took great
delight in courtly manners'; 17 *coppe* cup; 19 *raughte* reached; 20 *sikerly* certainly;
desport deportment; 21 *port* bearing; 22 *peyned hire* took pains;
23 *estatlich* dignified; 24 *digne* worthy; 26 *pitous* compassionate; 27 *saugh* saw;
30 *flessh* meat; *wastel-breed* fine white bread; 32 *smoot* hit; *yerde* stick;

Ful semyly hir wympul pynched was,
Hir nose tretys, hir eyen greye as glas,
Hir mouth ful smal, and therto softe and reed.
But sikerly she hadde a fair forheed;
It was almoost a spanne brood, I trowe;
For, hardily, she was nat undergrowe.
40 Ful fetys was hir cloke, as I was war.
Of smal coral aboute hire arm she bar
A peire of bedes, gauded al with grene,
And theron heng a brooch of gold ful sheene,
On which ther was first write a crowned A,
45 And after *Amor vincit omnia.*

Another Nonne with hire hadde she,
That was hir chapeleyne, and preestes thre.

from The Knight's Tale [The Temple of Mars]

Why sholde I noght as wel eek telle yow al
The portreiture that was upon the wal
Withinne the temple of myghty Mars the rede?
Al peynted was the wal, in lengthe and brede,
5 Lyk to the estres of the grisly place
That highte the grete temple of Mars in Trace,
In thilke colde, frosty regioun
Ther as Mars hath his sovereyn mansioun.

First on the wal was peynted a forest,
10 In which ther dwelleth neither man ne best,
With knotty, knarry, bareyne trees olde,
Of stubbes sharpe and hidtouse to biholde,
In which ther ran a rumbel in a swough,
As though a storm sholde bresten every bough.
15 And dounward from an hille, under a bente,
Ther stood the temple of Mars armypotente,

34 *pynched was* was pleated; 35 *tretys* well-formed; 36 *therto* moreover;
37 *sikerly* certainly; 38 *brood* broad; *trowe* believe; 40 *fetys* elegant; 42 *peire of
bedes* rosary; *gauded* decorated; 43 *sheene* beautiful; 44 *write* engraved; 45 *Amor
vincit omnia* Love conquers all

1 *eek* also; 3 *rede* red; 4 *brede* breadth; 5 *estres* interior apartments; 6 *highte* is
called; 7 *thilke* that; 8 *ther as* where; *sovereyn* finest; 11 *knarry* gnarled;
bareyne barren; 12 *stubbes* stumps; 13 *rumbel* rumbling; *swough* sound of wind;
14 *bresten* burst; 15 *under* close to; *bente* grassy slope; 16 *armypotente* powerful in
arms;

Wroght al of burned steel, of which the entree
Was long and streit, and gastly for to see.
And therout came a rage and swich a veze
20 That it made al the gate for to rese.
The northren lyght in at the dores shoon,
For wyndowe on the wal ne was ther noon,
Thurgh which men myghten any light discerne.
The dore was al of adamant eterne,
25 Yclenched overthwart and endelong
With iren tough; and for to make it strong,
Every pyler, the temple to sustene,
Was tonne-greet, of iren bright and shene.
       Ther saugh I first the derke ymaginyng
30 Of Felonye, and al the compassyng;
The crueel Ire, reed as any gleede;
The pykepurs, and eek the pale Drede;
The smylere with the knyf under the cloke;
The shepne brennynge with the blake smoke;
35 The tresoun of the mordrynge in the bedde;
The open werre, with woundes al bibledde;
Contek, with blody knyf and sharp manace.
Al ful of chirkyng was that sory place.
The sleere of hymself yet saugh I ther –
40 His herte-blood hath bathed al his heer –
The nayl ydryven in the shode anyght;
The colde deeth, with mouth gapyng upright.
Amyddes of the temple sat Meschaunce,
With disconfort and sory contenaunce.
45 Yet saugh I Woodnesse, laughynge in his rage,
Armed Compleint, Outhees, and fiers Outrage;
The careyne in the busk, with throte ycorve;
A thousand slayn, and nat of qualm ystorve;

---

17 *burned* burnished; 18 *streit* narrow; 19 *rage* rush of wind; *veze* blast;
20 *rese* shake; 25 *yclenched* bound; *overthwart* crosswise; *endelong* lengthwise;
27 *pyler* pillar; *sustene* support; 28 *tonne-greet* round as a great barrel;
29 *ymaginyng* plotting; 30 *compassyng* scheming; 31 *Ire* Anger; *gleede* glowing
coal; 32 *pykepurs* pick-purse; *Drede* Fear; 34 *shepne* stable; 35 *mordrynge* murder;
36 *werre* war; *bibledde* covered with blood; 37 *Contek* Strife; *manace* menace;
38 *chirkyng* groaning; 39 *sleere of hymself* suicide; 41 *shode* forehead; *anyght* by
night; 43 *Meschaunce* Misfortune; 45 *Woodnesse* Madness;
46 *Compleint* Grievance; *Outhees* Outcry; *Outrage* Violence; 47 *careyne* corpse;
busk woods; *ycorve* cut; 48 *and not of qualm ystorve* and not killed by the plague;

The tiraunt, with the pray by force yraft;
The toun destroyed, ther was no thyng laft.
Yet saugh I brent the shippes hoppesteres;
The hunte strangled with the wilde beres;
The sowe freten the child right in the cradel;
The cook yscalded, for al his longe ladel.
55 Noght was foryeten by the infortune of Marte.
The cartere overryden with his carte –
Under the wheel ful lowe he lay adoun.
Ther were also, of Martes divisioun,
The barbour, and the bocher, and the smyth,
60 That forgeth sharpe swerdes on his styth.
And al above, depeynted in a tour,
Saugh I Conquest, sittynge in greet honour,
With the sharpe swerd over his heed
Hangynge by a soutil twynes threed.

from **The Knight's Tale** [Saturn]

'My deere doghter Venus,' quod Saturne,
'My cours, that hath so wyde for to turne,
Hath moore power than woot any man.
Myn is the drenchyng in the see so wan;
5 Myn is the prison in the derke cote;
Myn is the stranglyng and hangyng by the throte,
The murmure and the cherles rebellyng,
The groynynge, and the pryvee empoysonyng;
I do vengeance and pleyn correccioun,
10 Whil I dwelle in the signe of the leoun.
Myn is the ruyne of the hye halles,
The fallynge of the toures and of the walles
Upon the mynour or the carpenter.
I slow Sampsoun, shakynge the piler;

49 *pray* prey; *yraft* taken away; 51 *brent* burnt; *hoppesteres* dancing (in the storm);
52 *hunte* hunter; *strangled with* killed by; 53 *freten* devour; 54 *ladel* ladle;
55 *foryeten* forgotten; *infortune of Marte* evil influence of Mars; 59 *bocher* butcher;
60 *styth* anvil; 61 *depeynted* painted; 64 *twynes threed* thread of twine

1 *quod* said; 2 *cours* orbit; 3 *woot* knows; 4 *drenchyng* drowning; *wan* dark;
5 *cote* cell; 7 *murmure* grumbling; *cherles* peasants'; 8 *groynynge* grumbling;
pryvee secret; 9 *correccioun* punishment; 10 *the leoun* Leo; 13 *mynour* miner;
14 *slow* slew;

15 And myne be the maladyes colde,
The derke tresons, and the castes olde;
My lookyng is the fader of pestilence.'

from **The Milleres Tale [Alysoun]**

This carpenter hadde wedded newe a wyf,
Which that he lovede moore than his lyf;
Of eighteteene yeer she was of age.
Jalous he was, and heeld hire narwe in cage,
5 For she was wylde and yong, and he was old
And demed hymself been lik a cokewold.
He knew nat Catoun, for his wit was rude,
That bad man sholde wedde his simylitude.
Men sholde wedden after hire estaat,
10 For youthe and elde is often at debaat.
But sith that he was fallen in the snare,
He moste endure, as oother folk, his care.
   Fair was this yonge wyf, and therwithal
As any wezele hir body gent and smal.
15 A ceynt she werede, barred al of silk,
A barmclooth as whit as morne milk
Upon hir lendes, ful of many a goore.
Whit was hir smok, and broyden al bifoore
And eek bihynde, on hir coler aboute,
20 Of col-blak silk, withinne and eek withoute.
The tapes of hir white voluper
Were of the same suyte of hir coler;
Hir filet brood of silk, and set ful hye.
And sikerly she hadde a likerous ye;
25 Ful smale ypulled were hire browes two,
And tho were bent and blake as any sloo.
She was ful moore blisful on to see
Than is the newe pere-jonette tree,

16 *castes* plots

4 *narwe* closely; 6 *been lik* likely to be; *cokewold* cuckold; 8 *simylitude* equal;
10 *elde* old age; 14 *wezele* weasel; *gent* delicate; *smal* slender; 15 *ceynt* belt;
16 *barmclooth* apron; *morne* morning; 17 *lendes* loins; *goore* flounce;
18 *broyden* embroidered; 19 *coler* collar; 21 *tapes* ribbons; *voluper* cap;
22 *suyte* colour; 23 *filet* headband; 24 *sikerly* truly; *likerous* flirtatious;
25 *ypulled* plucked; 26 *sloo* sloe; 27 *blisful* delightful; 28 *pere-jonette* early pear;

And softer than the wolle is of a wether.
And by hir girdel heeng a purs of lether,
Tasseled with silk and perled with latoun.
In al this world, to seken up and doun,
There nys no man so wys that koude thenche
So gay a popelote or swich a wenche.
35 Ful brighter was the shynyng of hir hewe
Than in the Tour the noble yforged newe.
But of hir song, it was as loude and yerne
As any swalwe sittynge on a berne.
Therto she koude skippe and make game,
40 As any kyde or calf folwynge his dame.
Hir mouth was sweete as bragot or the meeth,
Or hoord of apples leyd in hey or heeth.
Wynsynge she was, as is a joly colt,
Long as a mast, and upright as a bolt.
45 A brooch she baar upon hir lowe coler,
As brood as is the boos of a bokeler.
Hir shoes were laced on hir legges hye.
She was a prymerole, a piggesnye,
For any lord to leggen in his bedde,
50 Or yet for any good yeman to wedde.

from The Wife of Bath's Prologue

My fourthe housbonde was a revelour –
This is to seyn, he hadde a paramour –
And I was yong and ful of ragerye,
Stibourn and strong, and joly as a pye.
5 How koude I daunce to an harpe smale,
And synge, ywis, as any nyghtyngale,
Whan I had dronke a draughte of sweete wyn!
Metellius, the foule cherl, the swyn,

29 *wether* sheep; 31 *latoun* brass; 33 *thenche* imagine; 34 *popelote* little doll;
36 *Tour* the Mint (Tower of London); *noble* gold coin; 37 *yerne* lively;
38 *swalwe* swallow; *berne* barn; 41 *bragot* country drink; *meeth* mead; 42 *hey* hay;
43 *wynsynge* skittish; 46 *boos of a bokeler* raised centre of a shield;
48 *prymerole* primrose; *piggesnye* 'pig's eye' (flower); 49 *leggen* lay;
50 *yeman* yeoman

1 *revelour* profligate; 3 *ragerye* wantonness; 4 *stibourn* stubborn; *pye* magpie;
8 *cherl* villain; 9 *birafte* took away from;

That with a staf birafte his wyf hir lyf,

10   For she drank wyn, thogh I hadde been his wyf,
He sholde nat han daunted me fro drynke!
And after wyn on Venus moste I thynke,
For al so siker as cold engendreth hayl,
A likerous mouth moste han a likerous tayl.
15   In wommen vinolent is no defence –
This knowen lecchours by experience.
        But – Lord Crist! – whan that it remembreth me
Upon my yowthe, and on my jolitee,
It tikleth me aboute myn herte roote.
20   Unto this day it dooth myn herte boote
That I have had my world as in my tyme.
But age, allas, that al wole envenyme,
Hath me biraft my beautee and my pith.
Lat go. Farewel! The devel go therwith!
25   The flour is goon; ther is namoore to telle;
The bren, as I best kan, now moste I selle;
But yet to be right myrie wol I fonde.
Now wol I tellen of my fourthe housbonde.
        I seye, I hadde in herte greet despit
30   That he of any oother had delit.
But he was quit, by God and by Seint Joce!
I made hym of the same wode a croce;
Nat of my body, in no foul manere,
But certeinly, I made folk swich cheere
35   That in his owene grece I made hym frye
For angre, and for verray jalousye.
By God, in erthe I was his purgatorie,
For which I hope his soule be in glorie.
For, God it woot, he sat ful ofte and song,
40   Whan that his shoo ful bitterly hym wrong.
Ther was no wight, save God and he, that wiste,
In many wise, how soore I hym twiste.
He deyde whan I cam fro Jerusalem,
And lith ygrave under the roode beem,

13 *al so siker* as as sure as; 14 *likerous* gluttonous; 15 *vinolent* drunken; 17 *it remembreth me* I remember; 19 *herte root* the bottom of my heart; 20 *boote* good; 22 *envenyme* poison; 23 *biraft* taken away; 26 *bren* bran; 27 *fonde* try; 32 *croce* cross; 35 *grece* grease; 38 *hope* suppose; 40 *wrong* pinched; 42 *twiste* tormented; 43 *deyde* died; 44 *ygrave* buried; *roode beem* rood beam (in church);

Al is his tombe noght so curyus
As was the sepulcre of hym Daryus,
Which that Appelles wroghte subtilly;
It nys but wast to burye hym preciously.
Lat hym fare wel; God yeve his soule reste!
He is now in his grave and in his cheste.

from **The Pardoner's Tale**

Thise riotoures thre of whiche I telle,
Longe erst er prime rong of any belle,
Were set hem in a taverne to drynke,
And as they sat, they herde a belle clynke
Biforn a cors, was caried to his grave.
That oon of hem gan callen to his knave:
'Go bet,' quod he, 'and axe redily
What cors is this that passeth heer forby;
And looke that thou reporte his name weel.'

'Sire,' quod this boy, 'it nedeth never-a-deel;
It was me toold er ye cam heer two houres.
He was, pardee, an old felawe of youres,
And sodeynly he was yslayn to-nyght,
Fordronke, as he sat on his bench upright.
Ther cam a privee theef men clepeth Deeth,
That in this contree al the peple sleeth,
And with his spere he smoot his herte atwo,
And wente his wey withouten wordes mo.
He hath a thousand slayn this pestilence,
And, maister, er ye come in his presence,
Me thynketh that it were necessarie
For to be war of swich an adversarie.
Beth redy for to meete hym everemoore;
Thus taughte me my dame; I sey namoore.'
'By Seinte Marie!' seyde this taverner,
'The child seith sooth, for he hath slayn this yeer,

---

45 *curyus* elaborate; 48 *wast* waste; *preciously* expensively; 50 *cheste* coffin

1 *riotoures* debauchers; 2 *erst er* before; *prime* first hour of the day; 5 *cors* corpse; 7 *go bet* go quickly; 10 *it nedeth never-a-deel* there is no need; 14 *fordronke* very drunk; 15 *men clepeth* is called; 19 *this pestilence* during this plague; 24 *dame* mother;

Henne over a mile, withinne a greet village,

Bothe man and womman, child, and hyne, and page;
I trowe his habitacioun be there.
30 To been avysed greet wysdom it were,
Er that he dide a man a dishonour.'
    'Ye, Goddes armes!' quod this riotour,
'Is it swich peril with hym for to meete?
I shal hym seke by wey and eek by strete,
35 I make avow to Goddes digne bones!
Herkneth, felawes, we thre been al ones;
Lat ech of us holde up his hand til oother,
And ech of us bicomen otheres brother,
And we wol sleen this false traytour Deeth.
40 He shal be slayn, he that so manye sleeth,
By Goddes dignitee, er it be nyght!'
    Togidres han thise thre hir trouthes plight
To lyve and dyen ech of hem for oother,
As though he were his owene ybore brother.
45 And up they stirte, al dronken in this rage,
And forth they goon towardes that village
Of which the taverner hadde spoke biforn.
And many a grisly ooth thanne han they sworn,
And Cristes blessed body they torente –
50 Deeth shal be deed, if that they may hym hente!
    Whan they han goon nat fully half a mile,
Right as they wolde han troden over a stile,
An oold man and a povre with hem mette.
This olde man ful mekely hem grette,
55 And seyde thus, 'Now, lordes, God yow see!'
    The proudeste of thise riotoures three
Answerde agayn, 'What, carl, with sory grace!
Why artow al forwrapped save thy face?
Why lyvestow so longe in so greet age?'
60 This olde man gan looke in his visage,
And seyde thus: 'For I ne kan nat fynde
A man, though that I walked into Ynde,
Neither in citee ne in no village,
That wolde chaunge his youthe for myn age;

27 *henne* from here; 28 *hyne* farm worker; *page* serving boy;
30 *avysed* forewarned; 42 *plight* pledged; 49 *torente* tore to pieces; 50 *hente* seize;
53 *povre* poor; 55 *God yow see* may God look after you; 57 *carl* fellow;
58 *forwrapped* wrapped up; 62 *Ynde* India;

And therfore moot I han myn age stille,
As longe tyme as it is Goddes wille.
Ne Deeth, allas, ne wol nat han my lyf.
Thus walke I, lyk a restelees kaityf,
And on the ground, which is my moodres gate,
70   I knokke with my staf, bothe erly and late,
And seye "Leeve mooder, leet me in!
Lo how I vanysshe, flessh, and blood, and skyn!
Allas, whan shul my bones been at reste?
Mooder, with yow wolde I chaunge my cheste
75   That in my chambre longe tyme hath be,
Ye, for an heyre clowt to wrappe me!"
But yet to me she wol nat do that grace,
For which ful pale and welked is my face.
    'But, sires, to yow it is no curteisye
80   To speken to an old man vileynye,
But he trespasse in word or elles in dede.
In Hooly Writ ye may yourself wel rede:
"Agayns an oold man, hoor upon his heed,
Ye sholde arise;" wherfore I yeve yow reed,
85   Ne dooth unto an oold man noon harm now,
Namoore than that ye wolde men did to yow
In age, if that ye so longe abyde.
And God be with yow, where ye go or ryde!
I moot go thider as I have to go.'
90   'Nay, olde cherl, by God, thou shalt nat so,'
Seyde this oother hasardour anon;
'Thou partest nat so lightly, by Seint John!
Thou spak right now of thilke traytour Deeth.
That in this contree alle oure freendes sleeth.
95   Have heer my trouthe, as thou art his espye,
Telle where he is or thou shalt it abye,
By God and by the hooly sacrement!
For soothly thou art oon of his assent
To sleen us yonge folk, thou false theef!'
100   'Now, sires,' quod he, 'if that yow be so leef
To fynde Deeth, turne up this croked wey,
For in that grove I lafte hym, by my fey,

65 *han* have; 68 *kaityf* wretch; 69 *moodres* mother's; 74 *cheste* strongbox;
76 *heyre clowt* haircloth; 78 *welked* withered; 87 *abyde* remain alive;
91 *hasardour* gambler; 96 *abye* pay for; 98 *oon of his assent* in league with him;

Under a tree, and there he wole abyde;
Noght for youre boost he wole him no thyng hyde.
105 Se ye that ook? Right there ye shal hym fynde.
God save yow, that boghte agayn mankynde,
And yow amende!' Thus seyde this olde man;
And everich of thise riotoures ran
Til he cam to that tree, and ther they founde
110 Of floryns fyne of gold ycoyned rounde
Wel ny an eighte busshels, as hem thoughte.
No lenger thanne after Deeth they soughte,
But ech of hem so glad was of that sighte,
For that the floryns been so faire and brighte,
115 That doun they sette hem by this precious hoord.

(1478)

ANONYMOUS *from* Patience

[Jonah and the Whale]

Now is Jonas the Jwe jugged to drowne;
Of that schended schyp men schowved hym sone.
A wylde walterande whal, as Wyrde then schaped,
That was beten fro the abyme, bi that bot flotte
5 And was war of that wyye that the water soghte
And swyftely swenged hym to swepe and his swolw opened.
The folk yet haldande his fete, the fysch hym tyd hentes;
Withouten towche of any tothe he tult in his throte.
        Thenne he swenges and swayves to the se bothem,
10 Bi mony rokkes ful roghe and rydelande strondes,
Wyth the mon in his mawe, malskred in drede –
As lyttel wonder hit was yif he wo dreyed,
For nade the hyghe Heven-Kyng, thurgh his honde myght,
Warded this wrech man in warlowes guttes,

105 *ook* oak; 106 *boghte agayn* redeemed; 110 *floryns* gold coins

1 *jugged* doomed; 2 *schended* battered; *schyp* ship; *schowved* shoved;
3 *walterande* rolling; *Wyrde* Fate; *schaped* decreed; 4 *abyme* bottom of the sea;
bot boat; *flotte* floated; 5 *war* aware; *wyye* man; 6 *swenged hym to swepe* swung
round to swoop; *swolw* gullet; 7 *folk* sailors; *haldande* holding; *tyd hentes* seized
quickly; 8 *tult* tumbled; 9 *swayves* glides; 10 *rydelande strondes* swirling currents;
11 *malskred* dazed; 12 *dreyed* suffered; 13 *nade* had not; 14 *Warded* guarded;
warlowes the devil's;

What lede moght leve bi lawe of any kynde
That any lyf myght be lent so longe hym withinne?
Bot he was sokored by that Syre that syttes so highe,
Thagh were wanles of wele in wombe of that fissche,
And also dryven thurgh the depe and in derk walteres.

20   Lorde! colde was his cumfort and his care huge
For he knew uche a cace and kark that hym lymped,
How fro the bot into the blober was with a best lached
And thrwe in at hit throte withouten thret more,
As mote in at a munster-dor, so mukel wern his chawles.

25   He glydes in by the giles thugh glaym ande glette,
Relande in by a rop, a rode that hym thoght,
Ay hele over hed hourlande aboute,
Til he blunt in a blok as brod as a halle;
And ther he festnes the fete and fathmes aboute

30   And stod up in his stomak that stank as the devel.
Ther in saym and in sorwe that savoured as helle
Ther was bylded his bour that wyl no bale suffer.

And thenne he lurkkes and laytes where was le best
In uche a nok of his navel, bot nowhere he fyndes

35   No rest ne recoverer bot ramel ande myre
In wych gut so-ever he gos – bot ever is God swete!

And ther he lenged at the last and to the lede called:
'Now, Prynce, of thy prophete pite thou have!
Thagh I be fol and fykel and falce of my hert,

40   Devoyde now thy vengaunce, thurgh vertu of rauthe;
Thagh I be gulty of gyle, as gaule of prophetes,
Thou art God, and alle gowdes ar graythely thyn owen.
Haf now mercy of thy man and his mysdedes
And preve the lyghtly a Lorde in londe and in water.'

45   With that he hitte to a hyrne and helde hym therinne,

15 *lede* man; *leve* believe; 16 'that any living creature might survive so long inside
him'; 17 *sokored* succoured; 18 *wanles of wele* without hope of happiness;
21 *cace* misfortune; *kark* hardship; *lymped* happened to; 22 *bot* boat; *blober* seething
water; *lached* seized; 23 *thrwe* rushed; *hit* its; *thret* resistance; 24 *mote* speck of dust;
munster-dor cathedral door; *chawles* jaws; 25 *giles* gills; *glaym and glette* slime and
filth; 26 *Relande* tumbling; *by a rop* along a gut; *rode* road; 27 *hourlande* tumbling;
28 *blunt* came to a stop; *blok* cavern; 29 *festnes the fete* gains a foothold;
fathmes gropes; 31 *saym* grease; *sorwe* filth; 32 *bour* bower; 33 *lurkkes* lies low;
laytes looks; *le* shelter; 35 *recoverer* remedy; *ramel* muck; 37 *lenged* stood still;
lede Lord; 39 *thagh* though; 40 *Devoyde* withdraw; *rauthe* mercy; 41 *gaule* scum;
42 *gowdes* things; *graythely* truly; 44 *preve the lyghtly* prove yourself easily;
45 *hitte to a hyrne* hit upon a nook;

Ther no defoule of no fylthe was fest hym abute;
Ther he sete also sounde, saf for merk one,
As in the bulk of the bote ther he byfore sleped.
So in a bouel of that best he bides on lyve
50   Thre dayes and thre nyght, ay thenkande on Dryghtyn,
His myght and his merci, his mesure thenne:
Now he knawes hym in care that couthe not in sele.
   Ande ever walteres this whal bi wyldren depe
Thurgh mony a regioun ful roghe, thurgh ronk of his wylle;
55   For that mote in his mawe mad hym, I trowe,
Thagh hit lyttel were hym wyth, to wamel at his hert;
Ande as sayled the segge, ay sykerly he herde
The bygge borne on his bak and bete on his sydes.

(1864)

ANONYMOUS *from* Sir Gawain and the Green Knight

[Gawain Journeys North]

Now rides this renk thurgh the ryalme of Logres,
Sir Gawayn, on Godes halve, thagh him no game thoght.
Oft ledeles alone he lenges on nightes
There he fonde noght him before the fare that he liked.
5   Had he no fere bot his fole by frythes and downes,
Ne no gome bot God by gate with to carp,
Til that he neghed ful negh into the North Wales.
All the iles of Anglesay on lyft half he holdes
And fares over the fordes by the forlondes,
10   Over at the Holy Hede, til he had eft bonk

---

46 *fest* close; 47 *saf for merk one* except only for the darkness; 48 *bulk* hold;
byfore previously; 49 *best* beast; *on lyve* alive; 50 *thenkande* thinking; *Dryghtyn* the
Lord; 51 *mesure* moderation; 52 *care* misery; *sele* happiness; 53 *walteres* rolls;
54 *ronk of his wylle* rank pride; 56 'small though it was compared with him, to make
him feel queasy'; 57 *the segge* the man; *sykerly* constantly; 58 *the bygge* the great
flood

1 *renk* knight; *ryalme of Logres* (Arthur's kingdom); 2 *on Godes halve* for God's
sake; *thagh* though; 3 *ledeles* without company; *lenges* remains;
4 *fare* entertainment; 5 *fere* companion; *fole* horse; *frythes* woods; 6 *gome* man; *by
gate* on the road; *to carp* to speak to; 7 *neghed* approached; 9 *forlondes* headlands;
10 *Holy Hede* Holyhead; *eft* again; *bonk* reached the shore;

In the wyldrenesse of Wyrale: woned there bot lyte
That auther God auther gome with good hert lovied.
And ay he frayned as he ferde at frekes that he met
If thay had herd any carp of a knight grene,
15   In any grounde theraboute of the Grene Chapel;
And all nikked him with nay, that never in her live
Thay seye never no segge that was of such hewes
          Of grene.
     The knight toke gates straunge
20   In mony a bonk unbene;
     His chere ful oft con chaunge
     That chapel ere he myght sene.

Mony clyff he overclambe in contrayes straunge,
Fer floten fro his frendes fremedly he rides.
25   At uch warthe auther water there the wye passed
He fonde a foo him before, bot ferly hit were,
And that so foule and so felle that fyght him behoved.
So mony mervayl by mount there the mon findes
Hit were to tor for to telle of the tenthe dole.
30   Sumwhyle with wormes he werres and with wolves als,
Sumwhyle with wodwos that woned in the knarres,
Both with bulles and beres, and bores otherwhyle,
And etaynes that him anelede of the high felle.
Nad he bene doghty and drye and Dryghtyn had served,
35   Douteles he had bene ded and dreped ful oft;
For werre wrathed him not so much that wynter nas wors,
When the colde clere water fro the cloudes schadde
And fres ere hit falle myght to the fale erthe.
Nere slayn with the slete he slepte in his yrnes
40   Mo nightes then innogh in naked rokkes,
There as claterande fro the crest the colde borne rennes
And henged high over his hede in hard iisse-ikkles.

11 *Wyrale* Wirral; 11–12 'few lived there whom either God or good-hearted men loved'; 13 *frayned* asked; *ferde* journeyed; *frekes* men; 14 *carp* talk; 16 *nikked him with nay* said no to him; *seye* saw; *segge* man; *hewes* colour; 19 *gates* roads; 20 *bonk* hillside; *unbene* unpleasant; 21 *chere ... chaunge* looked this way and that; 24 *floten* travelled; *fremedly* as a stranger; 25 *uch* each; *warthe* ford; *auther* or; *wye* knight; 25 *bot ferly hit were* 'or else it was a wonder'; 27 *felle* fierce; 29 *to tor* too difficult; *dole* part; 30 *Sumwhyle* sometimes; *wormes* dragons; *als* also; 31 *wodwos* trolls; *woned* lived; *knarres* crags; 33 *etaynes* giants, ogres; *anelede* pursued; 34 *doghty* doughty; *drye* resolute; *Dryghtyn* the Lord God; 35 *dreped* killed; 36 *werre* fighting; *wrathed* afflicted; 38 *fres* froze; *fale* pale; 39 *slete* sleet; *yrnes* armour; 40 *innogh* enough; 41 *borne* burn, stream;

Thus in peryl and payne and plytes ful hard
By contray cayres this knight til Cristmasse even
45   All one.
    The knight wel that tyde
    To Mary made his mone
    That ho him rede to ride
    And wysse him to sum wone.

50 By a mount on the morn meryly he rides
    Into a forest ful depe that ferly was wylde,
    High hilles on uch a half and holtwodes under,
    Of hore okes ful huge a hundreth togeder.
    The hasel and the hawthorne were harled all samen,
55 With rogh raged mosse rayled aywhere,
    With mony bryddes unblythe upon bare twyges,
    That pitosly there piped for pine of the colde.
    The gome upon Gryngolet glydes hem under
    Thurgh mony misy and myre, mon all him one,
60 Carande for his costes lest he ne kever schulde
    To se the servyce of that syre that on that self night
    Of a burde was born oure baret to quelle.
    And therfore sykyng he sayd, 'I beseche the, Lord,
    And Mary, that is myldest moder so dere,
65 Of sum herber there highly I myght here masse
    And thy matynes tomorn, mekely I ask,
    And therto prestly I pray my pater and ave
            And crede.'
    He rode in his prayere
70 And cryed for his mysdede;
    He sayned him in sythes sere
    And sayd, 'Cros Cryst me spede!'

                                    (1839)

43 *plytes* hardships; 44 *cayres* rides; 45 *all one* all alone; 46 *tyde* time;
47 *mone* complaint; 48 'that she would direct him where to ride'; 49 *wysse* guide;
wone dwelling-place; 51 *ferly* truly; 52 *holtwodes* woods; 54 *harled all samen*
tangled together; 55 *rayled* arranged; 58 *gome* knight; *Gryngolet* (his horse);
glydes rides; 59 *misy* bog; *mon all him one* a man all alone; 60–2 'anxious about his
plight, lest he should not succeed in attending the service of that Lord who on that
very night was born of a maiden to end our strife'; 63 *sykyng* sighing;
65 *herber* lodge; 66 *matynes* matins; 67 *prestly* promptly; 70 *mysdede* sins;
71 *sayned* blessed; *sythes sere* several times

GEOFFREY CHAUCER Envoy to Scogan

Tobroken been the statutz hye in hevene
That creat were eternally to dure,
Syth that I see the bryghte goddis sevene
Mowe wepe and wayle, and passioun endure,
5   As may in erthe a mortal creature.
Allas, fro whennes may thys thing procede,
Of which errour I deye almost for drede?

By word eterne whilom was it shape
That fro the fyfte sercle, in no manere,
10   Ne myght a drope of teeres doun escape.
But now so wepith Venus in hir spere
That with hir teeres she wol drenche us here.
Allas! Scogan, this is for thyn offence;
Thow causest this diluge of pestilence.

15   Hastow not seyd, in blaspheme of the goddis,
Thurgh pride, or thrugh thy grete rekelnesse,
Swich thing as in the lawe of love forbode is,
That, for thy lady sawgh nat thy distresse,
Therfore thow yave hir up at Michelmesse?
20   Allas! Scogan, of olde folk ne yonge
Was never erst Scogan blamed for his tonge.

Thow drowe in skorn Cupide eke to record
Of thilke rebel word that thow hast spoken,
For which he wol no lenger be thy lord.
25   And, Scogan, though his bowe be nat broken,
He wol nat with his arwes been ywroken
On the, ne me, ne noon of oure figure;
We shul of him have neyther hurt ne cure.

1 *Tobroken* shattered; *statutz* edicts; 2 *creat* created; *dure* endure; 3 *goddis sevene*
the seven planets; 4 *Mowe* may; 7 *errour* confusion; 8 *shape* decreed;
9 *sercle* circle; 11 *spere* sphere; 16 *rekelnesse* rashness; 17 *forbode* forbidden;
18 *for* because; 21 *erst* previously; 22 'you also contemptuously called on Cupid as
your witness'; 23 *thilke* that same; 26 *ywroken* revenged; 27 *of oure figure* shaped
like us;

Now certes, frend, I dreed of thyn unhap,
30   Lest for thy gilt the wreche of Love procede
On alle hem that ben hoor and rounde of shap,
That ben so lykly folk in love to spede.
Than shal we for oure labour have no mede;
But wel I wot, thow wolt answere and saye,
35   'Lo, olde Grisel lyst to ryme and playe!'

Nay, Scogan, say not so, for I m'excuse –
God helpe me so! – in no rym, dowteles,
Ne thynke I never of slep to wake my muse,
That rusteth in my shethe stille in pees.
40   While I was yong, I put hir forth in prees;
But al shal passe that men prose or ryme;
Take every man hys turn, as for his tyme.

[*Envoy*]
Scogan, that knelest at the stremes hed
Of grace, of alle honour and worthynesse,
45   In th'ende of which strem I am dul as ded,
Forgete in solytarie wildernesse –
Yet, Scogan, thenke on Tullius kyndenesse;
Mynne thy frend, there it may fructyfye!
Far-wel, and loke thow never eft Love dyffye.

(1478)

JOHN GOWER *from* Confessio Amantis

[Pygmaleon]

I finde hou whilom ther was on,
Whos name was Pymaleon,
Which was a lusti man of yowthe:
The werkes of entaile he cowthe

---

29 *unhap* misfortune; 30 *wreche* vengeance; 31 *hem* them; *hoor* grey; 32 *so lykly* so
well qualified; *spede* succeed; 33 *mede* reward; 35 *olde Grisel* the old horse;
lyst likes; 36 *m'excuse* declare myself innocent; 37 *rym* rhyme; 40 *in prees* in
public; 43 *stremes hed* the head of the Thames [Windsor castle]; 45 *th'ende* the
mouth of the Thames [Greenwich]; 46 *forgete* forgotten; 47 *Tullius* Cicero;
48 *mynne* remember; 49 *eft* again; *dyffye* defy

1 *whilom* once; *on* one; 4 *entaile* sculpture; *cowthe* could (do);

Above alle othre men as tho;
And thurgh fortune it fell him so,
As he whom love schal travaile,
He made an ymage of entaile
Lich to a womman in semblance
Of feture and of contienance,
So fair yit nevere was figure.
Riht as a lyves creature
Sche semeth, for of yvor whyt
He hath hire wroght of such delit,
That sche was rody on the cheke
And red on bothe hire lippes eke;
Wherof that he himself beguileth.
For with a goodly lok sche smyleth,
So that thurgh pure impression
Of his ymaginacion
With al the herte of his corage
His love upon this faire ymage
He sette, and hire of love preide;
Bot sche no word ayeinward seide.
The longe day, what thing he dede,
This ymage in the same stede
Was evere bi, that ate mete
He wolde hire serve and preide hire ete,
And putte unto hire mowth the cuppe;
And whan the bord was taken uppe,
He hath hire into chambre nome,
And after, whan the nyht was come,
He leide hire in his bed al nakid.
He was forwept, he was forwakid,
He keste hire colde lippes ofte,
And wissheth that thei weren softe,
And ofte he rouneth in hire Ere,
And ofte his arm now hier now there
He leide, as he hir wolde embrace,
And evere among he axeth grace,
As thogh sche wiste what he mente:
And thus himself he gan tormente

5 *as tho* then; 7 *travaile* trouble; 10 *feture* feature; 12 *lyves* living; 13 *yvor* ivory;
23 *preide* prayed; 24 *ayeinward* in answer; 27 *ate mete* at dinner; 31 *nome* taken;
34 *forwept* exhausted with weeping; *forwakid* deprived of sleep;
37 *rouneth* whispers; 41 *wiste* knew;

With such desese of loves peine,
That noman mihte him more peine.

45 Bot how it were, of his penance
He made such continuance
Fro dai to nyht, and preith so longe,
That his preiere is underfonge,
Which Venus of hire grace herde;

50 Be nyhte and whan that he worst ferde,
And it lay in his nakede arm,
The colde ymage he fieleth warm
Of fleissh and bon and full of lif.

[The Rape of Lucrece]

Sche broghte him to his chambre tho
And tok hire leve, and forth is go
Into hire oghne chambre by,
As sche that wende certeinly

5 Have had a frend, and hadde a fo,
Wherof fel after mochel wo.
    This tirant, thogh he lyhe softe,
Out of his bed aros fulofte,
And goth aboute, and leide his Ere

10 To herkne, til that alle were
To bedde gon and slepten faste.
And thanne upon himself he caste
A mantell, and his swerd al naked
He tok in honde; and sche unwaked

15 Abedde lay, but what sche mette,
God wot; for he the Dore unschette
So prively that non it herde,
The softe pas and forth he ferde
Unto the bed wher that sche slepte,

20 Al sodeinliche and in he crepte,
And hire in bothe his Armes tok.
With that this worthi wif awok,
Which thurgh tendresce of wommanhiede
Hire vois hath lost for pure drede,

---

48 *underfonge* accepted; 50 ferde fared

1 *tho* then; 3 *oghne* own; 4 *wende* believed herself; 15 *mette* dreamed;
18 *ferde* fared;

That o word speke sche ne dar:
And ek he bad hir to be war,
For if sche made noise or cry,
He seide, his swerd lay faste by
To slen hire and hire fold aboute.

30 And thus he broghte hire herte in doute,
That lich a Lomb whanne it is sesed
In wolves mouth, so was desesed
Lucrece, which he naked fond:
Wherof sche swounede in his hond,

35 And, as who seith, lay ded oppressed.
And he, which al him hadde adresced
To lust, tok thanne what him liste,
And goth his wey, that non it wiste,
Into his oghne chambre ayein,

40 And clepede up his chamberlein,
And made him redi forto ryde.
And thus this lecherouse pride
To horse lepte and forth he rod;
And sche, which in hire bed abod,

45 Whan that sche wiste he was agon,
Sche clepede after liht anon
And up aros long er the day,
And caste awey hire freissh aray,
As sche which hath the world forsake,

50 And tok upon the clothes blake:
And evere upon continuinge,
Right as men sen a welle springe,
With yhen fulle of wofull teres,
Hire her hangende aboute hire Eres,

55 Sche wepte, and noman wiste why.

(1483)

25 *o word* one word; 29 *fold* family; 34 *swounede* swooned; 40 *clepede* called;
46 *liht* light; 53 *yhen* eyes

THOMAS HOCCLEVE *from* The Complaint of Hoccleve

Aftir that hervest inned had hise sheves
And that the broun sesoun of Mihelmesse
Was come, and gan the trees robbe of her leves
That grene had ben and in lusty freisshenesse,
5   And hem into colour of yelownesse
Had died and doun throwen undir foote,
That chaunge sanke into myn herte roote,

For freisshly broughte it to my remembraunce
That stablenesse in this worlde is ther noon:
10 Ther is nothing but chaunge and variaunce.
Howe welthi a man be or wel-begoon,
Endure it shal not, he shal it forgoon.
Deeth undir foote shal him thriste adoun:
That is every wightes conclucioun,

15 Whiche for to weyve is in no mannes myght,
Howe riche he be, stronge, lusty, freissh and gay.
And in the ende of Novembre uppon a night,
Sighynge sore as I in my bed lay,
For this and othir thoughtis wiche many a day
20 Byforne I tooke, sleep cam noon in myn ye,
So vexid me the thoughtful maladie.

I sy wel sithin I with siknesse last
Was scourgid, cloudy hath bene the favour
That shoon on me ful bright in times past.
25 The sunne abated and the dirke shour
Hilded doun right on me and in langour
Me made swymme, so that my spirite
To lyve no lust had ne no delite.

(...)

1 *inned* gathered in; 2 *Mihelmesse* Michaelmas; 6 *died* dyed; 7 *myn herte roote*
depths of my heart; 11 *wel begoon* well provided; 12 *forgoon* lose; 13 *thriste* thrust;
15 *weyve* waive, avoid; 16 *howe* however; 22 *sy* saw; *sithin* since;
26 *Hilded* poured;

Men seiden I loked as a wilde steer,
30 And so my looke aboute I gan to throwe.
Min heed to hie, anothir seide, I beer:
'Ful bukkissh is his brayn, wel may I trowe.'
And seide the thridde – and apt is in the rowe
To site of hem that a resounles reed
35 Can yeve – 'No sadnesse is in his heed.'

Chaunged had I my pas, somme seiden eke,
For here and there forthe stirte I as a roo,
Noon abood, noon areest, but al brain-seke.
Another spake and of me seide also,
40 My feet weren ay wavynge to and fro
Whanne that I stonde shulde and with men talke,
And that myn yen soughten every halke.

I leide an eere ay to as I by wente
And herde al, and thus in myn herte I caste:
45 'Of longe abidinge here I may me repente;
Lest that of hastinesse I at the laste
Answere amys, beste is hens hie faste,
For if I in this prees amys me gye,
To harme wole it me turne and to folie.'

50 And this I demed wel and knewe wel eke:
What-so that evere I shulde answere or seie
They wolden not han holde it worth a leke.
Forwhy, as I had lost my tunges keie,
Kepte I me cloos and trussid me my weie
55 Droupinge and hevy and al woo-bistaad.
Smal cause hadde I, me thoughte, to be glad.

---

29 *seiden* said; *as* as if; *steer* young ox; 30 *and so* and for this reason; 31 *heed* head;
to hie too high; *beer* carried; 32 *bukkissh* capricious; 33 *thridde* third; 33–5 'and is
fit for the company of those who give unreasonable advice'; 35 *sadnesse* seriousness;
36 *pas* way of walking; 37 *stirte* started; *roo* roe deer; 38 *noon abood, noon areest*
no resting, no stopping; 42 *yen* eyes; *halke* corner (of a room); 44 *caste* pondered;
47 *amys* amiss; *hens hie* go hence; 48 *prees* crowd; *amys me gye* conduct myself
badly; 52 *leke* leek; 53–4 'for which reason I kept quiet as if I had lost the key to my
tongue, and took myself off'; 55 *woo-bistaad* woebegone;

My spirites labouriden evere ful bisily
To peinte countenaunce, chere and look,
For that men spake of me so wondringly,
60 And for the verry shame and feer I qwook.
Though myn herte hadde be dippid in the brook
It weet and moist was ynow of my swoot,
Wiche was nowe frosty colde, nowe firy hoot.

And in my chaumbre at home whanne that I was
65 Mysilfe aloone, I in this wise wrought:
I streite unto my mirrour and my glas
To loke howe that me of my chere thought,
If any othir were it than it ought,
For fain wolde I, if it had not bene right,
70 Amendid it to my kunnynge and myght.

Many a saute made I to this mirrour,
Thinking, 'If that I looke in this manere
Amonge folke as I nowe do, noon errour
Of suspecte look may in my face appere.
75 This countinaunce, I am sure, and this chere,
If I it forthe use, is nothing reprevable
To hem that han conceitis resonable.'

And therwithal I thoughte thus anoon:
'Men in her owne cas bene blinde alday,
80 As I have herde seie manie a day agoon,
And in that same plite I stonde may.
Howe shal I do? Wiche is the beste way
My troublid spirit for to bringe in rest?
If I wiste howe, fain wolde I do the best.'

85 Sithen I recovered was, have I ful ofte
Cause had of anger and impacience,
Where I borne have it esily and softe,
Suffringe wronge be done to me and offence

---

58 *peinte* simulate; 59 *for that* because; 60 *qwook* trembled; 61 *though* as if;
62 *ynow* enough; *swoot* sweat; 65 *wise* manner; *wrought* acted; 66 *streite* hurried;
67 'to see how my demeanour looked to me'; 70 'have improved it to the best of my
ability'; 71 *saute* leap; 76 *if I it forthe use* if I go on using it;
reprevable reprehensible; 77 *conseitis* notions; 81 *plite* plight; 85 *Sithen* since;

And not answerid ayen but kepte scilence,
90 Leste that men of me deme wolde and sein,
'Se howe this man is fallen in ayein.'

As that I oones fro Westminstir cam,
Vexid ful grevously with thoughtful hete,
Thus thoughte I: 'A greet fool I am
95 This pavyment a-daies thus to bete
And in and oute laboure faste and swete,
Wondringe and hevinesse to purchace,
Sithen I stonde out of al favour and grace.'

And thane thoughte I on that othir side:
100 'If that I not be sen amonge the prees,
Men deme wole that I myn heed hide
And am werse than I am, it is no lees.'
O Lorde, so my spirit was restelees!
I soughte reste and I not it fonde,
105 But ay was trouble redy at myn honde.

(1892)

1440 CHARLES OF ORLEANS [Ballade]

In the forest of Noyous Hevynes
As I went wandryng in the moneth of May,
I mette of Love the myghti gret goddes,
Which axid me whithir I was away.
5 I hir answerid, 'As Fortune doth convey
As oon exylid from joy, al be me loth,
That passyng well all folke me clepyn may
The man forlost that wot not where he goth.'

89 *ayen* in reply; 90 *deme* judge; 91 *fallen in* relapsed; 93 *thoughtful hete* painful thoughts; 95 *pavyment* pavement; *a-daies* daily; *bete* beat; 96 *swete* sweat; 97 *wondringe* anxiety; 100 *prees* throng; 102 *lees* lie

1 *Noyous Hevynes* grievous sadness; 4 *whithir y was away* where I was going; 5 *convey* guide; 6 *al be me loth* although it is hateful to me; 7 'So that all people may fittingly call me'; 8 *forlost* completely lost;

Half in a smyle, ayen of hir humblesse
She seide, 'My frend, if so I wist, ma fay,
Wherfore that thou art brought in such distresse,
To shape thyn ese I wolde mysilf assay,
For here-tofore I sett thyn hert in way
Of gret plesere – I not who made thee wroth.
Hit grevith me thee see in suche aray,
The man forlost that wot not where he goth.'

'Allas!' I seide, 'most sovereyne good princesse,
Ye knowe my case: what nedith to yow say?
Hit is thorugh Deth, that shewith to all rudesse,
Hath fro me tane that I most lovyd ay,
In whom that all myn hope and comfort lay.
So passyng frendship was bitwene us both
That I was not, to fals Deth did hir day,
The man forlost that wot not where he goth.

'Thus am I blynd, allas and welaway!
Al fer myswent, with my staf grapsyng wey,
That nothyng axe but me a grave to cloth;
For pite is that I lyve thus a day,
The man forlost that wot not where he goth.'

CHARLES OF ORLEANS [Roundel]

Take, take this cosse, atonys, atonys, my hert!
That thee presentid is of thi maystres –
The goodly fayre so full of lustynes –
Only of grace to lessen with thi smert.
But to myn honoure loke thou well avert
That Daunger not parseyve my sotilnes.
    Take, take this cosse, atonys, atonys, my hert!
    That thee presentid is of thi maystres.

---

9 *ayen* in reply; *of hir humblesse* in her graciousness; 10 *if so I wist, ma fay* if I knew, indeed; 12 *shape* bring about; *ese* cure; 13 *here-tofore* formerly; 14 *not* know not; *wroth* sad; 15 *aray* state; 18 *what nedith to yow say* what need is there to tell you; 19 *rudesse* harshness; 20 *tane* taken; *ay* ever, always; 22 *passyng* great; 23 *to* till; *did hir day* caused her to die; 26 *al fer myswent* for fear of going astray; *grapsyng wey* groping my way; 27 *axe* ask; *to cloth* to cover me

1 *cosse* kiss; *atonys* at once; 2 *maystres* mistress; 5 *avert* pay attention; 6 *parseyve* perceive;

Daunger wacchith al nyght in his shert
10   To spye me, in a gery currisshenes;
So to have doon attones let se thee dresse
While in a slepe his eyen ben covert.
        Take, take this cosse, atonys, atonys, my hert!
        That thee presentid is of thi maystres.

CHARLES OF ORLEANS [Roundel]

Go forth myn hert wyth my lady,
Loke that ye spar no besynes
To serve hyr wyth seche lowlynes
That ye get hyr grace and mercy.
5   Pray hyr oftymes pryvely
That sche quippe trewly hyr promes.
        Go forth myn hert wyth my lady
        Loke that ye spar no besynes.
I most as a hertles body
10   Abyde alone in hevynes
And ye schal dowel wyth your maistres
In plesans glad and mery.
        Go forth myn hert wyth my lady
        Loke that ye spar no besynes.

                                        (1827)

1450   § [Sloane Lyrics]

ANONYMOUS

Adam lay y-bownden   bownden in a bond,
Fower thousand wynter   thought he not to long,

---

10 *gery* capricious; 11 *dresse* get ready; 12 *covert* covered

1 *myn* my; 2 *besynes* pains; 3 *seche* such; 6 *quippe* keep; 9 *hertles* without a heart; 11 *dowel* play; 12 *plesans* delight

1 *y-bownden* bound [in Hell]; 2 *to long* too long;

And al was for an appil   an appil that he took,
As clerkës fynden writen   in herë book.

5   Ne hadde the appil takë ben   the appil takë ben,
Ne haddë never our lady   have ben hevenë quen.

Blessëd be the tymë   that appil takë was,
Therefore we mown singen   'Deo gratias!'

ANONYMOUS

I syng of a mayden   that is makëles,
King of allë kingës   to here sone she ches.

He cam also styllë   ther his moder was,
As dew in Aprylle   that fallëth on the gras.

5   He cam also styllë   to his moderës bowr
As dew in Aprille   that fallëth on the flour.

He cam also stillë   ther his moder lay,
As dew in Aprille   that fallëth on the spray.

Moder and mayden   was never non but she –
10 Wel may swych a lady   Godës moder be!

(1856)

§   §   §

4 *clerkës fynden writen* scholars find written; *herë* their; 5 *ne hadde* had not; *takë ben* been taken; 6 'Our Lady would never have been Queen of Heaven'; 8 *mown singen* may sing

1 *makëles* matchless/mateless; 2 *to here sone she ches* as her son she chose; 3 *also styllë* as silently; *ther his moder was* where his mother was; 5 *bowr* bower; 6 *flour* flower; 8 *spray* branch; 9 *was never non* was never anyone; 10 *swych* such; *Godës* God's

ANONYMOUS

The merthe of alle this londe
Maketh the gode husbonde
   With erynge of his plowe;
Iblessyd be Cristes sonde
5 That hath us sent in honde
   Merthe and joye ynowe.

The plowe goth mony a gate
Both erly and eke late
   In wynter in the clay
10 Aboute barly and whete,
That maketh men to swete,
   God spede the plowe al day!

Browne, Morel and Gore
Drawen the plowe ful sore
15   Al in the morwenynge;
Rewarde hem therfore
With a shefe or more
   Al in the evenynge.

Whan men bygynne to sowe
20 Ful wel here corne they knowe
   In the monnthe of May.
Howe ever Janyver blowe,
Whether hye or lowe,
   God spede the plowe allway!

25 Whan men bygynneth to wede
The thystle fro the sede,
   In somer whan they may,
God lete hem wel to spede;
And longe gode lyfe to lede
30 All that for plowemen pray.

2 *husbonde* husbandman, farmer; 3 *erynge* ploughing; 4 *sonde* sending (gift); 5 *in honde* in hand; 6 *ynowe* enough, in abundance; 7 *gate* way; 10 *aboute* busy with; 11 *swete* sweat; 13 [horse names]; 14 *ful sore* with great difficulty; 15 *morwenynge* morning; 17 *shefe* sheave; 20 *knowe* judge; 22 *Janyver* January; 26 *sede* seed; 28 *lete* grant; 29 *lede* lead; 30 'all who pray for ploughmen'

ANONYMOUS [Christ Triumphant]

I have laborede sore and suffered deyyth,
And now I rest and draw my breyth;
But I schall come and call ryght sone
Hevene and erth and hell to dome;
And thane schall know both devyll and mane,
What I was and what I ame.

(1939)

ANONYMOUS [Holly against Ivy]

Nay, Ivy, nay, hyt shal not be, iwys;
Let Holy hafe the maystry, as the maner ys.

Holy stond in the hall, fayre to behold;
Ivy stond without the dore; she ys ful sore a-cold.

5   Holy and hys mery men, they dawnsyn and they syng;
Ivy and hur maydenys, they wepyn and they wryng.

Ivy hath a kybe; she kaght yt with the colde;
So mot they all haf ae that with Ivy hold.

Holy hat berys as rede as any rose;
10   The foster, the hunters kepe hem fro the doos.

Ivy hath berys as blake as any slo;
Ther com the oule and ete hym as she goo.

Holy hath byrdys, a ful fayre flok,
The nyghtyngale, the poppynguy, the gayntyl lavyrok.

15   Gode Ivy, what byrdys ast thou?
Non but the howlat, that kreye, 'How, how!'

3 *sone* soon; 4 *dome* the Last Judgement; 5 *mane* man

2 *maystry* mastery; 3 *stond* stands; 6 *maydenys* maidens; 7 *kybe* chilblain;
kaght caught; 8 *ae* always; 9 *berys* berries; 10 *foster* forester; *doos* does;
12 *oule* owl; 14 *poppynguy* green woodpecker; *gayntyl* gentle; *lavyrok* lark;
16 *howlat* owl; *kreye* cries

ANONYMOUS

Ther is no rose of swych vertu
As is the rose that bare Jesu.

Ther is no rose of swych vertu
As is the rose that bar Jesu;
5   *Alleluya.*

For in this rose conteynyd was
Heven and erthe in lytyl space,
       Res miranda.

Be that rose we may weel see
10   That he is God in personys thre,
       Pari forma.

The aungelys sungyn the sheperdes to:
'Gloria in excelcis Deo.'
       Gaudeamus.

15   Leve we al this wordly merthe,
And folwe we this joyful berthe;
       Transeamus.

1500   JOHN SKELTON *from* **Phyllyp Sparowe**

Whan I remembre agayn
How mi Philyp was slayn,
Never halfe the payne
Was betwene you twayne,
5   Pyramus and Thesbe,
As than befell to me.

1 *swych* such; 8 *Res miranda* 'Thing to be marvelled at'; 11 *Pari forma* 'In one substance'; 12 *to* too; 14 *Gaudeamus* 'Let us rejoice'; 17 *Transeamus* 'Let us proceed'

I wept and I wayled,
The tearys downe hayled,
But nothynge it avayled

10 To call Phylyp agayne
Whom Gyb our cat hath slayne.

(. . .)

  It had a velvet cap
And wold syt upon my lap
And seke after small wormes

15 And somtyme white bred-crommes;
And many tymes and ofte
Betwene my brestes softe
It wolde lye and rest –
It was propre and prest.

20 Somtyme he wolde gaspe
Whan he sawe a waspe;
A fly or a gnat,
He wold flye at that;
And prytely he wolde pant

25 Whan he saw an ant;
Lord, how he wolde pry
After the butterfly!
Lord, how he wolde hop
After the gressop!

30 And whan I sayd, 'Phyp, Phyp,'
Than he wold lepe and skyp,
And take me by the lyp.
Alas, it wyll me slo,
That Phillyp is gone me fro!

35 *Si in i qui ta tes*
Alas, I was evyll at ease!
De pro fun dis cla ma vi,
Whan I sawe my sparowe dye!

(. . .)

19 *propre and prest* decorous and well-behaved; 24 *prytely* prettily;
29 *gressop* grasshopper; 33 *slo* slay;

For it wold come and go,
40   And fly so to and fro;
      And on me it wolde lepe
      Whan I was aslepe,
      And his fethers shake,
      Wherewith he wolde make
45   Me often for to wake,
      And for to take him in
      Upon my naked skyn,
      God wot, we thought no syn.
      What though he crept so lowe?
50   It was no hurt, I trowe.
      He dyd nothynge, perde,
      But syt upon my kne.
      Phyllyp, though he were nyse,
      In him it was no vyse;
55   Phyllyp had leve to go
      To pyke my lytell too;
      Phillip myght be bolde
      And do what he wolde;
      Phillip wolde seke and take
60   All the flees blake
      That he coulde there espye
      With his wanton eye.

      (. . .)

      . . . Vengeaunce I aske and crye,
      By way of exclamacyon,
65   On all the hole nacyon
      Of cattes wylde and tame;
      God send them sorowe and shame!
      That cat specyally
      That slew so cruelly
70   My lytell prety sparowe
      That I brought up at Carowe.
         O cat of carlyshe kynde,
      The fynde was in thy mynde
      Whan thou my byrde untwynde!
75   I wold thou haddest ben blynde!

---

72 *carlyshe* churlish; 73 *fynde* fiend; 74 *untwynde* destroyed;

The leopardes savage,
The lyons in theyr rage,
Myght catche the in theyr pawes,
And gnawe the in theyr jawes!
80 The serpents of Lybany
Myght stynge the venymously!
The dragones with their tonges
Might poyson thy lyver and longes!
The mantycors of the montaynes
85 Myght fede them on thy braynes!
    Melanchates, that hounde
That plucked Actaeon to the grounde,
Gave hym his mortall wounde,
Chaunged to a dere,
90 The story doth appere –
Was chaunged to an harte:
So thou, foule cat that thou arte,
The selfe same hounde
Myght the confounde,
95 That his owne lorde bote,
Myght byte asondre thy throte!
    Of Inde the gredy grypes
Myght tere out all thy trypes!
Of Arcady the beares
100 Might plucke awaye thyne eares!
The wylde wolfe Lycaon
Byte asondre thy backe-bone!
Of Ethna the brennynge hyll
That day and night brenneth styl,
105 Set in thy tayle a blase
That all the world may gase
And wonder upon the.
From Occyan the great se
Unto the Iles of Orchady,
110 From Tyllbery fery
To the playne of Salysbery!
So trayterously my byrde to kyll
That never ought the evyll wyll!
    Was never byrde in cage
115 More gentle of corage
In doynge his homage

95 *bote* bit; 97 *grypes* griffins; 113 *ought the* bore thee;

Unto his soverayne.
Alas, I say agayne,
Deth hath departed us twayne:
120 The false cat hath the slayne!
Farewell, Phyllyp, adew:
Our Lorde thy soule reskew!
Farewell without restore,
Farewell for evermore!

ROBERT HENRYSON *from* **The Testament of Cresseid**

'O ladyis fair of Troy and Grece, attend
My miserie, quhilk nane may comprehend,
My frivoll fortoun, my infelicitie,
My greit mischeif, quhilk na man can amend.
5   Be war in tyme, approchis neir the end,
And in your mynd ane mirrour mak of me:
As I am now, peradventure that ye
For all your micht may cum to that same end,
Or ellis war, gif ony war may be.

10   'Nocht is your fairnes bot ane faiding flour,
Nocht is your famous laud and hie honour
Bot wind inflat in uther mennis eiris;
Your roising reid to rotting sall retour;
Exempill mak of me in your memour,
15   Quhilk of sic thingis wofull witnes beiris.
All welth in eird, away as wind it weiris;
Be war thairfoir, approchis neir the hour:
Fortoun is fikkill quhen scho beginnis and steiris!'

Thus chydand with hir drerie destenye,
20   Weiping scho woik the nicht fra end to end;
Bot all in vane – hir dule, hir cairfull cry,
Micht not remeid nor yit hir murning mend.

119 *departed* separated

2 *quhilk* which; 3 *frivoll* fickle; 9 *war* worse; 12 *inflat* puffed; 13 *roising* rosy;
14 *memour* memory; 15 *sic* such; 16 *weiris* passes away; 18 *steiris* gets moving;
19 *drerie* miserable; 20 *woik* stayed awake; 21 *dule* grief; 22 *remeid* bring relief;
mend provide a remedy;

Ane lipper lady rais and till hir wend,
And said: 'Quhy spurnis thow aganis the wall
25 To sla thyself and mend nathing at all?

'Sen thy weiping dowbillis bot thy wo,
I counsall the mak vertew of ane neid;
Go leir to clap thy clapper to and fro,
And leif efter the law of lipper leid.'
30 Thair was na buit, bot furth with thame scho yeid
Fra place to place, quhill cauld and hounger sair
Compellit hir to be ane rank beggair.

That samin tyme, of Troy the garnisoun,
Quhilk had to chiftane worthie Troylus,
35 Throw jeopardie of weir had strikken doun
Knichtis of Grece in number mervellous;
With greit tryumphe and laude victorious
Agane to Troy richt royallie thay raid
The way quhair Cresseid with the lipper baid.

40 Seing that companie, all with ane stevin
Thay gaif ane cry, and schuik coppis gude speid;
Said: 'Worthie lordis, for Goddis lufe of hevin,
To us lipper part of your almous deid!'
Than to thair cry nobill Troylus tuik heid,
45 Having pietie, neir by the place can pas
Quhair Cresseid sat, not witting quhat scho was.

Than upon him scho kest up baith hir ene –
And with ane blenk it come into his thocht
That he sumtime hir face befoir had sene.
50 Bot scho was in sic plye he knew hir nocht;
Yit than hir luik into his mynd it brocht
The sweit visage and amorous blenking
Of fair Cresseid, sumtyme his awin darling.

23 *lipper* leper; *rais* got up; *wend* went; 24 *spurnis* kick; 25 *sla* slay; 26 *sen* since;
dowbillis doubles; 27 *neid* necessity; 28 *leir* learn; *clapper* (leper's) rattle;
29 *leif* live; *leid* people; 30 *buit* remedy; *yeid* went; 31 *quhill* until;
32 *rank* downright; 33 *samin* same; *garnisoun* garrison; 35 *jeopardie of weir* fortune
of war; 38 *agane* back; *raid* rode; 39 *lipper* lepers; *bait* waited; 40 *ane stevin* one
voice; 41 *schuik* shook; *coppis* bowls; *gude speid* vigorously; 43 *deid* give;
45 *pietie* pity; *can pas* passed; 46 *witting* knowing; 47 *scho* she; *kest* cast; *ene* eyes;
48 *blenk* glance; *come* came; 50 *plye* condition; 52 *blenking* glances;

Na wonder was, suppois in mynd that he
55 Tuik hir figure sa sone – and lo, now quhy:
The idole of ane thing in cace may be
Sa deip imprentit in the fantasy
That it deludis the wittis outwardly,
And sa appeiris in forme and lyke estait
60 Within the mynd as it was figurait.

Ane spark of lufe than till his hart culd spring
And kendlit all his bodie in ane fyre:
With hait fewir, ane sweit and trimbling
Him tuik, quhill he was reddie to expyre;
65 To beir his scheild his breist began to tyre;
Within ane quhyle he changit mony hew,
And nevertheless not ane ane uther knew.

For knichtlie pietie and memoriall
Of fair Cresseid, ane gyrdill can he tak,
70 Ane purs of gold, and mony gay jowall,
And in the skirt of Cresseid doun can swak;
Than raid away and not ane word he spak,
Pensive in hart, quhill he come to the toun,
And for greit cair oftsyis almaist fell doun.

75 The lipper folk to Cresseid than can draw
To se the equall distributioun
Of the almous, bot quhen the gold thay saw,
Ilkane to uther prevelie can roun,
And said; 'Yone lord hes mair affectioun,
80 However it be, unto yone lazarous
Than to us all; we knaw be his almous.'

54–5 'It was no wonder if he conceived her image so quickly in his mind – and see
now why'; 56 *idole* image; *in cace* by chance; 57 *fantasy* imagination;
58 *wittis* senses; 59 *lyke estait* similar state; 60 'As it was shaped within the mind';
61 *culd spring* sprang; 62 *kendlit* kindled; 63 *hait* hot; *fewir* fever; *sweit* sweat;
trimbling trembling; 64 *quhill* until; 66 *ane quhyle* a short time; *he changit mony
hewe* his colour kept on changing; 67 *not ane ane uther knew* neither recognised the
other; 68 *pietie* pity; *memoriall* remembrance; 69 *gyrdill* belt; *can he tak* he took;
70 *jowall* jewel; 71 *can swak* flung; 73 *quhill* while; 74 *oftsyis* often; 75 *can draw*
drew near; 78 'each began to whisper secretly to the other'; 80 *however it be* for
whatever reason; *lazarous* leper; 81 *knaw* know;

'Quhat lord is yone,' quod scho, 'have ye na feill,
Hes done to us so greit humanitie?'
'Yes,' quod a lipper man, 'I knaw him weill;
85   Schir Troylus it is, gentill and fre.'
Quhen Cresseid understude that it was he,
Stiffer than steill thair stert ane bitter stound
Throwout hir hart, and fell doun to the ground.

Quhen scho ovircome, with siching sair and sad,
90   With mony cairfull cry and cald ochane:
'Now is my breist with stormie stoundis stad,
Wrappit in wo, ane wretch full will of wane!'
Than swounit scho oft or scho culd refrane,
And ever in hir swouning cryit scho thus;
95   'O fals Cresseid and trew knicht Troylus!

'Thy lufe, thy lawtie, and thy gentilnes
I countit small in my prosperitie,
Sa elevait I was in wantones,
And clam upon the fickill quheill sa hie.
100   All faith and lufe I promissit to the
Was in the self fickill and frivolous:
O fals Cresseid and trew knicht Troilus!

'For lufe of me thow keipt gude continence,
Honest and chaist in conversatioun;
105   Of all wemen protectour and defence
Thou was, and helpit thair opinioun;
My mynd in fleschelie foull affectioun
Was inclynit to lustis lecherous:
Fy, fals Cresseid! O trew knicht Troylus!

110   'Lovers be war and tak gude heid about
Quhome that ye lufe, for quhome ye suffer paine.
I lat yow wit, thair is richt few thairout

---

82 *scho* she; *feill* idea; 85 *gentill and fre* noble and generous; 87 *stiffer* stronger;
steill steel; *stert* sprang; *stound* pain; 89 *ouircome* revived; *siching* sighing; 90 *cald*
cold, mournful; *ochane* cry of sorrow; 91 *stoundis* pangs; *stad* beset; 92 *will of wane*
bewildered, hopeless; 93 *swounit* swooned; *or scho culd refane* before she ceased;
96 *lawtie* loyalty; 98 *elevait* raised high; 99 *clam* climbed; *quheill* wheel [of
Fortune]; *hie* high; 101 *the self* itself; 103 *continence* self-restraint;
104 *chaist* honourable; *conversatioun* conduct; 106 *opinioun* reputation; 112 *I lat
yow wit* I'd have you know; *thairout* in the world;

Quhome ye may traist to have trew lufe agane;
Preif quhen ye will, your labour is in vaine.
115 Thairfoir I reid ye tak thame as ye find,
For thay ar sad as widdercok in wind.

'Becaus I knaw the greit unstabilnes,
Brukkill as glas, into my self, I say,
Traisting in uther als greit unfaithfulnes,
120 Als unconstant, and als untrew of fay –
Thocht sum be trew, I wait richt few ar thay;
Quha findis treuth, lat him his lady ruse!
Nane but myself as now I will accuse.'

Quhen this was said, with paper scho sat doun,
125 And on this maneir maid hir testament:
'Heir I beteiche my corps and carioun
With wormis and with taidis to be rent;
My cop and clapper, and myne ornament,
And all my gold the lipper folk sall have
130 Quhen I am deid, to burie me in grave.

'This royall ring set with this rubie reid,
Quhilk Troylus in drowrie to me send,
To him agane I leif it quhen I am deid,
To mak my cairfull deid unto him kend.
135 Thus I conclude schortlie, and mak ane end:
My spreit I leif to Diane, quhair scho dwellis,
To walk with hir in waist woddis and wellis.

'O Diomeid, thou hes baith broche and belt
Quhilk Troylus gave me in takning
140 Of his trew lufe!' and with that word scho swelt.
And sone ane lipper man tuik of the ring,
Syne buryt hir withouttin tarying;
To Troylus furthwith the ring he bair,
And of Cresseid the deith he can declair.

113 *traist* trust; 114 *preif* try; 115 *reid* advise; 116 *sad* steadfast;
widdercok weathercock; 117 *knaw* know; 118 *brukkill* brittle; *into my self, I say*
'which I find by experience'; 119 *traisting* expecting; 120 *als* as; *fay* faith;
121 *thocht* though; *wait* know; 122 *ruse* praise; 126 *beteiche* commit; *carioun* corpse;
127 *taidis* toads; *rent* devoured; 132 *quhilk* which; *in drowrie* as a love-token;
134 *cairfull deid* sorrowful death; *kend* known; 136 *spreit* spirit; *Diane* Diana;
137 *waist* wild; *wellis* springs; 139 *in takning* as a token; 140 *swelt* died; 141 *tuik of*
took off; 142 *syne* then; *buryt hir* buried her; 143 *bair* bore; 144 *can declair* told of;

145 Quhen he had hard hir greit infirmitie,
    Hir legacie and lamentatioun,
    And how scho endit in sic povertie,
    He swelt for wo and fell doun in ane swoun;
    For greit sorrow his hart to brist was boun;
150 Siching full sadlie, said, 'I can no moir –
    Scho was untrew and wo is me thairfoir.'

    Sum said he maid ane tomb of merbell gray,
    And wrait hir name and superscriptioun,
    And laid it on hir grave quhair that scho lay,
155 In goldin letteris, conteining this ressoun:
    'Lo, fair ladyis! Cresseid of Troyis toun,
    Sumtyme countit the flour of womanheid,
    Under this stane, lait lipper, lyis deid.'

    Now, worthie wemen, in this ballet schort,
160 Maid for your worschip and instructioun,
    Of cheritie, I monische and exhort,
    Ming not your lufe with fals deceptioun.
    Beir in your mynd this schort conclusioun
    Of fair Cresseid, as I have said befoir.
165 Sen scho is deid, I speik of hir no moir.

WILLIAM DUNBAR Lament, When He Wes Seik

I that in heill wes and gladnes
Am trublit now with gret seiknes
And feblit with infermité;
Timor mortis conturbat me.

5 Our plesance heir is all vane glory,
This fals warld is bot transitory,
The flesch is brukle, the Fend is sle;
Timor mortis conturbat me.

---

145 *hard* heard; 147 *sic* such; 148 *swelt* swooned; *swoun* faint; 149 *to brist was boun* was ready to burst; 150 *I can no moir* there is no more I can do; 152 *merbell* marble; 153 *wrait* wrote; *superscriptioun* inscription; 155 *ressoun* statement; 158 *lait lipper* former leper; 159 *ballet* poem; 160 *worschip* honour; 161 *of cheritie* for the love of God; *monische* admonish; 162 *ming* mingle; 165 *sen* since

1 *heill* health; 4 'The fear of death confounds me'; 7 *brukle* brittle, fragile; *sle* sly;

The stait of man dois change and vary,
Now sound, now seik, now blith, now sary,
Now dansand mery, now like to dee;
Timor mortis conturbat me.

No stait in erd heir standis sickir;
As with the wynd wavis the wickir
Wavis this warldis vanité;
Timor mortis conturbat me.

On to the ded gois all estatis,
Princis, prelotis and potestatis,
Baith riche and pur of al degré;
Timor mortis conturbat me.

He takis the knychtis in to feild
Anarmyt undir helme and scheild,
Victour he is at all mellé;
Timor mortis conturbat me.

That strang unmercifull tyrand
Takis on the moderis breist sowkand
The bab full of benignité;
Timor mortis conturbat me.

He takis the campion in the stour,
The capitane closit in the tour,
The lady in bour full of bewté;
Timor mortis conturbat me.

He sparis no lord for his piscence,
Na clerk for his intelligence;
His awfull strak may no man fle;
Timor mortis conturbat me.

10 *sary* sorrowful; 11 *like* likely; 13 *erd* earth; *sickir* secure; 14 *wickir* willow
branch; 17 *the ded* death; 18 *potestatis* rulers; 21 *in to* in (the); 22 *anarmyt* armed;
23 *mellé* combat, skirmish; 26 *sowkand* sucking; 27 *benignité* graciousness,
meekness; 29 *campion* champion; *stour* battle; 30 *closit* enclosed (for defence);
31 *bour* bower; 33 *piscence* puissance, power; 34 *clerk* scholar; 35 *strak* stroke;

Art-magicianis and astrologgis,
Rethoris, logicianis and theologgis –
Thame helpis no conclusionis sle;
40 *Timor mortis conturbat me.*

In medicyne the most practicianis,
Lechis, surrigianis and phisicianis,
Thame self fra ded may not supplé;
Timor mortis conturbat me.

45 I se that makaris amang the laif
Playis heir ther pageant, syne gois to graif;
Sparit is nought ther faculté;
Timor mortis conturbat me.

He has done petuously devour
50 The noble Chaucer, of makaris flour,
The Monk of Bery, and Gower, all thre;
Timor mortis conturbat me.

The gude Syr Hew of Eglintoun
And eik Heryot, and Wyntoun
55 He has tane out of this cuntré;
Timor mortis conturbat me.

That scorpion fell has done infek
Maister Johne Clerk and James Afflek
Fra balat making and trigidé;
60 *Timor mortis conturbat me.*

Holland and Barbour he has berevit;
Allace, that he nought with us levit
Schir Mungo Lokert of the Le;
Timor mortis conturbat me.

39 'No subtle conclusions can help them'; 41 *most* greatest; 42 *lechis* physicians;
43 *supplé* deliver; 45 *laif* rest; 46 *pageant* pageant (of life); *syne* then; *graif* grave;
47 *faculté* profession; 50 *of makaris flour* the flower of makers (poets); 55 *cuntré*
country (i.e. Scotland); 57 *has done infek* infected; 59 *balat* song; *trigidé*
tragedy-writing; 61 *berevit* taken away by force; 62 *allace* alas; 63 *Schir* Sir;

Clerk of Tranent eik he has tane
That maid the anteris of Gawane;
Schir Gilbert Hay endit has he;
Timor mortis conturbat me.

He has Blind Hary and Sandy Traill
70   Slane with his schour of mortall haill
Quhilk Patrik Johnestoun mycht nought fle;
Timor mortis conturbat me.

He has reft Merseir his endite
That did in luf so lifly write,
75   So schort, so quyk, of sentence hie;
Timor mortis conturbat me.

He has tane Roull of Aberdene
And gentill Roull of Corstorphin –
Two bettir fallowis did no man se;
80   *Timor mortis conturbat me.*

In Dunfermelyne he has done roune
With Maister Robert Henrisoun;
Schir Johne the Ros enbrast has he;
Timor mortis conturbat me.

85   And he has now tane last of aw
Gud gentill Stobo and Quintyne Schaw
Of quham all wichtis has peté;
Timor mortis conturbat me.

Gud Maister Walter Kennedy
90   In poynt of dede lyis veraly –
Gret reuth it wer that so suld be;
Timor mortis conturbat me.

65 *eik* too; 66 *anteris* adventures; 70 *schour* shower; 71 *quhilk* which;
73 *reft* bereft; *endite* (power of) writing; 74 *lifly* vividly; 75 *quyk* vigorous; *of
sentence hie* of great pith; 79 *fallowis* fellows; 81 *done roun* whispered, had a
conversation; 83 *enbrast* embraced; 85 *aw* all; 87 'whom all men regret';
91 *reuth* pity; *so suld be* it should be so;

Sen he has all my brether tane
He will naught lat me lif alane;
On forse I man his nyxt pray be;
Timor mortis conturbat me.

Sen for the ded remeid is none,
Best is that we for dede dispone,
Eftir our deid that lif may we;
Timor mortis conturbat me.

WILLIAM DUNBAR

Done is a battell on the dragon blak;
Our campioun Chryst confoundit hes his force:
The yettis of hell ar brokin with a crak,
The signe triumphall rasit is of the croce,
The divillis trymmillis with hiddous voce,
The saulis ar borrowit and to the bliss can go,
Chryst with his blud our ransonis dois indoce:
Surrexit Dominus de sepulchro.

Dungin is the deidly dragon Lucifer,
The crewall serpent with the mortall stang,
The auld kene tegir with his teith on char
Quhilk in a wait hes lyne for us so lang
Thinking to grip us in his clowis strang;
The mercifull lord wald nocht that it wer so,
He maid him for to felye of that fang:
Surrexit Dominus de sepulchro.

He for our saik that sufferit to be slane
And lyk a lamb in sacrifice wes dicht
Is lyk a lyone rissin up agane
And as a gyane raxit him on hicht;

---

93 *sen* since; *brether* brothers, brethren; 94 *alane* alone; 95 'Of necessity I must be his next prey'; 97 *remeid* remedy; 98 *dispone* make ready; 99 *eftir* after

2 *campioun* champion; 3 *yettis* gates; 4 *croce* cross; 5 *divillis trymmillis* devils tremble; 6 *saulis* souls; *borrowit* ransomed; 7 *dois indoce* endorses; 8 'The Lord is risen from the tomb'; 9 *Dungin* struck down; 10 *stang* sting; 11 'the fierce old tiger with his teeth ajar'; 15 *to felye of that fang* to fall short of that prey; 18 *dicht* arrayed; 20 'and like a giant has stretched himself on high';

Sprungin is Aurora radius and bricht,
On loft is gone the glorius Appollo,
The blisfull day depairtit fro the nycht:
Surrexit Dominus de sepulchro.

25   The grit victour agane is rissin on hicht
That for our querrell to the deth wes woundit;
The sone that wox all paill now schynis bricht,
And dirknes clerit, our fayth is now refoundit;
The knell of mercy fra the hevin is soundit,
30   The Cristin ar deliverit of thair wo,
The Jowis and thair errour ar confoundit:
Surrexit Dominus de sepulchro.

The fo is chasit, the battell is done ceis,
The presone brokin, the jevellouris fleit and flemit;
35   The weir is gon, confermit is the peis,
The fetteris lowsit and the dungeoun temit,
The ransoun maid, the presoneris redemit;
The feild is win, ourcumin is the fo,
Dispulit of the tresur that he yemit:
40   *Surrexit Dominus de sepulchro.*

WILLIAM DUNBAR

In to thir dirk and drublie dayis
Quhone sabill all the hevin arrayis,
    With mystie vapouris, cluddis and skyis
    Nature all curage me denyis
5   Off sangis, ballattis and of playis.

21 *sprungin* risen; *Aurora* [the Dawn]; *radius* radiant; 22 *on loft* into the heavens;
26 *querrell* cause; 27 *sone* sun; *wox* grew; 28 *clerit* cleared; 31 *Jowis* Jews; 33 *done ceis* brought to an end; 34 *jevellouris* jailers; *fleit and flemit* scared away;
35 *weir* war; 36 *lowsit* loosed; *temit* emptied; 38 *ourcomin* overcome;
39 *dispulit* despoiled; *yemit* guarded

1 *In to thir* in these; *drublie* clouded; 2 *quhone* when; *sabill* sable, black;
arrayis cloaks; 3 *cluddis* clouds; 4 *curage . . . of* heart for;

Quhone that the nycht dois lenthin houris
With wind, with haill and havy schouris,
   My dulé spreit dois lurk for schoir;
   My hairt for langour dois forloir
10   For laik of Symmer with his flouris.

I walk, I turne, sleip may I nocht,
I vexit am with havie thocht;
   This warld all ovir I cast about,
   And ay the mair I am in dout
15   The mair that I remeid have socht.

I am assayit on everie syde;
Despair sayis, 'Ay in tyme provyde
   And get sum thing quhairon to leif,
   Or with grit trouble and mischeif
20   Thow sall in to this court abyd.'

Than Patience sayis, 'Be not agast;
Hald Hoip and Treuthe within the fast
   And lat Fortoun wirk furthe hir rage,
   Quhome that no rasoun may assuage
25   Quhill that hir glas be run and past.'

And Prudence in my eir sayis ay,
'Quhy wald thow hald that will away?
   Or craif that thow may have mo space,
   Thow tending to ane uther place
30   A journay going everie day?'

And than sayis Age, 'My freind, cum neir
And be not strange, I the requeir;
   Cum brodir, by the hand me tak;
   Remember thow hes compt to mak
35   Off all thi tyme thow spendit heir.'

---

6 *lenthin* length; 8 *dulé* doleful; *lurk for schoir* cower under the threat; 9 *dois forlore* is lost, becomes desolate; 14 *mair* more; 15 *remeid* remedy; 18 *quhairon* on which; *leif* live; 19 *mischeif* hardship; 20 *in to* in; *court* the royal court; 22 *the* thee; 24 *quhome* whom; 25 *quhill* until; *glass* i.e. Time's glass; 27 *that will away* what wishes to be off; 28 'or crave what you cannot keep for any length of time'; 30 *journay* journey; 32 *I the requeir* I beg you; 34 *compt* an account;

Syne Deid castis upe his yettis wyd
Saying, 'Thir oppin sall the abyd;
   Albeid that thow wer never sa stout,
   Undir this lyntall sall thow lowt –
40 Thair is nane uther way besyde.'

For feir of this all day I drowp:
No gold in kist nor wyne in cowp,
   No ladeis bewtie nor luiffis blys
   May lat me to remember this,
45 How glaid that ever I dyne or sowp.

Yit quhone the nycht begynnis to schort
It dois my spreit sum pairt confort
   Off thocht oppressit with the schowris;
   Cum lustie Symmer with thi flowris,
50 That I may leif in sum disport.

1515   GAVIN DOUGLAS / VIRGIL *from* The Aeneid

from Book I [Aeolus Looses the Winds]

Be this was said a grondyn dart leit he glide
And persit the boss hill as the braid syde
Furth at the ilke port wyndis brade in a rout
And with a quhirl blew all the erth about
5 Thai ombeset the seys bustuusly
Quhil fra the deip til every cost fast by
The huge wallis weltris apon hie,
Rollit at anys with storm of wyndis thre
Eurus, Nothus, and the wynd Affricus
10 Quhilkis est, south, and west wyndis hait with us.

---

36 'At which Death casts open his wide gates'; 37 'saying "These will stay open for you"'; 38 *stout* strong, brave; 39 *lowt* stoop; 42 *kist* chest; *coup* wine-cup; 43 *luiffis blys* love's joy; 44 *lat* prevent; 45 *sowp* sup; 46 *quhone* when; 50 *disport* merriment

1 *be* when; *grondyn* sharpened; 2 *boss* hollow; *braid* broad; 3 *ilke* same; *brade* burst forth; 5 *ombeset* beset; *bustuusly* violently; 7 *wallis weltris* waves roll; 8 *anys* once; 10 *hait* are called;

Sone efter this of men the clamour rayss,
The takillis, graslis, cabillis can fret and frays
Swith the clowdis hevyn, son, and days lycht
Hyd and byreft furth of the Troianys sycht.

15 Dyrknes as nycht beset the seys about
The firmament gan rummyling rair and rout
The skyis oft lychtnyt with fyry levin
And, schortly bath ayr, sey, and hevin
And every thing mannasit the men to de,

20 Schawand the ded present tofor that e.

from The Proloug of the Sevynt Buik of Eneados

As bryght Phebus, scheyn soverane hevynnys e,
The opposit held of hys chymmys hie,
Cleir schynand bemys, and goldyn symmyris hew,
In laton cullour alteryng haill of new,

5 Kythyng no syng of heyt be hys vissage,
So neir approchit he his wyntir stage;
Reddy he was to entyr the thrid morn
In clowdy skyis undre Capricorn;
All thocht he be the hart and lamp of hevyn,

10 Forfeblit wolx hys lemand gylty levyn,
Throu the declynyng of hys large round speir.
The frosty regioun ryngis of the yer,
The tyme and sesson bittir, cald and paill,
Tha schort days that clerkis clepe brumaill,

15 Quhen brym blastis of the northyn art
Ourquhelmyt had Neptunus in his cart,
And all to-schaik the levis of the treis,
The rageand storm ourweltrand wally seys.
Ryveris ran reid on spait with watir browne,

20 And burnys hurlys all thar bankis downe,
And landbrist rumland rudely with sik beir,
So lowd ne rumyst wild lyoun or ber;

---

12 *takillis* tackle, rigging; *graslis* harsh, grating noise; *cabillis* cables; *can fret* begin to
fret; 13 *Swith* swiftly; 17 *levin* lightning; 19 *mannasit* menaced; 20 *e* eye

1 *e* eye; 2 *chymmys* mansions; 3 *symmyris* summer's; 4 *laton* copper; *haill of new*
entirely; 5 *Kythyng no syng* showing no sign; 9 *all thocht* although;
10 *Forfeblit* enfeebled; *wolx* waxed; *lemand gylty levyn* gleaming golden light;
11 *speir* sphere; 12 *ryngis* reigns; 14 *brumaill* wintry; 15 *brym* fierce; *art* direction;
18 *ourweltrand* tossing about; *wally seys* stormy seas; 19 *reid* furiously;
20 *burnys* burns; 21 *landbrist rumland* surf roaring; *sik beir* such noise; 22 *rumyst* roared;

Fludis monstreis, sik as meirswyne or quhalis,
Fro the tempest law in the deip devalis.

25   Mars occident retrograde in his speir,
Provocand stryfe, regnyt as lord that yer;
Rany Oryon with his stormy face
Bewavit oft the schipman by hys race;
Frawart Saturn, chill of complexioun,

30   Throu quhais aspect darth and infectioun
Beyn causyt oft, and mortal pestilens,
Went progressyve the greis of his ascens;
And lusty Hebe, Junoys douchtir gay,
Stude spulyeit of hir office and array.

35   The soyl ysowpit into watir wak,
The firmament ourcast with rokis blak,
The grond fadyt, and fawch wolx all the feildis,
Montane toppis slekit with snaw ourheildis;
On raggit rolkis of hard harsk quhyn-stane

40   With frosyn frontis cauld clynty clewis schane.
Bewté was lost, and barrand schew the landis,
With frostis hair ourfret the feldis standis.
Seir bittir bubbis and the schowris snell
Semyt on the sward a symylitude of hell,

45   Reducyng to our mynd, in every sted,
Gousty schaddois of eild and grisly ded.
Thik drumly skuggis dyrknyt so the hevyn,
Dym skyis oft furth warpit feirfull levyn,
Flaggis of fire, and mony felloun flaw,

50   Scharpe soppys of sleit and of the snypand snaw.
The dolly dichis war all donk and wait,
The law vallé flodderit all with spait,
The plane stretis and every hie way
Full of floschis, dubbis, myre and clay.

---

23 *Fludis monstreis* sea-monsters; *meirswyne* porpoises; *quhalis* whales; 24 *law* low; *devalis* descend; 25 *occident* in the west; 28 *Bewavit* blew about; *by hys race* in his course; 29 *Frawart* ill-natured; 30 *quhais* whose; *darth* dearth; 32 *greis* degrees; 34 *spulyeit* despoiled; 35 *ysowpit* soaked; *wak* wet; 36 *rokis* clouds; 37 *fawch* yellowy-brown; *wolx* waxed; 38 *slekit* smooth; *ourheildis* are covered; 39 *rolkis* rocks; *quhyn-stane* whinstone; 40 *clynty clewis schane* fissured cliffs shone; 41 *barrand* barren; 42 *hair* hoar; *ourfret* patterned over; 43 *bubbis* squalls; *snell* bitter; 44 *sward* open field; 46 *eild* age; *ded* death; 47 *drumly skuggis* gloomy shadows; 48 *warpit* threw; *levyn* lightning; 49 *Flaggis* flashes; *felloun flaw* fierce blast; 50 *soppys* downpours; *snypand* biting; 51 *dolly* dismal; *donk* damp; 52 *flodderit* flooded; 54 *floschis* pools; *dubbis* puddles;

55   Laggerit leyis wallowit farnys schew,
Browne muris kythit thar wysnyt mossy hew,
Bank, bra and boddum blanchit wolx and bar.
For gurl weddir growit bestis hair.
The wynd maid waif the red wed on the dyke,
60   Bedowyn in donkis deip was every sike.
Our craggis and the front of rochis seir
Hang gret ische-schouchlis lang as ony speir.
The grond stud barrant, widderit, dosk or gray,
Herbis, flowris and gersis wallowyt away.
45   Woddis, forrestis, with nakyt bewis blowt,
Stude stripyt of thar weid in every howt.
So bustuusly Boreas his bugill blew,
The deyr full dern doun in the dalis drew;
Smale byrdis, flokkand throu thik ronys thrang,
70   In chyrmyng and with cheping changit thar sang,
Sekand hidlis and hyrnys thame to hyde
Fra feirfull thuddis of the tempestuus tyde;
The watir lynnys rowtis, and every lynd
Quhislit and brayt of the swouchand wynd.
75   Puyr lauboraris and bissy husband men
Went wait and wery draglit in the fen.
The silly scheip and thar litil hyrd gromys
Lurkis undre le of bankis, woddis and bromys;
And other dantit grettar bestiall,
80   Within thar stabillis sesyt into stall,
Sik as mulis, horssis, oxin and ky,
Fed tuskyt barys and fat swyne in sty,
Sustenyt war by mannys governance
On hervist and on symmeris purvyance.

(1553)

55 'meadows covered in mire are seen with withered ferns'; 56 *kythit* showed;
wysnyt wizened; 57 *boddum* valley; *blanchit* bleached; 58 *gurl* rough;
59 *waif* wave; 60 *bedowyn* immersed; *sike* stream; 61 *Our* over; *seir* many
62 *ische-schouchlis* icicles; 64 *gersis* grasses; *wallowyt* withered; 65 *bewis blowt*
bare boughs; 66 *weid* wood; *howt* copse; 68 *deyr* deer; *dern* timidly;
69 *ronys* brambles; *thrang* thronged; 70 *chyrmyng* chirping; 71 *hidlis and hyrnys*
hiding-places and nooks; 72 *thuddis* blasts; 73 *watir lynnys rowtis* waterfalls roar;
lynd lime-tree; 74 *brayt* roared; *swouchand* rushing; 76 *wait* wet;
draglit bedraggled; 77 *sheip* shepherds; *hyrd gromys* shepherd-lads; 78 *le* lee;
bromys broom; 79 *dantit* tamed; *grettar* greater; 80 *sesyt* settled; 81 *sik as* such as;
ky kine; 82 *barys* boars; 84 *symmeris* summer's

ANONYMOUS [The Corpus Christi Carol]

> *Lully, lulley; lully, lulley;*
> *The fawcon hath born my mak away.*

He bare hym up, he bare hym down;
He bare hym into an orchard brown.

5   In that orchard ther was an hall,
That was hangid with purpill and pall.

And in that hall ther was a bede;
Hit was hangid with gold so rede.

And yn that bed ther lythe a knyght,
10   His wowndes bledyng day and nyght.

By that bedes side ther kneleth a may,
And she wepeth both nyght and day.

And by that beddes side ther stondith a ston,
'Corpus Christi' wretyn theron.

(1908)

ANONYMOUS

Farewell, this world! I take my leve for evere;
    I am arested to apere at Goddes face.
O myghtyfull God, thou knowest that I had levere
    Than all this world to have oone houre space
5   To make asythe for all my grete trespace.
My hert, alas, is brokyne for that sorowe –
Som be this day that shall not be tomorow!

---

2 *born* carried; *mak* mate; 4 *brown* dark/shady; 6 *purpill and pall* purple cloth and
costly fabric; 7 *bede* [four-poster] bed; 9 *lythe* lies; 10 *wowndes* wounds;
11 *may* maiden; 13 *ston* altar-stone/sepulchre; *Corpus Christi* 'Body of Christ'

2 *at* before; 3 *levere* rather; 5 *asythe* amends; 7 'some are here today that shall not
be here tomorow';

This lyfe, I see, is but a cheyré feyre;
    All thyngis passene and so most I algate.
10 Today I sat full ryall in a cheyere,
    Tyll sotell Deth knokyd at my gate,
    And onavysed he seyd to me, 'Chek-mate!'
  Lo, how sotell he maketh a devors!
  And, wormys to fede, he hath here leyd my cors.

15 Speke softe, ye folk, for I am leyd aslepe!
    I have my dreme – in trust is moche treson.
  Fram dethes hold feyne wold I make a lepe,
    But my wysdom is turnyd into feble resoun:
    I see this worldis joye lastith but a season –
20 Wold to God I had remembyrd me beforne!
  I sey no more, but be ware of ane horne!

  This febyll world, so fals and so unstable,
    Promoteth his lovers for a lytell while,
  But at the last he yeveth hem a bable
25   When his peynted trowth is torned into gile.
    Experyence cawsith me the trowth to compile,
  Thynkyng this, to late, alas, that I began,
  For foly and hope disseyveth many a man.

  Farewell, my frendis! the tide abidith no man:
30   I moste departe hens, and so shall ye.
  But in this passage, the beste song that I can
    Is *Requiem eternam* – I pray God grant it me!
    Whan I have endid all myn adversité,
  Graunte me in Paradise to have a mancyon,
35 That shede his blode for my redempcion.

                            (1908)

8 *cheyré feyre* [fair held in cherry-orchards during the brief season]; 9 *algate* whatever I do; 10 *ryall* royal; *cheyere* throne; 11 *sotell* subtle, insidious; 12 *onavysed* without warning; 13 *devors* divorce [between soul and body]; 14 *cors* corpse; 17 *hold* stronghold; 21 *horne* horn [trumpet-blast]; 24 *yeveth* gives; *bable* bauble; 25 *trowth* truth; 26 *compile* formulate; 28 *foly* folly; 32 *Requiem eternam* 'Eternal rest (grant them, O Lord)'; 35 *that* he who

ANONYMOUS

Draw me nere, draw me nere,
Draw me nere, ye joly juggelere!

Here beside dwelleth
  A riche barons doughter;
5 She wold have no man
    That for her love had sought her.
      So nise she was.

She wold have no man
  That was made of molde,
10 But if he had a mouth of gold
    To kisse her whan she wold.
      So dangerus she was.

There of hard a joly juggeler
  That laid was on the grene,
15 And at this ladys wordës
    Iwis he had gret tene.
      An angred he was.

He juggeled to him a well good stede
  Of an old hors bone,
20 A sadill and a bridill both,
    And set himself thereon.
      A juggeler he was.

He priked and praunsëd both
  Beffore that lady's gate;
25 She wend he had ben an angell
    Was come for her sake.
      A prikker he was.

2 *juggelere* magician/conjuror; 5 *wold* would; 7 *nise* coy; 9 *molde* earth [mortal];
12 *dangerus* haughty; 13 *hard* heard; 16 *Iwis* indeed; *tene* vexation; 23 *priked* rode;
25 *wend* thought;

He priked and praunsëd
  Before that lady's bowr;
30 She wend he had ben an angel
  Come from heven towre.
    A praunser he was.

Four and twenty knightës
  Lade him into the hall,
35 And as many squirës
  His hors to the stall,
    And gaff him mete.

They gaff him ottës
  And also hay;
40 He was an old shrew
  And held his hed away.
    He wold not ete.

The day began to passe,
  The night began to come,
45 To bed was brought
  The fair jentell woman,
    And the juggeler also.

The night began to passe,
  The day began to springe,
50 All the birdës of her bowr
  They began to singe,
    And the cokoo also.

'Where be ye, my mery maidens,
  That ye come not me to?
55 The joly windows of my bowr
  Look that you undo,
    That I may see!

'For I have in mine armës
  A duke or elles an erle.'
60 But whan she lookëd him upon,
  He was a blere-eyed chorle.
    'Alas!' she said.

31 *heven towre* tower of Heaven; 56 *undo* open; 61 *chorle* churl;

She lade him to an hill,
   And hangëd shuld he be.
He juggeled himself to a mele-pok;
   The dust fell in her eye;
      Begiled she was.

God and our Lady
   And swetë Seint Johan
Send every giglot of this town
   Such another leman,
      Even as he was.

(1903)

1520 ANONYMOUS

Westron wynde when wyll thow blow
The smalle rayne downe can rayne –
Cryst, yf my love wer in my armys
And I in my bed agayne!

(1790)

1523 JOHN SKELTON *from* A Goodly Garlande or Chapelet of Laurell

[The Garden of the Muses: Iopas' Song]

There Cintheus sat twynklyng upon his harpe stringis;
And Iopas his instrument did avaunce,
The poemis and storis auncient inbryngis
Of Athlas astrology, and many noble thyngis,
Of wandryng of the mone, the course of the sun,
Of men and of bestis, and whereof they begone,

---

65 *mele-pok* meal-bag; 70 *giglot* wench/strumpet; 71 *leman* lover

2 *can* does

3 *inbryngis* performed;

What thynge occasionyd the showris of rayne,
Of fyre elementar in his supreme spere,
And of that pole artike whiche doth remayne
10 Behynde the taile of Ursa so clere;
Of Pliades he prechid with ther drowsy chere,
Immoysturid with mislyng and ay droppyng dry,
And where the two Trions a man shold aspy,

And of the winter days that hy them so fast,
15 And of the wynter nyghtes that tary so longe,
And of the somer days so longe that doth last,
And of their shorte nyghtes; he browght in his songe
How wronge was no ryght, and ryght was no wronge;
There was counteryng of carollis in meter and verse
20 So many, that longe it were to reherse.

To Maystres Isabell Pennell

By Saynt Mary, my lady,
Your mammy and your dady
Brought forth a godely babi!
    My mayden Isabell,
5   Reflaring rosabell,
The flagrant camamell;
    The ruddy rosary,
The soverayne rosemary,
The praty strawbery;
10   The columbyne, the nepte,
The jeloffer well set,
The propre vyolet;
    Enuwyd, your colowre
Is lyke the dasy flowre
15 After the Aprill showre;
    Sterre of the morow gray,
The blossom on the spray,
The fresshest flowre of May!

11 *chere* countenance; 12 *mislyng* drizzle; 19 *counteryng* improvisation

5 *Reflaring* odorous; 6 *camamell* camomile; 7 *rosay* rose-tree; 10 *nepte* catmint;
11 *jeloffer* gillyflower; 13 *Enuwyd* revived, freshened

Maydenly demure,
20 Of womanhode the lure;
Wherfore, I make you sure,
        It were an hevenly helth,
        It were an endeles welth,
        A lyfe for God hymselfe,
25   To here this nightingale
        Amonge the byrdes smale,
        Warbelynge in the vale:
        Dug, dug, jug, jug,
        Good yere and good luk,
30 With chuk, chuk, chuk, chuk.

JOHN SKELTON *from* Speke Parott

[Parrot's Complaint]

GALATHEA

Nowe, Parott, my swete byrde, speke owte yet ons agayn,
Sette asyde all sophysms, and speke now trew and playne.

PAROTTE

So many morall maters, and so lytell usyd;
So myche newe makyng, and so madd tyme spente;
5   So myche translacion into Englyshe confused;
So myche nobyll prechyng, and so lytell amendment;
So myche consultacion, almoste to none entente;
So myche provision, and so lytell wytte at nede –
Syns Dewcalyons flodde there can no clerkes rede.

10   So lytyll dyscressyon, and so myche reasonyng;
So myche hardy-dardy, and so lytell manlynes;
So prodigall expence, and so shamfull reconyng;
So gorgyous garmentes, and so myche wrechydnese,
So myche portlye pride, with pursys penyles;
15   So myche spente before, and so myche unpayd behynde –
Syns Dewcalyons flodde there can no clerkes fynde.

8 *provision* [of place-men for benefices]; 11 *hardy-dardy* rash daring;

So myche forcastyng, and so farre an after-dele;

So myche poletyke pratyng, and so lytell stondythe in stede;
So lytell secretnese, and so myche grete councell;
20 So manye bolde barons, there hertes as dull as lede;
So many nobyll bodyes, undyr on dawys hedd;
So royall a kyng, as reynythe uppon us all –
Syns Dewcalions flodde, was nevyr sene nor shall.

So many complayntes, and so smalle redresse;
25 So myche callyng on, and so smalle takyng hede;
So myche losse of merchaundyse, and so remedyles;
So lytell care for the comynweall, and so myche nede;
So myche dowghtfull daunger, and so lytell drede;
So myche pride of prelattes, so cruell and so kene –
30 Syns Dewcalyons flodde, I trowe, was nevyr sene.

So many thevys hangyd, and thevys neverthelesse;
So myche presonment, for matyrs not worth a hawe;
So myche papers weryng for ryghte a smalle exesse;
So myche pelory pajauntes undyr colowur of good lawe;
35 So myche towrnyng on the cooke-stole for every guy-gaw;
So myche mokkyshe makyng of statutes of array –
Syns Dewcalyons flodde was nevyr, I dar sey.

So braynles calvys hedes, so many shepis taylys;
So bolde a braggyng bocher, and flesshe sold so dere;
40 So many plucte partryches, and so fatte quaylles;
So mangye a mastyfe curre, the grete greyhoundes pere;
So bygge a bulke of brow-auntleres cabagyd that yere;
So many swannes dede, and so small revell –
Syns Dewcalyons flodde, I trow, no man can tell.

45 So many trusys takyn, and so lytyll perfyte trowthe;
So myche bely-joye, and so wastefull banketyng;
So pynchyng and sparyng, and so lytell profyte growth;
So many howgye howsys byldyng, and so small howse-holdyng;

---

17 *after-dele* consequence; 21 *dawys hedde* fool's head; 28 *dowghtfull* fearful;
32 *worth a hawe* worth a thing; 34 *pelory pajauntes* pillory-pageants; 35 *cooke-stole*
cucking stool; 36 *mokkyshe* scorneful, skittish; 39 *bocher* [Cardinal Wolsey was the
son of a butcher]; 42 *browe-auntleres* cuckold's horns; *cabagyd* grown;
45 *trusys* truces; 46 *bely-joye* gluttony; 48 *howgye howsys* huge houses;

Suche statutes apon diettes, suche pyllyng and pollyng –
50   So ys all thyng wrowghte wylfully withowte reson and skylle.
Syns Dewcalyons flodde the world was never so yll.

So many vacabondes, so many beggers bolde,
So myche decay of monesteries and relygious places;
So hote hatered agaynste the Chyrche, and cheryte so colde;
55   So myche of my lordes grace, and in hym no grace ys;
So many holow hartes, and so dowbyll faces;
So myche sayntuary brekyng, and prevylegidde barryd –
Syns Dewcalyons flodde was nevyr sene nor lyerd.

So myche raggyd ryghte of a rammes horne;
60   So rygorous revelyng, in a prelate specially;
So bold and so braggyng, and was so baselye borne;
So lordlye of hys lokes, and so dysdayneslye;
So fatte a magott, bred of a flesshe-flye;
Was nevyr suche a fylty gorgon, nor suche an epycure,
65   Syn Dewcalyons flodde, I make the faste and sure.

So myche prevye wachyng in cold wynters nyghtes;
So myche serchyng of loselles, and ys hym selfe so lewde;
So myche conjuracions for elvyshe myday sprettes;
So many bullys of pardon publysshed and shewyd;
70   So myche crossyng and blyssyng and hym all be shrewde;
Suche pollaxis and pyllers, suche mulys trapte with gold –
Sens Dewcalyons flodde, in no cronycle ys told.

(1554)

1530   WILLIAM CORNISH

Pleasure it is
To here, iwis,
The birdes sing;
The dere in the dale,
5   The shepe in the vale,
The corne springing.

49 *pyllyng and pollyng* plundering and extortion; 54 *hatered* hatred; *cheryte* charity;
56 *dowbyll* double; 58 *lyerd* heard of; 60 *rygorous* harsh; 64 *fylty* filthy;
67 *loselles* scoundrels; 68 *myday sprettes* noonday devils; 70 *all be shrewde* so
depraved; 71 *mulys* mules

2 *iwis* truly;

God's purveaunce
For sustenaunce
It is for man:
10 Then we always
To him give praise,
And thank him than,
And thank him than.

MYLES COVERDALE *from* **The Bible**   **1535**

Psalm 137: Super flumina

By the waters of Babylon we sat downe and weapte, when we
remembred the, O Syon. As for our harpes, we hanged them up
upon the trees, that are therin. Then they that led us awaye
captyve, required of us a songe and melody in our hevynes: synge
us one of the songes of Sion. How shall we synge the Lordes
songe in a straunge lande. If I forget the, O Jerusalem, let my
right hande be forgotten. If I do not remembre the, let my tongue
cleve to the rofe of my mouth: yee yf I preferre not Jerusalem in
my myrth. Remembre the chyldren of Edom, O Lorde, in the
daye of Jerusalem, how they sayd: downe with it, downe with
it, even to the grounde. O daughter of Babylon, thou shalt come
to misery thy selfe: yee, happy shall he be, that rewardeth the as
thou hast served us. Blessed shall he be, that taketh thy chyldren,
and throweth them agaynst the stones.

SIR THOMAS WYATT *from the Italian of Petrarch*   **1540**

The longe love that in my thought doeth harbar
    And in myn hert doeth kepe his residence,
    Into my face preseth with bold pretence,
    And therin campeth, spreding his baner.
She that me lerneth to love and suffre
    And will that my trust and lustes negligence
    Be rayned by reason, shame, and reverence,
    With his hardines taketh displeasure.

12 *than* then

Wherewithall, unto the hertes forrest he fleith,
    Leving his entreprise with payne and cry
    And there him hideth and not appereth.
What may I do, when my maister fereth,
    But in the felde with him to lyve and dye?
    For goode is the liff ending faithfully.

(1557)

SIR THOMAS WYATT *from the Italian of Petrarch*

Who so list to hount I knowe where is an hynde,
    But as for me, helas, I may no more;
    The vayne travaill hath weried me so sore,
    I ame of them that farthest cometh behinde;
Yet may I by no meanes my weried mynde
    Drawe from the Deere, but as she fleeth afore
    Faynting I followe. I leve of therefore
    Sithens in a nett I seke to hold the wynde.
Who list her hount, I put him owte of dowbte,
    As well as I may spend his tyme in vain.
    And graven with Diamondes in letters plain
There is written her faier neck rounde abowte:
    'Noli me tangere for Cesars I ame
    And wylde for to hold though I seme tame.'

(1815)

SIR THOMAS WYATT

They fle from me that sometyme did me seke
With naked fote stalking in my chambre.
I have sene theim gentill tame and meke
That nowe are wyld and do not remembre
That sometyme they put theimself in daunger
To take bred at my hand; and nowe they raunge
Besely seking with a continuell chaunge.

Thancked be fortune it hath ben othrewise
Twenty tymes better, but ons in special,
In thyn arraye after a pleasaunt gyse

When her lose gowne from her shoulders did fall
And she me caught in her armes long and small,
Therewithall swetely did me kysse
And softely said 'Dere hert, how like you this?'

It was no dreme: I lay brode waking.
But all is torned thorough my gentilnes
Into a straunge fasshion of forsaking;
And I have leve to goo of her goodenes
And she also to use new fangilnes.
But syns that I so kyndely ame served
I would fain knowe what she hath deserved.

(1557)

SIR THOMAS WYATT

My lute, awake! Perfourme the last
Labour that thou and I shall wast,
And end that I have now begon;
For when this song is sung and past,
My lute be still, for I have done.

As to be herd where ere is none,
As lede to grave in marbill stone,
My song may perse her hert as sone;
Should we then sigh or syng or mone?
No, no, my lute, for I have done.

The Rokkes do not so cruelly
Repulse the waves continuelly
As she my suyte and affection,
So that I ame past remedy,
Whereby my lute and I have done.

Prowd of the spoyll that thou hast gott
Of simple hertes thorough Loves shot,
By whome, unkynd, thou hast theim wone,
Thinck not he haith his bow forgot,
All tho my lute and I have done.

Vengeaunce shall fall on thy disdain
That makest but game on ernest pain;
Thinck not alone under the sonne
Unquyt to cause thy lovers plain,
All tho my lute and I have done.

Perchaunce thee lye wethered and old
The wynter nyghtes that are so cold,
Playnyng in vain unto the mone;
Thy wisshes then dare not be told;
Care then who lyst for I have done.

And then may chaunce the to repent
The tyme that thou hast lost and spent
To cause thy lovers sigh and swoune;
Then shalt thou knowe beacltie but lent
And wisshe and want as I have done.

Now cesse, my lute; this is the last
Labour that thou and I shall wast,
And ended is that we begon;
Now is this song boeth sung and past;
My lute, be still, for I have done.

(1557)

SIR THOMAS WYATT

Forget not yet the tryde entent
Of suche a truthe as I have ment,
My gret travayle so gladly spent
    Forget not yet.

Forget not yet when fyrst began
The wery lyffe ye know syns whan,
The sute, the servys none tell can,
    Forget not yet.

Forget not yet the gret assays,
The cruell wrong, the skornfull ways,
The paynfull pacyence in denays,
    Forgett not yet.

Forget not yet, forget not thys,
How long ago hathe bene and ys
The mynd that never ment amys,
        Forget not yet.

Forget not then thyn owne aprovyd
The whyche so long hathe the so lovyd,
Whose stedfast faythe yet never movyd,
        Forget not thys.

(1815)

SIR THOMAS WYATT *from the Italian of Alamanni*

Myne owne John Poyntz, sins ye delight to know
    The cawse why that homeward I me draw,
    And fle the presse of courtes wher soo they goo
Rather then to lyve thrall under the awe
    Of lordly lookes, wrappid within my cloke,
    To will and lust lerning to set a lawe,
It is not for becawsse I skorne or moke
    The power of them to whome fortune hath lent
    Charge over us, of Right to strike the stroke;
But trew it is that I have allwais ment
    Lesse to estime them then the common sort,
    Off owtward thinges that juge in their intent
Withowte Regarde what dothe inwarde resort.
    I grawnt sumtime that of glorye the fyar
    Dothe touche my hart; me lyst not to report
Blame by honowr and honour to desyar;
    But how may I this honour now atayne
    That cannot dy the coloure blake a lyer?
My Poyntz, I cannot frame my tune to fayne,
    To cloke the trothe for praisse, withowt desart,
    Of them that lyst all vice for to retayne.
I cannot honour them that settes their part
    With Venus and Baccus all their lyf long,
    Nor holld my pece of them alltho I smart.
I cannot crowche nor knelle to do so great a wrong
    To worship them like God on erthe alone
    That ar as wollffes thes sely lambes among.
I cannot with my wordes complayne and mone
    And suffer nought, nor smart wythout complaynt,

Nor torne the worde that from my mouthe is gone.

I cannot speke and loke lyke as a saynct,
   Use wyles for witt and make deceyt a plesure
   And call crafft counsell, for proffet styll to paint.

I cannot wrest the law to fill the coffer,
   With innocent blode to fede my sellff fat,
   And doo most hurt where most hellp I offer.

I am not he that can alow the state
   Off him Cesar and dam Cato to dye,
   That with his dethe dyd skape owt off the gate

From Cesares handes, if Lyvye do not lye,
   And wolld not lyve whar lyberty was lost,
   So did his hart the commonn wele aplye.

I am not he suche eloquence to boste
   To make the crow singing as the swanne,
   Nor call the lyon of cowarde bestes the moste

That cannot take a mows as the cat can;
   And he that diethe for hunger of the golld,
   Call him Alessaundre, and say that Pan

Passithe Apollo in musike manyfolld;
   Praysse Syr Thopas for a noble tale
   And skorne the story that the knyght tolld;

Praise him for counceill that is droncke of ale;
   Grynne when he laugheth that bereth all the swaye,
   Frowne when he frowneth and grone when he is pale,

On othres lust to hang boeth nyght and daye.
   None of these poyntes would ever frame in me.
   My wit is nought, I cannot lerne the waye.

And much the lesse of thinges that greater be,
   That asken helpe of colours of devise
   To joyne the mene with eche extremitie:

With the neryst vertue to cloke alway the vise
   And, as to pourpose like wise it shall fall,
   To presse the vertue that it may not rise.

As dronkenes good felloweshippe to call,
   The frendly foo with his dowble face
   Say he is gentill and courtois therewithall;

And say that Favell hath a goodly grace
   In eloquence; and crueltie to name
   Zele of Justice and chaunge in tyme and place;

And he that sufferth offence withoute blame
   Call him pitefull, and him true and playn
   That raileth rekles to every mans shame;

Say he is rude that cannot lye and fayn,

The letcher a lover, and tirannye
To be the right of a prynces reigne.
I cannot, I; no, no, it will not be!
  This is the cause that I could never yet
  Hang on their slevis that way, as thou maist se,
A chippe of chaunce more then a pownde of witt.
  This maketh me at home to hounte and to hawke
  And in fowle weder at my booke to sitt;
In frost and snowe then with my bow to stawke;
  No man doeth marke where so I ride or goo;
  In lusty lees at libertie I walke,
And of these newes I fele nor wele nor woo,
  Sauf that a clogg doeth hang yet at my hele:
  No force for that, for it is ordered so
That I may lepe boeth hedge and dike full well.
  I ame not now in Fraunce to judge the wyne,
  With saffry sauce the delicates to fele;
Nor yet in Spaigne where oon must him inclyne
  Rather then to be, owtewerdly to seme.
  I meddill not with wittes that be so fyne,
Nor Flaunders chiere letteth not my sight to deme
  Of black and white, nor taketh my wit awaye
  With bestlynes they, beestes, do so esteme;
Nor I ame not where Christe is geven in pray
  For mony, poisen and traison at Rome,
  A commune practise used nyght and daie.
But here I ame in Kent and Christendome
  Emong the muses where I rede and ryme,
  Where if thou list, my Poynz, for to come,
Thou shalt be judge how I do spend my tyme.

(1557)

HENRY HOWARD, EARL OF SURREY An Excellent   1542
Epitaffe of Syr Thomas Wyat

W. resteth here, that quick could never rest;
Whose heavenly giftes encreased by disdayn
And vertue sank the deper in his brest:
Such profit he by envy could obtain.

A hed, where wisdom misteries did frame;
Whose hammers bet styll in that lively brayn
As on a stithe, where that some work of fame
Was dayly wrought to turne to Britaines gayn.

A visage stern and myld; where bothe did grow
Vice to contemne, in vertue to rejoyce;
Amid great stormes whom grace assured so
To lyve upright and smile at fortunes choyce.

A hand that taught what might be sayd in ryme;
That reft Chaucer the glory of his wit;
A mark the which, unparfited for time,
Some may approche, but never none shall hit.

A toung that served in forein realmes his king;
Whose courteous talke to vertue did enflame
Eche noble hart; a worthy guide to bring
Our English youth by travail unto fame.

An eye, whose judgement none affect could blinde,
Frendes to allure, and foes to reconcile;
Whose persing loke did represent a mynde
With vertue fraught, reposed, voyd of gyle.

A hart, where drede was never so imprest
To hyde the thought that might the trouth avance;
In neyther fortune loft nor yet represt,
To swell in wealth, or yeld unto mischance.

A valiant corps, where force and beawty met;
Happy, alas, to happy, but for foes;
Lived and ran the race that nature set;
Of manhodes shape, where she the molde did lose.

But to the heavens that simple soule is fled,
Which left with such as covet Christ to know
Witnesse of faith that never shall be ded;
Sent for our helth, but not received so.

Thus, for our gilte, this jewel have we lost.
The earth his bones, the heavens possesse his gost.

ANNE ASKEW The Balade whych Anne Askewe made and sange whan she was in Newgate

Lyke as the armed knyght
Appoynted to the fielde
With thys world wyll I fyght
And fayth shall be my shielde.

5   Faythe is that weapon stronge
Whych wyll not fayle at nede
My foes therfor amonge
Therwith wyll I procede.

As it is had in strengthe
10   And force of Christes waye
It wyll prevayle at lengthe
Though all the devyls saye naye.

Faythe in the fathers olde
Obtayned ryghtwysnesse
15   Whych make me verye bolde
To feare no worldes dystresse.

I now rejoyce in hart
And hope byd me do so
For Christ wyll take my part
20   And ease me of my wo.

Thu sayst lorde, who so knocke
To them wylt thu attende
Undo therfor the locke
And thy stronge power sende.

25   More enmyes now I have
Than heeres upon my heed
Lete them not me deprave
But fyght thu in my steed.

On the my care I cast
30   For all their cruell spyght
I sett not by their hast
For thu art my delyght.

I am not she that lyst
My anker to lete fall
35   For everye dryslynge myst
My shyppe substancyall.

14 *ryghtwysnesse* righteousness; 27 *deprave* defame; 35 *dryslynge* drizzling;

Not oft use I to wryght
In prose nor yet in ryme
Yet wyll I shewe one syght
40   That I sawe in my tyme.
    I sawe a ryall trone
Where Justyce shuld have sytt
But in her stede was one
Of modye cruell wytt.
45   Absorpt was rygtwysnesse
As of the ragynge floude
Sathan in hys excesse
Sucte up the gyltelesse bloude.
    Then thought I, Jesus lorde
50   Whan thu shalt judge us all
Harde is it to recorde
On these men what wyll fall.
    Yet lorde I the desyre
For that they do to me
55   Lete them not tast the hyre
Of their inyquyte.

1557   § *from* **Tottel's Songes and Sonettes**

SIR THOMAS WYATT *from the Latin of Seneca* [Chorus from Thyestes]

Stond who so list upon the Slipper toppe
Of courtes estates, and lett me heare rejoyce
And use me quyet without lett or stoppe,
Unknowen in courte, that hath such brackish joyes.
In hidden place so lett my dayes forthe passe
That when my yeares be done, withouten noyse,
I may dye aged after the common trace.
For hym death greep'the right hard by the croppe
That is moch knowen of other, and of him self alas,
Doth dye unknowen, dazed, with dreadfull face.

44 *modye* angry; 55 *hyre* reward

HENRY HOWARD, EARL OF SURREY

O happy dames, that may embrace
The frute of your delight,
Help to bewaile the wofull case
And eke the heavy plight
Of me, that wonted to rejoyce
The fortune of my pleasant choyce:
Good Ladies, help to fill my moorning voyce.

In ship, freight with rememberance
Of thoughtes and pleasures past,
He sailes that hath in governance
My life, while it wil last;
With scalding sighes, for lack of gale,
Furdering his hope, that is his sail
Toward me, the swete port of his avail.

Alas, how oft in dreames I se
Those eyes, that were my food,
Which somtime so delited me,
That yet they do me good;
Wherwith I wake with his returne
Whose absent flame did make me burne.
But when I find the lacke, Lord how I mourne!

When other lovers in armes acrosse
Rejoyce their chief delight,
Drowned in teares to mourne my losse
I stand the bitter night
In my window, where I may see
Before the windes how the cloudes flee.
Lo, what a mariner love hath made me!

And in grene waves when the salt flood
Doth rise by rage of wind,
A thousand fansies in that mood
Assayle my restlesse mind.
Alas, now drencheth my swete fo,
That with the spoyle of my hart did go,
And left me; but, alas, why did he so?

And when the seas waxe calme againe,
To chase fro me annoye,
My doubtfull hope doth cause me plaine:
So dreade cuts of my joye.
Thus is my wealth mingled with wo,
And of ech thought a dout doth growe,
Now he comes, will he come? alas, no, no!

HENRY HOWARD, EARL OF SURREY

Alas, so all thinges nowe doe holde their peace,
Heaven and earth disturbed in nothing;
The beastes, the ayer, the birdes their song doe cease;
The nightes chare the starres aboute dothe bring.
Calme is the sea, the waves worke lesse and lesse;
So am not I, whom love alas doth wring,
Bringing before my face the great encrease
Of my desires, whereat I wepe and syng
In joye and wo as in a doutfull ease.
For my swete thoughtes sometyme doe pleasure bring,
But by and by the cause of my disease
Geves me a pang that inwardly dothe sting,
    When that I thinke what griefe it is againe
    To live and lacke the thing should ridde my paine.

HENRY HOWARD, EARL OF SURREY *from* Certayn
Bokes of Virgiles Aenaeis

[Aeneas Searches for his Wife]

'And first the walles and dark entrie I sought
Of the same gate wherat I issued out,
Holding backward the steppes where we had come
In the dark night, loking all round about.
In every place the ugsome sightes I saw,
The silence selfe of night agast my sprite.
From hense againe I past unto our house,
If she by chaunce had ben returned home.
The Grekes were there, and had it all beset.
The wasting fire blown up by drift of wind

Above the roofes; the blazing flame sprang up,
The sound wherof with furie pearst the skies.
To Priams palace and the castel then
I made; and there at Junous sanctuair,
In the void porches, Phenix, Ulisses eke,
Sterne guardens stood, watching of the spoile.
The richesse here were set, reft from the brent
Temples of Troy; the tables of the gods,
The vessells eke that were of massy gold,
And vestures spoild, were gatherd all in heap.
The children orderly and mothers pale for fright
Long ranged on a rowe stode round about.

  So bold was I to showe my voice that night,
With clepes and cries to fill the stretes throughout,
With Creuse name in sorrow, with vain teres,
And often sithes the same for to repete.
The town restlesse with furie as I sought,
Th'unlucky figure of Creusaes ghost,
Of stature more than wont, stood fore mine eyen.
Abashed then I woxe. Therwith my heare
Gan start right up, my voice stack in my throte.
When with such words she gan my hart remove:
"What helps to yeld unto such furious rage,
Sweet spouse?" quod she. "Without wil of the gods
This chaunced not; ne lefull was for thee
To lead away Creusa hense with thee:
The king of the hye heven suffreth it not.
A long exile thou art assigned to bere,
Long to furrow large space of stormy seas:
So shalt thou reach at last Hesperian land,
Wher Lidian Tiber with his gentle streme
Mildly doth flow along the frutfull felds.
There mirthful wealth, there kingdom is for thee,
There a kinges child preparde to be thy make.
For thy beloved Creusa stint thy teres.
For now shal I not see the proud abodes
Of Myrmidons, nor yet of Dolopes;
Ne I, a Troyan lady and the wife
Unto the sonne of Venus the goddesse,
Shall goe a slave to serve the Grekish dames.
Me here the gods great mother holdes.
And now farwell, and kepe in fathers brest
The tender love of thy yong son and myne."

  This having said, she left me all in teres,

And minding much to speake; but she was gone,
And suttly fled into the weightlesse aire.
Thrise raught I with mine arms t'accoll her neck,
Thrise did my handes vaine hold th'image escape,
Like nimble windes, and like the flieng dreame.
So night spent out, returne I to my feers.
And ther wondring I find together swarmd
A new number of mates, mothers and men,
A rout exiled, a wreched multitude,
From eche where flockte together, prest to passe,
With hart and goods, to whatsoever land
By sliding seas me listed them to lede.
And now rose Lucifer above the ridge
Of lusty Ide, and brought the dawning light.
The Grekes held th'entries of the gates beset;
Of help there was no hope. Then gave I place,
Toke up my sire, and hasted to the hill.'

§   §   §

1560   *from* The Geneva Bible, Ecclesiastes 3:1–8

To all things there is an appointed time, and a time to
    everie purpose under the heaven.
A time to be borne, and a time to dye: a time to plant, and
    a time to plucke up that, which is planted.
A time to slay, and a time to heale: a time to breake
    downe, and a time to buylde.
A time to wepe, and a time to laugh: a time to mourne, and
    a time to dance.
A time to cast away stones, and a time to gather stones: a
    time to embrace, and a time to be farre from embracing.
A time to seke, and a time to lose: a time to kepe, and a
    time to cast away.
A time to rent, and a time to sowe: a time to kepe
    silence, and a time to speake.
A time to love, and a time to hate: a time of warre, and a
    time of peace.

ROBERT WEEVER Of Youth He Singeth

In a herber green asleep whereas I lay,
The birds sang sweet in the middes of the day;
I dreamed fast of mirth and play:
    In youth is pleasure, in youth is pleasure.

Methought I walked still to and fro,
And from her company I could not go;
But when I waked it was not so:
    In youth is pleasure, in youth is pleasure.

Therefore my heart is surely pight
Of her alone to have a sight,
Which is my joy and heart's delight:
    In youth is pleasure, in youth is pleasure.

BARNABE GOOGE Commynge Home-warde out of Spayne   1563

O ragyng Seas,
and myghty Neptunes rayne,
In monstrous Hylles,
that throwest thy selfe so hye,
That wyth thy fludes,
doest beate the shores of Spayne:
And breake the Clyves,
that dare thy force envie.
Cease now thy rage,
and laye thyne Ire asyde,
And thou that hast,
the governaunce of all,
O myghty God,
grant Wether Wynd and Tyde,
Tyll on my Coun-
treye Coast, our Anker fall.

BARNABE GOOGE An Epytaphe of the Death of Nicolas Grimoald

Beholde this fle-
tyng world how al things fade
Howe every thyng
doth passe and weare awaye,
Eche state of lyfe,
by comon course and trade,
Abydes no tyme,
but hath a passyng daye.
For looke as lyfe,
that pleasaunt Dame hath brought,
The pleasaunt yeares,
and dayes of lustynes,
So Death our Foe,
consumeth all to nought,
Envyeng thefe,
with Darte doth us oppresse,
And that whiche is,
the greatest gryfe of all,
The gredye Grype,
doth no estate respect,
But wher he comes,
he makes them down to fall,
Ne stayes he at,
the hie sharpe wytted sect.
For if that wytt,
or worthy Eloquens,
Or learnyng deape,
coulde move hym to forbeare,
O *Grimoald* then,
thou hadste not yet gon hence
But heare hadest sene,
full many an aged yeare.
Ne had the Mu-
ses loste so fyne a Floure,
Nor had *Miner-*
va wept to leave thee so,
If wysdome myght
have fled the fatall howre,
Thou hadste not yet

ben suffred for to go,
A thousande doltysh
Geese we myght have sparde,
A thousande wytles
heads, death might have found
And taken them,
for whom no man had carde,
And layde them lowe,
in deepe oblivious grounde,
But Fortune fa-
vours Fooles as old men saye
And lets them lyve,
and take the wyse awaye.

ARTHUR GOLDING *from* The First Four Books of Ovid 1565

[Proserpine and Dis]

While in this garden *Proserpine* was taking hir pastime,
In gathering eyther Violets blew, or Lillies white as Lime,
And while of Maidenly desire she fillde hir Maund and Lap,
Endevoring to outgather hir companions there. By hap
Dis spide hir: lovde hir: caught hir up: and all at once well neere:
So hastie, hote, and swift a thing is Love, as may appeare.
The Ladie with a wailing voyce afright did often call
Hir Mother and hir waiting Maides, but Mother most of all
And as she from the upper part hir garment would have rent,
By chaunce she let her lap slip downe, and out the flowres went.
And such a sillie simplenesse hir childish age yet beares,
That even the verie losse of them did move hir more to teares.

[Daphne and Apollo]

I pray thee Nymph *Penaeis* stay, I chase not as a fo:
Stay Nymph: the Lambes so flee the Wolves, the Stags the Lions so:
With flittring fethers sielie Doves so from the Gossehauke flie,
And every creature from his foe. Love is the cause that I
Do followe thee: alas alas how woulde it grieve my heart,
To see thee fall among the briers, and that the bloud should start
Out of thy tender legges, I wretch the causer of thy smart.
The place is rough to which thou runst, take leysure I thee pray,
Abate thy flight, and I my selfe my running pace will stay.

Yet would I wishe thee take advise, and wisely for to viewe
What one he is that for thy grace in humble wise doth sewe.
I am not one that dwelles among the hilles and stonie rockes,
I am no sheepehearde with a Curre, attending on the flockes:
I am no Carle nor countrie Clowne, nor neathearde taking charge
Of cattle grazing here and there within this Forrest large.
Thou doest not know poore simple soule, God wote thou dost not
    knowe,
From whome thou fleest. For if thou knew, thou wouldste not flee
    me so.
In *Delphos* is my chiefe abode, my Temples also stande
At *Glaros* and at *Patara* within the *Lycian* lande.
And in the Ile of *Tenedos* the people honour mee.
The king of Gods himself is knowne my father for to bee.
By me is knowne that was, that is, and that that shall ensue,
By mee men learne to sundrie tunes to frame sweete ditties true.
In shooting I have stedfast hand, but surer hand had hee
That made this wound within my heart that heretofore was free.
Of Phisicke and of surgerie I found the Artes for neede
The powre of everie herbe and plant doth of my gift proceede.
Nowe wo is me that neare an herbe can heale the hurt of love
And that the Artes that others helpe their Lord doth helpelesse
    prove.
As *Phœbus* would have spoken more, away *Penaeis* stale
With fearefull steppes, and left him in the midst of all his tale.
And as shee ran the meeting windes hir garments backewarde blue,
So that hir naked skinne apearde behinde hir as she flue,
Hir goodly yellowe golden haire that hanged loose and slacke,
With every puffe of ayre did wave and tosse behind hir backe.
Hir running made hir seeme more fayre. The youthfull God
    therefore
Coulde not abyde to waste his wordes in dalyance any more.
But as his love advysed him he gan to mende his pace,
And with the better foote before the fleeing Nymph to chace.
And even as when the greedie Grewnde doth course the sielie Hare
Amiddes the plaine and champion fielde without all covert bare,
Both twaine of them do straine themselves and lay on footemanship,
Who may best runne with all his force the tother to outstrip,
The tone for safetie of his lyfe, the tother for his pray,
The Grewnde aye prest with open mouth to beare the Hare away,
Thrusts forth his snoute, and gyrdeth out, and at hir loynes doth
    snatch,
As though he would at everie stride betweene his teeth hir latch:

Againe in doubt of being caught the Hare aye shrinking slips,
Upon the sodaine from his Jawes, and from betweene his lips:
So farde *Apollo* and the Mayde: hope made *Apollo* swift,
And feare did make the Mayden fleete devising how to shift.
Howebeit he that did pursue of both the swifter went,
As furthred by the feathred wings that *Cupid* had him lent:
So that he would not let hir rest, but preased at hir heele
So neere that through hir scattred haire shee might his breathing
    feele.
But when she sawe hir breath was gone and strength began to fayle,
The colour faded in hir cheekes, and ginning for to quayle,
Shee looked too *Penæus* streame, and sayde, nowe Father dere,
And if yon streames have powre of Gods, then help your daughter
    here.
O let the earth devour me quicke, on which I seeme to fayre,
Or else this shape which is my harme by chaunging straight appayre.
This piteous prayer scarsly sed: hir sinewes waxed starke,
And therewithall about hir breast did grow a tender barke.
Hir haire was turned into leaves, hir armes in boughes did growe,
Hir feete that were ere while so swift, now rooted were as slowe.
Hir crowne became the toppe, and thus of that she earst had beene,
Remayned nothing in the worlde, but beautie fresh and greene.
Which when that *Phœbus* did beholde (affection did so move)
The tree to which his love was turnde he coulde no lesse but love.
And as he softly layde his hand upon the tender plant,
Within the barke newe overgrowne he felt hir heart yet pant.
And in his armes embracing fast hir boughes and braunches lythe,
He proferde kisses too the tree: the tree did from him writhe.
Well (quoth *Apollo*) though my Feere and spouse thou can not bee,
Assuredly from this time forth yet shalt thou be my tree.
Thou shalt adorne my golden lockes, and eke my pleasant Harpe,
Thou shalt adorne my Quyver full of shaftes and arrowes sharpe,
Thou shalt adorne the valiant knyghts and royall Emperours:
When for their noble feates of armes like mightie conquerours,
Triumphantly with stately pompe up to the Capitoll,
They shall ascende with solemne traine that doe their deedes extoll.
Before *Augustus* Pallace doore full duely shalt thou warde,
The Oke amid the Pallace yarde aye faythfully to garde,
And as my heade is never poulde nor never more without
A seemely bushe of youthfull haire that spreadeth rounde about:
Even so this honour give I thee continually to have
Thy braunches clad from time to tyme with leaves both fresh and
    brave.

Now when that *Pean* of this talke had fully made an ende,
The Lawrell to his just request did seeme to condescende,
By bowing of hir newe made boughes and tender braunches downe,
And wagging of hir seemely toppe, as if it were hir crowne.

1567   ARTHUR GOLDING *from* The Fifteen Books of Ovid

[Medea's Incantation]

Before the Moone should circlewise close both hir hornes in one
Three nightes were yet as then to come. Assoone as that she shone
Most full of light, and did behold the earth with fulsome face,
Medea with hir haire not trust so much as in a lace,
But flaring on hir shoulders twaine, and barefoote, with hir gowne
Ungirded, gate hir out of doores and wandred up and downe
Alone the dead time of the night: both Man, and Beast, and Bird
Were fast a sleepe: the Serpents slie in trayling forward stird
So softly as you would have thought they still a sleepe had bene.
The moysting Ayre was whist: no leafe ye could have moving sene.
The starres alonly faire and bright did in the welkin shine.
To which she lifting up hir handes did thrise hirselfe encline,
And thrice with water of the brooke hir haire besprincled shee:
And gasping thrise she opte hir mouth: and bowing downe hir knee
Upon the bare hard ground, she said: O trustie time of night
Most faithfull unto privities, O golden starres whose light
Doth jointly with the Moone succeede the beames that blaze by day
And thou three headed *Hecaté* who knowest best the way
To compasse this our great attempt and art our chiefest stay:
Ye Charmes and Witchcrafts, and thou Earth which both with herbe
     and weed
Of mightie working furnishest the Wizardes at their neede:
Ye Ayres and windes: ye Elves of Hilles, of Brookes, of Woods
     alone,
Of standing Lakes, and of the Night approche ye everychone.
Through helpe of whom (the crooked bankes much wondring at the
     thing)
I have compelled streames to run cleane backward to their spring.
By charmes I make the calme Seas rough, and make the rough Seas
     plaine
And cover all the Skie with Cloudes, and chase them thence againe.
By charmes I rayse and lay the windes, and burst the Vipers jaw,
And from the bowels of the Earth both stones and trees doe drawe.

Whole woods and Forestes I remove: I make the Mountaines shake,
And even the Earth it selfe to grone and fearfully to quake.
I call up dead men from their graves: and thee O lightsome Moone
I darken oft, though beaten brasse abate thy perill soone
Our Sorcerie dimmes the Morning faire, and darkes the Sun at
    Noone.

ALEXANDER SCOTT   **1568**

To luve unluvit it is ane pane
for scho that is my soverane
sum wantoun man so he hes set hir
that I can get no lufe agane
5   bot brekis my hairt and nocht the bettir.

Quhen that I went with that sweit may
to dance to sing to sport and pley
and oft times in my armis plet hir
I do now murne both nycht and day
10 and brekis my hart and nocht the bettir.

Quhair I wes wont to se hir go
rycht trymly passand to and fro
with cumly smylis quhen that I met hir –
and now I leif in pane and wo
15 and brekis my hairt and nocht the bettir.

Quhattane ane glaikit fule am I
to slay my self with malancoly
sen weill I ken I may nocht get hir
or quhat suld be the caus and quhy
20 to brek my hairt and nocht the bettir.

1 *To luve unluvit* to love unloved; 2 *scho* she; 3 *he* high, haughty; 6 *quhen* when;
may maiden; 8 *plet* pleated, clasped; 11 *quhair* where; 12 *trymly* trimly, smartly;
14 *leif* live; 16 *Quhattane* how like; *glaikit* foolish; 18 *sen* since;

My hairt, sen thou may nocht hir pleis
adew! – as gud lufe cumis as gais.
Go chus ane udir and foryet hir.
God gif him dolour and diseis
25   that brekis thair hairt and nocht the bettir.

ANONYMOUS

Christ was the word that spake it;
Hee tooke the bread and brake it;
And what that Word did make it,
I doe beleeve and take it.

(1960)

1579   EDMUND SPENSER *from* **The Shepheardes Calender**

[Roundelay]

Perigot	It fell upon a holly eve,
Willye	hey ho hollidaye,
Per.	When holly fathers wont to shrieve:
Wil.	now gynneth this roundelay.
5 *Per.*	Sitting upon a hill so hye
Wil.	hey ho the high hyll,
Per.	The while my flocke did feede thereby,
Wil.	the while the shepheard selfe did spill:
Per.	I saw the bouncing Bellibone,
10 *Wil.*	hey ho Bonibell,
Per.	Tripping over the dale alone,
Wil.	she can trippe it very well:
Per.	Well decked in a frocke of gray,
Wil.	hey ho gray is greete,
15 *Per.*	And in a Kirtle of greene saye,
Wil.	the greene is for maydens meete:

22 *gais* goes; 24 *diseis* trouble

3 *holly* holy; 8 *selfe did spill* wasted his time; 9 *Bellibone* girl; 15 *saye* good cloth;

Per.	A chapelet on her head she wore,
Wil.	hey ho chapelet,
Per.	Of sweete Violets therein was store,
20	*Wil.*	she sweeter then the Violet.
Per.	My sheepe did leave theyr wonted foode,
Wil.	hey ho seely sheepe,
Per.	And gazd on her, as they were wood,
Wil.	woode as he, that did them keepe.
25	*Per.*	As the bonilasse passed bye,
Wil.	hey ho bonilasse,
Per.	She rovde at me with glauncing eye,
Wil.	as cleare as the christall glasse:
Per.	All as the Sunnye beame so bright,
30	*Wil.*	hey ho the Sunne beame,
Per.	Glaunceth from *Phœbus* face forthright,
Wil.	so love into thy hart did streame:
Per.	Or as the thonder cleaves the cloudes,
Wil.	hey ho the Thonder,
35	*Per.*	Wherein the lightsome levin shroudes,
Wil.	so cleaves thy soule a sonder:
Per.	Or as Dame *Cynthias* silver raye
Wil.	hey ho the Moonelight,
Per.	Upon the glyttering wave doth playe:
40	*Wil.*	such play is a pitteous plight.
Per.	The glaunce into my heart did glide,
Wil.	hey ho the glyder,
Per.	Therewith my soule was sharply gryde,
Wil.	such woundes soone wexen wider.
45	*Per.*	Hasting to raunch the arrow out,
Wil.	hey ho Perigot,
Per.	I left the head in my hart roote:
Wil.	it was a desperate shot.
Per.	There it ranckleth ay more and more,
50	*Wil.*	hey ho the arrowe,
Per.	Ne can I find salve for my sore:
Wil.	love is a curelesse sorrowe.
Per.	And though my bale with death I bought,
Wil.	hey ho heavie cheere,
55	*Per.*	Yet should thilk lasse not from my thought:
Wil.	so you may buye gold to deare.

23 *wood* mad; 43 *gryde* pierced;

Per.	But whether in paynefull love I pyne,
Wil.	hey ho pinching payne,
Per.	Or thrive in welth, she shalbe mine.
60 Wil.	but if thou can her obteine.
Per.	And if for gracelesse greefe I dye,
Wil.	hey ho gracelesse griefe,
Per.	Witnesse, shee slewe me with her eye:
Wil.	let thy follye be the priefe.
65 Per.	And you, that sawe it, simple shepe,
Wil.	hey ho the fayre flocke,
Per.	For priefe thereof, my death shall weepe,
Wil.	and mone with many a mocke.
Per.	So learnd I love on a hollye eve,
70 Wil.	hey ho holidaye,
Per.	That ever since my hart did greve.
Wil.	now endeth our roundelay.

1580 EDMUND SPENSER Iambicum Trimetrum

Unhappie Verse, the witnesse of my unhappie state,
    Make thy selfe fluttring wings of thy fast flying thought,
    And fly forth unto my Love, whersoever she be:
Whether lying reastlesse in heavy bedde, or else,
    Sitting so cheerelesse at the cheerfull boorde, or else
    Playing alone carelesse on hir heavenlie Virginals.
If in Bed, tell hir, that my eyes can take no reste:
    If at Boorde, tell hir, that my mouth can eate no meate:
    If at hir Virginals, tel hir, I can heare no mirth.
Asked why? say: Waking Love suffereth no sleepe:
    Say, that raging Love dothe appall the weake stomacke:
    Say, that lamenting Love marreth the Musicall.
Tell hir, that hir pleasures were wonte to lull me asleepe:
    Tell hir, that hir beautie was wonte to feede mine eyes:
    Tell hir, that hir sweete Tongue was wonte to make me mirth.
Nowe doe I nightly waste, wanting my kindely reste:
    Nowe doe I dayly starve, wanting my lively foode:
    Nowe doe I alwayes dye, wanting thy timely mirth.
And if I waste, who will bewaile my heavy chaunce?
    And if I starve, who will record my cursed end?
    And if I dye, who will saye: *this was, Immerito*?

64 *priefe* proof

JASPER HEYWOOD *from the Latin of Seneca* [*Chorus from* **1581**
Hercules Furens]

Goe hurtles soules, whom mischiefe hath opprest
Even in first porch of life but lately had,
And fathers fury goe unhappy kind
O litle children, by the way ful sad
    Of journey knowen.
    Goe see the angry kynges.

THOMAS WATSON My Love is Past **1582**

Ye captive soules of blindefold Cyprians boate,
Marke with advise in what estate yee stande,
Your Boteman never whistles mearie noate,
And Folly keeping sterne, still puttes from lande,
    And makes a sport to tosse you to and froe
    Twixt sighing windes, and surging waves of woe.
On Beawties rocke she runnes you at her will,
And holdes you in suspense twixt hope and feare,
Where dying oft, yet are you living still,
But such a life, as death much better were;
    Be therefore circumspect, and follow me,
    When Chaunce, or chaunge of maners sets you free.
Beware how you returne to seas againe:
Hang up your votive tables in the quyre
Of Cupids Church, in witnesse of the paine
You suffer now by forced fond desire:
    Then hang your throughwett garmentes on the wall,
    And sing with me, that Love is mixt with gall.

ANONYMOUS A new Courtly Sonet, of the Lady Greensleeves. **1584**
To the new tune of Greensleeves

Alas my love, ye do me wrong,
    to cast me off discurteously:
And I have loved you so long,
    Delighting in your companie.

Greensleeves was all my joy,
      Greensleeves was my delight:
   Greensleeves was my heart of gold, –
      And who but my ladie Greensleeeves.

I have been readie at your hand,
   to grant what ever you would crave.
I have both waged life and land,
   your love and good will for to have.
      Greensleeves was all my joy, etc.,

I bought thee kerchers to thy head,
   that were wrought fine and gallantly:
I kept thee both at boord and bed,
   Which cost my purse wel favouredly,
      Greensleeves was all my joy, etc.

I bought thee peticotes of the best,
   the cloth so fine as fine might be:
I gave thee jewels for thy chest,
   and all this cost I spent on thee.
      Greensleeves was all my joy, etc.

Thy smock of silk, both faire and white,
   with gold embrodered gorgeously:
Thy peticote of Sendall right:
   and thus I bought thee gladly.
      Greensleeves was all my joy, etc.

Thy girdle of gold so red,
   with pearles bedecked sumptuously:
The like no other lasses had,
   and yet thou wouldst not love me,
      Greensleeves was all my joy, etc.

Thy purse and eke thy gay guilt knives,
   thy pincase gallant to the eie:
No better wore the Burgesse wives,
   and yet thou wouldst not love me.
      Greensleeves was all my joy, etc.

Thy crimson stockings all of silk,
　with golde all wrought above the knee,
Thy pumps as white as was the milk,
　and yet thou wouldst not love me.
　　Greensleeves was all my joy, etc.

Thy gown was of the grassie green,
　thy sleeves of Satten hanging by:
Which made thee be our harvest Queen,
　and yet thou wouldst not love me.
　　Greensleeves was all my joy, etc.

Thy garters fringed with the golde,
　And silver aglets hanging by,
Which made thee blithe for to beholde,
　And yet thou wouldst not love me.
　　Greensleeves was all my joy, etc.

My gayest gelding I thee gave,
　To ride where ever liked thee,
No Ladie ever was so brave,
　And yet thou wouldst not love me.
　　Greensleeves was all my joy, etc.

My men were clothed all in green,
　And they did ever wait on thee:
Al this was gallant to be seen,
　and yet thou wouldst not love me.
　　Greensleeves was all my joy, etc.

They set thee up, they took thee downe,
　they served thee with humilitie,
Thy foote might not once touch the ground
　and yet thou wouldst not love me.
　　Greensleeves was all my joy, etc.

For everie morning when thou rose,
　I sent thee dainties orderly:
To cheare thy stomack from all woes,
　and yet thou wouldst not love me.
　　Greensleeves was all my joy, etc.

Thou couldst desire no earthly thing,
    But stil thou hadst it readily:
Thy musicke still to play and sing,
    And yet thou wouldst not love me.
      Greensleeves was all my joy, etc.

And who did pay for all this geare,
    that thou didst spend when pleased thee
Even I that am rejected here,
    and thou disdainst to love me.
      Greensleeves was all my joy, etc.

Wel, I wil pray to God on hie,
    that thou my constancie maist see:
And that yet once before I die,
    thou wilt vouchsafe to love me.
      Greensleeves was all my joy, etc.

Greensleeves now farewel adue,
    God I pray to prosper thee:
For I am stil thy lover true,
    come once againe and love me.
      Greensleeves was all my joy, etc.

1586   CHIDIOCK TICHBORNE

My prime of youth is but a froste of cares:
My feaste of joy, is but a dishe of payne:
My cropp of corne, is but a field of tares:
And all my good is but vaine hope of gaine:
The daye is gone, and yet I sawe no sonn:
And nowe I live, and nowe my life is donn

The springe is paste, and yet it hath not sprong
The frute is deade, and yet the leaves are greene
My youth is gone, and yet I am but yonge
I sawe the woorld, and yet I was not seene
My threed is cutt, and yet it was not sponn
And nowe I lyve, and nowe my life is donn.

I saught my death, and founde it in my wombe
I lookte for life, and sawe it was a shade.
I trode the earth and knewe it was my Tombe
And nowe I die, and nowe I am but made
The glasse is full, and nowe the glass is rune
And nowe I live, and nowe my life is donn

ANONYMOUS

Constant *Penelope*, sends to thee carelesse *Ulisses*,
write not againe, but come sweet mate, thy self to revive me.
Troy we do much envie, we desolate lost ladies of *Greece*:
Not *Priamus*, nor yet all Troy can us recompence make.
Oh, that he had when he first toke shipping to Lacedemon,
that adulter I meane, had ben o'rewhelmed with waters:
Then had I not lien now all alone, thus quivering for cold,
nor used this complaint, nor have thought the day to be so long.

ANONYMOUS *from* Sixe Idillia . . . chosen out of . . . Theocritus

[Adonis]

When Venus first did see
Adonis dead to be,
With woeful tatterd heare
And cheekes so wan and seare,
The winged Loves she bad,
The Bore should straight be had.
Forthwith like birdes thay flie,
And through the wood thay hie,
The woefull beast thay finde,
And him with cordes thay binde.
One with a rope before
Doth lead the captive Bore.
Another on his backe
Doth make his bow to cracke.
The beast went wretchedly,
For Venus horribly
Hee fearde, who thus him curst:
    Of all the beasts the wurst,

Didst thou this thigh so wounde?
Didst thou my Love confounde?
   The beast thus spake in feare;
Venus, to thee I sweare,
By thee, and husband thine,
And by these bands of mine,
And by these hunters all,
Thy husband faire and tall
I minded not to kill,
But as an image still,
I him beheld for love,
Which made me forward shove
His thigh, that naked was,
Thinking to kisse, alas,
And that hath hurt me thus.
   Wherfore these teeth, Venus,
Or punish, or cut out.
Why beare I in my snowt
These needlesse teeth about?
If this maie not suffise,
Cut off my chaps likewise.
   To ruth he Venus moves,
And she commands the Loves
His bands for to untie.
After, he came not nie
The wood, but at her wil,
He followde Venus still.
And cumming to the fire,
He burnt up his desire.

1589   SIR PHILIP SIDNEY

My true love hath my hart, and I have his,
By just exchange, one for the other giv'ne.
I holde his deare, and myne he cannot misse:
There never was a better bargaine driv'ne.
My true love hath my hart and I have his.

His hart in me, keepes me and him in one,
My hart in him, his thoughtes and senses guides:
He loves my hart, for once it was his owne:
I cherish his, because in me it bides.
My true love hath my hart and I have his.

SIR WALTER RALEGH

As you came from the holy land
of Walsinghame
Mett you not with my true love
by the way as you came
How shall I know your trew love
That have mett many one
As I went to the holy lande
That have come that have gone
She is neyther whyte nor browne
Butt as the heavens fayre
There is none hathe a form so divine
In the earth or the ayre
Such an one did I meet good Sir
Suche an Angelyke face
Who lyke a queene lyke a nymph did appere
by her gate by her grace:
She hath lefte me here all alone
All allone as unknowne
Who somtymes did me lead with her selfe
And me lovde as her owne:
Whats the cause that she leaves you alone
And a new waye doth take:
Who loved you once as her owne
And her joye did you make:
I have lovde her all my youth
butt now ould as you see
Love lykes not the fallyng frute
From the wythered tree:
Know that love is a careless chylld
And forgets promysse paste:
He is blynd, he is deaff when he lyste
And in faythe never faste:
His desyre is a dureless contente
And a trustless joye
He is wonn with a world of despayre
And is lost with a toye:
Of women kynde suche indeed is the love

Or the word Love abused
Under which many chyldysh desyres
And conceytes are excusde:
Butt trwe Love is a durable fyre
In the mynde ever burnynge:
Never sycke never ould never dead
from itt selfe never turnynge.

(1628)

MARK ALEXANDER BOYD Sonet

Fra banc to banc fra wod to wod I rin
   Ourhailit with my feble fantasie
   Lyc til a leif that fallis from a trie
   Or til a reid ourblawin with the wind.
5 Twa gods gyds me the ane of tham is blind,
   Ye and a bairn brocht up in vanitie.
   The nixt a wyf ingenrit of the se,
   And lichter nor a dauphin with hir fin.
Unhappie is the man for evirmaire
10   That teils the sand and sawis in the aire,
   Bot twyse unhappier is he I lairn
That feidis in his hairt a mad desyre,
   And follows on a woman throw the fyre
   Led be a blind and teichit be a bairn

SIR HENRY LEE

His Golden lockes, Time hath to Silver turn'd,
O Time too swift, ô Swiftnesse never ceasing:
His Youth gainst Time and Age hath ever spurn'd
But spurn'd in vain, Youth waineth by increasing.
   Beauty Strength, Youth, are flowers, but fading seen,
   Dutie, Faith, Love are roots, and ever greene.

1 *wod* wood; 2 *Ourhailit* overcome; 7 *ingenrit* engendered, born; *se* sea;
8 *lichter nor* lighter than; *dauphin* dolphin; 10 *teils* tills; *sawis* sows; 14 *be* by

His Helmet now, shall make a hive for Bees,
And Lovers Sonets, turn'd to holy Psalmes:
A man at Armes must now serve on his knees,
And feede on praiers, which are Age his almes.
    But though from Court to Cottage he depart,
    His Saint is sure of his unspotted heart.

And when he saddest sits in homely Cell,
Heele teach his Swaines this Carroll for a Song,
Blest be the heartes that wish my Soveraigne well,
Curst be the soules that thinke her any wrong.
    Goddesse, allow this agèd man his right,
    To be your Beads-man now, that was your Knight.

EDMUND SPENSER *from* The Faerie Queene

from Book II, Canto XII [The Bower of Blisse Destroyed]

Eftsoones they heard a most melodious sound,
    Of all that mote delight a daintie eare,
    Such as attonce might not on living ground,
    Save in this Paradise, be heard elswhere:
    Right hard it was, for wight, which did it heare,
    To read, what manner musicke that mote bee:
    For all that pleasing is to living care,
    Was there consorted in one harmonee,
Birdes, voyces, instruments, windes, waters, all agree.

The joyous birdes shrouded in chearefull shade,
    Their notes unto the voyce attempred sweet;
    Th'Angelicall soft trembling voyces made
    To th'instruments divine respondence meet:
    The silver sounding instruments did meet
    With the base murmure of the waters fall:
    The waters fall with difference discreet,
    Now soft, now loud, unto the wind did call:
The gentle warbling wind low answered to all.

There, whence that Musick seemed heard to bee,
    Was the faire Witch her selfe now solacing,
    With a new Lover, whom through sorceree
    And witchcraft, she from farre did thither bring:
    There she had him now layd a slombering,

In secret shade, after long wanton joyes:
   Whilst round about them pleasauntly did sing
   Many faire Ladies, and lascivious boyes,
That ever mixt their song with light licentious toyes.

And all that while, right over him she hong,
   With her false eyes fast fixed in his sight,
   As seeking medicine, whence she was strong,
   Or greedily depasturing delight:
   And oft inclining downe with kisses light,
   For feare of waking him, his lips bedewd,
   And through his humid eyes did sucke his spright,
   Quite molten into lust and pleasure lewd;
Wherewith she sighed soft, as if his case she rewd.

The whiles some one did chaunt this lovely lay;
   Ah see, who so faire thing doest faine to see,
   In springing flowre the image of thy day;
   Ah see the Virgin Rose, how sweetly shee
   Doth first peepe forth with bashfull modestee,
   That fairer seemes, the lesse ye see her may;
   Lo see soone after, how more bold and free
   Her bared bosome she doth broad display;
Loe see soone after, how she fades, and falles away.

So passeth, in the passing of a day,
   Of mortall life the leafe, the bud, the flowre,
   Ne more doth flourish after first decay,
   That earst was sought to decke both bed and bowre,
   Of many a Ladie, and many a Paramowre:
   Gather therefore the Rose, whilest yet is prime,
   For soone comes age, that will her pride deflowre:
   Gather the Rose of love, whilest yet is time,
Whilest loving thou mayst loved be with equall crime.

He ceast, and then gan all the quire of birdes
   Their diverse notes t'attune unto his lay,
   As in approvance of his pleasing words.
   The constant paire heard all, that he did say,
   Yet swarved not, but kept their forward way,
   Through many covert groves, and thickets close,
   In which they creeping did at last display
   That wanton Ladie, with her lover lose,
Whose sleepie head she in her lap did soft dispose.

Upon a bed of Roses she was layd,
   As faint through heat, or dight to pleasant sin,
   And was arayd, or rather disarayd,
   All in a vele of silke and silver thin,
   That hid no whit her alablaster skin,
   But rather shewd more white, if more might bee:
   More subtle web *Arachne* can not spin,
   Nor the fine nets, which oft we woven see
Of scorched deaw, do not in th'aire more lightly flee.

Her snowy brest was bare to readie spoyle
   Of hungry eies, which n'ote therewith be fild,
   And yet through languour of her late sweet toyle,
   Few drops, more cleare then Nectar, forth distild,
   That like pure Orient perles adowne it trild,
   And her faire eyes sweet smyling in delight,
   Moystened their fierie beames, with which she thrild
   Fraile harts, yet quenched not; like starry light
Which sparckling on the silent waves, does seeme more bright.

The young man sleeping by her, seemd to bee
   Some goodly swayne of honorable place,
   That certes it great pittie was to see
   Him his nobilitie so foule deface;
   A sweet regard, and amiable grace,
   Mixed with manly sternnesse did appeare
   Yet sleeping, in his well proportiond face,
   And on his tender lips the downy heare
Did now but freshly spring, and silken blossomes beare.

His warlike armes, the idle instruments
   Of sleeping praise, were hong upon a tree,
   And his brave shield, full of old moniments,
   Was fowly ra'st, that none the signes might see;
   Ne for them, ne for honour cared hee,
   Ne ought, that did to his advauncement tend,
   But in lewd loves, and wastfull luxuree,
   His dayes, his goods, his bodie he did spend:
O horrible enchantment, that him so did blend.

The noble Elfe, and carefull Palmer drew
   So nigh them, minding nought, but lustfull game,
   That suddein forth they on them rusht, and threw
   A subtile net, which onely for the same

The skilfull Palmer formally did frame.
So held them under fast, the whiles the rest
Fled all away for feare of fowler shame.
The faire Enchauntresse, so unwares opprest,
Tryde all her arts, and all her sleights, thence out to wrest.

And eke her lover strove: but all in vaine;
For that same net so cunningly was wound,
That neither guile, nor force might it distraine.
They tooke them both, and both them strongly bound
In captive bandes, which there they readie found:
But her in chaines of adamant he tyde;
For nothing else might keepe her safe and sound;
But *Verdant* (so he hight) he soone untyde,
And counsell sage in steed thereof to him applyde.

But all those pleasant bowres and Pallace brave,
Guyon broke downe, with rigour pittilesse;
Ne ought their goodly workmanship might save
Them from the tempest of his wrathfulnesse,
But that their blisse he turn'd to balefulnesse:
Their groves he feld, their gardins did deface,
Their arbers spoyle, their Cabinets suppresse,
Their banket houses burne, their buildings race,
And of the fairest late, now made the fowlest place.

from Book III, Canto VI [The Gardin of Adonis]

In that same Gardin all the goodly flowres,
Wherewith dame Nature doth her beautifie,
And decks the girlonds of her paramoures,
Are fetcht: there is the first seminarie
Of all things, that are borne to live and die,
According to their kindes. Long worke it were,
Here to account the endlesse progenie
Of all the weedes, that bud and blossome there;
But so much as doth need, must needs be counted here.

It sited was in fruitfull soyle of old,
And girt in with two walles on either side;
The one of yron, the other of bright gold,
That none might thorough breake, nor over-stride:
And double gates it had, which opened wide,

By which both in and out men moten pas;
    Th'one faire and fresh, the other old and dride:
    Old *Genius* the porter of them was,
Old *Genius*, the which a double nature has.

He letteth in, he letteth out to wend,
    All that to come into the world desire;
    A thousand thousand naked babes attend
    About him day and night, which doe require,
    That he with fleshly weedes would them attire:
    Such as him list, such as eternall fate
    Ordained hath, he clothes with sinfull mire,
    And sendeth forth to live in mortall state,
Till they againe returne backe by the hinder gate.

After that they againe returned beene,
    They in that Gardin planted be againe;
    And grow afresh, as they had never seene
    Fleshly corruption, nor mortall paine.
    Some thousand yeares so doen they there remaine;
    And then of him are clad with other hew,
    Or sent into the chaungefull world againe,
    Till thither they returne, where first they grew:
So like a wheele around they runne from old to new.

Ne needs there Gardiner to set, or sow,
    To plant or prune: for of their owne accord
    All things, as they created were, doe grow,
    And yet remember well the mightie word,
    Which first was spoken by th'Almightie lord,
    That bad them to increase and multiply:
    Ne doe they need with water of the ford,
    Or of the clouds to moysten their roots dry;
For in themselves eternall moisture they imply.

Infinite shapes of creatures there are bred,
    And uncouth formes, which none yet ever knew,
    And every sort is in a sundry bed
    Set by it selfe, andranckt in comely rew:
    Some fit for reasonable soules t'indew,
    Some made for beasts, some made for birds to weare,
    And all the fruitfull spawne of fishes hew
    In endlesse rancks along enraunged were,
That seem'd the *Ocean* could not containe them there.

Daily they grow, and daily forth are sent
   Into the world, it to replenish more;
   Yet is the stocke not lessened, nor spent,
   But still remaines in everlasting store,
   As it at first created was of yore.
   For in the wide wombe of the world there lyes,
   In hatefull darkenesse and in deepe horrore,
   An huge eternall *Chaos*, which supplyes
The substances of natures fruitfull progenyes.

All things from thence doe their first being fetch,
   And borrow matter, whereof they are made,
   Which when as forme and feature it does ketch,
   Becomes a bodie, and doth then invade
   The state of life, out of the griesly shade.
   That substance is eterne, and bideth so,
   Ne when the life decayes, and forme does fade,
   Doth it consume, and into nothing go,
But chaunged is, and often altred to and fro.

The substance is not chaunged, nor altered,
   But th'only forme and outward fashion;
   For every substance is conditioned
   To change her hew, and sundry formes to don,
   Meet for her temper and complexion:
   For formes are variable and decay,
   By course of kind, and by occasion;
   And that faire flowre of beautie fades away,
As doth the lilly fresh before the sunny ray.

Great enimy to it, and to all the rest,
   That in the *Gardin* of *Adonis* springs,
   Is wicked *Time*, who with his scyth addrest,
   Does mow the flowring herbes and goodly things,
   And all their glory to the ground downe flings,
   Where they doe wither, and are fowly mard:
   He flyes about, and with his flaggy wings
   Beates down both leaves and buds without regard,
Ne ever pittie may relent his malice hard.

Yet pittie often did the gods relent,
   To see so faire things mard, and spoyled quight:
   And their great mother *Venus* did lament
   The losse of her deare brood, her deare delight;

Her hart was pierst with pittie at the sight,
When walking through the Gardin, them she spyde,
Yet no'te she find redresse for such despight.
For all that lives, is subject to that law:
All things decay in time, and to their end do draw.

But were it not, that *Time* their troubler is,
All that in this delightful Gardin growes,
Should happie be, and have immortall blis:
For here all plentie, and all pleasure flowes,
And sweet love gentle fits emongst them throwes,
Without fell rancor, or fond gealosie;
Franckly each paramour his leman knowes,
Each bird his mate, ne any does envie
Their goodly meriment, and gay felicitie.

There is continuall spring, and harvest there
Continuall, both meeting at one time:
For both the boughes doe laughing blossomes beare,
And with fresh colours decke the wanton Prime,
And eke attonce the heavy trees they clime,
Which seeme to labour under their fruits lode:
The whiles the joyous birdes make their pastime
Emongst the shadie leaves, their sweet abode,
And their true loves without suspition tell abrode.

from Book III, Canto XI [Britomart in the House of the Enchanter Busyrane]

And at the upper end of that faire rowme,
There was an Altar built of pretious stone,
Of passing valew, and of great renowme,
On which there stood an Image all alone,
Of massy gold, which with his owne light shone;
And wings it had with sundry colours dight,
More sundry colours, then the proud *Pavone*
Beares in his boasted fan, or *Iris* bright,
When her discolourd bow she spreds through heaven bright.

Blindfold he was, and in his cruell fist
A mortall bow and arrowes keene did hold,
With which he shot at random, when him list,
Some headed with sad lead, some with pure gold;
(A man beware, how thou those darts behold)

A wounded Dragon under him did ly,
  Whose hideous tayle his left foot did enfold,
  And with a shaft was shot through either eye,
That no man forth might draw, ne no man remedye.

And underneath his feet was written thus,
  Unto the Victor of the Gods this bee:
  And all the people in that ample hous
  Did to that image bow their humble knee,
  And oft committed fowle Idolatree.
  That wondrous sight faire *Britomart* amazed,
  Ne seeing could her wonder satisfie,
  But ever more and more upon it gazed,
The whiles the passing brightnes her fraile sences dazed.

Tho as she backward cast her busie eye,
  To search each secret of that goodly sted
  Over the dore thus written she did spye
  Be bold: she oft and oft it over-red,
  Yet could not find what sence it figured:
  But what so were therein or writ or ment,
  She was no whit thereby discouraged
  From prosecuting of her first intent,
But forward with bold steps into the next roome went.

Much fairer, then the former, was that roome,
  And richlier by many partes arayd:
  For not with arras made in painefull loome,
  But with pure gold it all was overlayd,
  Wrought with wilde Antickes, which their follies playd,
  In the rich metall, as they living were:
  A thousand monstrous formes therein were made,
  Such as false love doth oft upon him weare,
For love in thousand monstrous formes doth oft appeare.

And all about, the glistring walles were hong
  With warlike spoiles, and with victorious prayes,
  Of mighty Conquerours and Captaines strong,
  Which were whilome captived in their dayes
  To cruell love, and wrought their owne decayes:
  Their swerds and speres were broke, and hauberques rent;
  And their proud girlonds of tryumphant bayes
  Troden in dust with fury insolent,
To shew the victors might and mercilesse intent.

The warlike Mayde beholding earnestly
    The goodly ordinance of this rich place,
    Did greatly wonder ne could satisfie
    Her greedy eyes with gazing a long space,
    But more she mervaild that no footings trace,
    Nor wight appear'd, but wastefull emptinesse,
    And solemne silence over all that place:
    Straunge thing it seem'd, that none was to possesse
So rich purveyance, ne them keepe with carefulnesse.

And as she lookt about, she did behold,
    How over that same dore was likewise writ,
    Be bold, be bold, and every where *Be bold*,
    That much she muz'd, yet could not construe it
    By any ridling skill, or commune wit.
    At last she spyde at that roomes upper end,
    Another yron dore, on which was writ,
    Be not too bold; whereto though she did bend
Her earnest mind, yet wist not what it might intend.

Thus she there waited untill eventyde,
    Yet living creature none she saw appeare:
    And now sad shadowes gan the world to hyde,
    From mortall vew, and wrap in darkenesse dreare;
    Yet nould she d'off her weary armes, for feare
    Of secret daunger, ne let sleepe oppresse
    Her heavy eyes with natures burdein deare,
    But drew her selfe aside in sickernesse,
And her welpointed weapons did about her dresse.

§ SIR PHILIP SIDNEY *from* Astrophil and Stella   1591

I

Loving in truth, and faine in verse my love to show,
That she deare she might take some pleasure of my paine:
Pleasure might cause her reade, reading might make her know,
Knowledge might pitie winne, and pitie grace obtaine,
    I sought fit words to paint the blackest face of woe,
Studying inventions fine, her wits to entertaine:
Oft turning others' leaves, to see if thence would flow
Some fresh and fruitfull showers upon my sunne-burn'd braine.

But words came halting forth, wanting Invention's stay,
Invention, Nature's child, fled step-dame Studie's blowes,
And others' feete still seem'd but strangers in my way.
Thus great with child to speake, and helplesse in my throwes,
  Biting my trewand pen, beating my selfe for spite,
  'Foole,' said my Muse to me, 'looke in thy heart and write.'

31

With how sad steps, ô Moone, thou climb'st the skies,
  How silently, and with how wanne a face,
  What, may it be that even in heav'nly place
That busie archer his sharpe arrowes tries?
Sure, if that long with *Love* acquainted eyes
  Can judge of *Love*, thou feel'st a Lover's case;
  I reade it in thy lookes, thy languisht grace,
To me that feele the like, thy state descries.
  Then ev'n of fellowship, ô Moone, tell me
Is constant *Love* deem'd there but want of wit?
Are Beauties there as proud as here they be?
Do they above love to be lov'd, and yet
  Those Lovers scorne whom that *Love* doth possesse?
  Do they call *Vertue* there ungratefulnesse?

33

I might, unhappie word, ô me, I might,
And then would not, or could not see my blisse:
Till now, wrapt in a most infernall night,
I find how heav'nly day wretch I did misse.
  Hart rent thy selfe, thou doest thy selfe but right,
No lovely *Paris* made thy *Hellen* his:
No force, no fraud, robd thee of thy delight,
Nor Fortune of thy fortune author is:
  But to my selfe my selfe did give the blow,
While too much wit (forsooth) so troubled me,
That I respects for both our sakes must show:
And yet could not by rising Morne foresee
  How faire a day was neare, ô punisht eyes,
  That I had bene more foolish or more wise.

§   §   §

THOMAS CAMPION

Harke, al you ladies that do sleep;
   The fayry queen Proserpina
Bids you awake and pitie them that weep.
   You may doe in the darke
What the day doth forbid;
   Feare not the dogs that barke,
     Night will have all hid.

But if you let your lovers mone,
   The Fairie Queene Proserpina
Will send abroad her Fairies ev'ry one,
   That shall pinch blacke and blew
Your white hands and faire armes
   That did not kindly rue
     Your Paramours harmes.

In Myrtle Arbours on the downes
   The Fairie Queene Proserpina,
This night by moone-shine leading merrie rounds
   Holds a watch with sweet love,
Downe the dale, up the hill;
   No plaints or groanes may move
     Their holy vigill.

All you that will hold watch with love,
   The Fairie Queene Proserpina
Will make you fairer than Dione's dove;
   Roses red, Lillies white,
And the cleare damaske hue,
   Shall on your cheekes alight:
     Love will adorne you.

All you that love, or lov'd before,
   The Fairie Queene Proserpina
Bids you encrease that loving humour more:
   They that yet have not fed
On delight amorous,
   She vowes that they shall lead
     Apes in Avernus.

SIR JOHN HARINGTON *from* **Ariosto's Orlando Furioso, in English Heroical Verse**

[Astolfo flies by Chariot to the Moon, where he collects Orlando's lost wits]

I say although the fire were wondrous hot,
    Yet in their passage they no heat did feele,
    So that it burnd them, nor offends them not;
    Thence to the moone he guids the running wheele,
    The Moone was like a glasse all voyd of spot,
    Or like a peece of purelie burnisht steele,
    And lookt, although to us it seems so small,
    Well nye as bigg as earth, and sea and all.

Here had *Astolfo* cause of double wonder,
    One, that that region seemeth there so wyde,
    That unto us that are so far a sunder,
    Seems but a little circle, and beside,
    That to behold the ground that him lay under,
    A man had need to have been sharply eyd,
    And bend his brows, and marke ev'n all they might,
    It seemed so small, now chiefly wanting light.

Twere infinit to tell what wondrous things
    He saw, that passed ours not few degrees,
    What towns, what hills, what rivers and what springs
    What dales, what Pallaces, what goodly trees:
    But to be short, at last his guide him brings,
    Unto a goodlie vallie, where he sees,
    A mightie masse of things straungely confused,
    Things that on earth were lost, or were abused.

A store house straunge, that what on earth is lost,
    By fault, by time, by fortune, there is found,
    And like a marchaundise is there engrost,
    In straunger sort then I can well expound:
    Nor speake I sole of wealth, or things of cost,
    In which blind fortunes powre doth most abound,
    But ev'n of things quite out of fortunes powre,
    Which wilfullie we wast each day and houre.

The precious time that fools mispend in play,
    The vaine attempts that never take effect,
    The vows that sinners make, and never pay,
    The counsells wise that carelesse men neglect,
    The fond desires that lead us oft astray,
    The prayses that with pride the heart infect,
    And all we loose with follie and mispending,
    May there be found unto this place ascending.

Now, as *Astolfo* by those regions past,
    He asked many questions of his guide,
    And as he on tone side his eye did cast,
    A wondrous hill of bladders he espyde;
    And he was told they had been in time past,
    The pompous crowns and scepters, full of pride,
    Of Monarks of Assiria, and of Greece,
    Of which now scantlie there is left a peece.

He saw great store of baited hookes with gold,
    And those were gifts that foolish men prepard,
    To give to Princes covetous and old,
    With fondest hope of future vaine reward:
    Then were there ropes all in sweet garlands rold,
    And those were all false flatteries he hard,
    Then hard he crickets songs like to the verses,
    The servant in his masters prayse reherses.

There did he see fond loves, that men pursew,
    To looke like golden gyves with stones all set,
    Then things like Eagles talents he did vew,
    Those offices that favorites do get:
    Then saw he bellows large that much winde blew,
    Large promises that Lords make, and forget,
    Unto their Ganimeds in flowre of youth,
    But after nought but beggerie insewth.

He saw great Cities seated in fayre places,
    That overthrown quite topsie turvie stood,
    He askt and learnd, the cause of their defaces
    Was treason, that doth never turne to good:
    He saw fowle serpents, with fayre womens faces,
    Of coyners and of thieves the cursed brood,
    He saw fine glasses, all in peeces broken,
    Of service lost in court, a wofull token.

Of mingled broth he saw a mightie masse,
    That to no use, all spilt on ground did lye,
    He askt his teacher, and he heard it was,
    The fruitlesse almes that men geve when they dye:
    Then by a fayre green mountain he did passe,
    That once smelt sweet, but now it stinks perdye,
    This was that gift (be't said without offence)
    That *Constantin* gave *Silvester* long since.

Of birdlymd rodds, he saw no litle store,
    And these (O Ladies fayre) your bewties be,
    I do omit ten thousand things and more
    Like unto these, that there the Duke did see
    For all that here is lost, there evermore
    Is kept, and thither in a trise doth flee,
    Howbeit more nor lesse there was no folly,
    For still that here with us remaineth wholly.

He saw some of his own lost time and deeds,
    But yet he knew them not to be his own,
    They seemed to him disguisd in so straunge weeds,
    Till his instructer made them better known:
    But last, the thing which no man thinks he needs,
    Yet each man needeth most, to him was shown,
    By name mans wit, which here we leese so fast,
    As that one substance, all the other past.

It seemd to be a body moyst and soft,
    And apt to mount by ev'ry exhalation,
    And when it hither mounted was aloft,
    It there was kept in potts of such a fashion,
    As we call Jarrs, where oyle is kept in oft:
    The Duke beheld with no small admiration,
    The Jarrs of wit, amongst which one had writ,
    Upon the side thereof, *Orlandos wit.*

This vessell bigger was then all the rest,
    And ev'ry vessell had ingrav'n with art,
    His name, that earst the wit therein possest:
    There of his own, the Duke did finde a part,
    And much he musd, and much him selfe he blest,
    To see some names of men of great desart,
    That thinke they have great store of wit, and bost it,
    And here it playne appeard they quite had lost it.

Some loose their wit with love, some with ambition, [125
   Some running to the sea, great wealth to get,
   Some following Lords, and men of high condition,
   And some in fayre jewells ritch and costlie set,
   One hath desire to prove a rare magicion,
   And some with Poetrie their wit forget,
   An other thinks to be an Alcumist,
   Till all be spent, and he his number mist.

JOHN LYLY *from* Midas   **1592**

PAN

Pan's Syrinx was a Girle indeed,
Though now shee's turn'd into a Reed,
From that deare Reed *Pan's* Pipe does come,
A Pipe that strikes *Apollo* dumbe;
Nor Flute, nor Lute, nor Gitterne can
So chant it, as the Pipe of *Pan*;
Cross-gartred Swaines, and Dairie girles,
With faces smug, and round as Pearles,
When *Pans* shrill Pipe begins to play,
With dancing weare out Night and Day:
The Bag-pipes Drone his Hum layes by,
When *Pan* sounds up his Minstrelsie,
His Minstrelsie! O Base! This Quill
Which at my mouth with winde I fill,
Puts me in minde, though Her I misse,
That still my *Syrinx* lips I kisse.

SAMUEL DANIEL *from* Delia

45

   Care-charmer sleepe, sonne of the Sable night,
Brother to death, in silent darknes borne:
Relieve my languish, and restore the light,
With darke forgetting of my cares returne.

And let the day be time enough to morne,
The shipwrack of my ill-adventred youth:
Let waking eyes suffice to wayle theyr scorne,
Without the torment of the nights untruth.
    Cease dreames, th'ymagery of our day desires,
To modell foorth the passions of the morrow:
Never let rysing Sunne approve you lyers,
To adde more griefe to aggravat my sorrow.
        Still let me sleepe, imbracing clowdes in vaine;
        And never wake, to feele the dayes disdayne.

HENRY CONSTABLE

Deere to my soule, then leave me not forsaken,
    Flie not, my hart within thy bosome sleepeth:
    Even from my selfe and sense I have betaken
    Mee unto thee, for whom my spirit weepeth;
And on the shoare of that salt tearie sea,
    Couch'd in a bed of unseene seeming pleasure
    Where, in imaginarie thoughts thy faire selfe lay,
    But being wakt, robd of my lives best treasure,
I call the heavens, ayre, earth, and seas, to heare
    My love, my trueth, and black disdaind estate:
    Beating the rocks with bellowings of dispaire,
    Which stil with plaints my words reverbarate.
Sighing, 'Alas, what shall become of me?'
Whilst Eccho cryes, 'What shal become of me?'

SIR WALTER RALEGH The Lie

Goe soule the bodies guest
    upon a thankelesse arrant,
Feare not to touch the best
    the truth shall be thy warrant.
Goe since I needs must die
    and give the world the lie.

Say to the Court it glowes
    and shines like rotten wood,
Say to the Church it showes
    what's good, and doth noe good.
If Church and Court reply
    then give them both the lie.

Tell potentates they live
    acting by others action,
Not loved unlesse they give,
    not strong but by affection:
If potentates reply
    give potentates the lie.

Tell men of high condition,
    that manage the Estate,
Their purpose is ambition,
    their practise only hate,
And if they once reply
    then give them all the lie.

Tell them that brave it most,
    they beg for more by spending
Who in their greatest cost
    seek nothing, but commending.
And if they make reply,
    then give them all the lie.

Tell zeale it wants devotion
    tell love it is but lust,
Tell time it meets but motion
    tell flesh it is but dust.
And wish them not reply
    for thou must give the lie.

Tell age it daily wasteth,
    tell honor how it alters.
Tel beauty how she blasteth
    tell favour how it falters
And as they shall reply,
    give every one the lie.

Tell wit how much it wrangles
   in tickle points of nycenesse,
Tell wisedome she entangles
   her selfe in over-wisenesse.
And when they do reply
   straight give them both the lie.

Tell Phisick of her boldnes,
   tel skill it is prevention
Tel charity of coldnes,
   tell Law it is contention,
And as they doe reply
   so give them still the lie.

Tell Fortune of her blindnesse,
   tel nature of decay,
Tel friendship of unkindnesse,
   tel Justice of delay.
And if they wil reply,
   then give them all the lie.

Tell Arts they have no soundnes,
   but vary by esteeming,
Tel schooles they want profoundnes
   and stand to much on seeming.
If Arts and Schooles reply,
   give arts and schooles the lie.

Tell faith it's fled the Citie,
   tell how the country erreth
Tel manhood shakes of pitty
   tel vertue least preferreth,
And if they doe reply,
   spare not to give the lie.

So when thou hast as I,
   commanded thee, done blabbing,
Because to give the lie,
   deserves no lesse then stabbing,
Stab at thee, he that will,
   no stab thy soule can kill.

               (1608)

ANONYMOUS

Praisd be Dianas faire and harmles light,
Praisd be the dewes, wherwith she moists the ground;
Praisd be hir beames, the glorie of the night,
Praisd be hir powre, by which all powres abound.

Praisd be hir Nimphs, with whom she decks the woods,
Praisd be hir knights, in whom true honor lives,
Praisd be that force, by which she moves the floods,
Let that Diana shine, which all these gives.

In heaven Queene she is among the spheares,
In ay she Mistres-like makes all things pure,
Eternitie in hir oft chaunge she beares,
She beautie is, by hir the faire endure.

Time weares hir not, she doth his chariot guide,
Mortalitie belowe hir orbe is plaste,
By hir the vertue of the starrs downe slide,
In hir is vertues perfect image cast.

  A knowledge pure it is hir worth to kno,
  With Circes let them dwell that thinke not so.

THOMAS LODGE The Sheepheards Sorrow,
Being Disdained in Love

Muses helpe me, sorrow swarmeth,
Eies are fraught with seas of languish,
Haples hope my solace harmeth:
Mindes repast is bitter anguish.

Eie of daie regarded never,
Certaine trust in world untrustie,
Flattring hope beguileth ever:
Wearie olde, and wanton lustie.

Dawne of day, beholdes inthroned,
Fortunes darling proud and dreadles:
Darksome night doth heare him moned,
Who before was rich and needles.

Rob the spheare of lines united;
Make a sudden voide in nature:
Force the day to be benighted;
Reave the cause of time, and creature.

Ere the world will cease to varie:
This I weepe for, this I sorrow:
Muses if you please to tarie,
Further helpe I meane to borrow.

Courted once by fortunes favor,
Compast now with envies curses:
All my thoughts of sorrowes savor,
Hopes run fleeting like the Sourses.

Ay me wanton scorne hath maimed
All the joies my hart enjoied:
Thoughts their thinking have disclaimed,
Hate my hopes have quite annoied.

Scant regard my weale hath scanted:
Looking coie hath forst my lowring:
Nothing likte, where nothing wanted,
Weds mine eies to ceasles showring.

Former Love was once admired,
Present favor is estranged:
Loath'd the pleasure long desired;
Thus both men and thoughts are changed.

Lovely Swaine with luckie speeding,
Once (but now no more) so frended:
Thou my flocks hast had in feeding,
From the morne, till day was ended.

Drinke and fodder, foode and folding,
Had my lambes and ewes togeather:
I with them was still beholding,
Both in warmth, and winter weather.

Now they languish since refused,
Ewes and lambes are paind with pining:
I with ewes and lambes confused,
All unto our deathes declining.

Silence leave thy cave obscured,
Daine a dolefull Swaine to tender,
Though disdaines I have endured,
Yet I am no deepe offender.

Philips sonne can with his finger,
Hide his scar, it is so little:
Little sinne a day to linger,
Wise men wander in a tittle.

Trifles yet my Swaine have turned,
Tho my sonne he never showeth:
Tho I weepe, I am not mourned,
Tho I want, no pitie groweth.

Yet for pitie love my muses,
Gentle silence be their cover,
They must leave their wonted uses,
Since I leave to be a Lover.

They shall live with thee inclosed,
I will loath my pen and paper:
Art shall never be supposed,
Sloth shall quench the watching taper.

Kisse them silence, kisse them kindely,
Tho I leave them, yet I love them:
Tho my wit have led them blindely,
Yet my Swaine did once approve them.

I will travell soiles removed,
Night and morning never merie,
Thou shalt harbor that I loved,
I will love that makes me wearie.

If perchaunce the Shepherd straieth,
In thy walks and shades unhaunted,
Tell the Teene my hart betraieth,
How neglect my joyes have daunted.

§   §   §

BARNABE BARNES from Parthenophil and Parthenophe

[Sestina]

Then, first with lockes disheveled, and bare,
Straite guirded, in a chearefull calmie night:
Having a fier made of greene *Cypresse* woode,
And with male franckincense on alter kindled
I call on threefould *Hecate* with teares,
And here (with loude voyce) invocate the furies:

For their assistance, to me with their furies:
Whilst snowye steedes in coach bright *Phoebe* bare.
Ay me *Parthenophe* smiles at my teares,
I neither take my rest by day, or night:
Her cruell loves in me such heate have kindled.
Hence goate and bring her to me raging woode:

Hecate tell which way she comes through the woode.
This wine aboute this aulter, to the furies
I sprinkle, whiles the *Cypresse* bowes be kindled,
This brimstone earth within her bowelles bare,
And this blew incense sacred to the night.
This hand (perforce) from this bay this braunche teares.

So be she brought which pittied not my teares.
And as it burneth with the *Cypresse* woode
So burne she with desier by day and night.
You goddes of vengance, and avenge-full furies
Revenge, to whom I bende on my knees bare.
Hence goate, and bring her with loves outrage kindled.

Hecate make signes if she with love come kindled.
Thinke on my passions *Hec'ate*, and my teares:
This *Rosemariene* (whose braunche she cheefely bare
And loved best) I cut both barke and woode,
Broke with this brasen Axe, and in loves furies
I treade on it, rejoycing in this night:

And saying, let her her feele such woundes this night.
About this alter, and rich incense kindled
This lace and *Vervine* to loves bitter furies
I binde, and strewe, and with sadde sighes and teares
About I beare her Image raging woode.
Hence goate and bring her from her bedding bare:

(. . .)

Come blessed goate, that my sweet Lady bare:
Where hast thou beene (*Parthenophe*) this night?
What, cold? Sleepe by this fier of *Cypresse* woode
Which I much longing for thy sake have kindled,
Weepe not, come loves and wipe away her teares:
At length yet, wilt thou take away my furies?

Ay me, embrace me, see those ouglye furies.
Come to my bed, least they behold thee bare
And beare thee hence. They will not pittie teares,
And these still dwell in everlasting night:
Ah loves, sweet love, sweet fiers for us hath kindled,
But not inflam'd, with franckinsense, or woode,

The furies, they shall hence into the woode,
Whiles *Cupid* shall make calmer his hot furies,
And stand appeased at our fier's kindled.
Joyne; joyne (*Parthenophe*) thy selfe unbare,
None can perceive us in the silent night,
Now will I cease from sighes, lamentes, and teares,

And cease (*Parthenophe*) sweet cease thy teares:
Beare golden *Apples thornes* in every woode,
Joyne heavens, for we conjoyne this heavenly night:
Let *Alder* trees beare *Apricockes* (dye furies)
And *Thistles Peares*, which prickles lately bare.
Now both in one with equall flame be kindled:

Dye magicke bowes, now dye, which late were kindled:
Here is mine heaven: loves droppe in steede of teares.
It joynes, it joynes, ah both embracing bare.
Let *Nettles* bring forth *Roses* in each woode,
Last ever verdant woodes: hence former furies:
Oh dye, live, joye: what? last continuall night,

Sleepe *Phoebus* still with *Thetis*: rule still night.
I melt in love, loves marrow-flame is kindled:
Here will I be consum'd in loves sweet furies.
I melt, I melt, watche Cupid my love-teares:
If these be furies, oh let me be woode!
If all the fierie element I bare

Tis now acquitted: cease your former teares,
For as she once with rage my bodie kindled,
So in hers am I buried this night.

SIR PHILIP SIDNEY *from* The Countess of Pembroke's Arcadia

STREPHON

Yee Gote-heard Gods, that love the grassie mountaines,
Yee Nimphes which haunt the springs in pleasant vallies,
Ye Satyrs joyde with free and quiet forrests,
Vouchsafe your silent eares to playning musique,
Which to my woes gives still an early morning:
And drawes the dolor on till wery evening.

KLAIUS

O *Mercurie*, foregoer to the evening,
O heavenlie huntresse of the savage mountaines,
O lovelie starre, entitled of the morning,
While that my voice doth fill these wofull vallies,
Vouchsafe your silent eares to plaining musique,
Which oft hath *Echo* tir'd in secrete forrests.

STREPHON

I that was once free-burges of the forrests,
Where shade from Sunne, and sporte I sought in evening,
I that was once esteem'd for pleasant musique,

Am banisht now among the monstrous mountaines
Of huge despaire, and foule affliction's vallies,
Am growne a shrich-owle to my selfe each morning.

KLAIUS

I that was once delighted every morning,
Hunting the wilde inhabiters of forrests,
I that was once the musique of these vallies,
So darkened am, that all my day is evening,
Hart-broken so, that molehilles seeme high mountaines,
And fill the vales with cries in steed of musique.

STREPHON

Long since alas, my deadly Swannish musique
Hath made it selfe a crier of the morning,
And hath with wailing strength clim'd highest mountaines:
Long since my thoughts more desert be then forrests:
Long since I see my joyes come to their evening,
And state throwen downe to over-troden vallies.

KLAIUS

Long since the happie dwellers of these vallies,
Have praide me leave my strange exclaiming musique,
Which troubles their daye's worke, and joyes of evening:
Long since I hate the night, more hate the morning:
Long since my thoughts chase me like beasts in forrests,
And make me wish my selfe layd under mountaines.

STREPHON

Me seemes I see the high and stately mountaines,
Transforme themselves to lowe dejected vallies:
Me seemes I heare in these ill-changed forrests,
The Nightingales doo learne of Owles their musique:
Me seemes I feele the comfort of the morning
Turnde to the mortall serene of an evening.

KLAIUS

Me seemes I see a filthie clowdie evening,
As soon as Sunne begins to clime the mountaines:
Me seemes I feele a noysome sent, the morning
When I doo smell the flowers of these vallies:
Me seemes I heare, when I doo heare sweete musique,
The dreadfull cries of murdred men in forrests.

STREPHON

I wish to fire the trees of all these forrests;
I give the Sunne a last farewell each evening;
I curse the fidling finders out of Musicke:
With envie I doo hate the loftie mountaines;
And with despite despise the humble vallies:
I doo detest night, evening, day, and morning.

KLAIUS

Curse to my selfe my prayer is, the morning:
My fire is more, then can be made with forrests;
My state more base, then are the basest vallies:
I wish no evenings more to see, each evening;
Shamed I hate my selfe in sight of mountaines,
And stoppe mine eares, lest I growe mad with Musicke.

STREPHON

For she, whose parts maintainde a perfect musique,
Whose beawties shin'de more then the blushing morning,
Who much did passe in state the stately mountaines,
In straightnes past the Cedars of the forrests,
Hath cast me, wretch, into eternall evening,
By taking her two Sunnes from these darke vallies.

KLAIUS

For she, with whom compar'd, the Alpes are vallies,
She, whose lest word brings from the spheares their musique,
At whose approach the Sunne rase in the evening,
Who, where she went, bare in her forhead morning,
Is gone, is gone from these our spoyled forrests,
Turning to desarts our best pastur'de mountaines.

STREPHON

These mountaines witnesse shall, so shall these vallies,

KLAIUS

These forrests eke, made wretched by our musique,
Our morning hymne this is, and song at evening.

WILLIAM SHAKESPEARE *from* Love's Labours Lost   **1594**

ARMADO
Holla, Approach.
   Enter all.
This side is *Hiems*, Winter.
This *Ver*, the Spring: the one maintained by the Owle,
Th'other by the Cuckow.
Ver, begin.

Spring

> When Dasies pied, and Violets blew,
> And Cuckow-buds of yellow hew:
> And Ladie-smockes all silver white,
> Do paint the Medowes with delight.
> The Cuckow then on everie tree,
> Mockes married men, for thus sings he,
> Cuckow.
> Cuckow, Cuckow: O word of feare,
> Unpleasing to a married eare.

> When Shepherds pipe on Oaten strawes,
> And merrie Larkes are Ploughmens clockes:
> When Turtles tread, and Rookes and Dawes,
> And Maidens bleach their summer smockes:
> The Cuckow then on everie tree
> Mockes married men; for thus sings he,
>   Cuckow.
> Cuckow, Cuckow: O word of feare,
> Unpleasing to a married eare.

Winter

> When Isicles hang by the wall,
> And Dicke the Shepheard blowes his naile:
> And Tom beares logges into the hall,
> And Milke comes frozen home in paile:
> When blood is nipt, and waies be fowle,

Then nightly sings the staring Owle
Tu-whit to-who.
　　A merrie note,
　　While greasie Jone doth keele the pot.

When all aloud the winde doth blow,
And coffing drownes the Parsons saw:
And birds sit brooding in the snow,
And Marrians nose lookes red and raw:
When roasted Crabs hisse in the bowle,
Then nightly sings the staring Owle,
Tu-whit to who:
　　A merrie note,
　　While greasie Jone doth keele the pot.

ARMADO
The Words of Mercurie,
Are harsh after the songs of Apollo:
You that way; we this way.

　　　　　　　　　　　　　　Exeunt omnes.

　　　　　　　　　　　　　　　　　(1598)

ANONYMOUS

Weare I a Kinge I coude commande content;
Weare I obscure unknowne shoulde be my cares,
And weare I ded no thoughtes should me torment,
Nor wordes, nor wronges, nor loves, nor hopes, nor feares.
　　A dowtefull choyse of these thinges one to crave,
　　A Kingdom or a cottage or a grave.

1595　　§ EDMUND SPENSER *from* Amoretti

Sonnet LXVII

Lyke as a huntsman after weary chace,
　　Seeing the game from him escapt away,
　　sits downe to rest him in some shady place,
　　with panting hounds beguiled of their pray:

So after long pursuit and vaine assay,
    when I all weary had the chace forsooke,
    the gentle deare returnd the selfe-same way,
    thinking to quench her thirst at the next brooke.
There she beholding me with mylder looke,
    sought not to fly, but fearelesse still did bide:
    till I in hand her yet halfe trembling tooke,
    and with her owne goodwill hir fyrmely tyde.
Strange thing me seemd to see a beast so wyld,
    so goodly wonne with her owne will beguyld.

Sonnet LXVIII

Most glorious Lord of lyfe that on this day,
    Didst make thy triumph over death and sin:
    and having harrowd hell didst bring away
    captivity thence captive us to win:
This joyous day, deare Lord, with joy begin,
    and grant that we for whom thou diddest dye
    being with thy deare blood clene washt from sin,
    may live for ever in felicity.
And that thy love we weighing worthily,
    may likewise love thee for the same againe:
    and for thy sake that all lyke deare didst buy,
    with love may one another entertayne.
So let us love, deare love, lyke as we ought,
    love is the lesson which the Lord us taught.

§   §   §

ROBERT SOUTHWELL S.J. Decease Release

The pounded spice both tast and sent doth please,
In fading smoke the force doth incense shewe,
The perisht kernell springeth with encrease,
The lopped tree doth best and soonest growe.

Gods spice I was and pounding was my due,
In fadinge breath my incense savored best,
Death was the meane my kyrnell to renewe,
By loppinge shott I upp to heavenly rest.

Some thinges more perfect are in their decaye,
Like sparke that going out gives clerest light,
Such was my happ whose dolefull dying daye
Beganne my joy and termed fortunes spite.

Alive a Queene, now dead I am a Sainte,
Once Mary calld, my name nowe Martyr is,
From earthly raigne debarred by restraint,
In liew whereof I raigne in heavenly blisse.

My life my griefe, my death hath wrought my joye,
My frendes my foyle, my foes my weale procur'd,
My speedy death hath shortned longe annoye,
And losse of life an endles life assur'd.

My skaffold was the bedd where ease I founde,
The blocke a pillowe of Eternall reste,
My hedman cast me in a blisfull swounde,
His axe cutt off my cares from combred breste.

Rue not my death, rejoyce at my repose,
It was no death to me but to my woe,
The budd was opened to lett out the Rose,
The cheynes unloo'sd to lett the captive goe.

A prince by birth, a prisoner by mishappe,
From Crowne to crosse, from throne to thrall I fell,
My right my ruthe, my titles wrought my trapp,
My weale my woe, my worldly heaven my hell.

By death from prisoner to a prince enhaunc'd,
From Crosse to Crowne, from thrall to throne againe,
My ruth my right, my trapp my stile advaunc'd,
From woe to weale, from hell to heavenly raigne.

(1817)

ROBERT SOUTHWELL S.J. New Heaven, New Warre

This little Babe so few dayes olde,
Is come to ryfle sathans folde;
All hell doth at his presence quake,
Though he himselfe for cold doe shake:
For in this weake unarmed wise,
The gates of hell he will surprise.

With teares he fights and winnes the field,
His naked breast stands for a shield;
His battring shot are babish cryes,
His Arrowes lookes of weeping eyes,
His Martiall ensignes cold and neede,
And feeble flesh his warriers steede.

His Campe is pitched in a stall,
His bulwarke but a broken wall:
The Crib his trench, hay stalks his stakes,
Of Sheepheards he his Muster makes;
And thus as sure his foe to wound,
The Angells trumps alarum sound.

My soule with Christ joyne thou in fight,
Sticke to the tents that he hath pight;
Within his Crib is surest ward,
This little Babe will be thy guard:
If thou wilt foyle thy foes with joy,
Then flit not from this heavenly boy.

(1602)

ROBERT SOUTHWELL S.J. The Burning Babe

As I in hoarie Winters night stoode shivering in the snow,
Surpris'd I was with sodaine heate, which made my hart to glow;
And lifting up a fearefull eye, to view what fire was neare,
A pretty Babe all burning bright did in the ayre appeare;
Who scorched with excessive heate, such floods of teares did shed,
As though his floods should quench his flames, which with his teares
    were fed:

Alas (quoth he) but newly borne, in fierie heates I frie,
Yet none approach to warme their harts or feele my fire, but I;
My faultlesse breast the furnace is, the fuell wounding thornes:
Love is the fire, and sighs the smoake, the ashes, shame and
        scornes;
The fewell Justice layeth on, and Mercie blowes the coales,
The mettall in this furnace wrought, are mens defiled soules:
For which, as now on fire I am to worke them to their good,
So will I melt into a bath, to wash them in my blood.
With this he vanisht out of sight, and swiftly shrunk away,
And straight I called unto minde, that it was Christmasse day.

(1602)

GEORGE PEELE *from* The Old Wives Tale

When as the Rie reach to the chin,
And chopcherrie chopcherrie ripe within,
Strawberries swimming in the creame,
And schoole boyes playing in the streame:
Then O, then O, then O my true love said,
Till that time come againe,
Shee could not live a maid.

VOICE.
Gently dip: but not too deepe;
For feare you make the goulden beard to weepe.
    [*A head comes up with eares of Corne, and she combes them in her
    lap.*]
Faire maiden white and red,
Combe me smoothe, and stroke my head:
And thou shalt have some cockell bread.
Gently dippe, but not too deepe,
For feare thou make the goulden beard to weep.
    [*A head comes up full of golde, she combes it into her lap.*]
Faire maiden, white, and redde,
Combe me smooth, and stroke my head;
And every haire, a sheave shall be,
And every sheave a goulden tree.

EDMUND SPENSER Prothalamion

I

Calme was the day, and through the trembling ayre,
Sweete breathing *Zephyrus* did softly play
A gentle spirit, that lightly did delay
Hot *Titans* beames, which then did glyster fayre:
When I whom sullein care,
Through discontent of my long fruitlesse stay
In Princes Court, and expectation vayne
Of idle hopes, which still doe fly away,
Like empty shaddowes, did aflict my brayne,
Walkt forth to ease my payne
Along the shoare of silver streaming *Themmes*,
Whose rutty Bancke, the which his River hemmes,
Was paynted all with variable flowers,
And all the meades adornd with daintie gemmes,
Fit to decke maydens bowres,
And crowne their Paramours,
Against the Brydale day, which is not long:
   Sweete *Themmes* runne softly, till I end my Song.

2

There, in a Meadow, by the Rivers side,
A Flocke of *Nymphes* I chaunced to espy,
All lovely Daughters of the Flood thereby,
With goodly greenish locks all loose untyde,
As each had bene a Bryde,
And each one had a little wicker basket,
Made of fine twigs entrayled curiously,
In which they gathered flowers to fill their flasket:
And with fine Fingers, cropt full feateously
The tender stalkes on hye.
Of every sort, which in that Meadow grew,
They gathered some; the Violet pallid blew,
The little Dazie, that at evening closes,
The virgin Lillie, and the Primrose trew,
With store of vermeil Roses,
To decke their Bridegromes posies,
Against the Brydale day, which was not long:
   Sweete *Themmes* runne softly, till I end my Song.

3

With that I saw two Swannes of goodly hewe,
Come softly swimming downe along the Lee;
Two fairer Birds I yet did never see:
The snow which doth the top of *Pindus* strew,
Did never whiter shew,
Nor *Jove* himselfe when he a Swan would be
For love of *Leda*, whiter did appeare:
Yet *Leda* was they say as white as he,
Yet not so white as these, nor nothing neare;
So purely white they were,
That even the gentle streame, the which them bare,
Seem'd foule to them, and bad his billowes spare
To wet their silken feathers, least they might
Soyle their fayre plumes with water not so fayre,
And marre their beauties bright,
That shone as heavens light,
Against their Brydale day, which was not long:
   Sweete *Themmes* runne softly, till I end my Song.

4

Eftsoones the *Nymphes*, which now had Flowers their fill,
Ran all in haste, to see that silver brood,
As they came floating on the Christal Flood,
Whom when they sawe, they stood amazed still,
Their wondring eyes to fill.
Them seem'd they never saw a sight so fayre,
Of Fowles so lovely, that they sure did deeme
Them heavenly borne, or to be that same payre
Which through the Skie draw *Venus* silver Teeme,
For sure they did not seeme
To be begot of any earthly Seede,
But rather Angels or of Angels breede:
Yet were they bred of *Somers-heat* they say,
In sweetest Season, when each Flower and weede
The earth did fresh aray,
So fresh they seem'd as day,
Even as their Brydale day, which was not long:
   Sweete *Themmes* runne softly, till I end my Song.

Then forth they all out of their baskets drew
Great store of Flowers, the honour of the field,
That to the sense did fragrant odours yield,
All which upon those goodly Birds they threw,
And all the Waves did strew,
That like old *Peneus* Waters they did seeme,
When downe along by pleasant *Tempes* shore
Scattred with Flowres, through *Thessaly* they streeme,
That they appeare through Lillies plenteous store,
Like a Brydes Chamber flore:
Two of those *Nymphes*, meane while, two Garlands bound,
Of freshest Flowres which in that Mead they found,
The which presenting all in trim Array,
Their snowie Foreheads therewithall they crownd,
Whil'st one did sing this Lay,
Prepar'd against that Day,
Against their Brydale day, which was not long:
   Sweete *Themmes* runne softly, till I end my Song.

6

Ye gentle Birdes, the worlds faire ornament,
And heavens glorie, whom this happie hower
Doth leade unto your lovers blisfull bower,
Joy may you have and gentle hearts content
Of your loves couplement:
And let faire *Venus*, that is Queene of love,
With her heart-quelling Sonne upon you smile,
Whose smile they say, hath vertue to remove
All Loves dislike, and friendships faultie guile
For ever to assoile.
Let endlesse Peace your steadfast hearts accord,
And blessed Plentie wait upon your bord,
And let your bed with pleasures chast abound,
That fruitfull issue may to you afford,
Which may your foes confound,
And make your joyes redound,
Upon your Brydale day, which is not long:
   Sweete *Themmes* run softlie, till I end my Song.

So ended she; and all the rest around
To her redoubled that her undersong,
Which said, their bridale daye should not be long.
And gentle Eccho from the neighbour ground,
Their accents did resound.
So forth those joyous Birdes did passe along,
Adowne the Lee, that to them murmurde low,
As he would speake, but that he lackt a tong,
Yet did by signes his glad affection show,
Making his streame run slow.
And all the foule which in his flood did dwell
Gan flock about these twaine, that did excell
The rest, so far, as *Cynthia* doth shend
The lesser starres. So they enranged well,
Did on those two attend,
And their best service lend,
Against their wedding day, which was not long:
    Sweete *Themmes* run softly, till I end my song.

8

At length they all to mery *London* came,
To mery London, my most kyndly Nurse,
That to me gave this Lifes first native sourse:
Though from another place I take my name,
An house of auncient fame.
There when they came, whereas those bricky towres,
The which on *Themmes* brode aged backe doe ryde,
Where now the studious Lawyers have their bowers,
There whylome wont the Templer Knights to byde,
Till they decayd through pride:
Next whereunto there standes a stately place,
Where oft I gayned giftes and goodly grace
Of that great Lord, which therein wont to dwell,
Whose want too well, now feeles my freendles case:
But Ah here fits not well
Olde woes but joyes to tell
Against the bridale daye, which is not long:
    Sweete *Themmes* runne softly, till I end my Song.

9

Yet therein now doth lodge a noble Peer,
Great *Englands* glory and the Worlds wide wonder,
Whose dreadfull name, late through all *Spaine* did thunder,
And *Hercules* two pillors standing neere,
Did make to quake and feare:
Faire branch of Honor, flower of Chevalrie,
That fillest *England* with thy triumphes fame,
Joy have thou of thy noble victorie,
And endlesse happinesse of thine owne name
That promiseth the same:
That through thy prowesse and victorious armes,
Thy country may be freed from forraine harmes:
And great *Elisaes* glorious name may ring
Through al the world, fil'd with thy wide Alarmes,
Which some brave muse may sing
To ages following,
Upon the Brydale day, which is not long:
   Sweete *Themmes* runne softly, till I end my Song.

10

From those high Towers, this noble Lord issuing,
Like Radiant *Hesper* when his golden hayre
In th'*Ocean* billowes he hath Bathed fayre,
Descended to the Rivers open vewing,
With a great traine ensuing.
Above the rest were goodly to bee seene
Two gentle Knights of lovely face and feature
Beseeming well the bower of anie Queene,
With gifts of wit and ornaments of nature,
Fit for so goodly stature:
That like the twins of *Jove* they seem'd in sight,
Which decke the Bauldricke of the Heavens bright.
They two forth pacing to the Rivers side,
Received those two faire Brides, their Loves delight,
Which at th'appointed tyde,
Each one did make his Bryde,
Against their Brydale day, which is not long:
   Sweete *Themmes* runne softly, till I end my Song.

SIR JOHN DAVIES In Cosmum

Cosmus hath more discoursing in his head,
Then Jove, when Pallas issued from his braine,
And still he strives to be delivered,
Of all his thoughtes at once, but al in vaine.
For as we see at all the play house dores,
When ended is the play, the daunce, and song:
A thousand townesmen, gentlemen, and whores,
Porters and serving-men togither throng,
So thoughts of drinking, thriving, wenching, war,
And borrowing money, raging in his minde,
To issue all at once so forwarde are,
As none at all can perfect passage finde.

SIR JOHN DAVIES *from* Orchestra, or a Poeme of Dauncing

['The speach of Love persuading men to learn Dancing']

And now behold your tender Nurse the *Ayre*   *Of the Ayre.*
And common neighbour that *ay runns around*,
How many pictures and impressions faire
Within her emptie regions are there found,
Which to your sences Dauncing doe propound?
  For what are *Breath*, *Speech*, *Ecchos*, *Musick*, *Winds*,
  But Dauncings of the ayre in sundry kinds?

For when you breath, the *ayre* in order moves,
Now in, now out, in time and measure trew;
And when you speake, so well she dauncing loves,
That doubling oft, and oft redoubling new,
With thousand formes she doth her selfe endew:
  For all the words that from your lips repaire,
  Are nought but tricks and turnings of the aire.

Hence is her pratling daughter *Eccho* borne
That daunces to all voyces she can heare:
There is no sound so harsh that she doth scorne,
Nor any time wherein she will forbeare

The aiery pavement with her feete to weare.
And yet her hearing sence is nothing quick,
For after time she endeth every trick.

And thou sweet *Musick*, Dauncings only life,
The eares sole happines, the ayres best speach,
Loadstone of fellowship, charming rod of strife,
The soft minds Paradice, the sick minds Leach,
With thine owne tongue thou trees and stones canst teach
That when the Aire doth daunce her finest measure,
Then art thou borne the Gods and mens sweet pleasure.

Lastly, where keepe the *Winds* their revelry,
Their violent turnings and wild whirling hayes?
But in the Ayres tralucent gallery?
Where she her selfe is turnd a hundreth wayes,
While with those Maskers wantonly she playes;
Yet in this misrule, they such rule embrace
As two at once encomber not the place.

If then fier, ayre, wandring and fixed lights
In every province of th'imperiall skye,
Yeeld perfect formes of dauncing to your sights,
In vaine I teach the eare, that which the eye
With certaine view already doth descrie.
But for your eyes perceive not all they see,
In this I will your sences maister bee.

For loe the *Sea* that fleets about the Land,   *Of the Sea.*
And like a girdle clips her solide wast,
Musick and measure both doth understand:
For his great Christall eye is alwayes cast
Up to the Moone, and on her fixed fast.
And as she daunceth in her pallid spheere,
So daunceth he about the Center heere.

Sometimes his proud greene waves in order set,
One after other flow unto the shore,
Which when they have with many kisses wet,
They ebb away in order as before;
And to make knowne his Courtly Love the more,
He oft doth lay aside his three-forkt Mace,
And with his armes the timerous Earth embrace.

Onely the Earth doth stand for ever still,
Her rocks remove not, nor her mountaines meete,
(Although some witts enricht with Learnings skill
Say heav'n stands firme, and that the Earth doth fleete
And swiftly turneth underneath their feete)
Yet though the Earth is ever stedfast seene,
On her broad breast hath Dauncing ever beene.

For those blew vaines that through her body spred,   *Of the Rivers.*
Those saphire streams which from great hills do spring,
(The Earths great duggs: for every wight is fed
With sweet fresh moisture from them issuing)
Observe a daunce in their wide wandering:
　　And still their daunce begets a murmur sweete,
　　And still the murmur with the daunce doth meete.

Of all their wayes I love *Mæanders* path,
Which to the tunes of dying Swans doth daunce,
Such winding sleights, such turnes and tricks he hath,
Such Creekes, such wrenches, and such daliaunce,
That whether it be hap or heedlesse chaunce,
　　In this indented course and wriggling play
　　He seemes to daunce a perfect cunning *Hay.*

1597　　**ANONYMOUS**

Since Bonny-boots was dead, that so divinely
Could toot and foot it, (O he did it finely!)
　　We ne'er went more a-Maying
　　Nor had that sweet fa-laing. Fa la.

WILLIAM ALABASTER　Of the Reed That the Jews Set in Our
Saviour's Hand

Long time hath Christ, long time I must confess,
Held me a hollow reed within his hand,
That merited in hell to make a brand,
Had not his grace supplied mine emptiness.

Oft time with languor and newfangleness,
Had I been borne away like sifted sand,
When sin and Satan got the upper hand,
But that his steadfast mercy did me bless.
Still let me grow upon that living land,
Within that wound which iron did impress,
And made a spring of blood flow from thy hand.
Then will I gather sap and rise and stand,
That all that see this wonder may express,
Upon this ground how well grows barrenness.

(1938)

WILLIAM ALABASTER Of His Conversion

Away feare with thy projectes, noe false fyre
which thou doest make, can ought my courage quaile
or cause mee leward come, or strike my sayle;
what if the world doe frowne att my retyre,
what if denyall dash my wish'd desire
and purblind pitty doe my state bewaile
and wonder cross it selfe, and free speech raile
and greatnes take it not, and death shew nigher?
Tell them, my Soule, the feares that make mee quake:
the smouldering brimstone, and the burninge lake,
life feeding Death, Death ever life devowring,
tormentes not moved, unheard, yett still roaring,
God lost, hell fownd: ever, never begune:
now bidd mee into flame from smoake to runne.

(1831)

ROBERT SIDNEY, EARL OF LEICESTER

Forsaken woods, trees with sharpe storms opprest
whose leaves once hidd, the sun, now strew the grownd
once bred delight, now scorn, late usde to sownd
of sweetest birds, now of hoars crowes the nest

Gardens which once in thowsand coulers drest
shewed natures pryde: now in dead sticks abownd
in whome prowde summers treasure late was found
now but the rags, of winters torn coate rest

Medows whose sydes, late fayre brookes kist now slyme
embraced holds: feelds whose youth green and brave
promist long lyfe, now frosts lay in the grave

Say all and I with them: what doth not tyme!
But they whoe knew tyme, tyme will finde again
I that fayre tymes lost, on tyme call in vaine

(1975)

1598 SIR PHILIP SIDNEY

When to my deadlie pleasure,
When to my livelie torment,
Ladie mine eyes remained,
Joyned alas to your beames,

With violence of heav'nly
Beautie tied to vertue,
Reason abasht retyred,
Gladly my senses yeelded.

Gladly my senses yeelding,
Thus to betray my hart's fort,
Left me devoid of all life;

They to the beamie Sunnes went,
Where by the death of all deaths,
Finde to what harme they hastned,

Like to the silly *Sylvan*,
Burn'd by the light he best liked,
When with a fire he first met.

Yet, yet, a life to their death,
Lady you have reserved,
Lady the life of all love;

For though my sense be from me,
And I be dead who want sense,
Yet do we both live in you.

Turned anew by your meanes,
Unto the flowre that ay turnes,
As you, alas, my Sunne bends;

Thus do I fall to rise thus,
Thus do I dye to live thus,
Changed to a change, I change not.

Thus may I not be from you:
Thus be my senses on you:
Thus what I thinke is of you:
Thus what I seeke is in you:
    All what I am, it is you.

SIR PHILIP SIDNEY

Leave me ô Love, which reachest but to dust,
And thou my mind aspire to higher things:
Grow rich in that which never taketh rust:
What ever fades, but fading pleasure brings.

Draw in thy beames, and humble all thy might,
To that sweet yoke, where lasting freedomes be:
Which breakes the clowdes and opens forth the light,
That doth both shine and give us sight to see.

O take fast hold, let that light be thy guide,
In this small course which birth drawes out to death,
And thinke how evil becommeth him to slide,
Who seeketh heav'n, and comes of heav'nly breath.
    Then farewell world, thy uttermost I see,
    Eternall Love maintaine thy life in me.

MARY HERBERT, COUNTESS OF PEMBROKE
Psalm 58

And call yee this to utter what is just,
    You that of justice hold the sov'raign throne?
And call yee this to yeld, O sonnes of dust,
    To wronged brethren ev'ry man his own?
O no: it is your long malicious will
    Now to the world to make by practize known,
With whose oppression you the ballance fill,
    Just to your selves, indiff'rent else to none.

But what could they, who ev'n in birth declin'd,
    From truth and right to lies and injuries?
To shew the venim of their cancred mynd
    The adders image scarcly can suffice;
Nay scarce the aspick may with them contend,
    On whom the charmer all in vaine applies
His skillfull'st spells: ay missing of his end,
    While shee self-deff, and unaffected lies.

Lord crack their teeth, Lord crush these lions jawes,
    Soe lett them sinck as water in the sand:
When deadly bow their aiming fury drawes,
    Shiver the shaft er past the shooters hand.
So make them melt as the dishowsed snaile
    Or as the Embrio, whose vitall band
Breakes er it holdes, and formlesse eyes do faile
    To see the sun, though brought to lightfull land.

O let their brood, a brood of springing thornes,
    Be by untymely rooting overthrowne
Er bushes waxt, they push with pricking hornes,
    As fruites yet greene are oft by tempest blowne.
The good with gladness this reveng shall see,
    And bath his feete in bloud of wicked one
While all shall say: the just rewarded be,
    There is a God that carves to each his own.

(1823)

MARY HERBERT, COUNTESS OF PEMBROKE
from **Psalm 139**

Each inmost peece in me is thine:
   While yet I in my mother dwelt,
      All that me cladd
      From thee I hadd.
   Thou in my frame hast strangly delt:
Needes in my praise thy workes must shine
   So inly them my thoughts have felt.

Thou, how my back was beam-wise laid,
   And raftring of my ribbs, dost know:
      Know'st ev'ry point
      Of bone and joynt,
   How to this whole these partes did grow,
In brave embrod'ry faire araid,
   Though wrought in shopp both dark and low.

Nay fashionless, ere forme I tooke,
   Thy all and more beholding ey
      My shapelesse shape
      Could not escape:
   All these tyme fram'd successively
Ere one had beeing, in the booke
   Of thy foresight, enrol'd did ly.

My God, how I these studies prize,
   That doe thy hidden workings show!
      Whose summ is such,
      Noe suume soe much:
   Nay summ'd as sand they summlesse grow.
I lye to sleepe, from sleepe I rise,
   Yet still in thought with thee I goe.

(1823)

CHRISTOPHER MARLOWE *from* Hero and Leander

His bodie was as straight as *Circes* wand,
Jove might have sipt out *Nectar* from his hand.
Even as delicious meat is to the tast,
So was his necke in touching, and surpast
The white of *Pelops* shoulder. I could tell ye,
How smooth his brest was, and how white his bellie,
And whose immortall fingars did imprint,
That heavenly path, with many a curious dint,
That runs along his backe, but my rude pen,
Can hardly blazon foorth the loves of men,
Much lesse of powerfull gods. Let it suffise,
That my slacke muse, sings of *Leanders* eies,
Those orient cheekes and lippes, exceeding his
That leapt into the water for a kis
Of his owne shadow, and despising many,
Died ere he could enjoy the love of any.
Had wilde *Hippolitus, Leander* seene,
Enamoured of his beautie had he beene,
His presence made the rudest paisant melt,
That in the vast uplandish countrie dwelt,
The barbarous *Thratian* soldier moov'd with nought,
Was moov'd with him, and for his favour sought.
Some swore he was a maid in mans attire,
For in his lookes were all that men desire,
A pleasant smiling cheeke, a speaking eye,
A brow for Love to banquet roiallye,
And such as knew he was a man would say,
Leander, thou art made for amorous play:
Why art thou not in love, and lov'd of all?
Though thou be faire, yet be not thine owne thrall.

(. . .)

By this *Leander* being nere the land,
Cast downe his wearie feet, and felt the sand.
Breathlesse albeit he were, he rested not,
Till to the solitarie tower he got.
And knockt and cald, at which celestiall noise,
The longing heart of *Hero* much more joies

Then nymphs and sheapheards, when the timbrell rings,
Or crooked Dolphin when the sailer sings;
She stayd not for her robes, but straight arose,
And drunke with gladnesse, to the dore she goes.
Where seeing a naked man, she scriecht for feare,
Such sights as this, to tender maids are rare.
And ran into the darke her selfe to hide,
Rich jewels in the darke are soonest spide.
Unto her was he led, or rather drawne,
By those white limmes, which sparckled through the lawne.
The neerer that he came, the more she fled,
And seeking refuge, slipt into her bed.
Whereon *Leander* sitting, thus began,
Through numming cold, all feeble, faint and wan:
   If not for love, yet love for pittie sake,
Me in thy bed and maiden bosome take,
At least vouchsafe these armes some little roome,
Who hoping to imbrace thee, cherely swome.
This head was beat with manie a churlish billow,
And therefore let it rest upon thy pillow.
Herewith afrighted *Hero* shrunke away,
And in her luke-warme place *Leander* lay.
Whose lively heat like fire from heaven fet,
Would animate grosse clay, and higher set
The drooping thoughts of base declining soules,
Then drerie *Mars*, carowsing *Nectar* boules.
His hands he cast upon her like a snare,
She overcome with shame and sallow feare,
Like chast *Diana*, when *Acteon* spyde her,
Being sodainly betraide, dyv'd downe to hide her.
And as her silver body downeward went,
With both her hands she made the bed a tent,
And in her owne mind thought her selfe secure,
O'recast with dim and darksome coverture.
And now she lets him whisper in her eare,
Flatter, intreat, promise, protest and sweare,
Yet ever as he greedily assayd
To touch those dainties, she the *Harpey* playd,
And every lim did as a soldier stout,
Defend the fort, and keep the foe-man out.
For though the rising yv'rie mount he scal'd,
Which is with azure circling lines empal'd,
Much like a globe, (a globe may I tearme this,
By which love sailes to regions full of blis,)

Yet there with *Sysiphus* he toyld in vaine,
Till gentle parlie did the truce obtaine.
Wherein *Leander* on her quivering brest,
Breathlesse spoke some thing, and sigh'd out the rest;
Which so prevail'd, as he with small ado,
Inclos'd her in his armes and kist her to.
And everie kisse to her was as a charme,
And to *Leander* as a fresh alarme.
So that the truce was broke, and she alas,
(Poore sillie maiden) at his mercie was.
Love is not ful of pittie (as men say)
But deaffe and cruell, where he meanes to pray.
Even as a bird, which in our hands we wring,
Foorth plungeth, and oft flutters with her wing,
She trembling strove, this strife of hers (like that
Which made the world) another world begat,
Of unknowne joy. Treason was in her thought,
And cunningly to yeeld her selfe she sought.
Seeming not woon, yet woon she was at length,
In such warres women use but halfe their strength.
Leander now like Theban *Hercules*,
Entred the orchard of *Th'esperides*,
Whose fruit none rightly can describe, but hee
That puls or shakes it from the golden tree:
And now she wisht this night were never done,
And sigh'd to thinke upon th'approching sunne,
For much it greev'd her that the bright day-light,
Should know the pleasure of this blessed night,
And them like *Mars* and *Ericine* displayed,
Both in each others armes chaind as they layd.
Or speake to him who in a moment tooke,
That which so long so charily she kept,
And faine by stealth away she would have crept,
And to some corner secretly have gone,
Leaving *Leander* in the bed alone.
But as her naked feet were whipping out,
He on the suddaine cling'd her so about,
That Meremaid-like unto the floore she slid,
One halfe appear'd, the other halfe was hid.
Thus neere the bed she blushing stood upright,
And from her countenance behold ye might,
A kind of twilight breake, which through the heare,
As from an orient cloud, glymse here and there.

And round about the chamber this false morne,
Brought foorth the day before the day was borne.
So *Heroes* ruddie cheeke, *Hero* betrayd,
And her all naked to his sight displayd.

ANONYMOUS

Hark, all ye lovely saints above,
Diana hath agreed with Love
His fiery weapon to remove. Fa la.
    Do you not see
    How they agree?
Then cease, fair ladies; why weep ye? Fa la.

See, see, your mistress bids you cease,
And welcome Love, with love's increase;
Diana hath procured your peace. Fa la.
    Cupid hath sworn
    His bow forlorn
To break and burn, ere ladies mourn. Fa la.

§ CHRISTOPHER MARLOWE *from* All Ovids Elegies

Book I, Elegia 5

In summers heate and mid-time of the day
To rest my limbes upon a bed I lay,
One window shut, the other open stood,
Which gave such light, as twincles in a wood,
Like twilight glimps at setting of the Sunne
Or night being past, and yet not day begunne.
Such light to shamefast maidens must be showne,
Where they may sport, and seeme to be unknowne.
Then came *Corinna* in a long loose gowne,
Her white neck hid with tresses hanging downe:
Resembling fayre *Semiramis* going to bed
Or *Layis* of a thousand wooers sped,
I snacht her gowne: being thin, the harme was small,
Yet striv'd she to be covered there withall.

And striving thus as one that would be cast,
Betray'd her selfe, and yeelded at the last.
Starke naked as she stood before mine eye,
Not one wen in her body could I spie.
What armes and shoulders did I touch and see,
How apt her breasts were to be prest by me.
How smooth a belly under her wast saw I?
How large a legge, and what a lustie thigh?
To leave the rest all lik'd me passing well,
I cling'd her naked body, downe she fell,
Judge you the rest, being tirde she bad me kisse;
Jove send me more such after-noones as this.

Book III, Elegia 13

Seeing thou art faire, I barre not thy false playing,
But let not me poore soule know of thy straying.
Nor do I give thee counsell to live chaste,
But that thou wouldst dissemble, when 'tis paste.
She hath not trod awry, that doth deny it.
Such as confesse have lost their good names by it.
What madnesse ist to tell nights pranckes by day?
And hidden secrets openly to bewray?
The strumpet with the stranger will not doo,
Before the roome be cleere, and dore put too.
Will you make ship-wrack of your honest name?
And let the world be witnesse of the same.
Be more advisde, walke as a puritan,
And I shall think you chaste, do what you can.
Slip still, onely deny it, when 'tis done,
And before folke immodest speeches shunne.
The bed is for lascivious toyings meete,
There use all tricks, and tread shame under feete.
When you are up, and drest, be sage and grave,
And in the bed hide all the faults you have.
Be not asham'de to strip you being there,
And mingle thighes yours ever mine to beare.
There in your Rosie lips my tongue in-tombe,
Practise a thousand sports when there you come.
Forbeare no wanton words you there would speake,
And with your pastime let the bed-stead creake.

But with your robes put on an honest face,
And blush, and seeme as you were full of grace.
Deceive all, let me erre, and think I am right,
And like a Wittall think thee voide of slight.
Why see I lines so oft receiv'd, and given?
This bed and that by tumbling made uneven?
Like one start up your haire tost and displac'd,
And with a wantons tooth your neck new rac'd.
Graunt this, that what you doe I may not see,
If you weigh not ill speeches, yet weigh mee.
My soule fleetes, when I thinke what you have done,
And thorough every veine doth cold bloud runne.
Then thee whom I must love, I hate in vaine,
And would be dead, but dead with thee remaine.
Ile not sift much, but holde thee soone excusde,
Say but thou wert injuriously accusde.
Though while the deed be dooing you be tooke,
And I see when you ope the two leav'd booke,
Sweare I was blinde, deny, if you be wise,
And I will trust your words more then mine eyes.
From him that yeelds the palme is quickly got,
Teach but your tongue to say, I did it not,
And being justifide by two words thinke,
The cause acquits you not, but I that winke.

JOHN DONNE On His Mistris

By our first strange and fatall interview,
By all desires which thereof did ensue,
By our long sterving hopes, by that remorse
Which my words masculine perswasive force
Begot in thee, and by the memory
Of hurts which spies and rivalls threatned mee,
I calmely beg; but by thy parents wrath,
By all paines which want and divorcement hath,
I conjure thee; and all those oathes which I
And thou have sworne, to seal joint constancie,

Here I unsweare, and over-sweare them thus:
Thou shalt not love by meanes so dangerous.
Temper, oh faire Love, loves impetuous rage,
Be my true mistris still, not my feign'd page.
I'll goe, and, by thy kind leave, leave behinde
Thee, onely worthy to nurse in my minde
Thirst to come back; oh, if thou dye before,
From other lands my soule towards thee shall soare.
Thy (else Almighty) Beauty cannot move
Rage from the seas, nor thy love teach them love,
Nor tame wilde Boreas harshness; thou hast read
How roughly hee in peices shivered
Faire Orithea, whome he swore hee lov'd.
Fall ill or good, 'tis madness to have prov'd
Dangers unurg'd; feede on this flatterye,
That absent lovers one in th'other bee.
Dissemble nothing, not a boy, nor change
Thy bodies habit, nor mindes; bee not strange
To thy selfe onely; all will spye in thy face
A blushing womanly discovering grace.
Richly cloth'd Apes are call'd Apes, and as soone
Ecclips'd as bright, wee call the moone, the moone.
Men of France, changeable Camelions,
Spittles of diseases, shops of fashions,
Loves fuellers, and the rightest companie
Of Players which uppon the worlds stage bee,
Will quickly knowe thee, 'and knowe thee; and alas
Th'indifferent Italian, as wee passe
His warme land, well content to thinke thee page,
Will haunt thee, with such lust and hideous rage
As Lots faire guests were vext: But none of these,
Nor spungie hydroptique Dutch, shall thee displease,
If thou stay here. Oh stay here, for, for thee
England is only'a worthy gallerie,
To walk in expectation, till from thence
Our greate King call thee into his presence.
When I am gone, dreame mee some happinesse,
Nor let thy lookes our long hid love confesse,
Nor praise, nor dispraise mee, blesse, nor curse
Openly loves force; nor in bed fright thy nurse
With midnights startings, crying out, oh, oh,
Nurse, oh my love is slaine; I saw him goe

Ore the white Alpes, alone; I saw him, I,
Assayld, fight, taken, stabb'd, bleede, fall, and dye.
Augure mee better chance, except dreade Jove
Think it enough for mee, to'have had thy love.

(1635)

MICHAEL DRAYTON *from* Idea

1599

5

Nothing but No and I, and I and No,
How fals it out so strangely you reply?
I tell yee (Faire) ile not be answered so,
With this affirming No, denying I.
I say, I Love, you sleightly answere I:
I say, You Love, you peule me out a No:
I say, I Die, you Eccho me with I:
Save mee I Crie, you sigh me out a No;
Must Woe and I, have naught but No and I?
No I, am I, if I no more can have;
Answere no more, with Silence make reply,
And let me take my selfe what I doe crave,
    Let No and I, with I and you be so:
    Then answere No and I, and I and No.

ALEXANDER HUME *from* Of the Day Estivall

O perfite light, quhilk schaid away,
The darkenes from the light,
And set a ruler ou'r the day,
Ane uther ou'r the night.

5   Thy glorie when the day foorth flies,
Mair vively dois appeare,
Nor at midday unto our eyes,
The shining Sun is cleare.

1 *schaid away* separated; 6 *vively* vividly; 7 *nor* than;

The shaddow of the earth anon,
10 Remooves and drawes by,
Sine in the East, when it is gon,
Appeares a clearer sky.

Quhilk Sunne perceaves the little larks,
The lapwing and the snyp,
15 And tunes their sangs like natures clarks,
Ou'r midow, mure, and stryp.

Bot everie bais'd nocturnall beast,
Na langer may abide,
They hy away baith maist and least,
20 Them selves in houis to hide.

They dread the day fra thay it see,
And from the sight of men.
To saits, and covars fast they flee,
As Lyons to their den.

25 Oure Hemisphere is poleist clein,
And lightened more and more,
While everie thing be clearly sein,
Quhilk seemed dim before.

Except the glistering astres bright,
30 Which all the night were cleere,
Offusked with a greater light,
Na langer dois appeare.

The golden globe incontinent,
Sets up his shining head,
35 And ou'r the earth and firmament,
Displayes his beims abread.

11 *sine* then; 15 *clarks* choristers; 16 *mure* moor; *stryp* small stream;
17 *bais'd* fearful; 19 *hy* hie, hurry; *maist and least* the largest and the smallest;
21 *fra* when; 23 *saits* lairs; *covars* hiding places; 25 *poleist* polished; 27 *while* until;
29 *astres* stars; 31 *offusked* obscured; 33 *incontinent* at once;

For joy the birds with boulden throts,
Agains his visage shein,
Takes up their kindelie musicke nots,
40   In woods and gardens grein.

Up braids the carefull husbandman,
His cornes, and vines to see,
And everie tymous artisan,
In buith worke busilie.

45   The pastor quits the slouthfull sleepe,
And passis forth with speede,
His little camow-nosed sheepe,
And rowtting kie to feede.

The passenger from perrels sure,
50   Gangs gladly foorth the way:
Breife, everie living creature,
Takes comfort of the day,

The subtile mottie rayons light,
At rifts thay are in wonne,
55   The glansing thains, and vitre bright,
Resplends against the sunne.

The dew upon the tender crops,
Lyke pearles white and round,
Or like to melted silver drops,
60   Refreshes all the ground.

The mystie rocke, the clouds of raine,
From tops of mountaines skails,
Cleare are the highest hils and plaine,
The vapors takes the vails.

---

37 *boulden* swollen; 38 *shein* bright; 39 *kindelie* natural; 41 *braids* rises;
43 *tymous* early; 44 *buith* booth; 47 *camow* snub; 48 *rowtting kie* lowing cows;
53 *mottie rayons* dusty beams; 54 *rifts* chinks; *wonne* entered; 55 *glansing thains*
shimmering vanes; *vitre* window-glass; 56 *resplends* shines; 57 *crops* heads;
61 *rocke* steam; 62 *skails* disperses; 63 *begaried* ornamented; *pend* vault;

Begaried is the saphire pend,
With sprangs of skarlet hew,
And preciously from end till end,
Damasked white and blew.

The ample heaven of fabrik sure,
70   In cleannes dois surpas,
The chrystall and the silver pure,
Or clearest poleist glas.

The time sa tranquill is and still,
That na where sall ye find,
75   Saife on ane high, and barren hill,
Ane aire of peeping wind.

All trees and simples great and small,
That balmie leife do beir,
Nor thay were painted on a wall,
80   Na mair they move or steir.

Calme is the deepe, and purpour se,
Yee smuther nor the sand,
The wals that woltring wont to be,
Are stable like the land.

85   Sa silent is the cessile air,
That every cry and call,
The hils, and dails, and forrest fair,
Againe repeates them all.

The rivers fresh, the callor streames,
90   Ou'r rockes can softlie rin,
The water cleare like chrystall seames,
And makes a pleasant din.

The fields, and earthly superfice,
With verdure greene is spread,
95   And naturallie but artifice,
In partie coulors cled.

66 *sprangs* streaks;   75 *saife* except;   76 *peeping* piping;   77 *simples* herbs;   79 *nor*
than if;   81 *purpour se* purple sea;   82 *smuther nor* smoother than;   83 *wals* waves;
woltring weltering;   85 *cessile* yielding;   89 *callor* cool;   90 *rin* run;
93 *superfice* surface;   95 *but* without;

The flurishes and fragrant flowres,
Throw *Phoebus* fostring heit,
Refresht with dew and silver showres,
100   Casts up ane odor sweit.

The clogged busie bumming beis,
That never thinks to drowne,
On flowers and flourishes of treis,
Collects their liquor browne.

105   The Sunne maist like a speedie post,
With ardent course ascends,
The beautie of the heavenly host,
Up to our Zenith tends.

Nocht guided be na *Phaeton*,
110   Nor trained in a chyre,
Bot be the high and haly On,
Quhilk dois all where impire.

GEORGE PEELE *from* **David and Fair Bethsabe**

Hot sunne, coole fire, temperd with sweet aire,
Black shade, fair nurse, shadow my white haire.
Shine sun, burne fire, breathe aire, and ease mee,
Black shade, fair nurse, shroud me and please me.
Shadow (my sweet nurse) keep me from burning,
Make not my glad cause, cause of mourning.
Let not my beauties fire,
Enflame unstaied desire,
Nor pierce any bright eye,
That wandreth lightly.

97 *flurishes* blossoms; 101 *clogged* burdened; *bumming* humming;
102 *drowne* drone; 105 *post* courier; 110 *trained* drawn; *chyre* chariot; 111 *on* one
(God); 112 *quhilk* who; *impire* rule absolutely

SAMUEL DANIEL *from* Musophilus

[Stonehenge]

Where wil you have your vertuous names safe laid,
    In gorgeous tombes, in sacred Cels secure?
    Do you not see those prostrate heapes betraid
    Your fathers bones, and could not keepe them sure?
    And will you trust deceitfull stones faire laid:
    And thinke they will be to your honor truer?
No, no, unsparing time will proudly send
    A warrant unto wrath that with one frown
    Wil al these mock'ries of vaine glory rend,
    And make them as before, ungrac'd, unknown,
    Poore idle honors that can ill defend
    Your memories, that cannot keepe their own.
And whereto serve that wondrous *trophei* now,
    That on the goodly plaine neare *Wilton* stands?
    That huge domb heap, that cannot tel us how,
    Nor what, nor whence it is, nor with whose hands,
    Nor for whose glory, it was set to shew
    How much our pride mockes that of other lands?
Whereon when as the gazing passenger
    Hath greedy lookt with admiration,
    And faine would know his birth, and what he were,
    How there erected, and how long agone:
    Enquires and askes his fellow travailer
    What he hath heard and his opinion:
And he knowes nothing. Then he turnes againe
    And looks and sighs, and then admires afresh,
    And in himselfe with sorrow doth complaine
    The misery of darke forgetfulnesse;
    Angrie with time that nothing should remain,
    Our greatest wonders-wonder to expresse.
Then ignorance with fabulous discourse
    Robbing faire arte and cunning of their right,
    Tels how those stones were by the divels force
    From *Affricke* brought to Ireland in a night,
    And thence to Britannie by Magicke course,
    From giants hand redeem'd by *Merlins* sleight.

§ **FULKE GREVILLE, LORD BROOKE** *from* **Caelica**

Sonnet XLV

Absence, the noble truce
Of *Cupids* warre:
Where though desires want use,
They honoured are.
Thou art the just protection,
Of prodigall affection,
Have thou the praise;
When bankrupt *Cupid* braveth,
Thy mines his credit saveth,
With sweet delayes.

Of wounds which presence makes
With Beauties shot,
Absence the anguish slakes,
But healeth not:
Absence records the Stories,
Wherein Desire glories,
Although she burne;
She cherisheth the spirits
Where Constancy inherits
And Passions mourne.

Absence, like dainty Clouds,
On glorious-bright,
Natures weake senses shrowds,
From harming light.
Absence maintaines the treasure
Of pleasure unto pleasure,
Sparing with praise;
Absence doth nurse the fire,
Which starves and feeds desire
With sweet delayes.

Presence to every part
Of Beauty tyes,
Where Wonder rules the Heart
There Pleasure dyes:

Presence plagues minde and senses
With modesties defences,
Absence is free:
Thoughts doe in absence venter
On *Cupids* shadowed center,
They winke and see.

But Thoughts be not so brave,
With absent joy;
For you with that you have
Your selfe destroy:
The absence which you glory,
Is that which makes you sory,
And burne in vaine:
For Thought is not the weapon,
Wherewith *thoughts-ease* men cheapen,
Absence is paine.

(1633)

Sonnet LXXXIV

Farewell sweet Boy, complaine not of my truth;
Thy Mother lov'd thee not with more devotion;
For to thy Boyes play I gave all my youth,
Yong Master, I did hope for your promotion.

While some sought Honours, Princes thoughts observing,
Many woo'd *Fame, the child of paine and anguish*,
Others judg'd inward good a chiefe deserving,
I in thy wanton Visions joy'd to languish.

I bow'd not to thy image for succession,
Nor bound thy bow to shoot reformed kindnesse,
Thy playes of hope and feare were my confession,
The spectacles to my life was thy blindnesse;
   But *Cupid* now farewell, I will goe play me,
   With thoughts that please me lesse, and lesse betray me.

(1633)

Sonnet LXXXV

Love is the Peace, whereto all thoughts doe strive,
Done and begun with all our powers in one:
The first and last in us that is alive,
End of the good, and therewith pleas'd alone.

Perfections spirit, Goddesse of the minde,
Passed through hope, desire, griefe and feare,
A simple Goodnesse in the flesh refin'd,
Which of the joyes to come doth witnesse beare.

Constant, because it sees no cause to varie,
A Quintessence of Passions overthrowne,
Rais'd above all that change of objects carry,
A Nature by no other nature knowne:
   For Glorie's of eternitie a frame,
   That by all bodies else obscures her name.

(1633)

Sonnet XCIX

Downe in the depth of mine iniquity,
That ugly center of infernall spirits;
Where each sinne feeles her owne deformity,
In these peculiar torments she inherits,
   Depriv'd of humane graces, and divine,
   Even there appeares this *saving God* of mine.

And in this fatall mirrour of transgression,
Shewes man as fruit of his degeneration,
The errours ugly infinite impression,
Which beares the faithlesse downe to desperation;
   Depriv'd of humane graces and divine,
   Even there appeares this *saving God* of mine.

In power and truth, Almighty and eternall,
Which on the sinne reflects strange desolation,
With glory scourging all the Sprites infernall,
And uncreated hell with unprivation;
    Depriv'd of humane graces, not divine,
    Even there appeares this *saving God* of mine.

For on this sp'rituall Crosse condemned lying,
To paines infernall by eternall doome,
I see my Saviour for the same sinnes dying,
And from that hell I fear'd, to free me, come;
    Depriv'd of humane graces, not divine,
    Thus hath his death rais'd up this soule of mine.

                                  (1633)

Sonnet C

In Night when colours all to blacke are cast,
Distinction lost, or gone downe with the light;
The eye a watch to inward senses plac'd,
Not seeing, yet still having power of sight,

Gives vaine *Alarums* to the inward sense,
Where feare stirr'd up with witty tyranny,
Confounds all powers, and thorough selfe-offence,
Doth forge and raise impossibility:

Such as in thicke depriving darkenesses,
Proper reflections of the errour be,
And images of selfe-confusednesses,
Which hurt imaginations onely see;
    And from this nothing seene, tels newes of devils,
    Which but expressions be of inward evils.

                                  (1633)

§   §   §

⑤ from **Englands Helicon**

ANONYMOUS The Sheepheards Description of Love

MELIBEUS
Sheepheard, what's Love, I pray thee tell?
FAUSTUS
It is that Fountaine, and that Well,
Where pleasure and repentance dwell.
It is perhaps that sauncing bell,
    That toules all into heaven or hell,
    And this is Love as I heard tell.
MELI.
Yet what is Love, I pre-thee say?
FAU.
It is a worke on holy-day,
It is December match'd with May,
When lustie-bloods in fresh aray,
    Heare ten moneths after of the play,
    And this is Love, as I heare say.
MELI.
Yet what is Love, good Sheepheard saine?
FAU.
It is a Sun-shine mixt with raine,
It is a tooth-ach, or like paine,
It is a game where none dooth gaine,
    The Lasse saith no, and would full faine:
    And this is Love, as I heare saine.
MELI.
Yet Sheepheard, what is Love, I pray?
FAU.
It is a yea, it is a nay,
A pretty kind of sporting fray,
It is a thing will soone away,
    Then Nimphs take vantage while ye may:
    And this is love as I heare say.
MELI.
Yet what is love, good Sheepheard show?

A thing that creepes, it cannot goe,
A prize that passeth too and fro,
A thing for one, a thing for moe,
    And he that prooves shall finde it so;
    And Sheepheard this is love I troe.

CHRISTOPHER MARLOWE The Passionate Sheepheard to his Love

Come live with mee, and be my love,
And we will all the pleasures prove,
That Vallies, groves, hills and fieldes,
Woods, or steepie mountaine yeeldes.

And wee will sit upon the Rocks,
Seeing the Sheepheards feede theyr flocks,
By shallow Rivers, to whose falls,
Melodious byrds sing Madrigalls.

And I will make thee beds of Roses,
And a thousand fragrant poesies,
A cap of flowers, and a kirtle,
Imbroydred all with leaves of Mirtle.

A gowne made of the finest wooll,
Which from our pretty Lambes we pull,
Fayre lined slippers for the cold:
With buckles of the purest gold.

A belt of straw, and Ivie buds,
With Corall clasps and Amber studs,
And if these pleasures may thee move,
Come live with mee, and be my love.

The Sheepheards Swaines shall daunce and sing,
For thy delight each May-morning,
If these delights thy minde may move;
Then live with mee, and be my love.

SIR WALTER RALEGH The Nimphs Reply to the Sheepheard

If all the world and love were young,
And truth in every Sheepheards tongue,
These pretty pleasures might me move,
To live with thee, and be thy love.

Time drives the flocks from field to fold,
When Rivers rage, and Rocks grow cold,
And *Philomell* becommeth dombe,
The rest complaines of cares to come.

The flowers doe fade, and wanton fieldes,
To wayward winter reckoning yeeldes,
A honny tongue, a hart of gall,
Is fancies spring, but sorrowes fall.

Thy gownes, thy shooes, thy beds of Roses,
Thy cap, thy kirtle, and thy poesies,
Soone breake, soone wither, soone forgotten:
In follie ripe, in reason rotten.

Thy belt of straw and Ivie buddes,
Thy Corall claspes and Amber studdes,
All these in mee no meanes can move,
To come to thee, and be thy love.

But could youth last, and love still breede,
Had joyes no date, nor age no neede,
Then these delights my minde might move,
To live with thee, and be thy love.

THOMAS NASHE *from* Summers Last Will and Testament

Fayre Summer droops, droope men and beasts therefore:
So fayre a summer looke for never more.
All good things vanish, lesse then in a day,
Peace, plenty, pleasure, sodainely decay.
   Goe not yet away, bright soule of the sad yeare;
   The earth is hell when thou leav'st to appeare.

What, shall those flowres that deckt thy garland erst,
Upon thy grave be wastfully disperst?
O trees, consume your sap in sorrowes sourse;
Streames, turne to teares your tributary course.
   Goe not yet hence, bright soule of the sad yeare;
   The earth is hell, when thou leav'st to appeare.

*

Adieu, farewell earths blisse,
This world uncertaine is,
Fond are lifes lustfull joyes,
Death proves them all but toyes,
None from his darts can flye;
I am sick, I must dye:
   Lord, have mercy on us.

Rich men, trust not in wealth,
Gold cannot buy you health;
Phisick himselfe must fade.
All things to end are made,
The plague full swift goes bye;
I am sick, I must dye:
   Lord, have mercy on us.

Beauty is but a flowre,
Which wrinckles will devoure,
Brightness falls from the ayre,
Queenes have died yong and faire,
Dust hath closde *Helens* eye.
I am sick, I must dye:
   Lord, have mercy on us.

Strength stoopes unto the grave,
Wormes feed on *Hector* brave,
Swords may not fight with fate,
Earth still holds ope her gate.
Come, come, the bells do crye.
I am sick, I must dye:
   Lord, have mercy on us.

Wit with his wantonnesse
Tasteth deaths bitternesse:
Hels executioner
Hath no eares for to heare
What vaine art can reply.
I am sick, I must dye:
   Lord, have mercy on us.

Haste therefore eche degree,
To welcome destiny:
Heaven is our heritage
Earth but a players stage,
Mount wee unto the sky.
I am sick, I must dye:
   Lord, have mercy on us.

ANONYMOUS [A Lament for Our Lady's Shrine at Walsingham]

In the wrackes of Walsingam
  Whom should I chuse,
But the Queene of Walsingam
  to be guide to my muse
Then thou Prince of Walsingam
  graunt me to frame,
Bitter plaintes to rewe thy wronge,
  bitter wo for thy name,
Bitter was it oh to see,
  The seely sheepe
Murdred by the raveninge wolves
  While the sheephardes did sleep,
Bitter was it oh to vewe
  the sacred vyne,
Whiles the gardiners plaied all close,
  rooted up by the swine

Bitter bitter oh to behould,
   the grasse to growe
Where the walles of Walsingam
   so statly did shewe,
Such were the workes of Walsingam:
   while shee did stand
Such are the wrackes as now do shewe
   of that holy land,
Levell Levell with the ground
   the towres doe lye
Which with their golden glitteringe tops
   Pearsed once to the skye,
Wher weare gates no gates ar nowe,
   the waies unknowen
Wher the presse of peares did passe
   While her fame far was blowen
Oules do scrike wher the sweetest himnes
   lately weer songe
Toades and serpentes hold ther dennes,
   Wher the Palmers did thronge
Weepe weepe o Walsingam
   Whose dayes are nightes
Blessinges turned to blasphemies
   Holy deedes to dispites,
Sinne is wher our Ladie sate
   Heaven turned is to Hell.
Sathan sittes wher our Lord did swaye
   Walsingam oh farewell.

          (1868)

ANONYMOUS

Fine knacks for ladies, cheape choise brave and new,
Good penniworths but mony cannot move,
I keep a faier but for the faier to view,
A beggar may bee liberall of love,
Though all my wares bee trash the hart is true,
                The hart is true,
                The hart is true.

Great gifts are guiles and looke for gifts againe,
My trifles come, as treasures from my minde,
It is a precious Jewell to bee plaine,
Sometimes in shell th' orients pearles we finde,
Of others take a sheaf, of mee a graine,
     Of me a graine,
     Of me a graine.

Within this packe pinnes points laces and gloves,
And divers toies fitting a country faier,
But in my hart where duety serves and loves,
Turtels and twins, courts brood, a heavenly paier:
Happy the hart that thincks of no removes,
     Of no removes,
     Of no removes.

ANONYMOUS

Thule, the period of cosmography,
 Doth vaunt of Hecla, whose sulphurious fire
Doth melt the frozen clime and thaw the sky;
 Trinacrian Ætna's flames ascend not higher.
These things seem wondrous, yet more wondrous I,
Whose heart with fear doth freeze, with love doth fry.

The Andalusian merchant, that returns
 Laden with cochineal and China dishes,
Reports in Spain how strangely Fogo burns
 Amidst an ocean full of flying fishes.
These things seem wondrous, yet more wondrous I,
Whose heart with fear doth freeze, with love doth fry.

JOHN HOLMES   1601

Thus Bonny-boots the birthday celebrated
  Of her his lady dearest,
Fair Oriana, which to his heart was nearest:
  The nymphs and shepherds feasted

With clowted cream were, and to sing requested.
　　Lo here the fair created,
　　　Quoth he, the world's chief goddess.
Sing then, for she is Bonny-boots' sweet mistress.
　　Then sang the shepherds and nymphs of Diana:
　　　Long live fair Oriana.

WILLIAM SHAKESPEARE *from* Twelfth Night

Exeunt.

Clowne sings

When that I was and a little tiny boy,
　　with hey, ho, the winde and the raine:
A foolish thing was but a toy,
　　for the raine it raineth every day.

But when I came to mans estate,
　　with hey ho, the winde and the raine:
Gainst Knaves and Theeves men shut their gate,
　　for the raine it raineth every day.

But when I came alas to wive,
　　with hey ho, the winde and the raine:
By swaggering could I never thrive,
　　for the raine it raineth every day.

But when I came unto my beds,
　　with hey ho, the winde and the raine:
With tosspottes still had drunken heades,
　　for the raine it raineth every day.

A great while ago the world begon,
　　hey ho, the winde and the raine:
But that's all one, our play is done,
　　and wee'l strive to please you every day.

(1623)

WILLIAM SHAKESPEARE [The Phoenix and Turtle]

Let the bird of lowdest lay,
On the sole *Arabian* tree,
Herauld sad and trumpet be:
To whose sound chaste wings obay.

But thou shriking harbinger,
Foule precurrer of the fiend,
Augour of the fevers end,
To this troupe come thou not neere.

From this Session interdict
Every foule of tyrant wing,
Save the Eagle feath'red King,
Keepe the obsequie so strict.

Let the Priest in Surples white,
That defunctive Musicke can,
Be the death-devining Swan,
Lest the *Requiem* lacke his right.

And thou treble dated Crow,
That thy sable gender mak'st,
With the breath thou giv'st and tak'st,
Mongst our mourners shalt thou go.

Here the Antheme doth commence,
Love and Constancie is dead,
Phœnix and the *Turtle* fled,
In a mutuall flame from hence.

So they lov'd as love in twaine,
Had the essence but in one,
Two distincts, Division none,
Number there in love was slaine.

Hearts remote, yet not asunder;
Distance and no space was seene,
Twixt this *Turtle* and his Queene;
But in them it were a wonder.

So betweene them Love did shine,
That the *Turtle* saw his right,
Flaming in the *Phœnix* sight;
Either was the others mine.

Propertie was thus appalled,
That the selfe was not the same:
Single Natures double name,
Neither two nor one was called.

Reason in it selfe confounded,
Saw Division grow together,
To themselves yet either neither,
Simple were so well compounded,

That it cried, how true a twaine,
Seemeth this concordant one,
Love hath Reason, Reason none,
If what parts, can so remaine.

Whereupon it made this *Threne*,
To the *Phœnix* and the *Dove*,
Co-supremes and starres of Love.
As *Chorus* to their Tragique Scene.

Threnos

Beautie, Truth, and Raritie,
Grace in all simplicitie,
Here enclosde, in cinders lie.

Death is now the *Phœnix* nest,
And the *Turtles* loyall brest,
To eternitie doth rest.

Leaving no posteritie,
Twas not their infirmitie,
It was married Chastitie.

Truth may seeme, but cannot be,
Beautie bragge, but tis not she,
Truth and Beautie buried be.

To this urne let those repaire,
That are either true or faire,
For these dead Birds, sigh a prayer.

THOMAS CAMPION *from the Latin of Catullus*

My sweetest Lesbia, let us live and love,
And, though the sager sort our deedes reprove,
Let us not way them: heav'ns great lampes doe dive
Into their west, and strait againe revive,
But, soone as once set is our little light,
Then must we sleepe one ever-during night.

If all would lead their lives in love like mee,
Then bloudie swords and armour should not be,
No drum nor trumpet peaceful sleepes should move,
Unles alar'me came from the campe of love:
But fooles do live, and wast their little light,
And seeke with paine their ever-during night.

When timely death my life and fortune ends,
Let not my hearse be vext with mourning friends,
But let all lovers, rich in triumph, come,
And with sweet pastimes grace my happie tombe;
And, Lesbia, close up thou my little light,
And crowne with love my ever-during night.

THOMAS CAMPION

Followe thy faire sunne unhappy shaddowe,
Though thou be blacke as night
And she made all of light,
Yet follow thy faire sunne unhappie shaddowe.

Follow her whose light thy light depriveth,
Though here thou liv'st disgrac't,
And she in heaven is plac't,
Yet follow her whose light the world reviveth.

Follow those pure beames whose beautie burneth,
That so have scorched thee,
As thou still blacke must bee,
Til her kind beames thy black to brightnes turneth.

Follow her while yet her glorie shineth,
There comes a luckles night,
That will dim all her light,
And this the black unhappie shade devineth.

Follow still since so thy fates ordained,
The Sunne must have his shade,
Till both at once doe fade,
The Sun still prov'd the shadow still disdained.

THOMAS CAMPION *from the Latin of Propertius*

When thou must home to shades of under ground,
And there ariv'd, a newe admired guest,
The beauteous spirits do ingirt thee round,
White Iope, blith Hellen, and the rest,
To heare the stories of thy finisht love,
From that smoothe toong whose musicke hell can move:

Then wilt thou speake of banqueting delights,
Of masks and revels which sweete youth did make,
Of Turnies and great challenges of knights,
And all these triumphes for thy beauties sake:
When thou hast told these honours done to thee,
Then tell, O tell, how thou didst murther me.

1602   ANONYMOUS

The lowest trees have tops, the Ant her gall,
the flie her spleene, the little sparke his heate,
and slender haires cast shadowes though but small,
and Bees have stings although they be not great.
Seas have their source, and so have shallowe springs,
and love is love in beggers and in kings.

Where waters smoothest run, deep are the foords,
The diall stirres, yet none perceives it move:
The firmest faith is in the fewest words,
The Turtles cannot sing, and yet they love,
True hearts have eyes and eares, no tongues to speake:
They heare, and see, and sigh, and then they breake.

THOMAS CAMPION

   Rose-cheekt *Lawra* come
Sing thou smoothly with thy beawties
Silent musick, either other
       Sweetely gracing.
   Lovely formes do flowe
From concent devinely framed,
Heav'n is musick, and thy beawties
       Birth is heavenly.
   These dull notes we sing
Discords neede for helps to grace them,
Only beawty purely loving
       Knowes no discord:
   But still mooves delight
Like cleare springs renu'd by flowing,
Ever perfet, ever in them-
       selves eternall.

ANONYMOUS   1603

Weepe you no more sad fountaines,
   What need you flowe so fast,
Looke how the snowie mountaines,
   Heav'ns sunne doth gently waste.
But my sunnes heav'nly eyes
   View not your weeping,
   That nowe lies sleeping
Softly now softly lies sleeping.

Sleepe is a reconciling,
    A rest that peace begets:
Doth not the sunne rise smiling,
    When faire at ev'n he sets,
Rest you, then rest sad eyes,
    Melt not in weeping,
    While she lies sleeping
Softly now softly lies sleeping.

1604   ANONYMOUS The Passionate Mans Pilgrimage

Supposed to be Written by One at the Point of Death

Give me my Scallop shell of quiet,
My staffe of Faith to walke upon,
My Scrip of Joy, Immortall diet,
My bottle of salvation:
My Gowne of Glory, hopes true gage,
And thus Ile take my pilgrimage.

Blood must be my bodies balmer,
No other balme will there be given
Whilst my soule like a white Palmer
Travels to the land of heaven,
Over the silver mountaines,
Where spring the Nectar fountaines:
And there Ile kisse
The Bowle of blisse,
And drink my eternall fill
On every milken hill.
My soule will be a-dry before,
But after it, will nere thirst more.

And by the happie blisfull way
More peacefull Pilgrims I shall see,
That have shooke off their gownes of clay,
And goe apparel'd fresh like mee.
Ile bring them first
To slake their thirst,

And then to tast those Nectar suckets
At the cleare wells
Where sweetnes dwells,
Drawne up by Saints in Christall buckets.

And when our bottles and all we,
Are fill'd with immortalitie:
Then the holy paths we'll travell
Strewde with Rubies thicke as gravell,
Ceilings of Diamonds, Saphire floores,
High walles of Corall and Pearle Bowres.

From thence to heavens Bribeless hall
Where no corrupted voyces brall,
No Conscience molten into gold,
Nor forg'd accusers bought and sold,
No cause deferd, nor vaine spent Journey,
For there Christ is the Kings Atturney:
Who pleades for all without degrees,
And he hath Angells, but no fees.

When the grand twelve million Jury,
Of our sinnes and sinfull fury,
Gainst our soules blacke verdicts give,
Christ pleades his death, and then we live,
Be thou my speaker taintless pleader,
Unblotted Lawyer, true proceeder,
Thou movest salvation even for almes:
Not with a bribed Lawyers palmes.

And this is my eternall plea,
To him that made Heaven, Earth and Sea,
Seeing my flesh must die so soone,
And want a head to dine next noone,
Just at the stroke when my vaines start and spred
Set on my soule an everlasting head.
Then am I readie like a palmer fit,
To tread those blest paths which before I writ.

NICHOLAS BRETON *from* A Solemne Long Enduring Passion

Wearie thoughts doe waite upon me
Griefe hath to much over-gone me
Time doth howerly over-toyle me,
While deepe sorrowes seeke to spoile me
Wit and sences all amazéd,
In their Graces over-gazéd:
In exceeding torments tell me,
Never such a death befell mee.

(. . .)

Let mee thinke no more on thee,
Thou hast too much wounded me:
And that skarre upon thy throate,
No such starre on *Stellas* coate.
Let me chide, yet with that stay,
That did weare the skinne away:
But alas shall I goe lower,
In sweet similies to showe her?
When to touch her praises tittle,
Nature's sweetnes is to little:
Where each Sinow, Limme and joynt,
Perfect shape in every point,
From corruptions eye concealed,
But to vertue love revealed,
Binde my thoughts to silence speaking,
While my hart must lye a breaking.
Petrarche, in his thoughts divine,
Tasso in his highest line.
Ariosto's best invention.
Dante's best obscur'd intention.
Ovid in his sweetest vaine:
Pastor Fidos purest straine.
With the finest Poet's wit,
That of wonders ever writ:
Were they all but now alive,
And would for the Garland strive,

In the gratious praise of love,
Heere they might their passions proove.
On such excellences grownded;
That their wittes would be confounded.

(. . .)

I have neither Plummes nor Cherries,
Nuttes, nor Aples, nor Straw-berries;
Pinnes nor Laces, Pointes nor gloves,
Nor a payre of painted Doves:
Shuttle-Cocke nor trundle ball,
To present thy love with all:
But a heart as true and kinde,
As an honest faithfull minde
Can device for to invent,
To thy patience I present:
At thy fairest feete it lies:
Blesse it with thy blessèd eyes:
Take it up into thy handes,
At whose onely grace it standes,
To be comforted for ever,
Or to looke for comfort never:
Oh it is a strange affecte,
That my fancie doth effect.
I am caught and can not start,
Wit and reason, eye and heart:
All are witnesses to mee,
Love hath sworne me slave to thee,
Let me then be but thy slave,
And no further favour crave:
Send mee foorth to tende thy flocke,
On the highest Mountaine rocke.
Or commaund me but to goe,
To the valley grownd belowe:
All shall be a like to me,
Where it please thee I shall bee.
Let my face be what thou wilt:
Save my life, or see it spilt.
Keepe me fasting on thy Mountaine:
Charge me not come neere thy Fountaine.
In the stormes and bitter blastes,
Where the skie all overcasts.

In the coldest frost and snowe,
That the earth did ever knowe:
Let me sit and bite my thumbes,
Where I see no comfort comes.
All the sorrowes I can proove,
Cannot put me from my love.
Tell me that thou art content,
To beholde me passion-rente,
That thou know'st I deerely love thee,
Yet withall it cannot moove thee.
That thy pride doth growe so great,
Nothing can thy grace intreate,
That thou wilt so cruell bee,
As to kill my love and mee:
That thou wilt no foode reserve,
But my flockes and I shall sterve.
Be thy rage yet nere so great,
When my little Lambes doe bleate,
To beholde their Shepheard die:
Then will truth her passion trie.
How a Hart it selfe hath spent,
With concealing of content.

1607   BEN JONSON / CATULLUS *from* Volpone

[*Volpone sings.*]

Come my CELIA, let us prove,
While we may, the sports of love;
Time will not be ours, for ever:
He, at length, our good will sever.
Spend not then his guifts in vaine.
Sunnes, that set, may rise againe:
But if once we loose this light,
'Tis, with us, perpetuall night.
Why should we deferre our joyes?
Fame, and rumor are but toyes.
Cannot we delude the eyes
Of a few poore houshold spyes?
Or his easier eares beguile,
So removed by our wile?

'Tis no sinne, loves fruit to steale,
But the sweet theft to reveale:
To be taken, to be seene,
These have crimes accounted beene.

ANONYMOUS

Ay me, alas, heigh ho, heigh ho!
Thus doth Messalina go
Up and down the house a-crying,
For her monkey lies a-dying.
Death, thou art too cruel
To bereave her jewel,
Or to make a seizure
Of her only treasure.
If her monkey die,
She will sit and cry,
Fie fie fie fie fie!

BEN JONSON *from* Epicoene

Still to be neat, still to be drest,
As, you were going to a feast;
Still to be pou'dred, still perfum'd:
Lady, it is to be presum'd,
Though arts hid causes are not found,
All is not sweet, all is not sound.

Give me a looke, give me a face,
That makes simplicitie a grace;
Robes loosely flowing, haire as free:
Such sweet neglect more taketh me,
Then all th'adulteries of art.
They strike mine eyes, but not my heart.

(1616)

EDMUND SPENSER *from* Two Cantos of Mutabilitie

[Nature's Reply to Mutabilitie]

Then since within this wide great *Universe*
　　Nothing doth firme and permanent appeare,
　　But all things tost and turned by transverse:
　　What then should let, but I aloft should reare
　　My Trophee, and from all, the triumph beare?
　　Now judge then (ô thou greatest goddesse trew!)
　　According as thy selfe doest see and heare,
　　And unto me addoom that is my dew;
That is the rule of all, all being rul'd by you.

So having ended, silence long ensewed,
　　Ne *Nature* to or fro spake for a space,
　　But with firme eyes affixt, the ground still viewed.
　　Meanewhile, all creatures, looking in her face,
　　Expecting th'end of this so doubtfull case,
　　Did hang in long suspence what would ensew,
　　To whether side should fall the soveraigne place:
　　At length, she looking up with chearefull view,
The silence brake, and gave her doome in speeches few.

I well consider all that ye have sayd,
　　And find that all things stedfastnes doe hate
　　And changed be: yet being rightly wayd
　　They are not changed from their first estate;
　　But by their change their being doe dilate:
　　And turning to themselves at length againe,
　　Doe worke their owne perfection so by fate:
　　Then over them Change doth not rule and raigne;
But they raigne over change, and doe their states maintaine.

Cease therefore daughter further to aspire,
　　And thee content thus to be rul'd by me:
　　For thy decay thou seekst by thy desire;
　　But time shall come that all shall changed bee,
　　And from thenceforth, none no more change shall see.

So was the *Titaness* put downe and whist, [193]
And *Jove* confirm'd in his imperiall see.
Then was that whole assembly quite dismist,
And *Natur's* selfe did vanish, whither no man wist.

The VIII Canto, unperfite

When I bethinke me on that speech whyleare,
  Of *Mutability*, and well it way:
  Me seemes, that though she all unworthy were
  Of the Heav'ns Rule; yet very sooth to say,
  In all things else she beares the greatest sway.
  Which makes me loath this state of life so tickle,
  And love of things so vaine to cast away;
  Whose flowring pride, so fading and so fickle,
Short *Time* shall soon cut down with his consuming sickle.

Then gin I thinke on that which Nature sayd,
  Of that same time when no more *Change* shall be,
  But stedfast rest of all things firmely stayd
  Upon the pillours of Eternity,
  That is contrayr to *Mutabilitie*:
  For, all that moveth, doth in *Change* delight:
  But thence-forth all shall rest eternally
  With Him that is the God of Sabbaoth hight:
O that great Sabbaoth God, graunt me that Sabaoths sight.

§ WILLIAM SHAKESPEARE *from* Sonnets

18

Shall I compare thee to a Summers day?
Thou art more lovely and more temperate:
Rough windes do shake the darling buds of Maie,
And Sommers lease hath all too short a date:
Sometime too hot the eye of heaven shines,
And often is his gold complexion dimm'd,
And every faire from faire some-time declines,
By chance, or natures changing course untrim'd:

But thy eternall Sommer shall not fade,
Nor loose possession of that faire thou ow'st,
Nor shall death brag thou wandr'st in his shade,
When in eternall lines to time thou grow'st,
  So long as men can breath or eyes can see,
  So long lives this, and this gives life to thee.

55

Not marble, nor the guilded monuments
Of Princes shall out-live this powrefull rime,
But you shall shine more bright in these contents
Then unswept stone, besmeer'd with sluttish time.
When wastefull warre shall *Statues* over-turne,
And broiles roote out the worke of masonry,
Nor *Mars* his sword, nor warres quick fire shall burne
The living record of your memory.
Gainst death, and all oblivious enmity
Shall you pace forth, your praise shall stil finde roome,
Even in the eyes of all posterity
That weare this world out to the ending doome.
  So til the judgement that your selfe arise,
  You live in this, and dwell in lovers eies.

60

Like as the waves make towards the pibled shore,
So do our minuites hasten to their end,
Each changing place with that which goes before,
In sequent toile all forwards do contend.
Nativity once in the maine of light,
Crawles to maturity, wherewith being crown'd,
Crooked eclipses gainst his glory fight,
And time that gave, doth now his gift confound.
Time doth transfixe the florish set on youth,
And delves the paralels in beauties brow,
Feedes on the rarities of natures truth,
And nothing stands but for his sieth to mow.
  And yet to times in hope, my verse shall stand
  Praising thy worth, dispight his cruell hand.

66

Tyr'd with all these for restfull death I cry,
As to behold desert a begger borne,
And needie Nothing trimd in jollitie,
And purest faith unhappily forsworne,
And gilded honor shamefully misplast,
And maiden vertue rudely strumpeted,
And right perfection wrongfully disgrac'd,
And strength by limping sway disabled,
And arte made tung-tide by authoritie,
And Folly (Doctor-like) controuling skill,
And simple-Truth miscalde Simplicitie,
And captive-good attending Captaine ill.
   Tyr'd with all these, from these would I be gone,
    Save that to dye, I leave my love alone.

73

That time of yeeare thou maist in me behold,
When yellow leaves, or none, or few doe hange
Upon those boughes which shake against the could,
Bare ruin'd quiers, where late the sweet birds sang.
In me thou seest the twi-light of such day,
As after Sun-set fadeth in the West,
Which by and by blacke night doth take away,
Deaths second selfe that seals up all in rest.
In me thou seest the glowing of such fire,
That on the ashes of his youth doth lye,
As the death bed, whereon it must expire,
Consum'd with that which it was nurrisht by.
   This thou percev'st, which makes thy love more strong,
    To love that well, which thou must leave ere long.

94

They that have powre to hurt, and will doe none,
That doe not do the thing, they most do showe,
Who moving others, are themselves as stone,
Unmooved, could, and to temptation slow:
They rightly do inherrit heavens graces,
And husband natures ritches from expence,
They are the Lords and owners of their faces,
Others, but stewards of their excellence:
The sommers flowre is to the sommer sweet,
Though to it selfe, it onely live and die,
But if that flowre with base infection meete,
The basest weed out-braves his dignity:
    For sweetest things turne sowrest by their deedes,
    Lillies that fester, smell far worse then weeds.

107

Not mine owne feares, nor the prophetick soule,
Of the wide world, dreaming on things to come,
Can yet the lease of my true love controule,
Supposde as forfeit to a confin'd doome.
The mortall Moone hath her eclipse indur'de,
And the sad Augurs mock their owne presage,
Incertenties now crowne them-selves assur'de,
And peace proclaimes Olives of endlesse age.
Now with the drops of this most balmie time,
My love lookes fresh, and death to me subscribes,
Since spight of him Ile live in this poore rime,
While he insults ore dull and speachlesse tribes.
    And thou in this shalt finde thy monument,
    When tyrants crests and tombs of brasse are spent.

116

Let me not to the marriage of true mindes
Admit impediments, love is not love
Which alters when it alteration findes,
Or bends with the remover to remove.
O no, it is an ever fixed marke
That lookes on tempests and is never shaken;
It is the star to every wandring barke,
Whose worths unknowne, although his higth be taken.
Lov's not Times foole, though rosie lips and cheeks
Within his bending sickles compasse come,
Love alters not with his breefe houres and weekes,
But beares it out even to the edge of doome:
    If this be error and upon me proved,
    I never writ, nor no man ever loved.

124

Yf my deare love were but the childe of state,
It might for fortunes basterd be unfathered,
As subject to times love, or to times hate,
Weeds among weeds, or flowers with flowers gatherd.
No it was buylded far from accident,
It suffers not in smilinge pomp, nor falls
Under the blow of thralled discontent,
Whereto th'inviting time our fashion calls:
It feares not policy that *Heriticke*,
Which workes on leases of short numbred howers,
But all alone stands hugely pollitick,
That it nor growes with heat, nor drownes with showres.
    To this I witnes call the foles of time,
    Which die for goodnes, who have liv'd for crime.

129

Th'expence of Spirit in a waste of shame
Is lust in action, and till action, lust
Is perjurd, murdrous, blouddy full of blame,
Savage, extreame, rude, cruell, not to trust,
Injoyd no sooner but dispised straight,
Past reason hunted, and no sooner had
Past reason hated as a swollowed bayt,
On purpose layd to make the taker mad.
Made In pursut and in possession so,
Had, having, and in quest to have, extreame,
A blisse in proofe and prov'd a very wo,
Before a joy proposd behind a dreame,
    All this the world well knowes yet none knowes well,
    To shun the heaven that leads men to this hell.

138

When my love sweares that she is made of truth,
I do beleeve her though I know she lyes,
That she might thinke me some untuterd youth,
Unlearned in the worlds false subtilties.
Thus vainely thinking that she thinkes me young,
Although she knowes my dayes are past the best,
Simply I credit her false speaking tongue,
On both sides thus is simple truth supprest:
But wherefore sayes she not she is unjust?
And wherefore say not I that I am old?
O loves best habit is in seeming trust,
And age in love, loves not to have yeares told.
    Therefore I lye with her, and she with me,
    And in our faults by lyes we flattered be.

(1599)

144

Two loves I have of comfort and dispaire,
Which like two spirits do sugiest me still,
The better angell is a man right faire:
The worser spirit a woman collour'd il.
To win me soone to hell my femall evill,
Tempteth my better angel from my side,
And would corrupt my saint to be a divel:
Wooing his purity with her fowle pride.
And whether that my angel be turn'd finde,
Suspect I may, yet not directly tell,
But being both from me both to each friend,
I gesse one angel in an others hel.
     Yet this shal I nere know but live in doubt,
     Till my bad angel fire my good one out.

(1599)

     §   §   §

WILLIAM SHAKESPEARE *from* Cymbeline

GUIDERIUS
Pray you fetch him hither.
Thersites body is as good as *Ajax*,
When neyther are alive.
ARVIRAGUS
If you'll go fetch him,
Wee'l say our Song the whil'st: Brother begin.
GUID.
Nay Cadwall, we must lay his head to th'East,
My father hath a reason for't.
ARVI.
'Tis true.
GUID.
Come on then, and remove him.
ARVI.
So, begin.

GUID.
Feare no more the heate o'th'Sun,
Nor the furious Winters rages,
Thou thy worldly task hath don,
Home art gon and tane they wages.
> *Golden Lads, and Girles all must,*
> *As Chimney-sweepers come to dust.*

ARVI.
Fear no more the frowne o'th'Great,
Thou art past the Tirants stroake,
Care no more to cloath and eate,
To thee the Reede is as the Oake:
> *The Scepter, Learning, Physicke must,*
> *All follow this and come to dust.*

GUID.
Feare no more the Lightning flash.

ARVI.
Nor th'all-dreaded Thunder stone.

GUID.
Feare not Slander, Censure rash.

ARVI.
Thou hast finish'd Joy and mone.

BOTH
All Lovers young, all Lovers must,
Consigne to thee and come to dust.

GUID.
No Exorcisor harme thee,

ARVI.
Nor no witch-craft charme thee.

GUID.
Ghost unlaid forbeare thee.

ARVI.
Nothing ill come neare thee.

BOTH
Quiet consumation have,
And renowned be thy grave.

[*Enter Belarius with the body of Cloten*]

GUID.
We have done our obsequies: Come lay him downe.

(1623)

ANONYMOUS [*Inscription in Osmington Church, Dorset*]

  Man's Life

  Man is a Glas: Life is
  A water that's weakly
walled about: sinne bring
  es death: death breakes
    the Glas: so runnes
      the water out
        finis.

ANONYMOUS [*Inscription in St Mary Magdalene Church, Milk Street, London*]

Grass of levity,
Span in brevity,
Flowers' felicity,
Fire of misery,
Winds' stability,
Is mortality.

JOHN DAVIES OF HEREFORD The Author Loving These   **1610**
Homely Meats specially, viz.: cream, pancakes, buttered, pippin-pies
(laugh, good people) and tobacco; writ to that worthy and virtuous
gentlewoman, whom he calleth mistress, as followeth

If there were, oh! an Hellespont of cream
Between us, milk-white mistress, I would swim
To you, to show to both my love's extreme,
Leander-like, – yea! dive from brim to brim.
But met I with a buttered pippin-pie
Floating upon 't, that would I make my boat
To waft me to you without jeopardy,
Though sea-sick I might be while it did float.

Yet if a storm should rise, by night or day,
Of sugar-snows and hail of caraways,
Then, if I found a pancake in my way,
It like a plank should bring me to your kays;
    Which having found, if they tobacco kept,
    The smoke should dry me well before I slept.

1611   § *from* **The Authorized Version of the Bible**

2 Samuel 1: 19–27 David lamenteth the death of Jonathan

The beauty of Israel is slaine upon thy high places: how are the mightie fallen!

Tell it not in Gath, publish it not in the streetes of Askelon: lest the daughters of the Philistines rejoyce, lest the daughters of the uncircumcised triumph.

Yee mountaines of Gilboa, let there bee no dewe, neither let there *be* raine upon you, nor fields of offerings: for there the shield of the mightie is vilely cast away, the shield of Saul, *as though* hee had not beene annointed with oile.

From the blood of the slaine, from the fat of the mightie, the bow of Ionathan turned not backe, and the sword of Saul returned not emptie.

Saul and Jonathan were lovely and pleasant in their lives, and in their death they were not divided: they were swifter then Eagles, they were stronger then Lions.

Yee daughters of Israel, weepe over Saul, who clothed you in scarlet, with other delights, who put on ornaments of golde upon your apparell.

How are the mightie fallen in the midst of the battell! O Jonathan, thou wast slaine in thine high places.

I am distressed for thee, my brother Jonathan, very pleasant hast thou beene unto mee: thy love to mee was wonderfull, passing the love of women.

How are the mightie fallen, and the weapons of warre perished!

Job 3: 3–26 Job curseth the day, and services of his birth

Let the day perish, wherein I was borne, and the night in which it was said, There is a man-childe conceived.

Let that day bee darkenesse, let not God regard it from above, neither let the light shine upon it.

Let darkenes and the shadowe of death staine it, let a cloud dwell upon it, let the blacknes of the day terrifie it.

As for that night, let darkenesse seaze upon it, let it not be joyned unto the dayes of the yeere, let it not come into the number of the moneths.

Loe, let that night be solitarie, let no joyfull voice come therein.

Let them curse it that curse the day, who are ready to raise up their mourning.

Let the starres of the twilight thereof be darke, let it looke for light, but have none, neither let it see the dawning of the day:

Because it shut not up the doores of my mothers wombe, nor hid sorrowe from mine eyes.

Why died I not from the wombe? why did I not give up the ghost when I came out of the bellie?

Why did the knees prevent mee? or why the breasts, that I should sucke?

For now should I have lien still and beene quiet, I should have slept; then had I bene at rest,

With Kings and counsellers of the earth, which built desolate places for themselves,

Or with Princes that had golde, who filled their houses with silver:

Or as an hidden untimely birth, I had not bene; as infants which never saw light.

There the wicked cease from troubling: and there the wearie be at rest.

There the prisoners rest together, they heare not the voice of the oppressour.

The small and great are there, and the servant is free from his master.

Wherefore is light given to him that is in misery, and life unto the bitter in soule?

Which long for death, but it commeth not, and dig for it more then for hid treasures:

Which rejoice exceedingly, and are glad when they can finde the grave?

Why is light given to a man, whose way is hid, and whom God hath hedged in?

For my sighing commeth before I eate, and my roarings are powred out like the waters.

For the thing which I greatly feared is come upon me, and that which I was afraid of, is come unto me.

I was not in safetie, neither had I rest, neither was I quiet: yet trouble came.

Ecclesiastes 12: 1–8 The Creator is to be remembred in due time

Remember now thy Creatour in the days of thy youth, while the evil daies come not, nor the yeeres drawe nigh, when thou shalt say, I have no pleasure in them:

While the Sunne, or the light, or the moone, or the starres be not darkened, nor the cloudes returne after the raine:

In the day when the keepers of the house shall tremble, and the strong men shall bowe themselves, and the grinders cease, because they are fewe, and those that looke out of the windowes be darkened:

And the doores shal be shut in the streets, when the sound of the grinding is low, and he shall rise up at the voice of the bird, and all the daughters of musicke shall be brought low.

Also when they shalbe afraid of that which is high, and feares shall bee in the way, and the Almond tree shall flourish, and the grashopper shall be a burden, and desire shall faile: because man goeth to his long home, and the mourners goe about the streets:

Or ever the silver corde be loosed, or the golden bowle be broken, or the pitcher be broken at the fountaine, or the wheele broken at the cisterne.

Then shall the dust returne to the earth as it was: and the spirit shall returne unto God who gave it.

Vanitie of vanities (saith the preacher) all is vanitie.

§   §   §

GEORGE CHAPMAN *from* The Iliads of Homer

from The Third Booke [Helen and the Elders on the Ramparts]

And as in well-growne woods, on trees, cold spinie Grashoppers
Sit chirping and send voices out that scarce can pierce our eares
For softnesse and their weake faint sounds; so (talking on the towre)
These Seniors of the people sate, who, when they saw the powre
Of beautie in the Queene ascend, even those cold-spirited Peeres,
Those wise and almost witherd men, found this heate in their yeares
That they were forc't (though whispering) to say: 'What man can
    blame
The Greekes and Troyans to endure, for so admir'd a Dame,
So many miseries, and so long? In her sweet countenance shine
Lookes like the Goddesses'. And yet (though never so divine)
Before we boast, unjustly still, of her enforced prise
And justly suffer for her sake, with all our progenies,
Labor and ruine, let her go: the profit of our land
Must passe the beautie.' Thus, though these could beare so fit a hand
On their affections, yet when all their gravest powers were usde
They could not chuse but welcome her, and rather they accusde
The gods than beautie. For thus spake the most fam'd King of Troy:
'Come, loved daughter, sit by me, and take the worthy joy
Of thy first husband's sight, old friends' and Princes' neare allyed,
And name me some of these brave Greekes, so manly beautified.
Come: do not thinke I lay the warres, endur'd by us, on thee:
The gods have sent them, and the teares in which they swumme to
    me.'

from The Twelfth Booke [Sarpedon's Speech to Glaucus]

And as in winter time when Jove his cold-sharpe javelines throwes
Amongst us mortals and is mov'd to white earth with his snowes
(The winds asleepe) he freely poures, till highest Prominents,
Hill tops, low meddowes and the fields that crowne with most
    contents
The toiles of men, sea ports and shores are hid, and everie place
But floods (that snowe's faire tender flakes, as their owne brood,
    embrace):
So both sides coverd earth with stones, so both for life contend
To shew their sharpnesse. Through the wall, uprore stood up on
    end.

Nor had great Hector and his friends the rampire overrun
If heaven's great Counsellour, high Jove, had not inflam'd his sonne
Sarpedon (like the forrest's king when he on Oxen flies)
Against the Grecians: his round targe he to his arme applies,
Brasse-leav'd without and all within thicke Oxe-hides quilted hard,
The verge naild round with rods of gold; and with two darts prepard
He leades his people. As ye see a mountaine Lion fare,
Long kept from prey, in forcing which his high mind makes him dare
Assault upon the whole full fold, though guarded never so
With well-arm'd men and eager dogs – away he will not go
But venture on and either snatch a prey or be a prey:
So far'd divine Sarpedon's mind, resolv'd to force his way
Through all the fore-fights and the wall. Yet, since he did not see
Others as great as he in name, as great in mind as he,
He spake to Glaucus: 'Glaucus, say why are we honord more
Than other men of Lycia in place – with greater store
Of meates and cups, with goodlier roofes, delightsome gardens,
    walks,
More lands and better, so much wealth that Court and countrie
    talks
Of us and our possessions and every way we go
Gaze on us as we were their Gods? This where we dwell is so:
The shores of Xanthus ring of this: and shall not we exceed
As much in merit as in noise? Come, be we great in deed
As well as looke, shine not in gold but in the flames of fight,
That so our neat-arm'd Lycians may say: "See, these are right
Our kings, our Rulers: these deserve to eate and drinke the best;
These governe not ingloriously; these thus exceed the rest.
Do more than they command to do." O friend, if keeping backe
Would keepe backe age from us, and death, and that we might not
    wracke
In this life's humane sea at all, but that deferring now
We shund death ever – nor would I halfe this vaine valour show,
Nor glorifie a folly so, to wish thee to advance:
But, since we must go though not here, and that, besides the chance
Proposd now, there are infinite fates of other sort in death
Which (neither to be fled nor scap't) a man must sinke beneath –
Come, trie we if this sort be ours and either render thus
Glorie to others or make them resigne the like to us.'

ANONYMOUS A Belmans Song

Maides to bed, and cover coale,
Let the Mouse Out of her hole:
Crickets in the Chimney sing,
Whil'st the little Bell doth ring.
If fast asleepe, who can tell
When the Clapper hits the Bell.

WILLIAM SHAKESPEARE *from* The Winter's Tale

Enter Autolicus singing

When Daffadils begin to peere.
With heigh the Doxy over the dale,
Why then comes in the sweet o'the yeere,
For the red blood raigns in the winters pale.

The white sheete bleaching on the hedge,
With hey the sweet birds, O how they sing:
Doth set my pugging tooth on edge
For a quart of Ale is a dish for a King.

The Larke that tirra-Lyra chaunts,
With heigh, the Thrush and the Jay:
Are Summer songs for me and my Aunts
While we lye tumbling in the hay.

(. . .)

Enter Autolicus singing.

Lawne as white as driven Snow,
Cypresse black as ere was Crow,
Gloves as sweete as Damask Roses,
Maskes for faces, and for noses:
Bugle-bracelet, Necke-lace Amber,
Perfume for a Ladies Chamber:
Golden Quoifes, and Stomachers
For my Lads, to give their deers:

Pins, and poaking-stickes of steele.
What Maids lacke from head to heele:
　　Come buy of me, come: come buy, come buy,
　　Buy Lads, or else your Lasses cry: come buy.

(1623)

WILLIAM SHAKESPEARE *from* The Tempest

Enter Ferdinand & Ariel, invisible playing and singing.

Ariels Song.

Come unto these yellow sands,
　　and then take hands:
Curtsied when you have, and kist
　　The wilde waves whist:
Foote it featly heere, and there,
　　And Sweet Sprights beare
The burthen.

　　[*Burthern dispersedly.*] Bowgh-wawgh.

ARIEL
The watch-Dogges barke:

　　[*Burthen dispersedly.*] Bowgh-wawgh.

ARIEL
Hark, hark, I heare
The straine of strutting Chanticlere
　　Cry cockadidle-dowe.

FERDINAND
Where should this Musick be? I'th'aire, or th'earth?
It sounds no more: and sure it waytes upon
Some God o'th'Iland, sitting on a banke,
Weeping againe the King my Fathers wracke.
This Musicke crept by me upon the waters,
Allaying both their fury, and my passion
With its sweet ayre: thence have I follow'd it
(Or it hath drawne me rather) but 'tis gone.
No, it begins againe.

Full fadom five thy Father lies,
Of his bones are Corall made:
Those are pearles that were his eies,
Nothing of him that doth fade,
But doth suffer a Sea-change
Into something rich, and strange:
Sea Nimphs hourly ring his knell.
    [*Burthen*: ding dong.]

ARIEL
Harke now I heare them, ding-dong bell.

(1623)

JOHN WEBSTER *from* The White Divel   1612

FLAMINEO
I would I were from hence.
CORNELIA
                    Do you heere, sir?
Ile give you a saying which my grandmother
Was wont, when she heard the bell tolle, to sing ore
to her lute.
FLA.
            Doe, and you will, doe.

COR.
Call for the Robin-Red-brest and the wren,
Since ore shadie groves they hover,
And with leaves and flowres doe cover
The friendlesse bodies of unburied men.
Call unto his funerall Dole
The Ante, the field-mouse, and the mole
To reare him hillockes, that shall keepe him warme,
And (when gay tombes are rob'd) sustaine no harme,
But keepe the wolfe far thence, that's foe to men,
For with his nailes hee'l dig them up agen.

They would not bury him 'cause hee died in a quarrell
But I have an answere for them.
Let holie Church receive him duly
Since hee payd the Church tithes truly.

GEORGE CHAPMAN *from the Latin of Epictetus*

Pleasd with thy Place

God hath the whole world perfect made, and free;
His parts to th'use of all. Men then, that be
Parts of that all, must as the generall sway
Of that importeth, willingly obay
In everie thing, without their powres to change.
He that (unpleasd to hold his place) will range,
Can in no other be containd, thats fit:
And so resisting all, is crusht with it.
But he that knowing how divine a frame
The whole world is, and of it all can name
(Without selfe flatterie) no part so divine
As he himselfe, and therefore will confine
Freely, his whole powres, in his proper part:
Goes on most god-like. He that strives t'invert
The universall course, with his poore way:
Not onely, dustlike, shivers with the sway;
But (crossing God in his great worke) all earth
Beares not so cursed, and so damn'd a birth.
This then the universall discipline
Of manners comprehends: a man to joyne
Himselfe with th'universe, and wish to be
Made all with it, and go on, round as he.
Not plucking from the whole his wretched part,
And into streights, or into nought revert:
Wishing the complete universe might be
Subject to such a ragge of it, as he.
But to consider great necessitie,
All things, as well refract, as voluntarie
Reduceth to the high celestiall cause:
Which he that yeelds to, with a mans applause,
And cheeke by cheeke goes, crossing it, no breath,
But like Gods image followes to the death:
That man is perfect wise, and everie thing,
(Each cause and everie part distinguishing)
In nature, with enough Art understands,
And that full glorie merits at all hands,
That doth the whole world, at all parts adorne,
And appertaines to one celestiall borne.

THOMAS CAMPION

Never weather-beaten Saile more willing bent to shore,
Never tyred Pilgrims limbs affected slumber more,
Then my weary spright now longs to flye out of my troubled brest.
   O come quickly, sweetest Lord, and take my soule to rest.

Ever-blooming are the joyes of Heav'ns high paradice,
Cold age deafes not there our eares, nor vapour dims our eyes;
Glory there the Sun outshines, whose beames the blessed onely see:
   O come quickly, glorious Lord, and raise my spright to thee.

WILLIAM FOWLER

Ship-broken men whom stormy seas sore toss
Protests with oaths not to adventure more;
Bot all their perils, promises, and loss
They quite forget when they come to the shore:
Even so, fair dame, whiles sadly I deplore
The shipwreck of my wits procured by you,
Your looks rekindleth love as of before,
And dois revive which I did disavow;
So all my former vows I disallow,
And buries in oblivion's grave, but groans;
Yea, I forgive, hereafter, even as now
My fears, my tears, my cares, my sobs, and moans,
In hope if anes I be to shipwreck driven,
Ye will me thole to anchor in your heaven.

JOHN WEBSTER *from* The Dutchesse of Malfy   **1614**

BOSOLA
I am the common Bell-man,   [*Takes up the Bell.*]
That usually is sent to condemn'd persons
The night before they suffer:
DUCHESS
Even now thou said'st,
Thou wast a tombe-maker?

BOS.
'Twas to bring you
By degrees to mortification: Listen.   [*Rings his bell.*]

Hearke, now every thing is still—
The Schritch-Owle, and the whistler shrill,
Call upon our Dame, aloud,
And bid her quickly don her shrowd:
Much you had of Land and rent,
Your length in clay's now competent.
A long war disturb'd your minde,
Here your perfect peace is sign'd—
Of what is't fooles make such vaine keeping?
Sin their conception, their birth, weeping:
Their life, a generall mist of error,
Their death, a hideous storme of terror—
Strew your haire, with powders sweete:
Don cleane linnen, bath your feete,
And (the foule feend more to checke)
A crucifixe let blesse your necke,
'Tis now full tide, 'tweene night, and day,
End your groane, and come away.

CARIOLA
Hence villaines, tyrants, murderers: alas!
What will you do with my Lady? call for helpe.
DUCH.
To whom, to our next neighbours? they are mad-folkes.

1615   **SIR JOHN HARINGTON** Of Treason

Treason doth never prosper, what's the reason?
For if it prosper, none dare call it Treason.

ANONYMOUS [Tom o' Bedlam's Song]

From the hagg and hungrie goblin
That into raggs would rend ye,
And the spirit that stands by the naked man
In the Book of Moones defend yee,

That of your five sounde sences
You never be forsaken,
Nor wander from your selves with Tom
Abroad to begg your bacon.
   While I doe sing Any foode, any feeding,
   Feedinge, drinke or clothing
   Come dame or maid, be not afraid,
   Poor Tom will injure nothing.

Of thirty bare years have I
Twice twenty bin enragèd,
And of forty bin three tymes fifteene
In durance soundlie cagèd
On the lordlie loftes of Bedlam,
With stubble softe and dainty,
Brave braceletts strong, sweet whips ding dong,
With wholsome hunger plenty.
   And nowe I sing, etc.

With a thought I tooke for Maudlin,
And a cruse of cockle pottage,
With a thing thus tall, skie blesse you all,
I befell into this dotage.
I slept not since the Conquest,
Till then I never waked,
Till the rogysh boy of love where I lay
Mee found and strip't mee naked.
   And nowe I sing, etc.

When I short have shorne my sow's face
And swigg'd my horny barrel,
In an oaken inne I pound my skin
As a suite of guilt apparell.
The moon's my constant Mistrisse,
And the lowlie owle my marrowe,
The flaming Drake and the Nightcrowe make
Mee musicke to my sorrowe.
   While I doe sing, etc.

The palsie plagues my pulses
When I prigg your pigs or pullen,
Your culvers take, or matchles make
Your Chanticleare, or Sullen.

When I want provant, with Humfrie
I sup, and when benighted,
I repose in Powles with waking soules
Yet nevere am affrighted.
But I doe sing, etc.

I knowe more then Apollo,
For oft, when hee ly's sleeping,
I see the starres att bloudie warres
In the wounded welkin weeping;
The moone embrace her shepheard,
And the quene of Love her warryor,
While the first doth horne the star of morne,
And the next the heavenly Farrier.
While I doe sing, etc.

The Gipsie Snap and Pedro
Are none of Tom's comradoes,
The punk I skorne and the cut purse sworn
And the roaring boyes bravadoe.
The meeke, the white, the gentle,
Me handle touch and spare not
But those that crosse Tom Rynosseros
Doe what the panther dare not.
Although I sing, etc.

With an host of furious fancies,
Whereof I am commander,
With a burning speare, and a horse of aire,
To the wildernesse I wander.
By a knight of ghostes and shadowes
I summon'd am to tourney
Ten leagues beyond the wide world's end.
Me thinke it is noe journey.
Yet will I sing, etc.

§ BEN JONSON *from* Epigrammes

XIV To William Camden

Camden, most reverend head, to whom I owe
　　All that I am in arts, all that I know,
(How nothing's that?) to whom my countrey owes
　　The great renowne, and name wherewith shee goes.
Then thee the age sees not that thing more grave,
　　More high, more holy, that shee more would crave.
What name, what skill, what faith hast thou in things!
　　What sight in searching the most antique springs!
What weight, and what authoritie in thy speech!
　　Man scarse can make that doubt, but thou canst teach.
Pardon free truth, and let thy modestie,
　　Which conquers all, be once over-come by thee.
Many of thine this better could, then I,
　　But for their powers, accept my pietie.

XLV On My First Sonne

Farewell, thou child of my right hand, and joy;
　　My sinne was too much hope of thee, lov'd boy,
Seven yeeres tho'wert lent to me, and I thee pay,
　　Exacted by thy fate, on the just day.
O, could I loose all father, now. For why
　　Will man lament the state he should envie?
To have so soone scap'd worlds, and fleshes rage,
　　And, if no other miserie, yet age?
Rest in soft peace, and, ask'd, say here doth lye
　　BEN. JONSON his best piece of *poetrie*.
For whose sake, hence-forth, all his vowes be such,
　　As what he loves may never like too much.

LIX On Spies

Spies, you are lights in state, but of base stuffe,
    Who, when you'have burnt your selves downe to the snuffe,
Stinke, and are throwne away. End faire enough.

CI Inviting a Friend to Supper

To night, grave sir, both my poore house, and I
    Doe equally desire your companie:
Not that we thinke us worthy such a ghest,
    But that your worth will dignifie our feast,
With those that come; whose grace may make that seeme
    Something, which, else, could hope for no esteeme.
It is the faire acceptance, Sir, creates
    The entertaynment perfect: not the cates.
Yet shall you have, to rectifie your palate,
    An olive, capers, or some better sallade
Ushring the mutton; with a short-leg'd hen,
    If we can get her, full of egs, and then,
Limons, and wine for sauce: to these, a coney
    Is not to be despair'd of, for our money;
And, though fowle, now, be scarce, yet there are clarkes,
    The skie not falling, thinke we may have larkes.
Ile tell you of more, and lye, so you will come:
    Of partrich, pheasant, wood-cock, of which some
May yet be there; and godwit, if we can:
    Knat, raile, and ruffe too. How so ere, my man
Shall reade a piece of VIRGIL, TACITUS,
    LIVIE, or of some better booke to us,
Of which wee'll speake our minds, amidst our meate;
    And Ile professe no verses to repeate:
To this, if ought appeare, which I not know of,
    That will the pastrie, not my paper, show of.
Digestive cheese, and fruit there sure will bee;
    But that, which most doth take my *Muse*, and mee,
Is a pure cup of rich *Canary*-wine,
    Which is the *Mermaids*, now, but shall be mine:
Of which had HORACE, or ANACREON tasted,
    Their lives, as doe their lines, till now had lasted.

Tabacco, Nectar, or the *Thespian* spring,
Are all but LUTHERS beere, to this I sing.

Of this we will sup free, but moderately,
    And we will have no *Pooly'*, or *Parrot* by;
Nor shall our cups make any guiltie men:
    But, at our parting, we will be, as when
We innocently met. No simple word,
    That shall be utter'd at our mirthfull boord,
Shall make us sad next morning: or affright
    The libertie, that wee'll enjoy to night.

CXVIII On Gut

Gut eates all day, and lechers all the night,
    So all his meate he tasteth over, twise:
And, striving so to double his delight,
    He makes himselfe a thorough-fare of vice.
Thus, in his belly, can he change a sin,
    Lust it comes out, that gluttony went in.

§   §   §

BEN JONSON *from* The Forrest

To Heaven

Good, and great GOD, can I not thinke of thee,
    But it must, straight, my melancholy bee?
Is it interpreted in me disease,
    That, laden with my sinnes, I seeke for ease?
O, be thou witnesse, that the reynes dost know,
    And hearts of all, if I be sad for show,
And judge me after: if I dare pretend
    To ought but grace, or ayme at other end.
As thou art all, so be thou all to mee,
    First, midst, and last, converted one, and three;
My faith, my hope, my love: and in this state,
    My judge, my witnesse, and my advocate.

Where have I beene this while exil'd from thee?
    And whither rap'd, now thou but stoup'st to mee?
Dwell, dwell here still: O, being every-where,
    How can I doubt to finde thee ever, here?
I know my state, both full of shame, and scorne,
    Conceiv'd in sinne, and unto labour borne,
Standing with feare, and must with horror fall,
    And destin'd unto judgement, after all.
I feele my griefes too, and there scarce is ground,
    Upon my flesh to'inflict another wound.
Yet dare I not complaine, or wish for death
    With holy PAUL, lest it be thought the breath
Of discontent; or that these prayers bee
    For wearinesse of life, not love of thee.

WILLIAM DRUMMOND OF HAWTHORNDEN Sonnet

How many times *Nights silent Queene* her Face
Hath hid, how oft with Starres in silver Maske
In Heavens great Hall shee hath begunne her Taske,
And chear'd the waking Eye in lower Place:
How oft the *Sunne* hath made by Heavens swift Race
The happie Lover to forsake the Brest
Of his deare Ladie, wishing in the West
His golden Coach to runne had larger Space:
I ever count, and number, since alas
I bade Farewell to my Hearts dearest Guest,
The Miles I compasse, and in Minde I chase
The Flouds and Mountaines holde mee from my Rest:
    But (woe is mee) long count and count may I,
    Ere I see Her whose Absence makes mee die.

WILLIAM BROWNE *from* Britannia's Pastorals

[The Golden Age: Flower-weaving]

The *Pansie*, *Thistle*, all with prickles set,
The *Cowslip*, *Honisuckle*, *Violet*,
And many hundreds more that grac'd the Meades,
Gardens and Groves, (where beauteous *Flora* treads)

Were by the Shepheards Daughters (as yet are
Us'd in our Cotes) brought home with speciall care:
For bruising them they not alone would quell
But rot the rest, and spoile their pleasing smell.
Much like a Lad, who in his tender prime
Sent from his friends to learne the use of time,
As are his mates, or good or bad, so he
Thrives to the world, and such his actions be.

　　As in the *Rainbowes* many coloured hewe
Here see wee watchet deepned with a blewe,
There a darke tawny with a purple mixt,
Yealow and flame, with streakes of greene betwixt,
A bloudy streame into a blushing run
And ends still with the colour which begun,
Drawing the deeper to a lighter staine,
Bringing the lightest to the deep'st againe,
With such rare Art each mingleth with his fellow,
The blewe with watchet, greene and red with yealow;
Like to the changes which we daily see
About the Doves necke with varietie,
Where none can say (though he it strict attends)
Here one begins; and there the other ends:
So did the Maidens with their various flowres
Decke up their windowes, and make neate their bowres:
Using such cunning as they did dispose
The ruddy *Piny* with the lighter *Rose*,
The *Moncks-hood* with the *Buglosse*, and intwine
The white, the blewe, the flesh-like *Columbine*
With *Pinckes*, *Sweet-williams*; that farre off the eye
Could not the manner of their mixtures spye.

　　Then with those flowres they most of all did prise,
(With all their skill and in most curious wise
On tufts of Hearbs or Rushes) would they frame
A daintie border round their Shepheards name.
Or *Poesies* make, so quaint, so apt, so rare,
As if the *Muses* only lived there:
And that the after world should strive in vaine
What they then did to counterfeit againe.
Nor will the Needle nor the Loome e're be
So perfect in their best embroderie,
Nor such composures make of silke and gold,
As theirs, when *Nature* all her cunning told.

THOMAS CAMPION

There is a Garden in her face,
Where Roses and white Lillies grow;
  A heav'nly paradice is that place,
Wherein all pleasant fruits doe flow.
    There Cherries grow which none may buy
    Till Cherry ripe themselves doe cry.

    Those Cherries fayrely doe enclose
Of Orient Pearle a double row,
  Which when her lovely laughter showes,
They look like Rose-buds fill'd with snow.
    Yet them nor Peere, nor Prince can buy,
    Till Cherry ripe themselves doe cry.

    Her Eyes like Angels watch them still;
Her Browes like bended bowes doe stand,
  Threatning with piercing frownes to kill
All that attempt with eye or hand
    Those sacred Cherries to come nigh,
    Till Cherry ripe themselves doe cry.

THOMAS CAMPION

Now winter nights enlarge
  The number of their houres,
And clouds their stormes discharge
  Upon the ayrie towres,
Let now the chimneys blaze
  And cups o'erflow with wine:
Let well-tun'd words amaze
  With harmonie divine.
Now yellow waxen lights
  Shall waite on hunny Love,
While youthfull Revels, Masks, and Courtly sights,
  Sleepes leaden spels remove.

This time doth well dispence
    With lovers long discourse;
Much speech hath some defence,
    Though beauty no remorse.
All doe not all things well;
    Some measures comely tread;
Some knotted Ridles tell;
    Some Poems smoothly read.
The Summer hath his joyes,
    And Winter his delights;
Though Love and all his pleasures are but toyes,
    They shorten tedious nights.

SIR WALTER RALEGH [Sir Walter Ralegh to his Sonne]   **1618**

Three thinges there bee that prosper up apace
And flourish, whilest they growe asunder farr,
But on a day, they meet all in one place,
And when they meet, they one another marr;
And they bee theise: the wood, the weede, the wagg.
The wood is that, which makes the Gallow tree,
The weed is that, which stringes the Hangmans bagg,
The wagg my pritty knave betokeneth thee.
Marke well deare boy whilest theise assemble not,
Green springs the tree, hempe growes, the wagg is wilde,
But when they meet, it makes the timber rott,
It fretts the halter, and it choakes the childe.
    Then bless thee, and beware, and lett us praye,
    Wee part not with the at this meeting day.

                (1870)

SIR WALTER RALEGH *from* **The Ocean to Scinthia**

Butt stay my thoughts, make end, geve fortune way
harshe is the voice of woe and sorrows sounde
cumplaynts cure not, and teares do butt allay
greifs for a tyme, which after more abounde

to seeke for moysture in th'arabien sande
is butt a losse of labor, and of rest
the lincks which tyme did break of harty bands

words cannot knytt, or waylings make a new,
seeke not the soonn in cloudes, when it is sett ...
On highest mountaynes wher thos Sedars grew
agaynst whose bancks, the trobled ocean bett

and weare the markes to finde thy hoped port
into a soyle farr of them sealves remove
on Sestus shore, Leanders late resorte
Hero hath left no lampe to Guyde her love

Thow lookest for light in vayne, and stormes arize
Shee sleaps thy death, that erst thy danger syth-ed
strive then no more bow down thy weery eyes
eyes, which to all thes woes thy hart have guided

Shee is gonn, Shee is lost, shee is found, shee is ever faire,
Sorrow drawes weakly, wher love drawes not too
Woes cries, sound nothinge, butt only in loves eare
Do then by Diinge, what life cannot doo ...

Unfolde thy flockes, and leve them to the feilds
to feed on hylls, or dales, wher likes them best
of what the summer, or the springetyme yeildes
for love, and tyme, hath geven thee leve to rest

Thy hart which was their folde now in decay
by often stormes, and winters many blasts
all torne and rent becumes misfortunes pray,
falce hope, my shepherds staff now age hath brast

My pipe, which loves own hand, gave my desire
to singe her prayses, and my wo uppon
Dispaire hath often threatned to the fier
as vayne to keipe now all the rest ar gonn.

Thus home I draw, as deaths longe night drawes onn
yet every foot, olde thoughts turne back myne eyes
constraynt mee guides as old age drawes a stonn
agaynst the hill, which over wayghty lyes

for feebell armes, or wasted strenght to move
my steapps ar backwarde, gasinge onn my loss,
my minds affection, and my sowles sole love,
not mixte with fances chafe, or fortunes dross,

to god I leve it, who first gave it me,
and I her gave, and she returnd agayne,
as it was herrs, so lett his mercies bee,
of my last cumforts, the essentiall meane.

But be it so, or not, th'effects, ar past,
her love hath end, my woe must ever last.

(1870)

SIR WALTER RALEGH

Even suche is tyme that takes in trust
our youth, our joies and what we have
And paies us but with earth, and dust
which in the Darke and silent grave
when we have wandred all our waies
shutts up the storie of our daies:
But from this earth, this grave this dust
The Lord will raise me up I trust.

MICHAEL DRAYTON *from* Idea   **1619**

61

Since ther's no helpe, Come let us kisse and part,
Nay, I have done: You get no more of Me,
And I am glad, yea glad withall my heart,
That thus so cleanly, I my Selfe can free,
Shake hands for ever, Cancell all our Vowes,
And when We meet at any time againe,
Be it not seene in either of our Browes,
That We one jot of former Love reteyne;

Now at the last gaspe, of Loves latest Breath,
When his Pulse fayling, Passion speechlesse lies,
When Faith is kneeling by his bed of Death,
And Innocence is closing up his Eyes,
    Now if thou would'st, when all have given him over,
    From Death to Life, thou might'st him yet recover.

ANONYMOUS

Sweet Suffolk owl, so trimly dight
With feathers like a lady bright,
Thou sing'st alone, sitting by night,
    Te whit, te whoo, te whit, te whoo.
Thy note, that forth so freely rolls,
With shrill command the mouse controls,
And sings a dirge for dying souls,
    Te whit, te whoo, te whit, te whoo.

1620   JOHN DONNE **The Canonization**

For Godsake hold your tongue, and let me love,
    Or chide my palsie, or my gout,
My five gray haires, or ruin'd fortune flout,
    With wealth your state, your minde with Arts improve,
        Take you a course, get you a place,
        Observe his honour, or his grace,
Or the Kings reall, or his stamped face
    Contemplate, what you will, approve,
    So you will let me love.

Alas, alas, who's injur'd by my love?
    What merchants ships have my sighs drown'd?
Who saies my teares have overflow'd his ground?
    When did my colds a forward spring remove?
        When did the heats which my veines fill
        Adde one more, to the plaguie Bill?
Soldiers finde warres, and Lawyers finde out still
    Litigious men, which quarrels move,
    Though she and I do love.

Call us what you will, wee are made such by love;
    Call her one, mee another flye,
We'are Tapers too, and at our owne cost die,
    And wee in us finde the'Eagle and the dove;
        The Phœnix ridle hath more wit
        By us, we two being one, are it.
So, to one neutrall thing both sexes fit,
    Wee dye and rise the same, and prove
    Mysterious by this love.

Wee can dye by it, if not live by love,
    And if unfit for tombes and hearse
Our legend bee, it will be fit for verse;
    And if no peece of Chronicle wee prove,
        We'll build in sonnets pretty roomes;
        As well a well wrought urne becomes
The greatest ashes, as halfe-acre tombes,
    And by these hymnes, all shall approve
    Us *Canoniz'd* for Love.

And thus invoke us; You whom reverend love
    Made one anothers hermitage;
You, to whom love was peace, that now is rage;
    Who did the whole worlds soule contract, and drove
        Into the glasses of your eyes
        So made such mirrors, and such spies,
That they did all to you epitomize,
    Countries, Townes, Courts: Beg from above
    A patterne of your love.

(1633)

JOHN DONNE A Nocturnall upon S. *Lucies* Day, Being the Shortest Day

'Tis the yeares midnight, and it is the dayes,
Lucies, who scarce seaven houres herself unmaskes,
    The Sunne is spent, and now his flasks
    Send forth light squibs, no constant rayes;
        The world's whole sap is sunke:
The generall balme th'hydroptique earth hath drunk,
Whither, as to the beds-feet, life is shrunke,
Dead and enterr'd; yet all these seeme to laugh,
Compar'd with mee, who am their Epitaph.

Study me then, you who shall lovers bee
At the next world, that is, at the next Spring:
   For I am every dead thing,
   In whom love wrought new Alchimie.
     For his art did expresse
A quintessence even from nothingnesse,
From dull privations, and leane emptinesse:
He ruin'd mee, and I am re-begot
Of absence, darknesse, death; things which are not.

All others, from all things, draw all that's good,
Life, soule, forme, spirit, whence they beeing have;
   I, by loves limbecke, am the grave
   Of all, that's nothing. Oft a flood
     Have wee two wept, and so
Drownd the whole world, us two; oft did we grow
To be two Chaosses, when we did show
Care to ought else; and often absences
Withdrew our soules, and made us carcasses.

But I am by her death, (which word wrongs her)
Of the first nothing, the Elixer grown;
   Were I a man, that I were one,
   I needs must know; I should preferre,
     If I were any beast,
Some ends, some means; Yea plants, yea stones detest,
And love; all, all some properties invest;
If I an ordinary nothing were,
As shadow, a light, and body must be here.

But I am None; nor will my Sunne renew.
You lovers, for whose sake, the lesser Sunne
   At this time to the Goat is runne
   To fetch new lust, and give it you,
     Enjoy your summer all;
Since shee enjoyes her long nights festivall,
Let mee prepare towards her, and let mee call
This houre her Vigill, and her eve, since this
Both the yeares, and the dayes deep midnight is.

(1633)

JOHN DONNE Loves Growth

I scarce beleeve my love to be so pure
    As I had thought it was,
    Because it doth endure
Vicissitude, and season, as the grasse;
Me thinkes I lyed all winter, when I swore,
My love was infinite, if spring make'it more.
But if this medicine, love, which cures all sorrow
With more, not onely bee no quintessence,
But mixt of all stuffes, paining soule, or sense,
And of the Sunne his working vigour borrow,
Love's not so pure, and abstract, as they use
To say, which have no Mistresse but their Muse,
But as all else, being elemented too,
Love sometimes would contemplate, sometimes do.

And yet not greater, but more eminent,
    Love by the spring is growne;
    As, in the firmament,
Starres by the Sunne are not inlarg'd, but showne.
Gentle love deeds, as blossomes on a bough,
From loves awaken'd root do bud out now.
If, as in water stir'd more circles bee
Produc'd by one, love such additions take,
Those like to many spheares, but one heaven make,
For, they are all concentrique unto thee;
And though each spring doe adde to love new heate,
As princes doe in times of action get
New taxes, and remit them not in peace,
No winter shall abate the springs encrease.

(1633)

JOHN DONNE A Valediction: Forbidding Mourning

As virtuous men passe mildly away,
   And whisper to their soules, to goe,
Whilst some of their sad friends doe say,
   The breath goes now, and some say, no:

So let us melt, and make no noise,
    No teare-floods, nor sigh-tempests move,
'Twere prophanation of our joyes
    To tell the layetie our love.

Moving of th'earth brings harmes and feares,
    Men reckon what it did and meant,
But trepidation of the spheares,
    Though greater farre, is innocent.

Dull sublunary lovers love
    (Whose soule is sense) cannot admit
Absence, because it doth remove
    Those things which elemented it.

But we by a love, so much refin'd,
    That our selves know not what it is,
Inter-assured of the mind,
    Care lesse, eyes, lips, and hands to misse.

Our two soules therefore, which are one,
    Though I must goe, endure not yet
A breach, but an expansion,
    Like gold to ayery thinnesse beate.

If they be two, they are two so
    As stiffe twin compasses are two,
Thy soule the fixt foot, makes no show
    To move, but doth, if the'other doe.

And though it in the center sit,
    Yet when the other far doth rome,
It leanes, and hearkens after it,
    And growes erect, as that comes home.

Such wilt thou be to mee, who must
    Like th'other foot, obliquely runne;
Thy firmnes makes my circle just,
    And makes me end, where I begunne.

                                                     (1633)

JOHN DONNE The Exstasie

Where, like a pillow on a bed,
  A Pregnant banke swel'd up, to rest
The violets reclining head,
  Sat we two, one anothers best;
Our hands were firmely cimented
  With a fast balme, which thence did spring,
Our eye-beames twisted, and did thred
  Our eyes, upon one double string;
So to'entergraft our hands, as yet
  Was all our meanes to make us one,
And pictures in our eyes to get
  Was all our propagation.
As 'twixt two equal Armies, Fate
  Suspends uncertaine victorie,
Our soules, (which to advance their state,
  Were gone out,) hung 'twixt her, and mee.
And whil'st our soules negotiate there,
  Wee like sepulchrall statues lay;
All day, the same our postures were,
  And wee said nothing, all the day.
If any, so by love refin'd,
  That he soules language understood,
And by good love were growen all minde,
  Within convenient distance stood,
He (though he knew not which soule spake,
  Because both meant, both spake the same)
Might thence a new concoction take,
  And part farre purer then he came.
This Extasie doth unperplex
  (We said) and tell us what we love,
Wee see by this, it was not sexe,
  Wee see, we saw not what did move:
But as all severall soules containe
  Mixture of things, they know not what,
Love, these mixt soules, doth mixe againe,
  And makes both one, each this and that.
A single violet transplant,
  The strength, the colour, and the size,
(All which before was poore, and scant,)
  Redoubles still, and multiplies.

When love, with one another so
    Interinanimates two soules,
That abler soule, which thence doth flow,
    Defects of lonelinesse controules.
Wee then, who are this new soule, know,
    Of what we are compos'd, and made,
For, th'Atomies of which we grow,
    Are soules, whom no change can invade.
But O alas, so long, so farre
    Our bodies why doe wee forbeare?
They'are ours, though they'are not wee, Wee are
    Th'intelligences, they the spheare.
We owe them thankes, because they thus,
    Did us, to us, at first convay,
Yeelded their forces, sense, to us,
    Nor are drosse to us, but allay.
On man heavens influence workes not so,
    But that it first imprints the ayre,
Soe soule into the soule may flow,
    Though it to body first repaire.
As our blood labours to beget
    Spirits, as like soules as it can,
Because such fingers need to knit
    That subtile knot, which makes us man:
So must pure lovers soules descend
    T'affections, and to faculties,
Which sense may reach and apprehend,
    Else a great Prince in prison lies.
To'our bodies turne wee then, that so
    Weake men on love reveal'd may looke;
Loves mysteries in soules doe grow,
    But yet the body is his booke.
And if some lover, such as wee,
    Have heard this dialogue of one,
Let him still marke us, he shall see
    Small change, when we'are to bodies gone.

                          (1633)

§ JOHN DONNE *from* Holy Sonnets

VII

At the round earths imagin'd corners, blow
Your trumpets, Angells, and arise, arise
From death, you numberlesse infinities
Of soules, and to your scattred bodies goe,
All whom the flood did, and fire shall o'erthrow,
All whom warre, dearth, age, agues, tyrannies,
Despaire, law, chance, hath slaine, and you whose eyes,
Shall behold God, and never tast deaths woe.
But let them sleepe, Lord, and mee mourne a space,
For, if above all these, my sinnes abound,
'Tis late to aske abundance of thy grace,
When wee are there; here on this lowly ground,
Teach mee how to repent; for that's as good
As if thou'hadst seal'd my pardon, with thy blood.

X

Death be not proud, though some have called thee
Mighty and dreadfull, for, thou art not soe,
For, those, whom thou think'st, thou dost overthrow,
Die not, poore death, nor yet canst thou kill mee;
From rest and sleepe, which but thy pictures bee,
Much pleasure, then from thee, much more must flow,
And soonest our best men with thee doe goe,
Rest of their bones, and soules deliverie.
Thou'art slave to Fate, chance, kings, and desperate men,
And dost with poyson, warre, and sicknesse dwell,
And poppie,'or charmes can make us sleepe as well,
And better then thy stroake; why swell'st thou then?
One short sleepe past, wee wake eternally,
And death shall be no more, Death thou shalt die.

XIV

Batter my heart, three person'd God; for, you
As yet but knocke, breathe, shine, and seeke to mend;
That I may rise, and stand, o'erthrow mee,'and bend
Your force, to breake, blowe, burn and make me new.
I, like an usurpt towne, to'another due,
Labour to'admit you, but Oh, to no end,
Reason your viceroy in mee, mee should defend,
But is captiv'd, and proves weake or untrue,
Yet dearely'I love you, and would be lov'd faine,
But am betroth'd unto your enemie,
Divorce mee,'untie, or breake that knot againe,
Take mee to you, imprison mee, for I
Except you'enthrall mee, never shall be free,
Nor ever chast, except you ravish mee.

(1633)

§   §   §

JOHN DONNE A Hymne to Christ, at the Authors Last Going into Germany

In what torne ship soever I embarke,
That ship shall be my embleme of thy Arke;
What sea soever swallow mee, that flood
Shall be to mee an embleme of thy blood;
Though thou with clouds of anger do disguise
Thy face; yet through that maske I know those eyes,
    Which, though they turne away sometimes,
        They never will despise.

I sacrifice this Iland unto thee,
And all whom I lov'd there, and who lov'd mee;
When I have put our seas twixt them and mee,
Put thou thy sea betwixt my sinnes and thee.

As the trees sap doth seeke the root below
In winter, in my winter now I goe,
  Where none but thee, th'Eternall root
    Of true love I may know.

Nor thou nor thy religion dost controule,
The amorousnesse of an harmonious Soule,
But thou would'st have that love thy selfe: As thou
Art jealous, Lord, so I am jealous now,
Thou lov'st not, till from loving more, thou free
My soule: Who ever gives, takes libertie:
  O, if thou car'st not whom I love,
    Alas, thou lov'st not mee.

Seale then this bill of my Divorce to All,
On whom those fainter beames of love did fall;
Marry those loves, which in youth scatter'd bee
On Fame, Wit, Hopes (false mistresses) to thee.
Churches are best for Prayer, that have least light:
To see God only, I goe out of sight:
  And to scape stormy dayes, I chuse
    An everlasting night.

(1633)

JOHN DONNE A Hymne to God the Father

Wilt thou forgive that sinne where I begunne,
  Which is my sin, though it were done before?
Wilt thou forgive that sinne; through which I runne,
  And do run still: though still I doe deplore?
    When thou hast done, thou hast not done,
      For, I have more.

Wilt thou forgive that sinne which I'have wonne
  Others to sinne? and, made my sinne their doore?
Wilt thou forgive that sinne which I did shunne
  A yeare, or two: but wallow'd in, a score?
    When thou hast done, thou hast not done,
      For, I have more.

I have a sinne of feare, that when I'have spunne
 My last thred, I shall perish on the shore;
Sweare by thy selfe, that at my death thy Sonne
 Shall shine as he shines now, and heretofore;
  And, having done that, Thou hast done,
   I feare no more.

     (1633)

1621   KATHERINE, LADY DYER [Epitaph on Sir William Dyer]

My dearest dust could not thy hasty day
Afford thy drowzy patience leave to stay
One hower longer; so that we might either
  Sate up, or gone to bedd together?
But since thy finisht labor hath possest
  Thy weary limbs with early rest,
Enjoy it sweetly; and thy widdowe bride
Shall soone repose her by thy slumbring side;
Whose business, now is only to prepare
  My nightly dress, and call to prayre:
Mine eyes wax heavy and the day growes old
  The dew falls thick, my bloud growes cold;
Draw, draw the closed curtaynes: and make roome;
My deare, my dearest dust; I come, I come.

§ LADY MARY WROTH *from* **Pamphilia to Amphilanthus**

77

In this strang labourinth how shall I turne?
 wayes are on all sids while the way I miss:
 if to the right hand, ther, in love I burne;
 lett mee goe forward, therein danger is;

If to the left, suspition hinders bliss,
 lett mee turne back, shame cries I ought returne
 nor fainte though crosses with my fortunes kiss;
 stand still is harder, allthough sure to mourne;

Thus lett mee take the right, or left hand way;
   goe forward, or stand still, or back retire;
   I must thes doubts indure with out allay
   or help, butt traveile find for my best hire;

Yett that which most my troubled sence doth move
is to leave all, and take the thread of love.

96

Late in the Forest I did Cupid see
   colde, wett, and crying hee had lost his way,
   and beeing blind was farder like to stray:
   which sight a kind compassion bred in mee,

I kindly tooke, and dride him, while that hee
   poore child complain'd hee sterved was with stay,
   and pin'de for want of his accustom'd pray,
   for non in that wilde place his hoste would bee,

I glad was of his finding, thinking sure
   this service should my freedome still procure,
   and in my armes I tooke him then unharmde,

Carrying him safe unto a Mirtle bowre
   butt in the way hee made mee feele his powre,
   burning my hart who had him kindly warmd.

§   §   §

WILLIAM DRUMMOND OF HAWTHORNDEN [For the   1623
Baptiste]

The last and greatest Herauld of Heavens King,
Girt with rough Skinnes, hyes to the Desarts wilde,
Among that savage brood the Woods foorth bring,
Which hee than Man more harmlesse found and milde:

His food was Blossomes, and what yong doth spring,
With Honey that from virgine Hives distil'd;
Parcht Bodie, hollow Eyes, some uncouth thing
Made him appeare, long since from Earth exilde.
There burst hee foorth; All yee, whose Hopes relye
On GOD, with mee amidst these Desarts mourne,
Repent, repent, and from olde errours turne.
Who listned to his voyce, obey'd his crye?
  Onelie the Ecchoes which hee made relent,
  Rung from their Marble Caves, repent, repent.

WILLIAM DRUMMOND OF HAWTHORNDEN [Content and Resolute]

As when it hapneth that some lovely Towne
Unto a barbarous Besieger falles,
Who there by Sword and Flame himselfe enstalles,
And (Cruell) it in Teares and Blood doth drowne;
Her Beauty spoyl'd, her Citizens made Thralles,
His spight yet so cannot her all throw downe,
But that some Statue, Arch, Phan of renowne,
Yet lurkes unmaym'd within her weeping walles:
So after all the Spoile, Disgrace, and Wrake,
That Time, the World, and Death could bring combind,
Amidst that Masse of Ruines they did make,
Safe and all scarre-lesse yet remaines my Minde:
  From this so high transcending Rapture springes,
  That I, all else defac'd, not envie Kinges.

WILLIAM BROWNE On the Countesse *Dowager* of *Pembroke*

Underneth this Marble Hearse;
Lyes the subject of all verse,
Sidneys sister; *Pembrookes* mother,
Death, ere thou hast kill'd another,
Faire, and learn'd, and good as shee,
Time shall throw a dart at thee.

Marble Pyles let no man rayse
To her name; for after dayes;
Some kinde woman borne as she
Reading this; (Like Niobe,)
Shall turne Marble, and become
Both her mourner and her Tombe.

SIR HENRY WOTTON On his Mistress, the Queen of Bohemia **1624**

You meaner *Beauties* of the *Night*,
That poorly satisfie our *Eyes*
More by your *number*, than your *light*,
You *Common people* of the *Skies*;
   What are you when the *Sun* shall rise?

You curious Chanters of the Wood,
That warble forth *Dame Natures* layes,
Thinking your *Voices* understood
By your weak *accents*; what's your praise
   When *Philomel* her voice shall raise?

You *Violets*, that first appear,
By your *pure purple mantles* known,
Like the proud *Virgins* of the *year*,
As if the *Spring* were all your own;
   What are you when the *Rose is blown*?

So, when *my Mistress* shall be *seen*
In *Form* and *Beauty* of her *mind*,
By *Vertue* first, then *Choice a Queen*,
Tell me, if *she* were not design'd
   Th' *Eclipse* and *Glory* of her kind?

GEORGE SANDYS *from the Latin of Ausonius*
Echo   **1626**

Fond Painter, why woulds't thou my picture draw?
An unknowne Goddesse, whom none ever saw,
Daughter of aire and tongue: of judgment blind
The mother I; a voice without a mind.

I only with anothers language sport,
And but the last of dying speech retort.
Lowd Ecchos mansion in the eare is found:
If therefore thou wilt paint me, paint a sound.

1627   BEN JONSON My Picture left in Scotland

I now thinke, Love is rather deafe, then blind,
    For else it could not be,
                That she,
Whom I adore so much, should so slight me,
    And cast my love behind:
I'm sure my language to her, was as sweet,
        And every close did meet
        In sentence, of as subtile feet,
                As hath the youngest Hee,
        That sits in shadow of *Apollo's* tree.
    Oh, but my conscious feares,
            That flie my thoughts betweene,
            Tell me that she hath seene
            My hundred of gray haires,
            Told seven and fortie years,
    Read so much wast, as she cannot imbrace
        My mountaine belly, and my rockie face,
And all these through her eyes, have stopt her eares.

                                        (1640)

BEN JONSON An Ode. To Himselfe

Where do'st thou carelesse lie,
    Buried in ease and sloth?
Knowledge, that sleepes, doth die;
And this Securitie,
    It is the common Moath,
That eats on wits, and Arts, and oft destroyes them both.

Are all th' *Aonian* springs
    Dri'd up? lyes *Thespia* wast?
Doth *Clarius* Harp want strings,
That not a Nymph now sings?
    Or droop they as disgrac't,
To see their Seats and Bowers by chattring Pies defac't?

If hence thy silence be,
    As 'tis too just a cause;
Let this thought quicken thee,
Minds that are great and free,
    Should not on fortune pause,
'Tis crowne enough to vertue still, her owne applause.

What though the greedie Frie
    Be taken with false Baytes
Of worded Balladrie,
And thinke it Poësie?
    They die with their conceits,
And only pitious scorne, upon their folly waites.

Then take in hand thy Lyre,
    Strike in thy proper straine,
With *Japhets* lyne, aspire
Sols Chariot for new fire,
    To give the world againe:
Who aided him, will thee, the issue of *Joves* braine.

And since our Daintie age,
    Cannot indure reproofe,
Make not thy selfe a Page,
To that strumpet the Stage,
    But sing high and aloofe,
Safe from the wolves black jaw, and the dull Asses hoofe.

(1640)

MICHAEL DRAYTON *from* Nimphidia, The Court of Fayrie

[Queen Mab's Chariot]

Her Chariot ready straight is made,
Each thing therein is fitting layde,
That she by nothing might be stayde,
   For naught must her be letting,
Foure nimble Gnats the Horses were,
Their Harnasses of Gossamere,
Flye Cranion her Chariottere,
   Upon the Coach-box getting.

Her Chariot of a Snayles fine shell,
Which for the colours did excell:
The faire Queene *Mab*, becomming well,
   So lively was the limming:
The seate the soft wooll of the Bee;
The cover (gallantly to see)
The wing of a pyde Butterflee,
   I trowe t'was simple trimming.

The wheeles compos'd of Crickets bones,
And daintily made for the nonce,
For feare of ratling on the stones,
   With Thistle-downe they shod it;
For all her Maydens much did feare,
If *Oberon* had chanc'd to heare,
That *Mab* his Queene should have bin there,
   He would not have aboad it.

She mounts her Chariot with a trice,
Nor would she stay for no advice,
Untill her Maydes that were so nice,
   To wayte on her were fitted,
But ranne her selfe away alone;
Which when they heard there was not one,
But hasted after to be gone,
   As she had beene diswitted.

Hop, and *Mop*, and *Drop* so cleare,
Pip, and *Trip*, and *Skip* that were,
To *Mab* their Soveraigne ever deare:
   Her speciall Maydes of Honour;
Fib, and *Tib*, and *Pinck*, and *Pin*,
Tick, and *Quick*, and *Jill*, and *Jin*,
Tit, and *Nit*, and *Wap*, and *Win*,
   The Trayne that wayte upon her.

Upon a Grashopper they got,
And what with Amble, and with Trot,
For hedge nor ditch they spared not,
   But after her they hie them.
A Cobweb over them they throw,
To shield the winde if it should blowe,
Themselves they wisely could bestowe,
   Lest any should espie them.

MICHAEL DRAYTON These Verses weare Made by Michaell   **1631**
Drayton Esquier Poett Lawreatt the Night before Hee Dyed.

Soe well I love thee, as without thee I
Love Nothing, yf I might Chuse, I'de rather dye
Then bee one day debarde thy companye

Since Beasts, and plantes doe growe, and live and move
Beastes are those men, that such a life approve
Hee onlye Lives, that Deadly is in Love

The Corne that in the grownd is sowen first dies
And of one seed doe manye Eares arise
Love this worldes Corne, by dying Multiplies

The seeds of Love first by thy eyes weare throwne
Into a grownd untild, a harte unknowne
To beare such fruitt, tyll by thy handes t'was sowen

Looke as your Looking glass by Chance may fall
Devyde and breake in manye peyces smale
And yett shewes forth, the selfe same face in all

Proportions, Features Graces just the same
And in the smalest peyce as well the name
Of Fayrest one deserves, as in the richest frame

Soe all my Thoughts are peyces but of you
Whiche put together makes a Glass soe true
As I therin noe others face but yours can Veiwe

(1905)

ANONYMOUS Feltons Epitaph

Heere uninterr'd suspendes (though not to save
Surviving Frendes th'expences of a grave)
Feltons dead Earth; which to the world must bee
Its owne sadd Monument. His Elegie
As large as Fame; but whether badd or good
I say not: by himself 'twas writt in blood:
For which his bodie is entomb'd in Ayre,
Archt o're with heaven, sett with a thousand faire
And glorious Diamond Starrs. A Sepulchre
That time can never ruinate, and where
Th'impartiall Worme (which is not brib'd to spare
Princes corrupt in Marble) cannot share
His Flesh; which yf the charitable skies
Embalme with teares; doeing those Obsequies
Belong to men shall last; till pittying Fowle
Contend to beare his bodie to his soule.

(1658)

ANONYMOUS [Epitaph on the Duke of Buckingham]

This little Grave embraces
One Duke and twentie places.

Redemption

Having been tenant long to a rich Lord,
    Not thriving, I resolved to be bold,
    And make a suit unto him, to afford
A new small-rented lease, and cancell th' old.

In heaven at his manour I him sought:
    They told me there, that he was lately gone
    About some land, which he had dearly bought
Long since on earth, to take possession.

I straight return'd, and knowing his great birth,
    Sought him accordingly in great resorts;
    In cities, theatres, gardens, parks, and courts:
At length I heard a ragged noise and mirth

    Of theeves and murderers: there I him espied,
    Who straight, *Your suit is granted*, said, and died.

Prayer

Prayer the Churches banquet, Angels age,
    Gods breath in man returning to his birth,
    The soul in paraphrase, heart in pilgrimage,
The Christian plummet sounding heav'n and earth;

Engine against th' Almightie, sinners towre,
    Reversed thunder, Christ-side-piercing spear,
    The six-daies world-transposing in an houre,
A kinde of tune, which all things heare and fear;

Softnesse, and peace, and joy, and love, and blisse,
    Exalted Manna, gladnesse of the best,
    Heaven in ordinarie, man well drest,
The milkie way, the bird of Paradise,

    Church-bels beyond the starres heard, the souls bloud,
    The land of spices; something understood.

Church-monuments

While that my soul repairs to her devotion,
Here I intombe my flesh, that it betimes
May take acquaintance of this heap of dust;
To which the blast of deaths incessant motion,
Fed with the exhalation of our crimes,
Drives all at last. Therefore I gladly trust

My bodie to this school, that it may learn
To spell his elements, and finde his birth
Written in dustie heraldrie and lines;
Which dissolution sure doth best discern,
Comparing dust with dust, and earth with earth.
These laugh at Jeat and Marble put for signes,

To sever the good fellowship of dust,
And spoil the meeting. What shall point out them,
When they shall bow, and kneel, and fall down flat
To kisse those heaps, which now they have in trust?
Deare flesh, while I do pray, learn here thy stemme
And true descent; that when thou shalt grow fat,

And wanton in thy cravings, thou mayst know,
That flesh is but the glasse, which holds the dust
That measures all our time; which also shall
Be crumbled into dust. Mark here below
How tame these ashes are, how free from lust,
That thou mayst fit thy self against thy fall.

Deniall

When my devotions could not pierce
             Thy silent eares;
Then was my heart broken, as was my verse:
        My breast was full of fears
             And disorder:

My bent thoughts, like a brittle bow,
             Did flie asunder:
Each took his way; some would to pleasures go,
        Some to the warres and thunder
             Of alarms.

As good go any where, they say,
             As to benumme
Both knees and heart, in crying night and day,
        Come, come, my God, O come,
             But no hearing.

O that thou shouldst give dust a tongue
             To crie to thee,
And then not heare it crying! all day long
        My heart was in my knee,
             But no hearing.

Therefore my soul lay out of sight,
             Untun'd, unstrung:
My feeble spirit, unable to look right,
        Like a nipt blossome, hung
             Discontented.

O cheer and tune my heartlesse breast,
             Deferre no time;
That so thy favours granting my request,
        They and my minde may chime,
             And mend my ryme.

Hope

I gave to Hope a watch of mine: but he
               An anchor gave to me.
Then an old prayer-book I did present:
               And he an optick sent.
With that I gave a viall full of tears:
               But he a few green eares.
Ah Loyterer! I'le no more, no more I'le bring:
               I did expect a ring.

The Collar

I struck the board, and cry'd, No more.
               I will abroad.
     What? shall I ever sigh and pine?
My lines and life are free; free as the rode,
    Loose as the winde, as large as store.
          Shall I be still in suit?
    Have I no harvest but a thorn
    To let me bloud, and not restore
What I have lost with cordiall fruit?
          Sure there was wine
Before my sighs did drie it: there was corn
      Before my tears did drown it.
    Is the yeare onely lost to me?
        Have I no bayes to crown it?
No flowers, no garlands gay? all blasted?
         All wasted?
    Not so, my heart: but there is fruit,
        And thou hast hands.
    Recover all thy sigh-blown age
On double pleasures: leave thy cold dispute
Of what is fit, and not. Forsake thy cage,
        Thy rope of sands,
Which pettie thoughts have made, and made to thee
    Good cable, to enforce and draw,
        And be thy law,
    While thou didst wink and wouldst not see.
        Away; take heed:

I will abroad.
Call in thy deaths head there: tie up thy fears.
He that forbears
To suit and serve his need,
Deserves his load.
But as I rav'd and grew more fierce and wilde
At every word,
Me thoughts I heard one calling, *Childe*:
And I reply'd, *My Lord*.

The Flower

How fresh, O Lord, how sweet and clean
Are thy returns! ev'n as the flowers in spring;
To which, besides their own demean,
The late-past frosts tributes of pleasure bring.
Grief melts away
Like snow in May,
As if there were no such cold thing.

Who would have thought my shrivel'd heart
Could have recover'd greennesse? It was gone
Quite under ground; as flowers depart
To see their mother-root, when they have blown;
Where they together
All the hard weather,
Dead to the world, keep house unknown.

These are thy wonders, Lord of power,
Killing and quickning, bringing down to hell
And up to heaven in an houre;
Making a chiming of a passing-bell.
We say amisse,
This or that is:
Thy word is all, if we could spell.

O that I once past changing were,
Fast in thy Paradise, where no flower can wither!
Many a spring I shoot up fair,
Offring at heav'n, growing and groning thither:

Nor doth my flower
Want a spring-showre,
My sinnes and I joining together.

But while I grow in a straight line,
Still upwards bent, as if heav'n were mine own,
Thy anger comes, and I decline:
What frost to that? what pole is not the zone,
Where all things burn,
When thou dost turn,
And the least frown of thine is shown?

And now in age I bud again,
After so many deaths I live and write;
I once more smell the dew and rain,
And relish versing: O my onely light,
It cannot be
That I am he
On whom thy tempests fell all night.

These are thy wonders, Lord of love,
To make us see we are but flowers that glide:
Which when we once can finde and prove,
Thou hast a garden for us, where to bide.
Who would be more,
Swelling through store,
Forfeit their Paradise by their pride.

The Answer

My comforts drop and melt away like snow:
I shake my head, and all the thoughts and ends,
Which my fierce youth did bandie, fall and flow
Like leaves about me: or like summer friends,

Flyes of estates and sunne-shine. But to all,
Who think me eager, hot, and undertaking,
But in my prosecutions slack and small;
As a young exhalation, newly waking,

Scorns his first bed of dirt, and means the sky;
But cooling by the way, grows pursie and slow,
And setling to a cloud, doth live and die
In that dark state of tears: to all, that so

> Show me, and set me, I have one reply,
> Which they that know the rest, know more then I.

A Wreath

A wreathed garland of deserved praise,
Of praise deserved, unto thee I give,
I give to thee, who knowest all my wayes,
My crooked winding wayes, wherein I live,
Wherein I die, not live: for life is straight,
Straight as a line, and ever tends to thee,
To thee, who art more farre above deceit,
Then deceit seems above simplicitie.
Give me simplicitie, that I may live,
So live and like, that I may know, thy wayes,
Know them and practise them: then shall I give
For this poore wreath, give thee a crown of praise.

Love

Love bade me welcome: yet my soul drew back,
                    Guiltie of dust and sinne.
But quick-ey'd Love, observing me grow slack
                    From my first entrance in,
Drew nearer to me, sweetly questioning,
                    If I lack'd any thing.

A guest, I answer'd, worthy to be here:
                    Love said, You shall be he.
I the unkinde, ungratefull? Ah my deare,
                    I cannot look on thee.
Love took my hand, and smiling did reply,
                    Who made the eyes but I?

Truth Lord, but I have marr'd them: let my shame
    Go where it doth deserve.
And know you not, sayes Love, who bore the blame?
    My deare, then I will serve.
You must sit down, sayes Love, and taste my meat:
    So I did sit and eat.

    § § §

1635 FRANCIS QUARLES Embleme IV [Canticles 7.10. I am my
Beloved's, and his desire is towards me.]

Like to the Artick needle, that doth guide
 The wand'ring shade by his Magnetick pow'r,
And leaves his silken Gnomon to decide
 The question of the controverted houre;
First franticks up and down, from side to side,
  And restlesse beats his crystall'd Iv'ry case
  With vain impatience; jets from place to place,
And seeks the bosome of his frozen bride;
 At length he slacks his motion, and doth rest
His trembling point at his bright Pole's beloved brest.

Ev'n so my soul, being hurried here and there,
 By ev'ry object that presents delight,
Fain would be settled, but she knowes not where;
 She likes at morning what she loaths at night;
She bowes to honour; then she lends an eare
  To that sweet swan-like voyce of dying pleasure,
  Then tumbles in the scatter'd heaps of treasure;
Now flatter'd with false hope; now foyl'd with fear:
 Thus finding all the world's delights to be
But empty toyes, good God, she points alone to thee.

But hath the virtued steel a power to move?
 Or can the untouch'd needle point aright?
Or can my wandring thoughts forbear to rove,
 Unguided by the virtue of thy spirit?
O hath my leaden soul the art t' improve

Her wasted talent, and unrais'd, aspire
   In this sad moulting-time of her desire?
Not first belov'd have I the power to love?
   I cannot stirre, but as thou please to move me,
Nor can my heart return thee love, until thou love me.

The still Commandresse of the silent night
   Borrows her beams from her bright brother's eye;
His fair aspect filles her sharp horns with light;
   If he withdraw, her flames are quench'd and die:
Even so the beams of thy enlightning spirit
     Infus'd and shot into my dark desire,
     Inflame my thoughts, and fill my soul with fire,
That I am ravisht with a new delight;
     But if thou shroud thy face, my glory fades,
And I remain a *Nothing*, all compos'd of shades.

Eternall God, O thou that onely art
   The sacred Fountain of eternall light,
And blessed Loadstone of my better part;
   O thou my heart's desire, my soul's delight,
Reflect upon my soul, and touch my heart,
     And then my heart shall prize no good above thee;
     And then my soul shall know thee; knowing, love thee;
And then my trembling thoughts shall never start
     From thy commands, or swerve the least degree,
Or once presume to move, but as they move in thee.

Epigram

My soul, thy love is dear: 'Twas thought a good
And easie pen'worth of thy Saviour's bloud:
But be not proud; All matters rightly scann'd,
'Twas over-bought: 'Twas sold at second hand.

1637   EDWARD LORD HERBERT OF CHERBURY   Epitaph on
Sir Philip Sidney Lying in St Paul's without a Monument, to be
Fastned upon the Church Door

Reader,
Within this Church Sir *Philip Sidney* lies,
Nor is it fit that I should more acquaint,
    Lest superstition rise,
        And men adore,
Souldiers, their Martyr; Lovers, their Saint.

ROBERT SEMPILL OF BELTREES   The Life and Death of
Habbie Simson, the Piper of Kilbarchan

Kilbarchan now may say alas!
For she hath lost her game and grace,
Both *Trixie* and *The Maiden Trace*;
    But what remead?
5 For no man can supply his place:
      Hab Simson's dead.

Now who shall play *The Day it Dawis*,
Or *Hunt's Up*, when the cock he craws?
Or who can for our kirk-town cause
10   Stand us in stead?
On bagpipes now nobody blaws
      Sen Habbie's dead.

Or wha will cause our shearers shear?
Wha will bend up the brags of weir,
15 Bring in the bells, or good play-meir
    In time of need?
Hab Simson cou'd, what needs you speir?
      But now he's dead.

4 *remead* help; 14 'who will play the war-tunes'; 15 *play-meir* play more;
17 *speir* ask;

So kindly to his neighbours neast
20   At Beltan and St Barchan's feast
He blew, and then held up his breast,
        As he were weid:
But now we need not him arrest,
        For Habbie's dead.

25   At fairs he play'd before the spear-men
All gaily graithed in their gear men:
Steel bonnets, jacks, and swords so clear then
        Like any bead:
Now wha shall play before such weir-men
30   Sen Habbie's dead?

At clark-plays when he wont to come
His Pipe play'd trimly to the drum;
Like bikes of bees he gart it bum,
        And tun'd his reed:
35   Now all our pipers may sing dumb,
        Sen Habbie's dead.

And at horse races many a day,
Before the black, the brown, the gray,
He gart his pipe, when he did play,
40   Baith skirl and skreed:
Now all such pastime's quite away
        Sen Habbie's dead.

He counted was a weil'd wight-man,
And fiercely at football he ran:
45   At every game the gree he wan
        For pith and speed.
The like of Habbie was na than,
        But now he's dead.

19 *neast* nearest; 22 *weid* mad, feverish; 23 *arrest* stop; 26 *graithed* kitted-out;
28 *bead* ring of folk; 29 *weir-men* warriors; 31 *clark-plays* (acted by clerics);
33 *bikes* hives; *gart it bum* made it drone; 40 *skirl and skreed* shriek and screech;
43 *a weil'd wight-man* a chosen brave man; 45 *gree* prize;

And than, besides his valiant acts,
50   At bridals he won many placks;
He bobbed ay behind fo'k's backs
              And shook his head.
Now we want many merry cracks
              Sen Habbie's dead.

55   He was convoyer of the bride,
With Kittock hinging at his side;
About the kirk he thought a pride
              The ring to lead:
But now we may gae but a guide,
60   For Habbie's dead.

So well's he keeped his decorum
And all the stots of *Whip-meg-morum*;
He slew a man, and wae's me for him,
              And bure the fead!
65   But yet the man wan hame before him,
              And was not dead.

And whan he play'd, the lasses leugh
To see him teethless, auld, and teugh,
He wan his pipes besides Barcleugh,
70   Withouten dread!
Which after wan him gear eneugh;
              But now he's dead.

Ay when he play'd the gaitlings gedder'd,
And when he spake, the carl bledder'd,
75   On Sabbath days his cap was fedder'd,
              A seemly weid;
In the kirk-yeard his mare stood tedder'd
              Where he lies dead.

---

50 *placks* coins; 59 *but* without; 62 *stots* hops; 64 *bure the fead* put up with the
fiend; 65 *wan* got; *leugh* laughed; 71 *gear* wealth; 73 *gaitlings gedder'd* urchins
gathered; 74 *carl bledder'd* old man boasted; 76 *weid* outfit;

Alas! for him my heart is saur,
80 For of his spring I gat a skair,
    At every play, race, feast, and fair,
                    But guile or greed;
    We need not look for pyping mair,
                    Sen Habbie's dead.

THOMAS JORDAN A Double Acrostich on Mrs Svsanna Blvnt

Sweete   *Soule* of goodnesse, in whose *Saintlike* brest
Vertue   *Vowe's* dwelling, to make beauty blest;
Sure   *Sighing Cytherea* sits, your eyes
Are   *Altars* whereon shee might sacrifice;
Now   *None* will of the *Paphean* order be;
Natur's   *New* worke transcends a deity;
Arabia's *Aromatticks* court your scent;

Bright   *Beauty* makes your *gazers* eloquent,
Let   *Little Cupid* his lost eyes obtaine
(Vayl'd) *Viewing* you would strike him blinde againe;
Nay   *Never* thinke I flatter, if you be
Thus   *To* none else *(by love)* you are to me.

JOHN MILTON *from* A Mask Presented at Ludlow-Castle, 1634 [Comus]

Comus *enters with a Charming Rod in one hand, his Glass in the other, with him a rout of Monsters headed like sundry sorts of wilde Beasts, but otherwise like Men and Women, their Apparel glistring, they com in making a riotous and unruly noise, with Torches in their hands.*

COMUS
The Star that bids the Shepherd fold,
Now the top of Heav'n doth hold,
And the gilded Car of Day,
His glowing Axle doth allay

80 *spring* dance-tune; *skair* share; 82 *but* without

In the steep *Atlantick* stream,
And the slope Sun his upward beam
Shoots against the dusky Pole,
Pacing toward the other gole
Of his Chamber in the East.
Mean while welcom Joy, and Feast,
Midnight shout, and revelry,
Tipsie dance, and Jollity.
Braid your Locks with rosie Twine
Dropping odours, dropping Wine.
Rigor now is gon to bed,
And Advice with scrupulous head,
Strict Age, and sowre Severity,
With their grave Saws in slumber ly.
We that are of purer fire
Imitate the Starry Quire,
Who in their nightly watchfull Sphears,
Lead in swift round the Months and Years.
The Sounds, and Seas with all their finny drove
Now to the Moon in wavering Morrice move,
And on the Tawny Sands and Shelves,
Trip the pert Fairies and the dapper Elves;
By dimpled Brook, and Fountain brim,
The Wood-Nymphs deckt with Daisies trim,
Their merry wakes and pastimes keep:
What hath night to do with sleep?
Night hath better sweets to prove,
Venus now wakes, and wak'ns Love.
Com let us our rights begin,
'Tis onely day-light that makes Sin
Which these dun shades will ne're report.
Hail Goddesse of Nocturnal sport
Dark vaild *Cotytto*, t'whom the secret flame
Of mid-night Torches burns; mysterious Dame
That ne're art call'd, but when the Dragon woom
Of Stygian darknes spets her thickest gloom,
And makes one blot of all the ayr,
Stay thy cloudy Ebon chair,
Wherin thou rid'st with *Hecat'*, and befriend
Us thy vow'd Priests, till utmost end
Of all thy dues be done, and none left out,
Ere the blabbing Eastern scout,
The nice Morn on th' *Indian* steep
From her cabin'd loop hole peep,

And to the tel-tale Sun discry
Our conceal'd Solemnity.
Com, knit hands, and beat the ground,
In a light fantastick round.

THOMAS RANDOLPH A Gratulatory to Mr Ben. Johnson for   **1638**
his Adopting of Him to be his Son

I was not borne to *Helicon*, nor dare
Presume to thinke my selfe a *Muses* heire.
I have no title to *Parnassus* hill,
Nor any acre of it by the will
Of a dead Ancestour, nor could I bee
Ought but a tenant unto Poëtrie,
But thy Adoption quits me of all feare,
And makes me challenge a childs portion there.
I am a kinne to *Hero's* being thine,
And part of my alliance is divine.
Orpheus, *Musæus*, *Homer* too; beside
Thy Brothers by the *Roman* Mothers side;
As *Ovid*, *Virgil*, and the *Latine Lyre*,
That is so like thy *Horace*; the whole quire
Of Poets are by thy Adoption, all
My uncles; thou hast given me pow'r to call
Phœbus himselfe my grandsire, by this graunt
Each sister of the nine is made my Aunt.
Go you that reckon from a large descent
Your lineall Honours, and are well content
To glory in the age of your great name,
Though on a Herralds faith you build the same:
I do not envy you, nor thinke you blest
Though you may beare a Gorgon on your Crest
By direct line from *Perseus*; I will boast
No farther then my Father; that's the most
I can, or should be proud of; and I were
Unworthy his adoption, if that here
I should be dully modest; boast I must
Being sonne of his Adoption, not his lust.
And to say truth, that which is best in mee
May call you father, 'twas begot by thee.
Have I a sparke of that cœlestiall flame
Within me, I confesse I stole the same

Prometheus like, from thee; and may I feed
His vulture, when I dare deny the deed.
Many more moones thou hast, that shine by night,
All Bankrups, wer't not for a borrow'd light;
Yet can forsweare it; I the debt confesse,
And thinke my reputation ne're the lesse.
For Father let me be resolv'd by you;
Is't a disparagement from rich *Peru*
To ravish gold; or theft, for wealthy Ore
To ransack *Tagus*, or *Pactolus* shore?
Or does he wrong *Alcinous*, that for want
Doth take from him a sprig or two, to plant
A lesser Orchard? sure it cannot bee:
Nor is it theft to steale some flames from thee.
Grant this, and I'le cry guilty, as I am,
And pay a filiall reverence to thy name.
For when my Muse upon obedient knees,
Askes not a Fathers blessing, let her leese
The fame of this Adoption; 'tis a curse
I wish her 'cause I cannot thinke a worse.
And here, as Piety bids me, I intreat
Phœbus to lend thee some of his own heat,
To cure thy Palsie; else I will complaine
He has no skill in hearbs; Poets in vaine
Make him the God of Physicke; 'twere his praise
To make thee as immortall as thy Baies;
As his owne *Daphne*; 'twere a shame to see
The God, not love his Preist, more then his Tree.
　　But if heaven take thee, envying us thy Lyre,
　　'Tis to pen Anthems for an Angels quire.

SIR JOHN SUCKLING Song

Why so pale and wan fond Lover?
　　　　　Prithee why so pale?
Will, when looking well can't move her,
　　　　　Looking ill prevaile?
　　　　　Prithee why so pale?

Why so dull and mute young Sinner?
        Prithee why so mute?
Will, when speaking well can't win her,
        Saying nothing doo't?
        Prithee why so mute?

Quit, quit, for shame, this will not move,
        This cannot take her;
If of her selfe shee will not Love,
        Nothing can make her,
        The Devill take her.

JOHN MILTON Lycidas

In this Monody the Author bewails a learned Friend, unfortunatly
drown'd in his Passage from *Chester* on the *Irish* Seas, 1637. And by
occasion foretels the ruine of our corrupted Clergy then in their height.

Yet once more, O ye Laurels, and once more
Ye Myrtles brown, with Ivy never-sear,
I com to pluck your Berries harsh and crude,
And with forc'd fingers rude,
Shatter your leaves before the mellowing year.
Bitter constraint, and sad occasion dear,
Compels me to disturb your season due:
For *Lycidas* is dead, dead ere his prime
Young *Lycidas*, and hath not left his peer:
Who would not sing for *Lycidas*? he knew
Himself to sing, and build the lofty rhyme.
He must not flote upon his watry bear
Unwept, and welter to the parching wind,
Without the meed of som melodious tear.
   Begin then, Sisters of the sacred well,
That from beneath the seat of *Jove* doth spring,
Begin, and somwhat loudly sweep the string.
Hence with denial vain, and coy excuse,
So may som gentle Muse
With lucky words favour my destin'd Um,
And as he passes turn,
And bid fair peace be to my sable shrowd.
For we were nurst upon the self-same hill,
Fed the same flock, by fountain, shade, and rill.

Together both, ere the high Lawns appear'd
Under the opening eye-lids of the morn,
We drove a field, and both together heard
What time the Gray-fly winds her sultry horn,
Batt'ning our flocks with the fresh dews of night,
Oft till the Star that rose, at Ev'ning, bright
Toward Heav'ns descent had slop'd his westering wheel.
Mean while the Rural ditties were not mute,
Temper'd to th'Oaten Flute,
Rough *Satyrs* danc'd, and *Fauns* with clov'n heel,
From the glad sound would not be absent long,
And old *Damætas* lov'd to hear our song.

But O the heavy change, now thou art gon,
Now thou art gon, and never must return!
Thee Shepherd, thee the Woods, and desert Caves,
With wilde Thyme and the gadding Vine o'regrown,
And all their echoes mourn.
The Willows, and the Hazle Copses green,
Shall now no more be seen,
Fanning their joyous Leaves to thy soft layes.
As killing as the Canker to the Rose,
Or Taint-worm to the weanling Herds that graze,
Or Frost to Flowers, that their gay wardrop wear,
When first the White thorn blows;
Such, *Lycidas*, thy loss to Shepherds ear.

Where were ye Nymphs when the remorseless deep
Clos'd o're the head of your lov'd *Lycidas*?
For neither were ye playing on the steep,
Where your old *Bards*, the famous *Druids* ly,
Nor on the shaggy top of *Mona* high,
Nor yet where *Deva* spreads her wisard stream:
Ay me, I fondly dream!
Had ye bin there – for what could that have don?
What could the Muse her self that *Orpheus* bore,
The Muse her self, for her inchanting son
Whom Universal nature did lament,
When by the rout that made the hideous roar,
His goary visage down the stream was sent,
Down the swift *Hebrus* to the *Lesbian* shore.

Alas! What boots it with uncessant care
To tend the homely slighted Shepherds trade,
And strictly meditate the thankles Muse,
Were it not better don as others use,
To sport with *Amaryllis* in the shade,

Or with the tangles of *Neæra's* hair?

Fame is the spur that the clear spirit doth raise
(That last infirmity of Noble mind)
To scorn delights, and live laborious dayes;
But the fair Guerdon when we hope to find,
And think to burst out into sudden blaze,
Comes the blind *Fury* with th'abhorred shears,
And slits the thin-spun life. But not the praise,
Phœbus repli'd, and touch'd my trembling ears;
Fame is no plant that grows on mortal soil,
Nor in the glistering foil
Set off to th'world, nor in broad rumour lies,
But lives and spreds aloft by those pure eyes,
And perfet witnes of all-judging *Jove*;
As he pronounces lastly on each deed,
Of so much fame in Heav'n expect thy meed.

O Fountain *Arethuse*, and thou honour'd floud,
Smooth-sliding *Mincius*, crown'd with vocall reeds,
That strain I heard was of a higher mood:
But now my Oate proceeds,
And listens to the Herald of the Sea
That came in *Neptune's* plea,
He ask'd the Waves, and ask'd the Fellon winds,
What hard mishap hath doom'd this gentle swain?
And question'd every gust of rugged wings
That blows from off each beaked Promontory;
They knew not of his story,
And sage *Hippotades* their answer brings,
That not a blast was from his dungeon stray'd,
The Ayr was calm, and on the level brine,
Sleek *Panope* with all her sisters play'd.
It was that fatall and perfidious Bark
Built in th'eclipse, and rigg'd with curses dark,
That sunk so low that sacred head of thine.

Next *Camus*, reverend Sire, went footing slow,
His Mantle hairy, and his Bonnet sedge,
Inwrought with figures dim, and on the edge
Like to that sanguine flower inscrib'd with woe.
Ah! Who hath reft (quoth he) my dearest pledge?
Last came, and last did go,
The Pilot of the *Galilean* lake,
Two massy Keyes he bore of metals twain,
(The Golden opes, the Iron shuts amain)
He shook his Miter'd locks, and stern bespake,

How well could I have spar'd for thee young swain,
Anow of such as for their bellies sake,
Creep and intrude, and climb into the fold?
Of other care they little reck'ning make,
Then how to scramble at the shearers feast,
And shove away the worthy bidden guest;
Blind mouthes! that scarce themselves know how to hold
A Sheep-hook, or have learn'd ought els the least
That to the faithfull Herdmans art belongs!
What recks it them? What need they? They are sped;
And when they list, their lean and flashy songs
Grate on their scrannel Pipes of wretched straw,
The hungry Sheep look up, and are not fed,
But swoln with wind, and the rank mist they draw,
Rot inwardly, and foul contagion spread:
Besides what the grim Woolf with privy paw
Daily devours apace, and nothing sed,
But that two-handed engine at the door,
Stands ready to smite once, and smite no more.
       Return *Alpheus*, the dread voice is past,
That shrunk thy streams; Return *Sicilian* Muse,
And call the Vales, and bid them hither cast
Their Bels, and Flourets of a thousand hues.
Ye valleys low where the milde whispers use,
Of shades and wanton winds, and gushing brooks,
On whose fresh lap the swart Star sparely looks,
Throw hither all your quaint enameld eyes,
That on the green terf suck the honied showres,
And purple all the ground with vernal flowres.
Bring the rathe Primrose that forsaken dies,
The tufted Crow-toe, and pale Gessamine,
The white Pink, and the Pansie freakt with jeat,
The glowing Violet,
The Musk-rose, and the well attir'd Woodbine,
With Cowslips wan that hang the pensive hed,
And every flower that sad embroidery wears:
Bid *Amaranthus* all his beauty shed,
And Daffadillies fill their cups with tears,
To strew the Laureat Herse where *Lycid* lies.
For so to interpose a little ease,
Let our frail thoughts dally with false surmise.
Ay me! Whilst thee the shores, and sounding Seas
Wash far away, where ere thy bones are hurld,
Whether beyond the stormy *Hebrides*,

Where thou perhaps under the whelming tide
Visit'st the bottom of the monstrous world;
Or whether thou to our moist vows deny'd,
Sleep'st by the fable of *Bellerus* old,
Where the great vision of the guarded Mount
Looks toward *Namancos* and *Bayona's* hold;
Look homeward Angel now, and melt with ruth.
And, O ye *Dolphins*, waft the haples youth.

Weep no more, woful Shepherds weep no more,
For *Lycidas* your sorrow is not dead,
Sunk though he be beneath the watry floar,
So sinks the day-star in the Ocean bed,
And yet anon repairs his drooping head,
And tricks his beams, and with new spangled Ore,
Flames in the forehead of the morning sky:
So *Lycidas* sunk low, but mounted high,
Through the dear might of him that walk'd the waves;
Where other groves, and other streams along,
With *Nectar* pure his oozy Locks he laves,
And hears the unexpressive nuptiall Song,
In the blest Kingdoms meek of joy and love.
There entertain him all the Saints above,
In solemn troops, and sweet Societies
That sing, and singing in their glory move,
And wipe the tears for ever from his eyes.
Now *Lycidas* the Shepherds weep no more;
Henceforth thou art the Genius of the shore,
In thy large recompense, and shalt be good
To all that wander in that perilous flood.

Thus sang the uncouth Swain to th'Okes and rills,
While the still morn went out with Sandals gray,
He touch'd the tender stops of various Quills,
With eager thought warbling his *Dorick* lay:
And now the Sun had stretch'd out all the hills,
And now was dropt into the Western bay;
At last he rose, and twitch'd his Mantle blew:
To morrow to fresh Woods, and Pastures new.

1640   BEN JONSON *from* **A Celebration of Charis, in Ten Lyrick Peeces**

Her Triumph

See the Chariot at hand here of Love,
   Wherein my Lady rideth!
Each that drawes, is a Swan, or a Dove,
   And well the Carre Love guideth.
As she goes, all hearts doe duty
             Unto her beauty;
And enamour'd, doe wish, so they might
             But enjoy such a sight,
   That they still were to run by her side,
Thorough Swords, thorough Seas, whether she would ride.

Doe but looke on her eyes, they doe light
   All that Loves world compriseth!
Doe but looke on her Haire, it is bright
   As Loves starre when it riseth!
Doe but marke, her forehead's smoother
             Then words that sooth her!
And from her arched browes, such a grace
             Sheds it selfe through the face,
   As alone there triumphs to the life
All the Gaine, all the Good, of the Elements strife.

Have you seene but a bright Lillie grow,
   Before rude hands have touch'd it?
Have you mark'd but the fall o'the Snow
   Before the soyle hath smutch'd it?
Have you felt the wooll o' the Bever?
             Or Swans Downe ever?
Or have smelt o'the bud o'the Brier?
             Or the Nard i' the fire?
   Or have tasted the bag o'the Bee?
O so white! O so soft! O so sweet is she!

BEN JONSON [A Fragment of Petronius Arbiter]

Doing, a filthy pleasure is, and short;
And done, we straight repent us of the sport:
Let us not then rush blindly on unto it,
Like lustfull beasts, that onely know to doe it:
For lust will languish, and that heat decay.
But thus, thus, keeping endlesse Holy-day,
Let us together closely lie, and kisse,
There is no labour, nor no shame in this;
This hath pleas'd, doth please, and long will please; never
Can this decay, but is beginning ever.

SIDNEY GODOLPHIN

Faire Friend, 'tis true, your beauties move
    My heart to a respect:
Too little to bee paid with love,
    Too great for your neglect.

I neither love, nor yet am free,
    For though the flame I find
Be not intense in the degree,
    'Tis of the purest kind.

It little wants of love, but paine,
    Your beautie takes my sense,
And lest you should that price disdaine,
    My thoughts, too, feele the influence.

'Tis not a passions first accesse
    Readie to multiply,
But like Loves calmest State it is
    Possest with victorie.

It is like Love to Truth reduc'd,
    All the false values gone,
Which were created, and induc'd
    By fond imagination.

'Tis either Fancie, or 'tis Fate,
    To love you more then I;
I love you at your beauties rate,
    Lesse were an Injurie.

Like unstamp'd Gold, I weigh each grace,
    So that you may collect
Th'intrinsique value of your face
    Safely from my respect.

And this respect would merit love,
    Were not so faire a sight
Payment enough; for, who dare move
    Reward for his delight?

SIDNEY GODOLPHIN

Lord when the wise men came from Farr
Ledd to thy Cradle by A Starr,
Then did the shepheards too rejoyce,
Instructed by thy Angells voyce,
Blest were the wisemen in their skill,
And shepheards in their harmelesse will.

Wisemen in tracing Natures lawes
Ascend unto the highest cause,
Shepheards with humble fearefulnesse
Walke safely, though their light be lesse,
Though wisemen better know the way
It seemes noe honest heart can stray:

Ther is noe merrit in the wise
But love, (the shepheards sacrifice)
Wisemen all wayes of knowledge past,
To 'th shepheards wonder come at last,
To know, can only wonder breede,
And not to know, is wonders seede.

A wiseman at the Alter Bowes
And offers up his studied vowes
And is received, may not the teares,
Which spring too from a shepheards feares,
And sighs upon his fraylty spent,
Though not distinct, be eloquent.

Tis true, the object sanctifies
All passions which within us rise,
But since noe creature comprehends
The cause of causes, end of ends,
Hee who himselfe vouchsafes to know
Best pleases his creator soe.

When then our sorrowes wee applye
To our owne wantes and poverty,
When wee looke up in all distresse
And our owne misery confesse
Sending both thankes and prayers above
Then though wee doe not know, we love.

(1906)

HENRY KING An Exequy to His Matchlesse Never to be Forgotten Freind

Accept thou Shrine of my Dead Saint,
Instead of Dirges this Complaint,
And for sweet flowres to crowne thy Hearse
Receive a strew of weeping verse
From thy griev'd Friend; whome Thou might'st see
Quite melted into Teares for Thee
　　Deare Losse, since thy untimely fate
My task hath beene to meditate
On Thee, on Thee: Thou art the Book
The Library whereon I look
Though almost blind. For Thee (Lov'd Clay)
I Languish out, not Live the Day,
Using no other Exercise
But what I practise with mine Eyes.
By which wett glasses I find out
How lazily Time creepes about

To one that mournes: This, only This
My Exercise and bus'nes is:
So I compute the weary howres
With Sighes dissolved into Showres.

    Nor wonder if my time goe thus
Backward and most præposterous;
Thou hast Benighted mee. Thy Sett
This Eve of blacknes did begett
Who wast my Day (though overcast
Before thou hadst thy Noon-tide past)
And I remember must in teares,
Thou scarce hadst seene so many Yeeres
As Day tells Howres; By thy cleere Sunne
My Love and Fortune first did run;
But Thou wilt never more appeare
Folded within my Hemispheare:
Since both thy Light and Motion
Like a fledd Starr is fall'n and gone,
And 'twixt mee and my Soule's deare wish
The Earth now interposed is,
Which such a straunge Ecclipse doth make
As ne're was read in Almanake.

    I could allow Thee for a time
To darken mee and my sad Clime,
Were it a Month, a Yeere, or Ten,
I would thy Exile live till then;
And all that space my mirth adjourne
So Thou wouldst promise to returne,
And putting off thy ashy Shrowd
At length disperse this Sorrowes Cloud.

    But woe is mee! the longest date
To narrowe is to calculate
These empty hopes. Never shall I
Be so much blest as to descry
A glympse of Thee, till that Day come
Which shall the Earth to cinders doome,
And a fierce Feaver must calcine
The Body of this World like Thine,
(My Little World!) That fitt of Fire
Once off, our Bodyes shall aspire
To our Soules blisse: Then wee shall rise,
And view our selves with cleerer eyes
In that calme Region, where no Night
Can hide us from each others sight.

Meane time, thou hast Hir Earth: Much good
May my harme doe thee. Since it stood
With Heaven's will I might not call
Hir longer Mine; I give thee all
My short liv'd right and Interest
In Hir, whome living I lov'd best.
With a most free and bounteous grief,
I give thee what I could not keep.
Be kind to Hir: and prethee look
Thou write into thy Doomsday book
Each parcell of this Rarity
Which in thy Caskett shrin'd doth ly:
See that thou make thy reck'ning streight,
And yeeld Hir back againe by weight.
For thou must Auditt on thy trust
Each Grane and Atome of this Dust,
As thou wilt answere Him that leant,
Not gave thee, my deare Monument.

    So close the ground, and 'bout hir shade
Black Curtaines draw, My Bride is lay'd.

    Sleep on my Love in thy cold bed
Never to be disquieted.
My last Good-night! Thou wilt not wake
Till I Thy Fate shall overtake:
Till age, or grief, or sicknes must
Marry my Body to that Dust
It so much loves; and fill the roome
My heart keepes empty in Thy Tomb.
Stay for mee there: I will not faile
To meet Thee in that hollow Vale.
And think not much of my delay,
I am already on the way,
And follow Thee with all the speed
Desire can make, or Sorrowes breed.
Each Minute is a short Degree,
And e'ry Howre a stepp towards Thee.
At Night when I betake to rest,
Next Morne I rise neerer my West
Of Life, almost by eight Howres sayle,
Then when Sleep breath'd his drowsy gale.

    Thus from the Sunne my Bottome steares,
And my Dayes Compasse downward beares.
Nor labour I to stemme the Tide
Through which to Thee I swiftly glide.

Tis true, with shame and grief I yeild,
Thou like the Vann, first took'st the Field,
And gotten hast the Victory
In thus adventuring to Dy
Before Mee; whose more yeeres might crave
A just præcedence in the Grave.
But hark! My Pulse, like a soft Drum
Beates my Approach; Tells Thee I come;
And slowe howe're my Marches bee,
I shall at last sitt downe by Thee.

  The thought of this bids mee goe on,
And wait my dissolution
With Hope and Comfort. Deare (forgive
The Crime) I am content to live
Divided, with but half a Heart,
Till wee shall Meet, and Never part.

(1657)

THOMAS CAREW Song. Celia *singing*

Harke how my *Celia*, with the choyce
Musique of her hand and voyce
Stills the loude wind; and makes the wilde
Incensed Bore, and Panther milde!
Marke how those statues like men move,
Whilst men with wonder statues prove!
This stiffe rock bends to worship her,
That Idoll turnes Idolater.

  Now see how all the new inspir'd
Images, with love are fir'd!
Harke how the tender Marble grones,
And all the late transformed stones,
Court the faire Nymph with many a teare,
Which she (more stony then they were)
Beholds with unrelenting mind;
Whilst they amaz'd to see combin'd
Such matchlesse beautie, with disdaine,
Are all turn'd into stones againe.

THOMAS CAREW Epitaph on the Lady *Mary Villers*

The Lady *Mary Villers* lyes
Under this stone; with weeping eyes
The Parents that first gave her birth,
And their sad Friends, lay'd her in earth:
If any of them (Reader) were
Knowne unto thee, shed a teare,
Or if thyselfe possesse a gemme,
As deare to thee, as this to them;
Though a stranger to this place,
Bewayle in theirs, thine owne hard case;
For thou perhaps at thy returne
Mayest find thy Darling in an Urne.

THOMAS CAREW Maria Wentworth, Thomæ Comitis Cleveland, filia præmortua prima Virgineam animam exhalavit An. Dom. 1632 Æt. suæ 18.

And here the precious dust is layd;
Whose purely-tempered Clay was made
So fine, that it the guest betray'd.

Else the soule grew so fast within,
It broke the outward shell of sinne,
And so was hatch'd a Cherubin.

In heigth, it soar'd to God above;
In depth, it did to knowledge move,
And spread in breadth to generall love.

Before, a pious duty shind
To Parents, courtesie behind,
On either side an equall mind,

Good to the Poore, to kindred deare,
To servants kind, to friendship cleare,
To nothing but her selfe, severe.

So though a Virgin, yet a Bride
To every Grace, she justifi'd
A chaste Poligamie, and dy'd.

Learne from hence (Reader) what small trust
We owe this world, where vertue must
Fraile as our flesh, crumble to dust.

THOMAS CAREW A Song

Aske me no more whither doe stray,
The golden Atomes of the day:
For in pure love heaven did prepare,
Those powders to inrich your haire.

Aske me no more whither doth hast,
The Nightingale when *May* is past:
For in your sweet dividing throat,
She winters and keepes warme her note.

Aske me no more where *Jove* bestowes,
When *June* is past the fading rose:
For in your beauties orient deepe,
These flowers as in their causes, sleepe.

Aske me no more where those starres light,
That downewards fall in dead of night:
For in your eyes they sit and there,
Fixed become as in their sphere.

Aske me no more if East or West,
The Phenix builds her spicy nest:
For unto you at last shee flies,
And in your fragrant bosome dyes.

THOMAS CAREW Psalme 91

Make the greate God thy Fort, and dwell
  In him by Faith, and doe not Care
(Soe shaded) for the power of hell
  Or for the Cunning Fowlers snare
  Or poyson of th'infected Ayre.

His plumes shall make a downy bedd
  Where thou shalt rest, hee shall display
His wings of truth over thy head,
  Which like a shield shall drive away
  The feares of night, the darts of day.

The winged plague that flyes by night,
  The murdering sword that kills by day,
Shall not thy peacefull sleepes affright
  Though on thy right and left hand they
  A thousand and ten thousand slay.

Yet shall thine Eyes behould the fall
  Of Sinners, but because thy heart
Dwells with the Lord, not one of all
  Those ills, nor yett the plaguie dart
  Shall dare approach neere where thou art.

His angells shall direct thy leggs
  And guard them in the Stony streete;
On Lyons whelps, and Addars Eggs
  Thy Stepps shall March, and if thou meete
  With Draggons, they shall kiss thy feete.

When thou art troubled, hee shall heare
  And help thee, for thy Love embrast
And knewe his name, Therefore hee'l reare
  Thy honours high, and when thou hast
  Enjoyd them long, Save thee att last.

(1870)

WILLIAM HABINGTON *Nox nocti indicat Scientiam*

When I survay the bright
    Cœlestiall spheare:
So rich with jewels hung, that night
Doth like an Æthiop bride appeare.

My soule her wings doth spread
    And heaven-ward flies,
Th' Almighty's Mysteries to read
In the large volumes of the skies.

For the bright firmament
    Shootes forth no flame
So silent, but is eloquent
In speaking the Creators name.

No unregarded star
    Contracts its light
Into so small a Charactar,
Remov'd far from our humane sight:

But if we stedfast looke,
    We shall discerne
In it as in some holy booke,
How man may heavenly knowledge learne.

It tells the Conqueror,
    That farre-stretcht powre
Which his proud dangers traffique for,
Is but the triumph of an houre.

That from the farthest North,
    Some Nation may
Yet undiscovered issue forth,
And ore his new got conquest sway.

Some Nation yet shut in
    With hils of ice
May be let out to scourge his sinne
'Till they shall equall him in vice.

And then they likewise shall
    Their ruine have,
For as your selves your Empires fall,
And every Kingdome hath a grave.

    Thus those Cœlestiall fires,
        Though seeming mute
The fallacie of our desires
And all the pride of life confute.

    For they have watcht since first
        The World had birth:
And found sinne in it selfe accurst,
And nothing permanent on earth.

WILLIAM HABINGTON To *Castara*, Upon an Embrace

    'Bout th' Husband Oke, the Vine
Thus wreathes to kisse his leavy face:
    Their streames thus Rivers joyne,
And lose themselves in the embrace.
    But Trees want sence when they infold,
    And Waters when they meet, are cold.

    Thus Turtles bill, and grone
Their loves into each others eare:
    Two flames thus burne in one,
When their curl'd heads to heaven they reare.
    But Birds want soule though not desire:
    And flames materiall soone expire.

    If not prophane; we'll say
When Angels close, their joyes are such.
    For we no love obey
That's bastard to a fleshly touch.
    Let's close *Castara* then, since thus
    We patterne Angels, and they us.

1641   ANONYMOUS   On Francis Drake

Sir *Drake* whom well the world's end knew,
    Which thou did'st compass round,
And whom both Poles of heaven once saw
    Which North and South do bound,
The stars above, would make thee known,
    If men here silent were;
The Sun himself cannot forget
    His fellow traveller.

SIR HENRY WOTTON *from the Latin of Martial* Upon the
Death of Sir *Albert Morton's* Wife

He first deceas'd: She for a little tri'd
To live without Him: lik'd it not, and di'd.

1642   SIR JOHN DENHAM   *from* Coopers Hill

Here should my wonder dwell, and here my praise,
But my fixt thoughts my wandring eye betrays,
Viewing a neighbouring hill, whose top of late
A Chappel crown'd, till in the Common Fate,
The adjoyning Abby fell: (may no such storm
Fall on our times, where ruine must reform.)
Tell me (my Muse) what monstrous dire offence,
What crime could any Christian King incense
To such a rage? was't Luxury, or Lust?
Was he so temperate, so chast, so just?
Were these their crimes? they were his own much more:
But wealth is Crime enough to him that's poor,
Who having spent the Treasures of his Crown,
Condemns their Luxury to feed his own.
And yet this Act, to varnish o're the shame
Of sacriledge, must bear devotions name.
No Crime so bold, but would be understood
A real, or at least a seeming good.

Who fears not to do ill, yet fears the Name,
And free from Conscience, is a slave to Fame.
Thus he the Church at once protects, and spoils:
But Princes swords are sharper than their stiles.
And thus to th'ages past he makes amends,
Their Charity destroys, their Faith defends.
Then did Religion in a lazy Cell,
In empty, airy contemplations dwell;
And like the block, unmoved lay: but ours,
As much too active, like the stork devours.
Is there no temperate Region can be known,
Betwixt their Frigid, and our Torrid Zone?
Could we not wake from that Lethargick dream,
But to be restless in a worse extream?
And for that Lethargy was there no cure,
But to be cast into a Calenture?
Can knowledge have no bound, but must advance
So far, to make us wish for ignorance?
And rather in the dark to grope our way,
Than led by a false guide to erre by day?
Who sees these dismal heaps, but would demand
What barbarous Invader sackt the land?
But when he hears, no Goth, no Turk did bring
This desolation, but a Christian King;
When nothing, but the Name of Zeal, appears
'Twixt our best actions and the worst of theirs,
What does he think our Sacriledge would spare,
When such th'effects of our devotions are?
Parting from thence 'twixt anger, shame, and fear,
Those for whats past, and this for whats too near:
My eye descending from the Hill, surveys
Where *Thames* amongst the wanton vallies strays.
Thames, the most lov'd of all the Oceans sons,
By his old Sire to his embraces runs,
Hasting to pay his tribute to the Sea,
Like mortal life to meet Eternity.
Though with those streams he no resemblance hold,
Whose foam is Amber, and their Gravel Gold;
His genuine, and less guilty wealth t'explore,
Search not his bottom, but survey his shore;
Ore which he kindly spreads his spacious wing,
And hatches plenty for th'ensuing Spring.
Nor then destroys it with too fond a stay,
Like Mothers which their Infants overlay.

278]

Nor with a sudden and impetuous wave,
Like profuse Kings, resumes the wealth he gave.
No unexpected inundations spoyl
The mowers hopes, nor mock the plowmans toyl:
But God-like his unwearied Bounty flows;
First loves to do, then loves the Good he does.
Nor are his Blessings to his banks confin'd,
But free, and common, as the Sea or Wind;
When he to boast, or to disperse his stores
Full of the tributes of his grateful shores,
Visits the world, and in his flying towers
Brings home to us, and makes both *Indies* ours;
Finds wealth where 'tis, bestows it where it wants
Cities in deserts, woods in Cities plants.
So that to us no thing, no place is strange,
While his fair bosom is the worlds exchange.
O could I flow like thee, and make thy stream
My great example, as it is my theme!
Though deep, yet clear, though gentle, yet not dull,
Strong without rage, without ore-flowing full.

(1642–68)

1645 EDMUND WALLER Song

Go lovely Rose,
Tell her that wastes her time and me,
    That now she knows
When I resemble her to thee
    How sweet and fair she seems to be.

Tell her that's young,
And shuns to have her graces spy'd
    That hadst thou sprung
In desarts where no men abide,
    Thou must have uncommended dy'd.

Small is the worth
Of beauty from the light retir'd;
    Bid her come forth,
Suffer her self to be desir'd,
    And not blush so to be admir'd.

Then die that she,
The common fate of all things rare
   May read in thee
How small a part of time they share,
   That are so wondrous sweet and fair.

EDMUND WALLER Of the Marriage of the Dwarfs

Design, or chance, makes others wive:
But Nature did this match contrive;
Eve might as well have Adam fled,
As she denied her little bed
To him, for whom Heaven seemed to frame,
And measure out, this only dame.
   Thrice happy is that humble pair,
Beneath the level of all care!
Over whose heads those arrows fly
Of sad distrust and jealousy;
Secured in as high extreme,
As if the world held none but them.
   To him the fairest nymphs do show
Like moving mountains, topped with snow;
And every man a Polypheme
Does to his Galatea seem;
None may presume her faith to prove;
He proffers death that proffers love.
   Ah, Chloris, that kind Nature thus
From all the world had severed us;
Creating for ourselves us two,
As love has me for only you!

EDMUND WALLER To a Lady in a Garden

Sees not my love how Time resumes
The glory which he lent these flowers;
Though none should tast of their perfumes,
    Yet must they live but some few hours,
    Time what we forbear devours.

Had *Hellen*, or the Egyptian Queen,
Been nere so thrifty of their graces,
Those beauties must at length have been
      The spoyle of Age which finds out faces
      In the most retired places.

Should some malignant Planet bring
A barren drought, or ceaseless shower
Upon the Autumn, or the Spring,
      And spare us neither fruit nor flower;
      Winter would not stay an hour.

Could the resolve of loves neglect
Preserve you from the violation
Of comming years, then more respect
      Were due to so divine a fashion,
      Nor would I indulge my passion.

JOHN MILTON *from* On the Morning of Christs Nativity
Compos'd 1629

It was the Winter wilde,
While the Heav'n-born-childe,
  All meanly wrapt in the rude manger lies;
Nature in aw to him
Had doff't her gawdy trim,
  With her great Master so to sympathize:
It was no season then for her
To wanton with the Sun her lusty Paramour.

Onely with speeches fair
She woo's the gentle Air
  To hide her guilty front with innocent Snow,
And on her naked shame,
Pollute with sinfull blame,
  The Saintly Vail of Maiden white to throw,
Confounded, that her Makers eyes
Should look so neer upon her foul deformities.

But he her fears to cease,
Sent down the meek-eyd Peace,
   She crown'd with Olive green, came softly sliding
Down through the turning sphear
His ready Harbinger,
   With Turtle wing the amorous clouds dividing,
And waving wide her mirtle wand,
She strikes a universall Peace through Sea and Land.

No War, or Battails sound
Was heard the World around:
   The idle spear and shield were high up hung;
The hooked Chariot stood
Unstain'd with hostile blood,
   The Trumpet spake not to the armed throng,
And Kings sate still with awfull eye,
As if they surely knew their sovran Lord was by.

But peacefull was the night
Wherin the Prince of light
   His raign of peace upon the earth began:
The Windes with wonder whist,
Smoothly the waters kist,
   Whispering new joyes to the milde Ocean,
Who now hath quite forgot to rave,
While Birds of Calm sit brooding on the charmed wave.

The Stars with deep amaze
Stand fixt in stedfast gaze,
   Bending one way their pretious influence,
And will not take their flight,
For all the morning light,
   Or *Lucifer* that often warn'd them thence;
But in their glimmering Orbs did glow,
Untill their Lord himself bespake, and bid them go.

And though the shady gloom
Had given day her room,
   The Sun himself with-held his wonted speed,
And hid his head for shame,
As his inferiour flame,
   The new-enlightn'd world no more should need;
He saw a greater Sun appear
Then his bright Throne, or burning Axletree could bear.

The Shepherds on the Lawn,
Or ere the point of dawn,
   Sate simply chatting in a rustick row;
Full little thought they than,
That the mighty *Pan*
   Was kindly com to live with them below;
Perhaps their loves, or els their sheep,
Was all that did their silly thoughts so busie keep.

When such musick sweet
Their hearts and ears did greet,
   As never was by mortall finger strook,
Divinely-warbled voice
Answering the stringed noise,
   As all their souls in blisfull rapture took:
The Air such pleasure loth to lose,
With thousand echo's still prolongs each heav'nly close.

Nature that heard such sound
Beneath the hollow round
   Of *Cynthia's* seat, the Airy region thrilling,
Now was almost won
To think her part was don,
   And that her raign had here its last fulfilling;
She knew such harmony alone
Could hold all Heav'n and Earth in happier union.

At last surrounds their sight
A Globe of circular light,
   That with long beams the shame-fac't night array'd,
The helmed Cherubim
And sworded Seraphim,
   Are seen in glittering ranks with wings displaid,
Harping in loud and solemn quire,
With unexpressive notes to Heav'ns new-born Heir.

Such Musick (as 'tis said)
Before was never made,
   But when of old the sons of morning sung,
While the Creator Great
His constellations set,
   And the well-ballanc't world on hinges hung,
And cast the dark foundations deep,
And bid the weltring waves their oozy channel keep.

The Oracles are dumm,
No voice or hideous humm
   Runs through the arched roof in words deceiving.
Apollo from his shrine
Can no more divine,
   With hollow shreik the steep of *Delphos* leaving.
No nightly trance, or breathed spell,
Inspire's the pale-ey'd Priest from the prophetic cell.

The lonely mountains o're,
And the resounding shore,
   A voice of weeping heard, and loud lament;
From haunted spring, and dale
Edg'd with poplar pale,
   The parting Genius is with sighing sent,
With flowre-inwov'n tresses torn
The Nimphs in twilight shade of tangled thickets mourn.

In consecrated Earth,
And on the holy Hearth,
   The *Lars*, and *Lemures* moan with midnight plaint,
In Urns, and Altars round,
A drear, and dying sound
   Affrights the *Flamins* at their service quaint;
And the chill Marble seems to sweat,
While each peculiar power forgoes his wonted seat.

Peor, and *Baalim*,
Forsake their Temples dim,
   With that twise batter'd god of *Palestine*,
And mooned *Ashtaroth*,
Heav'ns Queen and Mother both,
   Now sits not girt with Tapers holy shine,
The Libyc *Hammon* shrinks his horn,
In vain the *Tyrian* Maids their wounded *Thamuz* mourn.

And sullen *Moloch* fled,
Hath left in shadows dred,
   His burning Idol all of blackest hue;
In vain with Cymbals ring,

They call the grisly king,
　　In dismall dance about the furnace blue;
The brutish gods of *Nile* as fast,
Isis and *Orus*, and the Dog *Anubis* hast.

Nor is *Osiris* seen
In *Memphian* Grove, or Green,
　　Trampling the unshowr'd Grasse with lowings loud:
Nor can he be at rest
Within his sacred chest,
　　Naught but profoundest Hell can be his shroud,
In vain with Timbrel'd Anthems dark
The sable-stoled Sorcerers bear his worshipt Ark.

He feels from *Juda's* Land
The dredded Infants hand,
　　The rayes of *Bethlehem* blind his dusky eyn;
Nor all the gods beside,
Longer dare abide,
　　Not *Typhon* huge ending in snaky twine:
Our Babe to shew his Godhead true,
Can in his swadling bands controul the damned crew.

So when the Sun in bed,
Curtain'd with cloudy red,
　　Pillows his chin upon an Orient wave,
The flocking shadows pale,
Troop to th'infernall jail,
　　Each fetter'd Ghost slips to his severall grave,
And the yellow-skirted *Fayes*,
Fly after the Night-steeds, leaving their Moon-lov'd maze.

But see the Virgin blest,
Hath laid her Babe to rest.
　　Time is our tedious Song should here have ending:
Heav'ns youngest teemed Star,
Hath fixt her polisht Car,
　　Her sleeping Lord with Handmaid Lamp attending.
And all about the Courtly Stable,
Bright-harnest Angels sit in order serviceable.

RICHARD CRASHAW *from* Divine Epigrams   **1646**

Upon Our Saviours Tombe Wherein Never Man was Laid

How Life and Death in Thee
        Agree?
Thou had'st a virgin Wombe
        And Tombe.
A *Joseph* did betroth
        Them both.

Upon the Infant Martyrs

To see both blended in one flood
The Mothers Milke, the Childrens blood,
Makes me doubt if Heaven will gather,
Roses hence, or *Lillies* rather.

RICHARD CRASHAW Musicks Duell

Now Westward *Sol* had spent the richest Beames
Of Noons high Glory, when hard by the streams
Of *Tiber*, on the sceane of a greene plat,
Under protection of an Oake; there sate
A sweet Lutes-master: in whose gentle aires
Hee lost the Dayes heat, and his owne hot cares.
   Close in the covert of the leaves there stood
A Nightingale, come from the neighbouring wood:
(The sweet inhabitant of each glad Tree,
Their Muse, their *Syren*. harmlesse *Syren* shee)
There stood she listning, and did entertaine
The Musicks soft report: and mold the same
In her owne murmures, that what ever mood
His curious fingers lent, her voyce made good:
The man perceiv'd his Rivall, and her Art,
Dispos'd to give the light-foot Lady sport
Awakes his Lute, and 'gainst the fight to come
Informes it, in a sweet *Præludium*
Of closer straines, and ere the warre begin,
Hee lightly skirmishes on every string

Charg'd with a flying touch: and streightway shee
Carves out her dainty voyce as readily,
Into a thousand sweet distinguish'd Tones,
And reckons up in soft divisions,
Quicke volumes of wild Notes; to let him know
By that shrill taste, shee could doe something too.

His nimble hands instinct then taught each string
A capring cheerefullnesse; and made them sing
To their owne dance; now negligently rash
Hee throwes his Arme, and with a long drawne dash
Blends all together; then distinctly tripps
From this to that; then quicke returning skipps
And snatches this againe, and pauses there.
Shee measures every measure, every where
Meets art with art; sometimes as if in doubt
Not perfect yet, and fearing to bee out
Trayles her playne Ditty in one long-spun note,
Through the sleeke passage of her open throat:
A cleare unwrinckled song, then doth shee point it
With tender accents, and severely joynt it
By short diminutives, that being rear'd
In controverting warbles evenly shar'd,
With her sweet selfe shee wrangles; Hee amazed
That from so small a channell should be rais'd
The torrent of a voyce, whose melody
Could melt into such sweet variety
Straines higher yet; that tickled with rare art
The tatling strings (each breathing in his part)
Most kindly doe fall out; the grumbling Base
In surly groanes disdaines the Trebles Grace.
The high-perch't treble chirps at this, and chides,
Untill his finger (Moderatour) hides
And closes the sweet quarrell, rowsing all
Hoarce, shrill, at once; as when the Trumpets call
Hot Mars to th' Harvest of Deaths field, and woo
Mens hearts into their hands; this lesson too
Shee gives him backe; her supple Brest thrills out
Sharpe Aires, and staggers in a warbling doubt
Of dallying sweetnesse, hovers ore her skill,
And folds in wav'd notes with a trembling bill,
The plyant Series of her slippery song.
Then starts shee suddenly into a Throng
Of short thicke sobs, whose thundring volleyes float,
And roule themselves over her lubricke throat

In panting murmurs, still'd out of her Breast
That ever-bubling spring; the sugred Nest

Of her delicious soule, that there does lye
Bathing in streames of liquid Melodie;
Musicks best seed-plot, whence in ripend Aires
A Golden-headed Harvest fairely reares
His Honey-dropping tops, plow'd by her breath
Which there reciprocally laboureth
In that sweet soyle. It seemes a holy quire
Founded to th' Name of great *Apollo's* lyre.
Whose sylver-roofe rings with the sprightly notes
Of sweet-lipp'd Angell-Imps, that swill their throats
In creame of Morning *Helicon*, and then
Preferre soft Anthems to the Eares of men,
To woo them from their Beds, still murmuring
That men can sleepe while they their Mattens sing:
(Most divine service) whose so early lay,
Prevents the Eye-lidds of the blushing day.
There might you heare her kindle her soft voyce,
In the close murmur of a sparkling noyse.
And lay the ground-worke of her hopefull song,
Still keeping in the forward streame, so long
Till a sweet whirle-wind (striving to gett out)
Heaves her soft Bosome, wanders round about,
And makes a pretty Earthquake in her Breast,
Till the fledg'd Notes at length forsake their Nest;
Fluttering in wanton shoales, and to the Sky
Wing'd with their owne wild Eccho's pratling fly.
Shee opes the floodgate, and lets loose a Tide
Of streaming sweetnesse, which in state doth ride
On the wav'd backe of every swelling straine,
Rising and falling in a pompous traine.
And while shee thus discharges a shrill peale
Of flashing Aires; shee qualifies their zeale
With the coole Epode of a graver Noat,
Thus high, thus low, as if her silver throat
Would reach the brasen voyce of warr's hoarce Bird;
Her little soule is ravisht: and so pour'd
Into loose extasies, that shee is plac't
Above her selfe, Musicks *Enthusiast*.
  Shame now and anger mixt a double staine
In the Musitians face; yet once againe
(Mistresse) I come; now reach a straine my Lute
Above her mocke, or bee for ever mute.

Or tune a song of victory to mee,
Or to thy selfe, sing thine owne Obsequie;
So said, his hands sprightly as fire hee flings,
And with a quavering coynesse tasts the strings.
The sweet-lip't sisters musically frighted,
Singing their feares are fearfully delighted.
Trembling as when *Appollo's* golden haires
Are fan'd and frizled, in the wanton ayres
Of his owne breath: which marryed to his lyre
Doth tune the *Sphæares*, and make Heavens selfe looke higher.
From this to that, from that to this hee flyes
Feeles Musicks pulse in all her Arteryes,
Caught in a net which there *Appollo* spreads,
His fingers struggle with the vocall threads,
Following those little rills, hee sinkes into
A Sea of *Helicon*; his hand does goe
Those parts of sweetnesse which with *Nectar* drop,
Softer then that which pants in *Hebe's* cup.
The humourous strings expound his learned touch,
By various Glosses; now they seeme to grutch,
And murmur in a buzzing dinne, then gingle
In shrill tongu'd accents: striving to bee single.
Every smooth turne, every delicious stroake
Gives life to some new Grace; thus doth h'invoke
Sweetnesse by all her Names; thus, bravely thus
(Fraught with a fury so harmonious)
The Lutes light *Genius* now does proudly rise,
Heav'd on the surges of swolne Rapsodyes.
Whose flourish (Meteor-like) doth curle the aire
With flash of high-borne fancyes: here and there
Dancing in lofty measures, and anon
Creeps on the soft touch of a tender tone:
Whose trembling murmurs melting in wild aires
Runs to and fro, complaining his sweet cares
Because those pretious mysteryes that dwell,
In musick's ravish't soule hee dare not tell,
But whisper to the world: thus doe they vary
Each string his Note, as if they meant to carry
Their Masters blest soule (snatcht out at his Eares
By a strong Extasy) through all the sphæares
Of Musicks heaven; and seat it there on high
In th' *Empyræum* of pure Harmony.
At length (after so long, so loud a strife
Of all the strings, still breathing the best life

Of blest variety attending on
His fingers fairest revolution
In many a sweet rise, many as sweet a fall)
A full-mouth *Diapason* swallowes all.

　　This done, hee lists what shee would say to this,
And shee although her Breath's late exercise
Had dealt too roughly with her tender throate,
Yet summons all her sweet powers for a Noate
Alas! in vaine! for while (sweet soule) shee tryes
To measure all those wild diversities
Of chatt'ring stringes, by the small size of one
Poore simple voyce, rais'd in a Naturall Tone;
Shee failes, and failing grieves, and grieving dyes.
Shee dyes; and leaves her life the Victors prise,
Falling upon his Lute; ô fit to have
(That liv'd so sweetly) dead, so sweet a Grave!

SIR JOHN SUCKLING [Loves Siege]

Tis now since I sate down before
　　That foolish Fort, a heart,
(Time strangely spent) a Year, and more,
　　And still I did my part:

Made my approaches, from her hand
　　Unto her lip did rise,
And did already understand
　　The language of her eyes;

Proceeded on with no lesse Art,
　　My Tongue was Engineer:
I thought to undermine the heart
　　By whispering in the ear.

When this did nothing, I brought down
　　Great Canon-oaths, and shot
A thousand thousand to the Town,
　　And still it yeelded not.

I then resolv'd to starve the place
   By cutting off all kisses,
Praysing and gazing on her face,
   And all such little blisses.

To draw her out, and from her strength,
   I drew all batteries in:
And brought my self to lie at length
   As if no siege had been.

When I had done what man could do,
   And thought the place mine owne,
The Enemy lay quiet too,
   And smil'd at all was done.

I sent to know from whence, and where,
   These hopes, and this relief?
A Spie inform'd, Honour was there,
   And did command in chief.

March, march, (quoth I) the word straight give,
   Lets lose no time, but leave her:
That Giant upon ayre will live,
   And hold it out for ever.

To such a place our Camp remove
   As will no siege abide;
I hate a fool that starves her Love
   Onely to feed her pride.

JOHN HALL An Epicurean Ode

Since that this thing we call the world
By chance on Atomes is begot,
Which though in dayly motions hurld,
                    Yet weary not,
                    How doth it prove
Thou art so fair and I in Love?

Since that the soul doth onely lie
Immers'd in matter, chaind in sense,
How can *Romira* thou and I
                     With both dispence?
                     And thus ascend
In higher flights then wings can lend.

Since man's but pasted up of Earth,
And ne're was cradled in the skies,
What *Terra Lemnia* gave thee birth?
                     What Diamond eyes?
                     Or thou alone
To tell what others were, came down?

JAMES SHIRLEY Epitaph on the Duke of *Buckingham*

Here lies the best and worst of Fate,
Two Kings delight, the peoples hate,
The Courtiers star, the Kingdoms eye,
A man to draw an Angel by.
  Fears despiser, *Villiers* glory,
  The Great mans volume, all times story.

JAMES SHIRLEY

The glories of our blood and state,
  Are shadows, not substantial things,
There is no armour against fate,
  Death lays his icy hand on Kings,
      Scepter and Crown,
      Must tumble down,
And in the dust be equal made,
With the poor crooked sithe and spade.

Some men with swords may reap the field,
  And plant fresh laurels where they kill,
But their strong nerves at last must yield,
  They tame but one another still;

Early or late,
They stoop to fate,
And must give up their murmuring breath,
When they pale Captives creep to death.

The Garlands wither on your brow,
    Then boast no more your mighty deeds,
Upon Deaths purple Altar now,
    See where the Victor-victim bleeds,
        Your heads must come,
        To the cold Tomb,
Onely the actions of the just
Smell sweet, and blossom in their dust.

(1659)

1647   JOHN CLEVELAND Epitaph on the Earl of *Strafford*

Here lies Wise and Valiant Dust,
Huddled up 'twixt Fit and Just:
STRAFFORD, who was hurried hence
'Twixt Treason and Convenience.
He spent his Time here in a Mist;
A *Papist*, yet a *Calvinist*.
His Prince's nearest Joy, and Grief.
He had, yet wanted all Reliefe.
The Prop and Ruine of the State;
The People's violent Love, and Hate:
One in extreames lov'd and abhor'd.
Riddles lie here; or in a word,
Here lies Blood; and let it lie
Speechlesse still, and never crie.

1648   SIR RICHARD FANSHAWE *from the Spanish of Gongora*
A Great Favorit Beheaded

The bloudy trunck of him who did possesse
    Above the rest a haplesse happy state,
    This little Stone doth Seale, but not depresse,
    And scarce can stop the rowling of his fate.

Brasse Tombes which justice hath deny'd t' his fault,
    The common pity to his vertues payes,
    Adorning an Imaginary vault,
    Which from our minds time strives in vaine to raze.

Ten yeares the world upon him falsly smild,
    Sheathing in fawning lookes the deadly knife
    Long aymed at his head: That so beguild
    It more securely might bereave his Life;

Then threw him to a Scaffold from a Throne.
Much Doctrine lyes under this little Stone.

§ ROBERT HERRICK *from* Hesperides

The Argument of His Book

I sing of *Brooks*, of *Blossomes, Birds*, and *Bowers*:
Of *April, May*, of *June*, and *July*-Flowers.
I sing of *May-poles, Hock-carts, Wassails, Wakes*,
Of *Bride-grooms, Brides*, and of their *Bridall-cakes*.
I write of *Youth*, of *Love*, and have Accesse
By these, to sing of cleanly-*Wantonnesse*.
I sing of *Dewes*, of *Raines*, and piece by piece
Of *Balme*, of *Oyle*, of *Spice*, and *Amber-Greece*.
I sing of *Times trans-shifting*; and I write
How *Roses* first came *Red*, and *Lillies White*.
I write of *Groves*, of *Twilights*, and I sing
The Court of *Mab*, and of the *Fairie-King*.
I write of *Hell*; I sing (and ever shall)
Of *Heaven*, and hope to have it after all.

Upon *Julia's* Voice

So smooth, so sweet, so silv'ry is thy voice,
As, could they hear, the Damn'd would make no noise,
But listen to thee, (walking in thy chamber)
Melting melodious words, to Lutes of Amber.

Delight in Disorder

A sweet disorder in the dresse
Kindles in cloathes a wantonnesse:
A Lawne about the shoulders thrown
Into a fine distraction:
An erring Lace, which here and there
Enthralls the Crimson Stomacher:
A Cuffe neglectfull, and thereby
Ribbands to flow confusedly:
A winning wave (deserving Note)
In the tempestuous petticote:
A carelesse shooe-string, in whose tye
I see a wilde civility:
Doe more bewitch me, then when Art
Is too precise in every part.

To the Virgins, to Make Much of Time

Gather ye Rose-buds while ye may,
    Old Time is still a flying:
And this same flower that smiles to day,
    To morrow will be dying.

The glorious Lamp of Heaven, the Sun,
    The higher he's a getting;
The sooner will his Race be run,
    And neerer he's to Setting.

That Age is best, which is the first,
    When Youth and Blood are warmer;
But being spent, the worse, and worst
    Times, still succeed the former.

Then be not coy, but use your time;
    And while ye may, goe marry:
For having lost but once your prime,
    You may for ever tarry.

The Comming of Good Luck

So Good-luck came, and on my roofe did light,
Like noyse-lesse Snow; or as the dew of night:
Not all at once, but gently, as the trees
Are, by the Sun-beams, tickel'd by degrees.

To Meddowes

Ye have been fresh and green,
    Ye have been fill'd with flowers:
And ye the Walks have been
    Where Maids have spent their houres.

You have beheld, how they
    With *Wicker Arks* did come
To kisse, and beare away
    The richer Couslips home.

Y'ave heard them sweetly sing,
    And seen them in a Round:
Each Virgin, like a Spring,
    With Hony-succles crown'd.

But now, we see, none here,
    Whose silv'rie feet did tread,
And with dishevell'd Haire,
    Adorn'd this smoother Mead.

Like Unthrifts, having spent,
    Your stock, and needy grown,
Y'are left here to lament
    Your poore estates, alone.

The Departure of the Good *Dæmon*

What can I do in Poetry,
Now the good Spirit's gone from me?
Why nothing now, but lonely sit,
And over-read what I have writ.

Upon *Prew* His Maid

In this little Urne is laid
Prewdence Baldwin (once my maid)
From whose happy spark here let
Spring the purple Violet.

On Himselfe

Lost to the world; lost to my selfe; alone
Here now I rest under this Marble stone:
In depth of silence, heard, and seene of none.

§   §   §

ROBERT HERRICK The White Island: Or Place of the Blest

In this world (the *Isle of Dreames*)
While we sit by sorrowes streames,
Teares and terrors are our theames
   Reciting:

But when once from hence we flie,
More and more approaching nigh
Unto young Eternitie
   Uniting:

In that *whiter Island*, where
Things are evermore sincere;
Candor here, and lustre there
             Delighting:

There no monstrous fancies shall
Out of hell an horrour call,
To create (or cause at all)
             Affrighting.

There in calm and cooling sleep
We our eyes shall never steep;
But eternall watch shall keep,
             Attending

Pleasures, such as shall pursue
Me immortaliz'd, and you;
And fresh joyes, as never too
             Have ending.

§ RICHARD LOVELACE *from* Lucasta   **1649**

Song. To Lucasta, Going to the Warres

Tell me not (Sweet) I am unkinde,
   That from the Nunnerie
Of thy chaste breast, and quiet minde,
   To Warre and Armes I flie.

True; a new Mistresse now I chase,
   The first Foe in the Field;
And with a stronger Faith imbrace
   A Sword, a Horse, a Shield.

Yet this Inconstancy is such,
   As you too shall adore;
I could not love thee (Deare) so much,
   Lov'd I not Honour more.

To Althea *from Prison*

When Love with unconfined wings
   Hovers within my Gates;
And my divine *Althea* brings
   To whisper at the Grates:
When I lye tangled in her haire,
   And fetterd to her eye;
The *Gods* that wanton in the Aire,
   Know no such Liberty.

When flowing Cups run swiftly round
   With no allaying *Thames*,
Our carelesse heads with Roses bound,
   Our hearts with Loyall Flames;
When thirsty griefe in Wine we steepe,
   When Healths and draughts go free,
Fishes that tipple in the Deepe,
   Know no such Libertie.

When (like committed Linnets) I
   With shriller throat shall sing
The sweetnes, Mercy, Majesty,
   And glories of my KING;
When I shall voyce aloud, how Good
   He is, how Great should be;
Inlarged Winds that curle the Flood,
   Know no such Liberty.

Stone Walls doe not a Prison make,
   Nor Iron bars a Cage;
Mindes innocent and quiet take
   That for an Hermitage;
If I have freedome in my Love,
   And in my soule am free;
Angels alone that sore above,
   Injoy such Liberty.

The Grasse-hopper

To My Noble Friend, Mr. CHARLES COTTON. *Ode*

Oh thou that swing'st upon the waving haire
   Of some well-filled Oaten Beard,
Drunke ev'ry night with a Delicious teare
   Dropt thee from Heav'n, where now th' art reard.

The Joyes of Earth and Ayre are thine intire,
   That with thy feet and wings dost hop and flye;
And when thy Poppy workes thou dost retire
   To thy Carv'd Acron-bed to lye.

Up with the Day, the Sun thou welcomst then,
   Sportst in the guilt-plats of his Beames,
And all these merry dayes mak'st merry men,
   Thy selfe, and Melancholy streames.

But ah the Sickle! Golden Eares are Cropt;
   Ceres and *Bacchus* bid good night;
Sharpe frosty fingers all your Flowr's have topt,
   And what sithes spar'd, Winds shave off quite.

Poore verdant foole! and now green Ice, thy Joys
   Large and as lasting, as thy Peirch of Grasse,
Bid us lay in 'gainst Winter, Raine, and poize
   Their flouds, with an o'reflowing glasse.

Thou best of *Men* and *Friends*! we will create
   A Genuine Summer in each others breast;
And spite of this cold Time and frosen Fate
   Thaw us a warme seate to our rest.

Our sacred harthes shall burne eternally
   As Vestall Flames, the North-wind, he
Shall strike his frost-stretch'd Winges, dissolve and flye
   This *Ætna* in Epitome.

Dropping *December* shall come weeping in,
   Bewayle th'usurping of his Raigne;
But when in show'rs of old Greeke we beginne
   Shall crie, he hath his Crowne againe!

Night as cleare *Hesper* shall our Tapers whip
    From the light Casements where we play,
And the darke Hagge from her black mantle strip,
    And sticke there everlasting Day.

Thus richer then untempted Kings are we,
    That asking nothing, nothing need:
Though Lord of all what Seas imbrace; yet he
    That wants himselfe, is poore indeed.

§   §   §

WILLIAM DRUMMOND OF HAWTHORNDEN *from the French of Jean Passerat*

Song

AMINTAS, DAPHNÈ

D. Shephard loveth thow me vell?
A. So vel that I cannot tell.
D. Like to vhat, good shephard, say?
A. Like to the, faire, cruell May.
D. Ah! how strange thy vords I find!
    But yet satisfie my mind;
    Shephard vithout flatterie,
    Beares thow any love to me,
    Like to vhat, good shephard, say?
A. Like to the, faire, cruell May.
D. Better answer had it beene
    To say, I love thee as mine eine.
A. Voe is me, I love them not,
    For be them love entress got,
    At the time they did behold
    Thy sveet face and haire of gold.
D. Like to vhat, good shephard, say?
A. Like to thee, faire cruell May.
D. But, deare shephard, speake more plaine,
    And I sal not aske againe;

For to end this gentle stryff
Doth thow love me as thy lyff?

A. No, for it doth eb and flow
Vith contrare teeds of grief and voe;
And now I thruch loves strange force
A man am not, but a dead corse.

D. Like to vhat, good shephard, say?

A. Like to thee, faire, cruel May.

D. This like to thee, O leave, I pray,
And as my selfe, good shephard, say.

A. Alas! I do not love my selff,
For I me split on beuties shelff.

D. Like to vhat, good shephard, say?

A. Like to the, faire, cruel May.

(1711)

JAMES GRAHAM, MARQUIS OF MONTROSE On Himself, upon Hearing What was His Sentence

1650

Let them bestow on ev'ry Airth a Limb;
Open all my Veins, that I may swim
To Thee my Saviour, in that Crimson Lake;
Then place my pur-boil'd Head upon a Stake;
Scatter my Ashes, throw them in the Air:
Lord (since Thou know'st where all these Atoms are)
I'm hopeful, once Thou'lt recollect my Dust,
And confident Thou'lt raise me with the Just.

(1711)

ANONYMOUS *from* The Second Scottish Psalter

Psalm 124

Now Israel
    may say, and that truly,
If that the Lord
    had not our cause maintain'd;
If that the Lord
    had not our right sustain'd,

When cruel men
   against us furiously
Rose up in wrath,
   to make of us their prey;

Then certainly
   they had devour'd us all,
And swallow'd quick,
   for ought that we could deem;
Such was their rage,
   as we might well esteem.
And as fierce floods
   before them all things drown,
So had they brought
   our soul to death quite down.

The raging streams,
   with their proud swelling waves,
Had then our soul
   o'erwhelmed in the deep.
But bless'd be God,
   who doth us safely keep.
And hath not giv'n
   us for a living prey
Unto their teeth,
   and bloody cruelty.

Ev'n as a bird
   out of the fowler's snare
Escapes away,
   so is our soul set free:
Broke are their nets,
   and thus escaped we.
Therefore our help
   is in the Lord's great name,
Who heav'n and earth
   by his great pow'r did frame.

⑨ HENRY VAUGHAN *from* Silex Scintillans, Or Sacred Poems

The Retreate

Happy those early dayes! when I
Shin'd in my Angell-infancy.
Before I understood this place
Appointed for my second race,
Or taught my soul to fancy ought
But a white, Celestiall thought,
When yet I had not walkt above
A mile, or two, from my first love,
And looking back (at that short space,)
Could see a glimpse of his bright-face;
When on some *gilded Cloud*, or *flowre*
My gazing soul would dwell an houre,
And in those weaker glories spy
Some shadows of eternity;
Before I taught my tongue to wound
My Conscience with a sinfull sound,
Or had the black art to dispence
A sev'rall sinne to ev'ry sence,
But felt through all this fleshly dresse
Bright *shootes* of everlastingnesse.
   O how I long to travell back
And tread again that ancient track!
That I might once more reach that plaine,
Where first I left my glorious traine,
From whence th' Inlightned spirit sees
That shady City of Palme trees;
But (ah!) my soul with too much stay
Is drunk, and staggers in the way.
Some men a forward motion love,
But I by backward steps would move,
And when this dust falls to the urn
In that state I came return.

¶

Silence, and stealth of dayes! 'tis now
        Since thou art gone,
Twelve hundred houres, and not a brow
        But Clouds hang on.
As he that in some Caves thick damp
        Lockt from the light,
Fixeth a solitary lamp,
        To brave the night
And walking from his Sun, when past
        That glim'ring Ray
Cuts through the heavy mists in haste
        Back to his day,
So o'r fled minutes I retreat
        Unto that hour
Which shew'd thee last, but did defeat
        Thy light, and pow'r,
I search, and rack my soul to see
        Those beams again,
But nothing but the snuff to me
        Appeareth plain;
That dark, and dead sleeps in its known,
        And common urn,
But those fled to their Makers throne,
        There shine, and burn;
O could I track them! but souls must
        Track one the other,
And now the spirit, not the dust
        Must be thy brother.
Yet I have one *Pearle* by whose light
        All things I see,
And in the heart of Earth, and night
        Find Heaven, and thee.

The World

I saw Eternity the other night
Like a great *Ring* of pure and endless light,
     All calm, as it was bright,
And round beneath it, Time in hours, days, years
          Driv'n by the spheres
Like a vast shadow mov'd, In which the world
          And all her train were hurl'd;
The doting Lover in his queintest strain
          Did their Complain,
Neer him, his Lute, his fancy, and his flights,
          Wits sour delights,
With gloves, and knots the silly snares of pleasure
          Yet his dear Treasure
All scatter'd lay, while he his eys did pour
          Upon a flowr.

The darksome States-man hung with weights and woe
Like a thick midnight-fog mov'd there so slow
     He did nor stay, nor go;
Condemning thoughts (like sad Ecclipses) scowl
          Upon his soul,
And Clouds of crying witnesses without
          Pursued him with one shout.
Yet dig'd the Mole, and lest his ways be found
          Workt under ground,
Where he did Clutch his prey, but one did see
          That policie,
Churches and altars fed him, Perjuries
          Were gnats and flies,
It rain'd about him bloud and tears, but he
          Drank them as free.

The fearfull miser on a heap of rust
Sate pining all his life there, did scarce trust
     His own hands with the dust,
Yet would not place one peece above, but lives
          In feare of theeves.
Thousands there were as frantick as himself
          And hug'd each one his pelf,

The down-right Epicure plac'd heav'n in sense
    And scornd pretence
While others slipt into a wide Excesse
    Said little lesse;
The weaker sort slight, triviall wares Inslave
    Who think them brave,
And poor, despised truth sate Counting by
    Their victory.

Yet some, who all this while did weep and sing,
And sing, and weep, soar'd up into the *Ring*,
    But most would use no wing.
O fools (said I,) thus to prefer dark night
    Before true light,
To live in grots, and caves, and hate the day
    Because it shews the way,
The way which from this dead and dark abode
    Leads up to God,
A way where you might tread the Sun, and be
    More bright than he.
But as I did their madnes so discusse
    One whisper'd thus,
This Ring the Bride-groome did for none provide
    But for his bride.

§   §   §

1651   WILLIAM CARTWRIGHT No Platonique Love

Tell me no more of minds embracing minds,
    And hearts exchang'd for hearts;
That Spirits Spirits meet, as Winds do Winds,
    And mix their subt'lest parts;
That two unbodi'd Essences may kiss,
And then like Angels, twist and feel one Bliss.

I was that silly thing that once was wrought
        To practice this thin Love;
I climb'd from Sex to Soul, from Soul to Thought;
        But thinking there to move,
Headlong, I rowl'd from Thought to Soul, and then
From Soul I lighted at the Sex agen.

As some strict down-look'd men pretend to fast
        Who yet in Closets Eat;
So Lovers who profess they Spirits taste,
        Feed yet on grosser meat;
I know they boast they Soules to Soules Convey,
How e'r they meet, the Body is the Way.

Come, I will undeceive thee, they that tread
        Those vain Aeriall waies,
Are like young Heyrs, and Alchymists misled
        To waste their wealth and Daies,
For searching thus to be for ever Rich,
They only find a Med'cine for the Itch.

JOHN CLEVELAND The Antiplatonick

For shame, thou everlasting Woer,
Still saying Grace and ne're fall to her!
Love that's in Contemplation plac't,
Is *Venus* drawn but to the Wast.
Unlesse your Flame confesse its Gender,
And your Parley cause surrender,
Y'are Salamanders of a cold desire,
That live untouch't amid the hottest fire.

What though she be a Dame of stone,
The Widow of *Pigmalion*;
As hard and un-relenting She,
As the new-crusted *Niobe*;
Or what doth more of Statue carry
A Nunne of the Platonick Quarrey?
Love melts the rigor which the rocks have bred,
A Flint will break upon a Feather-bed.

For shame you pretty Female Elves,
Cease for to Candy up your selves;
No more, you Sectaries of the Game,
No more of your calcining flame.
Women Commence by *Cupids* Dart,
As a Kings Hunting dubs a Hart.
Loves Votaries inthrall each others soul,
Till both of them live but upon Paroll.

Vertue's no more in Woman-kind
But the green-sicknesse of the mind.
Philosophy, their new delight,
A kind of Charcoal Appetite.
There is no Sophistry prevails,
Where all-convincing Love assails,
But the disputing Petticoat will Warp,
As skilfull Gamesters are to seek at Sharp.

The souldier, that man of Iron,
Whom Ribs of *Horror* all inviron,
That's strung with Wire, in stead of Veins,
In whose imbraces you're in chains,
Let a Magnetick Girle appear,
Straight he turns *Cupids* Cuiraseer.
Love storms his lips, and takes the Fortresse in,
For all the Brisled Turn-pikes of his chin.

Since Loves Artillery then checks
The Breast-works of the firmest Sex,
Come let us in Affections Riot,
Th'are sickly pleasures keep a Diet.
Give me a Lover bold and free,
Not Eunuch't with Formality;
Like an Embassador that beds a Queen,
With the Nice Caution of a sword between.

JOHN CLEVELAND A Song of Marke Anthony

When as the Nightingall chanted her Vesper,
And the wild Forrester coutch'd on the ground,
Venus invited me in th' Evening whisper,
Unto a fragrant field with Roses crown'd:

Where she before had sent
My wishes complement,
Who to my soules content
Plaid with me on the Green.
　Never Marke Anthony
　Dallied more wantonly
With the faire Egyptian Queen.

First on her cherry cheekes I mine eyes feasted,
Thence feare of surfetting made me retire
Unto her warmer lips, which, when I tasted,
My spirits dull were made active as fire.
　This heate againe to calme
　Her moyst hand yeilded balme,
　While we join'd palme to palme
　As if they one had beene.
　　Never Marke, &c.

Then in her golden hayre I my armes twined,
Shee her hands in my locks twisted againe,
As if our hayre had been fetters assigned,
Great litle Cupids loose captives to chaine.
　Then we did often dart
　Each at the others heart,
　Arrowes that knew no smart;
　Sweet lookes and smiles between.
　　Never Marke, &c.

Wanting a glasse to pleat those amber trasses,
Which like a bracelet deckt richly mine arme;
Gawdier than *Juno* weares, when as she blesses
Jove with embraces more stately than warme,
　Then did she peepe in mine
　Eyes humour Chrystaline;
　And by reflexive shine
　I in her eye was seene.
　　Never Marke, &c.

Mysticall Grammer of amorous glances,
Feeling of pulses, the Phisicke of Love,
Rhetoricall courtings, and Musicall Dances;
Numbring of kisses Arithmeticke prove.

Eyes like Astronomy,
Streight limbs Geometry,
In her arts ingeny
Our wits were sharpe and keene.
    Never Marke, &c.

THOMAS STANLEY The Snow-ball

Doris, I that could repell
All those darts about thee dwell,
And had wisely learn'd to fear,
Cause I saw a Foe so near;
I that my deaf ear did arm,
'Gainst thy voices powerful charm,
And the lightning of thine eye
Durst (by closing mine) defie,
Cannot this cold snow withstand
From the whiter of thy hand;
Thy deceit hath thus done more
Then thy open force before:
For who could suspect or fear
Treason in a face so clear,
Or the hidden fires descry
Wrapt in this cold out-side lie?
Flames might thus involv'd in ice
The deceiv'd world sacrifice;
Nature, ignorant of this
Strange Antiperistasis,
Would her falling frame admire,
That by snow were set on fire.

THOMAS STANLEY The Grassehopper

Grasshopper thrice-happy! who
Sipping the cool morning dew,
Queen-like chirpest all the day
Seated on some verdant spray;

Thine is all what ere earth brings,
Or the howrs with laden wings;
Thee, the Ploughman calls his Joy,
'Cause thou nothing dost destroy:
Thou by all art honour'd; All
Thee the Springs sweet Prophet call;
By the Muses thou admir'd,
By *Apollo* art inspir'd,
Agelesse, ever singing, good,
Without passion, flesh or blood;
Oh how near thy happy state
Comes the Gods to imitate!

SIR HENRY WOTTON Upon the Sudden Restraint of the *Earle* of *Somerset*, Then Falling from Favor

Dazel'd thus, with height of place,
Whilst our hopes our wits beguile,
No man markes the narrow space
'Twixt a prison, and a smile.

Then, since fortunes favours fade,
You, that in her armes doe sleep,
Learne to swim, and not to wade;
For, the Hearts of Kings are deepe.

But, if Greatness be so blind,
As to trust in towers of Aire,
Let it be with Goodness lin'd,
That at'least, the Fall be faire.

Then though darkned, you shall say,
When Friends faile, and Princes frowne,
Vertue is the roughest way,
But proves at night a *Bed of Downe*.

1652   SIR RICHARD FANSHAWE *from the Latin of Horace*

Odes. IV, 7 To L. Manlius Torquatus

The Snows are thaw'd, now grass new cloaths the earth,
  And Trees new hair thrust forth.
The Season's chang'd, and Brooks late swoln with rain,
  Their proper bankes contain.
Nymphs with the Graces (linkt) dare dance around
  Naked upon the ground.
That thou must dye, the *year* and *howers* say
  Which draw the winged *day*.
First *Spring*, then *Summer* that away doth chace,
  And must it self give place
To Apple-bearing *Autumne*, and that past
  Dull *Winter* comes at last.
But the decays of Time, *Time* doth repair:
  When *we* once plunged are
Where good *Æneas*, where rich *Ancus* wades,
  Ashes we are, and shades.
Who knows if *Jove* unto thy life's past score
  Will add one morning more?
When thou art dead, and *Rhadamanthus* just
  Sentence hath spoke thee dust,
Thy Blood, nor eloquence can ransome thee,
  No nor thy Piety,
For chast *Hippolytus* in Stygian night
  Diana cannot light:
Nor *Theseus* break with all his vertuous pains
  His dear *Perithous* chains.

RICHARD CRASHAW *from* The Flaming Heart. Upon the Book and Picture of the Seraphicall Saint Teresa

O sweet incendiary! shew here thy art,
Upon this carcasse of a hard, cold, hart,
Let all thy scatter'd shafts of light, that play
Among the leaves of thy larg Books of day,
Combin'd against this Brest at once break in
And take away from me my self and sin,

This gratious Robbery shall thy bounty be;
And my best fortunes such fair spoiles of me.
O thou undanted daughter of desires!
By all thy dowr of LIGHTS & FIRES;
By all the eagle in thee, all the dove;
By all thy lives and deaths of love;
By thy larg draughts of intellectuall day,
And by thy thirsts of love more large then they;
By all thy brim-fill'd Bowles of feirce desire
By thy last Morning's draught of liquid fire;
By the full kingdome of that finall kisse
That seiz'd thy parting Soul, and seal'd thee his;
By all the heav'ns thou hast in him
(Fair sister of the SERAPHIM!)
By all of HIM we have in THEE;
Leave nothing of my SELF in me.
Let me so read thy life, that I
Unto all life of mine may dy.

AURELIAN TOWNSHEND A Dialogue betwixt Time and a Pilgrime   1653

PILGRIM
    Aged man, that mowes these fields.
TIME
    Pilgrime speak, what is thy will?
PILGR.
Whose soile is this that such sweet Pasture yields?
Or who art thou whose Foot stand never still?
      Or where am I? TIME In love.
PILGR.
      His Lordship lies above.
TIME
  Yes and below, and round about
  Where in all sorts of flow'rs are growing
  Which as the early Spring puts out,
      Time falls as fast a mowing.
PILGR.
  If thou art Time, these Flow'rs have Lives,
      And then I fear,
  Under some Lilly she I love
      May now be growing there.

TIME

>   And in some Thistle or some spyre of grasse
>   My syth thy stalk before hers come may passe.

PILGR.

Wilt thou provide it may? TIME. No. PILGR. Allege the cause.

TIME

Because Time cannot alter but obey Fates laws.

CHORUS

Then happy those whom Fate, that is the stronger,
Together twists their threads, and yet draws hers the longer.

MARGARET CAVENDISH, DUCHESS OF NEWCASTLE Of Many *Worlds* in This *World*

Just like unto a *Nest* of *Boxes* round,
Degrees of *sizes* within each *Boxe* are found.
So in this *World*, may many *Worlds* more be,
Thinner, and lesse, and lesse still by degree;
Although they are not subject to our *Sense*,
A *World* may be no bigger then *two-pence*.
Nature is curious, and such *worke* may make,
That our dull *Sense* can never finde, but scape.
For *Creatures*, small as *Atomes*, may be there,
If every *Atome* a *Creatures Figure* beare.
If foure *Atomes* a *World* can make, then see,
What severall *Worlds* might in an *Eare-ring* bee.
For *Millions* of these *Atomes* may bee in
The *Head* of one *small*, little, *single Pin*.
And if thus *small*, then *Ladies* well may weare
A *World* of *Worlds*, as *Pendents* in each *Eare*.

1655   ❦ HENRY VAUGHAN *from* Silex Scintillans II

¶

They are all gone into the world of light!
>   And I alone sit lingring here;
Their very memory is fair and bright,
>   And my sad thoughts doth clear.

It glows and glitters in my cloudy brest
    Like stars upon some gloomy grove,
Or those faint beams in which this hill is drest,
    After the Sun's remove.

I see them walking in an Air of glory,
    Whose light doth trample on my days:
My days, which are at best but dull and hoary,
    Meer glimering and decays.

O holy hope! and high humility,
    High as the Heavens above!
These are your walks, and you have shew'd them me
    To kindle my cold love,

Dear, beauteous death! the Jewel of the Just,
    Shining nowhere, but in the dark;
What mysteries do lie beyond thy dust;
    Could man outlook that mark!

He that hath found some fledg'd birds nest, may know
    At first sight, if the bird be flown;
But what fair Well, or Grove he sings in now,
    That is to him unknown.

And yet, as Angels in some brighter dreams
    Call to the soul, when man doth sleep:
So some strange thoughts transcend our wonted theams,
    And into glory peep.

If a star were confin'd into a Tomb
    Her captive flames must needs burn there;
But when the hand that lockt her up, gives room,
    She'l shine through all the sphære.

O Father of eternal life, and all
    Created glories under thee!
Resume thy spirit from this world of thrall
    Into true liberty.

Either disperse these mists, which blot and fill
    My perspective (still) as they pass,
Or else remove me hence unto that hill,
    Where I shall need no glass.

Cock-crowing

Father of lights! what Sunnie seed,
What glance of day hast thou confin'd
Into this bird? To all the breed
This busie Ray thou hast assign'd;
  Their magnetisme works all night,
  And dreams of Paradise and light.

Their eyes watch for the morning hue,
Their little grain expelling night
So shines and sings, as if it knew
The path unto the house of light.
  It seems their candle, howe'r done,
  Was tinn'd and lighted at the sunne.

If such a tincture, such a touch,
So firm a longing can impowre
Shall thy own image think it much
To watch for thy appearing hour?
  If a meer blast so fill the sail,
  Shall not the breath of God prevail?

O thou immortall light and heat!
Whose hand so shines through all this frame,
That by the beauty of the seat,
We plainly see, who made the same.
  Seeing thy seed abides in me,
  Dwell thou in it, and I in thee.

To sleep without thee, is to die;
Yea, 'tis a death partakes of hell:
For where thou dost not close the eye
It never opens, I can tell.
  In such a dark, Ægyptian border,
  The shades of death dwell and disorder.

If joyes, and hopes, and earnest throws,
And hearts, whose Pulse beats still for light
Are given to birds; who, but thee, knows
A love-sick souls exalted flight?
  Can souls be track'd by any eye
  But his, who gave them wings to flie?

Onely this Veyle which thou hast broke,
And must be broken yet in me,
This veyle, I say, is all the cloke
And cloud which shadows thee from me.
    This veyle thy full-ey'd love denies,
    And onely gleams and fractions spies.

O take it off! make no delay,
But brush me with thy light, that I
May shine unto a perfect day,
And warme me at thy glorious Eye!
    O take it off! or till it flee,
    Though with no Lilie, stay with me!

The Night

John 3.2

Through that pure *Virgin-shrine*,
That sacred vail drawn o'r thy glorious noon
That men might look and live as Glo-worms shine,
    And face the Moon:
  Wise *Nicodemus* saw such light
  As made him know his God by night.

Most blest believer he!
Who in that land of darkness and blinde eyes
Thy long expected healing wings could see,
    When thou didst rise,
  And what can never more be done,
  Did at mid-night speak with the Sun!

O who will tell me, where
He found thee at that dead and silent hour!
What hallow'd solitary ground did bear
    So rare a flower,
  Within whose sacred leafs did lie
  The fulness of the Deity.

No mercy-seat of gold,
No dead and dusty *Cherub*, nor carv'd stone,
But his own living works did my Lord hold
    And lodge alone;
  Where *trees* and *herbs* did watch and peep
  And wonder, while the *Jews* did sleep.

    Dear night! this worlds defeat;
The stop to busie fools; cares check and curb;
The day of Spirits; my souls calm retreat
    Which none disturb!
  Christs progress, and his prayer time;
  The hours to which high Heaven doth chime.

    Gods silent, searching flight:
When my Lords head is fill'd with dew, and all
His locks are wet with the clear drops of night;
    His still, soft call;
  His knocking time; The souls dumb watch,
  When Spirits their fair kinred catch.

    Were all my loud, evil days
Calm and unhaunted as is thy dark Tent,
Whose peace but by some *Angels* wing or voice
    Is seldom rent;
  Then I in Heaven all the long year
  Would keep, and never wander here.

    But living where the Sun
Doth all things wake, and where all mix and tyre
Themselves and others, I consent and run
    To ev'ry myre,
  And by this worlds ill-guiding light,
  Erre more then I can do by night.

    There is in God (some say)
A deep, but dazling darkness; As men here
Say it is late and dusky, because they
    See not all clear;
  O for that night! where I in him
  Might live invisible and dim.

§   §   §

II Drinking

The thirsty *Earth* soaks up the *Rain*,
And drinks, and gapes for drink again.
The *Plants* suck in the *Earth*, and are
With constant drinking fresh and fair.
The *Sea* it self, which one would think
Should have but little need of *Drink*,
Drinks ten thousand *Rivers* up,
So fill'd that they or'eflow the *Cup*.
The busie *Sun* (and one would guess
By's drunken fiery face no less)
Drinks up the *Sea*, and when h'as done,
The *Moon* and *Stars* drink up the *Sun*.
They drink and dance by their own light,
They drink and revel all the night.
Nothing in *Nature's Sober* found,
But an eternal *Health* goes round.
Fill up the *Bowl* then, fill it high,
Fill all the *Glasses* there, for why
Should every creature drink but *I*,
Why, *Man* of *Morals*, tell me why?

X The Grashopper

Happy *Insect*, what can be
In happiness compar'd to Thee?
Fed with nourishment divine,
The dewy *Mornings* gentle *Wine*!
Nature waits upon thee still,
And thy verdant Cup does fill,
'Tis fill'd where ever thou dost tread,
Nature selfe's *thy Ganimed*.
Thou dost drink, and dance, and sing;
Happier then the happiest *King*!
All the *Fields* which thou dost see,
All the *Plants* belong to *Thee*,
All that *Summer Hours* produce,
Fertile made with early juice.

Man for thee does sow and plow;
Farmer He, and *Land-Lord Thou*!
Thou doest innocently joy;
Nor does thy *Luxury* destroy;
The *Shepherd* gladly heareth thee,
More *Harmonious* then *He*.
Thee Country Hindes with gladness hear,
Prophet of the ripened year!
Thee *Phœbus* loves, and does inspire;
Phœbus is himself thy *Sire*.
To thee of all things upon earth,
Life is no longer then thy *Mirth*.
Happy *Insect*, happy Thou,
Dost neither *Age*, nor *Winter* know.
But when thou'st drunk, and danc'd, and sung,
Thy fill, the flowry Leaves among
(*Voluptuous*, and *Wise* with all,
Epicuræan Animal!)
Sated with thy *Summer Feast*,
Thou retir'est to endless *Rest*.

ABRAHAM COWLEY *from* Davideis

[Lot's Wife]

Behind his wife stood, ever fixed alone;
No more a woman, not yet quite a stone.
A lasting death seized on her turning head;
One cheek was rough and white, the other red,
And yet a cheek; in vain to speak she strove;
Her lips, though stone, a little seemed to move.
One eye was closed, surprised by sudden night;
The other trembled still with parting light.
The wind admired, which her hair loosely bore,
Why it grew stiff, and now would play no more.
To Heav'n she lifted up her freezing hands,
And to this day a supplicant pillar stands.
She tried her heavy foot from ground to rear,
And raised the heel, but her toe's rooted there.
Ah, foolish woman, who must always be
A sight more strange than that she turned to see!

WILLIAM STRODE Song

I saw faire Cloris walke alone
When featherd raine came softly downe
And Jove descended from his Towre
To court her in a Silver showre.
The wanton Snow flew on her breast
As little birdes unto their nest
But overcome in whiteness there
For greife it thawd into a Teare
Then falling on her garments hemme
To deck her freezd into a Gemme.

WILLIAM STRODE On Westwell Downes

When Westwell Downes I gan to treade
    Where cleanly windes the Greene doe sweepe,
Me thought a Landskipp there was spread
    Here a bush and there a sheepe
The pleated wrinkles on the face
Of wave-swoln Earth did lend such grace
As shaddowings in Imagrie
Which both deceave and please the Eye.

The sheepe sometimes doe treade a Mase
    By often winding in and in,
And sometimes rounde about they trace,
    Which Milke-maids call a Fairy ring
Such Semicircles they have run,
Such lines acrosse soe trimly spun
That sheapheardes learne whenere they please
A new Geometry with Ease.

The slender foode upon the Downe
    Is allway even, allway bare
Which nether spring nor winters frowne
    Can ought improve or ought impayre
Such is the barren Eunuchs chin
Which thus doth ever more begin
With tender downe to be orecast
Which never comes to hayre at last.

Here and there two hilly Crests
 Amidst them hugg a pleasant Greene
And these are like two swelling breasts
 That close a tender Vale betweene
Here could I reade or sleepe or play
From Early morne till flight of Day
But harke a Sheeps-bell calls me up
Like Oxford Colledg bells to supp.

       (1907)

JOHN TAYLOR and ANONYMOUS Non-sense

Oh that my Lungs could bleat like butter'd pease;
But bleating of my lungs hath caught the itch,
And are as mangy as the Irish Seas,
That doth ingender windmills on a Bitch.

I grant that Rainbowes being lull'd asleep,
Snort like a woodknife in a Ladies eyes;
Which maks her grieve to see a pudding creep
For creeping puddings onely please the wise.

Not that a hard-row'd Herring should presum
To swing a tyth pig in a Cateskin purse;
For fear the hailstons which did fall at Rome
By lesning of the fault should make it worse.

For 'tis most certain Winter wool-sacks grow
From geese to swans, if men could keep them so,
Till that the sheep shorn Planets gave the hint
To pickle pancakes in Geneva print.

Some men there were that did supose the skie
Was made of Carbonado'd Antidotes;
But my opinion is a Whales left eye,
Need not be coyned all in King *Harry* groates

The reason's plain for *Charons* westerne barge
Running a tilt at the subjunctive mood,
Beckned to Bednal Green, and gave him charge
To fatten padlockes with Antartick food:

The end will be the Millponds must be laded,
To fish for whitepots in a Country dance;
So they that suffered wrong and were upbraded
Shal be made friends in a left-handed trance.

SIR JOHN SUCKLING

Out upon it, I have lov'd
    Three whole days together;
And am like to love three more,
    If it hold fair weather.

Time shall moult away his wings
    Ere he shall discover
In the whole wide world agen
    Such a constant Lover.

But a pox upon't, no praise
    There is due at all to me:
Love with me had made no stay,
    Had it any been but she.

Had it any been but she
    And that very very Face,
There had been at least ere this
    A dozen dozen in her place.

GEORGE DANIEL Ode. The Robin   **1657**

    Poore bird, I doe not envie thee;
    Pleas'd, in the gentle Melodie
            Of thy owne Song.
    Let crabbed winter Silence all
    The winged Quire; he never shall
            Chaine up thy Tongue.
                Poore Innocent,
When I would please my selfe, I looke on thee;
And guess some sparkes, of that Felicitie,
            That Selfe Content.

When the bleake Face, of winter Spreads
The Earth, and violates the Meads
    Of all their Pride;
When Saples Trees, and Flowers are fled
Backe, to their Causes; and lye dead
    To all beside;
        I see thee Sett,
Bidding defiance, to the bitter Ayre;
Upon a wither'd Spray, by cold made bare,
        And drooping yet.

There, full in notes, to ravish all
My Earth, I wonder what to call
    My dullness; when
I heare thee, prettye Creature, bring
Thy better odes of Praise, and Sing
    To pussle men.
        Poore pious Elfe!
I am instructed, by thy harmonie,
To sing away, the Times uncertaintie,
        Safe in my Selfe.

Poore Redbrest, caroll out thy Laye
And teach us mortalls what to saye.
    Here cease, the Quire
Of ayerie Choristers; noe more
Mingle your notes; but catch a Store
    From her Sweet Lire;
        You are but weake,
Meere summer Chanters; you have neither wing
Nor voice, in winter. Prettie Redbrest, Sing
        What I would speake.

1659   RICHARD LOVELACE The Snayl

Wise Emblem of our Politick World,
Sage Snayl, within thine own self curl'd;
Instruct me softly to make hast,
Whilst these my feet go slowly fast.
    Compendious Snayl! thou seem'st to me,
Large *Euclids* strickt Epitome;

And in each Diagram, dost Fling

Thee from the point unto the Ring.
A Figure now Triangulare,
An Oval now, and now a Square;
And then a Serpentine dost crawl
Now a straight Line, now crook'd, now all.

    Preventing Rival of the Day,
Th'art up and openest thy Ray,
And ere the Morn cradles the Moon,
Th'art broke into a Beauteous Noon.
Then when the Sun sups in the Deep,
Thy Silver Horns e're *Cinthia's* peep;
And thou from thine own liquid Bed
New *Phœbus* heav'st thy pleasant Head.

    Who shall a Name for thee create,
Deep Riddle of Mysterious State?
Bold Nature that gives common Birth
To all products of Seas and Earth,
Of thee, as Earth-quakes, is affraid,
Nor will thy dire Deliv'ry aid.

    Thou thine own daughter then, and Sire,
That Son and Mother art intire,
That big still with thy self dost go,
And liv'st an aged Embrio;
That like the Cubbs of *India*,
Thou from thy self a while dost play:
But frighted with a Dog or Gun,
In thine own Belly thou dost run,
And as thy House was thine own womb,
So thine own womb, concludes thy tomb.

    But now I must (analys'd King)
Thy Oeconomick Virtues sing;
Thou great stay'd Husband still within,
Thou, thee, that's thine dost Discipline;
And when thou art to progress bent,
Thou mov't thy self and tenement,
As Warlike *Scythians* travayl'd, you
Remove your Men and City too;
Then after a sad Dearth and Rain,
Thou scatterest thy Silver Train;
And when the Trees grow nak'd and old,
Thou cloathest them with Cloth of Gold,
Which from thy Bowels thou dost spin,
And draw from the rich Mines within.

Now hast thou chang'd thee Saint; and made
Thy self a Fane that's cupula'd;
And in thy wreathed Cloister thou
Walkest thine own Gray fryer too;
Strickt, and lock'd up, th'art Hood all ore
And ne'r Eliminat'st thy Dore.
On Sallads thou dost feed severe,
And 'stead of Beads thou drop'st a tear,
And when to rest, each calls the Bell,
Thou sleep'st within thy Marble Cell;
Where in dark contemplation plac'd,
The sweets of Nature thou dost tast;
Who now with Time thy days resolve,
And in a Jelly thee dissolve.
Like a shot Star, which doth repair
Upward, and Rarifie the Air.

1662   SAMUEL BUTLER *from* **Hudibras**

[The Presbyterian Knight]

He could raise Scruples dark and nice,
And after solve 'em in a trice:
As if Divinity had catch'd
The Itch, of purpose to be scratch'd;
Or, like a Mountebank, did wound
And stab her self with doubts profound,
Only to shew with how small pain
The sores of faith are cur'd again;
Although by woful proof we find,
They always leave a Scar behind.
He knew the Seat of Paradise,
Could tell in what degree it lies:
And as he was dispos'd, could prove it,
Below the Moon, or else above it.
What *Adam* dreamt of when his Bride
Came from her Closet in his side:
Whether the Devil tempted her
By a *High Dutch* Interpreter:
If either of them had a Navel;
Who first made Musick malleable:

Whether the Serpent at the fall
Had cloven Feet, or none at all.
All this without a Gloss or Comment,
He would unriddle in a moment:
In proper terms, such as men smatter
When they throw out and miss the matter.

For his *Religion* it was fit
To match his Learning and his Wit:
'Twas *Presbyterian* true blew,
For he was of that stubborn Crew
Of Errant Saints, whom all men grant
To be the true Church *Militant*:
Such as do build their Faith upon
The holy Test of *Pike* and *Gun*;
Decide all Controversies by
Infallible *Artillery*;
And prove their Doctrine Orthodox
By Apostolick *Blows* and *Knocks*;
Call Fire and Sword and Desolation,
A *godly-thorough-Reformation*,
Which always must be carry'd on,
And still be doing, never done:
As if Religion were intended
For nothing else but to be mended.
A Sect, whose chief Devotion lies
In odd perverse Antipathies;
In falling out with that or this,
And finding somewhat still amiss:
More peevish, cross, and splenetick,
Than Dog distract, or Monky sick.
That with more care keep Holy-day
The wrong, than others the right way:
Compound for Sins, they are inclin'd to;
By damning those they have no mind to;
Still so perverse and opposite,
As if they worshipp'd God for spight,
The self-same thing they will abhor
One way, and long another for.
Free-will they one way disavow,
Another, nothing else allow.
All Piety consists therein
In them, in other Men all Sin.

Rather than fail, they will defie
That which they love most tenderly,
Quarrel with *minc'd Pies*, and disparage
Their best and dearest friend, *Plum-porridge*;
Fat *Pig* and *Goose* it self oppose,
And blaspheme *Custard* through the *Nose*.
Th' Apostles of this fierce Religion,
Like *Mahomet*'s, were Ass and Widgeon,
To whom our Knight, by fast instinct
Of Wit and Temper was so linkt,
As if Hipocrise and Non-sence
Had got th' Advouson of his Conscience.

1663   ABRAHAM COWLEY Ode. *Upon* Dr. *Harvey*

I

Coy Nature, (which remain'd, though aged grown,
A Beauteous virgin still, injoy'd by none,
        Nor seen unveil'd by any one)
When *Harveys* violent passion she did see,
Began to tremble, and to flee,
Took Sanctuary like *Daphne* in a tree:
There *Daphnes* lover stop't, and thought it much
        The very Leaves of her to touch,
But *Harvey* our *Apollo*, stopt not so,
Into the Bark, and root he after her did goe:
        No smallest Fibres of a Plant,
For which the eiebeams Point doth sharpness want,
        His passage after her withstood.
What should she do? through all the moving wood
Of Lives indow'd with sense she took her flight,
Harvey persues, and keeps her still in sight.
But as the Deer long-hunted takes a flood,
She leap't at last into the winding streams of blood;
Of mans *Meander* all the Purple reaches made,
        Till at the heart she stay'd,
        Where turning head, and at a Bay,
Thus, by well-purged ears, was she o're-heard to say:

Here sure shall I be safe (said she)
None will be able sure to see
    This my retreat, but only He
    Who made both it and me.
The heart of Man, what Art can e're reveal?
    A wall impervious between
    Divides the very Parts within,
And doth the Heart of man ev'n from its self conceal.
    She spoke, but e're she was aware,
    Harvey was with her there,
And held this slippery *Proteus* in a chain,
Till all her mighty Mysteries she descry'd,
Which from his wit the attempt before to hide
Was the first Thing that Nature did in vain.

3

He the young Practise of New life did see,
    Whil'st to conceal its toilsome Poverty,
It for a living wrought, both hard, and privately.
    Before the Liver understood
    The noble Scarlet Dye of Blood,
    Before one drop was by it made,
Or brought into it, to set up the Trade;
Before the untaught Heart began to beat
The tuneful March to vital Heat,
From all the Souls that living Buildings rear,
Whether imply'd for Earth, or Sea, or Air,
Whether it in the Womb or Egg be wrought,
A strict account to him is hourly brought,
    How the Great Fabrick does proceed,
What time and what materials it does need.
He so exactly does the work survey,
As if he hir'd the workers by the day.

4

Thus *Harvey* sought for Truth in Truth's own Book
    The Creatures, which by God himself was writ;
    And wisely thought 'twas fit,
Not to read Comments only upon it,
But on th'original it self to look.
Methinks in Arts great Circle others stand
    Lock't up together, Hand in Hand,

Every one leads as he is led,
The same bare path they tread,
A Dance like Fairies a Fantastick round,
But neither change their motion, nor their ground:
Had *Harvey* to this Road confin'd his wit,
His noble Circle of the Blood, had been untroden yet.
Great Doctor! Th' Art of Curing's cur'd by thee,
We now thy patient Physick see,
From all inveterate diseases free,
Purg'd of old errors by thy care,
New dieted, put forth to clearer air,
It now will strong and healthful prove,
It self before Lethargick lay, and could not move.

5
These useful secrets to his Pen we owe,
And thousands more 'twas ready to bestow;
Of which a barb'rous Wars unlearned Rage
Has robb'd the ruin'd age;
O cruel loss! as if the Golden Fleece,
With so much cost, and labour bought,
And from a far by a Great *Heroe* brought
Had sunk ev'n in the Ports of *Greece*.
O cursed Warr! who can forgive thee this?
Houses and Towns may rise again,
And ten times easier it is
To rebuild *Pauls*, than any work of his.
That mighty Task none but himself can do,
Nay, scarce himself too now,
For though his Wit the force of Age withstand,
His Body alas! and Time it must command,
And Nature now, so long by him surpass't,
Will sure have her revenge on him at last.

ABRAHAM COWLEY The Country Mouse. A Paraphrase upon
Horace Book II, Satire 6

At the large foot of a fair hollow tree,
Close to plow'd ground, seated commodiously,
His antient and Hereditary House,
There dwelt a good substantial Country-Mouse:

Frugal, and grave, and careful of the main,
Yet, one, who once did nobly entertain
A City Mouse well coated, sleek, and gay,
A Mouse of high degree, which lost his way,
Wantonly walking forth to take the Air,
And arriv'd early, and belighted there,
For a days lodging: the good hearty Hoast,
(The antient plenty of his hall to boast)
Did all the stores produce, that might excite,
With various tasts, the Courtiers appetite.
Fitches and Beans, Peason, and Oats, and Wheat,
And a large Chesnut, the delicious meat
Which Jove himself, were he a Mouse, would eat.
And for a Haut goust there was mixt with these
The swerd of Bacon, and the coat of Cheese.
The precious Reliques, which at Harvest, he
Had gather'd from the Reapers luxurie.
Freely (said he) fall on and never spare,
The bounteous Gods will for to morrow care.
And thus at ease on beds of straw they lay,
And to their Genius sacrific'd the day.
Yet the nice guest's Epicurean mind,
(Though breeding made him civil seem and kind)
Despis'd this Country feast, and still his thought
Upon the Cakes and Pies of London wrought.
Your bounty and civility (said he)
Which I'm surpriz'd in these rude parts to see,
Shews that the Gods have given you a mind,
Too noble for the fate which here you find.
Why should a Soul, so virtuous and so great,
Lose it self thus in an Obscure retreat?
Let savage Beasts lodg in a Country Den,
You should see Towns, and Manners know, and men:
And taste the generous Lux'ury of the Court,
Where all the Mice of quality resort;
Where thousand beauteous shees about you move,
And by high fare, are plyant made to love.
We all e're long must render up our breath,
No cave or hole can shelter us from death.

Since Life is so uncertain, and so short,
Let's spend it all in feasting and in sport.
Come, worthy Sir, come with me, and partake,
All the great things that mortals happy make.

Alas, what virtue hath sufficient Arms,
T' oppose bright Honour, and soft Pleasures charms?
What wisdom can their magick force repel?
It draws this reverend Hermit from his Cel.
It was the time, when witty Poets tell,
That Phoebus into Thetis bosom fell:
She blusht at first, and then put out the light,
And drew the modest Curtains of the night.
Plainly, the troth to tell, the Sun was set,
When to the Town our wearied Travellers get,
To a Lords house, as Lordly as can be
Made for the use of Pride and Luxury,
They come; the gentle Courtier at the door
Stops and will hardly enter in before.
But 'tis, Sir, your command, and being so,
I'm sworn t' obedience, and so in they go.
Behind a hanging in a spacious room,
(The richest work of Mortclakes noble Loom)
They wait awhile their wearied limbs to rest,
Till silence should invite them to their feast.
About the hour that Cynthia's Silver light,
Had touch'd the pale Meridies of the night;
At last the various Supper being done,
It happened that the Company was gone,
Into a room remote, Servants and all,
To please their nobles fancies with a Ball.
Our host leads forth his stranger, and do's find,
All fitted to the bounties of his mind.
Still on the Table half fill'd dishes stood,
And with delicious bits the floor was strow'd.
The courteous mouse presents him with the best,
And both with fat varieties are blest,
Th' industrious Peasant every where does range,
And thanks the gods for his Life's happy change.
Loe, in the midst of a well fraited Pye,
They both at last glutted and wanton lye.
When see the sad Reverse of prosperous fate,
And what fierce storms on mortal glories wait.
With hideous noise, down the rude servants come,
Six dogs before run barking into th' room;
The wretched gluttons fly with wild affright,
And hate the fulness which retards their flight.
Our trembling Peasant wishes now in vain,
That Rocks and Mountains cover'd him again.

Oh how the change of his poor life he curst!
This, of all lives (said he) is sure the worst.
Give me again, ye gods, my Cave and wood;
With peace, let tares and acorns be my food.

EDWARD, LORD HERBERT OF CHERBURY Sonnet   1665

Made upon the Groves near *Merlou* Castle

You well compacted Groves, whose light and shade
   Mixt equally, produce nor heat, nor cold,
   Either to burn the young, or freeze the old,
But to one even temper being made,
Upon a Greene embroidering through each Glade
   An Airy Silver, and a Sunny Gold,
   So cloath the poorest that they do behold
Themselves, in riches which can never fade,
   While the wind whistles, and the birds do sing,
While your twigs clip, and while the leaves do friss,
   While the fruit ripens which those trunks do bring,
   Sensless to all but love, do you not spring
Pleasure of such a kind, as truly is
A self-renewing vegetable bliss?

(written 1620)

JOHN MILTON *from* Paradise Lost   1667

from Book I [Invocation]

OF Mans First Disobedience, and the Fruit
Of that Forbidd'n Tree, whose mortal tast
Brought Death into the World, and all our woe,
With loss of *Eden*, till one greater Man
Restore us, and regain the blissful Seat,
Sing Heav'nly Muse, that on the secret top
Of *Oreb*, or of *Sinai*, didst inspire
That Shepherd, who first taught the chosen Seed,
In the Beginning how the Heav'ns and Earth
Rose out of *Chaos*: Or if *Sion* Hill
Delight thee more, and *Siloa's* Brook that flowd
Fast by the Oracle of God; I thence

Invoke thy aid to my adventrous Song,
That with no middle flight intends to soar
Above th' *Aonian* Mount; while it persues
Things unattempted yet in Prose or Rime.
And chiefly Thou O Spirit, that dost preferr
Before all Temples th' upright heart and pure,
Instruct me, for Thou know'st; Thou from the first
Wast present, and with mighty wings outspred
Dove-like satst brooding on the vast Abyss
And mad'st it pregnant: What in mee is dark
Illumin, what is low raise and support;
That to the highth of this great Argument
I may assert Eternal Providence,
And justifie the wayes of God to men.

from Book I ['Satan with his Angels now fallen into Hell']

Is this the Region, this the Soil, the Clime,
Said then the lost Arch-Angel, this the seat
That we must change for Heav'n, this mournful gloom
For that celestial light? Be it so, since hee
Who now is Sovran can dispose and bid
What shall be right: fardest from him is best
Whom reason hath equald, force hath made supream
Above his equals. Farewel happy Fields
Where Joy for ever dwells: Hail horrours, hail
Infernal World, and thou profoundest Hell
Receive thy new Possessor: One who brings
A mind not to be chang'd by Place or Time.
The mind is its own place, and in it self
Can make a Heav'n of Hell, a Hell of Heav'n.
What matter where, if I be still the same,
And what I should be, all but less then hee
Whom Thunder hath made greater? Here at least
We shall be free; th' Almighty hath not built
Here for his envy, will not drive us hence:
Here we may reign secure, and in my choice
To reign is worth ambition though in Hell:
Better to reign in Hell, then serve in Heav'n.
But wherefore let we then our faithful friends,
Th' associats and copartners of our loss
Lye thus astonisht on th' oblivious Pool,
And call them not to share with us their part
In this unhappy Mansion; or once more

With rallied Arms to try what may be yet
Regaind in Heav'n, or what more lost in Hell?
    So *Satan* spake, and him *Bëëlzebub*
Thus answerd. Leader of those Armies bright,
Which but th' Omnipotent none could have foild,
If once they hear that voice, thir liveliest pledge
Of hope in fears and dangers, heard so oft
In worst extreams, and on the perilous edge
Of battel when it rag'd, in all assaults
Thir surest signal, they will soon resume
New courage and revive, though now they lye
Groveling and prostrate on yon Lake of Fire,
As wee erewhile, astounded and amaz'd:
No wonder, fall'n such a pernicious highth.
    He scarce had ceas't when the superiour Fiend
Was moving toward the shore; his ponderous shield
Ethereal temper, massy, large and round,
Behind him cast; the broad circumference
Hung on his shoulders like the Moon, whose Orb
Through Optic Glass the *Tuscan* Artist views
At Ev'ning from the top of *Fesole*,
Or in *Valdarno*, to descry new Lands,
Rivers or Mountains in her spotty Globe.
His Spear, to equal which the tallest Pine
Hewn on *Norwegian* hills, to be the Mast
Of some great Ammiral, were but a wand,
He walkd with, to support uneasie steps
Over the burning Marle, not like those steps
On Heavens Azure; and the torrid Clime
Smote on him sore besides, vaulted with Fire;
Nathless he so endur'd, till on the Beach
Of that inflamed Sea, he stood and calld
His Legions, Angel Forms, who lay intranst
Thick as Autumnal Leaves that strow the Brooks
In *Vallombrosa*, where th' *Etrurian* shades
High overarcht imbowr; or scatterd sedge
Afloat, when with fierce Winds *Orion* armd
Hath vext the Red-Sea Coast, whose waves orethrew
Busiris and his *Memphian* Chivalrie,
While with perfidious hatred they persu'd
The Sojourners of *Goshen*, who beheld
From the safe shore thir floating Carcasses
And brok'n Chariot Wheels. So thick bestrown
Abject and lost lay these, covering the Flood,

Under amazement of thir hideous change.
He calld so loud, that all the hollow deeps
Of Hell resounded.

from **Book IX** ['The Serpent finds Eve alone']

For now, and since first break of dawne the Fiend,
Meer Serpent in appearance, forth was come,
And on his Quest, where likeliest he might finde
The onely two of Mankinde, but in them
The whole included Race, his purposd prey.
In Bowre and Field he sought, where any tuft
Of Grove or Garden-Plot more pleasant lay,
Thir tendance or Plantation for delight,
By Fountain or by shadie Rivulet
He sought them both, but wishd his hap might find
Eve separate, he wishd, but not with hope
Of what so seldom chanc'd, when to his wish,
Beyond his hope, *Eve* separate he spies,
Veild in a Cloud of Fragrance, where she stood,
Half spi'd, so thick the Roses bushing round
About her glowd, oft stooping to support
Each Flour of slender stalk, whose head though gay
Carnation, Purple, Azure, or spect with Gold,
Hung drooping unsustaind, them she upstaies
Gently with Mirtle band, mindless the while,
Her self, though fairest unsupported Flour,
From her best prop so farr, and storm so nigh.
Neerer he drew, and many a walk travers'd
Of stateliest Covert, Cedar, Pine, or Palme,
Then voluble and bold, now hid, now seen
Among thick-woven Arborets and Flours
Imborderd on each Bank, the hand of *Eve*:
Spot more delicious then those Gardens feignd
Or of reviv'd *Adonis*, or renownd
Alcinous, host of old *Laertes* Son,
Or that, not Mystic, where the Sapient King
Held dalliance with his faire *Egyptian* Spouse.
Much he the Place admir'd, the Person more.
As one who long in populous City pent,
Where Houses thick and Sewers annoy the Aire,
Forth issuing on a Summers Morn to breathe
Among the pleasant Villages and Farmes
Adjoind, from each thing met conceaves delight,

The smell of Grain, or tedded Grass, or Kine,
Or Dairie, each rural sight, each rural sound;
If chance with Nymphlike step fair Virgin pass,
What pleasing seemd, for her now pleases more,
Shee most, and in her look summs all Delight.
Such Pleasure took the Serpent to behold
This Flourie Plat, the sweet recess of *Eve*
Thus earlie, thus alone; her Heav'nly forme
Angelic, but more soft, and Feminine,
Her graceful Innocence, her every Aire
Of gesture or lest action overawd
His Malice, and with rapin sweet bereav'd
His fierceness of the fierce intent it brought:
That space the Evil one abstracted stood
From his own evil, and for the time remaind
Stupidly good, of enmitie disarmd,
Of guile, of hate, of envie, of revenge;
But the hot Hell that alwayes in him burnes,
Though in mid Heav'n, soon ended his delight,
And tortures him now more, the more he sees
Of pleasure not for him ordaind: then soon
Fierce hate he recollects, and all his thoughts
Of mischief, gratulating, thus excites.

    Thoughts, whither have ye led me, with what sweet
Compulsion thus transported to forget
What hither brought us, hate, not love, nor hope
Of Paradise for Hell, hope here to taste
Of pleasure, but all pleasure to destroy,
Save what is in destroying, other joy
To mee is lost.

from Book XI ['Michael sets before Adam in vision what shall happ'n till the Flood']

    To whom thus *Michael*. Those whom last thou sawst
In triumph and luxurious wealth, are they
First seen in acts of prowess eminent
And great exploits, but of true vertu void;
Who having spilt much blood, and don much waste
Subduing Nations, and achievd thereby
Fame in the World, high titles, and rich prey,
Shall change thir course to pleasure, ease, and sloth,
Surfet, and lust, till wantonness and pride
Raise out of friendship hostil deeds in Peace.

The conquerd also, and enslav'd by Warr
Shall with thir freedom lost all vertu loose
And feare of God, from whom thir pietie feignd
In sharp contest of Battel found no aide
Against invaders; therefore coold in zeale
Thenceforth shall practice how to live secure,
Worldlie or dissolute, on what thir Lords
Shall leave them to enjoy; for th' Earth shall bear
More then anough, that temperance may be tri'd:
So all shall turn degenerat, all deprav'd,
Justice and Temperance, Truth and Faith forgot;
One Man except, the onely Son of light
In a dark Age, against example good,
Against allurement, custom, and a World
Offended; fearless of reproach and scorn,
Or violence, hee of thir wicked wayes
Shall them admonish, and before them set
The paths of righteousness, how much more safe,
And full of peace, denouncing wrauth to come
On thir impenitence; and shall returne
Of them derided, but of God observd
The one just Man alive; by his command
Shall build a wondrous Ark, as thou beheldst,
To save himself and houshold from amidst
A World devote to universal rack.
No sooner hee with them of Man and Beast
Select for life shall in the Ark be lodg'd,
And shelterd round, but all the Cataracts
Of Heav'n set op'n on the Earth shall powre
Raine day and night, all fountains of the Deep
Broke up, shall heave the Ocean to usurp
Beyond all bounds, till inundation rise
Above the highest Hills: then shall this Mount
Of Paradise by might of Waves be moovd
Out of his place, pusht by the horned floud,
With all his verdure spoild, and Trees adrift
Down the great River to the op'ning Gulf,
And there take root an Iland salt and bare,
The haunt of Seales and Orcs, and Sea-mews clang.

but now lead on;
In mee is no delay; with thee to goe,
Is to stay here; without thee here to stay,
Is to go hence unwilling; thou to mee
Art all things under Heav'n, all places thou,
Who for my wilful crime art banisht hence.
This furder consolation yet secure
I carry hence: though all by mee is lost,
Such favour I unworthie am voutsaft,
By mee the Promisd Seed shall all restore.
    So spake our Mother *Eve*, and *Adam* heard
Well pleas'd, but answerd not; for now too nigh
Th' Arch-Angel stood, and from the other Hill
To thir fixt Station, all in bright array
The Cherubim descended; on the ground
Gliding meteorous, as Ev'ning Mist
Ris'n from a River ore the marish glides,
And gathers ground fast at the Labourers heel
Homeward returning. High in Front advanc't,
The brandisht Sword of God before them blaz'd
Fierce as a Comet; which with torrid heat,
And vapour as the *Libyan* Air adust,
Began to parch that temperat Clime; whereat
In either hand the hastning Angel caught
Our lingring Parents, and to th' Eastern Gate
Led them direct, and down the Cliff as fast
To the subjected Plaine; then disappeerd.
They looking back, all th' Eastern side beheld
Of Paradise, so late thir happie seat,
Wav'd over by that flaming Brand, the Gate
With dreadful Faces throngd and fierie Armes:
Som natural tears they dropd, but wip'd them soon;
The World was all before them, where to choose
Thir place of rest, and Providence thir guide:
They hand in hand with wandring steps and slow,
Through *Eden* took thir solitarie way.

KATHERINE PHILIPS An Answer to Another Perswading a
Lady to Marriage

Forbear bold Youth, all's Heaven here,
    And what you do aver,
To others Courtship may appear,
    'Tis Sacriledge to her.

She is a publick Deity,
    And were't not very odd
She should depose her self to be
    A petty Houshold God?

First make the Sun in private shine,
    And bid the World adieu,
That so he may his beams confine
    In complement to you.

But if of that you do despair,
    Think how you did amiss,
To strive to fix her beams which are
    More bright and large than this.

KATHERINE PHILIPS To My Excellent Lucasia, on Our
Friendship. 17th. July 1651

I did not live until this time
    Crown'd my felicity,
When I could say without a crime,
    I am not Thine, but Thee.
This Carkasse breath'd, and walk'd, and slept,
    So that the world believ'd
There was a soule the motions kept;
    But they were all deceiv'd.
For as a watch by art is wound
    To motion, such was mine:
But never had Orinda found
    A Soule till she found thine;

Which now inspires, cures and supply's,
    And guides my darken'd brest:
For thou art all that I can prize,
    My Joy, my Life, my rest.
Nor Bridegroomes nor crown'd conqu'rour's mirth
    To mine compar'd can be:
They have but pieces of this Earth,
    I've all the world in thee.
Then let our flame still light and shine,
    (And no false feare controule)
As inocent as our design,
    Immortall as our Soule.

KATHERINE PHILIPS To my Lord Biron's Tune of — Adieu Phillis

'Tis true, our life is but a long disease,
Made up of reall pain and seeming ease;
You stars, who these entangled fortunes give,
    O tell me why
    It is so hard to dy,
      Yet such a task to live?
If with some pleasure we our griefs betray,
It costs us dearer then it can repay:
For time or fortune all things so devours;
    Our hopes are cross'd,
    Or els the object lost,
      Ere we can call it ours.

SIR JOHN DENHAM *Sarpedon's* Speech to *Glaucus* in the 12th Book of *Homer* **1668**

      Thus to *Glaucus* spake
Divine *Sarpedon*, since he did not find
Others as great in Place, as great in Mind.
Above the rest, why is our Pomp, our Power?
Our flocks, our herds, and our possessions more?
Why all the Tributes Land and Sea affords
Heap'd in great Chargers, load our sumptuous boards?

Our chearful Guests carowse the sparkling tears
Of the rich Grape, whilst Musick charms their ears.
Why as we pass, do those on *Xanthus* shore,
As Gods behold us, and as Gods adore?
But that as well in danger, as degree,
We stand the first; that when our *Lycians* see
Our brave examples, they admiring say,
Behold our Gallant Leaders! These are They
Deserve the Greatness; and un-envied stand:
Since what they act, transcends what they command.
Could the declining of this Fate (oh friend)
Our Date to Immortality extend?
Or if Death sought not them, who seek not Death,
Would I advance? Or should my vainer breath
With such a Glorious Folly thee inspire?
But since with Fortune Nature doth conspire,
Since Age, Disease, or some less noble End,
Though not less certain, doth our days attend;
Since 'tis decreed, and to this period lead,
A thousand ways the noblest path we'll tread;
And bravely on, till they, or we, or all,
A common Sacrifice to Honour fall.

JOHN MILTON *from* Samson Agonistes

                    but chief of all,
O loss of sight, of thee I most complain!
Blind among enemies, O worse then chains,
Dungeon, or beggery, or decrepit age!
Light the prime work of God to mee is extinct,
And all her various objects of delight
Annulld, which might in part my grief have eas'd,
Inferiour to the vilest now become
Of man or worm; the vilest here excell me,
They creep, yet see, I dark in light expos'd
To daily fraud, contempt, abuse and wrong,
Within doors, or without, still as a fool,
In power of others, never in my own;
Scarce half I seem to live, dead more then half.
O dark, dark, dark, amid the blaze of noon,
Irrecoverably dark, total Eclipse
Without all hope of day!

O first created Beam, and thou great Word,
Let ther be light, and light was over all;
Why am I thus bereav'd thy prime decree?
The Sun to me is dark
And silent as the Moon,
When she deserts the night
Hid in her vacant interlunar cave.
Since light so necessary is to life,
And almost life itself, if it be true
That light is in the Soul,
She all in every part; why was the sight
To such a tender ball as th' eye confin'd?
So obvious and so easie to be quencht,
And not as feeling through all parts diffus'd,
That she might look at will through every pore?
Then had I not bin thus exil'd from light;
As in the land of darkness yet in light,
To live a life half dead, a living death,
And buried; but O yet more miserable!
My self, my Sepulcher, a moving Grave,
Buried, yet not exempt
By priviledge of death and burial
From worst of other evils, pains and wrongs,
But made hereby obnoxious more
To all the miseries of life,
Life in captivity
Among inhuman foes.

(. . .)

CHORUS
Which shall I first bewail,
Thy Bondage or lost Sight,
Prison within Prison
Inseparably dark?
Thou art become (O worst imprisonment!)
The Dungeon of thy self; thy Soul
(Which Men enjoying sight oft without cause complain)
Imprisond now indeed;
In real darkness of the body dwells,
Shut up from outward light
To incorporate with gloomy night;
For inward light alas
Puts forth no visual beam.

O mirror of our fickle state,
Since man on earth unparalleld!
The rarer thy example stands,
By how much from the top of wondrous glory,
Strongest of mortal men,
To lowest pitch of abject fortune thou art fall'n.
For him I reckon'd not in high estate
Whom long descent of birth
Or the sphear of fortune raises;
But thee whose strength, while vertue was her mate,
Might have subdu'd the Earth,
Universally crowned with highest praises.

(. . .)

CHORUS

All is best, though we oft doubt,
What th' unsearchable dispose
Of highest wisdom brings about,
And ever best found in the close.
Oft he seems to hide his face,
But unexpectedly returns
And to his faithful Champion hath in place
Bore witness gloriously; whence *Gaza* mourns
And all that band them to resist
His uncontroulable intent;
His servants hee with new acquist
Of true experience from this great event
With peace and consolation hath dismist,
And calm of mind all passion spent.

1671   THOMAS TRAHERNE *from* Centuries of Meditations

The Corn was Orient and Immortal Wheat, which never should
be reaped, nor was ever sown. I thought it had stood from
Everlasting to Everlasting. The Dust and Stones of the Street
were as Precious as GOLD. The Gates were at first the End of
the World, The Green Trees when I saw them first through one
of the Gates Transported and Ravished me; their Sweetnes and
unusual Beauty made my Heart to leap, and almost mad with
Extasie, they were such strange and Wonderfull Things: The
Men! O what Venerable and Reverend Creatures did the Aged

seem! Immortal Cherubims! And yong Men Glittering and **1671** [345
Sparkling Angels and Maids strange Seraphick Pieces of Life and
Beauty! Boys and Girles Tumbling in the Street, and Playing,
were moving Jewels. I knew not that they were Born or should
Die. But all things abided Eternaly as they were in their Proper
Places. Eternity was Manifest in the Light of the Day, and som
thing infinit Behind evry thing appeared: which talked with my
Expectation and moved my Desire. The Citie seemed to stand in
Eden, or to be Built in Heaven. The Streets were mine, the
Temple was mine, the People were mine, their Clothes and Gold
and Silver was mine, as much as their Sparkling Eys fair Skins
and ruddy faces. The Skies were mine, and so were the Sun and
Moon and Stars, and all the World was mine, and I the only
Spectator and Enjoyer of it. I knew no Churlish Proprieties, nor
Bounds nor Divisions: but all Proprieties and Divisions were
mine: all Treasures and the Possessors of them. So that with
much adoe I was corrupted; and made to learn the Dirty Devices
of this World. Which now I unlearn, and becom as it were a
little Child again, that I may enter into the Kingdom of GOD.

(1908)

THOMAS TRAHERNE Wonder

How like an Angel came I down!
　　How Bright are all Things here!
When first among his Works I did appear
　　O how their GLORY me did Crown?
The World resembled his *Eternities*,
　　In which my Soul did Walk;
　　And evry Thing that I did see,
　　　　Did with me talk.

The Skies in their Magnificence,
　　The Lively, Lovely Air;
Oh how Divine, how soft, how Sweet, how fair!
　　The Stars did entertain my Sence,
And all the Works of GOD so Bright and pure,
　　So Rich and Great did seem,
　　As if they ever must endure,
　　　　In my Esteem.

A Native Health and Innocence
Within my Bones did grow,
And while my GOD did all his Glories shew,
I felt a Vigour in my Sence
That was all SPIRIT. I within did flow
With Seas of Life, like Wine;
I nothing in the World did know,
But 'twas Divine.

Harsh ragged Objects were conceald,
Oppressions Tears and Cries,
Sins, Griefs, Complaints, Dissentions, Weeping Eys,
Were hid: and only Things reveald,
Which Heav'nly Spirits, and the Angels prize.
The State of Innocence
And Bliss, not Trades and Poverties,
Did fill my Sence.

The Streets were pavd with Golden Stones,
The Boys and Girles were mine,
Oh how did all their Lovly faces shine!
The Sons of Men were Holy Ones.
Joy, Beauty, Welfare did appear to me,
And evry Thing which here I found,
While like an Angel I did see,
Adornd the Ground.

Rich Diamond and Pearl and Gold
In evry Place was seen;
Rare Splendors, Yellow, Blew, Red, White and Green,
Mine Eys did evrywhere behold,
Great Wonders clothd with Glory did appear,
Amazement was my Bliss.
That and my Wealth was evry where:
No Joy to this!

Cursd and Devisd Proprieties,
With Envy, Avarice
And Fraud, those Feinds that Spoyl even Paradice,
Fled from the Splendor of mine Eys.
And so did Hedges, Ditches, Limits, Bounds,
I dreamd not ought of those,
But wanderd over all mens Grounds,
And found Repose.

Proprieties themselvs were mine,
    And Hedges Ornaments;
Walls, Boxes, Coffers, and their rich Contents
    Did not Divide my Joys, but shine.
Clothes, Ribbans, Jewels, Laces, I esteemd
    My Joys by others worn;
    For me they all to wear them seemd
        When I was born.

(1903)

THOMAS TRAHERNE Shadows in the Water

In unexperienc'd Infancy
Many a sweet Mistake doth ly:
Mistake tho false, intending tru;
A *Seeming* somwhat more than *View*;
    That doth instruct the Mind
    In Things that ly behind,
And many Secrets to us show
Which afterwards we com to know.

Thus did I by the Water's brink
Another World beneath me think;
And while the lofty spacious Skies
Reversed there abus'd mine Eys,
    I fancy'd other Feet
    Came mine to touch and meet;
As by som Puddle I did play
Another World within it lay.

Beneath the Water Peeple drown'd.
Yet with another Hev'n crown'd,
In spacious Regions seem'd to go
Freely moving to and fro:
    In bright and open Space
    I saw their very face;
Eys, Hands, and Feet they had like mine;
Another Sun did with them shine.

'Twas strange that Peeple there should walk,
And yet I could not hear them talk:
That throu a little watry Chink,
Which one dry Ox or Horse might drink,

We other Worlds should see,
　　Yet not admitted be;
And other Confines there behold
Of Light and Darkness, Heat and Cold.

I call'd them oft, but call'd in vain;
No Speeches we could entertain:
Yet did I there expect to find
Som other World, to pleas my Mind.
　　　I plainly saw by these
　　　A new *Antipodes*,
Whom, tho they were so plainly seen,
A Film kept off that stood between.

By walking Men's reversed Feet
I chanc'd another World to meet;
Tho it did not to View exceed
A Phantasm, 'tis a World indeed,
　　　Where Skies beneath us shine,
　　　And Earth by Art divine
Another face presents below,
Where Peeple's feet against Ours go.

Within the Regions of the Air,
Compass'd about with Hev'ns fair,
Great Tracts of Land there may be found
Enricht with Fields and fertil Ground;
　　　Where many num'rous Hosts,
　　　In those far distant Coasts,
For other great and glorious Ends,
Inhabit, my yet unknown Friends.

O ye that stand upon the Brink,
Whom I so near me, throu the Chink,
With Wonder see: What Faces there,
Whose Feet, whose Bodies, do ye wear?
　　　I my Companions see
　　　In You, another Me.
They seemed Others, but are We;
Our second Selvs those Shadows be.

Look how far off those lower Skies
Extend themselvs! scarce with mine Eys
I can them reach. O ye my Friends,
What *Secret* borders on those Ends?
    Are lofty Hevens hurl'd
    'Bout your inferior World?
Are ye the Representatives
Of other Peopl's distant Lives?

Of all the Play-mates which I knew
That here I do the Image view
In other Selvs; what can it mean?
But that below the purling Stream
    Som unknown Joys there be
    Laid up in Store for me;
To which I shall, when that thin Skin
Is broken, be admitted in.

                              (1910)

RALPH KNEVET The Vote

The Helmett now an hive for Bees becomes,
And hilts of swords may serve for Spiders' loomes;
    Sharp pikes may make
    Teeth for a rake;
And the keene blade, th'arch enemy of life,
Shall bee digraded to a pruneing knife.
    The rusticke spade
    Which first was made
For honest agriculture, shall retake
Its primitive imployment, and forsake
    The rampire's steep
    And trenches deep.
Tame conyes in our brazen gunnes shall breed,
Or gentle Doves their young ones there shall feede.
    In musket barrells
    Mice shall raise quarrells
For their quarters. The ventriloquious drumme
Like Lawyers in vacations shall be dumme.
    Now all recrutes,
    (But those of fruites),

Shall bee forgott; and th'unarm'd Soldier
Shall onely boast of what Hee did whilere,
    In chimneys' ends
    Among his freinds.

If good effects shall happy signes ensue,
I shall rejoyce, and my prediction's true.

(1936)

1672   SIR WILLIAM DAVENANT Song. Endimion Porter, and
Olivia

OLIVIA
    Before we shall again behold
In his diurnal race the Worlds great Eye,
    We may as silent be and cold,
As are the shades where buried Lovers ly.

ENDIMION
    Olivia, 'tis no fault of Love
To loose our selves in death, but O, I fear,
    When Life and Knowledge is above
Restor'd to us, I shall not know thee there.

OLIVIA
    Call it not Heaven (my Love) where we
Our selves shall see, and yet each other miss:
    So much of Heaven I find in thee
As, thou unknown, all else privation is.

ENDIMION
    Why should we doubt, before we go
To find the Knowledge which shall ever last,
    That we may there each other know?
Can future Knowledge quite destroy the past?

OLIVIA
    When at the Bowers in the Elizian shade
I first arrive, I shall examine where
    They dwel, who love the highest Vertue made;
For I am sure to find *Endimion* there.

From this vext World when we shall both retire,
Where all are Lovers, and where all rejoyce;
    I need not seek thee in the Heavenly Quire;
For I shall know *Olivia* by her Voice.

SIR WILLIAM DAVENANT The Philosopher and the Lover; to a Mistress Dying. Song

LOVER
Your Beauty, ripe, and calm, and fresh,
    As Eastern Summers are,
Must now, forsaking Time and Flesh,
    Add light to some small Star.

PHILOSOPHER
Whilst she yet lives, were Stars decay'd,
    Their light by hers, relief might find:
But Death will lead her to a shade
    Where Love is cold, and Beauty blinde.

LOVER
Lovers (whose Priests all Poets are)
    Think ev'ry Mistress, when she dies,
Is chang'd at least into a Starr:
    And who dares doubt the Poets wise?

PHILOSOPHER
But ask not Bodies doom'd to die,
    To what abode they go;
Since Knowledge is but sorrows Spy,
    It is not safe to know.

JOHN MILTON   1673

Methought I saw my late espoused Saint
    Brought to me like *Alcestis* from the grave,
    Whom *Joves* great Son to her glad Husband gave,
    Rescu'd from death by force though pale and faint.

Mine as whom washt from spot of child-bed taint,
    Purification in the old Law did save,
    And such, as yet once more I trust to have
    Full sight of her in Heaven without restraint,
Came vested all in white, pure as her mind:
    Her face was vail'd, yet to my fancied sight,
    Love, sweetness, goodness, in her person shin'd
So clear, as in no face with more delight.
    But O as to embrace me she enclin'd
    I wak'd, she fled, and day brought back my night.

(written 1658)

JOHN MILTON

When I consider how my light is spent,
    Ere half my days, in this dark world and wide,
    And that one Talent which is death to hide,
    Lodg'd with me useless, though my Soul more bent
To serve therewith my Maker, and present
    My true account, least he returning chide,
    Doth God exact day-labour, light deny'd,
    I fondly ask; But patience to prevent
That murmur, soon replies, God doth not need
    Either man's work or his own gifts, who best
    Bear his milde yoak, they serve him best, his State
Is Kingly. Thousands at his bidding speed
    And post o're Land and Ocean without rest:
    They also serve who only stand and waite.

(written after 1652)

JOHN MILTON On the Late Massacher in Piemont

Avenge O Lord thy slaughter'd Saints, whose bones
    Lie scatter'd on the Alpine mountains cold,
    Ev'n them who kept thy truth so pure of old
    When all our Fathers worship't Stocks and Stones,
Forget not: in thy book record their groanes
    Who were thy Sheep and in their antient Fold
    Slayn by the bloody *Piemontese* that roll'd
    Mother with Infant down the Rocks. Their moans

The Vales redoubl'd to the Hills, and they
   To Heav'n. Their martyr'd blood and ashes sow
   O're all th'*Italian* fields where still doth sway
The triple Tyrant: that from these may grow
   A hunderd-fold, who having learnt thy way
   Early may fly the *Babylonian* wo.

JOHN MILTON To Mr. *Cyriack Skinner* upon His Blindness

Cyriack, this three years day these eys, though clear
   To outward view, of blemish or of spot;
   Bereft of light thir seeing have forgot,
   Nor to thir idle orbs doth sight appear
Of Sun or Moon or Starre throughout the year,
   Or man or woman. Yet I argue not
   Against heavns hand or will, nor bate a jot
   Of heart or hope; but still bear up and steer
Right onward. What supports me, dost thou ask?
   The conscience, Friend, to have lost them overply'd
   In libertyes defence, my noble task,
Of which all *Europe* talks from side to side.
   This thought might lead me through the worlds vain mask
   Content though blind, had I no better guide.

                                        (written 1655; 1694)

JOHN MILTON The Fifth Ode of *Horace*. Lib. I

Quis multa gracilis te puer in Rosa, Rendred almost word for word
without Rhyme according to the Latin Measure, as near as the Language
will permit.

What slender Youth bedew'd with liquid odours
Courts thee on Roses in some pleasant Cave,
      Pyrrha for whom bind'st thou
      In wreaths thy golden Hair,
Plain in thy neatness; O how oft shall he
On Faith and changed Gods complain: and Seas
      Rough with black winds and storms
      Unwonted shall admire:

Who now enjoyes thee credulous, all Gold,
Who alwayes vacant, alwayes amiable
    Hopes thee; of flattering gales
    Unmindfull. Hapless they
To whom thou untry'd seem'st fair. Me in my vow'd
Picture the sacred wall declares t' have hung
    My dank and dropping weeds
    To the stern God of Sea.

JOHN DRYDEN *from* **Marriage A-la-Mode**

Song

Whil'st *Alexis* lay prest
In her Arms he lov'd best,
With his hands round her neck,
And his head on her breast,
He found the fierce pleasure too hasty to stay,
And his soul in the tempest just flying away.

When *Cælia* saw this,
With a sigh, and a kiss,
She cry'd, Oh my dear, I am robb'd of my bliss;
'Tis unkind to your Love, and unfaithfully done,
To leave me behind you, and die all alone.

The Youth, though in haste,
And breathing his last,
In pity dy'd slowly, while she dy'd more fast;
Till at length she cry'd, Now, my dear, now let us go,
Now die, my *Alexis*, and I will die too.

Thus intranc'd they did lie,
Till *Alexis* did try
To recover new breath, that again he might die:
Then often they di'd; but the more they did so,
The Nymph di'd more quick, and the Shepherd more slow.

JOHN WILMOT, EARL OF ROCHESTER Love and Life. **1677**
A Song

All my past life is mine noe more
  The flying Houres are gon
Like transitory Dreames giv'n ore
Whose Images are kept in Store
  By Memory alone.

What ever is to come is not
  How can it then be mine,
The present Moment's all my Lott
And that as fast as it is got
  Phillis is wholy thine.

Then talke not of Inconstancy,
  False Hearts, and broken Vows,
If I, by Miracle can be,
This live-long Minute true to thee,
  Tis all that Heav'n allows.

APHRA BEHN Song. Love Arm'd

Love in Fantastique Triumph satt,
Whilst Bleeding Hearts a round him flow'd,
For whom Fresh paines he did Create,
And strange Tyranick power he show'd;
From thy Bright Eyes he took his fire,
Which round about, in sport he hurl'd;
But 'twas from mine, he took desire,
Enough to undo the Amorous World.

From me he took his sighs and tears,
From thee his Pride and Crueltie;
From me his Languishments and Feares,
And every Killing Dart from thee;
Thus thou and I, the God have arm'd,
And sett him up a Deity;
But my poor Heart alone is harm'd,
Whilst thine the Victor is, and free.

APHRA BEHN

A thousand martyrs I have made,
    All sacrific'd to my desire;
A thousand beauties have betray'd,
    That languish in resistless fire.
The untam'd heart to hand I brought,
And fixed the wild and wandering thought.

I never vow'd nor sigh'd in vain
    But both, tho' false, were well receiv'd.
The fair are pleas'd to give us pain,
    And what they wish is soon believ'd.
And tho' I talk'd of wounds and smart,
Love's pleasures only touched my heart.

Alone the glory and the spoil
    I always laughing bore away;
The triumphs, without pain or toil,
    Without the hell, the heav'n of joy.
And while I thus at random rove
Despis'd the fools that whine for love.

1679   **JOHN WILMOT, EARL OF ROCHESTER** *from* **A Letter from Artemiza in the Towne to Chloe in the Countrey**

Chloe, in Verse by your commande I write;
Shortly you'l bid mee ride astride, and fight.
These Talents better with our sexe agree,
Then lofty flights of dang'rous poetry.
Amongst the Men (I meane) the Men of Witt
(At least they passt for such, before they writt)
How many bold Advent'rers for the Bayes,
(Proudly designing large returnes of prayse)
Who durst that stormy pathlesse World explore,
Were soone dash't backe, and wreck't on the dull shore,
Broke of that little stocke, they had before?
How would a Womans tott'ring Barke be tost,
Where stoutest Ships (the Men of Witt) are lost?

When I reflect on this, I straight grow wise,
And my owne selfe thus gravely I advise.
Deare Artemiza, poetry's a snare:
Bedlam has many Mansions: have a Care.
Your Muse diverts you, makes the Reader sad;
You Fancy, you'r inspir'd, he thinkes, you mad.
Consider too, 'twill be discreetly done,
To make your Selfe the Fiddle of the Towne,
To fynd th'ill-humour'd pleasure att their need,
Curst, if you fayle, and scorn'd, though you succeede.
Thus, like an Arrant Woman, as I am, ⎫
Noe sooner well convinc'd, writing's a shame, ⎬
That Whore is scarce a more reproachfull name, ⎭
Then Poetesse;
Like Men, that marry, or like Maydes, that woe,
'Cause 'tis the very worst thing they can doe,
Pleas'd with the Contradiction, and the Sin,
Mee-thinkes, I stand on Thornes, till I begin.

(...)

Where I was visiting the other night,
Comes a fine Lady with her humble Knight,
Who had prevayl'd on her, through her owne skill,
At his request, though much against his will,
To come to London.
As the Coach stop't, wee heard her Voyce more loud,
Then a great belly'd Womans in a Crowd,
Telling the Knight, that her afayres require,
Hee for some houres obsequiously retire.
I thinke, shee was asham'd, to have him seene ⎫
(Hard fate of Husbands) the Gallant had beene, ⎬
Though a diseas'd ill-favour'd Foole, brought in. ⎭
'Dispatch,' sayes shee, 'that bus'nesse you pretend,
Your beastly visitt to your drunken freind;
A Bottle ever makes you looke soe fine!
Mee-thinkes I long, to smell you stinke of Wine.
Your Countrey-drinking-breath's enough, to kill
Sowre Ale corrected with a Lemmon pill.
Prithy farewell – wee'le meete againe anon';
The necessary thing bows, and is gone.
She flyes up stayres, and all the hast does show,
That fifty Antique postures will allow,

And then bursts out – 'Deare Madam, am not I
The alter'dst Creature breathing? Let me dye,
I fynde my selfe ridiculously growne
Embarassé with being out of Towne,
Rude, and untaught, like any Indian Queene;
My Countrey nakednesse is strangely seene.
How is Love govern'd? Love, that rules the State,
And, pray, who are the Men most worne of late?
When I was marry'd, Fooles were a la mode,
The Men of Witt were then held incommode,
Slow of beleife, and fickle in desire,   ⎫
Who e're they'l be persuaded, must inquire,   ⎬
As if they came to spye, not to admire.   ⎭
With searching Wisedome fatall to their ease
They still fynde out, why, what may, should not please;
Nay take themselves for injur'd, when Wee dare,
Make 'em thinke better of us, then Wee are:
And if Wee hide our frailtyes from their sights,
Call Us deceitefull Gilts, and Hypocrites.
They little guesse, who att Our Arts are greiv'd,
The perfect Joy of being well deceaved.
Inquisitive, as jealous Cuckolds, grow,   ⎫
Rather, then not bee knowing, they will know, ⎬
What being knowne creates their certaine woe. ⎭
Women should these of all Mankind avoyd;
For Wonder by cleare knowledge is destroy'd.
Woman, who is an Arrant Bird of night,   ⎫
Bold in the Duske, before a Fooles dull sight, ⎬
Should flye, when Reason brings the glaring light: ⎭
But the kinde easy Foole apt, to admire   ⎫
Himselfe, trusts us, his Follyes all conspire, ⎬
To flatter his, and favour Our desire.   ⎭
Vaine of his proper Meritt he with ease
Beleaves, wee love him best, who best can please.
On him Our grosse dull common Flatt'ries passe,
Ever most Joyfull, when most made an Asse.
Heavy, to apprehend, though all Mankinde
Perceave Us false, the Fopp concern'd is blinde,
Who doating on himselfe,
Thinkes ev'ry one, that sees him, of his mynde.
These are true Womens Men' – Here forc'd, to cease
Through Want of Breath, not Will, to hold her peace,
Shee to the Window runns, where she had spy'de
Her much esteem'd deare Freind the Monkey ti'de.

With fourty smiles, as many Antique bows,
As if 't had beene the Lady of the House,
The dirty chatt'ring Monster she embrac't,
And made it this fine tender speech att last
'Kisse mee, thou curious Miniature of Man;
How odde thou art! How pritty! How Japan!
Oh I could live, and dye with thee' – then on
For halfe an houre in Complement shee runne.
I tooke this tyme, to thinke, what Nature meant, }
When this mixt thinge into the World shee sent, }
Soe very wise, yet soe impertinent. }
One, who knew ev'ry thinge, who, God thought fitt,
Should bee an Asse through choyce, not want of Witt:
Whose Foppery, without the helpe of Sense,
Could ne're have rose to such an Excellence.
Nature's as lame, in making a true Fopp,
As a Philosopher; the very topp,
And Dignity of Folly wee attaine
By studious Search, and labour of the Braine,
By observation, Councell, and deepe thought:
God never made a Coxecombe worth a groate.
Wee owe that name to Industry, and Arts:
An Eminent Foole must bee a Foole of parts;
And such a one was shee, who had turn'd o're
As many Bookes, as Men, lov'd much, reade more,
Had a discerning Witt; to her was knowne
Ev'ry ones fault, and meritt, but her owne.
All the good qualityes, that ever blest }
A Woman, soe distinguisht from the rest, }
Except discretion onely, she possest. }

(. . .)

But now 'tis tyme, I should some pitty show }
To Chloe, synce I cannot choose, but know, }
Readers must reape the dullnesse, writers sow. }
By the next Post such storyes I will tell,
As joyn'd with these shall to a Volume swell,
As true, as Heaven, more infamous, then Hell;
But you are tyr'd, and soe am I. Farewell.

JOHN WILMOT, EARL OF ROCHESTER *from* A Satyr against Reason and Mankind

Were I (who to my cost already am
One of those strange prodigious Creatures *Man*)
A Spirit free, to choose for my own share,
What Case of Flesh, and Blood, I pleas'd to weare,
I'd be a *Dog*, a *Monkey*, or a *Bear*,
Or any thing but that vain *Animal*,
Who is so proud of being rational.
The senses are too gross, and he'll contrive
A Sixth, to contradict the other Five;
And before certain instinct, will preferr
Reason, which Fifty times for one does err.
Reason, an *Ignis fatuus*, in the *Mind*,
Which leaving light of *Nature*, sense behind;
Pathless and dang'rous wandring ways it takes,
Through errors Fenny – *Boggs*, and Thorny *Brakes*;
Whilst the misguided follower, climbs with pain,
Mountains of Whimseys, heap'd in his own *Brain*:
Stumbling from thought to thought, falls headlong down,
Into doubts boundless Sea, where like to drown,
Books bear him up awhile, and make him try,
To swim with Bladders of *Philosophy*;
In hopes still t'oretake th'escaping light,
The *Vapour* dances in his dazling sight,
Till spent, it leaves him to eternal Night.
Then Old Age, and experience, hand in hand,
Lead him to death, and make him understand,
After a search so painful, and so long,
That all his Life he has been in the wrong;
Hudled in dirt, the reas'ning *Engine* lyes,
Who was so proud, so witty, and so wise.

(. . .)

You see how far *Mans* wisedom here extends,
Look next, if humane Nature makes amends;
Whose Principles, most gen'rous are, and just,
And to whose *Moralls*, you wou'd sooner trust.
Be judge your self, I'le bring it to the test,
Which is the basest *Creature Man*, or *Beast*?

Birds, feed on *Birds*, *Beasts*, on each other prey,
But Savage *Man* alone, does *Man*, betray:
Prest by necessity, they Kill for Food,
Man, undoes *Man*, to do himself no good.
With Teeth, and Claws, by Nature arm'd they hunt,
Natures allowance, to supply their want.
But *Man*, with smiles, embraces, Friendships, praise,
Unhumanely his Fellows life betrays;
With voluntary pains, works his distress,
Not through necessity, but wantonness.
For hunger, or for Love, they fight, or tear,
Whilst wretched *Man*, is still in Arms for fear;
For fear he armes, and is of Armes afraid,
By fear, to fear, successively betray'd.
Base fear, the source whence his best passion came,
His boasted Honor, and his dear bought Fame.
That lust of *Pow'r*, to which he's such a *Slave*,
And for the which alone he dares be brave:
To which his various Projects are design'd,
Which makes him gen'rous, affable, and kind.
For which he takes such pains to be thought wise,
And screws his actions, in a forc'd disguise:
Leading a tedious life in Misery,
Under laborious, mean *Hypocrisie*.
Look to the bottom, of his vast design,
Wherein *Mans* Wisdom, Pow'r, and Glory joyn;
The good he acts, the ill he does endure,
'Tis all for fear, to make himself secure.
Meerly for safety, after Fame we thirst,
For all Men, wou'd be *Cowards* if they durst.
And honesty's against all common sense,
Men must be *Knaves*, 'tis in their own defence.
Mankind's dishonest, if you think it fair,
Amongst known *Cheats*, to play upon the square,
You'le be undone –
Nor can weak truth, your reputation save,
The *Knaves*, will all agree to call you *Knave*.
Wrong'd shall he live, insulted o're, opprest,
Who dares be less a *Villain*, than the rest.
Thus Sir you see what humane Nature craves,
Most Men are *Cowards*, all Men shou'd be *Knaves*:

The diff'rence lyes (as far as I can see)
Not in the thing it self, but the degree;
And all the subject matter of debate,
Is only who's a *Knave*, of the first *Rate*?

1680   NATHANIEL WANLEY The Resurrection

Can death be faithfull or the grave be just
Or shall my tombe restore my scattred dust?
Shall ev'ry haire find out its' proper pore
And crumbled bones be joined as before
Shall long unpractis'd pulses learne to beate
Victorious rottennesse a loud retreate
Or eyes Ecclipsed with a tedious night
May they once hope to resalute the light?
What if this flesh of mine be made the prey
Of Scaly Pirates Caniballs at sea
Shall living Sepulchres give up theire dead
Or is not flesh made fish then perished?
What if the working of a subtile flame
By an unkind embrace dissolve this frame
To ashes; and the whist'ling winds convey
Each atome to a quite contrary way
Shall the small Pilgrims that (perhaps) may passe
From grasse to flesh and thence from flesh to grasse
Travell untill they meet and then embrace
So strictly as to grow the former face?
My God I know thy pow'refull word did frame
Out of pure nothing all that hath a name
From the bright Angells bathing in full streames
Of deathlesse joyes to motes that dance in beames.
And shall I doubt but such a word can call
Flesh out of dust that out of lesse made all?
No no I am resolv'd, that when poore I
Shall slumbring in our mothers bosome lye
The circl'ing wormes shall loose theire fast embrace
And kinder turfes that cover mee give place
The bands of Death shall burst at the shrill sound
Of Heavens summons and I shall be found
Then will I rise and dresse mee lord for thee
Who did'st by Death undresse thee lord for mee.

(1928)

JOHN WILMOT, EARL OF ROCHESTER The Disabled
Debauchee

As some brave *Admiral*, in former *War*,
Depriv'd of force, but prest with courage still,
Two *Rival-Fleets*, appearing from a far,
Crawles to the top of an adjacent *Hill*:

From whence (with thoughts full of concern) he views
The wise, and daring Conduct of the fight,
And each bold Action, to his *Mind* renews,
His present glory, and his past delight;

From his fierce *Eyes*, flashes of rage he throws,
As from black *Clouds*, when *Lightning* breaks away,
Transported, thinks himself amidst his *Foes*,
And absent, yet enjoys the Bloody Day;

So when my *Days* of impotence approach,
And I'm by *Pox*, and *Wines* unlucky chance,
Forc'd from the pleasing *Billows* of debauch,
On the dull *Shore* of lazy temperance,

My pains at least some respite shall afford,
Whilst I behold the *Battails* you maintain,
When *Fleets* of *Glasses*, sail about the *Board*,
From whose Broad-sides *Volleys* of *Wit* shall rain.

Nor let the sight of *Honourable Scars*,
Which my too forward *Valour* did procure,
Frighten new-listed *Souldiers* from the Warrs,
Past joys have more than paid what I endure.

Shou'd any *Youth* (worth being drunk) prove nice,
And from his fair Inviter meanly shrink,
'Twill please the *Ghost*, of my departed *Vice*,
If at my Councel, he repent and drink.

Or shou'd some cold complexion'd *Sot* forbid,
With his dull *Morals*, our *Nights* brisk *Alarmes*,
I'll fire his Blood by telling what I did,
When I was strong, and able to bear Armes.

I'll tell of *Whores* attacqu'd, their Lords at home,
Bawds Quarters beaten up, and *Fortress* won,
Windows demolisht, *Watches* overcome,
And handsome ills, by my contrivance done.

Nor shall our *Love-fits Cloris* be forgot,
When each the well-look'd *Link-Boy*, strove t'enjoy,
And the best Kiss, was the deciding *Lot*,
Whether the *Boy* fuck'd you, or I the *Boy*.

With Tales like these, I will such thoughts inspire,
As to important mischief shall incline.
I'll make him long some *Antient Church* to fire,
And fear no lewdness he's called to by *Wine*.

Thus *States-man*-like, I'll sawcily impose,
And safe from Action valiantly advise,
Shelter'd in impotence, urge you to blows,
And being good for nothing else, be wise.

1681   ANDREW MARVELL An *Horatian* Ode upon *Cromwel's*
Return from *Ireland*

The forward Youth that would appear
Must now forsake his *Muses* dear,
    Nor in the Shadows sing
    His Numbers languishing.
'Tis time to leave the Books in dust,
And oyl th' unused Armours rust:
    Removing from the Wall
    The Corslet of the Hall.
So restless *Cromwel* could not cease
In the inglorious Arts of Peace,
    But through adventrous War
    Urged his active Star.
And, like the three-fork'd Lightning, first
Breaking the Clouds where it was nurst,
    Did thorough his own Side
    His fiery way divide.
For 'tis all one to Courage high
The Emulous or Enemy;

And with such to inclose
Is more then to oppose.
Then burning through the Air he went,
And Pallaces and Temples rent:
    And *Cæsars* head at last
    Did through his Laurels blast.
'Tis Madness to resist or blame
The force of angry Heavens flame:
    And, if we would speak true,
    Much to the Man is due.
Who, from his private Gardens, where
He liv'd reserved and austere,
    As if his highest plot
    To plant the Bergamot,
Could by industrious Valour climbe
To ruine the great Work of Time,
    And cast the Kingdome old
    Into another Mold.
Though Justice against Fate complain,
And plead the antient Rights in vain:
    But those do hold or break
    As Men are strong or weak.
Nature that hateth emptiness,
Allows of penetration less:
    And therefore must make room
    Where greater Spirits come.
What Field of all the Civil Wars,
Where his were not the deepest Scars?
    And *Hampton* shows what part
    He had of wiser Art.
Where, twining subtile fears with hope,
He wove a Net of such a scope,
    That *Charles* himself might chase
    To *Caresbrooks* narrow case.
That thence the *Royal Actor* born
The *Tragick Scaffold* might adorn:
    While round the armed Bands
    Did clap their bloody hands.
He nothing common did or mean
Upon that memorable Scene:
    But with his keener Eye
    The Axes edge did try:
Nor call'd the *Gods* with vulgar spight
To vindicate his helpless Right,

But bow'd his comely Head,
Down as upon a Bed.
This was that memorable Hour
Which first assur'd the forced Pow'r.
So when they did design
The *Capitols* first Line,
A bleeding Head where they begun,
Did fright the Architects to run;
And yet in that the *State*
Foresaw it's happy Fate.
And now the *Irish* are asham'd
To see themselves in one Year tam'd:
So much one Man can do,
That does both act and know.
They can affirm his Praises best,
And have, though overcome, confest
How good he is, how just,
And fit for highest Trust:
Nor yet grown stiffer with Command,
But still in the *Republick's* hand:
How fit he is to sway
That can so well obey.
He to the *Commons Feet* presents
A *Kingdome*, for his first years rents:
And, what he may, forbears
His Fame to make it theirs:
And has his Sword and Spoyls ungirt,
To lay them at the *Publick's* skirt.
So when the Falcon high
Falls heavy from the Sky,
She, having kill'd, no more does search,
But on the next green Bow to pearch;
Where, when he first does lure,
The Falckner has her sure.
What may not then our *Isle* presume
While Victory his Crest does plume!
What may not others fear
If thus he crown each Year!
A *Caesar* he ere long to *Gaul*,
To *Italy* an *Hannibal*,
And to all States not free
Shall *Clymacterick* be.
The *Pict* no shelter now shall find
Within his party-colour'd Mind;

But from this Valour sad
  Shrink underneath the Plad:
Happy if in the tufted brake
The *English Hunter* him mistake;
  Nor lay his Hounds in near
  The *Caledonian* Deer.
But thou the Wars and Fortunes Son
March indefatigably on;
  And for the last effect
  Still keep thy Sword erect:
Besides the force it has to fright
The Spirits of the shady Night,
  The same *Arts* that did *gain*
  A *Pow'r* must it *maintain*.

                      (written *c.* 1650)

ANDREW MARVELL Bermudas

Where the remote *Bermudas* ride
In th' Oceans bosome unespy'd,
From a small Boat, that row'd along,
The listning Winds receiv'd this Song.
  What should we do but sing his Praise
That led us through the watry Maze,
Unto an Isle so long unknown,
And yet far kinder than our own?
Where he the huge Sea-Monsters wracks,
That lift the Deep upon their Backs.
He lands us on a grassy Stage;
Safe from the Storms, and Prelat's rage.
He gave us this eternal Spring,
Which here enamells every thing;
And sends the Fowle to us in care,
On daily Visits through the Air.
He hangs in shades the Orange bright,
Like golden Lamps in a green Night.
And does in the Pomgranates close,
Jewels more rich than *Ormus* show's.
He makes the Figs our mouths to meet;
And throws the Melons at our feet.
But Apples plants of such a price,
No Tree could ever bear them twice.

With Cedars, chosen by his hand,
From *Lebanon*, he stores the Land.
And makes the hollow Seas, that roar,
Proclaime the Ambergris on shoar.
He cast (of which we rather boast)
The Gospels Pearl upon our Coast.
And in these Rocks for us did frame
A Temple, where to sound his Name.
Oh let our Voice his Praise exalt,
Till it arrive at Heavens Vault:
Which thence (perhaps) rebounding, may
Eccho beyond the *Mexique Bay*.
Thus sung they, in the *English* boat,
An holy and a chearful Note,
And all the way, to guide their Chime,
With falling Oars they kept the time.

ANDREW MARVELL To His Coy Mistress

Had we but World enough, and Time,
This coyness Lady were no crime.
We would sit down, and think which way
To walk, and pass our long Loves Day.
Thou by the *Indian Ganges* side
Should'st Rubies find: I by the Tide
Of *Humber* would complain. I would
Love you ten years before the Flood:
And you should if you please refuse
Till the Conversion of the *Jews*.
My vegetable Love should grow
Vaster then Empires, and more slow.
An hundred years should go to praise
Thine Eyes, and on thy Forehead Gaze.
Two hundred to adore each Breast:
But thirty thousand to the rest.
An Age at least to every part,
And the last Age should show your Heart.
For Lady you deserve this State;
Nor would I love at lower rate.
　　But at my back I alwaies hear
Times winged Charriot hurrying near:

And yonder all before us lye
Desarts of vast Eternity.
Thy Beauty shall no more be found;
Nor, in thy marble Vault, shall sound
My ecchoing Song: then Worms shall try
That long preserv'd Virginity:
And your quaint Honour turn to dust;
And into ashes all my Lust.
The Grave's a fine and private place,
But none I think do there embrace.

   Now therefore, while the youthful glew
Sits on thy skin like morning dew,
And while thy willing Soul transpires
At every pore with instant Fires,
Now let us sport us while we may;
And now, like am'rous birds of prey,
Rather at once our Time devour,
Than languish in his slow-chapt pow'r.
Let us roll all our Strength, and all
Our sweetness, up into one Ball:
And tear our Pleasures with rough strife,
Thorough the Iron gates of Life.
Thus, though we cannot make our Sun
Stand still, yet we will make him run.

ANDREW MARVELL The Mower to the Glo-Worms

Ye living Lamps, by whose dear light
The Nightingale does sit so late,
And studying all the Summer-night,
Her matchless Songs does meditate;

Ye Country Comets, that portend
No War, nor Princes funeral,
Shining unto no higher end
Then to presage the Grasses fall;

Ye Glo-worms, whose officious Flame
To wandring Mowers shows the way,
That in the Night have lost their aim,
And after foolish Fires do stray;

Your courteous Lights in vain you wast,
Since *Juliana* here is come,
For She my Mind hath so displac'd
That I shall never find my home.

(written 1651–2)

ANDREW MARVELL   The Mower against Gardens

Luxurious Man, to bring his Vice in use,
    Did after him the World seduce:
And from the fields the Flow'rs and Plants allure,
    Where Nature was most plain and pure.
He first enclos'd within the Gardens square
    A dead and standing pool of Air:
And a more luscious Earth for them did knead,
    Which stupifi'd them while it fed.
The Pink grew then as double as his Mind;
    The nutriment did change the kind.
With strange perfumes he did the Roses taint.
    And Flow'rs themselves were taught to paint.
The Tulip, white, did for complexion seek;
    And learn'd to interline its cheek:
Its Onion root they then so high did hold,
    That one was for a Meadow sold.
Another World was search'd, through Oceans new,
    To find the *Marvel of Peru*.
And yet these Rarities might be allow'd,
    To Man, that sov'raign thing and proud;
Had he not dealt between the Bark and Tree,
    Forbidden mixtures there to see.
No Plant now knew the Stock from which it came;
    He grafts upon the Wild the Tame:
That the uncertain and adult'rate fruit
    Might put the Palate in dispute.
His green *Seraglio* has its Eunuchs too;
    Lest any Tyrant him out-doe.
And in the Cherry he does Nature vex,
    To procreate without a Sex.
'Tis all enforc'd; the Fountain and the Grot;
    While the sweet Fields do lye forgot:

Where willing Nature does to all dispence
	A wild and fragrant Innocence:
And *Fauns* and *Faryes* do the Meadows till,
	More by their presence then their skill.
Their Statues polish'd by some ancient hand,
	May to adorn the Gardens stand:
But howso'ere the Figures do excel,
	The *Gods* themselves with us do dwell.

ANDREW MARVELL The Definition of Love

My Love is of a birth as rare
As 'tis for object strange and high:
It was begotten by despair
Upon Impossibility.

Magnanimous Despair alone
Could show me so divine a thing,
Where feeble Hope could ne'r have flown
But vainly flapt its Tinsel Wing.

And yet I quickly might arrive
Where my extended Soul is fixt,
But Fate does Iron wedges drive,
And alwaies crouds it self betwixt.

For Fate with jealous Eye does see
Two perfect Loves; nor lets them close:
Their union would her ruine be,
And her Tyrannick pow'r depose.

And therefore her Decrees of Steel
Us as the distant Poles have plac'd,
(Though Loves whole World on us doth wheel)
Not by themselves to be embrac'd.

Unless the giddy Heaven fall,
And Earth some new Convulsion tear;
And, us to joyn, the World should all
Be cramp'd into a *Planisphere*.

As Lines so Loves *oblique* may well
Themselves in every Angle greet:
But ours so truly *paralel*,
Though infinite can never meet.

Therefore the Love which us doth bind,
But Fate so enviously debarrs,
Is the Conjunction of the Mind,
And Opposition of the Stars.

ANDREW MARVELL The Garden

How vainly men themselves amaze
To win the Palm, the Oke, or Bayes;
And their uncessant Labours see
Crown'd from some single Herb or Tree.
Whose short and narrow verged Shade
Does prudently their Toyles upbraid;
While all Flow'rs and all Trees do close
To weave the Garlands of repose.

Fair quiet, have I found thee here,
And Innocence thy Sister dear!
Mistaken long, I sought you then
In busie Companies of Men.
Your sacred Plants, if here below,
Only among the Plants will grow.
Society is all but rude,
To this delicious Solitude.

No white nor red was ever seen
So am'rous as this lovely green.
Fond Lovers, cruel as their Flame,
Cut in these Trees their Mistress name.
Little, Alas, they know, or heed,
How far these Beauties Hers exceed!
Fair Trees! where s'eer your barkes I wound,
No Name shall but your own be found.

When we have run our Passions heat,
Love hither makes his best retreat.
The *Gods*, that mortal Beauty chase,
Still in a Tree did end their race.
Apollo hunted *Daphne* so,
Only that She might Laurel grow.
And *Pan* did after *Syrinx* speed,
Not as a Nymph, but for a Reed.

What wond'rous Life in this I lead!
Ripe Apples drop about my head;
The Luscious Clusters of the Vine
Upon my Mouth do crush their Wine;
The Nectaren, and curious Peach,
Into my hands themselves do reach;
Stumbling on Melons, as I pass,
Insnar'd with Flow'rs, I fall on Grass.

Mean while the Mind, from pleasure less,
Withdraws into its happiness:
The Mind, that Ocean where each kind
Does streight its own resemblance find;
Yet it creates, transcending these,
Far other Worlds, and other Seas;
Annihilating all that 's made
To a green Thought in a green Shade.

Here at the Fountains sliding foot,
Or at some Fruit-trees mossy root,
Casting the Bodies Vest aside,
My Soul into the boughs does glide:
There like a Bird it sits, and sings,
Then whets, and combs its silver Wings;
And, till prepar'd for longer flight,
Waves in its Plumes the various Light.

Such was that happy Garden-state,
While Man there walk'd without a Mate:
After a Place so pure, and sweet,
What other Help could yet be meet!
But 'twas beyond a Mortal's share
To wander solitary there:
Two Paradises 'twere in one
To live in Paradise alone.

How well the skilful Gardner drew
Of flow'rs and herbes this Dial new;
Where from above the milder Sun
Does through a fragrant Zodiack run;
And, as it works, th' industrious Bee
Computes its time as well as we.
How could such sweet and wholsome Hours
Be reckon'd but with herbs and flow'rs!

(written 1651–2)

JOHN OLDHAM *from* **An Imitation of Horace, Book I. Satyr IX**

As I was walking in the *Mall* of late,
Alone, and musing on I know not what;
Comes a familiar Fop, whom hardly I
Knew by his name, and rudely seizes me:
Dear Sir, I'm mighty glad to meet with you:
And pray, how have you done this Age, or two?
'Well I thank God (said I) as times are now:
'I wish the same to you. And so past on,
Hoping with this the Coxcomb would be gone.
But when I saw I could not thus get free;
I ask'd, what business else he had with me?
Sir (answer'd he) *if Learning, Parts, or Sence*
Merit your friendship; I have just pretence.
'I honor you (said I) *upon that score,*
'And shall be glad to serve you to my power.
Mean time, wild to get loose, I try all ways
To shake him off: Sometimes I walk apace,
Sometimes stand still: I frown, I chafe, I fret,
Shrug, turn my back, as in the *Bagnio*, sweat:
And shew all kind of signs to make him guess
At my impatience and uneasiness.
'*Happy the folk in* Newgate! (whisper'd I)
'*Who, tho in Chains are from this torment free:*
'*Wou'd I were like rough* Manly *in the Play,*
'*To send Impertinents with kicks away!*
   He all the while baits me with tedious chat,
Speaks much about the drought, and how the rate
Of Hay is rais'd, and what it now goes at:
Tells me of a new Comet at the *Hague*,
Portending God knows what, a Dearth, or Plague:

Names every Wench, that passes through the Park,
How much she is allow'd, and who the Spark
That keeps her: points, who lately got a Clap,
And who at the *Groom-Porters* had ill hap
Three nights ago in play with such a Lord:
When he observ'd, I minded not a word,
And did no answer to his trash afford;
Sir, I perceive you stand on Thorns (said he)
And fain would part: but, faith, it must not be:
Come let us take a Bottle. (I cried) 'No;
'*Sir, I am in a Course, and dare not now.*
Then tell me whether you design to go:
I'll wait upon you. 'Oh! *Sir, 'tis too far:*
'*I visit cross the Water: therefore spare*
'*Your needless trouble. Trouble! Sir, 'tis none:*
'*Tis more by half to leave you here alone.*
I have no present business to attend,
At least which I'll not quit for such a Friend:
Tell me not of the distance: for I vow,
I'll cut the Line, double the Cape for you,
Good faith, I will not leave you: make no words:
Go you to Lambeth? Is it to my Lords?
His Steward I most intimately know,
Have often drunk with his Comptroller too.
By this I found my wheadle would not pass,
But rather serv'd my suff'rings to increase:
And seeing 'twas in vain to vex, or fret,
I patiently submitted to my fate.
    Strait he begins again: *Sir, if you knew*
My worth but half so throughly as I do;
I'm sure, you would not value any Friend,
You have, like me: but that I won't commend
My self, and my own Talents; I might tell
How many ways to wonder I excel.
None has a greater gift in Poetry,
Or writes more Verses with more ease than I:
I'm grown the envy of the men of Wit,
I kill'd ev'n Rochester *with grief and spight:*
Next for the Dancing part I all surpass,
St. André *never mov'd with such a grace:*
And 'tis well known, when e're I sing, or set,
Humphreys, *nor* Blow *could ever match me yet.*
    Here I got room to interrupt: '*Have you*
'*A Mother, Sir, or Kindred living now?*

Not one: they are all dead. 'Troth, so I guest:
'The happier they (said I) who are at rest.
'Poor I am only left unmurder'd yet:
'Hast, I beseech you, and dispatch me quite:
'For I am well convinc'd, my time is come:
'When I was young, a Gypsie told my doom:
This Lad (said she, and look'd upon my hand)
Shall not by Sword, or Poison come to's end,
Nor by the Fever, Dropsie, Gout, or Stone,
But he shall die by an eternal Tongue:
Therefore, when he's grown up, if he be wise,
Let him avoid great Talkers, I advise.

    By this time we were got to *Westminster*,
Where he by chance a Trial had to hear,
And, if he were not there, his Cause must fall:
Sir, if you love me, step into the Hall
For one half hour. 'The Devil take me now,
'(Said I) if I know any thing of Law:
'Besides I told you whither I'm to go.
Hereat he made a stand, pull'd down his Hat
Over his eyes, and mus'd in deep debate:
I'm in a straight (said he) what I shall do:
Whether forsake my business, Sir, or you.
'Me by all means (say I). No (says my Sot)
I fear you'l take it ill, if I should do't:
I'm sure, you will. 'Not I, by all that's good.
'But I've more breeding, than to be so rude.
'Pray, don't neglect your own concerns for me:
'Your Cause, good Sir! My Cause be damn'd (says he)
I value't less than your dear Company.
With this he came up to me, and would lead
The way; I sneaking after hung my head.

JOHN DRYDEN *from* Absalom and Achitophel

[Monmouth]

In pious times, e'r Priest-craft did begin,
Before *Polygamy* was made a sin;
When man, on many, multiply'd his kind,
E'r one to one, was, cursedly, confin'd:

When Nature prompted, and no law deny'd
Promiscuous use of Concubine and Bride;
Then, *Israel*'s Monarch, after Heaven's own heart,
His vigorous warmth did, variously, impart
To Wives and Slaves: And, wide as his Command,
Scatter'd his Maker's Image through the Land.
Michal, of Royal blood, the Crown did wear,
A Soyl ungratefull to the Tiller's care:
Not so the rest; for several Mothers bore
To Godlike *David*, several Sons before.
But since like slaves his bed they did ascend,
No True Succession could their seed attend.
Of all this Numerous Progeny was none
So Beautifull, so brave as *Absolon*:
Whether, inspir'd by some diviner Lust,
His Father got him with a greater Gust;
Or that his Conscious destiny made way
By manly beauty to Imperiall sway.
Early in Foreign fields he won Renown,
With Kings and States ally'd to *Israel*'s Crown:
In Peace the thoughts of War he could remove,
And seem'd as he were only born for love.
What e'r he did was done with so much ease,
In him alone, 'twas Natural to please.
His motions all accompanied with grace;
And *Paradise* was open'd in his face.
With secret Joy, indulgent *David* view'd
His Youthfull Image in his Son renew'd:
To all his wishes Nothing he deny'd,
And made the Charming *Annabel* his Bride.
What faults he had (for who from faults is free?)
His Father could not, or he would not see.
Some warm excesses, which the Law forbore,
Were constru'd Youth that purg'd by boyling o'r:
And *Amnon*'s Murther, by a specious Name,
Was call'd a Just Revenge for injur'd Fame.
Thus Prais'd, and Lov'd, the Noble Youth remain'd,
While *David*, undisturb'd, in *Sion* raign'd.
But Life can never be sincerely blest:
Heaven punishes the bad, and proves the best.

(. . .)

This Plot, which fail'd for want of common Sense,
Had yet a deep and dangerous Consequence:
For, as when raging Fevers boyl the Blood,
The standing Lake soon floats into a Flood;
And every hostile Humour, which before
Slept quiet in its Channels, bubbles o'r:
So, several Factions from this first Ferment,
Work up to Foam, and threat the Government.
Some by their Friends, more by themselves thought wise,
Oppos'd the Power, to which they could not rise.
Some had in Courts been Great, and thrown from thence,
Like Feinds, were harden'd in Impenitence.
Some by their Monarch's fatal mercy grown,
From Pardon'd Rebels, Kinsmen to the Throne;
Were rais'd in Power and publick Office high:
Strong Bands, if Bands ungratefull men could tye.
    Of these the false *Achitophel* was first:
A Name to all succeeding Ages Curst.
For close Designs, and crooked Counsels fit;
Sagacious, Bold, and Turbulent of wit:
Restless, unfixt in Principles and Place;
In Power unpleas'd, impatient of Disgrace.
A fiery Soul, which working out its way, ⎫
Fretted the Pigmy body to decay: ⎬
And o'r inform'd the Tenement of Clay.   ⎭
A daring Pilot in extremity;
Pleas'd with the Danger, when the Waves went high
He sought the Storms; but for a Calm unfit,
Would Steer too nigh the Sands, to boast his Wit.
Great Wits are sure to Madness near ally'd;
And thin Partitions do their Bounds divide:
Else, why should he, with Wealth and Honour blest,
Refuse his Age the needful hours of Rest?
Punish a Body which he coud not please;
Bankrupt of Life, yet Prodigal of Ease?
And all to leave, what with his Toyl he won,
To that unfeather'd, two Leg'd thing, a Son:
Got, while his Soul did hudled Notions try;
And born a shapeless Lump, like Anarchy.
In Friendship False, Implacable in Hate:
Resolv'd to Ruine or to Rule the State.

To Compass this the Triple Bond he broke;
The Pillars of the publick Safety shook:
And fitted *Israel* for a Foreign Yoke.
Then, seiz'd with Fear, yet still affecting Fame,
Usurp'd a Patriott's All-attoning Name.
So easie still it proves in Factious Times,
With publick Zeal to cancel private Crimes:
How safe is Treason, and how sacred ill,
Where none can sin against the Peoples Will:
Where Crouds can wink; and no offence be known,
Since in anothers guilt they find their own.
Yet, Fame deserv'd, no Enemy can grudge;
The Statesman we abhor, but praise the Judge.
In *Israels* Courts ne'r sat an *Abbethdin*
With more discerning Eyes, or Hands more clean:
Unbrib'd, unsought, the Wretched to redress;
Swift of Dispatch, and easie of Access.
Oh, had he been content to serve the Crown,
With vertues only proper to the Gown;
Or, had the rankness of the Soyl been freed
From Cockle, that opprest the Noble seed:
David, for him his tunefull Harp had strung,
And Heaven had wanted one Immortal song.
But wilde Ambition loves to slide, not stand;
And Fortunes Ice prefers to Vertues Land:
Achitophel, grown weary to possess
A lawfull Fame, and lazy Happiness;
Disdain'd the Golden fruit to gather free,
And lent the Croud his Arm to shake the Tree.

JOHN BUNYAN *from* The Pilgrims Progress   1684

[Valiant-for-Truth's Song]

Who would true Valour see
Let him come hither;
One here will Constant be,
Come Wind, come Weather.
There's no *Discouragement*
Shall make him once *Relent*,
His first avow'd *Intent*,
To be a Pilgrim.

Who so beset him round,
With dismal *Storys*,
Do but themselves Confound;
His Strength the *more is*.
No *Lyon* can him fright,
He'l with a *Gyant* Fight,
But he will have a right,
To be a Pilgrim.

 Hobgoblin, nor foul *Fiend*,
Can *daunt* his Spirit:
He knows, he *at the end*,
Shall Life Inherit.
Then Fancies fly away,
He'l fear not what men say,
He'l labour Night and Day,
To be a Pilgrim.

JOHN DRYDEN To the Memory of Mr. *Oldham*

Farewel, too little and too lately known,
Whom I began to think and call my own;
For sure our Souls were near ally'd; and thine
Cast in the same Poetick mould with mine.
One common Note on either Lyre did strike,
And Knaves and Fools we both abhorr'd alike:
To the same Goal did both our Studies drive,
The last set out the soonest did arrive.
Thus *Nisus* fell upon the slippery place,
While his young Friend perform'd and won the Race.
O early ripe! to thy abundant store
What could advancing Age have added more?
It might (what Nature never gives the young)
Have taught the numbers of thy native Tongue.
But Satyr needs not those, and Wit will shine
Through the harsh cadence of a rugged line.
A noble Error, and but seldom made,
When Poets are by too much force betray'd.
Thy generous fruits, though gather'd ere their prime
Still shew'd a quickness; and maturing time
But mellows what we write to the dull sweets of Rime.

Once more, hail and farewel; farewel thou young, [381
But ah too short, *Marcellus* of our Tongue;
Thy Brows with Ivy, and with Laurels bound;
But Fate and gloomy Night encompass thee around.

JOHN DRYDEN Horat. Ode 29. Book 3 Paraphras'd in **1685**
Pindarique Verse

Descended of an ancient Line,
    That long the *Tuscan* Scepter sway'd,
Make haste to meet the generous wine,
    Whose piercing is for thee delay'd:
The rosie wreath is ready made;
    And artful hands prepare
The fragrant *Syrian* Oyl, that shall perfume thy hair.

When the Wine sparkles from a far,
    And the well-natur'd Friend cries, come away;
Make haste, and leave thy business and thy care,
    No mortal int'rest can be worth thy stay.

Leave for a while thy costly Country Seat;
    And, to be Great indeed, forget
The nauseous pleasures of the Great:
        Make haste and come:
Come and forsake thy cloying store;
    Thy Turret that surveys, from high,
The smoke, and wealth, and noise of *Rome*;
    And all the busie pageantry
That wise men scorn, and fools adore:
Come, give thy Soul a loose, and taste the pleasures of the poor.

Sometimes 'tis grateful to the Rich, to try
A short vicissitude, and fit of Poverty:
    A savoury Dish, a homely Treat,
    Where all is plain, where all is neat,
    Without the stately spacious Room,
The *Persian* Carpet, or the *Tyrian* Loom,
Clear up the cloudy foreheads of the Great.

The Sun is in the Lion mounted high;
  The *Syrian* Star
  Barks from a far;
 And with his sultry breath infects the Sky;
The ground below is parch'd, the heav'ns above us fry.
 The Shepheard drives his fainting Flock,
 Beneath the covert of a Rock;
 And seeks refreshing Rivulets nigh:
 The *Sylvans* to their shades retire,
Those very shades and streams, new shades and streams require;
And want a cooling breeze of wind to fan the rageing fire.

 Thou, what befits the new Lord May'r,
 And what the City Faction dare,
 And what the *Gallique* Arms will do,
 And what the Quiver bearing Foe,
 Art anxiously inquisitive to know:
But God has, wisely, hid from humane sight
 The dark decrees of future fate;
 And sown their seeds in depth of night;
 He laughs at all the giddy turns of State;
When Mortals search too soon, and fear too late.

 Enjoy the present smiling hour;
 And put it out of Fortunes pow'r:
 The tide of bus'ness, like the running stream,
 Is sometimes high, and sometimes low,
 A quiet ebb, or a tempestuous flow,
  And always in extream.
 Now with a noiseless gentle course
 It keeps within the middle Bed;
 Anon it lifts aloft the head,
And bears down all before it, with impetuous force:
 And trunks of Trees come rowling down,
 Sheep and their Folds together drown:
 Both House and Homested into Seas are borne,
 And Rocks are from their old foundations torn,
And woods made thin with winds, their scatter'd honours mourn.

 Happy the Man, and happy he alone,
 He, who can call to day his own:
 He, who secure within, can say
 To morrow do thy worst, for I have liv'd to day.

Be fair, or foul, or rain, or shine,
The joys I have possest, in spight of fate are mine.
    Not Heav'n it self upon the past has pow'r;
But what has been, has been, and I have had my hour.

        Fortune, that with malicious joy,
            Does Man her slave oppress,
        Proud of her Office to destroy,
            Is seldome pleas'd to bless.
    Still various and unconstant still;
But with an inclination to be ill;
    Promotes, degrades, delights in strife,
    And makes a Lottery of life.
    I can enjoy her while she's kind;
    But when she dances in the wind,
    And shakes her wings, and will not stay,
        I puff the Prostitute away:
The little or the much she gave, is quietly resign'd:
    Content with poverty, my Soul, I arm;
    And Vertue, tho' in rags, will keep me warm.

            What is't to me,
Who never sail in her unfaithful Sea,
    If Storms arise, and Clouds grow black;
    If the Mast split and threaten wreck,
    Then let the greedy Merchant fear
            For his ill gotten gain;
    And pray to Gods that will not hear,
While the debating winds and billows bear
            His Wealth into the Main.
    For me secure from Fortunes blows,
    (Secure of what I cannot lose,)
    In my small Pinnace I can sail,
        Contemning all the blustring roar;
            And running with a merry gale,
    With friendly Stars my safety seek
    Within some little winding Creek;
        And see the storm a shore.

JOHN DRYDEN *from* Latter Part of the Third Book of Lucretius. *Against the Fear of Death*

What has this Bugbear death to frighten Man,
If Souls can die, as well as Bodies can?
For, as before our Birth we felt no pain
When Punique arms infested Land and Mayn,
When Heav'n and Earth were in confusion hurl'd
For the debated Empire of the World,
Which aw'd with dreadful expectation lay,
Sure to be Slaves, uncertain who shou'd sway:
So, when our mortal frame shall be disjoyn'd,
The lifeless Lump, uncoupled from the mind,
From sense of grief and pain we shall be free;
We shall not feel, because we shall not *Be*.
Though Earth in Seas, and Seas in Heav'n were lost,
We shou'd not move, we only shou'd be tost.
Nay, ev'n suppose when we have suffer'd Fate,
The Soul cou'd feel in her divided state,
What's that to us, for we are only we
While Souls and bodies in one frame agree?
Nay, tho' our Atoms shou'd revolve by chance,
And matter leape into the former dance;
Tho' time our Life and motion cou'd restore,
And make our Bodies what they were before,
What gain to us wou'd all this bustle bring,
The new made man wou'd be another thing;
When once an interrupting pause is made,
That individual Being is decay'd.
We, who are dead and gone, shall bear no part
In all the pleasures, nor shall feel the smart,
Which to that other Mortal shall accrew,
Whom of our Matter Time shall mould anew.

And therefore if a Man bemoan his lot,
That after death his mouldring limbs shall rot,
Or flames, or jaws of Beasts devour his Mass,
Know he's an unsincere, unthinking Ass.
A secret Sting remains within his mind,
The fool is to his own cast offals kind;
He boasts no sense can after death remain, ⎫
Yet makes himself a part of life again: ⎬
As if some other He could feel the pain. ⎭

JOHN DRYDEN *from* **Fourth Book of Lucretius.** *Concerning the Nature of Love*

When Love its utmost vigour does imploy,
Ev'n then, 'tis but a restless wandring joy:
Nor knows the Lover, in that wild excess,
With hands or eyes, what first he wou'd possess:
But strains at all; and fast'ning where he strains,
Too closely presses with his frantique pains:
With biteing kisses hurts the twining fair,
Which shews his joyes imperfect, unsincere:
For stung with inward rage, he flings around,
And strives t' avenge the smart on that which gave the wound.
But love those eager bitings does restrain,
And mingling pleasure mollifies the pain.
For ardent hope still flatters anxious grief,
And sends him to his Foe to seek relief:
Which yet the nature of the thing denies;
For Love, and Love alone of all our joyes
By full possession does but fan the fire,
The more we still enjoy, the more we still desire.
Nature for meat, and drink provides a space;
And when receiv'd they fill their certain place;
Hence thirst and hunger may be satisfi'd,
But this repletion is to Love deny'd:
Form, feature, colour, whatsoe're delight
Provokes the Lovers endless appetite,
These fill no space, nor can we thence remove
With lips, or hands, or all our instruments of love:
In our deluded grasp we nothing find,
But thin aerial shapes, that fleet before the mind.
As he who in a dream with drought is curst,
And finds no real drink to quench his thirst,
Runs to imagin'd Lakes his heat to steep,
And vainly swills and labours in his sleep;
So Love with fantomes cheats our longing eyes,
Which hourly seeing never satisfies;
Our hands pull nothing from the parts they strain,
But wander o're the lovely limbs in vain:
Nor when the Youthful pair more clossely joyn,
When hands in hands they lock, and thighs in thighs they twine;

Just in the raging foam of full desire,
When both press on, both murmur, both expire,
They gripe, they squeeze, their humid tongues they dart,
As each wou'd force their way to t'others heart:
In vain; they only cruze about the coast,
For bodies cannot pierce, nor be in bodies lost:
As sure they strive to be, when both engage,
In that tumultuous momentary rage,
So 'tangled in the Nets of Love they lie,
Till Man dissolves in that excess of joy.
Then, when the gather'd bag has burst its way,
And ebbing tydes the slacken'd nerves betray,
A pause ensues; and Nature nods a while,
Till with recruited rage new Spirits boil;
And then the same vain violence returns,
With flames renew'd th' erected furnace burns.
Agen they in each other wou'd be lost,
But still by adamantine bars are crost;
All wayes they try, successeless all they prove,
To cure the secret sore of lingring love.

1686   EDMUND WALLER Of the Last Verses in the Book

When we for Age could neither read nor write,
The Subject made us able to indite.
The Soul with Nobler Resolutions deckt,
The Body stooping, does Herself erect:
No Mortal Parts are requisite to raise
Her, that Unbody'd can her Maker praise.

The Seas are quiet, when the Winds give o're;
So calm are we, when Passions are no more:
For then we know how vain it was to boast
Of fleeting Things, so certain to be lost.
Clouds of Affection from our younger Eyes
Conceal that emptiness, which Age descries.

The Soul's dark Cottage, batter'd and decay'd,
Lets in new Light thrò chinks that time has made;
Stronger by weakness, wiser Men become
As they draw near to their Eternal home:
Leaving the Old, both Worlds at once they view,
That stand upon the Threshold of the New.

Miratur Limen Olympi
Virgil

PHILIP AYRES *from the Greek of Theocritus*. **The Death of**   **1687**
Adonis

When VENUS her ADONIS found,
Just slain, and weltring on the Ground,
With Hair disorder'd, gastly Look,
And Cheeks their Roses had forsook;
She bad the Cupids fetch with speed,
The Boar that did this horrid Deed:
They, to revenge Adonis Blood,
As quick as Birds search'd all the Wood,
And straight the murd'rous Creature found,
Whom they, with Chains, securely bound;
And whilst his Net one o'er him flung,
To drag the Captive Boar along
Another follow'd with his Bow,
Pushing to make him faster go;
Who most unwillingly obey'd,
For he of VENUS was afraid.
    No sooner she the Boar espy'd,
But, Oh! Thou cruel Beast, she cry'd,
That hadst the Heart to wound this Thigh,
How couldst thou kill so sweet a Boy?
    Great Goddess (said the Boar, and stood
Trembling) I swear by all that's Good,
By thy Fair Self, by Him I've slain,
These pretty Hunters, and this Chain;
I did no Harm this Youth intend,
Much less had Thought to kill your Friend:
I gaz'd, and with my Passion strove,
For with his Charms I fell in Love:
At last that naked Thigh of his,
With Lovers Heat I ran to kiss;

Of Fatal Cause of all my Woe!
'Twas then I gave the heedless Blow.
These Tusks with utmost Rigour draw,
Cut, break, or tear them from my Jaw,
'Tis just I should these Teeth remove,
Teeth that can have a Sense of Love;
Or this Revenge, if yet too small,
Cut off the Kissing Lips and all.
    When Venus heard this humble Tale,
Pitty did o'er her Rage prevail,
She bad them straight his Chains unty,
And set the Boar at Liberty;
Who ne'er to Wood return'd again,
But follow'd Venus in her Train,
And when by Chance to Fire he came,
His Am'rous Tusks sing'd in the Flame.

1688   **JANE BARKER To Her Lovers Complaint**

A Song

If you complain your *Flames* are hot,
    'Tis 'cause they are *impure*
For strongest *Spirits* scorch us not,
Their Flames we can endure.

Love, like *Zeal* should be divine
    And *ardent* as the same;
Like *Stars*, which in cold Weather shine,
Or like a *Lambent* Flame.

It shou'd be like the Morning *Rays*
    Which quickens, but not burns;
Or th' innocence of Childrens plays,
Or *Lamps* in Antient urns.

CHARLES COTTON Evening Quatrains

The Day's grown old, the fainting Sun
Has but a little way to run,
And yet his Steeds, with all his skill,
Scarce lug the Chariot down the Hill.

With Labour spent, and Thirst opprest,
Whilst they strain hard to gain the West,
From Fetlocks hot drops melted light,
Which turn to Meteors in the Night.

The Shadows now so long do grow,
That Brambles like tall Cedars show,
Mole-hills seem Mountains, and the Ant
Appears a monstrous Elephant.

A very little little Flock
Shades thrice the ground that it would stock;
Whilst the small Stripling following them,
Appears a mighty *Polypheme*.

These being brought into the Fold,
And by the thrifty Master told,
He thinks his Wages are well paid,
Since none are either lost, or stray'd.

Now lowing Herds are each-where heard,
Chains rattle in the Villains Yard,
The Cart's on Tayl set down to rest,
Bearing on high the Cuckolds Crest.

The hedg is stript, the Clothes brought in,
Nought's left without should be within,
The Bees are hiv'd, and hum their Charm,
Whilst every House does seem a Swarm.

The Cock now to the Roost is prest:
For he must call up all the rest;
The Sow's fast pegg'd within the Sty,
To still her squeaking Progeny.

Each one has had his Supping Mess,
The Cheese is put into the Press,
The Pans and Bowls clean scalded all,
Rear'd up against the Milk-house Wall.

And now on Benches all are sat
In the cool Air to sit and chat,
Till *Phœbus*, dipping in the West,
Shall lead the World the way to Rest.

CHARLES COTTON An Epitaph on *M.H.*

In this cold *Monument* lies one,
That I know who has lain upon,
The happier *He*: her Sight would charm,
And Touch have kept *King David* warm.
Lovely, as is the dawning *East*,
Was this Marble's frozen *Guest*;
As soft, and Snowy, as that Down
Adorns the *Blow-balls* frizled Crown;
As straight and slender as the *Crest*,
Or *Antlet* of the one-beam'd Beast;
Pleasant as th'odorous *Month* of *May*:
As glorious, and as light as *Day*.

Whom I admir'd, as soon as knew,
And now her Memory pursue
With such a superstitious Lust,
That I could fumble with her Dust.

She all Perfections had, and more,
Tempting, as if design'd a *Whore*,
For so she was; and since there are
Such, I could wish them all as fair.

Pretty she was, and young, and wise,
And in her Calling so precise,
That Industry had made her prove
The sucking *School-Mistress* of *Love*:

And *Death*, ambitious to become
Her *Pupil*, left his Ghastly home,
And, seeing how we us'd her here,
The raw-bon'd *Rascal* ravisht her.

Who, pretty *Soul*, resign'd her Breath,
To seek new Letchery in Death.

CHARLES COTTON To My Dear and Most Worthy Friend, Mr. *Isaak Walton*

Whilst in this cold and blust'ring Clime,
        Where bleak winds howl, and Tempests roar,
We pass away the roughest time
        Has been of many years before;

Whilst from the most tempest'ous Nooks
        The chillest Blasts our peace invade,
And by great Rains our smallest Brooks
        Are almost navigable made;

Whilst all the ills are so improv'd
        Of this dead quarter of the year,
That even you, so much belov'd,
        We would not now wish with us here;

In this estate, I say, it is
        Some comfort to us to suppose,
That in a better Clime than this
        You our dear Friend have more repose;

And some delight to me the while,
        Though nature now does weep in Rain,
To think that I have seen her smile,
        And haply may I do again.

If the all-ruling Power please
        We live to see another *May*,
We'll recompence an Age of these
        Foul days in one fine fishing day:

We then shall have a day or two,
    Perhaps a week, wherein to try,
What the best Master's hand can doe
    With the most deadly killing Flie:

A day without too bright a Beam,
    A warm, but not a scorching Sun,
A Southern gale to curl the Stream,
    And (Master) half our work is done.

There whilst behind some bush we wait
    The Scaly People to betray,
We'll prove it just with treach'rous Bait
    To make the preying Trout our prey;

And think our selves in such an hour
    Happier than those, though not so high,
Who, like Leviathans, devour
    Of meaner men the smaller Fry.

This (my best Friend) at my poor Home
    Shall be our Pastime and our Theme,
But then should you not deign to come
    You make all this a flatt'ring Dream.

1691   JOHN WILMOT, EARL OF ROCHESTER A SONG of a
Young LADY. *To Her Ancient Lover*

Ancient Person, for whom I,
All the flattering Youth defy;
Long be it e're thou grow Old,
Aking, shaking, Crazy Cold.
But still continue as thou art,
Ancient Person of my Heart.

On thy withered Lips and dry,
Which like barren Furrows lye;
Brooding Kisses I will pour,
Shall thy youthful Heat restore.

Such kind Show'rs in Autumn fall,
And a second Spring recall:
Nor from thee will ever part,
Antient Person of my Heart.

Thy Nobler part, which but to name
In our Sex wou'd be counted shame,
By Ages frozen grasp possest,
From his Ice shall be releast:
And, sooth'd by my reviving hand,
In former Warmth and Vigor stand.
All a Lover's wish can reach,
For thy Joy my Love shall teach:
And for thy Pleasure shall improve,
All that Art can add to Love.
Yet still I love thee without Art,
Antient Person of my Heart.

JOHN WILMOT, EARL OF ROCHESTER A Song

Absent from thee I languish still,
　　Then ask me not, when I return?
The straying Fool 'twill plainly kill,
　　To wish all Day, all Night to Mourn.

Dear, from thine Arms then let me flie,
　　That my Fantastick mind may prove,
The Torments it deserves to try,
　　That tears my fixt Heart from my Love.

When wearied with a world of Woe,
　　To thy safe Bosom I retire
Where Love and Peace and Truth does flow,
　　May I contented there expire.

Lest once more wandring from that Heav'n
　　I fall on some base heart unblest;
Faithless to thee, False, unforgiv'n,
　　And lose my Everlasting rest.

JOHN WILMOT, EARL OF ROCHESTER The Mistress.
A Song

An Age in her Embraces past,
   Would seem a Winters day;
Where Life and Light, with envious hast,
   Are torn and snatch'd away.

But, oh how slowly Minutes rowl,
   When absent from her Eyes
That feed my Love, which is my Soul,
   It languishes and dyes.

For then no more a Soul but shade,
   It mournfully does move;
And haunts my Breast, by absence made
   The living Tomb of Love.

You Wiser men despise me not;
   Whose Love-sick Fancy raves,
On Shades of Souls, and Heaven knows what;
   Short Ages live in Graves.

When e're those wounding Eyes, so full
   Of Sweetness, you did see;
Had you not been profoundly dull,
   You had gone mad like me.

Nor Censure us You who perceive
   My best belov'd and me,
Sigh and lament, Complain and grieve,
   You think we disagree.

Alas! 'tis Sacred Jealousie,
   Love rais'd to an Extream;
The only Proof 'twixt her and me,
   We love, and do not dream.

Fantastick Fancies fondly move;
   And in frail Joys believe:
Taking false Pleasure for true Love;
   But Pain can ne're deceive.

Kind Jealous Doubts, tormenting Fears,
    And Anxious Cares, when past;
Prove our Hearts Treasure fixt and dear,
    And make us blest at last.

JOHN WILMOT, EARL OF ROCHESTER *from the Latin of* Lucretius. **De rerum natura, 1.44–9**

The *Gods*, by right of Nature, must possess
An Everlasting Age, of perfect Peace:
Far off, remov'd from us, and our Affairs:
Neither approach'd by *Dangers*, or by *Cares*:
Rich in themselves, to whom we cannot add:
Not pleas'd by *Good* Deeds; nor provok'd by *Bad*.

THOMAS HEYRICK On an Indian Tomineois, the Least of Birds

I'me made in sport by Nature, when
    Shee's tir'd with the stupendious weight
Of forming Elephants and Beasts of State;
Rhinoceros, that love the Fen;
    The Elkes, that scale the hills of Snow,
And Lions couching in their awfull Den:
    These do work Nature hard, and then,
    Her wearied Hand in Me doth show
What she can for her own Diversion doe.

    Man is a little World ('tis said),
    And I in Miniature am drawn,
A Perfect Creature, but in Short-hand shown.
    The Ruck, in Madagascar bred,
    (If new Discoveries Truth do speak)
Whom greatest Beasts and armed Horsemen dread,
    Both him and Me one Artist made:
    Nature in this Delight doth take,
That can so Great and Little Monsters make.

The Indians me a Sunbeam name,
    And I may be the Child of one:
So small I am, my Kind is hardly known.
    To some a sportive Bird I seem,
    And some believe me but a Fly;
Tho' me a Feather'd Fowl the Best esteem:
    What e're I am, I'me Nature's Gemm,
    And like a Sunbeam from the Sky,
I can't be follow'd by the quickest Eye.

I'me the true Bird of Paradise,
    And heavenly Dew's my only Meat:
My Mouth so small, 'twill nothing else admit.
    No Scales know how my weight to poise,
    So Light, I seem condensed Air;
And did at th'End of the Creation rise,
    When Nature wanted more Supplies,
    When she could little Matter spare,
But in Return did make the work more Rare.

1692   SIR CHARLES SEDLEY On a Cock at Rochester

Thou cursed Cock, with thy perpetual Noise,
May'st thou be Capon made, and lose thy Voice,
Or on a Dunghil may'st thou spend thy Blood,
And Vermin prey upon thy craven Brood;
May Rivals tread thy Hens before thy Face,
Then with redoubled Courage give thee chase;
May'st thou be punish'd for St. *Peter*'s Crime,
And on *Shrove-tuesday*, perish in thy Prime;
May thy bruis'd Carcass be some Beggar's Feast,
Thou first and worst Disturber of Man's Rest.

1693   JOHN DRYDEN *from* The Sixth Satyr of Juvenal

In *Saturn's* Reign, at Nature's Early Birth,
There was that Thing call'd Chastity on Earth;
When in a narrow Cave, their common shade,
The Sheep the Shepherds and their Gods were laid:

When Reeds and Leaves, and Hides of Beasts were spread
By Mountain Huswifes for their homely Bed,
And Mossy Pillows rais'd, for the rude Husband's head.
Unlike the Niceness of our Modern Dames
(Affected Nymphs with new Affected Names:)
The *Cynthia's* and the *Lesbia's* of our Years,
Who for a Sparrow's Death dissolve in Tears.
Those first unpolisht Matrons, Big and Bold,
Gave Suck to Infants of Gygantick Mold;
Rough as their Savage Lords who Rang'd the Wood,
And Fat with Akorns Belcht their windy Food.
For when the World was Bucksom, fresh, and young,
Her Sons were undebauch'd, and therefore strong;
And whether Born in kindly Beds of Earth,
Or strugling from the Teeming Oaks to Birth,
Or from what other Atoms they begun,
No Sires they had, or if a Sire the Sun.
Some thin Remains of Chastity appear'd
Ev'n under *Jove*, but *Jove* without a Beard:
Before the servile *Greeks* had learnt to Swear
By Heads of Kings; while yet the Bounteous Year
Her common Fruits in open Plains expos'd,
E're Thieves were fear'd, or Gardens were enclos'd:
At length uneasie Justice upwards flew,
And both the Sisters to the Stars withdrew;
From that Old *Æra* Whoring did begin,
So Venerably Ancient is the Sin.
Adult'rers next invade the Nuptial State,
And Marriage-Beds creak'd with a Foreign Weight;
All other Ills did Iron times adorn;
But Whores and Silver in one Age were Born.

JOHN DRYDEN *from* The First Book of *Ovid's* Metamorphoses

['Deucalion and Pyrrha, sole survivors of the Flood, renew Creation
by casting stones behind them']

This Earth our mighty Mother is, the Stones
In her capacious Body, are her Bones.
These we must cast behind: with hope and fear
The Woman did the new solution hear:

The Man diffides in his own Augury,
And doubts the Gods; yet both resolve to try.
Descending from the Mount, they first unbind
Their Vests, and veil'd, they cast the Stones behind:
The Stones (a Miracle to Mortal View,
But long Tradition makes it pass for true)
Did first the Rigour of their Kind expell,
And, suppl'd into softness, as they fell,
Then swell'd, and swelling, by degrees grew warm;
And took the Rudiments of Humane Form.
Imperfect shapes: in Marble such are seen
When the rude Chizzel does the Man begin;
While yet the roughness of the Stone remains,
Without the rising Muscles, and the Veins.
The sappy parts, and next resembling juice,
Were turn'd to moisture, for the Bodies use:
Supplying humours, blood, and nourishment;
The rest, (too solid to receive a bent;)
Converts to bones; and what was once a vein
Its former Name, and Nature did retain.
By help of Pow'r Divine, in little space
What the Man threw, assum'd a Manly face;
And what the Wife, renew'd the Female Race.
Hence we derive our Nature; born to bear
Laborious life; and harden'd into care.

1694   JOHN DRYDEN To My Dear Friend Mr. Congreve, on His
Comedy, Call'd The Double-Dealer

Well then; the promis'd hour is come at last;
The present Age of Wit obscures the past:
Strong were our Syres; and as they Fought they Writ,
Conqu'ring with force of Arms, and dint of Wit;
Theirs was the Gyant Race, before the Flood;
And thus, when *Charles* Return'd, our Empire stood.
Like *Janus* he the stubborn Soil manur'd,
With Rules of Husbandry the rankness cur'd:
Tam'd us to manners, when the Stage was rude;
And boistrous *English* Wit, with Art indu'd.
Our Age was cultivated thus at length;
But what we gain'd in skill we lost in strength.

Our Builders were, with want of Genius, curst;
The second Temple was not like the first:
Till You, the best *Vitruvius*, come at length;
Our Beauties equal; but excel our strength.
Firm *Dorique* Pillars found Your solid Base:
The Fair *Corinthian* Crowns the higher Space;
Thus all below is Strength, and all above is Grace.
In easie Dialogue is *Fletcher*'s Praise:
He mov'd the mind, but had not power to raise.
Great *Johnson* did by strength of Judgment please:
Yet doubling *Fletcher*'s Force, he wants his Ease.
In differing Tallents both adorn'd their Age;
One for the Study, t'other for the Stage.
But both to *Congreve* justly shall submit,
One match'd in Judgment, both o'er-match'd in Wit.
In Him all Beauties of this Age we see;
Etherege his Courtship, *Southern*'s Purity;
The Satire, Wit, and Strength of Manly *Witcherly*.
All this in blooming Youth you have Atchiev'd;
Nor are your foil'd Contemporaries griev'd;
So much the sweetness of your manners move,
We cannot envy you because we Love.
Fabius might joy in *Scipio*, when he saw
A Beardless Consul made against the Law,
And joyn his Suffrage to the Votes of *Rome*;
Though He with *Hannibal* was overcome.
Thus old *Romano* bow'd to *Raphel*'s Fame;
And Scholar to the Youth he taught, became.

  Oh that your Brows my Lawrel had sustain'd,
Well had I been Depos'd, if You had reign'd!
The Father had descended for the Son;
For only You are lineal to the Throne.
Thus when the State one *Edward* did depose;
A Greater *Edward* in his room arose.
But now, not I, but Poetry is curs'd;
For *Tom* the Second reigns like *Tom* the first.
But let 'em not mistake my Patron's part;
Nor call his Charity their own desert.
Yet this I Prophesy; Thou shalt be seen,
(Tho' with some short Parenthesis between:)
High on the Throne of Wit; and seated there,
Not mine (that's little) but thy Lawrel wear.
Thy first attempt an early promise made;
That early promise this has more than paid.

So bold, yet so judiciously you dare,
That Your least Praise, is to be Regular.
Time, Place, and Action, may with pains be wrought,
But Genius must be born; and never can be taught.
This is Your Portion; this Your Native Store;
Heav'n that but once was Prodigal before,
To *Shakespeare* gave as much; she cou'd not give him more.

 Maintain Your Post: That's all the Fame You need;
For 'tis impossible you shou'd proceed.
Already I am worn with Cares and Age;
And just abandoning th' Ungrateful Stage:
Unprofitably kept at Heav'ns expence,
I live a Rent-charge on his Providence:
But You, whom ev'ry Muse and Grace adorn,
Whom I foresee to better Fortune born,
Be kind to my Remains; and oh defend,
Against Your Judgment, Your departed Friend!
Let not the Insulting Foe my Fame pursue;
But shade those Lawrels which descend to You:
And take for Tribute what these Lines express:
You merit more; nor cou'd my Love do less.

1697   JOHN DRYDEN *from* Virgil's Aeneis

from The Second Book [The Death of Priam]

Perhaps you may of *Priam*'s Fate enquire.
He, when he saw his Regal Town on fire,
His ruin'd Palace, and his ent'ring Foes,
On ev'ry side inevitable woes;
In Arms, disus'd, invests his Limbs decay'd
Like them, with Age; a late and useless aid.
His feeble shoulders scarce the weight sustain:
Loaded, not arm'd, he creeps along, with pain;
Despairing of Success; ambitious to be slain!
Uncover'd but by Heav'n, there stood in view
An Altar; near the hearth a Lawrel grew;
Dodder'd with Age, whose Boughs encompass round
The Household Gods, and shade the holy Ground.
Here *Hecuba*, with all her helpless Train
Of Dames, for shelter sought, but sought in vain.

Driv'n like a Flock of Doves along the skie,
Their Images they hugg, and to their Altars fly.
The Queen, when she beheld her trembling Lord,
And hanging by his side a heavy Sword,
What Rage, she cry'd, has seiz'd my Husband's mind;
What Arms are these, and to what use design'd?
These times want other aids: were *Hector* here,
Ev'n *Hector* now in vain, like *Priam* wou'd appear.
With us, one common shelter thou shalt find,
Or in one common Fate with us be join'd.
She said, and with a last Salute embrac'd
The poor old Man, and by the Lawrel plac'd.
Behold *Polites*, one of *Priam*'s Sons,
Pursu'd by *Pyrrhus*, there for safety runs.
Thro Swords, and Foes, amaz'd and hurt, he flies
Through empty Courts, and open Galleries:
Him *Pyrrhus*, urging with his Lance, pursues;
And often reaches, and his thrusts renews.
The Youth transfix'd, with lamentable Cries
Expires, before his wretched Parent's Eyes.
Whom, gasping at his feet, when *Priam* saw,
The Fear of Death gave place to Nature's Law.
And shaking more with Anger, than with Age,
The Gods, said He, requite thy brutal Rage:
As sure they will, Barbarian, sure they must,
If there be Gods in Heav'n, and Gods be just:
Who tak'st in Wrongs an insolent delight;
With a Son's death t' infect a Father's sight.
Not He, whom thou and lying Fame conspire
To call thee his; Nor He, thy vaunted Sire,
Thus us'd my wretched Age: The Gods he fear'd,
The Laws of Nature and of Nations heard.
He chear'd my Sorrows, and for Sums of Gold
The bloodless Carcass of my *Hector* sold.
Pity'd the Woes a Parent underwent,
And sent me back in safety from his Tent.

This said, his feeble hand a Javelin threw,
Which flutt'ring, seem'd to loiter as it flew:
Just, and but barely, to the Mark it held,
And faintly tinckl'd on the Brazen Shield.

Then *Pyrrhus* thus: Go thou from me to Fate;
And to my Father my foul deeds relate.
Now dye: with that he dragg'd the trembling Sire,
Slidd'ring through clotter'd Blood, and holy Mire,

(The mingl'd Paste his murder'd Son had made,) ⎫
Haul'd from beneath the violated Shade; ⎬
And on the Sacred Pile, the Royal Victim laid. ⎭
His right Hand held his bloody Fauchion bare;
His left he twisted in his hoary Hair:
Then, with a speeding Thrust, his Heart he found: ⎫
The lukewarm Blood came rushing through the Wound, ⎬
And sanguine Streams distain'd the sacred Ground. ⎭
Thus *Priam* fell: and shar'd one common Fate
With *Troy* in Ashes, and his ruin'd State:
He, who the Scepter of all *Asia* sway'd,
Whom Monarchs like Domestick Slaves obey'd,
On the bleak Shoar now lies th' abandon'd King,
[1]A headless Carcass, and a nameless thing.

from **The Fourth Book [Fame]**

The loud Report through *Lybian* Cities goes;
Fame, the great Ill, from small beginnings grows.
Swift from the first; and ev'ry Moment brings
New Vigour to her flights, new Pinions to her wings.
Soon grows the Pygmee to Gygantic size;
Her Feet on Earth, her Forehead in the Skies:
Inrag'd against the Gods, revengeful Earth
Produc'd her last of the *Titanian* birth.
Swift is her walk, more swift her winged hast:
A monstrous Fantom, horrible and vast;
As many Plumes as raise her lofty flight,
So many piercing Eyes inlarge her sight:
Millions of opening Mouths to Fame belong; ⎫
And ev'ry Mouth is furnish'd with a Tongue: ⎬
And round with listning Ears the flying Plague is hung. ⎭
She fills the peaceful Universe with Cries;
No Slumbers ever close her wakeful Eyes.
By Day from lofty Tow'rs her Head she shews;
And spreads through trembling Crowds disastrous News.
With Court Informers haunts, and Royal Spyes,
Things done relates, not done she feigns; and mingles Truth with
    Lyes.
Talk is her business; and her chief delight
To tell of Prodigies, and cause affright.

---

[1] *This whole line is taken from Sir John Denham.* (Dryden's note)

Hence to deep *Acheron* they take their way;
Whose troubled Eddies, thick with Ooze and Clay,
Are whirl'd aloft, and in *Cocytus* lost:
There *Charon* stands, who rules the dreary Coast:
A sordid God; down from his hoary Chin
A length of Beard descends; uncomb'd, unclean:
His Eyes, like hollow Furnaces on Fire:
A Girdle, foul with grease, binds his obscene Attire.
He spreads his Canvas, with his Pole he steers;
The Freights of flitting Ghosts in his thin Bottom bears.
He look'd in Years; yet in his Years were seen
A youthful Vigour, and Autumnal green.
An Airy Crowd came rushing where he stood;
Which fill'd the Margin of the fatal Flood.
Husbands and Wives, Boys and unmarry'd Maids;
And mighty Heroes more Majestick Shades.
And Youths, intomb'd before their Fathers Eyes,
With hollow Groans, and Shrieks, and feeble Cries:
Thick as the Leaves in Autumn strow the Woods:
Or Fowls, by Winter forc'd, forsake the Floods,
And wing their hasty flight to happier Lands: ⎫
Such, and so thick, the shiv'ring Army stands: ⎬
And press for passage with extended hands. ⎭

JOHN DRYDEN Of the Pythagorean Philosophy, from Ovid's   **1700**
Metamorphoses, Book Fifteen

Time was, when we were sow'd, and just began
From some few fruitful Drops, the promise of a Man;
Then Nature's Hand (fermented as it was)
Moulded to Shape the soft, coagulated Mass;
And when the little Man was fully form'd,
The breathless Embryo with a Spirit warm'd;
But when the Mothers Throws begin to come,
The Creature, pent within the narrow Room,
Breaks his blind Prison, pushing to repair
His stiffled Breath, and draw the living Air;
Cast on the Margin of the World he lies,
A helpless Babe, but by Instinct he cries.

He next essays to walk, but downward press'd
On four Feet imitates his Brother Beast:
By slow degrees he gathers from the Ground
His Legs, and to the rowling Chair is bound;
Then walks alone; a Horseman now become
He rides a Stick, and travels round the Room:
In time he vaunts among his youthful Peers,
Strong-bon'd, and strung with Nerves, in pride of Years,
He runs with Mettle his first merry Stage,   ⎫
Maintains the next abated of his Rage,   ⎬
But manages his Strength, and spares his Age.   ⎭
Heavy the third, and stiff, he sinks apace,
And tho' 'tis down-hill all, but creeps along the Race.
Now sapless on the verge of Death he stands,
Contemplating his former Feet, and Hands;
And *Milo*-like, his slacken'd Sinews sees,   ⎫
And wither'd Arms, once fit to cope with *Hercules*, ⎬
Unable now to shake, much less to tear the Trees. ⎭
   So *Helen* wept when her too faithful Glass
Reflected to her Eyes the ruins of her Face:
Wondring what Charms her Ravishers cou'd spy,
To force her twice, or ev'n but once enjoy!
   Thy Teeth, devouring Time, thine, envious Age,
On Things below still exercise your Rage:
With venom'd Grinders you corrupt your Meat,
And then at lingring Meals, the Morsels eat.

(. . .)

All Things are alter'd, nothing is destroy'd,
The shifted Scene, for some new Show employ'd.
   Then to be born, is to begin to be
Some other Thing we were not formerly:
And what we call to Die, is not t'appear,
Or be the Thing that formerly we were.
Those very Elements which we partake,
Alive, when Dead some other Bodies make:
Translated grow, have Sense, or can Discourse,
But Death on deathless Substance has no force.
   That Forms are chang'd I grant; that nothing can
Continue in the Figure it began:
The Golden Age, to Silver was debas'd:
To Copper that; our Mettal came at last.
   The Face of Places, and their Forms decay;

And that is solid Earth, that once was Sea:
Seas in their turn retreating from the Shore,
Make solid Land, what Ocean was before;
And far from Strands are Shells of Fishes found,
And rusty Anchors fix'd on Mountain-Ground:
And what were Fields before, now wash'd and worn
By falling Floods from high, to Valleys turn,
And crumbling still descend to level Lands;
And Lakes, and trembling Bogs are barren Sands:
And the parch'd Desart floats in Streams unknown;
Wondring to drink of Waters not her own.

JOHN DRYDEN *from* The Secular Masque

Enter Janus.

JANUS
CHRONOS, *Chronos*, mend thy Pace,
An hundred times the rowling Sun
Around the Radiant Belt has run
In his revolving Race.
Behold, behold, the Goal in sight,
Spread thy Fans, and wing thy flight.

Enter Chronos, *with a Scythe in his hand, and a great Globe on his
Back, which he sets down at his entrance.*

CHRONOS
Weary, weary of my weight,
Let me, let me drop my Freight,
    And leave the World behind.
I could not bear
Another Year
The Load of Human-Kind.

(...)

JANUS
Then our Age was in it's Prime,
CHRONOS
Free from Rage.

And free from Crime.

MOMUS

A very Merry, Dancing, Drinking,
Laughing, Quaffing, and unthinking Time.

CHORUS OF ALL

Then our Age was in it's Prime,
Free from Rage, and free from Crime,
A very Merry, Dancing, Drinking,
Laughing, Quaffing, and unthinking Time.

(. . .)

CHRONOS

The World was then so light,
I scarcely felt the Weight;
Joy rul'd the Day, and Love the Night.
But since the Queen of Pleasure left the Ground,
   I faint, I lag,
   And feebly drag
The pond'rous Orb around.

MOMUS

All, all, of a piece throughout;
(Pointing to DIANA.)
Thy Chase had a Beast in View;
(to MARS.)
Thy Wars brought nothing about;
(to VENUS.)
Thy Lovers were all untrue.

JANUS

'Tis well an Old Age is out,

CHRONOS

And time to begin a New.

CHORUS OF ALL

All, all, of a piece throughout;
Thy Chase had a Beast in View;
Thy Wars brought nothing about;
Thy Lovers were all untrue.
'Tis well an Old Age is out,
And time to begin a New.

SIR CHARLES SEDLEY Song

Phillis, let's shun the common Fate,
And let our Love ne'r turn to Hate;
I'll dote no longer than I can,
Without being call'd a faithless Man.
When we begin to want Discourse,
And Kindness seems to tast of Force,
As freely as we met, we'll part,
Each one possest of their own Heart.
Thus whilst rash Fools themselves undo;
We'll Game, and give off Savers too;
So equally the Match we'll make,
Both shall be glad to draw the Stake.
A Smile of thine shall make my Bliss,
I will enjoy thee in a Kiss;
If from this Height our Kindness fall,
We'll bravely scorn to Love at all:
If thy Affection first decay,
I will the Blame on Nature lay.
Alas, what Cordial can remove
The hasty Fate of dying Love?
Thus we will all the World excel
In Loving, and in Parting well.

ANNE FINCH, COUNTESS OF WINCHILSEA *from* The Spleen. A Pindaric Poem

O'er me alas! thou dost too much prevail:
    I feel thy Force, whilst I against thee rail;
I feel my Verse decay, and my crampt Numbers fail.
Thro' thy black Jaundice I all Objects see,
    As Dark, and Terrible as Thee,
My Lines decry'd, and my Employment thought
An useless Folly, or presumptuous Fault:
    Whilst in the *Muses* Paths I stray,
Whilst in their Groves, and by their secret Springs
My Hand delights to trace unusual Things,
And deviates from the known, and common way;

Nor will in fading Silks compose
    Faintly th'inimitable *Rose*,
Fill up an ill-drawn *Bird*, or paint on Glass
The *Sov'reign's* blurr'd and undistinguish'd Face,
The threatning *Angel*, and the speaking *Ass*.

Patron thou art to ev'ry gross Abuse,
    The sullen *Husband's* feign'd Excuse,
When the ill Humour with his Wife he spends,
And bears recruited Wit, and Spirits to his Friends.
    The Son of *Bacchus* pleads thy Pow'r,
      As to the Glass he still repairs,
      Pretends but to remove thy Cares,
Snatch from thy Shades one gay, and smiling Hour,
And drown thy Kingdom in a purple Show'r.
When the *Coquette*, whom ev'ry Fool admires,
    Wou'd in Variety be Fair,
    And, changing hastily the Scene
    From Light, Impertinent, and Vain,
Assumes a soft, a melancholy Air,
And of her Eyes rebates the wand'ring Fires,
The careless Posture, and the Head reclin'd,
    The thoughtful, and composed Face,
Proclaiming the withdrawn, the absent Mind,
Allows the Fop more liberty to gaze,
Who gently for the tender Cause inquires;
The Cause, indeed, is a Defect in Sense,
Yet is the *Spleen* alledg'd, and still the dull Pretence.

    But these are thy fantastic Harms,
    The Tricks of thy pernicious Stage,
Which do the weaker Sort engage;
Worse are the dire Effects of thy more pow'rful Charms.
    By Thee *Religion*, all we know,
    That shou'd enlighten here below,
    Is veil'd in Darkness, and perplext
With anxious Doubts, with endless Scruples vext,
And some Restraint imply'd from each perverted Text.
    Whilst *Touch* not, *Taste* not, what is freely giv'n,
Is but thy niggard Voice, disgracing bounteous Heav'n,
    From Speech restrain'd, by thy Deceits abus'd,
    To Deserts banish'd, or in Cells reclus'd,

Mistaken Vot'ries to the Pow'rs Divine,
   Whilst they a purer Sacrifice design,
Do but the *Spleen* obey, and worship at thy Shrine.
   In vain to chase thee ev'ry Art we try,
   In vain all Remedies apply,
   In vain the *Indian* Leaf infuse,
   Or the parch'd *Eastern* Berry bruise;
Some pass, in vain, those Bounds, and nobler Liquors use.
   Now *Harmony*, in vain, we bring,
   Inspire the Flute, and touch the String.
   From Harmony no help is had;
Musick but soothes thee, if too sweetly sad,
And if too light, but turns thee gayly Mad.
     Tho' the Physician greatest Gains,
     Altho' his growing Wealth he sees
     Daily increas'd by Ladies Fees,
   Yet dost thou baffle all his studious Pains.
    Not skilful *Lower* thy Source cou'd find,
   Or thro' the well-dissected Body trace
   The secret, the mysterious ways,
By which thou dost surprise, and prey upon the Mind.
   Tho' in the Search, too deep for Humane Thought,
    With unsuccessful Toil he wrought,
  'Till thinking Thee to've catch'd, Himself by thee was caught,
   Retain'd thy Pris'ner, thy acknowledg'd Slave,
  And sunk beneath thy Chain to a lamented Grave.

WILLIAM CONGREVE Song   1704

Pious *Celinda* goes to Pray'rs,
   If I but ask the Favor;
And yet the tender Fool's in Tears,
   When she believes I'll leave her.

Wou'd I were free from this Restraint,
   Or else had Hopes to win her;
Wou'd she cou'd make of me a Saint,
   Or I of her a Sinner.

WILLIAM CONGREVE A Hue and Cry after Fair Amoret

Fair *Amoret* is gone astray;
   Pursue and seek her, ev'ry Lover;
I'll tell the Signs, by which you may
   The wand'ring Shepherdess discover.

Coquet and Coy at once her Air,
   Both study'd, tho both seem neglected;
Careless she is with artful Care,
   Affecting to seem unaffected.

With Skill her Eyes dart ev'ry Glance,
   Yet change so soon you'd ne'er suspect 'em;
For she'd persuade they wound by Chance,
   Tho' certain Aim and Art direct 'em.

She likes herself, yet others hates
   For that which in herself she prizes;
And while she laughs at them, forgets
   She is the Thing that she despises.

1706 ISAAC WATTS The Day of Judgement. An Ode. Attempted in English Sapphick

When the fierce *North* Wind with his airy Forces
Rears up the *Baltick* to a foaming Fury;
And the red Lightning, with a Storm of Hail comes
                        Rushing amain down.

How the poor Sailors stand amaz'd and tremble!
While the hoarse Thunder, like a bloody Trumpet,
Roars a loud Onset to the gaping Waters
                        Quick to devour them.

Such shall the Noise be, and the wild Disorder,
(If Things Eternal may be like these Earthly)
Such the dire Terror when the great Archangel
                        Shakes the Creation;

Tears the strong Pillars of the Vault of Heaven,
Breaks up old Marble, the Repose of Princes;
See the Graves open, and the Bones arising,
                    Flames all around em!

Hark, the shrill Outcries of the guilty Wretches!
Lively bright Horror, and amazing Anguish,
Stare thro their Eye-lids, while the living Worm lies
                    Gnawing within them.

Thoughts, like old Vultures, prey upon their Heart-strings,
And the Smart twinges, when the Eye beholds the
Lofty Judge frowning, and a Flood of Vengeance
                    Rolling afore him.

Hopeless Immortals! how they scream and shiver
While Devils push them to the Pit wide-yawning
Hideous and gloomy to receive them headlong
                    Down to the Centre.

Stop here, my Fancy: (all away, ye horrid
Doleful Ideas,) come, arise to *JESUS*,
How he sits God-like! and the Saints around him
                    Thron'd, yet adoring!

O may I sit there when he comes Triumphant,
Dooming the Nations! then ascend to Glory,
While our *Hosannas* all along the Passage
                    Shout the Redeemer.

ISAAC WATTS Crucifixion to the World by the Cross of Christ   **1707**
Gal. vi.14

When I survey the wond'rous Cross
Where the young Prince of Glory dy'd,
My richest Gain I count but Loss,
And pour Contempt on all my Pride.

Forbid it, Lord, that I should boast
Save in the Death of *Christ* my God;
All the vain things that charm me most,
I sacrifice them to his Blood.

See from his Head, his Hands, his Feet,
Sorrow and Love flow mingled down;
Did e'er such Love and Sorrow meet?
Or Thorns compose so rich a Crown?

His dying Crimson like a Robe
Spreads o'er his Body on the Tree,
Then am I dead to all the Globe,
And all the Globe is dead to me.

Were the whole Realm of Nature mine,
That were a Present far too small;
Love so amazing, so divine
Demand my Soul, my Life, my All.

1709   ANNE FINCH, COUNTESS OF WINCHILSEA **Adam Pos'd**

Cou'd our First Father, at his toilsome Plough,
Thorns in his Path, and Labour on his Brow,
Cloath'd only in a rude, unpolish'd Skin,
Cou'd he a vain Fantastick Nymph have seen,
5   In all her Airs, in all her antick Graces,
Her various Fashions, and more various Faces;
How had it pos'd that Skill, which late assign'd
Just Appellations to Each several Kind!
A right Idea of the Sight to frame;
10   T'have guest from what New Element she came;
T'have hit the wav'ring Form, or giv'n this Thing a Name.

MATTHEW PRIOR   **An Ode**

The Merchant, to secure his Treasure,
   Conveys it in a borrow'd Name:
EUPHELIA serves to grace my Measure;
   But CLOE is my real Flame.

7 *pos'd* puzzled

My softest Verse, my darling Lyre
    Upon EUPHELIA's Toylet lay;
When CLOE noted her Desire,
    That I should sing, that I should play.

My Lyre I tune, my Voice I raise;
    But with my Numbers mix my Sighs:
And whilst I sing EUPHELIA's Praise,
    I fix my Soul on CLOE's Eyes.

Fair CLOE blush'd: EUPHELIA frown'd:
    I sung and gaz'd: I play'd and trembl'd:
And VENUS to the LOVES around
    Remark'd, how ill We all dissembl'd.

AMBROSE PHILLIPS   A Winter-Piece

To the Earl of Dorset
                      Copenhagen, March 9, 1709

From Frozen Climes, and Endless Tracks of Snow,
From Streams that Northern Winds forbid to flow;
What Present shall the Muse to *Dorset* bring;
Or how, so near the Pole, attempt to sing?
The hoary Winter here conceals from Sight
All pleasing Objects that to Verse invite.
The Hills and Dales, and the Delightful Woods,
The Flowry Plains, and Silver Streaming Floods,
By Snow disguis'd, in bright Confusion lye,
And with one dazling Waste fatigue the Eye.
  No gentle breathing Breeze prepares the Spring,
No Birds within the Desart Region sing.
The Ships unmov'd the boist'rous Winds defy,
While rattling Chariots o'er the Ocean fly.
The vast *Leviathan* wants Room to play,
And spout his Waters in the Face of Day.
The starving Wolves along the main Sea prowl,
And to the Moon in Icy Valleys howl.
For many a shining League the level Main
Here spreads it self into a Glassy Plain:
There solid Billows of enormous Size,
Alpes of green Ice, in wild Disorder rise.

And yet but lately have I seen, e'en here,
The Winter in a lovely Dress appear.
E'er yet the Clouds let fall the treasur'd Snow,
Or Winds begun thro' hazy Skies to blow.
At Ev'ning a keen Eastern Breeze arose;
And the descending Rain unsullied froze.
Soon as the silent Shades of Night withdrew,
The ruddy Morn disclos'd at once to View
The Face of Nature in a rich Disguise,
And brighten'd ev'ry Object to my Eyes.
For ev'ry Shrub, and ev'ry Blade of Grass,
And ev'ry pointed Thorn, seem'd wrought in Glass.
In Pearls and Rubies rich the Hawthorns show,
While thro' the Ice the Crimson Berries glow.
The thick-sprung Reeds the watry Marshes yield,
Seem polish'd Lances in a hostile Field.
The Stag in limpid Currents with Surprize
Sees Chrystal Branches on his Forehead rise.
The spreading Oak, the Beech, and tow'ring Pine,
Glaz'd over, in the freezing Æther shine.
The frighted Birds the rattling Branches shun,
That wave and glitter in the distant Sun.
    When if a sudden Gust of Wind arise,
The brittle Forrest into Atoms flies:
The crackling Wood beneath the Tempest bends,
And in a spangled Show'r the Prospect ends.
Or if a Southern Gale the Region warm,
And by Degrees unbind the Wintry Charm;
The Traveller a miry Country sees,
And Journeys sad beneath the dropping Trees.
    Like some deluded Peasant, *Merlin* leads
Thro' fragrant Bow'rs, and thro' delicious Meads;
While here inchanted Gardens to him rise,
And airy Fabricks there attract his Eyes,
His wand'ring Feet the Magick Paths pursue;
And while he thinks the fair Illusion true,
The trackless Scenes disperse in fluid Air,
And Woods and Wilds, and thorny Ways appear:
A tedious Road the weary Wretch returns,
And, as He goes, the transient Vision mourns.

JONATHAN SWIFT A Description of a *City Shower*

Careful Observers may fortel the Hour
(By sure Prognosticks) when to dread a Show'r:
While Rain depends, the pensive Cat gives o'er
Her Frolicks, and pursues her Tail no more.
Returning Home at Night, you'll find the Sink
Strike your offended Sense with double Stink.
If you be wise, then go not far to Dine,
You spend in Coach-hire more than save in Wine.
A coming Show'r your shooting Corns presage,
Old Aches throb, your hollow Tooth will rage.
Sauntring in Coffee-house is *Dulman* seen;
He damns the Climate, and complains of Spleen.

Mean while the South rising with dabbled Wings,
A Sable Cloud a-thwart the Welkin flings,
That swill'd more Liquor than it could contain,
And like a Drunkard gives it up again.
Brisk *Susan* whips her Linen from the Rope,
While the first drizzling Show'r is born aslope,
Such is that Sprinkling which some careless Quean
Flirts on you from her Mop, but not so clean.
You fly, invoke the Gods; then turning, stop
To rail; she singing, still whirls on her Mop.
Not yet, the Dust had shun'd th' unequal Strife,
But aided by the Wind, fought still for Life;
And wafted with its Foe by violent Gust,
'Twas doubtful which was Rain, and which was Dust.
Ah! where must needy Poet seek for Aid,
When Dust and Rain at once his Coat invade;
Sole Coat, where Dust cemented by the Rain,
Erects the Nap, and leaves a cloudy Stain.

Now in contiguous Drops the Flood comes down,
Threat'ning with Deluge this *Devoted* Town.
To Shops in Crouds the dagled Females fly,
Pretend to cheapen Goods, but nothing buy.
The Templer spruce, while ev'ry Spout's a-broach,
Stays till 'tis fair, yet seems to call a Coach.
The tuck'd-up Sempstress walks with hasty Strides,
While Streams run down her oil'd Umbrella's Sides.

Here various Kinds by various Fortunes led,
Commence Acquaintance underneath a Shed.
Triumphant Tories, and desponding Whigs,
Forget their Fewds, and join to save their Wigs.
Box'd in a Chair the Beau impatient sits,
While Spouts run clatt'ring o'er the Roof by Fits;
And ever and anon with frightful Din
The Leather sounds, he trembles from within.
So when *Troy* Chair-men bore the Wooden Steed,
Pregnant with *Greeks*, impatient to be freed,
(Those Bully *Greeks*, who, as the Moderns do,
Instead of paying Chair-men, run them thro'.)
Laoco'n struck the Outside with his Spear,
And each imprison'd Hero quak'd for Fear.

Now from all Parts the swelling Kennels flow,
And bear their Trophies with them as they go:
Filth of all Hues and Odours seem to tell
What Streets they sail'd from, by the Sight and Smell.
They, as each Torrent drives, with rapid Force
From *Smithfield*, or St. *Pulchre*'s shape their Course,
And in huge Confluent join at *Snow-Hill* Ridge,
Fall from the *Conduit* prone to *Holborn-Bridge*.
Sweepings from Butchers Stalls, Dung, Guts, and Blood,
Drown'd Puppies, stinking Sprats, all drench'd in Mud,
Dead Cats and Turnip-Tops come tumbling down the Flood.

1712   JOSEPH ADDISON Ode

The Spacious Firmament on high,
With all the blue Etherial Sky,
And spangled Heav'ns, a Shining Frame,
Their great Original proclaim:
Th' unwearied Sun, from Day to Day,
Does his Creator's Power display,
And publishes to every Land
The Work of an Almighty Hand.

Soon as the Evening Shades prevail,
The Moon takes up the wondrous Tale,
And nightly to the listning Earth
Repeats the Story of her Birth:

Whilst all the Stars that round her burn,
And all the Planets, in their turn,
Confirm the Tidings as they rowl,
And spread the Truth from Pole to Pole.

What though, in solemn Silence, all
Move round the dark terrestrial Ball?
What tho' nor real Voice nor Sound
Amid their radiant Orbs be found?
In Reason's Ear they all rejoice,
And utter forth a glorious Voice,
For ever singing, as they shine,
'The Hand that made us is Divine.'

ANNE FINCH, COUNTESS OF WINCHILSEA
A Nocturnal Reverie

1713

In such a *Night*, when every louder Wind
Is to its distant Cavern safe confin'd;
And only gentle *Zephyr* fans his Wings,
And lonely *Philomel*, still waking, sings;
Or from some Tree, fam'd for the *Owl's* delight,
She, hollowing clear, directs the Wand'rer right:
In such a *Night*, when passing Clouds give place,
Or thinly vail the Heav'ns mysterious Face;
When in some River, overhung with Green,
The waving Moon and trembling Leaves are seen;
When freshen'd Grass now bears it self upright,
And makes cool Banks to pleasing Rest invite,
Whence springs the *Woodbind*, and the *Bramble*-Rose,
And where the sleepy *Cowslip* shelter'd grows;
Whilst now a paler Hue the *Foxglove* takes,
Yet checquers still with Red the dusky brakes
When scatter'd *Glow-worms*, but in Twilight fine,
Shew trivial Beauties watch their Hour to shine;
Whilst *Salisb'ry* stands the Test of every Light,
In perfect Charms, and perfect Virtue bright:
When Odours, which declin'd repelling Day,
Thro' temp'rate Air uninterrupted stray;
When darken'd Groves their softest Shadows wear,
And falling Waters we distinctly hear;

When thro' the Gloom more venerable shows
Some ancient Fabrick, awful in Repose,
While Sunburnt Hills their swarthy Looks conceal,
And swelling Haycocks thicken up the Vale:
When the loos'd *Horse* now, as his Pasture leads,
Comes slowly grazing thro' th' adjoining Meads,
Whose stealing Pace, and lengthen'd Shade we fear,
Till torn up Forage in his Teeth we hear:
When nibbling *Sheep* at large pursue their Food,
And unmolested Kine rechew the Cud;
When *Curlews* cry beneath the Village-walls,
And to her straggling Brood the *Partridge* calls;
Their shortliv'd Jubilee the Creatures keep,
Which but endures, whilst Tyrant-*Man* do's sleep;
When a sedate Content the Spirit feels,
And no fierce Light disturb, whilst it reveals;
But silent Musings urge the Mind to seek
Something, too high for Syllables to speak;
Till the free Soul to a compos'dness charm'd,
Finding the Elements of Rage disarm'd,
O'er all below a solemn Quiet grown,
Joys in th' inferiour World, and thinks it like her Own:
In such a *Night* let Me abroad remain,
Till Morning breaks, and All's confus'd again;
Our Cares, our Toils, our Clamours are renew'd,
Or Pleasures, seldom reach'd, again pursu'd.

1714   SAMUEL JONES The Force of Love

When Cleomira disbelieves
Her shepherd, when he swears he lives
Or dies i' th' smiles or frowns she gives,

The echo mourns him to the plain,
And pity moves in ev'ry swain,
And makes the nymphs partake his pain.

But pity and the fair ones prove,
When Cleomira hates his love,
Like strange embraces to a dove.

For Cleomira's hate can turn
Fresh youth and beauty to an urn:
Death sure than it's much easier borne!

But Cleomira's love can bless,
And turn t' a grove a wilderness,
A dungeon to a pleasant place.

Without it, Pleasure's self will show
The ghost of sorrow haunting you
In all the blissful things you do:

And with it, Nature's self may fall,
Old Night and Death frail men appal,
Without dismaying you at all.

ALEXANDER POPE *from* The Rape of the Lock

from Canto I

Sol thro' white Curtains shot a tim'rous Ray,
And op'd those Eyes that must eclipse the Day;
Now Lapdogs give themselves the rowzing Shake,
And sleepless Lovers, just at Twelve, awake:
Thrice rung the Bell, the Slipper knock'd the Ground,
And the press'd Watch return'd a silver Sound.
Belinda still her downy Pillow prest,
Her Guardian *Sylph* prolong'd the balmy Rest.
'Twas he had summon'd to her silent Bed
The Morning-Dream that hover'd o'er her Head.
A Youth more glitt'ring than a *Birth-night Beau*,
(That ev'n in Slumber caus'd her Cheek to glow)
Seem'd to her Ear his winning Lips to lay,
And thus in Whispers said, or seem'd to say.
    Fairest of Mortals, thou distinguish'd Care
Of thousand bright Inhabitants of Air!
If e'er one Vision touch'd thy infant Thought,
Of all the Nurse and all the Priest have taught,
Of airy Elves by Moonlight Shadows seen,
The silver Token, and the circled Green,
Or Virgins visited by Angel-Pow'rs,
With Golden Crowns and Wreaths of heav'nly Flow'rs,

Hear and believe! thy own Importance know,
Nor bound thy narrow Views to Things below.
Some secret Truths from Learned Pride conceal'd,
To Maids alone and Children are reveal'd:
What tho' no Credit doubting Wits may give?
The Fair and Innocent shall still believe.
Know then, unnumber'd Spirits round thee fly,
The light *Militia* of the lower Sky;
These, tho' unseen, are ever on the Wing,
Hang o'er the *Box*, and hover round the *Ring*.
Think what an Equipage thou hast in Air,
And view with scorn *Two Pages* and a *Chair*.
As now your own, our Beings were of old,
And once inclos'd in Woman's beauteous Mold;
Thence, by a soft Transition, we repair
From earthly Vehicles to these of Air.
Think not, when Woman's transient Breath is fled,
That all her Vanities at once are dead:
Succeeding Vanities she still regards,
And tho' she plays no more, o'erlooks the Cards.
Her Joy in gilded Chariots, when alive,
And Love of *Ombre*, after Death survive.
For when the Fair in all their Pride expire,
To their first Elements their Souls retire:
The Sprights of fiery Termagants in Flame
Mount up, and take a *Salamander*'s Name.
Soft yielding Minds to Water glide away,
And sip with *Nymphs*, their Elemental Tea.
The graver Prude sinks downward to a *Gnome*,
In search of Mischief still on Earth to roam.
The light Coquettes in *Sylphs* aloft repair,
And sport and flutter in the Fields of Air.

Know farther yet; Whoever fair and chaste
Rejects Mankind, is by some *Sylph* embrac'd:
For Spirits, freed from mortal Laws, with ease
Assume what Sexes and what Shapes they please.
What guards the Purity of melting Maids,
In Courtly Balls, and Midnight Masquerades,
Safe from the treach'rous Friend, the daring Spark,
The Glance by Day, the Whisper in the Dark;
When kind Occasion prompts their warm Desires,
When Musick softens, and when Dancing fires?

'Tis but their *Sylph*, the wise Celestials know,
Tho' *Honour* is the Word with Men below.

(...)

Of these am I, who thy Protection claim,
A watchful Sprite, and *Ariel* is my Name.
Late, as I rang'd the Crystal Wilds of Air,
In the clear Mirror of thy ruling *Star*
I saw, alas! some dread Event impend,
Ere to the Main this Morning Sun descend.
But Heav'n reveals not what, or how, or where:
Warn'd by thy *Sylph*, oh Pious Maid beware!
This to disclose is all thy Guardian can.
Beware of all, but most beware of Man!
   He said; when *Shock*, who thought she slept too long,
Leapt up, and wak'd his Mistress with his Tongue.
'Twas then *Belinda*! if Report say true,
Thy Eyes first open'd on a *Billet-doux*;
Wounds, Charms, and *Ardors*, were no sooner read,
But all the Vision vanish'd from thy Head.
   And now, unveil'd, the *Toilet* stands display'd,
Each Silver Vase in mystic Order laid.
First, rob'd in White, the Nymph intent adores
With Head uncover'd, the *Cosmetic* Pow'rs.
A heav'nly Image in the Glass appears,
To that she bends, to that her Eyes she rears;
Th'inferior Priestess, at her Altar's side,
Trembling, begins the sacred Rites of Pride.
Unnumber'd Treasures ope at once, and here
The various Off'rings of the World appear;
From each she nicely culls with curious Toil,
And decks the Goddess with the glitt'ring Spoil.
This Casket *India's* glowing Gems unlocks,
And all *Arabia* breathes from yonder Box.
The Tortoise here and Elephant unite,
Transform'd to *Combs*, the speckled and the white.
Here Files of Pins extend their shining Rows,
Puffs, Powders, Patches, Bibles, Billet-doux.
Now awful Beauty puts on all its Arms;
The Fair each moment rises in her Charms,
Repairs her Smiles, awakens ev'ry Grace,
And calls forth all the Wonders of her Face;

Sees by Degrees a purer Blush arise,
And keener Lightnings quicken in her Eyes.
The busy *Sylphs* surround their darling Care;
These set the Head, and those divide the Hair,
Some fold the Sleeve, while others plait the Gown;
And *Betty*'s prais'd for Labours not her own.

from **Canto V**

Then grave *Clarissa* graceful wav'd her Fan;
Silence ensu'd, and thus the Nymph began.
    Say, why are Beauties prais'd and honour'd most,
The wise Man's Passion, and the vain Man's Toast?
Why deck'd with all that Land and Sea afford,
Why Angels call'd, and Angel-like ador'd?
Why round our Coaches crowd the white-glov'd Beaus,
Why bows the Side-box from its inmost Rows?
How vain are all these Glories, all our Pains,
Unless good Sense preserve what Beauty gains:
That Men may say, when we the Front-box grace,
Behold the first in Virtue, as in Face!
Oh! if to dance all Night, and dress all Day,
Charm'd the Small-pox, or chas'd old Age away;
Who would not scorn what Huswife's Cares produce,
Or who would learn one earthly Thing of Use?
To patch, nay ogle, might become a Saint,
Nor could it sure be such a Sin to paint.
But since, alas! frail Beauty must decay,
Curl'd or uncurl'd, since Locks will turn to grey,
Since painted, or not painted, all shall fade,
And she who scorns a Man, must die a Maid;
What then remains, but well our Pow'r to use,
And keep good Humour still whate'er we lose?
And trust me, Dear! good Humour can prevail,
When Airs, and Flights, and Screams, and Scolding fail.
Beauties in vain their pretty Eyes may roll;
Charms strike the Sight, but Merit wins the Soul.
    So spoke the Dame, but no Applause ensu'd;
Belinda frown'd, *Thalestris* call'd her Prude.

JOHN GAY *from* **Trivia: Or The Art of Walking the Streets of London** **1716**

[Of the Weather]

O roving Muse, recal that wond'rous Year,   An Episode of the
When Winter reign'd in bleak *Britannia*'s Air;   Great Frost
When hoary *Thames*, with frosted Oziers crown'd,
Was three long Moons in icy Fetters bound.
The Waterman, forlorn along the Shore,
Pensive reclines upon his useless Oar,
Sees harness'd Steeds desert the stony Town;
And wander Roads unstable, not their own:
Wheels o'er the harden'd Waters smoothly glide,
And rase with whiten'd Tracks the slipp'ry Tide.
Here the fat Cook piles high the blazing Fire,
And scarce the Spit can turn the Steer entire.
Booths sudden hide the *Thames*, long Streets appear,
And num'rous Games proclaim the crouded Fair.
So when a Gen'ral bids the martial Train
Spread their Encampment o'er the spatious Plain;
Thick-rising Tents a Canvas City build,
And the loud Dice resound thro' all the Field.
'Twas here the Matron found a doleful Fate:
Let Elegiac Lay the Woe relate,
Soft, as the Breath of distant Flutes, at Hours,
When silent Ev'ning closes up the Flow'rs;
Lulling, as falling Water's hollow noise;
Indulging Grief, like *Philomela*'s Voice.

   Doll ev'ry Day had walk'd these treach'rous Roads;
Her Neck grew warpt beneath autumnal Loads
Of various Fruit; she now a Basket bore,
That Head, alas! shall Basket bear no more.
Each Booth she frequent past, in quest of Gain,
And Boys with pleasure heard her shrilling Strain.
Ah *Doll!* all Mortals must resign their Breath,
And Industry it self submit to Death!
The cracking Crystal yields, she sinks, she dyes,
Her Head, chopt off, from her lost Shoulders flies:
Pippins she cry'd, but Death her Voice confounds,
And Pip-Pip-Pip along the Ice resounds.

So when the *Thracian* Furies *Orpheus* tore,
And left his bleeding Trunk deform'd with Gore,
His sever'd Head floats down the silver Tide,
His yet warm Tongue for his lost Consort cry'd;
Eurydice, with quiv'ring Voice, he mourn'd,
And *Heber*'s Banks *Eurydice* return'd.

But now the western Gale the Flood unbinds,   A Thaw
And black'ning Clouds move on with warmer Winds,
The wooden Town its frail Foundation leaves,
And *Thames*' full Urn rolls down his plenteous Waves:
From ev'ry Penthouse streams the fleeting Snow,
And with dissolving Frost the Pavements flow.

Experienc'd Men, inur'd to City Ways,   How to Know the
Need not the *Calendar* to count their Days.   Days of the Week
When through the Town, with slow and solemn Air,
Led by the Nostril, walks the muzled Bear;
Behind him moves majestically dull,
The Pride of *Hockley-hole*, the surly Bull;
Learn hence the Periods of the Week to name,
Mondays and *Thursdays* are the Days of Game.

When fishy Stalls with double Store are laid;
The golden-belly'd Carp, the broad-finn'd Maid,
Red-speckled Trouts, the Salmon's silver Joul,
The jointed Lobster, and unscaly Soale,
And luscious 'Scallops, to allure the Tastes
Of rigid Zealots to delicious Fasts;
Wednesdays and *Fridays* you'll observe from hence,
Days, when our Sires were doom'd to Abstinence.

When dirty Waters from Balconies drop,
And dextrous Damsels twirle the sprinkling Mop,
And cleanse the spatter'd Sash, and scrub the Stairs;
Know *Saturday*'s conclusive Morn appears.

1717   ALEXANDER POPE **Epistle to Miss Blount, on Her Leaving the
Town, after the Coronation**

As some fond virgin, whom her mother's care
Drags from the town to wholsom country air,
Just when she learns to roll a melting eye,
And hear a spark, yet think no danger nigh;
From the dear man unwilling she must sever,
Yet takes one kiss before she parts for ever:

Thus from the world fair *Zephalinda* flew,
Saw others happy, and with sighs withdrew;
Not that their pleasures caus'd her discontent,
She sigh'd not that They stay'd, but that She went.

She went, to plain-work, and to purling brooks,
Old-fashion'd halls, dull aunts, and croaking rooks,
She went from Op'ra, park, assembly, play,
To morning walks, and pray'rs three hours a day;
To pass her time 'twixt reading and Bohea,
To muse, and spill her solitary Tea,
Or o'er cold coffee trifle with the spoon,
Count the slow clock, and dine exact at noon;
Divert her eyes with pictures in the fire,
Hum half a tune, tell stories to the squire;
Up to her godly garret after sev'n,
There starve and pray, for that's the way to heav'n.

Some Squire, perhaps, you take delight to rack;
Whose game is Whisk, whose treat a toast in sack,
Who visits with a gun, presents you birds,
Then gives a smacking buss, and cries – No words!
Or with his hound comes hollowing from the stable,
Makes love with nods, and knees beneath a table;
Whose laughs are hearty, tho' his jests are coarse,
And loves you best of all things – but his horse.

In some fair evening, on your elbow laid,
You dream of triumphs in the rural shade;
In pensive thought recall the fancy'd scene,
See Coronations rise on ev'ry green;
Before you pass th' imaginary sights
Of Lords, and Earls, and Dukes, and garter'd Knights;
While the spread Fan o'ershades your closing eyes;
Then give one flirt, and all the vision flies.
Thus vanish sceptres, coronets, and balls,
And leave you in lone woods, or empty walls.

So when your slave, at some dear, idle time,
(Not plagu'd with headachs, or the want of rhime)
Stands in the streets, abstracted from the crew,
And while he seems to study, thinks of you:
Just when his fancy points your sprightly eyes,
Or sees the blush of soft *Parthenia* rise,
Gay pats my shoulder, and you vanish quite;
Streets, chairs, and coxcombs rush upon my sight;
Vext to be still in town, I knit my brow,
Look sow'r, and hum a tune – as you may now.

MATTHEW PRIOR A Better Answer to Cloe Jealous

Dear Cloe, how blubber'd is that pretty Face?
   Thy Cheek all on Fire, and Thy Hair all uncurl'd:
Pr'ythee quit this Caprice; and (as Old FALSTAF says)
   Let Us e'en talk a little like Folks of This World.

How can'st Thou presume, Thou hast leave to destroy
   The Beauties, which VENUS but lent to Thy keeping?
Those Looks were design'd to inspire Love and Joy:
   More ord'nary Eyes may serve People for weeping.

To be vext at a Trifle or two that I writ,
   Your Judgment at once, and my Passion You wrong:
You take that for Fact, which will scarce be found Wit:
   Od's Life! must One swear to the Truth of a Song?

What I speak, my fair CLOE, and what I write, shews
   The Diff'rence there is betwixt Nature and Art:
I court others in Verse; but I love Thee in Prose:
   And They have my Whimsies; but Thou hast my Heart.

The God of us Verse-men (You know Child) the SUN,
   How after his Journeys He sets up his Rest:
If at Morning o'er Earth 'tis his Fancy to run;
   At Night he reclines on his THETIS's Breast.

So when I am weary'd with wand'ring all Day;
   To Thee my Delight in the Evening I come:
No Matter what Beauties I saw in my Way:
   They were but my Visits; but Thou art my Home.

Then finish, Dear CLOE, this Pastoral War;
   And let us like HORACE and LYDIA agree:
For Thou art a Girl as much brighter than Her,
   As He was a Poet sublimer than Me.

MATTHEW PRIOR The Lady Who Offers Her Looking-Glass to Venus

Venus, take my Votive Glass:
　Since I am not what I was;
What from this Day I shall be,
　VENUS, let Me never see.

MATTHEW PRIOR A True Maid

No, no; for my Virginity,
　When I lose that, says ROSE, I'll dye:
Behind the Elmes, last Night, cry'd DICK,
　ROSE, were You not extreamly Sick?

ISAAC WATTS Man Frail, and God Eternal   1719

Our God, our Help in Ages past,
　Our Hope for Years to come,
Our Shelter from the Stormy Blast,
　And our eternal Home.

Under the Shadow of thy Throne
　Thy Saints have dwelt secure;
Sufficient is thine Arm alone,
　And our Defence is sure.

Before the Hills in order stood,
　Or Earth receiv'd her Frame,
From everlasting Thou art God,
　To endless Years the same.

Thy Word commands our Flesh to Dust,
　Return, ye Sons of Men:
All Nations rose from Earth at first,
　And turn to Earth again.

A thousand Ages in thy Sight
　　Are like an Evening gone;
Short as the Watch that ends the Night
　　Before the rising Sun.

The busy Tribes of Flesh and Blood
　　With all their Lives and Cares
Are carried downwards by thy Flood,
　　And lost in following Years.

Time like an ever-rolling Stream
　　Bears all its Sons away;
They fly forgotten as a Dream
　　Dies at the opening Day.

Like flow'ry Fields the Nations stand
　　Pleas'd with the Morning-light;
The Flowers beneath the Mower's Hand
　　Ly withering e'er 'tis Night.

Our God, our Help in Ages past,
　　Our Hope for Years to come,
Be thou our Guard while Troubles last,
　　And our eternal Home.

1720　　ALLAN RAMSAY Polwart on the Green

At Polwart on the Green
If you'll meet me the Morn,
Where Lasses do conveen
To dance about the Thorn
5　　A kindly Welcome you shall meet
Frae her wha likes to view
A Lover and a Lad complete,
The Lad and Lover you.

Let dorty Dames say Na,
10　　As lang as e'er they please,
Seem caulder than the Sna',
While inwardly they bleeze;

9 *dorty* haughty; 12 *bleeze* blaze;

But I will frankly shaw my Mind,
And yield my Heart to thee;
15 Be ever to the Captive kind,
That langs na to be free.

At *Polwart* on the Green,
Among the new mawn Hay,
With Sangs and Dancing keen
20 We'll pass the heartsome Day,
At Night if Beds be o'er thrang laid,
And thou be twin'd of thine,
Thou shalt be welcome, my dear Lad,
To take a Part of mine.

JOHN GAY *My Own EPITAPH*

Life is a jest; and all things show it,
   I thought so once; but now I know it.

ALEXANDER POPE *To Mr. Gay,* Who Wrote Him a Congratulatory Letter on the Finishing His House

1722

Ah friend, 'tis true – this truth you lovers know –
In vain my structures rise, my gardens grow,
In vain fair Thames reflects the double scenes
Of hanging mountains, and of sloping greens:
Joy lives not here; to happier seats it flies,
And only dwells where WORTLEY casts her eyes.
What are the gay parterre, the chequer'd shade,
The morning bower, the ev'ning colonade,
But soft recesses of uneasy minds,
To sigh unheard in, to the passing winds?
So the struck deer in some sequester'd part
Lies down to die, the arrow at his heart;
There, stretch'd unseen in coverts hid from day,
Bleeds drop by drop, and pants his life away.

21 *o'er thrang* overcrowded; 22 *twin'd of* parted from

JONATHAN SWIFT A Satirical Elegy. On the Death of a Late Famous General

His Grace! impossible! what dead!
Of old age too, and in his bed!
And could that Mighty Warrior fall?
And so inglorious, after all!
Well, since he's gone, no matter how,
The last loud trump must wake him now:
And, trust me, as the noise grows stronger,
He'd wish to sleep a little longer.
And could he be indeed so old
As by the news-papers we're told?
Threescore, I think, is pretty high;
'Twas time in conscience he should die.
This world he cumber'd long enough;
He burnt his candle to the snuff;
And that's the reason, some folks think,
He left behind *so great a stink*.
Behold his funeral appears,
Nor widow's sighs, nor orphan's tears,
Wont at such times each heart to pierce,
Attend the progress of his herse.
But what of that, his friends may say,
He had those honours in his day.
True to his profit and his pride,
He made them weep before he dy'd.

    Come hither, all ye empty things,
Ye bubbles rais'd by breath of Kings;
Who float upon the tide of state,
Come hither, and behold your fate.
Let pride be taught by this rebuke,
How very mean a thing's a Duke;
From all his ill-got honours flung,
Turn'd to that dirt from whence he sprung.

                                             (1764)

WILLIAM DIAPER *from the Greek of* Oppian's Halieuticks

[The Loves of the Fishes]

   Strange the Formation of the *Eely* Race,
That know no Sex, yet love the close Embrace.
Their folded Lengths they round each other twine.
Twist am'rous Knots, and slimy Bodies joyn;
Till the close Strife brings off a frothy Juice,
The Seed that must the wriggling Kind produce.
Regardless They their future Offspring leave,
But porous Sands the spumy Drops receive,
That genial Bed impregnates all the Heap,
And little *Eelets* soon begin to creep.
Half-Fish, Half-Slime they try their doubtful strength,
And slowly trail along their wormy Length.
What great Effects from slender Causes flow!
Congers their Bulk to these Productions owe:
The Forms, which from the frothy Drop began.
Stretch out immense, and eddy all the Main.

   Justly might Female *Tortoises* complain,
To whom Enjoyment is the greatest Pain,
They dread the Tryal, and foreboding hate
The growing Passion of the cruel Mate.
He amorous pursues, They conscious fly
Joyless Caresses, and resolv'd deny.
Since partial Heav'n has thus restrain'd the Bliss,
The Males they welcome with a closer Kiss,
Bite angry, and reluctant Hate declare.
The *Tortoise*-Courtship is a State of War.
Eager they fight, but with unlike Design,
Males to obtain, and Females to decline.
The conflict lasts, till these by Strength o'ercome
All sorrowing yield to the resistless Doom.
Not like a Bride, but pensive Captive, led
To the loath'd Duties of an hated Bed.

(. . .)

Then from the teeming Filth, and putrid Heap,
Like Summer Grubs, the little *Slime-Fish* creep.
Devour'd by All the passive Curse they own,
Opprest by ev'ry Kind, but injure none.

Harmless they live, nor murd'rous Hunger know,
But to themselves their mutual Pleasures owe;
Each other lick, and the close Kiss repeat;
Thus loving thrive, and praise the luscious Treat.
When they in Throngs a safe Retirement seek,
Where pointed Rocks the rising Surges break,
Or where calm Waters in their Bason sleep,
While chalky Cliffs o'erlook the shaded Deep,
The Seas all gilded o'er the Shoal betray,
And shining Tracks inform their wand'ring Way.

　　As when soft Snows, brought down by Western Gales,
Silent descend and spread on all the Vales;
Add to the Plains, and on the Mountains shine,
While in chang'd Fields the starving Cattle pine;
Nature bears all one Face, looks coldly bright,
And mourns her lost Variety in White,
Unlike themselves the Objects glare around,
And with false Rays the dazzled Sight confound:
So, when the Shoal appears, the changing Streams
Lose their Sky-blew, and shine with silver Gleams.

1724　　LADY MARY WORTLEY MONTAGU Epistle from Mrs.
Y[onge] to her Husband

Think not this Paper comes with vain pretence
To move your Pity, or to mourn th'offence.
Too well I know that hard Obdurate Heart;
No soft'ning mercy there will take my part,
Nor can a Woman's Arguments prevail,
When even your Patron's wise Example fails,
But this last privelege I still retain,
Th'Oppress'd and Injur'd allways may complain.

　　Too, too severely Laws of Honour bind
The Weak Submissive Sex of Woman-kind.
If sighs have gain'd or force compell'd our Hand,
Deceiv'd by Art, or urg'd by stern Command,
What ever Motive binds the fatal Tye,
The Judging World expects our Constancy.

　　Just Heaven! (for sure in Heaven does Justice reign
Thô Tricks below that sacred Name prophane)
To you appealing I submit my Cause
Nor fear a Judgment from Impartial Laws.

All Bargains but conditional are made,
The Purchase void, the Creditor unpaid,
Defrauded Servants are from Service free,
A wounded Slave regains his Liberty.
For Wives ill us'd no remedy remains,
To daily Racks condemn'd, and to eternal Chains.

From whence is this unjust Distinction grown?
Are we not form'd with Passions like your own?
Nature with equal Fire our Souls endu'd,
Our Minds as Haughty, and as warm our blood,
O're the wide World your pleasures you persue,
The Change is justify'd by something new;
But we must sigh in Silence – and be true.
Our Sexes Weakness you expose and blame
(Of every Prattling Fop the common Theme),
Yet from this Weakness you suppose is due
Sublimer Virtu than your Cato knew.
Had Heaven design'd us Tryals so severe,
It would have form'd our Tempers then to bear.

And I have born (o what have I not born!)
The pang of Jealousie, th'Insults of Scorn.
Weary'd at length, I from your sight remove,
And place my Future Hopes, in Secret Love.
In the gay Bloom of glowing Youth retir'd,
I quit the Woman's Joy to be admir'd,
With that small Pension your hard Heart allows,
Renounce your Fortune, and release your Vows.
To Custom (thô unjust) so much is due,
I hide my Frailty, from the Public view.
My Conscience clear, yet sensible of Shame,
My Life I hazard, to preserve my Fame.
And I prefer this low inglorious State,
To vile dependance on the Thing I hate –
– But you persue me to this last retreat.
Dragg'd into Light, my tender Crime is shown
And every Circumstance of Fondness known.
Beneath the Shelter of the Law you stand,
And urge my Ruin with a cruel Hand.
While to my Fault thus rigidly severe,
Tamely Submissive to the Man you fear.

This wretched Out-cast, this abandonn'd Wife,
Has yet this Joy to sweeten shamefull Life,
By your mean Conduct, infamously loose,
You are at once m'Accuser, and Excuse.

Let me be damn'd by the Censorious Prude
(Stupidly Dull, or Spiritually Lewd),
My hapless Case will surely Pity find
From every Just and reasonable Mind,
When to the final Sentence I submit,
The Lips condemn me, but their Souls acquit.

No more my Husband, to your Pleasures go,
The Sweets of your recover'd Freedom know,
Go; Court the brittle Freindship of the Great,
Smile at his Board, or at his Levée wait
And when dismiss'd to Madam's Toilet fly,
More than her Chambermaids, or Glasses, Lye,
Tell her how Young she looks, how heavenly fair,
Admire the Lillys, and the Roses, there,
Your high Ambition may be gratify'd,
Some Cousin of her own be made your Bride,
And you the Father of a Glorious Race
Endow'd with Ch—l's strength and Low – r's face.

(1972)

1725   EDWARD YOUNG *from* Love of Fame. Satire V

The *languid* lady next appears in state,
Who was not born to carry her own weight;
She lolls, reels, staggers, 'till some foreign aid
To her own stature lifts the feeble maid.
Then, if ordain'd to so *severe* a doom,
She, by just stages, *journeys* round the room:
But knowing her own weakness, she despairs
To scale the *Alps* – that is, ascend the *stairs*.
My fan! let others say who laugh at toil;
Fan! hood! glove! scarf! is her *laconick* style.
And that is spoke with such a dying fall,
That *Betty* rather *sees*, than *hears* the call:
The motion of her lips, and meaning eye
Piece out the Idea her faint words deny.
O listen with attention most profound!
Her voice is but the shadow of a sound.
And help! O help! her spirits are so dead,
One hand scarce lifts the other to her head.

If, there, a stubborn pin it triumphs o'er,
She pants! she sinks away! and is no more.
Let the robust, and the gygantick *carve*,
Life is not worth so much, she'd rather *starve*;
But *chew* she must herself, ah cruel fate!
That *Rosalinda* can't by *proxy* eat.

HENRY CAREY *from* **Namby-Pamby.** *A Panegyric on the New Versification, Address'd to A— P—, Esq.*

Naughty Paughty Jack-a-Dandy,
Stole a Piece of Sugar Candy
From the Grocer's Shoppy-Shop,
And away did hoppy-hop.

  All ye poets of the age,
All ye witlings of the stage,
Learn your jingles to reform,
Crop your numbers and conform.
Let your little verses flow
Gently, sweetly, row by row;
Let the verse the subject fit,
Little subject, little wit.
Namby-Pamby is your guide,
Albion's joy, Hibernia's pride.
Namby-Pamby, pilly-piss,
Rhimy-pim'd on Missy Miss
Tartaretta Tartaree,
From the navel to the knee;
That her father's gracy grace
Might give him a placy place.

  He no longer writes of Mammy
Andromache and her lammy,
Hanging-panging at the breast
Of a matron most distress'd.
Now the venal poet sings
Baby clouts and baby things,
Baby dolls and baby houses,
Little misses, little spouses,
Little playthings, little toys,
Little girls and little boys.

As an actor does his part,
So the nurses get by heart
Namby-Pamby's little rhimes,
Little jingle, little chimes,
To repeat to missy-miss,
Piddling ponds of pissy-piss;
Cacking-packing like a lady,
Or bye-bying in the crady.
Namby-Pamby ne'er will die
While the nurse sings lullaby.
Namby-Pamby's doubly mild,
Once a man, and twice a child;
To his hanging sleeves restor'd,
Now he foots it like a lord;
Now he pumps his little wits,
Sh . . . ing writes, and writing sh . . . ts,
All by little tiny bits.
Now methinks I hear him say,
Boys and girls, come out to play!
Moon do's shine as bright as day.

1726   **ABEL EVANS On Sir John Vanbrugh (The Architect). An
Epigrammatical Epitaph**

Under this stone, Reader, survey
Dead Sir John Vanbrugh's House of Clay.
Lie heavy on him, Earth! for he
Laid many Heavy Loads on thee!

JOHN DYER *from* **Grongar Hill**

Now, I gain the Mountain's Brow,
What a Landskip lies below!
No Clouds, no Vapours intervene,
But the gay, the open Scene
Does the Face of Nature show,
In all the Hues of Heaven's Bow!
And, swelling to embrace the Light,
Spreads around beyond the Sight.

Old Castles on the Cliffs arise,
Proudly tow'ring in the Skies!
Rushing from the Woods, the Spires
Seem from hence ascending Fires!
Half his Beams *Apollo* sheds,
On the yellow Mountain-Heads!
Gilds the Fleeces of the Flocks;
And glitters on the broken Rocks!

Below me Trees unnumber'd rise,
Beautiful in various Dies:
The gloomy Pine, the Poplar blue,
The yellow Beech, the sable Yew,
The slender Firr, that taper grows,
The sturdy Oak with broad-spread Boughs.
And beyond the purple Grove,
Haunt of *Phillis*, Queen of Love!
Gawdy as the op'ning Dawn,
Lies a long and level Lawn,
On which a dark Hill, steep and high,
Holds and charms the wand'ring Eye!
Deep are his Feet in *Towy*'s Flood,
His Sides are cloath'd with waving Wood,
And antient Towers crown his Brow,
That cast an awful Look below;
Whose ragged Walls the Ivy creeps,
And with her Arms from falling keeps.
So both a Safety from the Wind
On mutual Dependance find.

'Tis now the Raven's bleak Abode;
'Tis now th' Apartment of the Toad;
And there the Fox securely feeds;
And there the pois'nous Adder breeds,
Conceal'd in Ruins, Moss and Weeds:
While, ever and anon, there falls,
Huge heaps of hoary moulder'd Walls.
Yet Time has seen, that lifts the low,
And level lays the lofty Brow,
Has seen this broken Pile compleat,
Big with the Vanity of State;
But transient is the Smile of Fate!
A little Rule, a little Sway,
A Sun-beam in a Winter's Day
Is all the Proud and Mighty have,
Between the Cradle and the Grave.

438] **1726**

ALLAN RAMSAY *from the Latin of Horace*

What young Raw Muisted Beau Bred at his Glass
now wilt thou on a Rose's Bed Carress
wha niest to thy white Breasts wilt thow intice
with hair unsnooded and without thy Stays
5   O Bonny Lass wi' thy Sweet Landart Air
how will thy fikle humour gie him care
when e'er thou takes the fling strings, like the wind
that Jaws the Ocean – thou'lt disturb his Mind
when thou looks smirky kind and claps his cheek
10   to poor friends then he'l hardly look or speak
the Coof belivest-na but Right soon he'll find
thee Light as Cork and wavring as the Wind
on that slid place where I 'maist brake my Bains
to be a warning I Set up twa Stains
15   that nane may venture there as I hae done
unless wi' frosted Nails he Clink his Shoon.

                       (1961)

JAMES THOMSON *from* Summer

['Forenoon. Summer Insects Described']

            The daw,
The rook, and magpie, to the grey-grown oaks
(That the calm village in their verdant arms,
Sheltering, embrace) direct their lazy flight;
Where on the mingling boughs they sit embowered
All the hot noon, till cooler hours arise.
Faint underneath the household fowls convene;
And, in a corner of the buzzing shade,
The house-dog with the vacant greyhound lies
Out-stretched and sleepy. In his slumbers one
Attacks the nightly thief, and one exults

1 *Muisted* perfumed with musk; 5 *Landart* rustic; 7 *takes the fling strings* goes into a sulk; 11 *Coof* fool; 13 *'maist* almost; 16 *Clink his Shoon* stud his shoes

O'er hill and dale; till, wakened by the wasp,
They starting snap. Nor shall the muse disdain
To let the little noisy summer-race
Live in her lay and flutter through her song:
Not mean though simple – to the sun allied,
From him they draw their animating fire.

Waked by his warmer ray, the reptile young
Come winged abroad, by the light air upborne,
Lighter, and full of soul. From every chink
And secret corner, where they slept away
The wintry storms, or rising from their tombs
To higher life, by myriads forth at once
Swarming they pour, of all the varied hues
Their beauty-beaming parent can disclose.
Ten thousand forms, ten thousand different tribes
People the blaze. To sunny waters some
By fatal instinct fly; where on the pool
They sportive wheel, or, sailing down the stream,
Are snatched immediate by the quick-eyed trout
Or darting salmon. Through the green-wood glade
Some love to stray; there lodged, amused, and fed
In the fresh leaf. Luxurious, others make
The meads their choice, and visit every flower
And every latent herb: for the sweet task
To propagate their kinds, and where to wrap
In what soft beds their young, yet undisclosed,
Employs their tender care. Some to the house,
The fold, and dairy hungry bend their flight;
Sip round the pail, or taste the curdling cheese:
Oft, inadvertent, from the milky stream
They meet their fate; or, weltering in the bowl,
With powerless wings around them wrapt, expire.

(...)

Resounds the living surface of the ground:
Nor undelightful is the ceaseless hum
To him who muses through the woods at noon,
Or drowsy shepherd as he lies reclined,
With half-shut eyes, beneath the floating shade
Of willows grey, close-crowding o'er the brook,
Gradual from these what numerous kinds descend,
Evading even the microscopic eye!
Full Nature swarms with life; one wondrous mass

Of animals, or atoms organized
Waiting the vital breath when Parent-Heaven
Shall bid his spirit blow. The hoary fen
In putrid streams emits the living cloud
Of pestilence. Through subterranean cells,
Where searching sunbeams scarce can find a way,
Earth animated heaves. The flowery leaf
Wants not its soft inhabitants. Secure
Within its winding citadel the stone
Holds multitudes. But chief the forest boughs,
That dance unnumbered to the playful breeze,
The downy orchard, and the melting pulp
Of mellow fruit the nameless nations feed
Of evanescent insects. Where the pool
Stands mantled o'er with green, invisible
Amid the floating verdure millions stray.
Each liquid too, whether it pierces, soothes,
Inflames, refreshes, or exalts the taste,
With various forms abounds. Nor is the stream
Of purest crystal, nor the lucid air,
Though one transparent vacancy it seems,
Void of their unseen people. These, concealed
By the kind art of forming Heaven, escape
The grosser eye of man: for, if the worlds
In worlds inclosed should on his senses burst,
From cates ambrosial and the nectared bowl
He would abhorrent turn; and in dead night,
When Silence sleeps o'er all, be stunned with noise.

['Night. Summer Meteors. A Comet']

Among the crooked lanes, on every hedge,
The glow-worm lights his gem; and, through the dark,
A moving radiance twinkles. Evening yields
The world to Night; not in her winter robe
Of massy Stygian woof, but loose arrayed
In mantle dun. A faint erroneous ray,
Glanced from the imperfect surfaces of things,
Flings half an image on the straining eye;
While wavering woods, and villages, and streams,
And rocks, and mountain-tops that long retained
The ascending gleam are all one swimming scene,
Uncertain if beheld. Sudden to heaven
Thence weary vision turns; where, leading soft

The silent hours of love, with purest ray
Sweet Venus shines; and, from her genial rise,
When daylight sickens, till it springs afresh,
Unrivalled reigns, the fairest lamp of night.
As thus the effulgence tremulous I drink,
With cherished gaze, the lambent lightnings shoot
Across the sky, or horizontal dart
In wondrous shapes – by fearful murmuring crowds
Portentous deemed. Amid the radiant orbs
That more than deck, that animate the sky,
The life-infusing suns of other worlds,
Lo! from the dread immensity of space
Returning with accelerated course,
The rushing comet to the sun descends;
And, as he sinks below the shading earth,
With awful train projected o'er the heavens,
The guilty nations tremble. But, above
Those superstitious horrors that enslave
The fond sequacious herd, to mystic faith
And blind amazement prone, the enlightened few,
Whose godlike minds philosophy exalts,
The glorious stranger hail. They feel a joy
Divinely great; they in their powers exult,
That wondrous force of thought, which mounting spurns
This dusky spot, and measures all the sky;
While, from his far excursion through the wilds
Of barren ether, faithful to his time,
They see the blazing wonder rise anew,
In seeming terror clad, but kindly bent,
To work the will of all-sustaining love –
From his huge vapoury train perhaps to shake
Reviving moisture on the numerous orbs
Through which his long ellipsis winds, perhaps
To lend new fuel to declining suns,
To light up worlds, and feed the eternal fire.

1727   JOHN GAY *from* **Fables**

The *Wild Boar* and the *Ram*

Against an elm a sheep was ty'd,
   The butcher's knife in blood was dy'd;
The patient flock, in silent fright,
From far beheld the horrid sight;
A savage Boar, who near them stood,
Thus mock'd to scorn the fleecy brood.
   All cowards should be serv'd like you.
See, see, your murd'rer is in view;
With purple hands and reeking knife
He strips the skin yet warm with life:
Your quarter'd sires, your bleeding dams,
The dying bleat of harmless lambs
Call for revenge. O stupid race!
The heart that wants revenge is base.
   I grant, an ancient Ram replys,
We bear no terror in our eyes,
Yet think us not of soul so tame,
Which no repeated wrongs inflame,
Insensible of ev'ry ill,
Because we want thy tusks to kill.
Know, Those who violence pursue
Give to themselves the vengeance due,
For in these massacres they find
The two chief plagues that waste mankind.
Our skin supplys the wrangling bar,
It wakes their slumbring sons to war,
And well revenge may rest contented,
Since drums and parchment were invented.

THOMAS SHERIDAN Tom Punsibi's Letter to *Dean Swift*

When to my House you come dear Dean,
Your humble Friend to entertain,
Thro' Dirt and Mire, along the Street,
You find no Scraper for your Feet:

At this, you storm, and stamp, and swell,
Which serves to clean your Feet as well:
By steps ascending to the Hall,
All torn to rags, with Boys and Ball.
Fragments of Lime about the Floor,
A sad uneasy Parlor Door,
Besmear'd with Chalk, and nick'd with Knives,
(A Pox upon all careless Wives!)
Are the next Sights you must expect;
But do not think they're my Neglect:
Ah! that these Evils were the worst,
The Parlor still is further curst;
To enter there if you advance,
If in you get, it is by Chance:
How oft in Turns have you and I
Said thus – let me, – no, let me try,
This Turn will open it I engage,
You push me from it in a Rage!
Twisting, turning, trifling, rumbling,
Scolding, stairing, fretting, grumbling;
At length it opens, in we go,
How glad are we to find it so!
Conquests, thro' Pains and Dangers, please,
Much more than those we gain with Ease.

If you're dispos'd to take a Seat,
The Moment that it feels your Weight,
Nay take the best in all the Room,
Out go it's Legs, and down you come.
Hence learn and see old Age display'd,
When Strength and Vigour are decay'd,
The Joints relaxing with their Years;
Then what are mortal Men, but Chairs.

The Windows next offend your Sight,
Now they are dark, now they are light,
The Shuts a working too and fro,
With quick Succession come and go.
So have I seen in human Life,
The same in an uneasy Wife,
By Turns, affording Joy and Sorrow,
Devil to day, and Saint to morrow.

Now to the Fire, if such there be,
But now 'tis rather Smoke you see:
In vain you seek the Poker's Aid,
Or Tongs, for they are both mislaid.

The Bellice, take their batter'd Nose,
Will serve for Poker, I suppose,
Now you begin to rake, – a-lack!
The Grate is tumbled from its Back:
The Coals upon the Hearth are laid,
Stay Sir, I'll run and call the Maid;
She'll make our Fire again compleat,
She knows the Humour of the Grate.

Deux take your Maid and you together,
This is cold Comfort in cold Weather.

Now all you see is well again,
Come be in Humour Mr. Dean,
And take the Bellice, use them so –
These Bellice were not made to blow,
Their leathern Lungs are in Decay;
They can't e'en puff the Smoke away. –

And is your Rev'rence vex'd at that?
Get up a-God's Name, take your Hat –
Hang 'em say I, that have no Shift;
Come blow the Fire good Doctor *Swift*. –

Trifles like these, if they must teize you,
Pox take those Fools that strive to please you,
Therefore no longer be a Quarr'ler,
Either with me, Sir, or my Parlor.

If you can relish ought of mine,
A Bit of Meat, a Glass of Wine,
You're welcome to't and you shall fare,
As well as dining with the May'r.
You saucy Scab, you tell me so,
You Booby Face, I'd have you know,
I'd rather see your Things in Order,
Than dine in state with the *Recorder*.

For Water I must keep a Clutter,
Then chide your Wife for stinking Butter
Or getting such a Deal of Meat,
As if you'd half the Town to eat;
That Wife of yours the Devil's in her –
I've told her of this Way of Dinner,
Five hundred Times, but all in vain,
Here comes a Leg of Beef again!

O that! that Wife of yours wou'd burst –
Get out and serve the Lodgers first,

Pox take them all for me – I fret
So much, I cannot eat my Meat.
You know I'd rather have a Slice –
I know Dear Sir, you're always Nice;
You'll see them bring it in a Minute,
Here comes the Plate, and Slices in it.
Therefore sit down and take your Place,
Do you fall to, and I'll say Grace.

HENRY CAREY A Lilliputian Ode on their Majesties' Accession

Smile, smile,
Blest isle!
Grief past,
At last,
Halcyon
Comes on.

New King,
Bells ring;
New Queen,
Blest scene!
Britain
Again
Revives
And thrives;
Fear flies,
Stocks rise;
Wealth flows,
Art grows.
Strange pack
Sent back;
Own folks
Crack jokes.
Those out
May pout;
Those in
Will grin.

Great, small,
Pleas'd all.

God send
No end
To line
Divine
Of George and Caroline.

1728   JOHN GAY *from* The Beggar's Opera

MACHEATH
Were I laid on *Greenland*'s Coast,
    And in my Arms embrac'd my Lass;
Warm amidst eternal Frost,
    Too soon the Half Year's Night would pass.
POLLY
Were I sold on *Indian* Soil,
    Soon as the burning Day was clos'd,
I could mock the sultry Toil,
    When on my Charmer's Breast repos'd.
MACHEATH
And I would love you all the Day,
POLLY
Every Night would kiss and play,
MACHEATH
If with me you'd fondly stray
POLLY
Over the Hills and far away.

1731   ALEXANDER POPE *from* An Epistle to Burlington

At Timon's Villa let us pass a day,
Where all cry out, 'What sums are thrown away!'
So proud, so grand, of that stupendous air,
Soft and Agreeable come never there.
Greatness, with Timon, dwells in such a draught
As brings all Brobdignag before your thought.
To compass this, his building is a Town,
His pond an Ocean, his parterre a Down:
Who but must laugh, the Master when he sees,
A puny insect, shiv'ring at a breeze!

Lo, what huge heaps of littleness around!
The whole, a labour'd Quarry above ground.
Two Cupids squirt before: a Lake behind
Improves the keenness of the Northern wind.
His Gardens next your admiration call,
On ev'ry side you look, behold the Wall!
No pleasing Intricacies intervene,
No artful wildness to perplex the scene;
Grove nods at grove, each Alley has a brother,
And half the platform just reflects the other.
The suff'ring eye inverted Nature sees,
Trees cut to Statues, Statues thick as trees,
With here a Fountain, never to be play'd,
And there a Summer-house, that knows no shade;
Here Amphitrite sails thro' myrtle bowers;
There Gladiators fight, or die, in flow'rs;
Un-water'd see the drooping sea-horse mourn,
And swallows roost in Nilus' dusty Urn.

My Lord advances with majestic mien,
Smit with the mighty pleasure, to be seen:
But soft – by regular approach – not yet –
First thro' the length of yon hot Terrace sweat,
And when up ten steep slopes you've dragg'd your thighs,
Just at his Study-door he'll bless your eyes.

His Study! with what Authors is it stor'd?
In Books, not Authors, curious is my Lord;
To all their dated Backs he turns you round,
These Aldus printed, those Du Suëil has bound.
Lo some are Vellom, and the rest as good
For all his Lordship knows, but they are Wood.
For Locke or Milton 'tis in vain to look,
These shelves admit not any modern book.

And now the Chapel's silver bell you hear,
That summons you to all the Pride of Pray'r:
Light quirks of Musick, broken and uneven,
Make the soul dance upon a Jig to Heaven.
On painted Cielings you devoutly stare,
Where sprawl the Saints of Verrio or Laguerre,
On gilded clouds in fair expansion lie,
And bring all Paradise before your eye.
To rest, the Cushion and soft Dean invite,
Who never mentions Hell to ears polite.

But hark! the chiming Clocks to dinner call;
A hundred footsteps scrape the marble Hall:

The rich Buffet well-colour'd Serpents grace,
And gaping Tritons spew to wash your face.
Is this a dinner? this a Genial room?
No, 'tis a Temple, and a Hecatomb.
A solemn Sacrifice, perform'd in state,
You drink by measure, and to minutes eat.
So quick retires each flying course, you'd swear
Sancho's dread Doctor and his Wand were there.
Between each Act the trembling salvers ring,
From soup to sweet-wine, and God bless the King.
In plenty starving, tantaliz'd in state,
And complaisantly help'd to all I hate,
Treated, caress'd, and tir'd, I take my leave,
Sick of his civil Pride from Morn to Eve;
I curse such lavish cost, and little skill,
And swear no Day was ever past so ill.

Yet hence the Poor are cloath'd, the Hungry fed;
Health to himself, and to his Infants bread
The Lab'rer bears: What his hard Heart denies,
His charitable Vanity supplies.

Another age shall see the golden Ear
Imbrown the Slope, and nod on the Parterre,
Deep Harvests bury all his pride has plann'd,
And laughing Ceres re-assume the land.

JONATHAN SWIFT The Day of Judgement

With a Whirl of Thought oppress'd,
I sink from Reverie to Rest.
An horrid Vision seiz'd my Head,
I saw the Graves give up their Dead.
Jove, arm'd with Terrors, burst the Skies,
And Thunder roars, and Light'ning flies!
Amaz'd, confus'd, its Fate unknown,
The World stands trembling at his Throne.
While each pale Sinner hangs his Head,
Jove, nodding, shook the Heav'ns, and said,
'Offending Race of Human Kind,
By Nature, Reason, Learning, blind;
You who thro' Frailty step'd aside,
And you who never fell – *thro' Pride*;

You who in different Sects have shamm'd,
And come to see each other damn'd;
(So some Folks told you, but they knew
No more of Jove's Designs than you)
The World's mad Business now is o'er,
And I resent these Pranks no more.
I to such Blockheads set my Wit!
I damn such Fools! – Go, go, you're bit.'

JONATHAN SWIFT An *Epigram* on *Scolding*

Great Folks are of a finer Mold;
Lord! how politely they can scold;
While a coarse *English* Tongue will itch,
For Whore and Rogue; and Dog and Bitch.

(1746)

JONATHAN SWIFT *Mary* the Cook-Maid's Letter to Dr. **1732**
Sheridan

Well; if ever I saw such another Man since my Mother bound my
    Head,
You a Gentleman! marry come up, I wonder where you were bred?
I am sure such Words does not become a Man of your Cloth,
I would not give such Language to a Dog, faith and troth.
Yes; you call'd my Master a Knave: Fie Mr. *Sheridan*, 'tis a Shame
For a Parson, who shou'd know better Things, to come out with
    such a Name.
Knave in your Teeth, Mr. *Sheridan*, 'tis both a Shame and a Sin,
And the Dean my Master is an honester Man than you and all your
    kin:
He has more Goodness in his little Finger, than you have in your
    whole Body,
My Master is a parsonable Man, and not a spindle-shank'd hoddy
    doddy.
And now whereby I find you would fain make an Excuse,
Because my Master one Day in anger call'd you Goose.

Which, and I am sure I have been his Servant four Years since
    October,
And he never call'd me worse than Sweet-heart drunk or sober:
Not that I know his Reverence was ever concern'd to my knowledge,
Tho' you and your Come-rogues keep him out so late in your wicked
    Colledge.

You say you will eat Grass on his Grave: a Christian eat Grass!
Whereby you now confess your self to be a Goose or an Ass:
But that's as much as to say, that my Master should die before ye,
Well, well, that's as God pleases, and I don't believe that's a true
    Story,
And so say I told you so, and you may go tell my Master; what care
    I?
And I don't care who knows it, 'tis all one to *Mary*.
Every body knows, that I love to tell Truth and shame the Devil,
I am but a poor Servant, but I think Gentle folks should be civil.
Besides, you found fault with our Vittles one Day that you was here,
I remember it was upon a *Tuesday*, of all Days in the Year.
And *Saunders* the Man says, you are always jesting and mocking,
Mary said he, (one Day, as I was mending my Master's Stocking,)
My Master is so fond of that Minister that keeps the School;
I thought my Master a wise Man, but that Man makes him a Fool.
Saunders said I, I would rather than a Quart of Ale,
He would come into our Kitchin, and I would pin a Dishclout to his
    Tail.
And now I must go, and get *Saunders* to direct this Letter,
For I write but a sad Scrawl, but my Sister *Marget* she writes better.
Well, but I must run and make the Bed before my Master comes
    from Pray'rs,
And see now, it strikes ten, and I hear him coming up Stairs:
Whereof I cou'd say more to your Verses, if I could write written
    hand,
And so I remain in a civil way, your Servant to command,

                                   Mary.

1733   LADY MARY WORTLEY MONTAGU [A Summary of Lord
Lyttleton's 'Advice to a lady']

Be plain in Dress and sober in your Diet;
In short my Dearee, kiss me, and be quiet.

ALEXANDER POPE *from* An Epistle to Bathurst

[Sir Balaam]

Where London's column, pointing at the skies,
Like a tall bully, lifts the head, and lyes;
There dwelt a Citizen of sober fame,
A plain good man, and Balaam was his name;
Religious, punctual, frugal, and so forth;
His word would pass for more than he was worth.
One solid dish his week-day meal affords,
An added pudding solemniz'd the Lord's:
Constant at Church, and Change; his gains were sure,
His givings rare, save farthings to the poor.
    The Dev'l was piqu'd such saintship to behold,
And long'd to tempt him like good Job of old:
But Satan now is wiser than of yore,
And tempts by making rich, not making poor.
    Rouz'd by the Prince of Air, the whirlwinds sweep
The surge, and plunge his Father in the deep;
Then full against his Cornish lands they roar,
And two rich ship-wrecks bless the lucky shore.
    Sir Balaam now, he lives like other folks,
He takes his chirping pint, and cracks his jokes:
'Live like yourself,' was soon my Lady's word;
And lo! two puddings smoak'd upon the board.
    Asleep and naked as an Indian lay,
An honest factor stole a Gem away:
He pledg'd it to the knight; the knight had wit,
So kept the Diamond, but the rogue was bit.
Some scruple rose, but thus he eas'd his thought,
'I'll now give six-pence where I gave a groat,
'Where once I went to church, I'll now go twice –
'And am so clear too of all other vice.'
    The Tempter saw his time; the work he ply'd;
Stocks and Subscriptions pour on ev'ry side,
'Till all the Daemon makes his full descent,
In one abundant show'r of Cent. per Cent.,
Sinks deep within him, and possesses whole,
Then dubs Director, and secures his soul.
    Behold Sir Balaam, now a man of spirit,
Ascribes his gettings to his parts and merit,

What late he call'd a Blessing, now was Wit,
And God's good Providence, a lucky Hit.
Things change their titles, as our manners turn:
His Compting-house employ'd the Sunday-morn:
Seldom at Church ('twas such a busy life)
But duly sent his family and wife.
There (so the Dev'l ordain'd) one Christmas-tide
My good old Lady catch'd a cold, and dy'd.

A Nymph of Quality admires our Knight;
He marries, bows at Court, and grows polite:
Leaves the dull Cits, and joins (to please the fair)
The well-bred cuckolds in St. James's air:
First, for his Son a gay Commission buys,
Who drinks, whores, fights, and in a duel dies:
His daughter flaunts a Viscount's tawdry wife;
She bears a Coronet and P-x for life.
In Britain's Senate he a seat obtains,
And one more Pensioner St. Stephen gains.
My Lady falls to play; so bad her chance,
He must repair it; takes a bribe from France;
The House impeach him; Coningsby harangues;
The Court forsake him, and Sir Balaam hangs:
Wife, son, and daughter, Satan, are thy own,
His wealth, yet dearer, forfeit to the Crown:
The Devil and the King divide the prize,
And sad Sir Balaam curses God and dies.

GEORGE FAREWELL   Quaerè

Whether at Doomsday (tell, ye reverend wise)
My friend Priapus with myself shall rise?

1734   ### JONATHAN SWIFT A Beautiful Young Nymph Going to Bed

Corinna, Pride of *Drury-Lane*,
For whom no Shepherd sighs in vain;
Never did *Covent Garden* boast
So bright a batter'd, strolling Toast;
No drunken Rake to pick her up,
No Cellar where on Tick to sup;

Returning at the Midnight Hour;
Four Stories climbing to her Bow'r;
Then, seated on a three-legg'd Chair,
Takes off her artificial Hair:
Now, picking out a Crystal Eye,
She wipes it clean, and lays it by.
Her Eye-Brows from a Mouse's Hyde,
Stuck on with Art on either Side,
Pulls off with Care, and first displays 'em,
Then in a Play-Book smoothly lays 'em.
Now dextrously her Plumpers draws,
That serve to fill her hollow Jaws.
Untwists a Wire; and from her Gums
A Set of Teeth completely comes.
Pulls out the Rags contriv'd to prop
Her flabby Dugs and down they drop.
Proceeding on, the lovely Goddess
Unlaces next her Steel-Rib'd Bodice;
Which by the Operator's Skill,
Press down the Lumps, the Hollows fill,
Up goes her Hand, and off she slips
The Bolsters that supply her Hips.
With gentlest Touch, she next explores
Her Shankers, Issues, running Sores,
Effects of many a sad Disaster;
And then to each applies a Plaister.
But must, before she goes to Bed,
Rub off the Dawbs of White and Red;
And smooth the Furrows in her Front,
With greasy Paper stuck upon't.
She takes a *Bolus* e'er she sleeps;
And then between two Blankets creeps.
With Pains of Love tormented lies;
Or if she chance to close her Eyes,
Of *Bridewell* and the *Compter* dreams,
And feels the Lash, and faintly screams;
Or, by a faithless Bully drawn,
At some Hedge-Tavern lies in Pawn;
Or to *Jamaica* seems transported,
Alone, and by no Planter courted;
Or, near *Fleet-Ditch*'s oozy Brinks,
Surrounded with a Hundred Stinks,
Belated, seems on watch to lye,
And snap some Cully passing by;

Or, struck with Fear, her Fancy runs
On Watchmen, Constables and Duns,
From whom she meets with frequent Rubs;
But, never from Religious Clubs;
Whose Favour she is sure to find,
Because she pays them all in Kind.
    CORINNA wakes. A dreadful Sight!
Behold the Ruins of the Night!
A wicked Rat her Plaister stole,
Half eat, and dragg'd it to his Hole.
The Crystal Eye, alas, was miss't;
And *Puss* had on her Plumpers pisst.
A Pigeon pick'd her Issue-Peas;
And *Shock* her Tresses fill'd with Fleas.
    The Nymph, tho' in this mangled Plight,
Must ev'ry Morn her Limbs unite.
But how shall I describe her Arts
To recollect the scatter'd Parts?
Or shew the Anguish, Toil, and Pain,
Of gath'ring up herself again?
The bashful Muse will never bear
In such a Scene to interfere.
Corinna in the Morning dizen'd,
Who sees, will spew; who smells, be poison'd.

1735   ALEXANDER POPE *from* Of the Characters of Women: An
Epistle to a Lady

Nothing so true as what you once let fall,
'Most Women have no Characters at all'.
Matter too soft a lasting mark to bear,
And best distinguish'd by black, brown, or fair.
    How many pictures of one Nymph we view,
All how unlike each other, all how true!

(...)

    Papillia, wedded to her doating spark,
Sighs for the shades – 'How charming is a Park!'
A Park is purchas'd, but the Fair he sees
All bath'd in tears – 'Oh odious, odious Trees!'

Ladies, like variegated Tulips, show,
'Tis to their Changes that their charms they owe;
Their happy Spots the nice admirer take,
Fine by defect, and delicately weak.
'Twas thus Calypso once each heart alarm'd,
Aw'd without Virtue, without Beauty charm'd;
Her Tongue bewitch'd as odly as her Eyes,
Less Wit than Mimic, more a Wit than wise:
Strange graces still, and stranger flights she had,
Was just not ugly, and was just not mad;
Yet ne'er so sure our passion to create,
As when she touch'd the brink of all we hate.

(. . .)

'Yet Cloe sure was form'd without a spot –'
Nature in her then err'd not, but forgot.
'With ev'ry pleasing, ev'ry prudent part,
Say, what can Cloe want?' – she wants a Heart.
She speaks, behaves, and acts just as she ought;
But never, never, reach'd one gen'rous Thought.
Virtue she finds too painful an endeavour,
Content to dwell in Decencies for ever.
So very reasonable, so unmov'd,
As never yet to love, or to be lov'd.
She, while her Lover pants upon her breast,
Can mark the figures on an Indian chest;
And when she sees her Friend in deep despair,
Observes how much a Chintz exceeds Mohair.
Forbid it Heav'n, a Favour or a Debt
She e'er should cancel – but she may forget.
Safe is your Secret still in Cloe's ear;
But none of Cloe's shall you ever hear.
Of all her Dears she never slander'd one,
But cares not if a thousand are undone.
Would Cloe know if you're alive or dead?
She bids her Footman put it in her head.
Cloe is prudent – would you too be wise?
Then never break your heart when Cloe dies.

(. . .)

Men, some to Bus'ness, some to Pleasure take;
But ev'ry Woman is at heart a Rake:
Men, some to Quiet, some to public Strife;
But ev'ry Lady would be Queen for life.

Yet mark the fate of a whole Sex of Queens!
Pow'r all their end, but Beauty all the means.
In Youth they conquer, with so wild a rage,
As leaves them scarce a Subject in their Age:
For foreign glory, foreign joy, they roam;
No thought of Peace of Happiness at home.
But Wisdom's Triumph is well-tim'd Retreat,
As hard a science to the Fair as Great!
Beauties, like Tyrants, old and friendless grown,
Yet hate to rest, and dread to be alone,
Worn out in public, weary ev'ry eye,
Nor leave one sigh behind them when they die.

Pleasures the sex, as children Birds, pursue,
Still out of reach, yet never out of view,
Sure, if they catch, to spoil the Toy at most,
To covet flying, and regret when lost:
At last, to follies Youth could scarce defend,
'Tis half their Age's prudence to pretend;
Asham'd to own they gave delight before,
Reduc'd to feign it, when they give no more:
As Hags hold Sabbaths, less for joy than spight,
So these their merry, miserable Night;
Still round and round the Ghosts of Beauty glide,
And haunt the places where their Honour dy'd.

See how the World its Veterans rewards!
A Youth of frolicks, an old Age of Cards,
Fair to no purpose, artful to no end,
Young without Lovers, old without a Friend,
A Fop their Passion, but their Prize a Sot,
Alive, ridiculous, and dead, forgot!

ALEXANDER POPE *from* An Epistle from Mr. Pope, to Dr. Arbuthnot

You think this cruel? take it for a rule,
No creature smarts so little as a Fool.
Let Peals of Laughter, *Codrus!* round thee break,
Thou unconcern'd canst hear the mighty Crack.

Pit, Box and Gall'ry in convulsions hurl'd,
Thou stand'st unshook amidst a bursting World.
Who shames a Scribler? break one cobweb thro',
He spins the slight, self-pleasing thread anew;
Destroy his Fib, or Sophistry; in vain,
The Creature's at his dirty work again;
Thron'd in the Centre of his thin designs;
Proud of a vast Extent of flimzy lines.
Whom have I hurt? has Poet yet, or Peer,
Lost the arch'd eye-brow, or *Parnassian* sneer?
And has not *Colly* still his Lord, and Whore?
His Butchers *Henley*, his Free-masons *Moor*?
Does not one Table *Bavius* still admit?
Still to one Bishop *Philips* seem a Wit?
Still *Sapho* – 'Hold! for God-sake – you'll offend:
No Names – be calm – learn Prudence of a Friend:
I too could write, and I am twice as tall,
But Foes like these!' – One Flatt'rer's worse than all;
Of all mad Creatures, if the Learn'd are right,
It is the Slaver kills, and not the Bite.
A Fool quite angry is quite innocent;
Alas! 'tis ten times worse when they *repent*.

(...)

Peace to all such! but were there One whose fires
True Genius kindles, and fair Fame inspires,
Blest with each Talent and each Art to please,
And born to write, converse, and live with ease:
Shou'd such a man, too fond to rule alone,
Bear, like the *Turk*, no brother near the throne,
View him with scornful, yet with jealous eyes,
And hate for Arts that caus'd himself to rise;
Damn with faint praise, assent with civil leer,
And without sneering, teach the rest to sneer;
Willing to wound, and yet afraid to strike,
Just hint a fault, and hesitate dislike;
Alike reserv'd to blame, or to commend,
A tim'rous foe, and a suspicious friend,
Dreading ev'n fools, by Flatterers besieg'd,
And so obliging that he ne'er oblig'd;
Like *Cato*, give his little Senate laws,
And sit attentive to his own applause;

While Wits and Templers ev'ry sentence raise,
And wonder with a foolish face of praise.
Who but must laugh, if such a man there be?
Who would not weep, if *Atticus* were he!

(. . .)

A Lash like mine no honest man shall dread,
But all such babling blockheads in his stead.
   Let *Sporus* tremble – 'What? that Thing of silk,
Sporus, that mere white Curd of Ass's milk?
Satire or Sense alas! can *Sporus* feel?
Who breaks a Butterfly upon a Wheel?'
Yet let me flap this Bug with gilded wings,
This painted Child of Dirt that stinks and stings;
Whose Buzz the Witty and the Fair annoys,
Yet Wit ne'er tastes, and Beauty ne'er enjoys,
So well-bred Spaniels civilly delight
In mumbling of the Game they dare not bite.
Eternal Smiles his Emptiness betray,
As shallow streams run dimpling all the way.
Whether in florid Impotence he speaks,
And, as the Prompter breathes, the Puppet squeaks;
Or at the Ear of *Eve*, familiar Toad,
Half Froth, half Venom, spits himself abroad,
In Puns, or Politicks, or Tales, or Lyes,
Or Spite, or Smut, or Rymes, or Blasphemies.
His Wit all see-saw between *that* and *this*,
Now high, now low, now Master up, now Miss,
And he himself one vile Antithesis.
Amphibious Thing! that acting either Part,
The trifling Head, or the corrupted Heart!
Fop at the Toilet, Flatt'rer at the Board,
Now trips a Lady, and now struts a Lord.
Eve's Tempter thus the Rabbins have exprest,
A Cherub's face, a Reptile all the rest;
Beauty that shocks you, Parts that none will trust,
Wit that can creep, and Pride that licks the dust.

ALEXANDER POPE

EPITAPH.
Intended for Sir ISAAC NEWTON,
In Westminster-Abbey.
ISAACUS NEWTONIUS
Quem Immortalem,
Testantur Tempus, Natura, Cœlum:
Mortalem
Hoc Marmor fatetur.

Nature, and Nature's Laws lay hid in Night.
God said, *Let Newton be!* and All was *Light.*

JOHN DYER My Ox Duke

'Twas on a summer noon, in Stainsford mead
New mown and tedded, while the weary swains,
Louting beneath an oak, their toils relieved;
And some with wanton tale the nymphs beguiled,
And some with song, and some with kisses rude;
Their scythes hung o'er their heads: when my brown ox,
Old labourer Duke, in awkward haste I saw
Run stumbling through the field to reach the shade
Of an old open barn, whose gloomy floor
The lash of sounding flails had long forgot.
In vain his eager haste: sudden old Duke
Stopped; a soft ridge of snow-white little pigs
Along the sacred threshold sleeping lay.
Burnt in the beam, and stung with swarming flies,
He stood tormented on the shadow's edge:
What should he do? What sweet forbearance held
His heavy foot from trampling on the weak,
To gain his wishes? Hither, hither all,
Ye vain, ye proud! see, humble heaven attends;
The fly-teased brute with gentle pity stays,
And shields the sleeping young. O gracious Lord!
Aid of the feeble, cheerer of distress,
In his low labyrinth each small reptile's guide!
God of unnumbered worlds! Almighty power!

Assuage our pride. Be meek, thou child of man:
Who gives thee life, gives every worm to live,
Thy kindred of the dust. – Long waiting stood
The good old labourer, in the burning beam,
And breathed upon them, nosed them, touched them soft,
With lovely fear to hurt their tender sides;
Again soft touched them; gently moved his head
From one to one; again, with touches soft,
He breathed them o'er, till gruntling waked and stared
The merry little young, their tails upcurled,
And gambolled off with scattered flight. Then sprung
The honest ox, rejoiced, into the shade.

(1855)

1737   MATTHEW GREEN *from* **The Spleen**

To cure the mind's wrong biass, spleen,
Some recommend the bowling-green;
Some, hilly walks; all, exercise;
Fling but a stone, the giant dies;
Laugh and be well; monkeys have been
Extreme good doctors for the spleen;
And kitten, if the humour hit,
Has harlequin'd away the fit.

(. . .)

Sometimes I dress, with women sit,
And chat away the gloomy fit,
Quit the stiff garb of serious sense,
And wear a gay impertinence,
Nor think, nor speak with any pains,
But lay on fancy's neck the reins;
Talk of unusual swell of waist
In maid of honour loosely lac'd,
And beauty borr'wing Spanish red,
And loving pair with sep'rate bed,
And jewels pawn'd for loss of game,
And then redeem'd by loss of fame,
Of Kitty (aunt left in the lurch
By grave pretence to go to church)

Perceiv'd in hack with lover fine,
Like Will and Mary on the coin:
And thus in modish manner we
In aid of sugar sweeten tea.

Permit, ye fair, your idol form,
Which e'en the coldest heart can warm,
May with its beauties grace my line,
While I bow down before it's shrine,
And your throng'd altars with my lays
Perfume, and get by giving praise.
With speech so sweet, so sweet a mien
You excommunicate the spleen.

SAMUEL JOHNSON from *London:* A Poem in Imitation of
the Third Satire of Juvenal

Tho' grief and fondness in my breast rebel,
When injur'd THALES bids the town farewell,
Yet still my calmer thoughts his choice commend,
I praise the hermit, but regret the friend,
Resolved at length, from vice and LONDON far,
To breathe in distant fields a purer air,
And, fix'd on Cambria's solitary shore,
Give to St David one true Briton more.
    For who would leave, unbrib'd, Hibernia's land,
Or change the rocks of Scotland for the Strand?
There none are swept by sudden fate away,
But all whom hunger spares, with age decay:
Here malice, rapine, accident, conspire,
And now a rabble rages, now a fire;
Their ambush here relentless ruffians lay,
And here the fell attorney prowls for prey;
Here falling houses thunder on your head,
And here a female atheist talks you dead.

(. . .)

    By numbers here from shame or censure free,
All crimes are safe, but hated poverty.
This, only this, the rigid law pursues,
This, only this, provokes the snarling muse.

The sober trader at a tatter'd cloak,
Wakes from his dream, and labours for a joke;
With brisker air the silken courtiers gaze,
And turn the varied taunt a thousand ways.
Of all the griefs that harrass the distress'd,
Sure the most bitter is a scornful jest;
Fate never wounds more deep the gen'rous heart,
Than when a blockhead's insult points the dart.

Has heaven reserv'd, in pity to the poor,
No pathless waste, or undiscover'd shore;
No secret island in the boundless main?
No peaceful desart yet unclaim'd by SPAIN?
Quick let us rise, the happy seats explore,
And bear oppression's insolence no more.
This mournful truth is ev'ry where confess'd,
SLOW RISES WORTH, BY POVERTY DEPRESS'D:
But here more slow, where all are slaves to gold,
Where looks are merchandise, and smiles are sold;
Where won by bribes, by flatteries implor'd,
The groom retails the favours of his lord.

ALEXANDER POPE *from* Epilogue to the Satires

from Dialogue I

Virtue may chuse the high or low Degree,
'Tis just alike to Virtue, and to me;
Dwell in a Monk, or light upon a King,
She's still the same, belov'd, contented thing.
Vice is undone, if she forgets her Birth,
And stoops from Angels to the Dregs of Earth:
But 'tis the *Fall* degrades her to a Whore;
Let *Greatness* own her, and she's mean no more:
Her Birth, her Beauty, Crowds and Courts confess,
Chaste Matrons praise her, and grave Bishops bless:
In golden Chains the willing World she draws,
And hers the Gospel is, and hers the Laws:
Mounts the Tribunal, lifts her scarlet head,
And sees pale Virtue carted in her stead!
Lo! at the Wheels of her Triumphal Car,
Old *England*'s Genius, rough with many a Scar,

Dragg'd in the Dust! his Arms hang idly round,
His Flag inverted trails along the ground!
Our Youth, all liv'ry'd o'er with foreign Gold,
Before her dance; behind her crawl the Old!
See thronging Millions to the Pagod run,
And offer Country, Parent, Wife, or Son!
Hear her black Trumpet thro' the Land proclaim,
That 'Not to be corrupted is the Shame.'
In Soldier, Churchman, Patriot, Man in Pow'r,
'Tis Av'rice all, Ambition is no more!
See, all our Nobles begging to be Slaves!
See, all our Fools aspiring to be Knaves!
The Wit of Cheats, the Courage of a Whore,
Are what ten thousand envy and adore.
All, all look up, with reverential Awe,
On Crimes that scape, or triumph o'er the Law:
While Truth, Worth, Wisdom, daily they decry –
'Nothing is Sacred now but Villany.'

ALEXANDER POPE Epitaph for One Who Would Not Be Buried in Westminster Abbey.

Heroes, and Kings! your distance keep:
In peace let one poor Poet sleep,
Who never flatter'd Folks like you:
Let Horace blush, and Virgil too.

JONATHAN SWIFT *from* **Verses on the Death of Dr. Swift** **1739**

The Time is not remote, when I
Must by the Course of Nature dye:
When I foresee my special Friends,
Will try to find their private Ends:
Tho' it is hardly understood,
Which way my Death can do them good;
Yet, thus methinks, I hear 'em speak;
See, how the Dean begins to break:
Poor Gentleman, he droops apace,
You plainly find it in his Face:

That old Vertigo in his Head,
Will never leave him, till he's dead:
Besides, his Memory decays,
He recollects not what he says;
He cannot call his Friends to Mind;
Forgets the Place where last he din'd:
Plyes you with Stories o'er and o'er,
He told them fifty Times before.
How does he fancy we can sit,
To hear his out-of-fashion'd Wit?
But he takes up with younger Fokes,
Who for his Wine will bear his Jokes:
Faith, he must make his Stories shorter,
Or change his Comrades once a Quarter:
In half the Time, he talks them round;
There must another Sett be found.

For Poetry, he's past his Prime,
He takes an Hour to find a Rhime:
His Fire is out, his Wit decay'd,
His Fancy sunk, his Muse a Jade.
I'd have him throw away his Pen;
But there's no talking to some Men.

And, then their Tenderness appears,
By adding largely to my Years:
'He's older than he would be reckon'd,
'And well remembers *Charles* the Second.

'He hardly drinks a Pint of Wine;
'And that, I doubt, is no good Sign.
'His Stomach too begins to fail:
'Last Year we thought him strong and hale;
'But now, he's quite another Thing;
'I wish he may hold out till Spring.'

Then hug themselves, and reason thus;
'It is not yet so bad with us.'

In such a Case they talk in Tropes,
And, by their Fears express their Hopes:
Some great Misfortune to portend,
No Enemy can match a Friend;

With all the Kindness they profess,
The Merit of a lucky Guess,
(When daily Howd'y's come of Course,
And Servants answer; *Worse and Worse)*
Wou'd please 'em better than to tell,
That, GOD be prais'd, the Dean is well.
Then he who prophecy'd the best,
Approves his Foresight to the rest:
'You know, I always fear'd the worst,
'And often told you so at first:'
He'd rather chuse that I should dye,
Than his Prediction prove a Lye.
Not one foretels I shall recover;
But, all agree, to give me over.

Yet shou'd some Neighbour feel a Pain,
Just in the Parts, where I complain;
How many a Message would he send?
What hearty Prayers that I should mend?
Enquire what Regimen I kept;
What gave me Ease, and how I slept?
And more lament, when I was dead,
Than all the Sniv'llers round my Bed.

My good Companions, never fear,
For though you may mistake a Year;
Though your Prognosticks run too fast,
They must be verify'd at last.

'Behold the fatal Day arrive!
'How is the Dean? He's just alive.
'Now the departing Prayer is read:
'He hardly breathes. The Dean is dead.
'Before the Passing-Bell begun,
'The News thro' half the Town has run.
'O, may we all for Death prepare!
'What has he left? And who's his Heir?
'I know no more than what the News is,
''Tis all bequeath'd to publick Uses.
'To publick Use! A perfect Whim!
'What had the Publick done for him!
'Meer Envy, Avarice, and Pride!
'He gave it all: – But first he dy'd.

'And had the Dean, in all the Nation,
'No worthy Friend, no poor Relation?
'So ready to do Strangers good,
'Forgetting his own Flesh and Blood?'

Now Grub-Street Wits are all employ'd;
With Elegies, the Town is cloy'd:
Some Paragraph in ev'ry Paper,
To *curse* the *Dean*, or *bless* the *Drapier*.

The Doctors tender of their Fame,
Wisely on me lay all the Blame:
'We must confess his Case was nice;
'But he would never take Advice:
'Had he been rul'd, for ought appears,
'He might have liv'd these Twenty Years:
'For when we open'd him we found,
'That all his vital Parts were sound.'

From *Dublin* soon to *London* spread,
'Tis told at Court, the Dean is dead.

Kind Lady *Suffolk* in the Spleen,
Runs laughing up to tell the Queen.
The Queen, so Gracious, Mild, and Good,
Cries, 'Is he gone? 'Tis time he shou'd.
'He's dead you say; why let him rot;
'I'm glad the Medals were forgot.
'I promis'd them, I own; but when?
'I only was the Princess then;
'But now as Consort of the King,
'You know 'tis quite a different Thing.'

(. . .)

Here shift the Scene, to represent
How those I love, my Death lament.
Poor POPE will grieve a Month; and GAY
A Week; and ARBUTHNOTT a Day.

ST JOHN himself will scarce forbear,
To bite his Pen, and drop a Tear.
The rest will give a Shrug and cry
I'm sorry; but we all must dye.

Indifference clad in Wisdom's Guise,
All Fortitude of Mind supplies:
For how can stony Bowels melt,
In those who never Pity felt;
When *We* are lash'd, *They* kiss the Rod;
Resigning to the Will of God.

The Fools, my Juniors by a Year,
Are tortur'd with Suspence and Fear.
Who wisely thought my Age a Screen,
When Death approach'd, to stand between:
The Screen remov'd, their Hearts are trembling,
They mourn for me without dissembling.

My female Friends, whose tender Hearts
Have better learn'd to act their Parts.
Receive the News in *doleful Dumps*,
'The Dean is dead, (*and what is Trumps?*)
'Then Lord have Mercy on his Soul.
'(Ladies I'll venture for the *Vole*.)
'Six Deans they say must bear the Pall.
'(I wish I knew what *King* to call.)
'Madam, your Husband will attend
'The Funeral of so good a Friend.
'No Madam, 'tis a shocking Sight,
'And he's engag'd To-morrow Night!
'My Lady *Club* wou'd take it ill,
'If he shou'd fail her at *Quadrill*.
'He lov'd the Dean. (*I lead a Heart*.)
'But dearest Friends, they say, must part.
'His Time was come, he ran his Race;
'We hope he's in a better Place.'

ALEXANDER POPE On Queen *Caroline's* Death-bed   **1740**

Here lies wrapt up in forty thousand towels
    The only proof that C*** had bowels.

SAMUEL JOHNSON An Epitaph on Claudy Phillips, a Musician

Phillips! whose touch harmonious could remove
The pangs of guilty pow'r, and hapless love,
Rest here distrest by poverty no more,
Find here that calm thou gav'st so oft before;
Sleep undisturb'd within this peaceful shrine,
Till angels wake thee with a note like thine.

CHARLES WESLEY Morning Hymn

Christ, whose Glory fills the Skies,
   CHRIST, the true, the only Light,
Sun of Righteousness, arise,
   Triumph o'er the Shades of Night:
Day-spring from on High, be near:
Day-star, in my Heart appear.

Dark and Chearless is the Morn
   Unaccompanied by Thee,
Joyless is the Day's Return,
   Till thy Mercy's Beams I see;
Till they Inward Light impart,
Glad my Eyes, and warm my Heart.

Visit then this Soul of mine,
   Pierce the Gloom of Sin, and Grief,
Fill me, Radiancy Divine,
   Scatter all my Unbelief,
More and more Thyself display
Shining to the Perfect Day.

ALEXANDER POPE *from* **The Dunciad**   **1742**

[The Tribe of Fanciers]

  Then thick as Locusts black'ning all the ground,
A tribe, with weeds and shells fantastic crown'd,
Each with some wond'rous gift approach'd the Pow'r,
A Nest, a Toad, a Fungus, or a Flow'r.
But far the foremost, two, with earnest zeal,
And aspect ardent to the Throne appeal.
  The first thus open'd: 'Hear thy suppliant's call,
Great Queen, and common Mother of us all!
Fair from its humble bed I rear'd this Flow'r,
Suckled, and chear'd, with air, and sun, and show'r,
Soft on the paper ruff its leaves I spread,
Bright with the gilded button tipt its head,
Then thron'd in glass, and nam'd it CAROLINE:
Each Maid cry'd, charming! and each Youth, divine!
Did Nature's pencil ever blend such rays,
Such vary'd light in one promiscuous blaze?
Now prostrate! dead! behold that Caroline:
No Maid cries, charming! and no Youth, divine!
And lo the wretch! whose vile, whose insect lust
Lay'd this gay daughter of the Spring in dust.
Oh punish him, or to th' Elysian shades
Dismiss my soul, where no Carnation fades.'
  He ceas'd, and wept. With innocence of mien,
Th' Accus'd stood forth, and thus address'd the Queen.
  'Of all th' enamel'd race, whose silv'ry wing
Waves to the tepid Zephyrs of the spring,
Or swims along the fluid atmosphere,
Once brightest shin'd this child of Heat and Air.
I saw, and started from its vernal bow'r
The rising game, and chac'd from flow'r to flow'r.
It fled, I follow'd; now in hope, now pain;
It stopt, I stopt; it mov'd, I mov'd again.
At last it fix'd, 'twas on what plant it pleas'd,
And where it fix'd, the beauteous bird I seiz'd:
Rose or Carnation was below my care;
I meddle, Goddess! only in my sphere.
I tell the naked fact without disguise,
And, to excuse it, need but shew the prize;

Whose spoils this paper offers to your eye,
Fair ev'n in death! this peerless *Butterfly*.'

'My sons! (she answer'd) both have done your parts:
Live happy both, and long promote our arts.
But hear a Mother, when she recommends
To your fraternal care, our sleeping friends.
The common Soul, of Heav'n's more frugal make,
Serves but to keep fools pert, and knaves awake:
A drowzy Watchman, that just gives a knock,
And breaks our rest, to tell us what's a clock.
Yet by some object ev'ry brain is stirr'd;
The dull may waken to a Humming-bird;
The most recluse, discreetly open'd, find
Congenial matter in the Cockle-kind;
The mind, in Metaphysics at a loss,
May wander in a wilderness of Moss;
The head that turns at super-lunar things,
Poiz'd with a tail, may steer on Wilkins' wings.

'O! would the Sons of Men once think their Eyes
And Reason giv'n them but to study *Flies!*
See Nature in some partial narrow shape,
And let the Author of the Whole escape:
Learn but to trifle; or, who most observe,
To wonder at their Maker, not to serve.'

(...)

[The Triumph of Dullness]

Then blessing all, 'Go Children of my care!
To Practice now from Theory repair.
All my commands are easy, short, and full:
My Sons! be proud, be selfish, and be dull.
Guard my Prerogative, assert my Throne:
This Nod confirms each Privilege your own.
The Cap and Switch be sacred to his Grace;
With Staff and Pumps the Marquis lead the Race;
From Stage to Stage the licens'd Earl may run,
Pair'd with his Fellow-Charioteer the Sun;
The learned Baron Butterflies design,
Or draw to silk Arachne's subtile line;
The Judge to dance his brother Sergeant call;
The Senator at Cricket urge the Ball;

The Bishop stow (Pontific Luxury!)
An hundred Souls of Turkeys in a pye;
The sturdy Squire to Gallic masters stoop,
And drown his Lands and Manors in a Soupe.
Others import yet nobler arts from France,
Teach Kings to fiddle, and make Senates dance.
Perhaps more high some daring son may soar,
Proud to my list to add one Monarch more;
And nobly conscious, Princes are but things
Born for First Ministers, as Slaves for Kings,
Tyrant supreme! shall three Estates command,
And MAKE ONE MIGHTY DUNCIAD OF THE LAND!'

   More she had spoke, but yawn'd – All Nature nods:
What Mortal can resist the Yawn of Gods?
Churches and Chapels instantly it reach'd;
(St. James's first, for leaden Gilbert preach'd)
Then catch'd the Schools; the Hall scarce kept awake;
The Convocation gap'd, but could not speak:
Lost was the Nation's Sense, nor could be found,
While the long solemn Unison went round:
Wide, and more wide, it spread o'er all the realm;
Ev'n Palinurus nodded at the Helm:
The Vapour mild o'er each Committee crept;
Unfinish'd Treaties in each Office slept;
And Chiefless Armies doz'd out the Campaign;
And Navies yawn'd for Orders on the Main.

   O Muse! relate (for you can tell alone,
Wits have short Memories, and Dunces none)
Relate, who first, who last resign'd to rest;
Whose Heads she partly, whose completely blest;
What Charms could Faction, what Ambition lull,
The Venal quiet, and intrance the Dull;
'Till drown'd was Sense, and Shame, and Right, and Wrong –
O sing, and hush the Nations with thy Song!

*   *   *   *   *   *

   In vain, in vain, – the all-composing Hour
Resistless falls: The Muse obeys the Pow'r.
She comes! she comes! the sable Throne behold
Of *Night* Primæval, and of *Chaos* old!
Before her, *Fancy*'s gilded clouds decay,
And all its varying Rain-bows die away.

Wit shoots in vain its momentary fires,
The meteor drops, and in a flash expires.
As one by one, at dread Medea's strain,
The sick'ning stars fade off th'ethereal plain;
As Argus' eyes by Hermes' wand opprest,
Clos'd one by one to everlasting rest;
Thus at her felt approach, and secret might,
Art after *Art* goes out, and all is Night.
See skulking *Truth* to her old Cavern fled,
Mountains of Casuistry heap'd o'er her head!
Philosophy, that lean'd on Heav'n before,
Shrinks to her second cause, and is no more.
Physic of *Metaphysic* begs defence,
And *Metaphysic* calls for aid on *Sense!*
See *Mystery* to *Mathematics* fly!
In vain! they gaze, turn giddy, rave, and die.
Religion blushing veils her sacred fires,
And unawares *Morality* expires.
Nor *public* Flame, nor *private*, dares to shine;
Nor *human* Spark is left, nor Glimpse *divine!*
Lo! thy dread Empire, CHAOS! is restor'd;
Light dies before thy uncreating word:
Thy hand, great Anarch! lets the curtain fall;
And Universal Darkness buries All.

(1728-42)

1744   ANONYMOUS On the Death of Mr. Pope

Seal up the Book, all Vision's at an end,
For who durst now to Poetry pretend?
Since Pope is dead, it must be sure confessed
The Muse's sacred Inspiration's ceased;
And we may only what is writ rehearse:
His Works are the Apocalypse of Verse.

§ *from* **Tommy Thumb's Pretty Song Book**

ANONYMOUS Cock Robbin

Who did kill Cock Robbin?
I, said the Sparrow,
With my bow and Arrow,
And I did kill Cock Robbin.

Who did see him die?
I, said the Fly,
With my little Eye,
And I did see him die.

And who did catch his blood?
I, said the Fish,
With my little Dish,
And I did catch his blood.

And who did make his shroud?
I, said the Beetle,
With my little Needle,
And I did make his shroud.

Who'll dig his grave?
I, said the Owl,
With my pick and shovel,
I'll dig his grave.

Who'll be the parson?
I, said the Rook,
With my little book,
I'll be the parson.

Who'll be the clerk?
I, said the Lark,
If it's not in the dark,
I'll be the clerk.

Who'll carry the link?
I, said the Linnet,
I'll fetch it in a minute,
I'll carry the link.

Who'll be chief mourner?
I, said the Dove,
I mourn for my love,
I'll be chief mourner.

Who'll carry the coffin?
I, said the Kite,
If it's not through the night,
I'll carry the coffin.

Who'll bear the pall?
We, said the Wren,
Both the cock and the hen,
We'll bear the pall.

Who'll sing a psalm?
I, said the Thrush,
As she sat on a bush,
I'll sing a psalm.

Who'll toll the bell?
I, said the Bull,
Because I can pull,
I'll toll the bell.

All the birds of the air
Fell a-sighing and a-sobbing,
When they heard the bell toll
For poor Cock Robbin.

ANONYMOUS London Bridge

London Bridge is broken down,
    Dance o'er my lady lee,
London Bridge is broken down,
    With a gay lady.

How shall we build it up again?
    Dance o'er my lady lee,
How shall we build it up again?
    With a gay lady.

Build it up with silver and gold,
    Dance o'er my lady lee,
Build it up with silver and gold,
    With a gay lady.

Silver and gold will be stole away,
    Dance o'er my lady lee,
Silver and gold will be stole away,
    With a gay lady.

Build it up with iron and steel,
    Dance o'er my lady lee,
Build it up with iron and steel,
    With a gay lady.

Iron and steel will bend and bow,
    Dance o'er my lady lee,
Iron and steel will bend and bow,
    With a gay lady.

Build it up with wood and clay,
    Dance o'er my lady lee,
Build it up with wood and clay,
    With a gay lady.

Wood and clay will wash away,
    Dance o'er my lady lee,
Wood and clay will wash away,
    With a gay lady.

Build it up with stone so strong,
    Dance o'er my lady lee,
Huzza! 'twill last for ages long,
    With a gay lady.

§   §   §

1745   CHARLES WESLEY

Let Earth and Heaven combine,
   Angels and Men agree
To praise in Songs divine
   Th'Incarnate Deity,
Our GOD contracted to a Span,
Incomprehensibly made Man.

He laid his Glory by,
   He wrap'd Him in our Clay,
Unmark'd by Human Eye
   The latent Godhead lay;
Infant of Days He here became,
And bore the lov'd IMMANUEL's Name.

See in that Infant's Face
   The Depths of Deity,
And labour while ye gaze
   To sound the Mystery:
In vain; ye Angels gaze no more,
But fall, and silently adore.

Unsearchable the Love
   That hath the Saviour brought,
The Grace is far above
   Or Men or Angels Thought;
Suffice for Us, that GOD, we know,
Our GOD is manifest below.

He deigns in Flesh t'appear,
   Widest Extremes to join,
To bring our Vileness near,
   And make us All divine;
And we the Life of GOD shall know,
For GOD is manifest below.

Made perfect first in Love,
   And sanctified by Grace,
We shall from Earth remove,
   And see his glorious Face;
His Love shall then be fully shew'd,
And Man shall be lost in GOD.

WILLIAM COLLINS Ode, Written in the Beginning of the Year 1746

How sleep the Brave, who sink to Rest,
By all their Country's Wishes blest!
When *Spring*, with dewy Fingers cold,
Returns to deck their hallow'd Mold,
She there shall dress a sweeter Sod,
Than *Fancy's* Feet have ever trod.

By Fairy Hands their Knell is rung,
By Forms unseen their Dirge is sung;
There *Honour* comes, a Pilgrim grey,
To bless the Turf that wraps their Clay,
And *Freedom* shall a-while repair,
To dwell a weeping Hermit there!

WILLIAM COLLINS Ode to Evening

If ought of Oaten Stop, or Pastoral Song,
May hope, chaste *Eve*, to sooth thy modest Ear,
    Like thy own solemn Springs,
    Thy Springs, and dying Gales,
O *Nymph* reserv'd, while now the bright-hair'd Sun
Sits in yon western Tent, whose cloudy Skirts,
    With Brede ethereal wove,
    O'erhang his wavy Bed:
Now Air is hush'd, save where the weak-ey'd Bat,
With short shrill Shriek flits by on leathern Wing,
    Or where the Beetle winds
    His small but sullen Horn,
As oft he rises 'midst the twilight Path,
Against the Pilgrim born in heedless Hum:
    Now teach me, *Maid* compos'd,
    To breathe some soften'd Strain,
Whose Numbers stealing thro' thy darkning Vale,
May not unseemly with its Stillness suit,
    As musing slow, I hail
    Thy genial lov'd Return!

For when thy folding Star arising shews
His paly Circlet, at his warning Lamp
    The fragrant *Hours*, and *Elves*
    Who slept in Flow'rs the Day,
And many a *Nymph* who wreaths her Brows with Sedge,
And sheds the fresh'ning Dew, and lovelier still,
    The *Pensive Pleasures* sweet
    Prepare thy shadowy Car.
Then lead, calm *Vot'ress*, where some sheety Lake
Cheers the lone Heath, or some time-hallow'd Pile,
    Or up-land Fallows grey
    Reflect it's last cool Gleam.
But when chill blustring Winds, or driving Rain,
Forbid my willing Feet, be mine the Hut,
    That from the Mountain's Side,
    Views Wilds, and swelling Floods,
And Hamlets brown, and dim-discover'd Spires,
And hears their simple Bell, and marks o'er all
    Thy Dewy Fingers draw
    The gradual dusky Veil.
While *Spring* shall pour his Show'rs, as oft he wont,
And bathe thy breathing Tresses, meekest *Eve!*
    While *Summer* loves to sport,
    Beneath thy ling'ring Light:
While sallow *Autumn* fills thy Lap with Leaves,
Or *Winter* yelling thro' the troublous Air,
    Affrights thy shrinking Train,
    And rudely rends thy Robes.
So long, sure-found beneath the Sylvan Shed,
Shall *Fancy*, *Friendship*, *Science*, rose-lip'd *Health*,
    Thy gentlest Influence own,
    And hymn thy fav'rite Name!

1747   **WILLIAM SHENSTONE Lines Written on a Window at
the Leasowes at a Time of Very Deep Snow**

In this small fort, besieged with snow,
When every studious pulse beats low,
   What does my wish require?
Some sprightly girls beneath my roof,
Some friends sincere and winter-proof,
   A bottle and a fire.

Prolong, O snow, prolong thy siege!
With these, thou wilt but more oblige,
   And bless me with thy stay;
Extend, extend thy frigid reign,
My few sincerer friends detain,
   And keep false friends away.

LADY MARY WORTLEY MONTAGU A Receipt to Cure the Vapours   1748

Why will Delia thus retire
   And languish Life away?
While the sighing Crowds admire
   'Tis too soon for Hartshorn Tea.

All these dismal looks and fretting
   Cannot Damon's life restore,
Long ago the Worms have eat him,
   You can never see him more.

Once again consult your Toilet,
   In the Glass your Face review,
So much weeping soon will spoil it
   And no Spring your Charms renew.

I like you was born a Woman –
   Well I know what Vapours mean,
The Disease alas! is common,
Single we have all the Spleen.

All the Morals that they tell us
   Never cur'd Sorrow yet,
Chuse among the pretty Fellows
   One of humour, Youth, and Wit.

Prithee hear him ev'ry Morning
   At least an hour or two,
Once again at Nights returning,
   I beleive the Dose will do.

MARY LEAPOR Mira's Will

Imprimis – My departed Shade I trust
To Heav'n – My Body to the silent Dust;
My Name to publick Censure I submit,
To be dispos'd of as the World thinks fit;
My Vice and Folly let Oblivion close,
The World already is o'erstock'd with those;
My Wit I give, as Misers give their Store,
To those who think they had enough before.
Bestow my Patience to compose the Lives
Of slighted Virgins and neglected Wives;
To modish Lovers I resign my Truth,
My cool Reflexion to unthinking Youth;
And some Good-nature give ('tis my Desire)
To surly Husbands, as their Needs require;
And first discharge my Funeral – and then
To the small Poets I bequeath my Pen.

Let a small Sprig (true Emblem of my Rhyme)
Of blasted Laurel on my Hearse recline;
Let some grave Wight, that struggles for Renown,
By chanting Dirges through a Market-Town,
With gentle Step precede the solemn Train;
A broken Flute upon his Arm shall lean.
Six comick Poets may the Corse surround,
And All Free-holders, if they can be found:
Then follow next the melancholy Throng,
As shrewd Instructors, who themselves are wrong.
The Virtuoso, rich in Sun-dry'd Weeds,
The Politician, whom no Mortal heeds,
The silent Lawyer, chamber'd all the Day,
And the stern Soldier that receives no Pay.
But stay – the Mourners shou'd be first our Care,
Let the freed Prentice lead the Miser's Heir;
Let the young Relict wipe her mournful Eye,
And widow'd Husbands o'er their Garlick cry.

All this let my Executors fulfil,
And rest assured that this is *Mira*'s Will,
Who was, when she these Legacies design'd,
In Body healthy, and compos'd in Mind.

CHRISTOPHER SMART A Morning Piece, Or, An Hymn for the Hay-Makers

Quinetiam Gallum noctem explaudentibus alis
Auroram clara consuetum voce vocare.

LUCRET.

Brisk chaunticleer his mattins had begun,
    And broke the silence of the night,
  And thrice he call'd aloud the tardy sun,
    And thrice he hail'd the dawn's ambiguous light;
Back to their graves the fear-begotten phantoms run.

  Strong Labour got up. – With his pipe to his mouth,
    He stoutly strode over the dale,
  He lent new perfumes to the breath of the south,
    On his back hung his wallet and flail.
Behind him came Health from her cottage of thatch,
Where never physician had lifted the latch.

First of the village Colin was awake,
And thus he sung, reclining on his rake.
  Now the rural graces three
  Dance beneath yon maple tree;
  First the vestal Virtue, known
  By her adamantine zone;
  Next to her in rosy pride,
  Sweet Society, the bride;
  Last Honesty, full seemly drest
  In her cleanly home-spun vest.

The abby bells in wak'ning rounds
  The warning peal have giv'n;
And pious Gratitude resounds
  Her morning hymn to heav'n.

All nature wakes – the birds unlock their throats,
And mock the shepherd's rustic notes.
  All alive o'er the lawn,
  Full glad of the dawn,
    The little lambkins play,
Sylvia and Sol arise, – and all is day –

Come, my mates, let us work,
And all hands to the fork,
While the Sun shines, our Hay-cocks to make,
So fine is the Day,
And so fragrant the Hay,
That the Meadow's as blithe as the Wake.

Our voices let's raise
In Phœbus's praise,
Inspir'd by so glorious a theme,
Our musical words
Shall be join'd by the birds,
And we'll dance to the tune of the stream.

1749   SAMUEL JOHNSON *from* The Vanity of Human Wishes, The
Tenth Satire of Juvenal

When first the College Rolls receive his Name,
The young Enthusiast quits his Ease for Fame;
Through all his Veins the fever of Renown
Burns from the strong Contagion of the Gown;
O'er *Bodley*'s Dome his future Labours spread,
And *Bacon*'s Mansion trembles o'er his Head;
Are these thy Views? proceed, illustrious Youth,
And Virtue guard thee to the Throne of Truth,
Yet should thy Soul indulge the gen'rous Heat,
Till captive Science yields her last Retreat;
Should Reason guide thee with her brightest Ray,
And pour on misty Doubt resistless Day;
Should no false Kindness lure to loose Delight,
Nor Praise relax, nor Difficulty fright;
Should tempting Novelty thy Cell refrain,
And Sloth effuse her opiate Fumes in vain;
Should Beauty blunt on Fops her fatal Dart,
Nor claim the triumph of a letter'd Heart;
Should no Disease thy torpid Veins invade,
Nor Melancholy's Phantoms haunt thy Shade;
Yet hope not Life from Grief or Danger free,
Nor think the Doom of Man revers'd for thee:
Deign on the passing World to turn thine Eyes,
And pause awhile from Letters to be wise;
There mark what Ills the Scholar's Life assail,
Toil, Envy, Want, the Patron, and the Jail.

The festal Blazes, the triumphal Show,
The ravish'd Standard, and the captive Foe,
The Senate's Thanks, the Gazette's pompous Tale,
With Force resistless o'er the Brave prevail.
Such Bribes the rapid *Greek* o'er *Asia* whirl'd,
For such the steady *Romans* shook the World;
For such in distant Lands the *Britons* shine,
And stain with Blood the *Danube* or the *Rhine*;
This Pow'r has Praise, that Virtue scarce can warm,
Till Fame supplies the universal Charm.
Yet Reason frowns on War's unequal Game,
Where wasted Nations raise a single Name,
And mortgag'd States their Grandsires Wreaths regret
From Age to Age in everlasting Debt;
Wreaths which at last the dear-bought Right convey
To rust on Medals, or on Stones decay.
    On what Foundation stands the Warrior's Pride?
How just his Hopes let *Swedish Charles* decide;
A Frame of Adamant, a Soul of Fire,
No Dangers fright him, and no Labours tire;
O'er Love, o'er Fear, extends his wide Domain,
Unconquer'd Lord of Pleasure and of Pain;
No Joys to him pacific Scepters yield,
War sounds the Trump, he rushes to the Field;
Behold surrounding Kings their Pow'r combine,
And One capitulate, and One resign;
Peace courts his Hand, but spreads her Charms in vain;
'Think Nothing gain'd, he cries, till nought remain,
'On *Moscow*'s Walls till *Gothic* Standards fly,
'And all be Mine beneath the Polar Sky.'
The March begins in Military State,
And Nations on his Eye suspended wait;
Stern Famine guards the solitary Coast,
And Winter barricades the Realms of Frost;
He comes, not Want and Cold his Course delay; –
Hide, blushing Glory, hide *Pultowa*'s Day:
The vanquish'd Hero leaves his broken Bands,
And shews his Miseries in distant Lands;
Condemn'd a needy Supplicant to wait,
While Ladies interpose, and Slaves debate.
But did not Chance at length her Error mend?
Did no subverted Empire mark his End?

Did rival Monarchs give the fatal Wound?
Or hostile Millions press him to the Ground?
His Fall was destin'd to a barren Strand,
A petty Fortress, and a dubious Hand;
He left the Name, at which the World grew pale,
To point a Moral, or adorn a Tale.

1751   THOMAS GRAY Elegy Written in a Country Church Yard

The Curfew tolls the knell of parting day,
The lowing herd wind slowly o'er the lea,
The plowman homeward plods his weary way,
And leaves the world to darkness and to me.

Now fades the glimmering landscape on the sight,
And all the air a solemn stillness holds,
Save where the beetle wheels his droning flight,
And drowsy tinklings lull the distant folds;

Save that from yonder ivy-mantled tow'r
The mopeing owl does to the moon complain
Of such, as wand'ring near her secret bow'r,
Molest her ancient solitary reign.

Beneath those rugged elms, that yew-tree's shade,
Where heaves the turf in many a mould'ring heap,
Each in his narrow cell for ever laid,
The rude Forefathers of the hamlet sleep.

The breezy call of incense-breathing Morn,
The swallow twitt'ring from the straw-built shed,
The cock's shrill clarion, or the ecchoing horn,
No more shall rouse them from their lowly bed.

For them no more the blazing hearth shall burn,
Or busy housewife ply her evening care:
No children run to lisp their sire's return,
Or climb his knees the envied kiss to share.

Oft did the harvest to their sickle yield,
Their furrow oft the stubborn glebe has broke;
How jocund did they drive their team afield!
How bow'd the woods beneath their sturdy stroke!

Let not Ambition mock their useful toil,
Their homely joys, and destiny obscure;
Nor Grandeur hear with a disdainful smile,
The short and simple annals of the poor.

The boast of heraldry, the pomp of pow'r,
And all that beauty, all that wealth e'er gave,
Awaits alike th' inevitable hour.
The paths of glory lead but to the grave.

Nor you, ye Proud, impute to These the fault,
If Mem'ry o'er their Tomb no Trophies raise,
Where thro' the long-drawn isle and fretted vault
The pealing anthem swells the note of praise.

Can storied urn or animated bust
Back to its mansion call the fleeting breath?
Can Honour's voice provoke the silent dust,
Or Flatt'ry sooth the dull cold ear of Death?

Perhaps in this neglected spot is laid
Some heart once pregnant with celestial fire,
Hands, that the rod of empire might have sway'd,
Or wak'd to extasy the living lyre.

But Knowledge to their eyes her ample page
Rich with the spoils of time did ne'er unroll;
Chill Penury repress'd their noble rage,
And froze the genial current of the soul.

Full many a gem of purest ray serene,
The dark unfathom'd caves of ocean bear:
Full many a flower is born to blush unseen,
And waste its sweetness on the desert air.

Some village-Hampden, that with dauntless breast
The little Tyrant of his fields withstood;
Some mute inglorious Milton here may rest,
Some Cromwell guiltless of his country's blood.

Th' applause of list'ning senates to command,
The threats of pain and ruin to despise,
To scatter plenty o'er a smiling land,
And read their hist'ry in a nation's eyes

Their lot forbad: nor circumscrib'd alone
Their growing virtues, but their crimes confin'd;
Forbad to wade through slaughter to a throne,
And shut the gates of mercy on mankind,

The struggling pangs of conscious truth to hide,
To quench the blushes of ingenuous shame,
Or heap the shrine of Luxury and Pride
With incense kindled at the Muse's flame.

Far from the madding crowd's ignoble strife,
Their sober wishes never learn'd to stray;
Along the cool sequester'd vale of life
They kept the noiseless tenor of their way.

Yet ev'n these bones from insult to protect
Some frail memorial still erected nigh,
With uncouth rhimes and shapeless sculpture deck'd,
Implores the passing tribute of a sigh.

Their name, their years, spelt by th' unletter'd muse,
The place of fame and elegy supply:
And many a holy text around she strews,
That teach the rustic moralist to die.

For who to dumb Forgetfulness a prey,
This pleasing anxious being e'er resign'd,
Left the warm precincts of the chearful day,
Nor cast one longing ling'ring look behind?

On some fond breast the parting soul relies,
Some pious drops the closing eye requires;
Ev'n from the tomb the voice of Nature cries,
Ev'n in our Ashes live their wonted Fires.

For thee, who mindful of th' unhonour'd Dead
Dost in these lines their artless tale relate;
If chance, by lonely contemplation led,
Some kindred Spirit shall inquire thy fate,

Haply some hoary-headed Swain may say,
'Oft have we seen him at the peep of dawn
'Brushing with hasty steps the dews away
'To meet the sun upon the upland lawn.

'There at the foot of yonder nodding beech
'That wreathes its old fantastic roots so high,
'His listless length at noontide wou'd he stretch,
'And pore upon the brook that babbles by.

'Hard by yon wood, now smiling as in scorn,
'Mutt'ring his wayward fancies he wou'd rove,
'Now drooping, woeful wan, like one forlorn,
'Or craz'd with care, or cross'd in hopeless love.

'One morn I miss'd him on the custom'd hill,
'Along the heath and near his fav'rite tree;
'Another came; nor yet beside the rill,
'Nor up the lawn, nor at the wood was he,

'The next with dirges due in sad array
'Slow thro' the church-way path we saw him born[e].
'Approach and read (for thou can'st read) the lay,
'Grav'd on the stone beneath yon aged thorn.'

The Epitaph

Here rests his head upon the lap of Earth
A Youth to Fortune and to Fame unknown,
Fair Science frown'd not on his humble birth,
And Melancholy mark'd him for her own.

Large was his bounty, and his soul sincere,
Heav'n did a recompence as largely send:
He gave to Mis'ry all he had, a tear,
He gain'd from Heav'n ('twas all he wish'd) a friend.

No farther seek his merits to disclose,
Or draw his frailties from their dread abode,
(There they alike in trembling hope repose)
The bosom of his Father and his God.

1755 ANONYMOUS This is the House That Jack Built

This is the farmer sowing his corn,
That kept the cock that crowed in the morn,
That waked the priest all shaven and shorn,
That married the man all tattered and torn,
That kissed the maiden all forlorn,
That milked the cow with the crumpled horn,
That tossed the dog,
That worried the cat,
That killed the rat,
That ate the malt
That lay in the house that Jack built.

1761 CHRISTOPHER SMART *from* Jubilate Agno

For the doubling of flowers is the improvement of the gardners
    talent.
For the flowers are great blessings.
For the Lord made a Nosegay in the meadow with his disciples and
    preached upon the lily.
For the angels of God took it out of his hand and carried it to the
    Height.
For a man cannot have publick spirit, who is void of private
    benevolence.
For there is no Height in which there are not flowers.
For flowers have great virtues for all the senses.
For the flower glorifies God and the root parries the adversary.
For the flowers have their angels even the words of God's Creation.
For the warp and woof of flowers are worked by perpetual moving
    spirits.
For flowers are good both for the living and the dead.
For there is a language of flowers.
For there is a sound reasoning upon all flowers.
For elegant phrases are nothing but flowers.
For flowers are peculiarly the poetry of Christ.
For flowers are medicinal.
For flowers are musical in ocular harmony.
For the right names of flowers are yet in heaven. God make
    gard'ners better nomenclators.
For the Poorman's nosegay is an introduction to a Prince.

For I will consider my Cat Jeoffry.

For he is the servant of the Living God duly and daily serving him.

For at the first glance of the glory of God in the East he worships in his way.

For is this done by wreathing his body seven times round with elegant quickness.

For then he leaps up to catch the musk, which is the blessing of God upon his prayer.

For he rolls upon prank to work it in.

For having done duty and received blessing he begins to consider himself.

For this he performs in ten degrees.

For first he looks upon his fore-paws to see if they are clean.

For secondly he kicks up behind to clear away there.

For thirdly he works it upon stretch with the fore paws extended.

For fourthly he sharpens his paws by wood.

For fifthly he washes himself.

For Sixthly he rolls upon wash.

For Seventhly he fleas himself, that he may not be interrupted upon the beat.

For Eighthly he rubs himself against a post.

For Ninthly he looks up for his instructions.

For Tenthly he goes in quest of food.

For having consider'd God and himself he will consider his neighbour.

For if he meets another cat he will kiss her in kindness.

For when he takes his prey he plays with it to give it chance.

For one mouse in seven escapes by his dallying.

For when his day's work is done his business more properly begins.

For he keeps the Lord's watch in the night against the adversary.

For he counteracts the powers of darkness by his electrical skin and glaring eyes.

For he counteracts the Devil, who is death, by brisking about the life

For in his morning orisons he loves the sun and the sun loves him.

For he is of the tribe of Tiger.

For the Cherub Cat is a term of the Angel Tiger.

For he has the subtlety and hissing of a serpent, which in goodness he suppresses.

For he will not do destruction, if he is well-fed, neither will he spit without provocation.

For he purrs in thankfulness, when God tells him he's a good Cat.

For he is an instrument for the children to learn benevolence upon.

For every house is incompleat without him and a blessing is lacking
in the spirit.

For the Lord commanded Moses concerning the cats at the
departure of the Children of Israel from Egypt.

For every family had one cat at least in the bag.

For the English Cats are the best in Europe.

For he is the cleanest in the use of his fore-paws of any quadrupede.

For the dexterity of his defence is an instance of the love of God to
him exceedingly.

For he is the quickest to his mark of any creature.

For he is tenacious of his point.

For he is a mixture of gravity and waggery.

For he knows that God is his Saviour.

For there is nothing sweeter than his peace when at rest.

For there is nothing brisker than his life when in motion.

For he is of the Lord's poor and so indeed is he called by
benevolence-perpetuall – Poor Jeoffry! poor Jeoffry! the rat
has bit thy throat.

For I bless the name of the Lord Jesus that Jeoffry is better.

For the divine spirit comes about his body to sustain it in compleat
cat.

For his tongue is exceeding pure so that it has in purity what it wants
in musick.

For he is docile and can learn certain things.

For he can set up with gravity which is patience upon approbation.

For he can fetch and carry, which is patience in employment.

For he can jump over a stick which is patience upon proof positive.

For he can spraggle upon waggle at the word of command.

For he can jump from an eminence into his master's bosom.

For he can catch the cork and toss it again.

For he is hated by the hypocrite and miser.

For the former is affraid of detection.

For the latter refuses the charge.

For he camels his back to bear the first notion of business.

For he is good to think on, if a man would express himself neatly.

For he made a great figure in Egypt for his signal services.

For he killed the Ichneumon-rat very pernicious by land.

For his ears are so acute that they sting again.

For from this proceeds the passing quickness of his attention.

For by stroaking of him I have found out electricity.

For I perceived God's light about him both wax and fire.

For the Electrical fire is the spiritual substance, which God sends
from heaven to sustain the bodies both of man and beast.

For God has blessed him in the variety of his movements.

For, tho he cannot fly, he is an excellent clamberer.

For his motions upon the face of the earth are more than any other
        quadrupede.

For he can tread to all the measures upon the musick.

For he can swim for life.

For he can creep.

(1939)

CHRISTOPHER SMART *from* A Song to David   **1763**

O DAVID, highest in the list
Of worthies, on God's ways insist,
   The genuine word repeat:
Vain are the documents of men,
And vain the flourish of the pen
   That keeps the fool's conceit.

PRAISE above all – for praise prevails;
Heap up the measure, load the scales,
   And good to goodness add:
The gen'rous soul her Saviour aids,
But peevish obloquy degrades;
   The Lord is great and glad.

For ADORATION all the ranks
Of angels yield eternal thanks,
   And DAVID in the midst;
With God's good poor, which, last and least
In man's esteem, thou to thy feast,
   O blessed bride-groom, bidst.

For ADORATION seasons change,
And order, truth, and beauty range,
   Adjust, attract, and fill:
The grass the polyanthus cheques;
And polish'd porphyry reflects,
   By the descending rill.

Rich almonds colour to the prime
For ADORATION; tendrils climb,
   And fruit-trees pledge their gems;
And Ivis with her gorgeous vest
Builds for her eggs her cunning nest,
   And bell-flowers bow their stems.

With vinous syrup cedars spout;
From rocks pure honey gushing out,
   For ADORATION springs:
All scenes of painting croud the map
Of nature; to the mermaid's pap
   The scaled infant clings.

The spotted ounce and playsome cubs
Run rustling 'mongst the flow'ring shrubs,
   And lizards feed the moss;
For ADORATION beasts embark,
While waves upholding halcyon's ark
   No longer roar and toss.

While Israel sits beneath his fig,
With coral root and amber sprig
   The wean'd advent'rer sports;
Where to the palm the jasmin cleaves,
For ADORATION 'mongst the leaves
   The gale his peace reports.

Increasing days their reign exalt,
Nor in the pink and mottled vault
   Th' opposing spirits tilt;
And, by the coasting reader spied,
The silverlings and crusions glide
   For ADORATION gilt.

For ADORATION rip'ning canes
And cocoa's purest milk detains
   The western pilgrim's staff;
Where rain in clasping boughs inclos'd,
And vines with oranges dispos'd,
   Embow'r the social laugh.

Now labour his reward receives,
For ADORATION counts his sheaves
   To peace, her bounteous prince;
The nectarine his strong tint imbibes,
And apples of ten thousand tribes,
   And quick peculiar quince.

The wealthy crops of whit'ning rice,
'Mongst thyine woods and groves of spice,
   For ADORATION grow;
And, marshall'd in the fenced land,
The peaches and pomegranates stand,
   Where wild carnations blow.

The laurels with the winter strive;
The crocus burnishes alive
   Upon the snow-clad earth:
For ADORATION myrtles stay
To keep the garden from dismay,
   And bless the sight from dearth.

The pheasant shows his pompous neck;
And ermine, jealous of a speck,
   With fear eludes offence:
The sable, with his glossy pride,
For ADORATION is descried,
   Where frosts the wave condense.

The chearful holly, pensive yew,
And holy thorn, their trim renew;
   The squirrel hoards his nuts:
All creatures batten o'er their stores,
And careful nature all her doors
   For ADORATION shuts.

For ADORATION, DAVID's psalms
Lift up the heart to deeds of alms;
   And he, who kneels and chants,
Prevails his passions to controul,
Finds meat and med'cine to the soul,
   Which for translation pants.

1764 OLIVER GOLDSMITH *from* **The Traveller, Or a Prospect of Society**

[Britain]

Creation's mildest charms are there combin'd,
Extremes are only in the master's mind;
Stern o'er each bosom reason holds her state.
With daring aims, irregularly great,
Pride in their port, defiance in their eye,
I see the lords of human kind pass by
Intent on high designs, a thoughtful band,
By forms unfashion'd, fresh from Nature's hand;
Fierce in their native hardiness of soul,
True to imagin'd right above controul,
While even the peasant boasts these rights to scan,
And learns to venerate himself as man.

Thine, Freedom, thine the blessings pictur'd here,
Thine are those charms that dazzle and endear;
Too blest indeed, were such without alloy,
But foster'd even by Freedom ills annoy:
That independence Britons prize too high,
Keeps man from man, and breaks the social tie;
The self dependent lordlings stand alone,
All claims that bind and sweeten life unknown;
Here by the bonds of nature feebly held,
Minds combat minds, repelling and repell'd;
Ferments arise, imprison'd factions roar,
Represt ambition struggles round her shore,
Till over-wrought, the general system feels
Its motions stopt, or phrenzy fire the wheels.

Nor this the worst. As nature's ties decay,
As duty, love, and honour fail to sway,
Fictitious bonds, the bonds of wealth and law,
Still gather strength, and force unwilling awe.
Hence all obedience bows to these alone,
And talent sinks, and merit weeps unknown;
Till Time may come, when, stript of all her charms,
The land of scholars, and the nurse of arms;

Where noble stems transmit the patriot flame,
Where kings have toil'd, and poets wrote for fame;
One sink of level avarice shall lie,
And scholars, soldiers, kings unhonor'd die.

SAMUEL JOHNSON [Lines contributed to Goldsmith's 'The Traveller']

How small, of all that human hearts endure,
That part which laws or kings can cause or cure.

§ from **Mother Goose's Melody, or Sonnets for the Cradle**   1765

ANONYMOUS High Diddle Diddle

High diddle diddle,
The cat and the fiddle,
  The cow jump'd over the moon;
The little dog laugh'd
To see such craft,
  And the dish ran away with the spoon.

§   §   §

§ from **THOMAS PERCY's Reliques of Ancient English Poetry**

ANONYMOUS Sir Patrick Spence

The king sits in Dumferling toune,
  Drinking the blude-reid wine:
O quhar will I get guid sailor,
  To sail this schip of mine?

Up and spak an eldern knicht,
    Sat at the kings richt kne:
Sir Patrick Spence is the best sailor,
    That sails upon the se.

The king has written a braid letter,
10   And sign'd it wi' his hand;
And sent it to Sir Patrick Spence,
    Was walking on the sand.

The first line that Sir Patrick red,
    A loud lauch lauched he:
15 The next line that Sir Patrick red,
    The teir blinded his e'e.

O quha is this has don this deid,
    This ill deid don to me;
To send me out this time o' the yeir,
20   To sail upon the se?

Mak haste, mak haste, my mirry men all,
    Our guid schip sails the morne.
O say na sae, my master deir,
    For I feir a deadlie storme.

25 Late, late yestreen I saw the new moone
    Wi' the auld moone in hir arme;
And I feir, I feir, my deir master,
    That we will com to harme.

O our Scots nobles wer richt laith
30   To weet their cork-heil'd schoone;
Bot lang owre a' the play wer play'd,
    Thair hats they swam aboone.

O lang, lang may thair ladies sit
    Wi' thair fans into their hand,
35 Or eir they se Sir Patrick Spence
    Cum sailing to the land.

9 *braid* long; 29 *laith* loath; 32 *aboone* above;

O lang, lang may the ladies stand
   Wi' thair gold kems in their hair,
Waiting for thair ain deir lords,
40   For they'll se thame na mair.

Haf owre, haf owre to Aberdour,
   It's fiftie fadom deip:
And thair lies guid Sir Patrick Spence,
   Wi' the Scots lords at his feit.

ANONYMOUS Edward, Edward

Quhy dois your brand sae drop wi' bluid,
        Edward, Edward?
Quhy dois your brand sae drop wi' bluid?
   And quhy sae sad gang yee, O?
5 O, I hae killed my hauke sae guid,
        Mither, mither:
O, I hae killed my hauke sae guid:
   And I had nae mair bot hee, O.

Your haukis bluid was nevir sae reid,
10   Edward, Edward.
Your haukis bluid was nevir sae reid,
   My deir son I tell thee, O.
O, I hae killed my reid-roan steid,
        Mither, mither:
15 O, I hae killed my reid-roan steid,
   That erst was sae fair and free, O.

Your steid was auld, and ye hae gat mair,
        Edward, Edward:
Your steid was auld, and ye hae gat mair,
20   Sum other dule ye drie, O.
O, I hae killed my fadir deir,
        Mither, mither:
O, I hae killed my fadir deir,
   Alas! and wae is me, O!

41 *haf owre* half over

20 *dule ye drie* sorrow you suffer

And quhatten penance wul ye drie for that,
　　　　　Edward, Edward?
And quhatten penance will ye drie for that?
　　My deir son, now tell me, O.
Ile set my feit in yonder boat,
30　　　　　Mither, mither:
Ile set my feit in yonder boat,
　　And Ile fare ovir the sea, O.

And quhat wul ye doe wi' your towirs and your ha',
　　　　　Edward, Edward?
35　And quhat wul ye doe wi' your towirs and your ha',
　　That were sae fair to see, O?
Ile let them stand til they doun fa',
　　　　　Mither, mither:
Ile let them stand til they doun fa',
40　　For here nevir mair maun I bee, O.

And quhat wul ye leive to your bairns and your wife,
　　　　　Edward, Edward?
And quhat wul ye leive to your bairns and your wife,
　　Quhan ye gang ovir the sea, O?
45　The warldis room, let thame beg thrae life,
　　　　　Mither, mither:
The warldis room, let thame beg thrae life,
　　For thame nevir mair wul I see, O.

And quhat wul ye leive to your ain mither deir,
50　　　　　Edward, Edward?
And quhat wul ye leive to your ain mither deir?
　　My deir son, now tell me, O.
The curse of hell frae me sall ye beir,
　　　　　Mither, mither:
55　The curse of hell frae me sall ye beir,
　　Sic counseils ye gave to me, O.

ANONYMOUS　Lord Thomas and Fair Annet

Lord Thomas and Fair Annet
　Sate a' day on a hill;
Whan night was cum, and sun was sett,
　They had not talkt their fill.

5   Lord Thomas said a word in jest,
      Fair Annet took it ill:
  'A, I will nevir wed a wife
    Against my ain friends' will.'

  'Gif ye wull nevir wed a wife,
10   A wife wull neir wed yee:'
  Sae he is hame to tell his mither,
    And knelt upon his knee.

  'O rede, O rede, mither,' he says,
    'A gude rede gie to mee;
15 O sall I take the nut-browne bride,
    And let Faire Annet bee?'

  'The nut-browne bride haes gowd and gear,
    Fair Annet she has gat nane;
  And the little beauty Fair Annet haes
20   O it wull soon be gane.'

  And he has till his brother gane:
    'Now, brother, rede ye mee;
  A, sall I marrie the nut-browne bride,
    And let Fair Annet bee?'

25 'The nut-browne bride has oxen, brother,
    The nut-browne bride has kye;
  I wad hae ye marrie the nut-browne bride,
    And cast Fair-Annet bye.'

  'Her oxen may dye i the house, billie,
30   And her kye into the byre,
  And I sall hae nothing to mysell
    Bot a fat fadge by the fyre.'

  And he has till his sister gane:
    'Now, sister, rede ye mee;
35 O sall I marrie the nut-browne bride,
    And set Fair Annet free?'

13 *rede* advice; 26 *kye* cattle; 29 *billie* brother; 32 *fadge* dumpy person;

'I'se rede ye tak Fair Annet, Thomas,
   And let the browne bride alane;
Lest ye sould sigh, and say, Alace,
40   What is this we brought hame!'

'No, I will tak my mither's counsel,
   And marrie me owt o hand;
And I will tak the nut-browne bride,
   Fair Annet may leive the land.'

45 Up then rose Fair Annet's father,
    Twa hours or it wer day,
And he is gane into the bower
   Wherein Fair Annet lay.

'Rise up, rise up, Fair Annet,' he says,
50   'Put on your silken sheene;
Let us gae to St Marie's kirke,
   And see that rich weddeen.'

'My maides, gae to my dressing-roome,
   And dress to me my hair;
55 Whaireir yee laid a plait before,
   See yee lay ten times mair.

'My maids, gae to my dressing-room,
   And dress to me my smock;
The one half is o the holland fine,
60   The other o needle-work.'

The horse Fair Annet rade upon,
   He amblit like the wind;
Wi siller he was shod before,
   Wi burning gowd behind.

65 Four and twenty siller bells
    Wer a' tyed till his mane,
And yae tift o the norland wind,
   They tinkled ane by ane.

59 *holland* linen; 67 *yae tift* every puff;

Four and twenty gay gude knichts
70   Rade by Fair Annet's side,
And four and twenty fair ladies,
    As gin she had bin a bride.

And whan she came to Marie's kirk,
    She sat on Marie's stean:
75 The cleading that Fair Annet had on
    It skinkled in their een.

And whan she cam into the kirk,
    She shimmerd like the sun;
The belt that was about her waist
80   Was a' wi pearles bedone.

She sat her by the nut-browne bride,
    And her een they wer sae clear,
Lord Thomas he clean forgat the bride,
    Whan Fair Annet drew near.

85 He had a rose into his hand,
    He gae it kisses three,
And reaching by the nut-browne bride,
    Laid it on Fair Annet's knee.

Up than spak the nut-brown bride,
90   She spak wi meikle spite:
'And whair gat ye that rose-water,
    That does mak yee sae white?'

'O I did get the rose-water
    Whair ye wull neir get nane,
95 For I did get that very rose-water
    Into my mither's wame.'

The bride she drew a long bodkin
    Frae out her gay head-gear,
And strake Fair Annet unto the heart,
100   That word spak nevir mair.

75 *cleading* clothing; 76 *skinkled* sparkled; 80 *bedone* ornamented;
96 *wame* womb;

Lord Thomas he saw Fair Annet wex pale,
    And marvelit what more bee;
But whan he saw her dear heart's blude,
    A' wood-wroth wexed hee.

105 He drew his dagger, that was sae sharp,
    That was sae sharp and meet,
And drave it into the nut-browne bride,
    That fell deid at his feit.

'Now stay for me, dear Annet,' he sed,
110   'Now stay, my dear,' he cry'd;
Then strake the dagger untill his heart,
    And fell deid by her side.

Lord Thomas was buried without kirk-wa,
    Fair Annet within the quiere,
115 And o the tane thair grew a birk,
    The other a bonny briere.

And ay they grew, and ay they threw,
    As they wad faine be neare;
And by this ye may ken right weil
120   They were twa luvers deare.

§   §   §

CHRISTOPHER SMART HYMN. The Nativity of Our Lord and Saviour Jesus Christ

Where is this stupendous stranger,
    Swains of Solyma, advise,
Lead me to my Master's manger,
    Shew me where my Saviour lies?

O Most Mighty! O MOST HOLY!
    Far beyond the seraph's thought,
Art thou then so mean and lowly
    As unheeded prophets taught?

104 *wood-wroth* mad; 114 *quiere* choir; 115 *birk* birch; 117 *threw* intertwined

O the magnitude of meekness!
    Worth from worth immortal sprung;
O the strength of infant weakness,
    If eternal is so young!

If so young and thus eternal,
    Michael tune the shepherd's reed,
Where the scenes are ever vernal,
    And the loves be love indeed!

See the God blasphem'd and doubted
    In the schools of Greece and Rome;
See the pow'rs of darkness routed,
    Taken at their utmost gloom.

Nature's decorations glisten
    Far above their usual trim;
Birds on box and laurels listen,
    As so near the cherubs hymn.

Boreas now no longer winters
    On the desolated coast;
Oaks no more are riv'n in splinters
    By the whirlwind and his host.

Spinks and ouzles sing sublimely,
    'We too have a Saviour born;'
Whiter blossoms burst untimely
    On the blest Mosaic thorn.

God all-bounteous, all-creative,
    Whom no ills from good dissuade,
Is incarnate, and a native
    Of the very world he made.

OLIVER GOLDSMITH *from* **The Vicar of Wakefield**   1766

When lovely woman stoops to folly,
    And finds too late that men betray,
What charm can sooth her melancholy,
    What art can wash her guilt away?

The only art her guilt to cover,
   To hide her shame from every eye,
To give repentance to her lover,
   And wring his bosom, is – to die.

1769   THOMAS GRAY On L[or]d H[olland']s Seat near M[argat]e, K[en]t

Old and abandon'd by each venal friend
   Here H[olland] took the pious resolution
To smuggle some few years and strive to mend
   A broken character and constitution.
On this congenial spot he fix'd his choice,
   Earl Godwin trembled for his neighbouring sand,
Here Seagulls scream and cormorants rejoice,
   And Mariners tho' shipwreckt dread to land,
Here reign the blustring north and blighting east,
   No tree is heard to whisper, bird to sing,
Yet nature cannot furnish out the feast,
   Art he invokes new horrors still to bring;
Now mouldring fanes and battlements arise,
   Arches and turrets nodding to their fall,
Unpeopled palaces delude his eyes,
   And mimick desolation covers all.
Ah, said the sighing Peer, had Bute been true
   Nor Shelburn's, Rigby's, Calcraft's friendship vain,
Far other scenes than these had bless'd our view
   And realis'd the ruins that we feign.
Purg'd by the sword and beautifyd by fire,
   Then had we seen proud London's hated walls,
Owls might have hooted in St. Peters Quire,
   And foxes stunk and litter'd in St. Pauls.

1770   OLIVER GOLDSMITH *from* **The Deserted Village**

   Sweet was the sound when oft at evening's close,
Up yonder hill the village murmur rose;
There as I past with careless steps and slow,
The mingling notes came softened from below;

The swain responsive as the milk-maid sung,
The sober herd that lowed to meet their young;
The noisy geese that gabbled o'er the pool,
The playful children just let loose from school;
The watch-dog's voice that bayed the whispering wind,
And the loud laugh that spoke the vacant mind,
These all in sweet confusion sought the shade,
And filled each pause the nightingale had made.
But now the sounds of population fail,
No chearful murmurs fluctuate in the gale,
No busy steps the grass-grown foot-way tread,
For all the bloomy flush of life is fled.
All but yon widowed, solitary thing
That feebly bends beside the plashy spring;
She, wretched matron, forced, in age, for bread,
To strip the brook with mantling cresses spread,
To pick her wintry faggot from the thorn,
To seek her nightly shed, and weep till morn;
She only left of all the harmless train,
The sad historian of the pensive plain.

　　Near yonder copse, where once the garden smil'd,
And still where many a garden flower grows wild;
There, where a few torn shrubs the place disclose,
The village preacher's modest mansion rose.
A man he was, to all the country dear,
And passing rich with forty pounds a year;
Remote from towns he ran his godly race,
Nor ere had changed, nor wish'd to change his place;
Unpractised he to fawn, or seek for power,
By doctrines fashioned to the varying hour;
Far other aims his heart had learned to prize,
More skilled to raise the wretched than to rise.
His house was known to all the vagrant train,
He chid their wanderings, but relieved their pain;
The long remembered beggar was his guest,
Whose beard descending swept his aged breast;
The ruined spendthrift, now no longer proud,
Claimed kindred there, and had his claims allowed;
The broken soldier, kindly bade to stay,
Sate by his fire, and talked the night away;
Wept o'er his wounds, or tales of sorrow done,
Shouldered his crutch, and shewed how fields were won.

Pleased with his guests, the good man learned to glow,
And quite forgot their vices in their woe;
Careless their merits, or their faults to scan,
His pity gave ere charity began.

Thus to relieve the wretched was his pride,
And even his failings leaned to Virtue's side;
But in his duty prompt at every call,
He watched and wept, he prayed and felt, for all.
And, as a bird each fond endearment tries,
To tempt its new fledged offspring to the skies;
He tried each art, reproved each dull delay,
Allured to brighter worlds, and led the way.

Beside the bed where parting life was layed,
And sorrow, guilt, and pain, by turns dismayed,
The reverend champion stood. At his control,
Despair and anguish fled the struggling soul;
Comfort came down the trembling wretch to raise,
And his last faultering accents whispered praise.

At church, with meek and unaffected grace,
His looks adorned the venerable place;
Truth from his lips prevailed with double sway,
And fools, who came to scoff, remained to pray.
The service past, around the pious man,
With steady zeal each honest rustic ran;
Even children followed with endearing wile,
And plucked his gown, to share the good man's smile.
His ready smile a parent's warmth exprest,
Their welfare pleased him, and their cares distrest;
To them his heart, his love, his griefs were given,
But all his serious thoughts had rest in Heaven.
As some tall cliff that lifts its awful form
Swells from the vale, and midway leaves the storm,
Tho' round its breast the rolling clouds are spread,
Eternal sunshine settles on its head.
Beside yon straggling fence that skirts the way,
With blossomed furze unprofitably gay,
There, in his noisy mansion, skill'd to rule,
The village master taught his little school;
A man severe he was, and stern to view,
I knew him well, and every truant knew;

Well had the boding tremblers learned to trace

The day's disasters in his morning face;
Full well they laugh'd with counterfeited glee,
At all his jokes, for many a joke had he;
Full well the busy whisper circling round,
Conveyed the dismal tidings when he frowned;
Yet he was kind, or if severe in aught,
The love he bore to learning was in fault;
The village all declared how much he knew;
'Twas certain he could write, and cypher too;
Lands he could measure, terms and tides presage,
And even the story ran that he could gauge.
In arguing too, the parson owned his skill,
For even tho' vanquished, he could argue still;
While words of learned length, and thundering sound,
Amazed the gazing rustics ranged around,
And still they gazed, and still the wonder grew,
That one small head could carry all he knew.

　　But past is all his fame. The very spot
Where many a time he triumphed, is forgot.
Near yonder thorn, that lifts its head on high,
Where once the sign-post caught the passing eye,
Low lies that house where nut-brown draughts inspired,
Where grey-beard mirth and smiling toil retired,
Where village statesmen talked with looks profound,
And news much older than their ale went round.
Imagination fondly stoops to trace
The parlour splendours of that festive place;
The white-washed wall, the nicely sanded floor,
The varnished clock that clicked behind the door;
The chest contrived a double debt to pay,
A bed by night, a chest of drawers by day;
The pictures placed for ornament and use,
The twelve good rules, the royal game of goose;
The hearth, except when winter chill'd the day,
With aspen boughs, and flowers, and fennel gay,
While broken tea-cups, wisely kept for shew,
Ranged o'er the chimney, glistened in a row.

　　Vain transitory splendours! Could not all
Reprieve the tottering mansion from its fall!
Obscure it sinks, nor shall it more impart
An hour's importance to the poor man's heart;

Thither no more the peasant shall repair
To sweet oblivion of his daily care;
No more the farmer's news, the barber's tale,
No more the wood-man's ballad shall prevail;
No more the smith his dusky brow shall clear,
Relax his ponderous strength, and lean to hear;
The host himself no longer shall be found
Careful to see the mantling bliss go round;
Nor the coy maid, half willing to be prest,
Shall kiss the cup to pass it to the rest.

Yes! let the rich deride, the proud disdain,
These simple blessings of the lowly train,
To me more dear, congenial to my heart,
One native charm, than all the gloss of art.

1772   JOHN BYROM On the Origin of Evil

Evil, if rightly understood,
Is but the Skeleton of Good,
Divested of its Flesh and Blood.

While it remains without Divorce
Within its hidden, secret Source,
It is the Good's own Strength and Force.

As Bone has the supporting Share
In human Form Divinely fair,
Altho' an Evil when laid bare;

As Light and Air are fed by Fire,
A shining Good, while all conspire,
But, – separate, – dark, raging Ire;

As Hope and Love arise from Faith,
Which then admits no Ill, nor hath;
But, if alone, it would be Wrath;

Or any Instance thought upon,
In which the Evil can be none,
Till Unity of Good is gone;

So, by Abuse of Thought and Skill
The greatest Good, to wit, *Free-will*
Becomes the *Origin* of Ill.

Thus, when rebellious Angels fell,
The very Heav'n where good ones dwell
Became th' apostate Spirits' Hell.

Seeking, against Eternal Right,
A Force without a Love and Light,
They found and felt its evil Might.

Thus Adam, biting at their Bait
Of Good and Evil when he ate,
Died to his first thrice-happy State;

Fell to the Evils of this Ball,
Which in harmonious Union all
Were *Paradise* before his Fall;

And, when the Life of Christ in Men
Revives its faded Image, then
Will all be *Paradise* again.

ROBERT FERGUSSON The Daft-Days

Now mirk December's dowie face
Glours our the rigs wi' sour grimace,
While, thro' his *minimum* of space,
                    The bleer-ey'd sun,
5   Wi' blinkin light and stealing pace,
                    His race doth run.

From naked groves nae birdie sings,
To shepherd's pipe nae hillock rings,
The breeze nae od'rous flavour brings
10   From *Borean* cave,
And dwyning nature droops her wings,
                    Wi' visage grave.

1 *dowie* dismal; 2 *rigs* ridges; 11 *dwyning* declining;

Mankind but scanty pleasure glean
Frae snawy hill or barren plain,
15 Whan Winter, 'midst his nipping train,
    Wi' frozen spear,
Sends drift owr a' his bleak domain,
    And guides the weir.

Auld Reikie! thou'rt the canty hole,
20 A bield for mony caldrife soul,
Wha snugly at thine ingle loll,
    Baith warm and couth;
While round they gar the bicker roll
    To weet their mouth.

25 When merry *Yule-day* comes, I trow
You'll scantlins find a hungry mou';
Sma' are our cares, our stamacks fou
    O' gusty gear,
And kickshaws, strangers to our view,
30 Sin Fairn-year.

Ye browster wives, now busk ye bra,
And fling your sorrows far awa';
Then come and gies the tither blaw
    Of reaming ale,
35 Mair precious than the well of *Spa*,
    Our hearts to heal.

Then, tho' at odds wi' a' the warl',
Amang oursells we'll never quarrel;
Tho' Discord gie a canker'd snarl
40 To spoil our glee,
As lang's there's pith into the barrel
    We'll drink and 'gree.

Fidlers, your pins in temper fix,
And roset weel your fiddle-sticks,
45 But banish vile Italian tricks

19 *Auld Reikie* Edinburgh; *canty* merry; 20 *bield* haven; *caldrife* cold;
22 *couth* sociable; 23 *bicker* cup; 26 *scantlins* scarcely; 28 *gusty gear* tasty liquor;
29 *kickshaws* novelties; 30 *Fairn-year* yesteryear; 31 *browster* brewer; *busk* dress;
bra handsomely; 33 *tither blaw* next draught; 34 *reaming* foaming; 44 *roset* put
rosin on;

From out your quorum:
Nor *fortes* wi' *pianos* mix,
                    Gie's *Tulloch Gorum*.

For nought can cheer the heart sae weil
50 As can a canty Highland reel,
It even vivifies the heel
                    To skip and dance:
Lifeless is he wha canna feel
                    Its influence.

55 Let mirth abound, let social cheer
Invest the dawning of the year;
Let blithesome innocence appear
                    To crown our joy,
Nor envy wi' sarcastic sneer
60   Our bliss destroy.

And thou, great god of *Aqua Vitæ!*
Wha sways the empire of this city,
When fou we're sometimes capernoity,
                    Be thou prepar'd
65 To hedge us frae that black banditti,
                    The City-Guard.

WILLIAM COWPER Light Shining out of Darkness   **1774**

God moves in a mysterious way,
His wonders to perform,
He plants his footsteps in the Sea,
And rides upon the Storm.

Deep in unfathomable Mines,
Of never failing Skill,
He treasures up his bright designs,
And works his Sovereign Will.

63 *fou* drunk; *capernoity* quarrelsome

Ye fearfull Saints fresh courage take,
The clouds ye so much dread,
Are big with Mercy, and shall break
In blessings on your head.

Judge not the Lord by feeble sense,
But trust him for his Grace,
Behind a frowning Providence
He hides a Smiling face.

His purposes will ripen fast,
Unfolding every hour,
The Bud may have a bitter taste,
But *wait*, to *Smell the flower*.

Blind unbelief is sure to err,
And scan his work in vain,
God is his own Interpreter,
And he will make it plain.

WILLIAM COWPER

Hatred and vengeance, my eternal portion,
Scare can endure delay of execution: –
Wait, with impatient readiness, to seize my
      Soul in a moment.
Damn'd below Judas; more abhorr'd than he was,
Who, for a few pence, sold his holy master.
Twice betray'd, Jesus me, the last delinquent,
      Deems the profanest.
Man disavows, and Deity disowns me.
Hell might afford my miseries a shelter;
Therefore hell keeps her everhungry mouths all
      Bolted against me.
Hard lot! Encompass'd with a thousand dangers,
Weary, faint, trembling with a thousand terrors,
Fall'n, and if vanquish'd, to receive a sentence
      Worse than Abiram's:
Him, the vindictive rod of angry justice
Sent, quick and howling, to the centre headlong;
I, fed with judgments, in a fleshly tomb, am
      Buried above ground.

(1816)

ANONYMOUS [Epitaph for Thomas Johnson, huntsman. Charlton, Sussex]

Here Johnson lies; what human can deny
Old honest Tom the tribute of a sigh?
Deaf is that ear which caught the opening sound;
Dumb that tongue which cheer'd the hills around.
Unpleasing truth: Death hunts us from our birth
In view, and men, like foxes, take to earth.

OLIVER GOLDSMITH *from* Retaliation

[Edmund Burke]

Here lies our good Edmund, whose genius was such,
We scarcely can praise it, or blame it too much;
Who, born for the Universe, narrow'd his mind,
And to party gave up, what was meant for mankind.
Tho' fraught with all learning, kept straining his throat,
To persuade Tommy Townsend to lend him a vote;
Who, too deep for his hearers, still went on refining,
And thought of convincing, while they thought of dining;
Tho' equal to all things, for all things unfit,
Too nice for a statesman, too proud for a wit:
For a patriot too cool; for a drudge, disobedient,
And too fond of the *right* to pursue the *expedient*.
In short, 'twas his fate, unemploy'd, or in place, Sir,
To eat mutton cold, and cut blocks with a razor.

[David Garrick]

Here lies David Garrick, describe me who can,
An abridgment of all that was pleasant in man;
As an actor, confest without rival to shine,
As a wit, if not first, in the very first line,
Yet with talents like these, and an excellent heart,
The man had his failings, a dupe to his art;
Like an ill judging beauty, his colours he spread,
And beplaister'd, with rouge, his own natural red.

On the stage he was natural, simple, affecting,
'Twas only that, when he was off, he was acting:
With no reason on earth to go out of his way,
He turn'd and he varied full ten times a day;
Tho' secure of our hearts, yet confoundedly sick,
If they were not his own by finessing and trick,
He cast off his friends, as a huntsman his pack;
For he knew when he pleased he could whistle them back.
Of praise, a mere glutton, he swallowed what came,
And the puff of a dunce, he mistook it for fame;
'Till his relish grown callous, almost to disease,
Who pepper'd the highest, was surest to please.
But let us be candid, and speak out our mind,
If dunces applauded, he paid them in kind.
Ye Kenricks, ye Kellys, and Woodfalls so grave,
What a commerce was yours, while you got and you gave?
How did Grub-street re-echo the shouts that you rais'd,
While he was beroscius'd, and you were beprais'd?
But peace to his spirit, wherever it flies,
To act as an angel, and mix with the skies:
Those poets, who owe their best fame to his skill,
Shall still be his flatterers, go where he will.
Old Shakespeare, receive him, with praise and with love,
And Beaumonts and Bens be his Kellys above.

[Joshua Reynolds]

Here Reynolds is laid, and to tell you my mind,
He has not left a better or wiser behind;
His pencil was striking, resistless and grand,
His manners were gentle, complying and bland;
Still born to improve us in every part,
His pencil our faces, his manners our heart:
To coxcombs averse, yet most civilly staring,
When they judged without skill he was still hard of hearing:
When they talk'd of their Raphaels, Corregios and stuff,
He shifted his trumpet, and only took snuff.

RICHARD BRINSLEY SHERIDAN On Lady Anne Hamilton 1777

Pray how did she look? Was she pale, was she wan?
She was blooming and red as a cherry – poor Anne.

Did she eat? Did she drink? Yes, she drank up a can,
And ate very near a whole partridge – poor Anne.

Pray what did she do? Why, she talked to each man
And flirted with Morpeth and Breanebie – poor Anne.

Pray how was she drest? With a turban and fan,
With ear-rings, with chains, and with bracelets – poor Anne.

And how went she home? In a good warm sedan
With a muff and a cloak and a tippet – poor Anne!

SAMUEL JOHNSON Prologue to Hugh Kelly's 'A Word to the Wise'

This night presents a play, which publick rage,
Or right, or wrong, once hooted from the stage;
From zeal or malice now no more we dread,
For English vengeance *wars not with the dead*.
A generous foe regards, with pitying eye,
The man whom fate has laid, where all must lye.
To wit, reviving from its author's dust,
Be kind, ye judges, or at least be just:
Let no resentful petulance invade
Th' oblivious grave's inviolable shade.
Let one great payment every claim appease,
And him who cannot hurt, allow to please;
To please by scenes unconscious of offence,
By harmless merriment, or useful sense.
Where aught of bright, or fair, the piece displays,
Approve it only – 'tis too late to praise.
If want of skill, or want of care appear,
Forbear to hiss – the Poet cannot hear.

By all, like him, must praise and blame be found;
At best, a fleeting gleam, or empty sound.
Yet then shall calm reflection bless the night,
When liberal pity dignify'd delight;
When pleasure fired her torch at Virtue's flame,
And mirth was bounty with a humbler name.

SAMUEL JOHNSON [Lines Contributed to Hawkesworth's 'The Rival']

Thy mind which Voluntary doubts molest
Asks but its own permission to be blest.

RICHARD BRINSLEY SHERIDAN *from* The School for Scandal

Song and Chorus

Here's to the maiden of Bashful fifteen
    Here's to the Widow of Fifty
Here's to the flaunting, Extravagant Quean,
    And here's to the House Wife that's thrifty.
Chorus. Let the toast pass –
        Drink to the Lass –
I'll warrant She'll prove an Excuse for the Glass!

Here's to the Charmer whose Dimples we Prize!
    Now to the Maid who has none Sir;
Here's to the Girl with a pair of blue Eyes,
    – And Here's to the Nymph with but one Sir!
Chorus. Let the Toast pass etc.

Here's to the Maid with a Bosom of Snow,
    Now to her that's as brown as a berry:
Here's to the Wife with a face full of Woe,
    And now for the Damsel that's Merry.
Chorus. Let the Toast pass etc.

For let 'Em be Clumsy, or let 'Em be Slim
    Young or Ancient, I care not a Feather:
– So fill a Pint Bumper Quite up to the brim
    And let us E'en toast 'Em together!
Chorus. Let the toast pass –
        Drink to the Lass –
I'll warrant She'll prove an Excuse for the Glass!

WILLIAM COWPER The Contrite Heart   **1779**

Isaiah lvii.15

The LORD will happiness divine
   On contrite hearts bestow:
Then tell me, gracious GOD, is mine
   A contrite heart, or no?

I hear, but seem to hear in vain,
   Insensible as steel;
If ought is felt, 'tis only pain,
   To find I cannot feel.

I sometimes think myself inclin'd
   To love thee, if I could;
But often feel another mind,
   Averse to all that's good.

My best desires are faint and few,
   I fain would strive for more;
But when I cry, 'My strength renew,'
   Seem weaker than before.

Thy saints are comforted I know
   And love thy house of pray'r;
I therefore go where others go,
   But find no comfort there.

O make this heart rejoice, or ach;
   Decide this doubt for me;
And if it be not broken, break,
   And heal it, if it be.

ROBERT FERGUSSON *from the Latin of Horace* Odes. I. II

Ne'er fash your *thumb* what *gods* decree
To be the *weird* o' you or me,
Nor deal in *cantrup's* kittle cunning
To speir how fast your days are running,
5   But patient lippen for the *best*
Nor be in *dowy thought* opprest,
Whether we see mare winters come
Than this that spits wi' canker'd foam.

  Now moisten weel your *geyzen'd wa'as*
10 Wi' couthy friends and *hearty blaws*;
Ne'er lat your *hope* o'ergang your *days*,
For *eild* and *thraldom* never stays;
The day looks *gash*, toot aff your *horn*,
Nor care yae *strae* about the *morn*.

1780   SAMUEL JOHNSON   A Short Song of Congratulation

Long-expected one and twenty
Ling'ring year, at last is flown,
Pomp and Pleasure, Pride and Plenty
Great Sir John, are all your own.

Loosen'd from the Minor's tether,
Free to mortgage or to sell,
Wild as wind, and light as feather
Bid the slaves of thrift farewel.

Call the Bettys, Kates, and Jennys
Ev'ry name that laughs at Care,
Lavish of your Grandsire's guineas,
Show the Spirit of an heir.

2 *weird* fate; 3 *cantrup's* magic's; *kittle* unreliable; 4 *speir* ask; 5 *lippen for* expect;
6 *dowy* dismal; 8 *canker'd* stormy; 9 *gevzen'd* dry; 10 *couthy* kindly; *blaws*
draughts [of drink]; 12 *eild* old age; *thraldom* servitude; 13 *gash* grim; 14 *strae* straw

All that prey on vice and folly
Joy to see their quarry fly,
Here the Gamester light and jolly,
There the Lender grave and sly.

Wealth, Sir John, was made to wander,
Let it wander as it will;
See the Jocky, see the Pander,
Bid them come, and take their fill.

When the bonny Blade carouses,
Pockets full, and Spirits high,
What are acres? What are houses?
Only dirt, or wet or dry.

If the Guardian or the Mother
Tell the woes of wilful waste,
Scorn their counsel and their pother,
You can hang or drown at last.

SAMUEL JOHNSON On the Death of *Dr. Robert Levet*   **1783**

Condemn'd to hope's delusive mine,
    As on we toil from day to day,
By sudden blasts, or slow decline,
    Our social comforts drop away.

Well tried through many a varying year,
    See LEVET to the grave descend;
Officious, innocent, sincere,
    Of ev'ry friendless name the friend.

Yet still he fills affection's eye,
    Obscurely wise, and coarsely kind;
Nor, letter'd arrogance, deny
    Thy praise to merit unrefin'd.

When fainting nature call'd for aid,
    And hov'ring death prepar'd the blow,
His vig'rous remedy display'd
    The power of art without the show.

In misery's darkest caverns known,
     His useful care was ever nigh,
Where hopeless anguish pour'd his groan,
     And lonely want retir'd to die.

No summons mock'd by chill delay,
     No petty gain disdain'd by pride,
The modest wants of ev'ry day
     The toil of ev'ry day supplied.

His virtues walk'd their narrow round,
     Nor made a pause, nor left a void;
And sure th' Eternal Master found
     The single talent well employ'd.

The busy day, the peaceful night,
     Unfelt, uncounted, glided by;
His frame was firm, his powers were bright,
     Tho' now his eightieth year was nigh.

Then with no throbbing fiery pain,
     No cold gradations of decay,
Death broke at once the vital chain,
     And free'd his soul the nearest way.

WILLIAM BLAKE To the Evening Star

Thou fair-hair'd angel of the evening,
Now, while the sun rests on the mountains, light
Thy bright torch of love; thy radiant crown
Put on, and smile upon our evening bed!
Smile on our loves; and, while thou drawest the
Blue curtains of the sky, scatter thy silver dew
On every flower that shuts its sweet eyes
In timely sleep. Let thy west wind sleep on
The lake; speak silence with thy glimmering eyes,
And wash the dusk with silver. Soon, full soon,
Dost thou withdraw; then the wolf rages wide,
And the lion glares thro' the dun forest:
The fleeces of our flocks are cover'd with
Thy sacred dew: protect them with thine influence.

WILLIAM COWPER *from* The Task

[The Winter Evening]

Just when our drawing-rooms begin to blaze
With lights by clear reflection multiplied
From many a mirrour, in which he of Gath
Goliath, might have seen his giant bulk
Whole without stooping, tow'ring crest and all,
My pleasures too begin. But me perhaps
The glowing hearth may satisfy awhile
With faint illumination that uplifts
The shadow to the cieling, there by fits
Dancing uncouthly to the quiv'ring flame.
Not undelightful is an hour to me
So spent in parlour twilight; such a gloom
Suits well the thoughtfull or unthinking mind,
The mind contemplative, with some new theme
Pregnant, or indisposed alike to all.
Laugh ye, who boast your more mercurial pow'rs
That never feel a stupor, I know no pause
Nor need one. I am conscious, and confess
Fearless, a soul that does not always think.
Me oft has fancy ludicrous and wild
Sooth'd with a waking dream of houses, tow'rs,
Trees, churches, and strange visages express'd
In the red cinders, while with poring eye
I gazed, myself creating what I saw.
Nor less amused have I quiescent watch'd
The sooty films that play upon the bars
Pendulous, and foreboding in the view
Of superstition prophesying still
Though still deceived, some stranger's near approach.
'Tis thus the understanding takes repose
In indolent vacuity of thought,
And sleeps and is refresh'd. Meanwhile the face
Conceals the mood lethargic with a mask
Of deep deliberation, as the man
Were task'd to his full strength, absorb'd and lost.
Thus oft reclin'd at ease, I lose an hour
At evening, till at length the freezing blast
That sweeps the bolted shutter, summons home

The recollected powers, and snapping short
The glassy threads with which the fancy weaves
Her brittle toys, restores me to myself.
How calm is my recess, and how the frost
Raging abroad, and the rough wind, endear
The silence and the warmth enjoy'd within.

(. . .)

[The Winter Walk at Noon]

Where now the vital energy that moved
While summer was, the pure and subtle lymph
Through th' imperceptible mæandring veins
Of leaf and flow'r? It sleeps; and the icy touch
Of unprolific winter has impress'd
A cold stagnation on th' intestine tide.
But let the months go round, a few short months,
And all shall be restored. These naked shoots
Barren as lances, among which the wind
Makes wintry music, sighing as it goes,
Shall put their graceful foliage on again,
And more aspiring and with ampler spread
Shall boast new charms, and more than they have lost.
Then, each in its peculiar honors clad,
Shall publish even to the distant eye
Its family and tribe. Laburnum rich
In streaming gold; syringa iv'ry-pure;
The scented and the scentless rose; this red
And of an humbler growth, the ¹other tall,
And throwing up into the darkest gloom
Of neighb'ring cypress or more sable yew
Her silver globes, light as the foamy surf
That the wind severs from the broken wave.
The lilac various in array, now white,
Now sanguine, and her beauteous head now set
With purple spikes pyramidal, as if
Studious of ornament, yet unresolved
Which hue she most approved, she chose them all.
Copious of flow'rs the woodbine, pale and wan,

1. The Guelder-rose.

But well compensating their sickly looks
With never-cloying odours, early and late.
Hypericum all bloom, so thick a swarm
Of flow'rs like flies cloathing her slender rods
That scarce a leaf appears. Mezerion too
Though leafless well attired, and thick beset
With blushing wreaths investing ev'ry spray.
Althæa with the purple eye, the broom,
Yellow and bright as bullion unalloy'd
Her blossoms, and luxuriant above all
The jasmine, throwing wide her elegant sweets,
The deep dark green of whose unvarnish'd leaf
Makes more conspicuous, and illumines more
The bright profusion of her scatter'd stars. –
These have been, and these shall be in their day.
And all this uniform uncoloured scene
Shall be dismantled of its fleecy load,
And flush into variety again.

ROBERT BURNS To a Mouse, on Turning Her Up in Her Nest, 1786 with the Plough, November, 1785

Wee, sleeket, cowran, tim'rous *beastie*,
O, what a panic 's in thy breastie!
Thou need na start awa sae hasty,
     Wi' bickering brattle!
5 I wad be laith to rin an' chase thee,
     Wi' murd'ring *pattle*!

I'm truly sorry Man's dominion
Has broken Nature's social union,
An' justifies that ill opinion,
10   Which makes thee startle,
At me, thy poor, earth-born companion,
     An' *fellow-mortal*!

1 *sleeket* glossy; 4 *bickering brattle* scurrying haste; 5 *laith* loath; 6 *pattle* spade;

I doubt na, whyles, but thou may *thieve*;
What then? poor beastie, thou maun live!
15 A *daimen-icker* in a *thrave*
    'S a sma' request:
    I'll get a blessin wi' the lave,
        An' never miss't!

    Thy wee-bit *housie*, too, in ruin!
20 It's silly wa's the win's are strewin!
    An' naething, now, to big a new ane,
        O' foggage green!
    An' bleak *December's winds* ensuin,
        Baith snell an' keen!

25 Thou saw the fields laid bare an' wast,
    An' weary *Winter* comin fast,
    An' cozie here, beneath the blast,
        Thou thought to dwell,
    Till crash! the cruel *coulter* past
30   Out thro' thy cell.

    That wee-bit heap o' leaves an' stibble,
    Has cost thee monie a weary nibble!
    Now thou 's turn'd out, for a' thy trouble,
        But house or hald,
35 To thole the Winter's *sleety dribble*,
        An' *cranreuch* cauld!

    But Mousie, thou art no thy-lane,
    In proving *foresight* may be vain:
    The best laid schemes o' *Mice* an' *Men*,
40   Gang aft agley,
    An' lea'e us nought but grief an' pain,
        For promis'd joy!

13 *whyles* at times; 15 *daimen-icker* odd ear of corn; *thrave* two stooks;
17 *lave* remainder; 21 *big* build; 22 *foggage* grass; 24 *snell* bitter; 34 *But* without;
hald refuge; 35 *thole* endure; 36 *cranreuch* frost; 37 *no thy-lane* not alone;
40 *agley* away

Still, thou art blest, compar'd wi' *me*!
The *present* only toucheth thee:
45 But Och! I *backward* cast my e'e,
   On prospects drear!
An' *forward*, tho' I canna *see*,
   I *guess* an' *fear*!

ROBERT BURNS Address to the Unco Guid, Or the Rigidly Righteous 1787

My Son, these maxims make a rule,
 And lump them ay thegither;
The Rigid Righteous *is a fool,*
 The Rigid Wise *anither:*
5 *The cleanest corn that e'er was dight*
 May hae some pyles o' caff in;
So ne'er a fellow-creature slight
 For random fits o' daffin.
SOLOMON. – Eccles. ch. vii. vers. 16.

O ye wha are sae guid yoursel,
 Sae pious and sae holy,
Ye've nought to do but mark and tell
 Your Neebours' fauts and folly!
5 Whase life is like a weel-gaun mill,
 Supply'd wi' store o' water,
The heaped happer 's ebbing still,
 And still the clap plays clatter.

Hear me, ye venerable Core,
10 As counsel for poor mortals,
That frequent pass douce Wisdom's door
 For glaikit Folly's portals;
I, for their thoughtless, careless sakes
 Would here propone defences,
15 Their donsie tricks, their black mistakes,
 Their failings and mischances.

5 *dight* cleaned from chaff; 8 *daffin* merriment

5 *weel-gaun* well-going; 7 *happer* hopper; 8 *clap* clapper; 11 *douce* steady;
12 *glaikit* inattentive; 15 *donsie* unlucky;

Ye see your state wi' theirs compar'd,
    And shudder at the niffer,
But cast a moment's fair regard
20   What maks the mighty differ;
Discount what scant occasion gave,
    That purity ye pride in,
And (what 's aft mair than a' the lave)
    Your better art o' hiding.

25 Think, when your castigated pulse
    Gies now and then a wallop,
What ragings must his veins convulse,
    That still eternal gallop:
Wi' wind and tide fair i' your tail,
30   Right on ye scud your sea-way;
But, in the teeth o' baith to sail,
    It maks an unco leeway.

See Social-life and Glee sit down,
    All joyous and unthinking,
35 Till, quite transmugrify'd, they're grown
    Debauchery and Drinking:
O would they stay to calculate
    Th' eternal consequences;
Or your more dreaded h-ll to state,
40   D-mnation of expences!

Ye high, exalted, virtuous Dames,
    Ty'd up in godly laces,
Before ye gie poor *Frailty* names,
    Suppose a change o' cases;
45 A dear-lov'd lad, convenience snug,
    A treacherous inclination –
But, let me whisper i' your lug,
    Ye're aiblins nae temptation.

Then gently scan your brother Man,
50   Still gentler sister Woman;
Tho' they may gang a kennin wrang,
    To step aside is human:

18 *niffer* exchange; 23 *lave* rest; 32 *unco* strange; 48 *aiblins* perhaps; 51 *a kennin* a little

One point must still be greatly dark,
 The moving *Why* they do it;
55 And just as lamely can ye mark,
 How far perhaps they rue it.

Who made the heart, 'tis *He* alone
 Decidedly can try us,
He knows each chord its various tone,
60 Each spring its various bias:
Then at the balance let's be mute,
 We never can adjust it;
What 's *done* we partly may compute,
 But know not what 's *resisted*.

WILLIAM BLAKE *from* Songs of Innocence   **1789**

Holy Thursday

Twas on a Holy Thursday their innocent faces clean
The children walking two & two in red & blue & green
Grey headed beadles walkd before with wands as white as snow
Till into the high dome of Pauls they like Thames waters flow

O what a multitude they seemd these flowers of London town
Seated in companies they sit with radiance all their own
The hum of multitudes was there but multitudes of lambs
Thousands of little boys & girls raising their innocent hands

Now like a mighty wind they raise to heaven the voice of song
Or like harmonious thunderings the seats of heaven among
Beneath them sit the aged men wise guardians of the poor
Then cherish pity, lest you drive an angel from your door

CHARLOTTE SMITH Sonnet. Written in the Church-yard at Middleton in Sussex

Pressed by the Moon, mute arbitress of tides,
 While the loud equinox its power combines,
 The sea no more its swelling surge confines,
But o'er the shrinking land sublimely rides.

The wild blast, rising from the Western cave,
   Drives the huge billows from their heaving bed,
   Tears from their grassy tombs the village dead,
And breaks the silent sabbath of the grave!
With shells and seaweed mingled, on the shore
Lo! their bones whiten in the frequent wave;
   But vain to them the winds and waters rave;
They hear the warring element no more:
While I am doomed – by life's long storm oppressed,
To gaze with envy on their gloomy rest.

ELIZABETH HANDS On an Unsociable Family

O what a strange parcel of creatures are we,
Scarce ever to quarrel, or even agree;
We all are alone, though at home altogether,
Except to the fire constrained by the weather;
Then one says, ''Tis cold,' which we all of us know,
And with unanimity answer, ''Tis so':
With shrugs and with shivers all look at the fire,
And shuffle ourselves and our chairs a bit nigher;
Then quickly, preceded by silence profound,
A yawn epidemical catches around:
Like social companions we never fall out,
Nor ever care what one another's about;
To comfort each other is never our plan,
For to please ourselves, truly, is more than we can.

1791 ROBERT BURNS Tam o' Shanter. A Tale

Of Brownyis and of Bogillis full is this buke.
                GAWIN DOUGLAS.

When chapman billies leave the street,
And drouthy neebors, neebors meet,
As market-days are wearing late,
An' folk begin to tak the gate;

1 *chapman billies* pedlars; 2 *drouthy* thirsty; 4 *gate* road;

While we sit bousing at the nappy,
And getting fou and unco happy,
We think na on the lang Scots miles,
The mosses, waters, slaps, and styles,
That lie between us and our hame,
Whare sits our sulky sullen dame,
Gathering her brows like gathering storm,
Nursing her wrath to keep it warm.

   This truth fand honest *Tam o' Shanter*,
As he frae Ayr ae night did canter,
(Auld Ayr, wham ne'er a town surpasses,
For honest men and bonny lasses.)

   O *Tam*! hadst thou but been sae wise,
As ta'en thy ain wife *Kate*'s advice!
She tauld thee weel thou was a skellum,
A blethering, blustering, drunken blellum;
That frae November till October,
Ae market-day thou was nae sober;
That ilka melder, wi' the miller,
Thou sat as lang as thou had siller;
That every naig was ca'd a shoe on,
The smith and thee gat roaring fou on;
That at the L – d's house, even on Sunday,
Thou drank wi' Kirkton Jean till Monday.
She prophesied that late or soon,
Thou would be found deep drown'd in Doon;
Or catch'd wi' warlocks in the mirk,
By *Alloway*'s auld haunted kirk.

   Ah, gentle dames! it gars me greet,
To think how mony counsels sweet,
How mony lengthen'd sage advices,
The husband frae the wife despises!

   But to our tale: Ae market-night,
Tam had got planted unco right;
Fast by an ingle, bleezing finely,
Wi' reaming swats, that drank divinely;
And at his elbow, Souter *Johnny*,
His ancient, trusty, drouthy crony;

5 *nappy* ale; 6 *fou* drunk; 8 *slaps* gaps in walls; 19 *skellum* good-for-nothing;
20 *blellum* windbag; 23 *melder* meal-grinding; 24 *siller* silver; 25 *naig* horse;
ca'd driven; 33 *gars me greet* makes me weep; 38 *unco* uncommonly; 39 *bleezing*
talking loudly; 40 *reaming swats* foaming ale; 41 *Souter* cobbler;

Tam lo'ed him like a vera brither;
They had been fou for weeks thegither.

45   The night drave on wi' sangs and clatter;
And ay the ale was growing better:
The landlady and *Tam* grew gracious,
Wi' favours, secret, sweet, and precious:
The Souter tauld his queerest stories;
50   The landlord's laugh was ready chorus:
The storm without might rair and rustle,
Tam did na mind the storm a whistle.

    Care, mad to see a man sae happy,
E'en drown'd himsel amang the nappy:
55   As bees flee hame wi' lades o' treasure,
The minutes wing'd their way wi' pleasure:
Kings may be blest, but *Tam* was glorious,
O'er a' the ills o' life victorious!

    But pleasures are like poppies spread,
60   You seize the flower, its bloom is shed;
Or like the snow falls in the river,
A moment white – then melts for ever;
Or like the borealis race,
That flit ere you can point their place;
65   Or like the rainbow's lovely form
Evanishing amid the storm. –
Nae man can tether time or tide;
The hour approaches *Tam* maun ride;
That hour, o' night's black arch the key-stane,
70   That dreary hour he mounts his beast in;
And sic a night he taks the road in,
As ne'er poor sinner was abroad in.

    The wind blew as 'twad blawn its last;
The rattling showers rose on the blast;
75   The speedy gleams the darkness swallow'd;
Loud, deep, and lang, the thunder bellow'd:
That night, a child might understand,
The Deil had business on his hand.

    Weel mounted on his gray mare, *Meg*,
80   A better never lifted leg,
Tam skelpit on thro' dub and mire,
Despising wind, and rain, and fire;

51 *rair* roar; 55 *lades* loads; 78 *Deil* devil; 81 *skelpit* hurried; *dub* puddle;

Whiles holding fast his gude blue bonnet;
Whiles crooning o'er some auld Scots sonnet;
85 Whiles glowring round wi' prudent cares,
Lest bogles catch him unawares:
Kirk-Alloway was drawing nigh,
Whare ghaists and houlets nightly cry. –
    By this time he was cross the ford,
90 Whare, in the snaw, the chapman smoor'd;
And past the birks and meikle stane,
Whare drunken *Charlie* brak's neck-bane;
And thro' the whins, and by the cairn,
Whare hunters fand the murder'd bairn;
95 And near the thorn, aboon the well,
Whare *Mungo*'s mither hang'd hersel. –
Before him *Doon* pours all his floods;
The doubling storm roars thro' the woods;
The lightnings flash from pole to pole;
100 Near and more near the thunders roll:
When, glimmering thro' the groaning trees,
Kirk-Alloway seem'd in a bleeze;
Thro' ilka bore the beams were glancing;
And loud resounded mirth and dancing. –
105   Inspiring bold *John Barleycorn*!
What dangers thou canst make us scorn!
Wi' tippeny, we fear nae evil;
Wi' usquabae, we'll face the devil! –
The swats sae ream'd in *Tammie*'s noddle,
110 Fair play, he car'd na deils a boddle.
But *Maggie* stood right sair astonish'd,
Till, by the heel and hand admonish'd,
She ventured forward on the light;
And, vow! *Tam* saw an unco sight!
115 Warlocks and witches in a dance;
Nae cotillion brent new frae *France*,
But hornpipes, jigs, strathspeys, and reels,
Put life and mettle in their heels.
A winnock-bunker in the east,
120 There sat auld Nick, in shape o' beast;

---

85 *glowring* staring; 88 *houlets* owls; 90 *smoor'd* smothered; 91 *birks* birches;
meikle stane great stone; 95 *aboon* above; 102 *bleeze* blaze; 103 *bore* chink;
107 *tippeny* twopenny ale; 109 *swats* ale; *ream'd* foamed; 110 *boddle* farthing;
116 *cotillion* dance; *brent* brand; 119 *winnock-bunker* window-seat;

A towzie tyke, black, grim, and large,
To gie them music was his charge:
He screw'd the pipes and gart them skirl,
Till roof and rafters a' did dirl. –

125 Coffins stood round, like open presses,
That shaw'd the dead in their last dresses;
And by some devilish cantraip slight
Each in its cauld hand held a light. –
By which heroic *Tam* was able

130 To note upon the haly table,
A murderer's banes in gibbet airns;
Twa span-lang, wee, unchristen'd bairns;
A thief, new-cutted frae a rape,
Wi' his last gasp his gab did gape;

135 Five tomahawks, wi' blude red-rusted;
Five scymitars, wi' murder crusted;
A garter, which a babe had strangled;
A knife, a father's throat had mangled,
Whom his ain son o' life bereft,

140 The grey hairs yet stack to the heft;
Wi' mair o' horrible and awefu',
Which even to name wad be unlawfu'.

As *Tammie* glow'rd, amaz'd, and curious,
The mirth and fun grew fast and furious:

145 The piper loud and louder blew;
The dancers quick and quicker flew;
They reel'd, they set, they cross'd, they cleekit,
Till ilka carlin swat and reekit,
And coost her duddies to the wark,

150 And linket at it in her sark!

Now, *Tam*, O *Tam*! had thae been queans,
A' plump and strapping in their teens,
Their sarks, instead o' creeshie flannen,
Been snaw-white seventeen hunder linnen!

155 Thir breeks o' mine, my only pair,
That ance were plush, o' gude blue hair,
I wad hae gi'en them off my hurdies,
For ae blink o' the bonie burdies!

---

121 *towzie* tousled; *tyke* dog; 123 *gart* made; *skirl* shriek; 124 *dirl* ring;
127 *cantraip* weird; *slight* trick; 134 *gab* mouth; 147 *cleekit* joined hands; 148 *carlin*
old woman; *swat and reekit* sweated and steamed; 149 *coost* cast off; *duddies* rags;
150 *linket* tripped nimbly; *sark* shift; 151 *queans* girls; 153 *creeshie* greasy;
155 *thir* these; 157 *hurdies* buttocks;

But wither'd beldams, auld and droll,
160 Rigwoodie hags wad spean a foal,
Lowping and flinging on a crummock,
I wonder didna turn thy stomach.

But *Tam* kend what was what fu' brawlie,
There was ae winsome wench and wawlie,
165 That night enlisted in the core,
(Lang after kend on *Carrick* shore;
For mony a beast to dead she shot,
And perish'd mony a bony boat,
And shook baith meikle corn and bear,
170 And kept the country-side in fear:)
Her cutty sark, o' Paisley harn,
That while a lassie she had worn,
In longitude tho' sorely scanty,
It was her best, and she was vauntie. –
175 Ah! little kend thy reverend grannie,
That sark she coft for her wee Nannie,
Wi' twa pund Scots, ('twas a' her riches),
Wad ever grac'd a dance of witches!

But here my Muse her wing maun cour;
180 Sic flights are far beyond her pow'r;
To sing how Nannie lap and flang,
(A souple jade she was, and strang),
And how *Tam* stood, like ane bewitch'd,
And thought his very een enrich'd;
185 Even Satan glowr'd, and fidg'd fu' fain,
And hotch'd and blew wi' might and main:
Till first ae caper, syne anither,
Tam tint his reason a' thegither,
And roars out, 'Weel done, Cutty-sark!'
190 And in an instant all was dark:
And scarcely had he Maggie rallied,
When out the hellish legion sallied.

As bees bizz out wi' angry fyke,
When plundering herds assail their byke;

160 *rigwoodie* scrawny; *spean* wean; 161 *lowping* leaping; *crummock* staff;
163 *fu' brawlie* very well; 164 *wawlie* buxom; 165 *core* company; 166 *kend* known;
169 *bear* barley; 171 *cutty sark* short smock; *harn* cloth; 176 *coft* bought;
179 *cour* stoop; 181 *lap* leaped; 185 *fidg'd* wriggled; *fain* fond; 186 *hotch'd* hitched
himself; 187 *syne* then; 188 *tint* lost; 193 *fyke* fuss; 194 *herds* shepherds;
byke hive;

195 As open pussie's mortal foes,
When, pop! she starts before their nose;
As eager runs the market-crowd,
When 'Catch the thief!' resounds aloud;
So Maggie runs, the witches follow,
200 Wi' mony an eldritch skreech and hollow.

    Ah, *Tam*! Ah, *Tam*! thou'll get thy fairin!
In hell they'll roast thee like a herrin!
In vain thy *Kate* awaits thy comin!
Kate soon will be a woefu' woman!

205 Now, do thy speedy utmost, Meg,
And win the key-stane of the brig;
There at them thou thy tail may toss,
A running stream they dare na cross.
But ere the key-stane she could make,
210 The fient a tail she had to shake!
For Nannie, far before the rest,
Hard upon noble Maggie prest,
And flew at *Tam* wi' furious ettle;
But little wist she Maggie's mettle –
215 Ae spring brought off her master hale,
But left behind her ain gray tail:
The carlin claught her by the rump,
And left poor Maggie scarce a stump.

    Now, wha this tale o' truth shall read,
220 Ilk man and mother's son, take heed:
Whene'er to drink you are inclin'd,
Or cutty-sarks run in your mind,
Think, ye may buy the joys o'er dear,
Remember Tam o' Shanter's mare.

1792   **ROBERT BURNS** Song

    Ae fond kiss, and then we sever;
    Ae fareweel, and then for ever!
    Deep in heart-wrung tears I'll pledge thee,
    Warring sighs and groans I'll wage thee. –

195 *open* bay; *pussie's* the hare's; 201 *fairin* punishment; 206 *brig* bridge; 210 *fient a* devil-a; 213 *ettle* purpose; 215 *hale* whole; 217 *carlin* old woman

Who shall say that Fortune grieves him,
While the star of hope she leaves him:
Me, nae chearful twinkle lights me;
Dark despair around benights me. –

I'll ne'er blame my partial fancy,
Naething could resist my Nancy:
But to see her, was to love her;
Love but her, and love for ever. –

Had we never lov'd sae kindly,
Had we never lov'd sae blindly!
Never met – or never parted,
We had ne'er been broken-hearted. –

Fare-thee-weel, thou first and fairest!
Fare-thee-weel, thou best and dearest!
Thine be ilka joy and treasure,
Peace, Enjoyment, Love and Pleasure! –

Ae fond kiss, and then we sever!
Ae fareweel, Alas, for ever!
Deep in heart-wrung tears I'll pledge thee,
Warring sighs and groans I'll wage thee. –

WILLIAM BLAKE *from* Visions of the Daughters of Albion   1793

Then Oothoon waited silent all the day. and all the night,
PLATE 5
But when the morn arose, her lamentation renewd,
The Daughters of Albion hear her woes, & eccho back her sighs.

O Urizen! Creator of men! mistaken Demon of heaven:
Thy joys are tears! thy labour vain, to form men to thine image.
How can one joy absorb another? are not different joys
Holy, eternal, infinite! and each joy is a Love.

Does not the great mouth laugh at a gift? & the narrow eyelids
    mock
At the labour that is above payment, and wilt thou take the ape
For thy councellor? or the dog, for a schoolmaster to thy children?
Does he who contemns poverty, and he who turns with abhorrence

From usury feel the same passion or are they moved alike?
How can the giver of gifts experience the delights of the merchant?
How the industrious citizen the pains of the husbandman.
How different far the fat fed hireling with hollow drum;
Who buys whole corn fields into wastes, and sings upon the heath:
How different their eye and ear! how different the world to them!
With what sense does the parson claim the labour of the farmer?
What are his nets & gins & traps. & how does he surround him
With cold floods of abstraction, and with forests of solitude,
To build him castles and high spires. where kings & priests may
    dwell.

Till she who burns with youth. and knows no fixed lot; is bound
In spells of law to one she loaths: and must she drag the chain
Of life, in weary lust: must chilling murderous thoughts, obscure
The clear heaven of her eternal spring? to bear the wintry rage
Of a harsh terror driv'n to madness, bound to hold a rod
Over her shrinking shoulders all the day; & all the night
To turn the wheel of false desire: and longings that wake her
    womb
To the abhorred birth of cherubs in the human form
That live a pestilence & die a meteor & are no more.
Till the child dwell with one he hates. and do the deed he loaths
And the impure scourge force his seed into its unripe birth
E'er yet his eyelids can behold the arrows of the day.

Does the whale worship at thy footsteps as the hungry dog?
Or does he scent the mountain prey, because his nostrils wide
Draw in the ocean? does his eye discern the flying cloud
As the ravens eye? or does he measure the expanse like the vulture?
Does the still spider view the cliffs where eagles hide their young?
Or does the fly rejoice, because the harvest is brought in?
Does not the eagle scorn the earth & despise the treasures beneath?
But the mole knoweth what is there, & the worm shall tell it thee.
Does not the worm erect a pillar in the mouldering church yard?

PLATE 6

And a palace of eternity in the jaws of the hungry grave
Over his porch these words are written: Take thy bliss O Man!
And sweet shall be thy taste & sweet thy infant joys renew!

(. . .)

PLATE 7   **1793** [537

The moment of desire! the moment of desire! The virgin
That pines for man; shall awaken her womb to enormous joys
In the secret shadows of her chamber; the youth shut up from
The lustful joy. shall forget to generate. & create an amorous image
In the shadows of his curtains and in the folds of his silent pillow.
Are not these the places of religion? the rewards of continence?
The self enjoyings of self denial? Why dost thou seek religion?
Is it because acts are not lovely, that thou seekest solitude,
Where the horrible darkness is impressed with reflections of desire.

Father of Jealousy. be thou accursed from the earth!
Why hast thou taught my Theotormon this accursed thing?
Till beauty fades from off my shoulders darken'd and cast out,
A solitary shadow wailing on the margin of non-entity.

I cry, Love! Love! Love! happy happy Love! free as the mountain
    wind!
Can that be Love, that drinks another as a sponge drinks water?
That clouds with jealousy his nights, with weepings all the day:
To spin a web of age around him, grey and hoary! dark!
Till his eyes sicken at the fruit that hangs before his sight.
Such is self-love that envies all! a creeping skeleton
With lamplike eyes watching around the frozen marriage bed.

But silken nets and traps of adamant will Oothoon spread,
And catch for thee girls of mild silver, or of furious gold;
I'll lie beside thee on a bank & view their wanton play
In lovely copulation bliss on bliss with Theotormon:
Red as the rosy morning, lustful as the first born beam,
Oothoon shall view his dear delight, nor e'er with jealous cloud
Come in the heaven of generous love; nor selfish blightings bring.

WILLIAM BLAKE

Never seek to tell thy love
Love that never told can be
For the gentle wind does move
Silently invisibly

I told my love I told my love
I told her all my heart
Trembling cold in ghastly fears
Ah she doth depart

Soon as she was gone from me
A traveller came by
Silently invisibly
He took her with a sigh

(1863)

1794   § **WILLIAM BLAKE** *from* **Songs of Innocence and of Experience**

Introduction

Hear the voice of the Bard!
Who Present, Past, & Future sees
Whose ears have heard,
The Holy Word,
That walk'd among the ancient trees.

Calling the lapsed Soul
And weeping in the evening dew:
That might controll,
The starry pole;
And fallen fallen light renew!

O Earth O Earth return!
Arise from out the dewy grass;
Night is worn,
And the morn
Rises from the slumberous mass.

Turn away no more:
Why wilt thou turn away
The starry floor
The watry shore
Is giv'n thee till the break of day.

The Clod and the Pebble

Love seeketh not Itself to please,
Nor for itself hath any care;
But for another gives its ease,
And builds a Heaven in Hells despair.

　So sang a little Clod of Clay,
　Trodden with the cattles feet:
　But a Pebble of the brook,
　Warbled out these metres meet.

Love seeketh only Self to please,
To bind another to its delight;
Joys in anothers loss of ease,
And builds a Hell in Heavens despite.

The Sick Rose

O Rose thou art sick.
The invisible worm,
That flies in the night
In the howling storm:

Has found out thy bed
Of crimson joy:
And his dark secret love
Does thy life destroy.

The Tyger

Tyger Tyger, burning bright,
In the forests of the night:
What immortal hand or eye,
Could frame thy fearful symmetry?

In what distant deeps or skies
Burnt the fire of thine eyes!
On what wings dare he aspire?
What the hand, dare sieze the fire?

And what shoulder, & what art,
Could twist the sinews of thy heart?
And when thy heart began to beat,
What dread hand? & what dread feet?

What the hammer? what the chain,
In what furnace was thy brain?
What the anvil? what dread grasp,
Dare its deadly terrors clasp?

When the stars threw down their spears
And water'd heaven with their tears:
Did he smile his work to see?
Did he who made the Lamb make thee?

Tyger, Tyger burning bright,
In the forests of the night:
What immortal hand or eye,
Dare frame thy fearful symmetry?

Ah! Sun-Flower

Ah Sun-flower! weary of time.
Who countest the steps of the Sun:
Seeking after that sweet golden clime
Where the travellers journey is done.

Where the Youth pined away with desire,
And the pale Virgin shrouded in snow:
Arise from their graves and aspire,
Where my Sun-flower wishes to go.

The Garden of Love

I went to the Garden of Love.
And saw what I never had seen:
A Chapel was built in the midst,
Where I used to play on the green.

And the gates of this Chapel were shut,
And Thou shalt not. writ over the door;
So I turn'd to the Garden of Love,
That so many sweet flowers bore.

And I saw it was filled with graves,
And tomb-stones where flowers should be:
And Priests in black gowns, were walking their rounds,
And binding with briars, my joys & desires.

London

I wander thro' each charter'd street,
Near where the charter'd Thames does flow.
And mark in every face I meet
Marks of weakness, marks of woe.

In every cry of every Man,
In every Infants cry of fear,
In every voice: in every ban,
The mind-forg'd manacles I hear

How the Chimney-sweepers cry
Every blackning Church appalls,
And the hapless Soldiers sigh,
Runs in blood down Palace walls

But most thro' midnight streets I hear
How the youthful Harlots curse
Blasts the new-born Infants tear
And blights with plagues the Marriage hearse

A Poison Tree

I was angry with my friend:
I told my wrath, my wrath did end.
I was angry with my foe:
I told it not, my wrath did grow.

And I watered it in fears.
Night & morning with my tears:
And I sunned it with smiles.
And with soft deceitful wiles.

And it grew both day and night.
Till it bore an apple bright.
And my foe beheld it shine.
And he knew that it was mine.

And into my garden stole.
When the night had veild the pole;
In the morning glad I see;
My foe outstretched beneath the tree.

§   §   §

1796   SAMUEL TAYLOR COLERIDGE The Eolian Harp

Composed at Clevedon, Somersetshire

My pensive Sara! thy soft cheek reclined
Thus on mine arm, most soothing sweet it is
To sit beside our Cot, our Cot o'ergrown
With white-flower'd Jasmin, and the broad-leav'd Myrtle,
(Meet emblems they of Innocence and Love!)
And watch the clouds, that late were rich with light,
Slow saddening round, and mark the star of eve
Serenely brilliant (such should Wisdom be)

Shine opposite! How exquisite the scents
Snatch'd from yon bean-field! and the world *so* hush'd!
The stilly murmur of the distant Sea
Tells us of silence.

            And that simplest Lute,
Placed length-ways in the clasping casement, hark!
How by the desultory breeze caress'd,
Like some coy maid half yielding to her lover,
It pours such sweet upbraiding, as must needs
Tempt to repeat the wrong! And now, its strings
Boldlier swept, the long sequacious notes
Over delicious surges sink and rise,
Such a soft floating witchery of sound
As twilight Elfins make, when they at eve
Voyage on gentle gales from Fairy-Land,
Where Melodies round honey-dropping flowers,
Footless and wild, like birds of Paradise,
Nor pause, nor perch, hovering on untam'd wing!
[O! the one Life within us and abroad,
Which meets all motion and becomes its soul,
A light in sound, a sound-like power in light,
Rhythm in all thought, and joyance every where –
Methinks, it should have been impossible
Not to love all things in a world so fill'd;
Where the breeze warbles, and the mute still air
Is Music slumbering on her instrument.][1]

   And thus, my Love! as on the midway slope
Of yonder hill I stretch my limbs at noon,
Whilst through my half-clos'd eye-lids I behold
The sunbeams dance, like diamonds, on the main,
And tranquil muse upon tranquillity;
Full many a thought uncall'd and undetain'd,
And many idle flitting phantasies,
Traverse my indolent and passive brain,
As wild and various as the random gales
That swell and flutter on this subject Lute!

1. [lines first published in 1817]

And what if all of animated nature
Be but organic Harps diversely fram'd,
That tremble into thought, as o'er them sweeps
Plastic and vast, one intellectual breeze,
At once the Soul of each, and God of all?

But thy more serious eye a mild reproof
Darts, O belovéd Woman! nor such thoughts
Dim and unhallow'd dost thou not reject,
And biddest me walk humbly with my God.
Meek Daughter in the family of Christ!
Well hast thou said and holily disprais'd
These shapings of the unregenerate mind;
Bubbles that glitter as they rise and break
On vain Philosophy's aye-babbling spring.
For never guiltless may I speak of him,
The Incomprehensible! save when with awe
I praise him, and with Faith that inly *feels*;
Who with his saving mercies healéd me,
A sinful and most miserable man,
Wilder'd and dark, and gave me to possess
Peace, and this Cot, and thee, heart-honour'd Maid!

(1796, 1817)

ROBERT BURNS A Red, Red Rose

My luve is like a red, red rose,
    That's newly sprung in June:
My luve is like the melodie,
    That's sweetly play'd in tune.
As fair art thou, my bonie lass,
    So deep in luve am I,
And I will luve thee still, my dear,
    Till a' the seas gang dry.

Till a' the seas gang dry, my dear,
    And the rocks melt wi' the sun!
And I will luve thee still, my dear,
    While the sands o' life shall run.
And fare-thee-weel, my only luve,
    And fare-thee-weel a while!
And I will come again, my luve,
    Tho' it were ten-thousand mile.

GEORGE CANNING and JOHN HOOKHAM
FRERE Sapphics

The Friend of Humanity and the Knife-Grinder

FRIEND OF HUMANITY

'Needy Knife-grinder! whither are you going?
Rough is the Road, your Wheel is out of order –
Bleak blows the blast; – your hat has got a hole in't,
        So have your breeches!

'Weary Knife-grinder! little think the proud ones,
Who in their coaches roll along the turnpike-
-road, what hard work 'tis crying all day 'Knives and
        'Scissars to grind O!'

'Tell me, Knife-grinder, how you came to grind knives?
Did some rich man tyrannically use you?
Was it the 'Squire? or Parson of the Parish?
        Or the Attorney?

'Was it the 'Squire for killing of his Game? or
Covetous Parson for his Tythes distraining?
Or roguish Lawyer made you lose your little
        All in a law-suit?

'(Have you not read the Rights of Man, by TOM PAINE?)
Drops of compassion tremble on my eye-lids,
Ready to fall, as soon as you have told your
        Pitiful story.'

KNIFE-GRINDER

'Story! God bless you! I have none to tell, Sir,
Only last night a-drinking at the Chequers,
This poor old hat and breeches, as you see, were
        Torn in a scuffle.

'Constables came up for to take me into
Custody; they took me before the Justice;
Justice OLDMIXON put me in the Parish-
        Stocks for a Vagrant.

'I should be glad to drink your Honour's health in
A Pot of Beer, if you will give me Sixpence;
But for my part, I never love to meddle
                                    With Politics, Sir.'

FRIEND OF HUMANITY

'*I* give thee Sixpence! I will see thee damn'd first –
Wretch! whom no sense of wrongs can rouse to vengeance –
Sordid, unfeeling, reprobate, degraded,
                                    Spiritless outcast!'

  *(Kicks the Knife-grinder, overturns his Wheel, and exit in a
transport of republican enthusiasm and universal philanthropy.)*

**CHARLOTTE SMITH Sonnet. On being Cautioned against
Walking on a Headland Overlooking the Sea, Because It was
Frequented by a Lunatic**

Is there a solitary wretch who hies
To the tall cliff, with starting pace or slow,
And, measuring, views with wild and hollow eyes
Its distance from the waves that chide below;
Who, as the sea-born gale with frequent sighs
Chills his cold bed upon the mountain turf,
With hoarse, half-utter'd lamentation, lies
Murmuring responses to the dashing surf?
In moody sadness, on the giddy brink,
I see him more with envy than with fear;
He has no *nice felicities* that shrink
From giant horrors; wildly wandering here,
He seems (uncursed with reason) not to know
The depth or the duration of his woe.

§ *from* **Lyrical Ballads**   **1798**

SAMUEL TAYLOR COLERIDGE *from* **The Rime of the Ancyent Marinere, in Seven Parts**

ARGUMENT

How a Ship having passed the Line was driven by Storms to the cold Country towards the South Pole; and how from thence she made her course to the Tropical Latitude of the Great Pacific Ocean; and of the strange things that befell; and in what manner the Ancyent Marinere came back to his own Country.

I

It is an ancyent Marinere,
     And he stoppeth one of three:
'By thy long grey beard and thy glittering eye
     Now wherefore stoppest me?

'The Bridegroom's doors are open'd wide,
     And I am next of kin;
The Guests are met, the Feast is set, –
     May'st hear the merry din.'

But still he holds the wedding-guest –
     There was a Ship, quoth he –
'Nay, if thou'st got a laughsome tale,
     'Marinere! come with me.'

He holds him with his skinny hand,
     Quoth he, there was a Ship –
'Now get thee hence, thou grey-beard Loon!
     'Or my Staff shall make thee skip.'

He holds him with his glittering eye –
     The wedding guest stood still
And listens like a three year's child;
     The Marinere hath his will.

The wedding-guest sate on a stone,
　　He cannot chuse but hear:
And thus spake on that ancyent man,
　　The bright-eyed Marinere.

The Ship was cheer'd, the Harbour clear'd –
　　Merrily did we drop
Below the Kirk, below the Hill,
　　Below the Light-house top.

The Sun came up upon the left,
　　Out of the Sea came he:
And he shone bright, and on the right
　　Went down into the Sea.

Higher and higher every day,
　　Till over the mast at noon –
The wedding-guest here beat his breast,
　　For he heard the loud bassoon.

The Bride hath pac'd into the Hall,
　　Red as a rose is she;
Nodding their heads before her goes
　　The merry Minstralsy.

The wedding-guest he beat his breast,
　　Yet he cannot chuse but hear:
And thus spake on that ancyent Man,
　　The bright-eyed Marinere.

Listen, Stranger! Storm and Wind,
　　A Wind and Tempest strong!
For days and weeks it play'd us freaks –
　　Like Chaff we drove along.

Listen, Stranger! Mist and Snow,
　　And it grew wond'rous cauld:
And Ice mast-high came floating by
　　As green as Emerauld.

And thro' the drifts the snowy clifts
　　Did send a dismal sheen;
Ne shapes of men ne beasts we ken –
　　The Ice was all between.

The Ice was here, the Ice was there,
   The Ice was all around:
It crack'd and growl'd, and roar'd and howl'd –
   Like noises of a swound.

At length did cross an Albatross,
   Thorough the Fog it came;
And an it were a Christian Soul,
   We hail'd it in God's name.

The Marineres gave it biscuit-worms,
   And round and round it flew:
The Ice did split with a Thunder-fit,
   The Helmsman steer'd us thro'.

And a good south wind sprung up behind,
   The Albatross did follow;
And every day for food or play
   Came to the Marinere's hollo!

In mist or cloud on mast or shroud,
   It perch'd for vespers nine,
Whiles all the night thro' fog-smoke white,
   Glimmer'd the white moon-shine.

'God save thee, ancyent Marinere!
   From the fiends that plague thee thus –
Why look'st thou so?' – with my cross bow
   I shot the Albatross.

II

The Sun came up upon the right,
   Out of the Sea came he;
And broad as a weft upon the left
   Went down into the Sea.

And the good south wind still blew behind,
   But no sweet Bird did follow
Ne any day for food or play
   Came to the Marinere's hollo!

And I had done an hellish thing
　　And it would work 'em woe:
For all averr'd, I had kill'd the Bird
　　That made the Breeze to blow.

Ne dim ne red, like God's own head,
　　The glorious Sun uprist:
Then all averr'd, I had kill'd the Bird
　　That brought the fog and mist.
'Twas right, said they, such birds to slay
　　That bring the fog and mist.

The breezes blew, the white foam flew,
　　The furrow follow'd free:
We were the first that ever burst
　　Into that silent Sea.

Down dropt the breeze, the Sails dropt down,
　　'Twas sad as sad could be
And we did speak only to break
　　The silence of the Sea.

And in a hot and copper sky
　　The bloody sun at noon,
Right up above the mast did stand,
　　No bigger than the moon.

Day after day, day after day,
　　We stuck, ne breath ne motion,
As idle as a painted Ship
　　Upon a painted Ocean.

Water, water, every where,
　　And all the boards did shrink;
Water, water, everywhere,
　　Ne any drop to drink.

The very deeps did rot: O Christ!
　　That ever this should be!
Yea, slimy things did crawl with legs
　　Upon the slimy Sea.

About, about, in reel and rout,
    The Death-fires danc'd at night;
The water, like a witch's oils,
    Burnt green and blue and white.

And some in dreams assured were
    Of the Spirit that plagued us so:
Nine fathom deep he had follow'd us
    From the Land of Mist and Snow.

And every tongue thro' utter drouth
    Was wither'd at the root;
We could not speak no more than if
    We had been choked with soot.

Ah wel-a-day! what evil looks
    Had I from old and young;
Instead of the Cross the Albatross
    About my neck was hung.

III

I saw a something in the Sky
    No bigger than my fist;
At first it seem'd a little speck
    And then it seem'd a mist:
It mov'd and mov'd, and took at last
    A certain shape, I wist.

A speck, a mist, a shape, I wist!
    And still it ner'd and ner'd;
And, an it dodg'd a water-sprite,
    It plung'd and tack'd and veer'd.

With throat unslack'd, with black lips bak'd
    Ne could we laugh, ne wail:
Then while thro' drouth all dumb they stood
I bit my arm and suck'd the blood
    And cry'd, A sail! a sail!

With throat unslack'd, with black lips bak'd
 Agape they hear'd me call:
Gramercy! they for joy did grin
And all at once their breath drew in
 As they were drinking all.

She doth not tack from side to side –
 Hither to work us weal
Withouten wind, withouten tide
 She steddies with upright keel.

The western wave was all a flame,
 The day was well nigh done!
Almost upon the western wave
 Rested the broad bright Sun;
When that strange shape drove suddenly
 Betwixt us and the Sun.

And strait the Sun was fleck'd with bars
 (Heaven's mother send us grace)
As if thro' a dungeon grate he peer'd
 With broad and burning face.

Alas! (thought I, and my heart beat loud)
 How fast she neres and neres!
Are those *her* Sails that glance in the Sun
 Like restless gossameres?

Are those *her* naked ribs, which fleck'd
 The sun that did behind them peer?
And are these two all, all the crew,
 That woman and her fleshless Pheere?

His bones were black with many a crack,
 All black and bare, I ween;
Jet-black and bare, save where with rust
Of mouldy damps and charnel crust
 They're patch'd with purple and green.

Her lips are red, *her* looks are free,
 Her locks are yellow as gold:
Her skin is as white as leprosy,
And she is far liker Death than he;
 Her flesh makes the still air cold.

The naked Hulk alongside came
   And the Twain were playing dice;
'The Game is done! I've won, I've won!'
   Quoth she, and whistled thrice.

A gust of wind sterte up behind
   And whistled thro' his bones;
Thro' the holes of his eyes and the hole of his mouth
   Half-whistles and half-groans.

With never a whisper in the Sea
   Off darts the Spectre-ship;
While clombe above the Eastern bar
The horned Moon, with one bright Star
   Almost atween the tips.

One after one by the horned Moon
   (Listen, O Stranger! to me)
Each turn'd his face with a ghastly pang
   And curs'd me with his ee.

Four times fifty living men,
   With never a sigh or groan,
With heavy thump, a lifeless lump
   They dropp'd down one by one.

Their souls did from their bodies fly, –
   They fled to bliss or woe;
And every soul it pass'd me by,
   Like the whiz of my Cross-bow.

WILLIAM WORDSWORTH Old Man Travelling. Animal
Tranquillity and Decay, A Sketch

       The little hedge-row birds,
That peck along the road, regard him not.
He travels on, and in his face, his step,
His gait, is one expression; every limb,
His look and bending figure, all bespeak
A man who does not move with pain, but moves
With thought – He is insensibly subdued
To settled quiet: he is one by whom

All effort seems forgotten, one to whom
Long patience has such mild composure given,
That patience now doth seem a thing, of which
He hath no need. He is by nature led
To peace so perfect, that the young behold
With envy, what the old man hardly feels.
– I asked him whither he was bound, and what
The object of his journey; he replied
'Sir! I am going many miles to take
A last leave of my son, a mariner,
Who from a sea-fight has been brought to Falmouth,
And there is dying in an hospital. –'

WILLIAM WORDSWORTH Lines Written a Few Miles above
Tintern Abbey, on Revisiting the Banks of the Wye during a Tour,
July 13, 1798

Five years have passed; five summers, with the length
Of five long winters! and again I hear
These waters, rolling from their mountain-springs
With a sweet inland murmur. – Once again
Do I behold these steep and lofty cliffs,
Which on a wild secluded scene impress
Thoughts of more deep seclusion; and connect
The landscape with the quiet of the sky.
The day is come when I again repose
Here, under this dark sycamore, and view
These plots of cottage-ground, these orchard-tufts,
Which, at this season, with their unripe fruits,
Among the woods and copses lose themselves,
Nor, with their green and simple hue, disturb
The wild green landscape. Once again I see
These hedge-rows, hardly hedge-rows, little lines
Of sportive wood run wild; these pastoral farms
Green to the very door; and wreathes of smoke
Sent up, in silence, from among the trees,
With some uncertain notice, as might seem,
Of vagrant dwellers in the houseless woods,
Or of some hermit's cave, where by his fire
The hermit sits alone.

These forms of beauty have not been to me,
As is a landscape to a blind man's eye:
But oft, in lonely rooms, and mid the din
Of towns and cities, I have owed to them,
In hours of weariness, sensations sweet,
Felt in the blood, and felt along the heart,
And passing even into my purer mind
With tranquil restoration: – feelings too
Of unremembered pleasure; such, perhaps,
As may have had no trivial influence
On that best portion of a good man's life;
His little, nameless, unremembered acts
Of kindness and of love. Nor less, I trust,
To them I may have owed another gift,
Of aspect more sublime; that blessed mood,
In which the burthen of the mystery,
In which the heavy and the weary weight
Of all this unintelligible world
Is lightened: – that serene and blessed mood,
In which the affections gently lead us on,
Until, the breath of this corporeal frame,
And even the motion of our human blood
Almost suspended, we are laid asleep
In body, and become a living soul:
While with an eye made quiet by the power
Of harmony, and the deep power of joy,
We see into the life of things.
                                        If this
Be but a vain belief, yet, oh! how oft,
In darkness, and amid the many shapes
Of joyless day-light; when the fretful stir
Unprofitable, and the fever of the world,
Have hung upon the beatings of my heart,
How oft, in spirit, have I turned to thee
O sylvan Wye! Thou wanderer through the wood
How often has my spirit turned to thee!

And now, with gleams of half-extinguished thought,
With many recognitions dim and faint,
And somewhat of a sad perplexity,
The picture of the mind revives again:
While here I stand, not only with the sense
Of present pleasure, but with pleasing thoughts

That in this moment there is life and food
For future years. And so I dare to hope
Though changed, no doubt, from what I was, when first
I came among these hills; when like a roe
I bounded o'er the mountains, by the sides
Of the deep rivers, and the lonely streams,
Wherever nature led; more like a man
Flying from something that he dreads, than one
Who sought the thing he loved. For nature then
(The coarser pleasures of my boyish days,
And their glad animal movements all gone by,)
To me was all in all. – I cannot paint
What then I was. The sounding cataract
Haunted me like a passion: the tall rock,
The mountain, and the deep and gloomy wood,
Their colours and their forms, were then to me
An appetite: a feeling and a love,
That had no need of a remoter charm,
By thought supplied, or any interest
Unborrowed from the eye. – That time is past,
And all its aching joys are now no more,
And all its dizzy raptures. Not for this
Faint I, nor mourn nor murmur: other gifts
Have followed, for such loss, I would believe,
Abundant recompence. For I have learned
To look on nature, not as in the hour
Of thoughtless youth, but hearing oftentimes
The still, sad music of humanity,
Not harsh nor grating, though of ample power
To chasten and subdue. And I have felt
A presence that disturbs me with the joy
Of elevated thoughts; a sense sublime
Of something far more deeply interfused,
Whose dwelling is the light of setting suns,
And the round ocean, and the living air,
And the blue sky, and in the mind of man,
A motion and a spirit, that impels
All thinking things, all objects of all thought,
And rolls through all things. Therefore am I still
A lover of the meadows and the woods,
And mountains; and of all that we behold
From this green earth; of all the mighty world
Of eye and ear, both what they half-create,
And what perceive; well pleased to recognize

In nature and the language of the sense,
The anchor of my purest thoughts, the nurse,
The guide, the guardian of my heart, and soul
Of all my moral being.

                  Nor, perchance,
If I were not thus taught, should I the more
Suffer my genial spirits to decay:
For thou art with me, here, upon the banks
Of this fair river; thou, my dearest Friend,
My dear, dear Friend, and in thy voice I catch
The language of my former heart, and read
My former pleasures in the shooting lights
Of thy wild eyes. Oh! yet a little while
May I behold in thee what I was once,
My dear, dear Sister! And this prayer I make,
Knowing that Nature never did betray
The heart that loved her; 'tis her privilege,
Through all the years of this our life, to lead
From joy to joy: for she can so inform
The mind that is within us, so impress
With quietness and beauty, and so feed
With lofty thoughts, that neither evil tongues,
Rash judgments, nor the sneers of selfish men,
Nor greetings where no kindness is, nor all
The dreary intercourse of daily life,
Shall e'er prevail against us, or disturb
Our cheerful faith that all which we behold
Is full of blessings. Therefore let the moon
Shine on thee in thy solitary walk;
And let the misty mountain winds be free
To blow against thee: and in after years,
When these wild ecstasies shall be matured
Into a sober pleasure, when thy mind
Shall be a mansion for all lovely forms,
Thy memory be as a dwelling-place
For all sweet sounds and harmonies; Oh! then,
If solitude, or fear, or pain, or grief,
Should be thy portion, with what healing thoughts
Of tender joy wilt thou remember me,
And these my exhortations! Nor, perchance,
If I should be, where I no more can hear
Thy voice, nor catch from thy wild eyes these gleams
Of past existence, wilt thou then forget

That on the banks of this delightful stream
We stood together; and that I, so long
A worshipper of Nature, hither came,
Unwearied in that service: rather say
With warmer love, oh! with far deeper zeal
Of holier love. Nor wilt thou then forget,
That after many wanderings, many years
Of absence, these steep woods and lofty cliffs,
And this green pastoral landscape, were to me
More dear, both for themselves, and for thy sake.

§   §   §

SAMUEL TAYLOR COLERIDGE Frost at Midnight

The Frost performs its secret ministry,
Unhelped by any wind. The owlet's cry
Came loud – and hark, again! loud as before.
The inmates of my cottage, all at rest,
Have left me to that solitude, which suits
Abstruser musings: save that at my side
My cradled infant slumbers peacefully.
'Tis calm indeed! so calm, that it disturbs
And vexes meditation with its strange
And extreme silentness. Sea, hill, and wood,
This populous village! Sea, and hill, and wood,
With all the numberless goings-on of life,
Inaudible as dreams! the thin blue flame
Lies on my low-burnt fire, and quivers not;
Only that film, which fluttered on the grate,
Still flutters there, the sole unquiet thing.
Methinks, its motion in this hush of nature
Gives it dim sympathies with me who live,
Making it a companionable form,
Whose puny flaps and freaks the idling Spirit
By its own moods interprets, every where
Echo or mirror seeking of itself,
And makes a toy of Thought.

How oft, at school, with most believing mind,
Presageful, have I gazed upon the bars,
To watch that fluttering *stranger*! and as oft
With unclosed lids, already had I dreamt
Of my sweet birth-place, and the old church-tower,
Whose bells, the poor man's only music, rang
From morn to evening, all the hot Fair-day,
So sweetly, that they stirred and haunted me
With a wild pleasure, falling on mine ear
Most like articulate sounds of things to come!
So gazed I, till the soothing things, I dreamt,
Lulled me to sleep, and sleep prolonged my dreams!
And so I brooded all the following morn,
Awed by the stern preceptor's face, mine eye
Fixed with mock study on my swimming book:
Save if the door half opened, and I snatched
A hasty glance, and still my heart leaped up,
For still I hoped to see the *stranger's* face,
Townsman, or aunt, or sister more beloved,
My play-mate when we both were clothed alike!

Dear Babe, that sleepest cradled by my side,
Whose gentle breathings, heard in this deep calm,
Fill up the interspersèd vacancies
And momentary pauses of the thought!
My babe so beautiful! it thrills my heart
With tender gladness, thus to look at thee,
And think that thou shalt learn far other lore,
And in far other scenes! For I was reared
In the great city, pent 'mid cloisters dim,
And saw nought lovely but the sky and stars.
But *thou*, my babe! shalt wander like a breeze
By lakes and sandy shores, beneath the crags
Of ancient mountain, and beneath the clouds,
Which image in their bulk both lakes and shores
And mountain crags: so shalt thou see and hear
The lovely shapes and sounds intelligible
Of that eternal language, which thy God
Utters, who from eternity doth teach
Himself in all, and all things in himself.
Great universal Teacher! he shall mould
Thy spirit, and by giving make it ask.

Therefore all seasons shall be sweet to thee,
Whether the summer clothe the general earth
With greenness, or the redbreast sit and sing
Betwixt the tufts of snow on the bare branch
Of mossy apple-tree, while the nigh thatch
Smokes in the sun-thaw; whether the eave-drops fall
Heard only in the trances of the blast,
Or if the secret ministry of frost
Shall hang them up in silent icicles,
Quietly shining to the quiet Moon.

1799   WILLIAM WORDSWORTH *from* The Two-Part *Prelude* of
1799

Was it for this
That one, the fairest of all rivers, loved
To blend his murmurs with my nurse's song,
And from his alder shades and rocky falls,
And from his fords and shallows, sent a voice
That flowed along my dreams? For this didst thou,
O Derwent, travelling over the green plains
Near my 'sweet birthplace', didst thou, beauteous stream,
Make ceaseless music through the night and day,
Which with its steady cadence tempering
Our human waywardness, composed my thoughts
To more than infant softness, giving me
Among the fretful dwellings of mankind
A knowledge, a dim earnest, of the calm
Which nature breathes among the fields and groves?
Beloved Derwent, fairest of all streams,
Was it for this that I, a four years' child,
A naked boy, among thy silent pools
Made one long bathing of a summer's day,
Basked in the sun, or plunged into thy streams,
Alternate, all a summer's day, or coursed
Over the sandy fields, and dashed the flowers
Of yellow groundsel – or, when crag and hill,
The woods, and distant Skiddaw's lofty height,
Were bronzed with a deep radiance, stood alone
A naked savage in the thunder-shower?

And afterwards ('twas in a later day,
Though early), when upon the mountain-slope
The frost and breath of frosty wind had snapped
The last autumnal crocus, 'twas my joy
To wander half the night among the cliffs
And the smooth hollows where the woodcocks ran
Along the moonlight turf. In thought and wish
That time, my shoulder all with springes hung,
I was a fell destroyer. Gentle powers,
Who give us happiness and call it peace,
When scudding on from snare to snare I plied
My anxious visitation, hurrying on,
Still hurrying, hurrying onward, how my heart
Panted; among the scattered yew-trees and the crags
That looked upon me, how my bosom beat
With expectation! Sometimes strong desire
Resistless overpowered me, and the bird
Which was the captive of another's toils
Became my prey, and when the deed was done
I heard among the solitary hills
Low breathings coming after me, and sounds
Of undistinguishable motion, steps
Almost as silent as the turf they trod.

Nor less in springtime, when on southern banks
The shining sun had from his knot of leaves
Decoyed the primrose flower, and when the vales
And woods were warm, was I a rover then
In the high places, on the lonesome peaks,
Among the mountains and the winds. Though mean,
And though inglorious, were my views, the end
Was not ignoble. Oh, when I have hung
Above the raven's nest, by knots of grass
Or half-inch fissures in the slippery rock
But ill sustained, and almost (as it seemed)
Suspended by the blast which blew amain
Shouldering the naked crag, oh, at that time,
While on the perilous ridge I hung alone,
With what strange utterance did the loud dry wind
Blow through my ears! The sky seemed not a sky
Of earth – and with what motion moved the clouds!

The mind of man is fashioned and built up
Even as a strain of music. I believe
That there are spirits which, when they would form
A favoured being, from his very dawn
Of infancy do open out the clouds
As at the touch of lightning, seeking him
With gentle visitation – quiet powers,
Retired, and seldom recognized, yet kind,
And to the very meanest not unknown –
With me, though, rarely in my early days
They communed. Others too there are, who use,
Yet haply aiming at the self-same end,
Severer interventions, ministry
More palpable – and of their school was I.

They guided me: one evening led by them
I went alone into a shepherd's boat,
A skiff that to a willow-tree was tied
Within a rocky cave, its usual home.
The moon was up, the lake was shining clear
Among the hoary mountains; from the shore
I pushed, and struck the oars, and struck again
In cadence, and my little boat moved on
Just like a man who walks with stately step
Though bent on speed. It was an act of stealth
And troubled pleasure. Not without the voice
Of mountain echoes did my boat move on,
Leaving behind her still on either side
Small circles glittering idly in the moon
Until they melted all into one track
Of sparkling light.

                              A rocky steep uprose
Above the cavern of the willow-tree,
And now, as suited one who proudly rowed
With his best skill, I fixed a steady view
Upon the top of that same craggy ridge,
The bound of the horizon – for behind
Was nothing but the stars and the grey sky.
She was an elfin pinnace; twenty times
I dipped my oars into the silent lake,
And as I rose upon the stroke my boat
Went heaving through the water like a swan –

When, from behind that rocky steep (till then
The bound of the horizon) a huge cliff,
As if with voluntary power instinct,
Upreared its head. I struck, and struck again,
And, growing still in stature, the huge cliff
Rose up between me and the stars, and still,
With measured motion, like a living thing
Strode after me. With trembling hands I turned
And through the silent water stole my way
Back to the cavern of the willow-tree.
There in her mooring-place I left my bark,
And through the meadows homeward went with grave
And serious thoughts; and after I had seen
That spectacle, for many days my brain
Worked with a dim and undetermined sense
Of unknown modes of being. In my thoughts
There was a darkness – call it solitude,
Or blank desertion. No familiar shapes
Of hourly objects, images of trees,
Of sea or sky, no colours of green fields,
But huge and mighty forms that do not live
Like living men moved slowly through my mind
By day, and were the trouble of my dreams.

(. . .)

                    Ere I had seen
Eight summers – and 'twas in the very week
When I was first transplanted to thy vale,
Belovèd Hawkshead, when thy paths, thy shores
And brooks, were like a dream of novelty
To my half-infant mind – I chanced to cross
One of those open fields which, shaped like ears,
Make green peninsulas on Esthwaite's lake.
Twilight was coming on, yet through the gloom
I saw distinctly on the opposite shore,
Beneath a tree and close by the lake side,
A heap of garments, as if left by one
Who there was bathing. Half an hour I watched
And no one owned them; meanwhile the calm lake
Grew dark with all the shadows on its breast,
And now and then a leaping fish disturbed
The breathless stillness. The succeeding day
There came a company, and in their boat

Sounded with iron hooks and with long poles.
At length the dead man, mid that beauteous scene
Of trees and hills and water, bolt upright
Rose with his ghastly face. I might advert
To numerous accidents in flood or field,
Quarry or moor, or mid the winter snows,
Distresses and disasters, tragic facts
Of rural history that impressed my mind
With images to which in following years
Far other feelings were attached – with forms
That yet exist with independent life,
And, like their archetypes, know no decay.

There are in our existence spots of time
Which with distinct preeminence retain
A fructifying virtue, whence, depressed
By trivial occupations and the round
Of ordinary intercourse, our minds –
Especially the imaginative power –
Are nourished and invisibly repaired;
Such moments chiefly seem to have their date
In our first childhood.

I remember well
('Tis of an early season that I speak,
The twilight of rememberable life),
While I was yet an urchin, one who scarce
Could hold a bridle, with ambitious hopes
I mounted, and we rode towards the hills.
We were a pair of horsemen: honest James
Was with me, my encourager and guide.
We had not travelled long ere some mischance
Disjoined me from my comrade, and, through fear
Dismounting, down the rough and stony moor
I led my horse, and stumbling on, at length
Came to a bottom where in former times
A man, the murderer of his wife, was hung
In irons. Mouldered was the gibbet-mast;
The bones were gone, the iron and the wood;
Only a long green ridge of turf remained
Whose shape was like a grave. I left the spot,
And reascending the bare slope I saw
A naked pool that lay beneath the hills,
The beacon on the summit, and more near
A girl who bore a pitcher on her head

And seemed with difficult steps to force her way
Against the blowing wind. It was in truth
An ordinary sight, but I should need
Colours and words that are unknown to man
To paint the visionary dreariness
Which, while I looked all round for my lost guide,
Did at that time invest the naked pool,
The beacon on the lonely eminence,
The woman and her garments vexed and tossed
By the strong wind.

(1973)

ROBERT BURNS *from* Love and Liberty. A Cantata

See the smoking bowl before us,
    Mark our jovial, ragged ring!
Round and round take up the Chorus,
    And in raptures let us sing –

Chorus –
        A fig for those by law protected!
            LIBERTY's a glorious feast!
        Courts for Cowards were erected,
            Churches built to please the PRIEST.

What is TITLE, what is TREASURE,
    What is REPUTATION's care?
If we lead a life of pleasure,
    'Tis no matter HOW or WHERE.
        A fig, &c.

With the ready trick and fable
    Round we wander all the day;
And at night, in barn or stable,
    Hug our doxies on the hay.
        A fig for &c.

Does the train-attended CARRIAGE
    Thro' the country lighter rove?
Does the sober bed of MARRIAGE
    Witness brighter scenes of love?
        A fig for &c.

Life is all a VARIORUM,
   We regard not how it goes;
Let them cant about DECORUM,
   Who have character to lose.
      A fig for &c.

Here 's to BUDGETS, BAGS and WALLETS!
   Here 's to all the wandering train!
Here 's our ragged BRATS and CALLETS!
   One and all cry out, AMEN!
      A fig for those by LAW protected,
         LIBERTY's a glorious feast!
      COURTS for Cowards were erected,
         CHURCHES built to please the Priest.

                                             (written 1785)

1800   § WILLIAM WORDSWORTH *from* Lyrical Ballads

A slumber did my spirit seal,
   I had no human fears:
She seemed a thing that could not feel
   The touch of earthly years.

No motion has she now, no force
   She neither hears nor sees
Rolled round in earth's diurnal course
   With rocks and stones and trees!

Song

She dwelt among th' untrodden ways
   Beside the springs of Dove,
A Maid whom there were none to praise
   And very few to love.

A Violet by a mossy stone
 Half-hidden from the Eye!
– Fair, as a star when only one
 Is shining in the sky!

She *lived* unknown, and few could know
 When Lucy ceased to be;
But she is in her Grave, and Oh!
 The difference to me.

§ § §

ROBERT BURNS

Oh wert thou in the cauld blast,
 On yonder lea, on yonder lea;
My plaidie to the angry airt,
 I'd shelter thee, I'd shelter thee:
5 Or did misfortune's bitter storms
 Around thee blaw, around thee blaw,
Thy bield should be my bosom,
 To share it a', to share it a'.

Or were I in the wildest waste,
10 Sae black and bare, sae black and bare,
The desart were a paradise,
 If thou wert there, if thou wert there.
Or were I monarch o' the globe,
 Wi' thee to reign, wi' thee to reign;
15 The brightest jewel in my crown,
 Wad be my queen, wad be my queen.

3 *plaidie* plaid; *airt* point of the compass; 7 *bield* shelter

ROBERT BURNS The Fornicator. A New Song

Ye jovial boys who love the joys,
   The blissful joys of Lovers;
Yet dare avow with dauntless brow,
   When th' bony lass discovers;
5 I pray draw near and lend an ear,
   And welcome in a Frater,
For I've lately been on quarantine,
   A proven Fornicator.

Before the Congregation wide
10   I pass'd the muster fairly,
My handsome Betsey by my side,
   We gat our ditty rarely;
But my downcast eye by chance did spy
   What made my lips to water,
15 Those limbs so clean where I, between,
   Commenc'd a Fornicator.

With rueful face and signs of grace
   I pay'd the buttock-hire,
The night was dark and thro' the park
20   I could not but convoy her;
A parting kiss, what could I less,
   My vows began to scatter,
My Betsey fell – lal de dal lal lal,
   I am a Fornicator.

25 But for her sake this vow I make,
   And solemnly I swear it,
That while I own a single crown,
   She's welcome for to share it;
And my roguish boy his Mother's joy,
30   And the darling of his Pater,
For him I boast my pains and cost,
   Although a Fornicator.

Ye wenching blades whose hireling jades
   Have tipt you off blue-boram,
35 I tell ye plain, I do disdain
   To rank you in the Quorum;
But a bony lass upon the grass
   To teach her esse Mater,
And no reward but for regard,
40   O that's a Fornicator.

Your warlike Kings and Heros bold,
   Great Captains and Commanders;
Your mighty Cèsars fam'd of old,
   And Conquering Alexanders;
45 In fields they fought and laurels bought
   And bulwarks strong did batter,
But still they grac'd our noble list
   And ranked Fornicator!!!

(written 1785)

SAMUEL TAYLOR COLERIDGE Dejection. An Ode,   1802
Written April 4, 1802

'Late, late yestreen I saw the New Moon,
With the Old Moon in her arms;
And I fear, I fear, my master dear,
We shall have a deadly storm.'
    Ballad of Sir Patrick Spence

Well! if the Bard was weather-wise, who made
   The grand Old Ballad of Sir PATRICK SPENCE,
   This night, so tranquil now, will not go hence
Unrous'd by winds, that ply a busier trade
Than those, which mould yon clouds in lazy flakes,
Or this dull sobbing draft, that drones and rakes
Upon the strings of this Œolian lute,
Which better far were mute.
For lo! the New Moon, winter-bright!
And overspread with phantom light,

---

34 *tipt you off blue-boram* given you syphilis; 38 *esse Mater* to be a mother

(With swimming phantom light o'erspread,
But rimm'd and circled by a silver thread)
I see the Old Moon in her lap, foretelling
   The coming on of rain and squally blast:
And O! that even now the gust were swelling,
   And the slant night-show'r driving loud and fast!
Those sounds which oft have rais'd me, while they aw'd,
And sent my soul abroad,
Might now perhaps their wonted impulse give,
Might startle this dull pain, and make it move and live!

II

A grief without a pang, void, dark, and drear,
   A stifled, drowsy, unimpassion'd grief,
   Which finds no nat'ral outlet, no relief
In word, or sigh, or tear –
O EDMUND! in this wan and heartless mood,
To other thoughts by yonder throstle woo'd,
All this long eve, so balmy and serene,
   Have I been gazing on the Western sky,
And its peculiar tint of yellow-green:
   And still I gaze – and with how blank an eye!
And those thin clouds above, in flakes and bars,
That give away their motion to the stars;
Those stars, that glide behind them, or between,
Now sparkling, now bedimm'd, but always seen;
Yon crescent moon, as fix'd as if it grew,
In its own cloudless, starless lake of blue,
A boat becalm'd! a lovely sky-canoe!
I see them all, so excellently fair –
I *see*, not *feel*, how beautiful they are!

III

   My genial spirits fail,
   And what can these avail,
To lift the smoth'ring weight from off my breast!
   It were a vain endeavour,
   Tho' I should gaze for ever
On that green light that lingers in the west:
I may not hope from outward forms to win
The passion and the life, whose fountains are within!

IV

O EDMUND! we receive but what we give,
And in *our* life alone does Nature live:
Ours is her wedding-garment, ours her shroud!
And would we aught behold, of higher worth,
Than that inanimate cold world, *allow'd*
To the poor loveless ever-anxious crowd,
Ah from the soul itself must issue forth,
A light, a glory, a fair luminous cloud
Enveloping the earth –
And from the soul itself must there be sent
A sweet and potent voice, of its own birth,
Of all sweet sounds the life and element!
O pure of heart! Thou need'st not ask of me
What this strong music in the soul may be?
What, and wherein it doth exist,
This light, this glory, this fair luminous mist,
This beautiful and beauty-making pow'r?
JOY, virtuous EDMUND! joy, that ne'er was given,
Save to the pure, and in their purest hour,
Joy, EDMUND! is the spirit and the pow'r,
Which wedding Nature to us gives in dow'r
  A new earth and new Heaven,
Undream'd of by the sensual and the proud –
JOY is the sweet voice, JOY the luminous cloud –
    We, we ourselves rejoice!
And thence flows all that charms or ear or sight,
All melodies the echoes of that voice
All colours a suffusion from that light.

V

Yes, dearest EDMUND, yes!
  There was a time when, tho' my path was rough,
    This joy within me dallied with distress,
  And all misfortunes were but as the stuff
    Whence fancy made me dreams of happiness:
For hope grew round me, like the twining vine,
And fruits and foliage, not my own, seem'd mine.
But now afflictions bow me down to earth:
Nor care I, that they rob me of my mirth,
  But O! each visitation
Suspends what nature gave me at my birth,
  My shaping spirit of imagination.

[The sixth and seventh Stanzas omitted.]¹

* * * * * *

* * * * * *

* * * * * *

VIII

O wherefore did I let it haunt my mind,
　　This dark distressful dream?
I turn from it and listen to the wind
　　Which long has rav'd unnotic'd. What a scream
Of agony, by torture, lengthen'd out,
That lute sent forth! O wind, that rav'st without,
　Bare crag, or mountain tairn, or blasted tree,
Or pine-grove, whither woodman never clomb,
Or lonely house, long held the witches' home,
　Methinks were fitter instruments for thee,
Mad Lutanist! who, in this month of show'rs,
Of dark-brown gardens, and of peeping flow'rs,
Mak'st devil's yule, with worse than wintry song,
The blossoms, buds, and tim'rous leaves among.
　Thou Actor, perfect in all tragic sounds!
　　Thou mighty Poet, ev'n to frenzy bold!
What tell'st thou now about?
'Tis of the rushing of an host in rout,
　With many groans of men with smarting wounds –
　　At once they groan with pain, and shudder with the cold!
But hush! there is a pause of deepest silence!
　And all that noise, as of a rushing crowd,
　　With groans and tremulous shudderings – all is over!
It tells another tale, with sounds less deep and loud –
　　A tale of less affright,
　　And temper'd with delight,
As EDMUND's self had fram'd the tender lay –
　　'Tis of a little child,
　　Upon a lonesome wild,
Not far from home; but she has lost her way –
And now moans low, in utter grief and fear;
And now screams loud, and hopes to make her mother *hear*!

1. [Coleridge's note.]

'Tis midnight, and small thoughts have I of sleep;
Full seldom may my friend such vigils keep!
Visit him, gentle Sleep, with wings of healing,
   And may this storm be but a mountain birth,
May all the stars hang bright above his dwelling,
    Silent, as tho' they *watch'd* the sleeping earth!
      With light heart may he rise,
       Gay fancy, cheerful eyes,
And sing his lofty song, and teach me to rejoice!
O EDMUND, friend of my devoutest choice,
O rais'd from anxious dread and busy care,
By the immenseness of the good and fair
Which thou see'st ev'ry where
Joy lifts thy spirit, joy attunes thy voice,
To thee do all things live from pole to pole,
Their life the eddying of thy living soul!
O simple spirit, guided from above,
O lofty Poet, full of light and love,
Brother and friend of my devoutest choice,
Thus may'st thou ever evermore rejoice!

§ **SIR WALTER SCOTT** (editor) *from* **Minstrelsy of the Scottish Border**

ANONYMOUS The Wife of Usher's Well

There lived a wife at Usher's Well,
   And a wealthy wife was she;
She had three stout and stalwart sons,
   And sent them oer the sea.

5   They hadna been a week from her,
   A week but barely ane,
Whan word came to the carline wife
   That her three sons were gane.

7 *carline wife* old woman;

They hadna been a week from her,
    A week but barely three,
Whan word came to the carlin wife
    That her sons she'd never see.

'I wish the wind may never cease,
    Nor fashes in the flood,
Till my three sons come hame to me,
    In earthly flesh and blood.'

It fell about the Martinmass,
    When nights are lang and mirk,
The carlin wife's three sons came hame,
    And their hats were o the birk.

It neither grew in syke nor ditch,
    Nor yet in ony sheugh;
But at the gates o Paradise,
    That birk grew fair eneugh.

    *   *   *   *   *   *

'Blow up the fire, my maidens,
    Bring water from the well;
For a' my house shall feast this night,
    Since my three sons are well.'

And she has made to them a bed,
    She's made it large and wide,
And she's taen her mantle her about,
    Sat down at the bed-side.

    *   *   *   *   *   *

Up then crew the red, red cock,
    And up then crew the gray;
The eldest to the youngest said,
    'T is time we were away.

The cock he hadna crawd but once,
    And clappd his wings at a',
When the youngest to the eldest said,
    Brother, we must awa.

14 *fashes* troubles; 20 *birk* birch; 21 *syke* trench; 22 *sheugh* furrow;

'The cock doth craw, the day doth daw,
    The channerin' worm doth chide;
Gin we be mist out o our place,
    A sair pain we maun bide.

45 'Fare ye weel, my mother dear!
    Fareweel to barn and byre!
And fare ye weel, the bonny lass
    That kindles my mother's fire!'

ANONYMOUS Thomas Rhymer

True Thomas lay on Huntlie bank,
    A ferlie he spied wi' his ee,
And there he saw a lady bright,
    Come riding down by the Eildon Tree.

5 Her shirt was o the grass-green silk,
    Her mantle o the velvet fyne,
At ilka tett of her horse's mane
    Hang fifty siller bells and nine.

True Thomas, he pulld aff his cap,
10   And louted low down to his knee:
'All hail, thou mighty Queen of Heaven!
    For thy peer on earth I never did see.'

'O no, O no, Thomas,' she said,
    'That name does not belang to me:
15 I am but the queen of fair Elfland,
    That am hither come to visit thee.

'Harp and carp, Thomas,' she said,
    'Harp and carp along wi me,
And if ye dare to kiss my lips,
20   Sure of your bodie I will be.'

42 *channerin'* grumbling

2 *ferlie* marvel; 7 *ilka tett* each lock; 17 *Harp and carp* play and sing;

'Betide me weal, betide me woe,
    That weird shall never daunton me;'
Syne he has kissed her rosy lips,
    All underneath the Eildon Tree.

25   'Now, ye maun go wi me,' she said,
    'True Thomas, ye maun go wi me,
And ye maun serve me seven years,
    Thro weal or woe, as may chance to be.'

She mounted on her milk-white steed,
30   She's taen True Thomas up behind,
And aye wheneer her bridle rung,
    The steed flew swifter than the wind.

O they rade on, and farther on –
    The steed gaed swifter than the wind –
35   Untill they reached a desart wide,
    And living land was left behind.

'Light down, light down, now, True Thomas,
    And lean your head upon my knee;
Abide and rest a little space,
40   And I will shew you ferlies three.

'O see ye not yon narrow road,
    So thick beset with thorns and briers?
That is the path of righteousness,
    Tho after it but few enquires.

45   'And see not ye that braid braid road,
    That lies across that lily leven?
That is the path of wickedness,
    Tho some call it the road to heaven.

'And see not ye that bonny road,
50   That winds about the fernie brae?
That is the road to fair Elfland,
    Where thou and I this night maun gae.

22 *daunton* intimidate; 46 *lily leven* fair plain;

'But, Thomas, ye maun hold your tongue,
    Whatever ye may hear or see,
55 For, if you speak word in Elflyn land,
    Ye'll neer get back to your ain countrie.'

O they rade on, and farther on,
    And they waded thro rivers aboon the knee,
And they saw neither sun nor moon,
60   But they heard the roaring of the sea.

It was mirk mirk night, and there was nae stern light,
    And they waded thro red blude to the knee;
For a' the blude that's shed on earth
    Rins thro the springs o that countrie.

65 Syne they came on to a garden green,
    And she pu'd an apple frae a tree:
'Take this for thy wages, True Thomas,
    It will give thee the tongue that can never lie.'

'My tongue is mine ain,' True Thomas said;
70   'A gudely gift ye wad gie to me!
I neither dought to buy nor sell,
    At fair or tryst where I may be.

'I dought neither speak to prince or peer,
    Nor ask of grace from fair ladye:'
75 'Now hold thy peace,' the lady said,
    'For as I say, so must it be.'

He has gotten a coat of the even cloth,
    And a pair of shoes of velvet green,
And till seven years were gane and past
80   True Thomas on earth was never seen.

71 *dought to* could

ANONYMOUS Lord Randal

O where ha' you been, Lord Randal my son?
And where ha' you been, my handsome young man?
I ha' been at the greenwood; mother, mak my bed soon,
For I'm wearied wi' hunting and fain wad lie down.

An' wha met ye there, Lord Randal my son?
An' wha met you there, my handsome young man?
O I met wi my true-love; mother, mak my bed soon,
For I'm wearied wi' huntin' an' fain wad lie down.

And what did she give you, Lord Randal my son?
And what did she give you, my handsome young man?
Eels fried in a pan; mother, mak my bed soon,
For I'm wearied wi' huntin' and fain wad lie down.

And wha gat your leavins, Lord Randal my son?
And wha gat your leavins, my handsom young man?
My hawks and my hounds; mother, mak my bed soon,
For I'm wearied wi' hunting and fain wad lie down.

And what becam of them, Lord Randal my son?
And what becam of them, my handsome young man?
They stretched their legs out an' died; mother, mak my bed soon,
For I'm wearied wi' huntin' and fain wad lie down.

O I fear you are poisoned, Lord Randal my son,
I fear you are poisoned, my handsome young man.
O yes, I am poisoned; mother, mak my bed soon,
For I'm sick at the heart and I fain wad lie down.

What d'ye leave to your mother, Lord Randal my son?
What d'ye leave to your mother, my handsome young man?
Four and twenty milk kye; mother, mak my bed soon,
For I'm sick at the heart and I fain wad lie down.

What d'ye leave to your sister, Lord Randal my son?
What d'ye leave to your sister, my handsome young man?
My gold and my silver; mother, make my bed soon,
For I'm sick at the heart an' I fain wad lie down.

What d'ye leave to your brother, Lord Randal my son?
What d'ye leave to your brother, my handsome young man?
My houses and my lands; mother, mak my bed soon,
For I'm sick at the heart and I fain wad lie down.

What d'ye leave to your true-love, Lord Randal my son?
What d'ye leave to your true-love, my handsome young man?
I leave her hell and fire; mother, mak my bed soon,
For I'm sick at the heart and I fain wad lie down.

A Lyke-Wake Dirge

This ae nighte, this ae nighte,
   – *Every nighte and alle*,
Fire and fleet and candle-lighte,
   And Christe receive thy saule.

5   When thou from hence away art past,
   – *Every nighte and alle*,
To Whinny-muir thou com'st at last;
   And Christe receive thy saule.

If ever thou gavest hosen and shoon,
10   – *Every nighte and alle*,
Sit thee down and put them on;
   And Christe receive thy saule.

If hosen and shoon thou ne'er gav'st nane
   – *Every nighte and alle*,
15   The whinnes sall prick thee to the bare bane;
   And Christe receive thy saule.

From Whinny-muir when thou may'st pass,
   – *Every nighte and alle*,
To Brig o' Dread thou com'st at last;
20   *And Christe receive thy saule*.

3 *fleet* house-room; 7 *Whinny-muir* furze-moor; 15 *whinnes* thorns; 19 *Brig* bridge

From Brig o' Dread when thou may'st pass,
    – *Every nighte and alle,*
To Purgatory fire thou com'st at last;
    And Christe receive thy saule.

25 If ever thou gavest meat or drink,
    – *Every nighte and alle,*
The fire sall never make thee shrink;
    And Christe receive thy saule.

If meat or drink thou ne'er gav'st nane,
30   – *Every nighte and alle,*
The fire will burn theee to the bare bane;
    And Christe receive thy saule.

This ae nighte, this ae nighte,
    – *Every nighte and alle,*
35 Fire and fleet and candle-lighte,
    And Christe receive thy saule.

1803   ANONYMOUS The Twa Corbies

As I was walking all alane,
I heard twa corbies making a mane;
The tane unto the t'other say,
'Where sall we gang and dine to-day?'

5 'In behint yon auld fail dyke,
I wot there lies a new slain knight;
And naebody kens that he lies there,
But his hawk, his hound, and lady fair.

'His hound is to the hunting gane,
10 His hawk to fetch the wild-fowl hame,
His lady's ta'en another mate,
So we may mak our dinner sweet.

2 *corbies* ravens; *making a mane* talking together; 5 *fail* turf;

'Ye'll sit on his white hause-bane,
And I'll pike out his bonny blue een;
15 Wi ae lock o his gowden hair
We'll theek our nest when it grows bare.

'Mony a one for him makes mane,
But nane sall ken where he is gane;
Oer his white banes, when they are bare,
20 The wind sall blaw for evermair.'

§ § §

WILLIAM COWPER The Snail

To grass, or leaf, or fruit, or wall
The snail sticks close, nor fears to fall,
As if he grew there, house and all,
                              Together.

Within that house secure he hides
When danger imminent betides
Of storm, or other harm besides
                              Of Weather.

Give but his horns the slightest touch,
His self-collecting pow'r is such,
He shrinks into his house with much
                              Displeasure.

Where'er he dwells, he dwells alone,
Except himself has chatells none,
Well satisfied to be his own
                              whole treasure.

13 *hause-bane* collar-bone; 16 *theek* thatch; 17 *makes mane* laments

Thus hermit-like his life he leads,
Nor partner of his banquet needs,
And if he meet one, only feeds
                The faster.

Who seeks him, must be worse than blind,
(He and his house are so combined),
If, finding it, he fail to find
                Its master.

WILLIAM COWPER The Cast-away

Obscurest night involved the sky,
  Th' Atlantic billows roar'd,
When such a destin'd wretch as I
  Wash'd headlong from on board
Of friends, of hope, of all bereft,
His floating home for ever left.

No braver Chief could Albion boast
  Than He with whom he went,
Nor ever ship left Albion's coast
  With warmer wishes sent,
He loved them both, but both in vain,
Nor Him beheld, nor Her again.

Not long beneath the whelming brine
  Expert to swim, he lay,
Nor soon he felt his strength decline
  Or courage die away;
But waged with Death a lasting strife
Supported by despair of life.

He shouted, nor his friends had fail'd
  To check the vessels' course,
But so the furious blast prevail'd
  That, pitiless perforce,
They left their outcast mate behind,
And scudded still before the wind.

Some succour yet they could afford,
    And, such as storms allow,
The cask, the coop, the floated cord
    Delay'd not to bestow;
But He, they knew, nor ship nor shore,
Whate'er they gave, should visit more.

Nor, cruel as it seem'd, could He
    Their haste, himself, condemn,
Aware that flight in such a sea
    Alone could rescue *them*;
Yet bitter felt it still to die
Deserted, and his friends so nigh.

He long survives who lives an hour
    In ocean, self-upheld,
And so long he with unspent pow'r
    His destiny repell'd,
And ever, as the minutes flew,
Entreated help, or cried, Adieu!

At length, his transient respite past,
    His comrades, who before
Had heard his voice in ev'ry blast,
    Could catch the sound no more;
For then, by toil subdued, he drank
The stifling wave, and then he sank.

No poet wept him, but the page
    Of narrative sincere
That tells his name, his worth, his age,
    Is wet with Anson's tear,
And tears by bards or heroes shed
Alike immortalize the Dead.

I, therefore, purpose not or dream,
    Descanting on his fate,
To give the melancholy theme
    A more enduring date,
But Mis'ry still delights to trace
Its semblance in another's case.

No voice divine the storm allay'd,
   No light propitious shone,
When, snatch'd from all effectual aid,
   We perish'd, each, alone;
But I, beneath a rougher sea,
And whelm'd in deeper gulphs than he.

1804   WILLIAM BLAKE *from* **Milton** [Preface]

And did those feet in ancient time.
Walk upon Englands mountains green:
And was the holy Lamb of God,
On Englands pleasant pastures seen!

And did the Countenance Divine,
Shine forth upon our clouded hills?
And was Jerusalem builded here,
Among these dark Satanic Mills?

Bring me my Bow of burning gold:
Bring me my Arrows of desire:
Bring me my Spear: O clouds unfold!
Bring me my Chariot of fire!

I will not cease from Mental Fight,
Nor shall my Sword sleep in my hand:
Till we have built Jerusalem,
In Englands green & pleasant Land.

WILLIAM BLAKE

Mock on Mock on Voltaire Rousseau
Mock on Mock on tis all in vain
You throw the sand against the wind
And the wind blows it back again

And every sand becomes a Gem
Reflected in the beams divine
Blown back they blind the mocking Eye
But still in Israels paths they shine

The Atoms of Democritus
And Newtons Particles of light
Are sands upon the Red sea shore
Where Israels tents do shine so bright

WILLIAM BLAKE The Crystal Cabinet

The Maiden caught me in the Wild
Where I was dancing merrily
She put me into her Cabinet
And Lockd me up with a golden Key

This Cabinet is formd of Gold
And Pearl & Crystal shining bright
And within it opens into a World
And a little lovely Moony Night

Another England there I saw
Another London with its Tower
Another Thames & other Hills
And another pleasant Surrey Bower

Another Maiden like herself
Translucent lovely shining clear
Threefold each in the other closd
O what a pleasant trembling fear

O what a smile a threefold Smile
Filld me that like a flame I burnd
I bent to Kiss the lovely Maid
And found a Threefold Kiss returnd

I strove to sieze the inmost Form
With ardor fierce & hands of flame
But burst the Crystal Cabinet
And like a Weeping Babe became

A weeping Babe upon the wild
And Weeping Woman pale reclind
And in the outward air again
I filld with woes the passing Wind

WILLIAM BLAKE *from* Auguries of Innocence

To see a World in a Grain of Sand
And a Heaven in a Wild Flower
Hold Infinity in the palm of your hand
And Eternity in an hour
A Robin Red breast in a Cage
Puts all Heaven in a Rage
A dove house filld with doves & Pigeons
Shudders Hell thro all its regions
A dog starvd at his Masters Gate
Predicts the ruin of the State
A Horse misusd upon the Road
Calls to Heaven for Human blood
Each outcry of the hunted Hare
A fibre from the Brain does tear
A Skylark wounded in the wing
A Cherubim does cease to sing
The Game Cock clipd & armd for fight
Does the Rising Sun affright
Every Wolfs & Lions howl
Raises from Hell a Human Soul
The wild deer wandring here & there
Keeps the Human Soul from Care
The Lamb misusd breeds Public strife
And yet forgives the Butchers Knife
The Bat that flits at close of Eve
Has left the Brain that wont Believe
The Owl that calls upon the Night
Speaks the Unbelievers fright
He who shall hurt the little Wren
Shall never be belovd by Men
He who the Ox to wrath has movd
Shall never be by Woman lovd
The wanton Boy that kills the Fly
Shall feel the Spiders enmity
He who torments the Chafers sprite
Weaves a Bower in endless Night
The Catterpiller on the Leaf
Repeats to thee thy Mothers grief
Kill not the Moth nor Butterfly
For the Last Judgment draweth nigh

He who shall train the Horse to War
Shall never pass the Polar Bar
The Beggers Dog & Widows Cat
Feed them & thou wilt grow fat
The Gnat that sings his Summers song
Poison gets from Slanders tongue
The poison of the Snake & Newt
Is the sweat of Envys Foot
The Poison of the Honey Bee
Is the Artists Jealousy
The Princes Robes & Beggars Rags
Are Toadstools on the Misers Bags
A truth thats told with bad intent
Beats all the Lies you can invent

(1863)

ANONYMOUS Lamkin

1806

It's Lamkin was a mason good
  As ever built wi stane;
He built Lord Wearie's castle,
  But payment got he nane.

5 'O pay me, Lord Wearie,
  Come, pay me my fee:'
'I canna pay you, Lamkin,
  For I maun gang oer the sea.'

'O pay me now, Lord Wearie,
10   Come, pay me out o hand:'
'I canna pay you, Lamkin,
  Unless I sell my land.'

'O gin ye winna pay me,
  I here sall mak a vow,
15 Before that ye come hame again,
  Ye sall hae cause to rue.'

Lord Wearie got a bonny ship,
  To sail the saut sea faem;
Bade his lady weel the castle keep,
20   Ay till he should come hame.

But the nourice was a fause limmer
 As eer hung on a tree;
She laid a plot wi Lamkin,
 Whan her lord was oer the sea.

25 She laid a plot wi Lamkin,
 When the servants were awa,
Loot him in at a little shot-window,
 And brought him to the ha.

'O whare's a' the men o this house,
30 That ca me Lamkin?'
'They're at the barn-well thrashing;
 'T will be lang ere they come in.'

'And whare's the women o this house,
 That ca me Lamkin?'
35 'They're at the far well washing;
 'T will be lang ere they come in.'

'And whare's the bairns o this house,
 That ca me Lamkin?'
'They're at the school reading;
40 'T will be night or they come hame.'

'O whare's the lady o this house,
 That ca's me Lamkin?'
'She's up in her bower sewing,
 But we soon can bring her down.'

45 Then Lamkin's tane a sharp knife,
 That hang down by his gaire,
And he has gien the bonny babe
 A deep wound and a sair.

Then Lamkin he rocked,
50 And the fause nourice sang,
Till frae ilkae bore o the cradle
 The red blood out sprang.

21 *nourice* nurse; *limmer* wretch; 46 *gaire* garment; 51 *bore* hole;

Then out it spak the lady,
    As she stood on the stair:
55 'What ails my bairn, nourice,
    That he's greeting sae sair?

'O still my bairn, nourice,
    O still him wi the pap!'
'He winna still, lady,
60   For this nor for that.'

'O still my bairn, nourice,
    O still him wi the wand!'
'He winna still, lady,
    For a' his father's land.'

65 'O still my bairn, nourice,
    O still him wi the bell!'
'He winna still, lady,
    Till ye come down yoursel.'

O the firsten step she steppit,
70   She steppit on a stane;
But the neisten step she steppit,
    She met him Lamkin.

'O mercy, mercy, Lamkin,
    Hae mercy upon me!
75 Though you've taen my young son's life,
    Ye may let mysel be.'

'O sall I kill her, nourice,
    Or sall I lat her be?'
'O kill her, kill her, Lamkin,
80   For she neer was good to me.'

'O scour the bason, nourice,
    And mak it fair and clean,
For to keep this lady's heart's blood,
    For she's come o noble kin.'

85 'There need nae bason, Lamkin,
    Lat it run through the floor;
What better is the heart's blood
    O the rich than o the poor?'

But ere three months were at an end,
90   Lord Wearie came again;
But dowie, dowie was his heart
   When first he came hame.

'O wha's blood is this,' he says,
   'That lies in the chamer?'
95 'It is your lady's heart's blood;
   'T is as clear as the lamer.'

'And wha's blood is this,' he says,
   'That lies in my ha?'
'It is your young son's heart's blood;
100   'T is the clearest ava.'

O sweetly sang the black-bird
   That sat upon the tree;
But sairer grat Lamkin,
   When he was condemned to die.

105 And bonny sang the mavis,
   Out o the thorny brake;
But sairer grat the nourice,
   When she was tied to the stake.

1807   **WILLIAM WORDSWORTH Composed upon Westminster Bridge**

Sept. 3, 1802

Earth has not any thing to shew more fair:
Dull would he be of soul who could pass by
A sight so touching in its majesty:
This City now doth like a garment wear
The beauty of the morning; silent, bare,
Ships, towers, domes, theatres, and temples lie
Open unto the fields, and to the sky;
All bright and glittering in the smokeless air.

91 *dowie* melancholy; 96 *lamer* amber; 103 *grat* cried; 105 *mavis* thrush

Never did sun more beautifully steep
In his first splendor valley, rock, or hill;
Ne'er saw I, never felt, a calm so deep!
The river glideth at his own sweet will:
Dear God! the very houses seem asleep;
And all that mighty heart is lying still!

WILLIAM WORDSWORTH Elegiac Stanzas Suggested by a Picture of Peele Castle, in a Storm, Painted by Sir George Beaumont

I was thy neighbour once, thou rugged Pile!
Four summer weeks I dwelt in sight of thee:
I saw thee every day; and all the while
Thy Form was sleeping on a glassy sea.

So pure the sky, so quiet was the air!
So like, so very like, was day to day!
Whene'er I looked, thy Image still was there;
It trembled, but it never passed away.

How perfect was the calm! it seemed no sleep;
No mood, which season takes away, or brings:
I could have fancied that the mighty Deep
Was even the gentlest of all gentle Things.

Ah! THEN, if mine had been the Painter's hand,
To express what then I saw; and add the gleam,
The light that never was, on sea or land,
The consecration, and the Poet's dream;

I would have planted thee, thou hoary Pile
Amid a world how different from this!
Beside a sea that could not cease to smile;
On tranquil land, beneath a sky of bliss.

Thou shouldst have seemed a treasure-house divine
Of peaceful years; a chronicle of heaven; –
Of all the sunbeams that did ever shine
The very sweetest had to thee been given.

A Picture had it been of lasting ease,
Elysian quiet, without toil or strife;
No motion but the moving tide, a breeze,
Or merely silent Nature's breathing life.

Such, in the fond illusion of my heart,
Such Picture would I at that time have made:
And seen the soul of truth in every part,
A stedfast peace that might not be betrayed.

So once it would have been, – 'tis so no more;
I have submitted to a new control:
A power is gone, which nothing can restore;
A deep distress hath humanized my Soul.

Not for a moment could I now behold
A smiling sea, and be what I have been:
The feeling of my loss will ne'er be old;
This, which I know, I speak with mind serene.

Then, Beaumont, friend! who would have been the Friend,
If he had lived, of Him whom I deplore,
This work of thine I blame not, but commend;
This sea in anger, and that dismal shore.

O 'tis a passionate Work! – yet wise and well,
Well chosen is the spirit that is here;
That Hulk which labours in the deadly swell,
This rueful sky, this pageantry of fear!

And this huge Castle, standing here sublime,
I love to see the look with which it braves,
Cased in the unfeeling armour of old time,
The lightning, the fierce wind, and trampling waves.

Farewell, farewell the heart that lives alone,
Housed in a dream, at distance from the Kind!
Such happiness, wherever it be known,
Is to be pitied; for 'tis surely blind.

But welcome fortitude, and patient cheer,
And frequent sights of what is to be borne!
Such sights, or worse, as are before me here. –
Not without hope we suffer and we mourn.

WILLIAM WORDSWORTH The Small Celandine

There is a Flower, the Lesser Celandine,
That shrinks, like many more, from cold and rain;
And, the first moment that the sun may shine,
Bright as the sun himself, 'tis out again!

When hailstones have been falling swarm on swarm,
Or blasts the green field and the trees distrest,
Oft have I seen it muffled up from harm,
In close self-shelter, like a Thing at rest.

But lately, one rough day, this Flower I passed,
And recognized it, though an altered Form,
Now standing forth an offering to the Blast,
And buffetted at will by Rain and Storm.

I stopped, and said with inly muttered voice,
'It doth not love the shower, nor seek the cold:
This neither is its courage nor its choice,
But its necessity in being old.

'The sunshine may not bless it, nor the dew;
It cannot help itself in its decay;
Stiff in its members, withered, changed of hue.'
And, in my spleen, I smiled that it was grey.

To be a Prodigal's Favorite – then, worse truth,
A Miser's Pensioner – behold our lot!
O Man! that from thy fair and shining youth
Age might but take the things Youth needed not!

WILLIAM WORDSWORTH Ode (Intimations of Immortality from Recollections of Early Childhood)

Paulò majora canamus

There was a time when meadow, grove, and stream,
The earth, and every common sight,
       To me did seem
      Apparelled in celestial light,
The glory and the freshness of a dream.
It is not now as it has been of yore; –
      Turn wheresoe'er I may,
       By night or day,
The things which I have seen I now can see no more.

      The Rainbow comes and goes,
      And lovely is the Rose,
      The Moon doth with delight
Look round her when the heavens are bare;
      Waters on a starry night
      Are beautiful and fair;
      The sunshine is a glorious birth;
      But yet I know, where'er I go,
That there hath passed away a glory from the earth.

Now, while the Birds thus sing a joyous song,
      And while the young Lambs bound
      As to the tabor's sound,
To me alone there came a thought of grief:
A timely utterance gave that thought relief,
      And I again am strong.
The Cataracts blow their trumpets from the steep,
No more shall grief of mine the season wrong;
I hear the Echoes through the mountains throng,
The Winds come to me from the fields of sleep,
      And all the earth is gay,
       Land and sea
      Give themselves up to jollity,
       And with the heart of May
      Doth every Beast keep holiday,
       Thou Child of Joy,
Shout round me, let me hear thy shouts, thou happy Shepherd Boy!

Ye blessed Creatures, I have heard the call
    Ye to each other make; I see
The heavens laugh with you in your jubilee;
    My heart is at your festival,
    My head hath its coronal,
The fullness of your bliss, I feel – I feel it all.
      Oh evil day! if I were sullen
      While the Earth herself is adorning,
        This sweet May-morning,
      And the Children are pulling,
        On every side,
    In a thousand vallies far and wide,
    Fresh flowers; while the sun shines warm,
And the Babe leaps up on his mother's arm: –
    I hear, I hear, with joy I hear!
    – But there's a Tree, of many one,
A single Field which I have looked upon,
Both of them speak of something that is gone:
      The Pansy at my feet
      Doth the same tale repeat:
Whither is fled the visionary gleam?
Where is it now, the glory and the dream?

Our birth is but a sleep and a forgetting:
The Soul that rises with us, our life's Star,
      Hath had elsewhere its setting,
      And cometh from afar:
    Not in entire forgetfulness,
    And not in utter nakedness,
But trailing clouds of glory do we come
      From God, who is our home:
Heaven lies about us in our infancy!
Shades of the prison-house begin to close
      Upon the growing Boy,
But He beholds the light, and whence it flows,
      He sees it in his joy;
The Youth, who daily farther from the East
    Must travel, still is Nature's Priest,
      And by the vision splendid
      Is on his way attended;
At length the Man perceives it die away,
And fade into the light of common day.

Earth fills her lap with pleasures of her own;
Yearnings she hath in her own natural kind,
And, even with something of a Mother's mind,
   And no unworthy aim,
  The homely Nurse doth all she can
To make her Foster-child, her Inmate Man,
   Forget the glories he hath known,
And that imperial palace whence he came.

Behold the Child among his new-born blisses,
A four year's Darling of a pigmy size!
See, where mid work of his own hand he lies,
Fretted by sallies of his Mother's kisses,
With light upon him from his Father's eyes!
See, at his feet, some little plan or chart,
Some fragment from his dream of human life,
Shaped by himself with newly-learned art;
   A wedding or a festival,
   A mourning or a funeral;
    And this hath now his heart,
    And unto this he frames his song:
    Then will he fit his tongue
To dialogues of business, love, or strife;
   But it will not be long
   Ere this be thrown aside,
   And with new joy and pride
The little Actor cons another part,
Filling from time to time his 'humorous stage'
With all the Persons, down to palsied Age,
That Life brings with her in her Equipage;
   As if his whole vocation
   Were endless imitation.

Thou, whose exterior semblance doth belie
   Thy Soul's immensity;
Thou best Philosopher, who yet dost keep
Thy heritage, thou Eye among the blind,
That, deaf and silent, read'st the eternal deep,
Haunted for ever by the eternal mind, –
   Mighty Prophet! Seer blest!
   On whom those truths do rest,
Which we are toiling all our lives to find;

Thou, over whom thy Immortality
Broods like the Day, a Master o'er a Slave,
A Presence which is not to be put by;
             To whom the grave
Is but a lonely bed without the sense or sight
             Of day or the warm light,
A place of thought where we in waiting lie;
Thou little Child, yet glorious in the might
Of untamed pleasures, on thy Being's height,
Why with such earnest pains dost thou provoke
The Years to bring the inevitable yoke,
Thus blindly with thy blessedness at strife?
Full soon thy Soul shall have her earthly freight,
And custom lie upon thee with a weight,
Heavy as frost, and deep almost as life!

             O joy! that in our embers
             Is something that doth live,
             That nature yet remembers
             What was so fugitive!
The thought of our past years in me doth breed
Perpetual benedictions: not indeed
For that which is most worthy to be blest;
Delight and liberty, the simple creed
Of Childhood, whether fluttering or at rest,
With new-born hope for ever in his breast: –
             Not for these I raise
             The song of thanks and praise;
        But for those obstinate questionings
             Of sense and outward things,
             Fallings from us, vanishings;
             Blank misgivings of a Creature
Moving about in worlds not realized,
High instincts, before which our mortal Nature
Did tremble like a guilty Thing surprized:
             But for those first affections,
             Those shadowy recollections,
             Which, be they what they may,
Are yet the fountain light of all our day,
Are yet a master light of all our seeing;
             Uphold us, cherish us, and make
Our noisy years seem moments in the being
Of the eternal Silence: truths that wake,

To perish never;
Which neither listlessness, nor mad endeavour,
                    Nor Man nor Boy,
Nor all that is at enmity with joy,
Can utterly abolish or destroy!
        Hence, in a season of calm weather,
                Though inland far we be,
Our Souls have sight of that immortal sea
                Which brought us hither,
                Can in a moment travel thither,
And see the Children sport upon the shore,
And hear the mighty waters rolling evermore.

Then, sing ye Birds, sing, sing a joyous song!
                And let the young Lambs bound
                As to the tabor's sound!
        We in thought will join your throng,
                Ye that pipe and ye that play,
                Ye that through your hearts to day
                Feel the gladness of the May!
What though the radiance which was once so bright
Be now for ever taken from my sight,
        Though nothing can bring back the hour
Of splendour in the grass, of glory in the flower;
                We will grieve not, rather find
                Strength in what remains behind,
                In the primal sympathy
                Which having been must ever be,
                In the soothing thoughts that spring
                Out of human suffering,
                In the faith that looks through death,
In years that bring the philosophic mind.

And oh ye Fountains, Meadows, Hills, and Groves,
Think not of any severing of our loves!
Yet in my heart of hearts I feel your might;
I only have relinquished one delight
To live beneath your more habitual sway.
I love the Brooks which down their channels fret,
Even more than when I tripped lightly as they;
The innocent brightness of a new-born Day
                Is lovely yet;

The Clouds that gather round the setting sun
Do take a sober colouring from an eye
That hath kept watch o'er man's mortality;
Another race hath been, and other palms are won.
Thanks to the human heart by which we live,
Thanks to its tenderness, its joys, and fears,
To me the meanest flower that blows can give
Thoughts that do often lie too deep for tears.

THOMAS MOORE

1808

Oh! blame not the bard, if he fly to the bowers,
    Where pleasure lies carelessly smiling at fame;
He was born for much more, and in happier hours,
    His soul might have burn'd with a holier flame.
The string that now languishes loose on the lyre,
    Might have bent a proud bow to the warrior's dart;
And the lip which now breathes but the song of desire,
    Might have pour'd the full tide of the patriot's heart!

But alas! for his country – her pride is gone by,
    And that spirit is broken which never would bend;
O'er the ruin her children in secret must sigh,
    For 'tis treason to love her, and death to defend.
Unpriz'd are her sons, till they've learn'd to betray;
    Undistinguish'd they live, if they shame not their sires;
And the torch that would light them through dignity's way,
    Must be caught from the pile where their country expires.

Then blame not the bard, if in pleasure's soft dream
    He should try to forget what he never can heal;
Oh! give but a hope – let a vista but gleam
    Through the gloom of his country, and mark how he'll feel!
That instant, his heart at her shrine would lay down
    Every passion it nurs'd, every bliss it ador'd;
While the myrtle, now idly entwin'd with his crown,
    Like the wreath of Harmodius, should cover his sword.

But though glory be gone, and though hope fade away,
    Thy name, lov'd Erin! shall live in his songs:
Not even in the hour when his heart is most gay,
    Will he lose the remembrance of thee and thy wrongs.

The stranger shall hear thy lament on his plains,
    The sigh of thy harp shall be sent o'er the deep,
Till thy masters themselves, as they rivet thy chains,
    Shall pause at the song of their captive and weep!

1810   GEORGE CRABBE *from* **The Borough**

from **Prisons [The Condemned Man]**

Yes! e'en in Sleep th'impressions all remain,
He hears the Sentence and he feels the Chain;
He sees the Judge and Jury, when he shakes,
And loudly cries, 'Not guilty,' and awakes:
Then chilling Tremblings o'er his Body creep,
Till worn-out Nature is compell'd to sleep.

Now comes the Dream again: it shows each Scene,
With each small Circumstance that comes between –
The Call to Suffering and the very Deed –
There Crowds go with him, follow and precede;
Some heartless shout, some pity, all condemn,
While he in fancied Envy looks at them:
He seems the Place for that sad Act to see,
And dreams the very Thirst which then will be:
A Priest attends – it seems the one he knew
In his best days, beneath whose care he grew.

At this his Terrors take a sudden flight,
He sees his native Village with delight;
The House, the Chamber, where he once array'd
His youthful Person; where he knelt and pray'd:
Then too the Comforts he enjoy'd at home,
The Days of Joy; the Joys themselves are come; –
The Hours of Innocence; – the timid Look
Of his lov'd Maid, when first her hand he took
And told his hope; her trembling Joy appears, –
Her forc'd Reserve and his retreating Fears.

All now is present; – 'tis a moment's gleam
Of former Sunshine – stay, delightful Dream!
Let him within his pleasant Garden walk,
Give him her Arm, of Blessings let them talk.

Yes! all are with him now, and all the while
Life's early Prospects and his *Fanny*'s Smile:
Then come his Sister and his Village Friend,
And he will now the sweetest Moments spend
Life has to yield: – No! never will he find
Again on Earth such Pleasure in his Mind:
He goes through shrubby Walks these Friends among,
Love in their Looks and Honour on the Tongue;
Nay, there's a Charm beyond what Nature shows,
The Bloom is softer and more sweetly glows; –
Pierc'd by no Crime, and urg'd by no desire
For more than true and honest Hearts require,
They feel the calm Delight, and thus proceed
Through the green Lane, – then linger in the Mead, –
Stray o'er the Heath in all its purple bloom, –
And pluck the Blossom where the Wild-bees hum;
Then through the broomy Bound with ease they pass,
And press the sandy Sheep-walk's slender Grass,
Where dwarfish Flowers among the Gorse are spread,
And the Lamb brouzes by the Linnet's Bed;
Then 'cross the bounding Brook they make their way
O'er its rough Bridge – and there behold the Bay! –
The Ocean smiling to the fervid Sun –
The Waves that faintly fall and slowly run –
The Ships at distance and the Boats at hand:
And now they walk upon the Sea-side Sand,
Counting the number and what kind they be,
Ships softly sinking in the sleepy Sea:
Now arm in arm, now parted, they behold
The glitt'ring Waters on the Shingles roll'd:
The timid Girls, half-dreading their design,
Dip the small Foot in the retarded Brine,
And search for crimson Weeds, which spreading flow,
Or lie like Pictures on the Sand below;
With all those bright red Pebbles, that the Sun
Through the small Waves so softly shines upon;
And those live lucid Jellies which the eye
Delights to trace as they swim glitt'ring by:
Pearl-shells and rubied Star-fish they admire,
And will arrange above the Parlour-fire, –
Tokens of Bliss! – 'Oh! horrible! – a Wave
Roars as it rises – save me, *Edward!* save!'
She cries: – Alas! the Watchman on his way
Calls and lets in – Truth, Terror, and the Day.

Alas! for *Peter* not an helping Hand,
So was he hated, could he now command;
Alone he row'd his Boat, alone he cast
His Nets beside, or made his Anchor fast;
To hold a Rope or hear a Curse was none, –
He toil'd and rail'd; he groan'd and swore alone.

Thus by himself compell'd to live each day,
To wait for certain hours the Tide's delay;
At the same times the same dull views to see,
The bounding Marsh-bank and the blighted Tree;
The Water only, when the Tides were high,
When low, the Mud half-cover'd and half-dry;
The Sun-burnt Tar that blisters on the Planks,
And Bank-side Stakes in their uneven ranks;
Heaps of entangled Weeds that slowly float,
As the Tide rolls by the impeded Boat.

When Tides were neap, and, in the sultry day,
Through the tall bounding Mud-banks made their way,
Which on each side rose swelling, and below
The dark warm Flood ran silently and slow;
There anchoring, *Peter* chose from Man to hide,
There hang his Head, and view the lazy Tide
In its hot slimy Channel slowly glide;
Where the small Eels that left the deeper way
For the warm Shore, within the Shallows play;
Where gaping Muscles, left upon the Mud,
Slope their slow passage to the fallen Flood; –
Here dull and hopeless he'll lie down and trace
How sidelong Crabs had scrawl'd their crooked race;
Or sadly listen to the tuneless cry
Of fishing *Gull* or clanging *Golden-eye*;
What time the Sea-birds to the Marsh would come,
And the loud *Bittern*, from the Bull-rush home,
Gave from the Salt-ditch side the bellowing Boom:
He nurst the Feelings these dull Scenes produce,
And lov'd to stop beside the opening Sluice;
Where the small Stream, confin'd in narrow bound,
Ran with a dull, unvaried, sad'ning sound;
Where all presented to the Eye or Ear,
Oppress'd the Soul! with Misery, Grief, and Fear.

SIR WALTER SCOTT *from* The Lady of the Lake

Coronach

He is gone on the mountain,
   He is lost to the forest,
Like a summer-dried fountain,
   When our need was the sorest.
5   The font, reappearing,
   From the rain-drops shall borrow,
But to us comes no cheering,
   To Duncan no morrow!

The hand of the reaper
10   Takes the ears that are hoary,
But the voice of the weeper
   Wails manhood in glory.
The autumn winds rushing
   Waft the leaves that are searest,
15   But our flower was in flushing,
   When blighting was nearest.

Fleet foot on the correi,
   Sage counsel in cumber,
Red hand in the foray,
20   How sound is thy slumber!
Like the dew on the mountain,
   Like the foam on the river,
Like the bubble on the fountain,
   Thou art gone, and for ever!

17 *correi* lee hillside; 18 *cumber* trouble

1815   GEORGE GORDON, LORD BYRON Stanzas for Music

There's not a joy the world can give like that it takes away,
When the glow of early thought declines in feeling's dull decay;
'Tis not on youth's smooth cheek the blush alone, which fades so
  fast,
But the tender bloom of heart is gone, ere youth itself be past.

Then the few whose spirits float above the wreck of happiness,
Are driven o'er the shoals of guilt or ocean of excess:
The magnet of their course is gone, or only points in vain
The shore to which their shiver'd sail shall never stretch again.

Then the mortal coldness of the soul like death itself comes down;
It cannot feel for others' woes, it dare not dream its own;
That heavy chill has frozen o'er the fountain of our tears,
And tho' the eye may sparkle still, 'tis where the ice appears.

Tho' wit may flash from fluent lips, and mirth distract the breast,
Through midnight hours that yield no more their former hope of
  rest;
'Tis but as ivy-leaves around the ruin'd turret wreath,
All green and wildly fresh without but worn and grey beneath.

Oh could I feel as I have felt, – or be what I have been,
Or weep as I could once have wept, o'er many a vanished scene:
As springs in deserts found seem sweet, all brackish though they be,
So midst the wither'd waste of life, those tears would flow to me.

1816   SAMUEL TAYLOR COLERIDGE Kubla Khan Or, A Vision
in a Dream. A Fragment

In Xanadu did Kubla Khan
A stately pleasure-dome decree:
Where Alph, the sacred river, ran
Through caverns measureless to man
 Down to a sunless sea.
So twice five miles of fertile ground
With walls and towers were girdled round:

And there were gardens bright with sinuous rills,
Where blossomed many an incense-bearing tree;
And here were forests ancient as the hills,
Enfolding sunny spots of greenery.

But oh! that deep romantic chasm which slanted
Down the green hill athwart a cedarn cover!
A savage place! as holy and enchanted
As e'er beneath a waning moon was haunted
By woman wailing for her demon-lover!
And from this chasm, with ceaseless turmoil seething,
As if this earth in fast thick pants were breathing,
A mighty fountain momently was forced:
Amid whose swift half-intermitted burst
Huge fragments vaulted like rebounding hail,
Or chaffy grain beneath the thresher's flail:
And 'mid these dancing rocks at once and ever
It flung up momently the sacred river.
Five miles meandering with a mazy motion
Through wood and dale the sacred river ran,
Then reached the caverns measureless to man,
And sank in tumult to a lifeless ocean:
And 'mid this tumult Kubla heard from far
Ancestral voices prophesying war!
   The shadow of the dome of pleasure
   Floated midway on the waves;
   Where was heard the mingled measure
   From the fountain and the caves.
It was a miracle of rare device,
A sunny pleasure-dome with caves of ice!

   A damsel with a dulcimer
   In a vision once I saw:
   It was an Abyssinian maid,
   And on her dulcimer she played,
   Singing of Mount Abora.
   Could I revive within me
   Her symphony and song,
   To such a deep delight 'twould win me,
That with music loud and long,
I would build that dome in air,

That sunny dome! those caves of ice!
And all who heard should see them there,
And all should cry, Beware! Beware!
His flashing eyes, his floating hair!
Weave a circle round him thrice,
And close your eyes with holy dread,
For he on honey-dew hath fed,
And drunk the milk of Paradise.

(written 1798)

JOHN KEATS On First Looking into Chapman's Homer

Much have I travell'd in the realms of gold,
    And many goodly states and kingdoms seen;
    Round many western islands have I been
Which bards in fealty to Apollo hold.
Oft of one wide expanse had I been told
    That deep-brow'd Homer ruled as his demesne;
    Yet did I never breathe its pure serene
Till I heard Chapman speak out loud and bold:
Then felt I like some watcher of the skies
    When a new planet swims into his ken;
Or like stout Cortez when with eagle eyes
    He star'd at the Pacific – and all his men
Look'd at each other with a wild surmise –
    Silent, upon a peak in Darien.

PERCY BYSSHE SHELLEY To Wordsworth

Poet of Nature, thou hast wept to know
That things depart which never may return:
Childhood and youth, friendship and love's first glow,
Have fled like sweet dreams, leaving thee to mourn.
These common woes I feel. One loss is mine
Which thou too feel'st, yet I alone deplore.
Thou wert as a lone star, whose light did shine
On some frail bark in winter's midnight roar:

Thou hast like to a rock-built refuge stood
Above the blind and battling multitude:
In honoured poverty thy voice did weave
Songs consecrate to truth and liberty, –
Deserting these, thou leavest me to grieve,
Thus having been, that thou shouldst cease to be.

SAMUEL TAYLOR COLERIDGE *from* The Rime of the Ancient Mariner   **1817**

PART IV

'I fear thee, ancient Mariner!
I fear thy skinny hand!
And thou art long, and lank, and brown,
As is the ribbed sea-sand.

The Wedding Guest feareth that a Spirit is talking to him.

I fear thee and thy glittering eye,
And thy skinny hand, so brown.' –
Fear not, fear not, thou Wedding-Guest!
This body dropt not down.

But the ancient Mariner assureth him of his bodily life, and proceedeth to relate his horrible penance.

Alone, alone, all, all alone,
Alone on a wide wide sea!
And never a saint took pity on
My soul in agony.

The many men, so beautiful!
And they all dead did lie:
And a thousand thousand slimy things
Lived on; and so did I.

He despiseth the creatures of the calm.

I looked upon the rotting sea,
And drew my eyes away;
I looked upon the rotting deck,
And there the dead men lay.

And envieth that they should live, and so many lie dead.

I looked to heaven, and tried to pray;
But or ever a prayer had gusht,
A wicked whisper came, and made
My heart as dry as dust.

I closed my lids, and kept them close,
And the balls like pulses beat;
For the sky and the sea, and the sea and the sky
Lay like a load on my weary eye,
And the dead were at my feet.

The cold sweat melted from their limbs,
Nor rot nor reek did they:
The look with which they looked on me
Had never passed away.

> But the curse liveth
> for him in the eye of
> the dead men.

An orphan's curse would drag to hell
A spirit from on high;
But oh! more horrible than that
Is the curse in a dead man's eye!
Seven days, seven nights, I saw that curse,
And yet I could not die.

The moving Moon went up the sky,
And no where did abide:
Softly she was going up,
And a star or two beside –

> In his loneliness and fixedness
> he yearneth towards the journeying
> Moon, and the stars that still
> sojourn, yet still move onward;
> and every where the blue sky
> belongs to them, and is their
> appointed rest, and their native country and their own natural homes, which
> they enter unannounced, as lords that are certainly expected and yet there is a
> silent joy at their arrival.

Her beams bemocked the sultry main,
Like April hoar-frost spread;
But where the ship's huge shadow lay,
The charmèd water burnt alway
A still and awful red.

Beyond the shadow of the ship,
I watched the water-snakes:
They moved in tracks of shining white,
And when they reared, the elfish light
Fell off in hoary flakes.

> By the light of the Moon he
> beholdeth God's creatures of
> the great calm.

Within the shadow of the ship
I watched their rich attire:
Blue, glossy green, and velvet black,
They coiled and swam; and every track
Was a flash of golden fire.

O happy living things! no tongue
Their beauty might declare:
A spring of love gushed from my heart,
And I blessed them unaware:
Sure my kind saint took pity on me,
And I blessed them unaware.

Their beauty and their happiness. [609

He blesseth them in his heart.

The selfsame moment I could pray;
And from my neck so free
The Albatross fell off, and sank
Like lead into the sea.

The spell begins to break.

JOHN KEATS

After dark vapours have oppress'd our plains
   For a long dreary season, comes a day
   Born of the gentle South, and clears away,
From the sick heavens all unseemly stains.
The anxious month, relieving from its pains,
   Takes as a long-lost right the feel of May,
   The eyelids with the passing coolness play,
Like rose leaves with the drip of summer rains.
The calmest thoughts come round us – as of leaves
   Budding, – fruit ripening in stillness, – autumn suns
Smiling at eve upon the quiet sheaves, –
Sweet Sappho's cheek, – a sleeping infant's breath, –
   The gradual sand that through an hour-glass runs, –
A woodland rivulet, – a Poet's death.

JOHN KEATS *from* Endymion

1818

       But there are
Richer entanglements, enthralments far
More self-destroying, leading, by degrees,
To the chief intensity: the crown of these
Is made of love and friendship, and sits high
Upon the forehead of humanity.
All its more ponderous and bulky worth
Is friendship, whence there ever issues forth

A steady splendour; but at the tip-top,
There hangs by unseen film, an orbèd drop
Of light, and that is love: its influence,
Thrown in our eyes, genders a novel sense,
At which we start and fret; till in the end,
Melting into its radiance, we blend,
Mingle, and so become a part of it –
Nor with aught else can our souls interknit
So wingedly. When we combine therewith,
Life's self is nourished by its proper pith,
And we are nurtured like a pelican brood.
Ay, so delicious is the unsating food,
That men, who might have towered in the van
Of all the congregated world, to fan
And winnow from the coming step of time
All chaff of custom, wipe away all slime
Left by men-slugs and human serpentry,
Have been content to let occasion die,
Whilst they did sleep in love's elysium.
And, truly, I would rather be struck dumb,
Than speak against this ardent listlessness:
For I have ever thought that it might bless
The world with benefits unknowingly,
As does the nightingale, up-perchèd high,
And cloistered among cool and bunchèd leaves –
She sings but to her love, nor e'er conceives
How tip-toe Night holds back her dark-grey hood.
Just so may love, although 'tis understood
The mere commingling of passionate breath,
Produce more than our searching witnesseth –
What I know not: but who, of men, can tell
That flowers would bloom, or that green fruit would swell
To melting pulp, that fish would have bright mail,
The earth its dower of river, wood, and vale,
The meadows runnels, runnels pebble-stones,
The seed its harvest, or the lute its tones,
Tones ravishment, or ravishment its sweet,
If human souls did never kiss and greet?

PERCY BYSSHE SHELLEY Ozymandias

I met a traveller from an antique land
Who said: 'Two vast and trunkless legs of stone
Stand in the desert. Near them, on the sand,
Half sunk, a shattered visage lies, whose frown,
And wrinkled lip, and sneer of cold command,
Tell that its sculptor well those passions read
Which yet survive, stamped on these lifeless things,
The hand that mocked them and the heart that fed;
And on the pedestal these word appear:
"My name is Ozymandias, king of kings:
Look on my works, ye Mighty, and despair!"
Nothing beside remains. Round the decay
Of that colossal wreck, boundless and bare
The lone and level sands stretch far away.'

SIR WALTER SCOTT *from* The Heart of Mid-Lothian

[*Madge Wildfire sings:*]

'Proud Maisie is in the wood,
   Walking so early;
Sweet Robin sits on the bush,
   Singing so rarely.

" 'Tell me, thou bonny bird,
   When shall I marry me?" –
"When six braw gentlemen
   Kirkward shall carry ye."

*   *   *

" 'Who makes the bridal bed,
   Birdie, say truly?"
"The gray-headed sexton
   That delves the grave duly."

*   *   *

'The glow-worm o'er grave and stone
   Shall light thee steady;
The owl from the steeple sing,
   "Welcome, proud lady."''

1819   SIR WALTER SCOTT *from* The Bride of Lammermoor

[Lucy Ashton's song]

'Look not thou on Beauty's charming, –
Sit thou still when Kings are arming, –
Taste not when the wine-cup glistens, –
Speak not when the people listens, –
Stop thine ear against the singer, –
From the red gold keep thy finger, –
Vacant heart, and hand, and eye, –
Easy live and quiet die.'

GEORGE CRABBE *from* Tales of the Hall

from **Delay has Danger**

Three weeks had past, and Richard rambles now
Far as the dinners of the day allow;
He rode to Farley Grange and Finley Mere,
That house so ancient, and that lake so clear:
He rode to Ripley through that river gay,
Where in the shallow stream the loaches play,
And stony fragments stay the winding stream,
And gilded pebbles at the bottom gleam,
Giving their yellow surface to the sun,
And making proud the waters as they run:
It is a lovely place, and at the side
Rises a mountain-rock in rugged pride;
And in that rock are shapes of shells, and forms
Of creatures in old worlds, of nameless worms,
Whose generations lived and died ere man,
A worm of other class, to crawl began.

There is a town call'd Silford, where his steed
Our traveller rested – He the while would feed
His mind by walking to and fro, to meet,
He knew not what adventure, in the street:
A stranger there, but yet a window-view
Gave him a face that he conceived he knew;
He saw a tall, fair, lovely lady, dress'd
As one whom taste and wealth had jointly bless'd;
He gazed, but soon a footman at the door
Thundering, alarm'd her, who was seen no more.

'This was the lady whom her lover bound
In solemn contract, and then proved unsound:
Of this affair I have a clouded view,
And should be glad to have it clear'd by you.'
So Richard spake, and instant George replied,
'I had the story from the injured side,
But when resentment and regret were gone,
And pity (shaded by contempt) came on.

'Frail was the hero of my tale, but still
Was rather drawn by accident than will;
Some without meaning into guilt advance,
From want of guard, from vanity, from chance;
Man's weakness flies his more immediate pain,
A little respite from his fears to gain;
And takes the part that he would gladly fly,
If he had strength and courage to deny.

'But now my tale, and let the moral say,
When hope can sleep, there's Danger in delay.
Not that for rashness, Richard, I would plead,
For unadvised alliance: No, indeed:
Think ere the contract – but, contracted, stand
No more debating, take the ready hand:
When hearts are willing, and when fears subside,
Trust not to time, but let the knot be tied;
For when a lover has no more to do,
He thinks in leisure, what shall I pursue?
And then who knows what objects come in view?
For when, assured, the man has nought to keep
His wishes warm and active, then they sleep:

Hopes die with fears; and then a man must lose
All the gay visions, and delicious views,
Once his mind's wealth! He travels at his ease,
Nor horrors now nor fairy-beauty sees;
When the kind goddess gives the wish'd assent,
No mortal business should the deed prevent;
But the blest youth should legal sanction seek
Ere yet th' assenting blush has fled the cheek.

'And – hear me, Richard, – man has reptile-pride
That often rises when his fears subside;
When, like a trader feeling rich, he now
Neglects his former smile, his humble bow,
And, conscious of his hoarded wealth, assumes
New airs, nor thinks how odious he becomes.
There is a wandering, wavering train of thought
That something seeks where nothing should be sought,
And will a self-delighted spirit move
To dare the danger of pernicious love.'

WILLIAM BLAKE To the Accuser Who is the God of This World

Truly My Satan thou art but a Dunce
And dost not know the Garment from the Man
Every Harlot was a Virgin once
Nor canst thou ever change Kate into Nan

Tho thou art Worshipd by the Names Divine
Of Jesus & Jehovah: thou art still
The Son of Morn in weary Nights decline
The lost Travellers Dream under the Hill

PERCY BYSSHE SHELLEY *from* The Mask of Anarchy

Written on the Occasion of the Massacre at Manchester

As I lay asleep in Italy
There came a voice from over the Sea,
And with great power it forth led me
To walk in the visions of Poesy.

I met Murder on the way –
He had a mask like Castlereagh –
Very smooth he looked, yet grim;
Seven bloodhounds followed him:

All were fat; and well they might
Be in admirable plight,
For one by one, and two by two,
He tossed them human hearts to chew
Which from his wide cloak he drew.

Next came Fraud, and he had on,
Like Eldon, an ermined gown;
His big tears, for he wept well,
Turned to mill-stones as they fell.

And the little children, who
Round his feet played to and fro,
Thinking every tear a gem,
Had their brains knocked out by them.

Clothed with the Bible, as with light,
And the shadows of the night,
Like Sidmouth, next, Hypocrisy
On a crocodile rode by.

And many more Destructions played
In this ghastly masquerade,
All disguised, even to the eyes,
Like Bishops, lawyers, peers, or spies.

Last came Anarchy: he rode
On a white horse, splashed with blood;
He was pale even to the lips,
Like Death in the Apocalypse.

And he wore a kingly crown,
And in his grasp a sceptre shone;
On his brow this mark I saw –
'I AM GOD, AND KING, AND LAW!'

With a pace stately and fast,
Over English land he past,
Trampling to a mire of blood
The adoring multitude.

And a mighty troop around,
With their trampling shook the ground,
Waving each a bloody sword,
For the service of their Lord.

And with glorious triumph, they
Rode through England proud and gay
Drunk as with intoxication
Of the wine of desolation.

O'er fields and towns, from sea to sea.
Passed the Pageant swift and free,
Tearing up, and trampling down;
Till they came to London town.

And each dweller, panic-stricken,
Felt his heart with terror sicken
Hearing the tempestuous cry
Of the triumph of Anarchy.

For with pomp to meet him came
Clothed in arms like blood and flame,
The hired Murderers, who did sing
'Thou art God, and Law, and King.

'We have waited, weak and lone
For thy coming, Mighty One!
Our purses are empty, our swords are cold
Give us glory, and blood, and gold.'

Lawyers and priests, a motley crowd,
To the earth their pale brows bowed;
Like a bad prayer not over loud,
Whispering – 'Thou art Law and God.' –

Then all cried with one accord;
'Thou art King, and God, and Lord;
Anarchy, to Thee we bow,
Be thy name made holy now!'

And Anarchy, the Skeleton,
Bowed and grinned to every one,
As well as if his education
Had cost ten millions to the Nation.

For he knew the Palaces
Of our Kings were rightly his;
His the sceptre, crown, and globe,
And the gold-inwoven robe.

(1832)

GEORGE GORDON, LORD BYRON *from* Don Juan

from Canto I [Juan's Puberty]

So much for Julia. Now we'll turn to Juan,
    Poor little fellow! he had no idea
Of his own case, and never hit the true one;
    In feelings quick as Ovid's Miss Medea,
He puzzled over what he found a new one,
    But not as yet imagined it could be a
Thing quite in course, and not at all alarming,
Which, with a little patience, might grow charming.

Silent and pensive, idle, restless, slow,
    His home deserted for the lonely wood,
Tormented with a wound he could not know,
    His, like all deep grief, plunged in solitude:
I'm fond myself of solitude or so,
    But then, I beg it may be understood,
By solitude I mean a sultan's, not
A hermit's, with a haram for a grot.

'Oh Love! in such a wilderness as this,
    Where transport and security entwine,
Here is the empire of thy perfect bliss,
    And here thou art a god indeed divine.'
The bard I quote from does not sing amiss,
    With the exception of the second line,
For that same twining 'transport and security'
Are twisted to a phrase of some obscurity.

The poet meant, no doubt, and thus appeals
    To the good sense and senses of mankind,
The very thing which every body feels,
    As all have found on trial, or may find,
That no one likes to be disturb'd at meals
    Or love. – I won't say more about 'entwined'
Or 'transport', as we knew all that before,
But beg 'Security' will bolt the door.

Young Juan wander'd by the glassy brooks
    Thinking unutterable things; he threw
Himself at length within the leafy nooks
    Where the wild branch of the cork forest grew;
There poets find materials for their books,
    And every now and then we read them through,
So that their plan and prosody are eligible,
Unless, like Wordsworth, they prove unintelligible.

He, Juan, (and not Wordsworth) so pursued
    His self-communion with his own high soul,
Until his mighty heart, in its great mood,
    Had mitigated part, though not the whole
Of its disease; he did the best he could
    With things not very subject to control,
And turn'd, without perceiving his condition,
Like Coleridge, into a metaphysician.

He thought about himself, and the whole earth,
    Of man the wonderful, and of the stars,
And how the deuce they ever could have birth;
    And then he thought of earthquakes, and of wars,
How many miles the moon might have in girth,
    Of air-balloons, and of the many bars
To perfect knowledge of the boundless skies;
And then he thought of Donna Julia's eyes.

In thoughts like these true wisdom may discern
   Longings sublime, and aspirations high,
Which some are born with, but the most part learn
   To plague themselves withal, they know not why:
'Twas strange that one so young should thus concern
   His brain about the action of the sky;
If *you* think 'twas philosophy that this did,
I can't help thinking puberty assisted.

He pored upon the leaves, and on the flowers,
   And heard a voice in all the winds; and then
He thought of wood nymphs and immortal bowers,
   And how the goddesses came down to men:
He miss'd the pathway, he forgot the hours,
   And when he look'd upon his watch again,
He found how much old Time had been a winner –
He also found that he had lost his dinner.

Sometimes he turn'd to gaze upon his book,
   Boscan, or Garcilasso; – by the wind
Even as the page is rustled while we look,
   So by the poesy of his own mind
Over the mystic leaf his soul was shook,
   As if 'twere one whereon magicians bind
Their spells, and give them to the passing gale,
According to some good old woman's tale.

Thus would he while his lonely hours away
   Dissatisfied, nor knowing what he wanted;
Nor glowing reverie, nor poet's lay,
   Could yield his spirit that for which it panted,
A bosom whereon he his head might lay,
   And hear the heart beat with the love it granted,
With – several other things, which I forget,
Or which, at least, I need not mention yet.

from **Canto II [The Shipwreck]**

At half-past eight o'clock, booms, hencoops, spars,
   And all things, for a chance, had been cast loose,
That still could keep afloat the struggling tars,
   For yet they strove, although of no great use:

There was no light in heaven but a few stars,
   The boats put off o'ercrowded with their crews;
She gave a heel, and then a lurch to port,
And, going down head foremost – sunk, in short.

Then rose from sea to sky the wild farewell,
   Then shriek'd the timid, and stood still the brave,
Then some leap'd overboard with dreadful yell,
   As eager to anticipate their grave;
And the sea yawn'd around her like a hell,
   And down she suck'd with her the whirling wave,
Like one who grapples with his enemy,
And strives to strangle him before he die.

And first one universal shriek there rush'd,
   Louder than the loud ocean, like a crash
Of echoing thunder; and then all was hush'd,
   Save the wild wind and the remorseless dash
Of billows; but at intervals there gush'd,
   Accompanied with a convulsive splash,
A solitary shriek, the bubbling cry
Of some strong swimmer in his agony.

The boats, as stated, had got off before,
   And in them crowded several of the crew;
And yet their present hope was hardly more
   Than what it had been, for so strong it blew
There was slight chance of reaching any shore;
   And then they were too many, though so few –
Nine in the cutter, thirty in the boat,
Were counted in them when they got afloat.

All the rest perish'd; near two hundred souls
   Had left their bodies; and, what's worse, alas!
When over Catholics the ocean rolls,
   They must wait several weeks before a mass
Takes off one peck of purgatorial coals,
   Because, till people know what's come to pass,
They won't lay out their money on the dead –
It costs three francs for every mass that's said.

Juan got into the long-boat, and there
    Contrived to help Pedrillo to a place;
It seem'd as if they had exchanged their care,
    For Juan wore the magisterial face
Which courage gives, while poor Pedrillo's pair
    Of eyes were crying for their owner's case:
Battista, though, (a name call'd shortly Tita)
Was lost by getting at some aqua-vita.

Pedro, his valet, too, he tried to save,
    But the same cause, conducive to his loss,
Left him so drunk, he jump'd into the wave
    As o'er the cutter's edge he tried to cross,
And so he found a wine-and-watery grave;
    They could not rescue him although so close,
Because the sea ran higher every minute,
And for the boat – the crew kept crowding in it.

A small old spaniel, – which had been Don Jóse's,
    His father's, whom he loved, as ye may think,
For on such things the memory reposes
    With tenderness, – stood howling on the brink,
Knowing, (dogs have such intellectual noses!)
    No doubt, the vessel was about to sink;
And Juan caught him up, and ere he stepp'd
Off, threw him in, then after him he leap'd.

(. . .)

'Tis thus with people in an open boat,
    They live upon the love of life, and bear
More than can be believed, or even thought,
    And stand like rocks the tempest's wear and tear;
And hardship still has been the sailor's lot,
    Since Noah's ark went cruising here and there;
She had a curious crew as well as cargo,
Like the first old Greek privateer, the Argo.

But man is a carnivorous production,
    And must have meals, at least one meal a day;
He cannot live, like woodcocks, upon suction,
    But, like the shark and tiger, must have prey,

Although his anatomical construction
   Bears vegetables in a grumbling way,
Your labouring people think beyond all question,
Beef, veal, and mutton, better for digestion.

And thus it was with this our hapless crew,
   For on the third day there came on a calm,
And though at first their strength it might renew,
   And lying on their weariness like balm,
Lull'd them like turtles sleeping on the blue
   Of ocean, when they woke they felt a qualm,
And fell all ravenously on their provision,
Instead of hoarding it with due precision.

The consequence was easily foreseen –
   They ate up all they had, and drank their wine,
In spite of all remonstrances, and then
   On what, in fact, next day were they to dine?
They hoped the wind would rise, these foolish men!
   And carry them to shore; these hopes were fine,
But as they had but one oar, and that brittle,
It would have been more wise to save their victual.

The fourth day came, but not a breath of air,
   And Ocean slumber'd like an unwean'd child:
The fifth day, and their boat lay floating there,
   The sea and sky were blue, and clear, and mild –
With their one oar (I wish they had had a pair)
   What could they do? and hunger's rage grew wild:
So Juan's spaniel, spite of his entreating,
Was kill'd, and portion'd out for present eating.

On the sixth day they fed upon his hide,
   And Juan, who had still refused, because
The creature was his father's dog that died,
   Now feeling all the vulture in his jaws,
With some remorse received (though first denied)
   As a great favour one of the fore-paws,
Which he divided with Pedrillo, who
Devour'd it, longing for the other too.

The seventh day, and no wind – the burning sun
    Blister'd and scorch'd, and, stagnant on the sea,
They lay like carcases; and hope was none,
    Save in the breeze that came not; savagely
They glared upon each other – all was done,
    Water, and wine, and food, – and you might see
The longings of the cannibal arise
(Although they spoke not) in their wolfish eyes.

At length one whisper'd his companion, who
    Whisper'd another, and thus it went round,
And then into a hoarser murmur grew,
    An ominous, and wild, and desperate sound,
And when his comrade's thought each sufferer knew,
    'Twas but his own, suppress'd till now, he found:
And out they spoke of lots for flesh and blood,
And who should die to be his fellow's food.

But ere they came to this, they that day shared
    Some leathern caps, and what remain'd of shoes;
And then they look'd around them, and despair'd,
    And none to be the sacrifice would choose;
At length the lots were torn up, and prepared,
    But of materials that much shock the Muse –
Having no paper, for the want of better,
They took by force from Juan Julia's letter.

The lots were made, and mark'd, and mix'd, and handed,
    In silent horror, and their distribution
Lull'd even the savage hunger which demanded,
    Like the Promethean vulture, this pollution;
None in particular had sought or plann'd it,
    'Twas nature gnaw'd them to this resolution,
By which none were permitted to be neuter –
And the lot fell on Juan's luckless tutor.

He but requested to be bled to death:
    The surgeon had his instruments, and bled
Pedrillo, and so gently ebb'd his breath,
    You hardly could perceive when he was dead.
He died as born, a Catholic in faith,
    Like most in the belief in which they're bred,
And first a little crucifix he kiss'd,
And then held out his jugular and wrist.

The surgeon, as there was no other fee,
     Had his first choice of morsels for his pains;
But being thirstiest at the moment, he
     Preferr'd a draught from the fast-flowing veins:
Part was divided, part thrown in the sea,
     And such things as the entrails and the brains
Regaled two sharks, who follow'd o'er the billow –
The sailors ate the rest of poor Pedrillo.

The sailors ate him, all save three or four,
     Who were not quite so fond of animal food;
To these were added Juan, who, before
     Refusing his own spaniel, hardly could
Feel now his appetite increased much more;
     'Twas not to be expected that he should,
Even in extremity of their disaster,
Dine with them on his pastor and his master.

'Twas better that he did not; for, in fact,
     The consequence was awful in the extreme;
For they, who were most ravenous in the act,
     Went raging mad – Lord! how they did blaspheme!
And foam and roll, with strange convulsions rack'd,
     Drinking salt-water like a mountain-stream,
Tearing and grinning, howling, screeching, swearing,
And, with hyaena laughter, died despairing.

JOHN KEATS The Eve of St. Agnes

St. Agnes' Eve – Ah, bitter chill it was!
The owl, for all his feathers, was a-cold;
The hare limp'd trembling through the frozen grass,
And silent was the flock in woolly fold;
Numb were the Beadsman's fingers, while he told
His rosary, and while his frosted breath,
Like pious incense from a censer old,
Seem'd taking flight for heaven, without a death,
Past the sweet Virgin's picture, while his prayer he saith.

His prayer he saith, this patient, holy man;
Then takes his lamp, and riseth from his knees,
And back returneth, meagre, barefoot, wan,
Along the chapel aisle by slow degrees:
The sculptur'd dead, on each side, seem to freeze,
Emprison'd in black, purgatorial rails:
Knights, ladies, praying in dumb orat'ries,
He passeth by; and his weak spirit fails
To think how they may ache in icy hoods and mails.

Northward he turneth through a little door,
And scarce three steps, ere Music's golden tongue
Flatter'd to tears this aged man and poor;
But no – already had his deathbell rung;
The joys of all his life were said and sung:
His was harsh penance on St. Agnes' Eve:
Another way he went, and soon among
Rough ashes sat he for his soul's reprieve,
And all night kept awake, for sinners' sake to grieve.

That ancient Beadsman heard the prelude soft;
And so it chanc'd, for many a door was wide,
From hurry to and fro. Soon, up aloft,
The silver, snarling trumpets 'gan to chide:
The level chambers, ready with their pride,
Were glowing to receive a thousand guests:
The carved angels, ever eager-eyed,
Star'd, where upon their heads the cornice rests,
With hair blown back, and wings put cross-wise on their breasts.

At length burst in the argent revelry,
With plume, tiara, and all rich array,
Numerous as shadows haunting fairily
The brain, new stuff'd, in youth, with triumphs gay
Of old romance. These let us wish away,
And turn, sole-thoughted, to one Lady there,
Whose heart had brooded, all that wintry day,
On love, and wing'd St. Agnes' saintly care,
As she had heard old dames full many times declare.

They told her how, upon St. Agnes' Eve,
Young virgins might have visions of delight,
And soft adorings from their loves receive
Upon the honey'd middle of the night,

If ceremonies due they did aright;
    As, supperless to bed they must retire,
    And couch supine their beauties, lily white;
    Nor look behind, nor sideways, but require
Of Heaven with upward eyes for all that they desire.

    Full of this whim was thoughtful Madeline:
    The music, yearning like a God in pain,
    She scarcely heard: her maiden eyes divine,
    Fix'd on the floor, saw many a sweeping train
    Pass by – she heeded not at all: in vain
    Came many a tiptoe, amorous cavalier,
    And back retir'd; not cool'd by high disdain,
    But she saw not: her heart was otherwise:
She sigh'd for Agnes' dreams, the sweetest of the year.

    She danc'd along with vague, regardless eyes,
    Anxious her lips, her breathing quick and short:
    The hallow'd hour was near at hand: she sighs
    Amid the timbrels, and the throng'd resort
    Of whisperers in anger, or in sport;
    'Mid looks of love, defiance, hate, and scorn,
    Hoodwink'd with faery fancy; all amort,
    Save to St. Agnes and her lambs unshorn,
And all the bliss to be before to-morrow morn.

    So, purposing each moment to retire,
    She linger'd still. Meantime, across the moors,
    Had come young Porphyro, with heart on fire
    For Madeline. Beside the portal doors,
    Buttress'd from moonlight, stands he, and implores
    All saints to give him sight of Madeline,
    But for one moment in the tedious hours,
    That he might gaze and worship all unseen;
Perchance speak, kneel, touch, kiss – in sooth such things have been.

    He ventures in: let not buzz'd whisper tell:
    All eyes be muffled, or a hundred swords
    Will storm his heart, Love's fev'rous citadel:
    For him, those chambers held barbarian hordes,

Hyena foemen, and hot-blooded lords,
Whose very dogs would execrations howl
Against his lineage: not one breast affords
Him any mercy, in that mansion foul,
Save one old beldame, weak in body and in soul.

Ah, happy chance! the aged creature came,
Shuffling along with ivory-headed wand,
To where he stood, hid from the torch's flame,
Behind a broad hall-pillar, far beyond
The sound of merriment and chorus bland:
He startled her; but soon she knew his face,
And grasp'd his fingers in her palsied hand,
Saying, 'Mercy, Porphyro! hie thee from this place;
'They are all here to-night, the whole blood-thirsty race!

'Get hence! get hence! there's dwarfish Hildebrand;
'He had a fever late, and in the fit
'He cursed thee and thine, both house and land:
'Then there's that old Lord Maurice, not a whit
'More tame for his gray hairs – Alas me! flit!
'Flit like a ghost away.' 'Ah, gossip dear,
'We're safe enough; here in this arm-chair sit,
'And tell me how' – 'Good Saints! not here, not here;
'Follow me, child, or else these stones will be thy bier.'

He follow'd through a lowly arched way,
Brushing the cobwebs with his lofty plume,
And as she mutter'd 'Well-a – well-a-day!'
He found him in a little moonlight room,
Pale, lattic'd, chill, and silent as a tomb.
'Now tell me where is Madeline,' said he,
'O tell me, Angela, by the holy loom
'Which none but secret sisterhood may see,
'When they St. Agnes' wool are weaving piously.'

'St. Agnes! Ah! it is St. Agnes' Eve –
'Yet men will murder upon holy days:
'Thou must hold water in a witch's sieve,
'And be liege-lord of all the Elves and Fays,

'To venture so: it fills me with amaze
'To see thee, Porphyro! – St. Agnes' Eve!
'God's help! my lady fair the conjuror plays
'This very night: good angels her deceive!
'But let me laugh awhile, I've mickle time to grieve.'

Feebly she laugheth in the languid moon,
While Porphyro upon her face doth look,
Like puzzled urchin on an aged crone
Who keepeth clos'd a wond'rous riddle-book,
As spectacled she sits in chimney nook.
But soon his eyes grew brilliant, when she told
His lady's purpose; and he scarce could brook
Tears, at the thought of those enchantments cold
And Madeline asleep in lap of legends old.

Sudden a thought came like a full-blown rose,
Flushing his brow, and in his pained heart
Made purple riot: then doth he propose
A stratagem, that makes the beldame start:
'A cruel man and impious thou art:
'Sweet lady, let her pray, and sleep, and dream
'Alone with her good angels, far apart
'From wicked men like thee. Go, go! – I deem
'Thou canst not surely be the same that thou didst seem.'

'I will not harm her, by all saints I swear,'
Quoth Porphyro: 'O may I ne'er find grace
'When my weak voice shall whisper its last prayer,
'If one of her soft ringlets I displace,
'Or look with ruffian passion in her face:
'Good Angela, believe me by these tears;
'Or I will, even in a moment's space,
'Awake, with horrid shout, my foemen's ears,
'And beard them, though they be more fang'd than wolves and
        bears.'

'Ah! why wilt thou affright a feeble soul?
'A poor, weak, palsy-stricken, churchyard thing,
'Whose passing-bell may ere the midnight toll;
'Whose prayers for thee, each morn and evening,

'Were never miss'd.' – Thus plaining, doth she bring
A gentler speech from burning Porphyro;
So woful, and of such deep sorrowing,
That Angela gives promise she will do
Whatever he shall wish, betide her weal or woe.

Which was, to lead him, in close secrecy,
Even to Madeline's chamber, and there hide
Him in a closet, of such privacy
That he might see her beauty unespied,
And win perhaps that night a peerless bride,
While legion'd fairies pac'd the coverlet,
And pale enchantment held her sleepy-eyed.
Never on such a night have lovers met,
Since Merlin paid his Demon all the monstrous debt.

'It shall be as thou wishest,' said the Dame:
'All cates and dainties shall be stored there
'Quickly on this feast-night: by the tambour frame
'Her own lute thou wilt see: no time to spare,
'For I am slow and feeble, and scarce dare
'On such a catering trust my dizzy head.
'Wait here, my child, with patience; kneel in prayer
'The while: Ah! thou must needs the lady wed,
'Or may I never leave my grave among the dead.'

So saying, she hobbled off with busy fear.
The lover's endless minutes slowly pass'd;
The dame return'd, and whisper'd in his ear
To follow her; with aged eyes aghast
From fright of dim espial. Safe at last,
Through many a dusky gallery, they gain
The maiden's chamber, silken, hush'd, and chaste;
Where Porphyro took covert, pleas'd amain.
His poor guide hurried back with agues in her brain.

Her falt'ring hand upon the balustrade,
Old Angela was feeling for the stair,
When Madeline, St Agnes' charmed maid,
Rose, like a mission'd spirit, unaware:

With silver taper's light, and pious care,
    She turn'd, and down the aged gossip led
To a safe level matting. Now prepare,
    Young Porphyro, for gazing on that bed;
She comes, she comes again, like ring-dove fray'd and fled.

Out went the taper as she hurried in;
    Its little smoke, in pallid moonshine, died:
She clos'd the door, she panted, all akin
    To spirits of the air, and visions wide:
No uttered syllable, or, woe betide!
    But to her heart, her heart was voluble,
Paining with eloquence her balmy side;
    As though a tongueless nightingale should swell
Her throat in vain, and die, heart-stifled, in her dell.

A casement high and triple-arch'd there was,
    All garlanded with carven imag'ries
Of fruits, and flowers, and bunches of knot-grass,
    And diamonded with panes of quaint device,
Innumerable of stains and splendid dyes,
    As are the tiger-moth's deep-damask'd wings;
And in the midst, 'mong thousand heraldries,
    And twilight saints, and dim emblazonings,
A shielded scutcheon blush'd with blood of queens and kings.

Full on this casement shone the wintry moon,
    And threw warm gules on Madeline's fair breast,
As down she knelt for heaven's grace and boon;
    Rose-bloom fell on her hands, together prest,
And on her silver cross soft amethyst,
    And on her hair a glory, like a saint:
She seem'd a splendid angel, newly drest,
    Save wings, for heaven: – Porphyro grew faint:
She knelt, so pure a thing, so free from mortal taint.

Anon his heart revives: her vespers done,
    Of all its wreathed pearls her hair she frees;
Unclasps her warmed jewels one by one;
    Loosens her fragrant boddice; by degrees

Her rich attire creeps rustling to her knees:
Half-hidden, like a mermaid in sea-weed,
Pensive awhile she dreams awake, and sees,
In fancy, fair St Agnes in her bed,
But dares not look behind, or all the charm is fled.

Soon, trembling in her soft and chilly nest,
In sort of wakeful swoon, perplex'd she lay,
Until the poppied warmth of sleep oppress'd
Her soothed limbs, and soul fatigued away;
Flown, like a thought, until the morrow-day;
Blissfully haven'd both from joy and pain;
Clasp'd like a missal where swart Paynims pray;
Blinded alike from sunshine and from rain,
As though a rose should shut, and be a bud again.

Stol'n to this paradise, and so entranced,
Porphyro gazed upon her empty dress,
And listen'd to her breathing, if it chanced
To wake into a slumberous tenderness;
Which when he heard, that minute did he bless,
And breath'd himself: then from the closet crept,
Noiseless as fear in a wide wilderness,
And over the hush'd carpet, silent, stept,
And 'tween the curtains peep'd, where, lo! – how fast she slept.

Then by the bed-side, where the faded moon
Made a dim, silver twilight, soft he set
A table, and, half anguish'd, threw thereon
A cloth of woven crimson, gold, and jet: –
O for some drowsy Morphean amulet!
The boisterous, midnight, festive clarion,
The kettle-drum, and far-heard clarionet,
Affray his ears, though but in dying tone: –
The hall door shuts again, and all the noise is gone.

And still she slept an azure-lidded sleep,
In blanched linen, smooth, and lavender'd,
While he from forth the closet brought a heap
Of candied apple, quince, and plum, and gourd

With jellies soother than the creamy curd,
And lucent syrops, tinct with cinnamon;
Manna and dates, in argosy transferr'd
From Fez; and spiced dainties, every one,
From silken Samarcand to cedar'd Lebanon.

These delicates he heap'd with glowing hand
On golden dishes and in baskets bright
Of wreathed silver: sumptuous they stand
In the retired quiet of the night,
Filling the chilly room with perfume light. –
'And now, my love, my seraph fair, awake!
'Thou art my heaven, and I thine eremite:
'Open thine eyes, for meek St. Agnes' sake,
'Or I shall drowse beside thee, so my soul doth ache.'

Thus whispering, his warm, unnerved arm
Sank in her pillow. Shaded was her dream
By the dusk curtains: – 'twas a midnight charm
Impossible to melt as iced stream:
The lustrous salvers in the moonlight gleam;
Broad golden fringe upon the carpet lies:
It seem'd he never, never could redeem
From such a stedfast spell his lady's eyes;
So mus'd awhile, entoil'd in woofed phantasies.

Awakening up, he took her hollow lute, –
Tumultuous, – and, in chords that tenderest be,
He play'd an ancient ditty, long since mute,
In Provence call'd, 'La belle dame sans mercy:'
Close to her ear touching the melody; –
Wherewith disturb'd, she utter'd a soft moan:
He ceased – she panted quick – and suddenly
Her blue affrayed eyes wide open shone:
Upon his knees he sank, pale as smooth-sculptured stone.

Her eyes were open, but she still beheld,
Now wide awake, the vision of her sleep:
There was a painful change, that nigh expell'd
The blisses of her dream so pure and deep

At which fair Madeline began to weep,
And moan forth witless words with many a sigh;
While still her gaze on Porphyro would keep;
Who knelt, with joined hands and piteous eye,
Fearing to move or speak, she look'd so dreamingly.

'Ah, Porphyro!' said she, 'but even now
'Thy voice was at sweet tremble in mine ear,
'Made tuneable with every sweetest vow;
'And those sad eyes were spiritual and clear:
'How chang'd thou art! how pallid, chill, and drear!
Give me that voice again, my Porphyro,
Those looks immortal, those complainings dear!
Oh leave me not in this eternal woe,
For if thou diest, my Love, I know not where to go.'

Beyond a mortal man impassion'd far
At these voluptuous accents, he arose,
Ethereal, flush'd, and like a throbbing star
Seen mid the sapphire heaven's deep repose
Into her dream he melted, as the rose
Blendeth its odour with the violet, –
Solution sweet: meantime the frost-wind blows
Like Love's alarum pattering the sharp sleet
Against the window-panes; St. Agnes' moon hath set.

'Tis dark: quick pattereth the flaw-blown sleet:
'This is no dream, my bride, my Madeline!'
'Tis dark: the iced gusts still rave and beat:
'No dream, alas! alas! and woe is mine!
Porphyro will leave me here to fade and pine. –
Cruel! what traitor could thee hither bring?
I curse not, for my heart is lost in thine
Though thou forsakest a deceived thing; –
A dove forlorn and lost with sick unpruned wing.'

'My Madeline! sweet dreamer! lovely bride!
Say, may I be for aye thy vassal blest?
Thy beauty's shield, heart-shap'd and vermeil dyed?
Ah, silver shrine, here will I take my rest

　　　After so many hours of toil and quest,
　　　　A famish'd pilgrim, – saved by miracle.
　　　Though I have found, I will not rob thy nest
　　　Saving of thy sweet self; if thou think'st well
To trust, fair Madeline, to no rude infidel.'

　　　'Hark! 'tis an elfin-storm from faery land,
　　　　Of haggard seeming, but a boon indeed:
　　　Arise – arise! the morning is at hand; –
　　　The bloated wassaillers will never heed: –
　　　Let us away, my love, with happy speed;
　　　There are no ears to hear, or eyes to see, –
　　　Drown'd all in Rhenish and the sleepy mead:
　　　Awake! arise! my love, and fearless be,
For o'er the southern moors I have a home for thee.'

　　　She hurried at his words, beset with fears,
　　　　For there were sleeping dragons all around,
　　　At glaring watch, perhaps, with ready spears –
　　　Down the wide stairs a darkling way they found. –
　　　In all the house was heard no human sound.
　　　A chain-droop'd lamp was flickering by each door;
　　　The arras, rich with horseman, hawk, and hound,
　　　Flutter'd in the besieging wind's uproar;
And the long carpets rose along the gusty floor.

　　　They glide, like phantoms, into the wide hall;
　　　　Like phantoms, to the iron porch, they glide;
　　　Where lay the Porter, in uneasy sprawl,
　　　With a huge empty flaggon by his side:
　　　The wakeful bloodhound rose, and shook his hide,
　　　But his sagacious eye an inmate owns:
　　　By one, and one, the bolts full easy slide: –
　　　The chains lie silent on the footworn stones; –
The key turns, and the door upon its hinges groans.

　　　And they are gone: ay, ages long ago
　　　　These lovers fled away into the storm.
　　　That night the Baron dreamt of many a woe,
　　　And all his warrior-guests, with shade and form
　　　Of witch, and demon, and large coffin-worm,
　　　Were long be-nightmar'd. Angela the old
　　　Died palsy-twitch'd, with meagre face deform;
　　　The Beadsman, after thousand aves told,
For aye unsought for slept among his ashes cold.

JOHN KEATS Ode to a Nightingale

My heart aches, and a drowsy numbness pains
   My sense, as though of hemlock I had drunk,
Or emptied some dull opiate to the drains
   One minute past, and Lethe-wards had sunk:
'Tis not through envy of thy happy lot,
   But being too happy in thine happiness, –
      That thou, light-winged Dryad of the trees,
         In some melodious plot
   Of beechen green, and shadows numberless,
    Singest of summer in full-throated ease.

O, for a draught of vintage! that hath been
   Cool'd a long age in the deep-delved earth,
Tasting of Flora and the country green,
   Dance, and Provençal song, and sunburnt mirth!
O for a beaker full of the warm South,
   Full of the true, the blushful Hippocrene,
      With beaded bubbles winking at the brim,
         And purple-stained mouth;
   That I might drink, and leave the world unseen,
    And with thee fade away into the forest dim:

Fade far away, dissolve, and quite forget
   What thou among the leaves hast never known,
The weariness, the fever, and the fret
   Here, where men sit and hear each other groan;
Where palsy shakes a few, sad, last gray hairs,
   Where youth grows pale, and spectre-thin, and dies;
      Where but to think is to be full of sorrow
         And leaden-eyed despairs,
   Where Beauty cannot keep her lustrous eyes,
    Or new Love pine at them beyond to-morrow.

Away! away! for I will fly to thee,
   Not charioted by Bacchus and his pards,
But on the viewless wings of Poesy,
   Though the dull brain perplexes and retards:

Already with thee! tender is the night,
   And haply the Queen-Moon is on her throne,
     Cluster'd around by all her starry Fays;
      But here there is no light,
   Save what from heaven is with the breezes blown
     Through verdurous glooms and winding mossy ways.

I cannot see what flowers are at my feet,
   Nor what soft incense hangs upon the boughs,
But, in embalmed darkness, guess each sweet
   Wherewith the seasonable month endows
The grass, the thicket, and the fruit-tree wild;
   White hawthorn, and the pastoral eglantine;
     Fast fading violets cover'd up in leaves;
      And mid-May's eldest child,
   The coming musk-rose, full of dewy wine,
     The murmurous haunt of flies on summer eves.

Darkling I listen; and, for many a time
   I have been half in love with easeful Death,
Call'd him soft names in many a mused rhyme,
   To take into the air my quiet breath;
Now more than ever seems it rich to die,
   To cease upon the midnight with no pain,
     While thou art pouring forth thy soul abroad
      In such an ecstasy!
   Still wouldst thou sing, and I have ears in vain –
     To thy high requiem become a sod.

Thou wast not born for death, immortal Bird!
   No hungry generations tread thee down;
The voice I hear this passing night was heard
   In ancient days by emperor and clown:
Perhaps the self-same song that found a path
   Through the sad heart of Ruth, when, sick for home,
     She stood in tears amid the alien corn;
      The same that oft-times hath
   Charm'd magic casements, opening on the foam
     Of perilous seas, in faery lands forlorn.

Forlorn! the very word is like a bell
   To toll me back from thee to my sole self!
Adieu! the fancy cannot cheat so well
   As she is fam'd to do, deceiving elf.

Adieu! adieu! thy plaintive anthem fades
    Past the near meadows, over the still stream,
      Up the hill-side; and now 'tis buried deep
        In the next valley-glades:
    Was it a vision, or a waking dream?
      Fled is that music: – Do I wake or sleep?

JOHN KEATS Ode on a Grecian Urn

Thou still unravish'd bride of quietness,
    Thou foster-child of silence and slow time,
Sylvan historian, who canst thus express
    A flowery tale more sweetly than our rhyme:
What leaf-fring'd legend haunts about thy shape
    Of deities or mortals, or of both,
      In Tempe or the dales of Arcady?
What men or gods are these? What maidens loth?
    What mad pursuit? What struggle to escape?
      What pipes and timbrels? What wild ecstasy?

Heard melodies are sweet, but those unheard
    Are sweeter; therefore, ye soft pipes, play on;
Not to the sensual ear, but, more endear'd,
    Pipe to the spirit ditties of no tone:
Fair youth, beneath the trees, thou canst not leave
    Thy song, nor ever can those trees be bare;
      Bold Lover, never, never canst thou kiss,
Though winning near the goal – yet, do not grieve;
    She cannot fade, though thou hast not thy bliss,
      For ever wilt thou love, and she be fair!

Ah, happy, happy boughs! that cannot shed
    Your leaves, nor ever bid the Spring adieu;
And, happy melodist, unwearied,
    For ever piping songs for ever new;
More happy love! more happy, happy love!
    For ever warm and still to be enjoy'd,
      For ever panting, and for ever young;
All breathing human passion far above,
    That leaves a heart high-sorrowful and cloy'd,
      A burning forehead, and a parching tongue.

Who are these coming to the sacrifice?
    To what green altar, O mysterious priest,
Lead'st thou that heifer lowing at the skies,
    And all her silken flanks with garlands drest?
What little town by river or sea shore,
    Or mountain-built with peaceful citadel,
        Is emptied of this folk, this pious morn?
And, little town, thy streets for evermore
    Will silent be; and not a soul to tell
        Why thou art desolate, can e'er return.

O Attic shape! Fair attitude! with brede
    Of marble men and maidens overwrought,
With forest branches and the trodden weed;
    Thou, silent form, dost tease us out of thought
As doth eternity: Cold Pastoral!
    When old age shall this generation waste,
        Thou shalt remain, in midst of other woe
Than ours, a friend to man, to whom thou say'st,
    Beauty is truth, truth beauty, – that is all
        Ye know on earth, and all ye need to know.

JOHN KEATS To Autumn

Season of mists and mellow fruitfulness,
    Close bosom-friend of the maturing sun;
Conspiring with him how to load and bless
    With fruit the vines that round the thatch-eves run;
To bend with apples the moss'd cottage-trees,
    And fill all fruit with ripeness to the core;
        To swell the gourd, and plump the hazel shells
With a sweet kernel; to set budding more,
    And still more, later flowers for the bees,
        Until they think warm days will never cease,
        For Summer has o'er-brimm'd their clammy cells.

Who hath not seen thee oft amid thy store?
    Sometimes whoever seeks abroad may find
Thee sitting careless on a granary floor,
    Thy hair soft-lifted by the winnowing wind;
Or on a half-reap'd furrow sound asleep,
    Drows'd with the fume of poppies, while thy hook

Spares the next swath and all its twined flowers:
And sometimes like a gleaner thou dost keep
  Steady thy laden head across a brook;
    Or by a cyder-press, with patient look,
      Thou watchest the last oozings hours by hours.

Where are the songs of Spring? Ay, where are they?
  Think not of them, thou hast thy music too, –
While barred clouds bloom the soft-dying day,
  And touch the stubble-plains with rosy hue;
Then in a wailful choir the small gnats mourn
  Among the river shallows, borne aloft
    Or sinking as the light wind lives or dies;
And full-grown lambs loud bleat from hilly bourn;
  Hedge-crickets sing; and now with treble soft
  The red-breast whistles from a garden-croft;
    And gathering swallows twitter in the skies.

JOHN KEATS   Ode on Melancholy

No, no, go not to Lethe, neither twist
  Wolf's-bane, tight-rooted, for its poisonous wine;
Nor suffer thy pale forehead to be kiss'd
  By nightshade, ruby grape of Proserpine;
Make not your rosary of yew-berries,
  Nor let the beetle, nor the death-moth be
    Your mournful Psyche, nor the downy owl
A partner in your sorrow's mysteries;
  For shade to shade will come too drowsily,
    And drown the wakeful anguish of the soul.

But when the melancholy fit shall fall
  Sudden from heaven like a weeping cloud,
That fosters the droop-headed flowers all,
  And hides the green hill in an April shroud;
Then glut thy sorrow on a morning rose,
  Or on the rainbow of the salt sand-wave,
    Or on the wealth of globed peonies;
Or if thy mistress some rich anger shows,
  Emprison her soft hand, and let her rave,
    And feed deep, deep upon her peerless eyes.

She dwells with Beauty – Beauty that must die;
    And Joy, whose hand is ever at his lips
Bidding adieu; and aching Pleasure nigh,
    Turning to poison while the bee-mouth sips:
Ay, in the very temple of Delight
    Veil'd Melancholy has her sovran shrine,
        Though seen of none save him whose strenuous tongue
Can burst Joy's grape against his palate fine;
    His soul shall taste the sadness of her might,
        And be among her cloudy trophies hung.

JOHN KEATS

Bright star! would I were steadfast as thou art –
    Not in lone splendour hung aloft the night
And watching, with eternal lids apart,
    Like nature's patient, sleepless Eremite,
The moving waters at their priestlike task
    Of pure ablution round earth's human shores,
Or gazing on the new soft fallen mask
    Of snow upon the mountains and the moors –
No – yet still steadfast, still unchangeable,
    Pillow'd upon my fair love's ripening breast,
To feel for ever its soft fall and swell,
    Awake for ever in a sweet unrest,
Still, still to hear her tender-taken breath,
And so live ever – or else swoon to death.

(1838)

1820 JOHN KEATS La Belle Dame sans Merci. A Ballad

O what can ail thee, knight-at-arms,
    Alone and palely loitering?
The sedge has withered from the lake,
    And no birds sing.

O what can ail thee, knight-at-arms,
    So haggard and so woe-begone?
The squirrel's granary is full,
    And the harvest's done.

I see a lily on thy brow,
   With anguish moist and fever-dew,
And on thy cheeks a fading rose
   Fast withereth too.

I met a lady in the meads,
   Full beautiful – a faery's child,
Her hair was long, her foot was light,
   And her eyes were wild.

I made a garland for her head,
   And bracelets too, and fragrant zone;
She looked at me as she did love,
   And made sweet moan.

I set her on my pacing steed,
   And nothing else saw all day long,
For sidelong would she bend, and sing
   A faery's song.

She found me roots of relish sweet,
   And honey wild, and manna-dew,
And sure in language strange she said –
   'I love thee true'.

She took me to her elfin grot,
   And there she wept and sighed full sore,
And there I shut her wild wild eyes
   With kisses four.

And there she lullèd me asleep
   And there I dreamed – Ah! woe betide! –
The latest dream I ever dreamt
   On the cold hill side.

I saw pale kings and princes too,
   Pale warriors, death-pale were they all:
They cried – 'La Belle Dame sans Merci
   Thee hath in thrall!'

I saw their starved lips in the gloam,
   With horrid warning gapèd wide,
And I awoke and found me here.
   On the cold hill's side.

And this is why I sojourn here
    Alone and palely loitering,
Though the sedge is withered from the lake,
    And no birds sing.

PERCY BYSSHE SHELLEY Ode to the West Wind

I

O wild West Wind, thou breath of Autumn's being,
Thou, from whose unseen presence the leaves dead
Are driven, like ghosts from an enchanter fleeing,

Yellow, and black, and pale, and hectic red,
Pestilence-stricken multitudes: O Thou,
Who chariotest to their dark wintry bed

The winged seeds, where they lie cold and low,
Each like a corpse within its grave, until
Thine azure sister of the Spring shall blow

Her clarion o'er the dreaming earth, and fill
(Driving sweet buds like flocks to feed in air)
With living hues and odours plain and hill:

Wild Spirit, which art moving everywhere;
Destroyer and Preserver; hear O hear!

II

Thou on whose stream, 'mid the steep sky's commotion,
Loose clouds like Earth's decaying leaves are shed,
Shook from the tangled boughs of Heaven and Ocean,

Angels of rain and lightning: there are spread
On the blue surface of thine aery surge,
Like the bright hair uplifted from the head

Of some fierce Mænad, even from the dim verge
Of the horizon to the zenith's height,
The locks of the approaching storm. Thou Dirge

Of the dying year, to which this closing night
Will be the dome of a vast sepulchre,
Vaulted with all thy congregated might

Of vapours, from whose solid atmosphere
Black rain and fire and hail will burst: O hear!

III

Thou who didst waken from his summer dreams
The blue Mediterranean, where he lay,
Lulled by the coil of his chrystalline streams,

Beside a pumice isle Baiæ's bay,
And saw in sleep old palaces and towers
Quivering within the wave's intenser day,

All overgrown with azure moss and flowers
So sweet, the sense faints picturing them! Thou
For whose path the Atlantic's level powers

Cleave themselves into chasms, while far below
The sea-blooms and the oozy woods which wear
The sapless foliage of the ocean, know

Thy voice, and suddenly grow grey with fear,
And tremble and despoil themselves: O hear!

IV

If I were a dead leaf thou mightest bear;
If I were a swift cloud to fly with thee;
A wave to pant beneath thy power, and share

The impulse of thy strength, only less free
Than thou, O Uncontrollable! If even
I were as in my boyhood, and could be

The comrade of thy wanderings over Heaven,
As then, when to outstrip thy skiey speed
Scarce seemed a vision; I would ne'er have striven

As thus with thee in prayer in my sore need.
Oh! lift me as a wave, a leaf, a cloud!
I fall upon the thorns of life! I bleed!

A heavy weight of hours has chained and bowed
One too like thee: tameless, and swift, and proud.

v

Make me thy lyre, even as the forest is:
What if my leaves are falling like its own!
The tumult of thy mighty harmonies

Will take from both a deep, autumnal tone,
Sweet though in sadness. Be thou, Spirit fierce,
My spirit! Be thou me, impetuous one!

Drive my dead thoughts over the universe
Like withered leaves to quicken a new birth!
And, by the incantation of this verse,

Scatter, as from an unextinguished hearth
Ashes and sparks, my words among mankind!
Be through my lips to unawakened Earth

The trumpet of a prophecy! O Wind,
If Winter comes, can Spring be far behind?

PERCY BYSSHE SHELLEY *from* **The Sensitive-Plant**

[Conclusion]

Whether the Sensitive-plant, or that
Which within its boughs like a spirit sat
Ere its outward form had known decay,
Now felt this change, – I cannot say.

Whether that Lady's gentle mind,
No longer with the form combined
Which scattered love – as stars do light,
Found sadness, where it left delight,

I dare not guess; but in this life
Of error, ignorance and strife –
Where nothing is – but all things seem,
And we the shadows of the dream,

It is a modest creed, and yet
Pleasant if one considers it,
To own that death itself must be,
Like all the rest, – a mockery.

That garden sweet, that lady fair
And all sweet shapes and odours there
In truth have never past away –
'Tis we, 'tis ours, are changed – not they.

For love, and beauty, and delight
There is no death nor change: their might
Exceeds our organs – which endure
No light – being themselves obscure.

PERCY BYSSHE SHELLEY *from* Adonais   **1821**

The One remains, the many change and pass;
Heaven's light forever shines, Earth's shadows fly;
Life, like a dome of many-coloured glass,
Stains the white radiance of Eternity,
Until Death tramples it to fragments. – Die,
If thou wouldst be with that which thou dost seek!
Follow where all is fled! – Rome's azure sky,
Flowers, ruins, statues, music, words, are weak
The glory they transfuse with fitting truth to speak.

Why linger, why turn back, why shrink, my Heart?
Thy hopes are gone before: from all things here
They have departed; thou shouldst now depart!
A light is past from the revolving year,
And man, and woman; and what still is dear
Attracts to crush, repels to make thee wither.
The soft sky smiles, – the low wind whispers near:
'Tis Adonais calls! oh, hasten thither,
No more let Life divide what Death can join together.

That Light whose smile kindles the Universe,
That Beauty in which all things work and move,
That Benediction which the eclipsing Curse
Of birth can quench not, that sustaining Love
Which through the web of being blindly wove
By man and beast and earth and air and sea,
Burns bright or dim, as each are mirrors of
The fire for which all thirst; now beams on me,
Consuming the last clouds of cold mortality.

The breath whose might I have invoked in song
Descends on me; my spirit's bark is driven,
Far from the shore, far from the trembling throng
Whose sails were never to the tempest given;
The massy earth and sphered skies are riven!
I am borne darkly, fearfully, afar;
Whilst burning through the inmost veil of Heaven,
The soul of Adonais, like a star,
Beacons from the abode where the Eternal are.

1822   GEORGE GORDON, LORD BYRON *from* **The Vision of Judgment**

Saint Peter sat by the celestial gate:
　　His keys were rusty, and the lock was dull,
So little trouble had been given of late;
　　Not that the place by any means was full,
But since the Gallic era 'eighty-eight'
　　The devils had ta'en a longer, stronger pull,
And 'a pull altogether,' as they say
At sea – which drew most souls another way.

The angels all were singing out of tune,
　　And hoarse with having little else to do,
Excepting to wind up the sun and moon,
　　Or curb a runaway young star or two,
Or wild colt of a comet, which too soon
　　Broke out of bounds o'er the ethereal blue,
Splitting some planet with its playful tail,
As boats are sometimes by a wanton whale.

The guardian seraphs had retired on high,
   Finding their charges past all care below;
Terrestrial business fill'd nought in the sky
   Save the recording angel's black bureau;
Who found, indeed, the facts to multiply
   With such rapidity of vice and wo,
That he had stripp'd off both his wings in quills,
And yet was in arrear of human ills.

His business so augmented of late years,
   That he was forced, against his will, no doubt,
(Just like those cherubs, earthly ministers,)
   For some resource to turn himself about
And claim the help of his celestial peers,
   To aid him ere he should be quite worn out
By the increased demand for his remarks;
Six angels and twelve saints were named his clerks.

This was a handsome board – at least for heaven;
   And yet they had even then enough to do,
So many conquerors' cars were daily driven,
   So many kingdoms fitted up anew;
Each day too slew its thousands six or seven,
   Till at the crowning carnage, Waterloo,
They threw their pens down in divine disgust –
The page was so besmear'd with blood and dust.

This by the way; 'tis not mine to record
   What angels shrink from: even the very devil
On this occasion his own work abhorr'd,
   So surfeited with the infernal revel:
Though he himself had sharpen'd every sword,
   It almost quench'd his innate thirst of evil.
(Here Satan's sole good work deserves insertion –
'Tis that he has both generals in reversion.)

Let's skip a few short years of hollow peace,
   Which peopled earth no better, hell as wont,
And heaven none – they form the tyrant's lease,
   With nothing but new names subscribed upon't;
'Twill one day finish: meantime they increase,
   'With seven heads and ten horns,' and all in front,
Like Saint John's foretold beast; but ours are born
Less formidable in the head than horn.

In the first year of freedom's second dawn
    Died George the Third; although no tyrant, one
Who shielded tyrants, till each sense withdrawn
    Left him nor mental nor external sun:
A better farmer ne'er brush'd dew from lawn,
    A worse king never left a realm undone!
He died – but left his subjects still behind,
One half as mad – and t'other no less blind.

He died! – his death made no great stir on earth;
    His burial made some pomp; there was profusion
Of velvet, gilding, brass, and no great dearth
    Of aught but tears – save those shed by collusion.
For these things may be bought at their true worth;
    Of elegy there was the due infusion –
Bought also; and the torches, cloaks, and banners,
Heralds, and relics of old Gothic manners,

Form'd a sepulchral melodrame. Of all
    The fools who flock'd to swell or see the show,
Who cared about the corpse? The funeral
    Made the attraction, and the black the woe.
There throbb'd not there a thought which pierced the pall;
    And when the gorgeous coffin was laid low,
It seem'd the mockery of hell to fold
The rottenness of eighty years in gold.

So mix his body with the dust! It might
    Return to what it *must* far sooner, were
The natural compound left alone to fight
    Its way back into earth, and fire, and air;
But the unnatural balsams merely blight
    What nature made him at his birth, as bare
As the mere million's base unmummied clay –
Yet all his spices but prolong decay.

He's dead – and upper earth with him has done;
    He's buried; save the undertaker's bill,
Or lapidary scrawl, the world is gone
    For him, unless he left a German will;
But where's the proctor who will ask his son?
    In whom his qualities are reigning still,
Except that household virtue, most uncommon,
Of constancy to a bad, ugly woman.

GEORGE GORDON, LORD BYRON Aristomenes. Canto First **1823**

The Gods of old are silent on their shore
Since the great Pan expired, and through the roar
Of the Ionian waters broke a dread
Voice which proclaimed 'the Mighty Pan is dead.'
How much died with him! false or true, the dream
Was beautiful which peopled every stream
With more than finny tenants, and adorned
The woods and waters with coy nymphs that scorned
Pursuing Deities, or in the embrace
Of gods brought forth the high heroic race
Whose names are on the hills and o'er the seas.

(1904)

GEORGE GORDON, LORD BYRON January 22nd 1824. **1824**
Messalonghi. On This Day I Complete My Thirty Sixth Year

'Tis time this heart should be unmoved
   Since others it hath ceased to move,
Yet though I cannot be beloved
      Still let me love.

My days are in the yellow leaf
   The flowers and fruits of love are gone –
The worm, the canker and the grief
      Are mine alone.

The fire that on my bosom preys
   Is lone as some Volcanic Isle,
No torch is kindled at its blaze
      A funeral pile!

The hope, the fear, the jealous care
   The exalted portion of the pain
And power of Love I cannot share
      But wear the chain.

But 't is not *thus* – and 't is not *here*
   Such thoughts should shake my soul, nor *now*
Where glory decks the hero's bier
      Or binds his brow.

The Sword – the Banner – and the Field
   Glory and Greece around us see!
The Spartan borne upon his shield
      Was not more free!

Awake! (*not* Greece – She *is* awake!)
   Awake my spirit – think through *whom*
Thy Life blood tracks its parent lake
      And then strike home!

Tread those reviving passions down
   Unworthy Manhood; – unto thee
Indifferent should the smile or frown
      Of Beauty be.

If thou regret'st thy youth, why *live*?
   The Land of honourable Death
Is here – up to the Field! and give
      Away thy Breath.

Seek out – less often sought than found,
   A Soldier's Grave – for thee the best,
Then look around and choose thy ground
      And take thy Rest.

GEORGE GORDON, LORD BYRON Remember Thee, Remember Thee!

Remember thee, remember thee!
   Till Lethe quench life's burning stream,
Remose and shame shall cling to thee,
   And haunt thee like a feverish dream!

Remember thee! Ay, doubt it not;
    Thy husband too shall think of thee;
By neither shalt thou be forgot,
    Thou *false* to him, thou *fiend* to me!

(written 1813)

PERCY BYSSHE SHELLEY To Jane. The Invitation

Best and brightest, come away –
Fairer far than this fair day
Which like thee to those in sorrow
Comes to bid a sweet good-morrow
To the rough year just awake
In its cradle on the brake. –
The brightest hour of unborn spring
Through the winter wandering
Found, it seems, this halcyon morn
To hoar February born;
Bending from Heaven in azure mirth
It kissed the forehead of the earth
And smiled upon the silent sea,
And bade the frozen streams be free
And waked to music all their fountains,
And breathed upon the frozen mountains,
And like a prophetess of May
Strewed flowers upon the barren way,
Making the wintry world appear
Like one on whom thou smilest, dear.

Away, away from men and towns
To the wild wood and the downs,
To the silent wilderness
Where the soul need not repress
Its music lest it should not find
An echo in another's mind,
While the touch of Nature's art
Harmonizes heart to heart. –
I leave this notice on my door
For each accustomed visitor –

'I am gone into the fields
To take what this sweet hour yields.
Reflexion, you may come tomorrow,
Sit by the fireside with Sorrow –
You, with the unpaid bill, Despair,
You, tiresome verse-reciter Care,
I will pay you in the grave,
Death will listen to your stave –
Expectation too, be off!
To-day is for itself enough –
Hope, in pity mock not woe
With smiles, nor follow where I go;
Long having lived on thy sweet food,
At length I find one moment's good
After long pain – with all your love
This you never told me of.'

Radiant Sister of the day,
Awake, arise and come away
To the wild woods and the plains
And the pools where winter-rains
Image all their roof of leaves,
Where the pine its garland weaves
Of sapless green and ivy dun
Round stems that never kiss the Sun –
Where the lawns and pastures be
And the sandhills of the sea –
Where the melting hoar-frost wets
The daisy-star that never sets,
And wind-flowers, and violets
Which yet join not scent to hue
Crown the pale year weak and new,
When the night is left behind
In the deep east dun and blind
And the blue noon is over us,
And the multitudinous
Billows murmur at our feet
Where the earth and ocean meet,
And all things seem only one
In the universal Sun. –

PERCY BYSSHE SHELLEY *from* **Julian and Maddalo. A Conversation**

The meadows with fresh streams, the bees with thyme,
The goats with the green leaves of budding spring,
Are saturated not – nor Love with tears.

VIRGIL's *Gallus.*

I rode one evening with Count Maddalo
Upon the bank of land which breaks the flow
Of Adria towards Venice: – a bare strand
Of hillocks, heaped from ever-shifting sand,
Matted with thistles and amphibious weeds,
Such as from earth's embrace the salt ooze breeds,
Is this; – an uninhabitable sea-side
Which the lone fisher, when his nets are dried,
Abandons; and no other object breaks
The waste, but one dwarf tree and some few stakes
Broken and unrepaired, and the tide makes
A narrow space of level sand thereon, –
Where 'twas our wont to ride while day went down.
This ride was my delight. – I love all waste
And solitary places; where we taste
The pleasure of believing what we see
Is boundless, as we wish our souls to be:
And such was this wide ocean, and this shore
More barren than its billows; – and yet more
Than all, with a remembered friend I love
To ride as then I rode; – for the winds drove
The living spray along the sunny air
Into our faces; the blue heavens were bare,
Stripped to their depths by the awakening North;
And, from the waves, sound like delight broke forth
Harmonizing with solitude, and sent
Into our hearts aërial merriment . . .
So, as we rode, we talked; and the swift thought,
Winging itself with laughter, lingered not,
But flew from brain to brain, – such glee was ours –
Charged with light memories of remembered hours,
None slow enough for sadness: till we came
Homeward, which always makes the spirit tame.

This day had been cheerful but cold, and now
The sun was sinking, and the wind also.
Our talk grew somewhat serious, as may be
Talk interrupted with such raillery
As mocks itself, because it cannot scorn
The thoughts it would extinguish: – 'twas forlorn
Yet pleasing, such as once, so poets tell,
The devils held within the dales of Hell
Concerning God, freewill and destiny:
Of all that earth has been or yet may be,
All that vain men imagine or believe,
Or hope can paint or suffering may atchieve,
We descanted, and I (for ever still
Is it not wise to make the best of ill?)
Argued against despondency, but pride
Made my companion take the darker side.
The sense that he was greater than his kind
Had struck, methinks, his eagle spirit blind
By gazing on its own exceeding light.
– Meanwhile the sun paused ere it should alight,
Over the horizon of the mountains; – Oh,
How beautiful is sunset, when the glow
Of Heaven descends upon a land like thee,
Thou Paradise of exiles, Italy!
Thy mountains, seas and vineyards and the towers
Of cities they encircle! – it was ours
To stand on thee, beholding it; and then
Just where we had dismounted, the Count's men
Were waiting for us with the gondola. –
As those who pause on some delightful way
Though bent on pleasant pilgrimage, we stood
Looking upon the evening and the flood
Which lay between the city and the shore
Paved with the image of the sky . . . the hoar
And aery Alps towards the North appeared
Through mist, an heaven-sustaining bulwark reared
Between the East and West; and half the sky
Was roofed with clouds of rich emblazonry
Dark purple at the zenith, which still grew
Down the steep West into a wondrous hue
Brighter than burning gold, even to the rent
Where the swift sun yet paused in his descent
Among the many folded hills: they were
Those famous Euganean hills, which bear

As seen from Lido through the harbour piles
The likeness of a clump of peaked isles –
And then – as if the Earth and Sea had been
Dissolved into one lake of fire, were seen
Those mountains towering as from waves of flame
Around the vaporous sun, from which there came
The inmost purple spirit of light, and made
Their very peaks transparent. 'Ere it fade,'
Said my Companion, 'I will shew you soon
A better station' – so, o'er the lagune
We glided, and from that funereal bark
I leaned, and saw the City, and could mark
How from their many isles, in evening's gleam,
Its temples and its palaces did seem
Like fabrics of enchantment piled to Heaven.
I was about to speak, when – 'We are even
Now at the point I meant,' said Maddalo,
And bade the gondolieri cease to row.
'Look, Julian, on the West, and listen well
If you hear not a deep and heavy bell.'
I looked, and saw between us and the sun
A building on an island; such a one
As age to age might add, for uses vile,
A windowless, deformed and dreary pile;
And on the top an open tower, where hung
A bell, which in the radiance swayed and swung;
We could just hear its hoarse and iron tongue:
The broad sun sunk behind it, and it tolled
In strong and black relief. – 'What we behold
Shall be the madhouse and its belfry tower,'
Said Maddalo, 'and ever at this hour
Those who may cross the water, hear that bell
Which calls the maniacs each one from his cell
To vespers.' – 'As much skill as need to pray
In thanks or hope for their dark lot have they
To their stern maker,' I replied. 'O ho!
You talk as in years past,' said Maddalo.
''Tis strange men change not. You were ever still
Among Christ's flock a perilous infidel,
A wolf for the meek lambs – if you can't swim
Beware of Providence.' I looked on him,
But the gay smile had faded in his eye.
'And such,' – he cried, 'is our mortality

And this must be the emblem and the sign
Of what should be eternal and divine! –
And like that black and dreary bell, the soul,
Hung in a heaven-illumined tower, must toll
Our thoughts and our desires to meet below
Round the rent heart and pray – as madmen do
For what? they know not, – till the night of death
As sunset that strange vision, severeth
Our memory from itself, and us from all
We sought and yet were baffled!' I recall
The sense of what he said, although I mar
The force of his expressions. The broad star
Of day meanwhile had sunk behind the hill
And the black bell became invisible
And the red tower looked grey, and all between
The churches, ships and palaces were seen
Huddled in gloom; – into the purple sea
The orange hues of heaven sunk silently.
We hardly spoke, and soon the gondola
Conveyed me to my lodging by the way.

PERCY BYSSHE SHELLEY *from* The Triumph of Life

As in that trance of wondrous thought I lay
   This was the tenour of my waking dream.
Methought I sate beside a public way

   Thick strewn with summer dust, and a great stream
Of people there was hurrying to and fro
   Numerous as gnats upon the evening gleam,

All hastening onward, yet none seemed to know
   Whither he went, or whence he came, or why
He made one of the multitude, yet so

   Was borne amid the crowd as through the sky
One of the million leaves of summer's bier. –
   Old age and youth, manhood and infancy,

Mixed in one mighty torrent did appear,
   Some flying from the thing they feared and some
Seeking the object of another's fear,

And others as with steps towards the tomb
Pored on the trodden worms that crawled beneath,
   And others mournfully within the gloom

Of their own shadow walked, and called it death . . .
   And some fled from it as it were a ghost,
Half fainting in the affliction of vain breath.

   But more with motions which each other crost
Pursued or shunned the shadows the clouds threw
   Or birds within the noonday ether lost,

Upon that path where flowers never grew;
   And weary with vain toil and faint for thirst
Heard not the fountains whose melodious dew

   Out of their mossy cells forever burst
Nor felt the breeze which from the forest told
   Of grassy paths, and wood lawns interspersed

With overarching elms and caverns cold,
   And violet banks where sweet dreams brood, but they
Pursued their serious folly as of old. . . .

   And as I gazed methought that in the way
The throng grew wilder, as the woods of June
   When the South wind shakes the extinguished day. –

And a cold glare, intenser than the noon
   But icy cold, obscured with light
The Sun as he the stars. Like the young Moon

   When on the sunlit limits of the night
Her white shell trembles amid crimson air
   And whilst the sleeping tempest gathers might

Doth, as a herald of its coming, bear
   The ghost of her dead Mother, whose dim form
Bends in dark ether from her infant's chair,

   So came a chariot on the silent storm
Of its own rushing splendour, and a Shape
   So sate within as one whom years deform

Beneath a dusky hood and double cape
    Crouching within the shadow of a tomb,
And o'er what seemed the head a cloud like crape

    Was bent, a dun and faint etherial gloom
Tempering the light; upon the chariot's beam
    A Janus-visaged Shadow did assume

The guidance of that wonder-winged team.
    The Shapes which drew it in thick lightnings
Were lost: I heard alone on the air's soft stream

    The music of their ever moving wings.
All the four faces of that charioteer
    Had their eyes banded . . . little profit brings

Speed in the van and blindness in the rear,
    Nor then avail the beams that quench the Sun
Or that these banded eyes could pierce the sphere

    Of all that is, has been, or will be done. –
So ill was the car guided, but it past
    With solemn speed majestically on . . .

The crowd gave way, and I arose aghast,
    Or seemed to rise, so mighty was the trance,
And saw like clouds upon the thunder blast

    The million with fierce song and maniac dance
Raging around; such seemed the jubilee
    As when to greet some conqueror's advance

Imperial Rome poured forth her living sea
    From senatehouse and prison and theatre
When Freedom left those who upon the free

    Had bound a yoke which soon they stooped to bear.
Nor wanted here the just similitude
    Of a triumphal pageant, for where'er

The chariot rolled a captive multitude
    Was driven; all those who had grown old in power
Or misery, – all who have their age subdued,

By action or by suffering, and whose hour
Was drained to its last sand in weal or woe,
  So that the trunk survived both fruit and flower;

All those whose fame or infamy must grow
  Till the great winter lay the form and name
Of their own earth with them forever low –

  All but the sacred few who could not tame
Their spirits to the Conqueror, but as soon
  As they had touched the world with living flame

Fled back like eagles to their native noon,
  Or those who put aside the diadem
Of earthly thrones or gems, till the last one

  Were there; for they of Athens and Jerusalem
Were neither mid the mighty captives seen
  Nor mid the ribald crowd that followed them

Or fled before. . . . Swift, fierce and obscene
  The wild dance maddens in the van, and those
Who lead it, fleet as shadows on the green,

  Outspeed the chariot and without repose
Mix with each other in tempestuous measure
  To savage music. . . . Wilder as it grows,

They, tortured by the agonizing pleasure,
  Convulsed and on the rapid whirlwinds spun
Of that fierce spirit, whose unholy leisure

  Was soothed by mischief since the world begun,
Throw back their heads and loose their streaming hair,
  And in their dance round her who dims the Sun

Maidens and youths fling their wild arms in air
  As their feet twinkle; now recede and now
Bending within each other's atmosphere

  Kindle invisibly; and as they glow
Like moths by light attracted and repelled,
  Oft to new bright destruction come and go,

Till like two clouds into one vale impelled
 That shake the mountains when their lightnings mingle
And die in rain, – the fiery band which held

 Their natures, snaps . . . ere the shock cease to tingle
One falls and then another in the path
 Senseless, nor is the desolation single,

Yet ere I can say *where* the chariot hath
 Past over them; nor other trace I find
But as of foam after the Ocean's wrath

 Is spent upon the desert shore. – Behind,
Old men, and women foully disarrayed
 Shake their grey hair in the insulting wind,

Limp in the dance and strain with limbs decayed
 To reach the car of light which leaves them still
Farther behind and deeper in the shade.

 But not the less with impotence of will
They wheel, though ghastly shadows interpose
 Round them and round each other, and fulfill

Their work and to the dust whence they arose
 Sink and corruption veils them as they lie –
And frost in these performs what fire in those.

CAROLINE OLIPHANT, BARONESS NAIRNE The Laird o' Cockpen

The laird o'Cockpen, he's proud and he's great
His mind is ta'en up wi' the things o' the State;
He wanted a wife, his braw house to keep,
But favour wi' wooin' was fashious to seek.

Down by the dyke-side a lady did dwell,
At his table head he thought she'd look well,
McClish's ae daughter o' Clavers-ha' Lee,
A penniless lass wi' a lang pedigree.

His wig was weel pouther'd and as gude as new,
His waistcoat was white, his coat it was blue;
He put on a ring, a sword, and cock'd hat,
And wha could refuse the laird wi' a' that?

He took his grey mare and he rade cannily,
An' rapp'd at the yett o' Clavers-ha' Lee;
'Gae tell Mistress Jean to come speedily ben, –
She's wanted to speak to the Laird o' Cockpen'.

Mistress Jean was makin' the elderflower wine;
'An' what brings the laird at sic a like time?'
She put aff her apron, and on her silk gown,
Her mutch wi' red ribbons, and gaed awa' down.

An' when she cam' ben he bowed fu' low,
An' what was his errand he soon let her know;
Amazed was the laird when the lady said 'Na',
And wi' a laigh curtsie she turned awa'.

Dumfounder'd was he, nae sigh did he gie,
He mounted his mare – he rade cannily;
An' aften he thought, as he gaed through the glen,
She's daft to refuse the laird o' Cockpen.

CAROLINE OLIPHANT, BARONESS NAIRNE The Land o' the Leal

I'm wearin' awa', John,
Like snaw-wreaths in thaw, John,
I'm wearin' awa'
    To the land o' the leal.
There's nae sorrow there, John,
There's neither cauld nor care, John,
The day's aye fair
    In the land o' the leal.

Our bonnie bairn's there, John,
She was baith gude and fair, John,
And oh! we grudged her sair
    To the land o' the leal.

But sorrow's sel' wears past, John,
And joy's a-comin' fast, John,
The joy that's aye to last,
    In the land o' the leal.

Sae dear's that joy was bought, John,
Sae free the battle fought, John,
That sinfu' man e'er brought
    To the land o' the leal.
Oh! dry your glist'ning e'e, John,
My saul langs to be free, John,
And angels beckon me
    To the land o' the leal.

Oh! haud ye leal and true, John,
Your day it's wearin' through, John,
And I'll welcome you
    To the land o' the leal.
Now fare-ye-weel, my ain John,
This warld's cares are vain, John,
We'll meet, and we'll be fain,
    In the land o' the leal.

1826   ANONYMOUS [A Metrical Adage]

The Robin and the Wren
Are God's cock and hen,
The Martin and the Swallow,
Are God's mate and marrow.

ANONYMOUS Tweed and Till

Says Tweed to Till,
What gars ye rin sae still?
Says Till to Tweed,
Though ye rin wi' speed

2 *gars* makes;

And I rin slaw,
For ae man that ye droun
I droun twa.

ANONYMOUS A Rhyme from Lincolnshire

Sad is the burying in the sunshine,
But bless'd is the corpse that goeth home in rain.

WINTHROP MACKWORTH PRAED Good-night to the Season

Thus runs the world away.
                    HAMLET

Good-night to the Season! 'tis over!
    Gay dwellings no longer are gay;
The courtier, the gambler, the lover,
    Are scatter'd like swallows away:
There's nobody left to invite one,
    Except my good uncle and spouse;
My mistress is bathing at Brighton,
    My patron is sailing at Cowes:
For want of a better employment,
    Till Ponto and Don can get out,
I'll cultivate rural enjoyment,
    And angle immensely for trout.

Good-night to the Season! – the lobbies,
    Their changes, and rumours of change,
Which startled the rustic Sir Bobbies,
    And made all the Bishops look strange:
The breaches, and battles, and blunders,
    Perform'd by the Commons and Peers;
The Marquis's eloquent thunders,
    The Baronet's eloquent ears:

6 *droun* drown

Denouncings of Papists and treasons,
   Of foreign dominion and oats;
Misrepresentations of reasons,
   And misunderstandings of notes.

Good-night to the Season! – the buildings
   Enough to make Inigo sick;
The paintings, and plasterings, and gildings
   Of stucco, and marble, and brick;
The orders deliciously blended,
   From love of effect, into one;
The club-houses only intended,
   The palaces only begun;
The hell where the fiend, in his glory,
   Sits staring at putty and stones,
And scrambles from story to story,
   To rattle at midnight his bones.

Good-night to the Season! – the dances,
   The fillings of hot little rooms,
The glancings of rapturous glances,
   The fancyings of fancy costumes;
The pleasures which Fashion makes duties,
   The praisings of fiddles and flutes,
The luxury of looking at beauties,
   The tedium of talking to mutes;
The female diplomatists, planners
   Of matches for Laura and Jane,
The ice of her Ladyship's manners,
   The ice of his Lordship's champagne.

Good-night to the Season! – the rages
   Led off by the chiefs of the throng,
The Lady Matilda's new pages,
   The Lady Eliza's new song;
Miss Fennel's macaw, which at Boodle's
   Is held to have something to say;
Mrs. Splenetic's musical poodles,
   Which bark 'Batti Batti' all day;
The pony Sir Araby sported,
   As hot and as black as a coal,
And the Lion his mother imported,
   In bearskins and grease, from the Pole.

Good-night to the Season! – the Toso,
  So very majestic and tall;
Miss Ayton, whose singing was so-so,
  And Pasta, divinest of all;
The labour in vain of the Ballet,
  So sadly deficient in stars;
The foreigners thronging the Alley,
  Exhaling the breath of cigars;
The 'loge' where some heiress, how killing,
  Environ'd with Exquisites sits,
The lovely one out of her drilling,
  The silly ones out of their wits.

Good-night to the Season! – the splendour
  That beam'd in the Spanish Bazaar;
Where I purchased – my heart was so tender –
  A card-case, – a pasteboard guitar, –
A bottle of perfume, – a girdle, –
  A lithograph'd Riego full-grown,
Whom Bigotry drew on a hurdle
  That artists might draw him on stone, –
A small panorama of Seville, –
  A trap for demolishing flies, –
A caricature of the Devil, –
  And a look from Miss Sheridan's eyes.

Good-night to the Season! – the flowers
  Of the grand horticultural fête,
When boudoirs were quitted for bowers,
  And the fashion was not to be late;
When all who had money and leisure
  Grew rural o'er ices and wines,
All pleasantly toiling for pleasure,
  All hungrily pining for pines,
And making of beautiful speeches,
  And marring of beautiful shows,
And feeding on delicate peaches,
  And treading on delicate toes.

Good-night to the Season! – another
  Will come with its trifles and toys,
And hurry away, like its brother,
  In sunshine, and odour, and noise.

Will it come with a rose or a briar?
    Will it come with a blessing or curse?
Will its bonnets be lower or higher?
    Will its morals be better or worse?
Will it find me grown thinner or fatter,
    Or fonder of wrong or of right,
Or married, – or buried? – no matter,
    Good-night to the Season, Good-night!

1828   THOMAS HOOD Death in the Kitchen

'Are we not here now?' – continued the corporal (striking the end of his
stick perpendicularly on the floor, so as to give an idea of health and
stability) – 'and are we not' (dropping his hat upon the ground) 'gone!
– in a moment?'   TRISTRAM SHANDY

Trim, thou are right! – 'Tis sure that I,
And all who hear thee, are to die.
    The stoutest lad and wench
Must lose their places at the will
Of Death, and go at last to fill
    The sexton's gloomy trench!

The dreary grave! – Oh, when I think
How close ye stand upon its brink,
    My inward spirit groans!
My eyes are fill'd with dismal dreams
Of coffins, and this kitchen seems
    A charnel full of bones!

Yes, jovial butler, thou must fail,
As sinks the froth on thine own ale;
    Thy days will soon be done!
Alas! the common hours that strike
Are knells; for life keeps wasting, like
    A cask upon the run.

Ay, hapless scullion! 'tis thy case:
Life travels at a scouring pace,
    Far swifter than thy hand.

The fast decaying frame of man
Is but a kettle, or a pan,
  Time wears away – with sand!

Thou needst not, mistress cook! be told,
The meat to-morrow will be cold
  That now is fresh and hot:
E'en thus our flesh will, by the by,
Be cold as stone: – Cook, thou must die!
  There's death within the pot!

Susannah, too, my lady's maid!
Thy pretty person once must aid
  To swell the buried swarm!
The 'glass of fashion' thou wilt hold
No more, but grovel in the mould
  That's not the 'mould of form'!

Yes, Jonathan, that drives the coach,
He too will feel the fiend's approach –
  The grave will pluck him down:
He must in dust and ashes lie,
And wear the churchyard livery,
  Grass-green, turn'd up with brown.

How frail is our uncertain breath!
The laundress seems full hale, but Death
  Shall her 'last linen' bring.
The groom will die, like all his kind;
And e'en the stable-boy will find
  His life no stable thing.

Nay, see the household dog – e'en *that*
The earth shall take! – The very cat
  Will share the common fall;
Although she hold (the proverb saith)
A ninefold life, one single death
  Suffices for them all!

Cook, butler, Susan, Jonathan,
The girl that scours the pot and pan,
  And those that tend the steeds –
All, all shall have another sort
Of service after this – in short,
  The one the parson reads!

The dreary grave! – Oh, when I think
How close ye stand upon its brink,
    My inward spirit groans!
My ears are fill'd with dismal dreams
Of coffins, and this kitchen seems
    A charnel full of bones!

SAMUEL TAYLOR COLERIDGE Duty Surviving Self-Love

Unchanged within, to see all changed without,
Is a blank lot and hard to bear, no doubt.
Yet why at others' wanings should'st thou fret?
Then only might'st thou feel a just regret,
Hadst thou withheld thy love or hid thy light
In selfish forethought of neglect and slight.
O wiselier then, from feeble yearnings freed,
While, and on whom, thou may'st – shine on! nor heed
Whether the object by reflected light
Return thy radiance or absorb it quite:
And though thou notest from thy safe recess
Old Friends burn dim, like lamps in noisome air,
Love them for what they are; nor love them less,
Because to thee they are not what they were.

1829   ## FELICIA DOROTHEA HEMANS Casabianca

Young Casabianca, a boy about thirteen years old, son to the admiral
of the Orient, remained at his post (in the battle of the Nile), after the
ship had taken fire, and all the guns had been abandoned; and perished
in the explosion of the vessel, when the flames had reached the powder.

The boy stood on the burning deck,
    Whence all but he had fled;
The flame that lit the battle's wreck,
    Shone round him o'er the dead.

Yet beautiful and bright he stood,
    As born to rule the storm;
A creature of heroic blood,
    A proud, though child-like form.

The flames roll'd on – he would not go,
    Without his father's word;
That father, faint in death below,
    His voice no longer heard.

He call'd aloud – 'Say, father, say
    If yet my task is done?'
He knew not that the chieftain lay
    Unconscious of his son.

'Speak, Father!' once again he cried,
    'If I may yet be gone!'
– And but the booming shots replied,
    And fast the flames roll'd on.

Upon his brow he felt their breath
    And in his waving hair;
And look'd from that lone post of death,
    In still, yet brave despair.

And shouted but once more aloud,
    'My father! must I stay?'
While o'er him fast, through sail and shroud,
    The wreathing fires made way.

They wrapt the ship in splendor wild,
    They caught the flag on high,
And stream'd above the gallant child,
    Like banners in the sky.

There came a burst of thunder sound –
    The boy – oh! where was he?
– Ask of the winds that far around
    With fragments strew'd the sea!

With mast, and helm, and pennon fair,
    That well had borne their part –
But the noblest thing that perish'd there,
    Was that young faithful heart.

DOROTHY WORDSWORTH Floating Island

Harmonious powers with nature work
On sky, earth, river, lake and sea
Sunshine and cloud, whirlwind and breeze,
All in one duteous task agree.

Once did I see a slip of earth
By throbbing waves long undermined,
Loosed from its hold – how, no one knew,
But all might see it float, obedient to the wind,

Might see it from the mossy shore
Dissevered, float upon the lake,
Float with its crest of trees adorned
On which the warbling birds their pastime take.

Food, shelter, safety, there they find;
There berries ripen, flowerets bloom;
There insects live their lives – and die:
A peopled world it is, in size a tiny room.

And thus through many seasons' space
This little island may survive,
But nature (though we mark her not)
Will take away, may cease to give.

Perchance when you are wandering forth
Upon some vacant sunny day
Without an object, hope, or fear,
Thither your eyes may turn – the isle is passed away,

Buried beneath the glittering lake,
Its place no longer to be found.
Yet the lost fragments shall remain
To fertilize some other ground.

                                                    (1842)

LAETITIA ELIZABETH LANDON Lines of Life

Orphan in my first years, I early learnt
To make my heart suffice itself, and seek
Support and sympathy in its own depths.

Well, read my cheek, and watch my eye, –
   Too strictly school'd are they,
One secret of my soul to show,
   One hidden thought betray.

I never knew the time my heart
   Look'd freely from my brow;
It once was check'd by timidness,
   'Tis taught by caution now.

I live among the cold, the false,
   And I must seem like them;
And such I am, for I am false
   As those I most condemn.

I teach my lip its sweetest smile,
   My tongue its softest tone;
I borrow others' likeness, till
   Almost I lose my own.

I pass through flattery's gilded sieve,
   Whatever I would say;
In social life, all, like the blind,
   Must learn to feel their way.

I check my thoughts like curbed steeds
   That struggle with the rein;
I bid my feelings sleep, like wrecks
   In the unfathom'd main.

I hear them speak of love, the deep,
   The true, and mock the name;
Mock at all high and early truth,
   And I too do the same.

I hear them tell some touching tale,
    I swallow down the tear;
I hear them name some generous deed,
    And I have learnt to sneer.

I hear the spiritual, the kind,
    The pure, but named in mirth;
Till all of good, ay, even hope,
    Seems exiled from our earth.

And one fear, withering ridicule,
    Is all that I can dread;
A sword hung by a single hair
    For ever o'er the head.

We bow to a most servile faith,
    In a most servile fear;
While none among us dares to say
    What none will choose to hear.

And if we dream of loftier thoughts,
    In weakness they are gone;
And indolence and vanity
    Rivet our fetters on.

Surely I was not born for this!
    I feel a loftier mood
Of generous impulse, high resolve,
    Steal o'er my solitude!

I gaze upon the thousand stars
    That fill the midnight sky;
And wish, so passionately wish,
    A light like theirs on high.

I have such eagerness of hope
    To benefit my kind;
And feel as if immortal power
    Were given to my mind.

I think on that eternal fame,
    The sun of earthly gloom,
Which makes the gloriousness of death,
    The future of the tomb –

That earthly future, the faint sign
    Of a more heavenly one;
– A step, a word, a voice, a look, –
    Alas! my dream is done.

And earth, and earth's debasing stain,
    Again is on my soul;
And I am but a nameless part
    Of a most worthless whole.

Why write I this? because my heart
    Towards the future springs,
That future where it loves to soar
    On more than eagle wings.

The present, it is but a speck
    In that eternal time,
In which my lost hopes find a home,
    My spirit knows its clime.

Oh! not myself, – for what am I? –
    The worthless and the weak,
Whose every thought of self should raise
    A blush to burn my cheek.

But song has touch'd my lips with fire,
    And made my heart a shrine;
For what, although alloy'd, debased,
    Is in itself divine.

I am myself but a vile link
    Amid life's weary chain;
But I have spoken hallow'd words,
    Oh do not say in vain!

My first, my last, my only wish,
    Say will my charmed chords
Wake to the morning light of fame,
    And breathe again my words?

Will the young maiden, when her tears
    Alone in moonlight shine –
Tears for the absent and the loved –
    Murmur some song of mine?

Will the pale youth by his dim lamp,
    Himself a dying flame,
From many an antique scroll beside,
    Choose that which bears my name?

Let music make less terrible
    The silence of the dead;
I care not, so my spirit last
    Long after life has fled.

LAETITIA ELIZABETH LANDON Revenge

Ay, gaze upon her rose-wreathed hair,
    And gaze upon her smile;
Seem as you drank the very air
    Her breath perfumed the while:

And wake for her the gifted line,
    That wild and witching lay,
And swear your heart is as a shrine,
    That only owns her sway.

'Tis well: I am revenged at last, –
    Mark you that scornful cheek, –
The eye averted as you pass'd,
    Spoke more than words could speak.

Ay, now by all the bitter tears
    That I have shed for thee, –
The racking doubts, the burning fears, –
    Avenged they well may be –

By the nights pass'd in sleepless care,
    The days of endless woe;
All that you taught my heart to bear,
    All that yourself will know.

I would not wish to see you laid
    Within an early tomb;
I should forget how you betray'd,
    And only weep your doom:

But this is fitting punishment,
 To live and love in vain, –
Oh my wrung heart, be thou content,
 And feed upon his pain.

Go thou and watch her lightest sigh, –
 Thine own it will not be;
And bask beneath her sunny eye, –
 It will not turn on thee.

'Tis well: the rack, the chain, the wheel,
 Far better had'st thou proved;
Ev'n I could almost pity feel,
 For thou art not beloved.

THOMAS LOVE PEACOCK The War-Song of Dinas Vawr

The mountain sheep are sweeter,
But the valley sheep are fatter;
We therefore deem'd it meeter
To carry off the latter.
We made an expedition;
We met a host and quell'd it;
We forced a strong position,
And kill'd the men who held it.

On Dyfed's richest valley,
Where herds of kine were browsing,
We made a mighty sally,
To furnish our carousing.
Fierce warriors rushed to meet us;
We met them, and o'erthrew them:
They struggled hard to beat us;
But we conquer'd them, and slew them.

As we drove our prize at leisure,
The king march'd forth to catch us:
His rage surpass'd all measure,
But his people could not match us.

He fled to his hall-pillars;
And, ere our force we led off,
Some sack'd his house and cellars,
While others cut his head off.

We there, in strife bewild'ring,
Spilt blood enough to swim in:
We orphan'd many children,
And widow'd many women.
The eagles and the ravens
We glutted with our foemen:
The heroes and the cravens,
The spearmen and the bowmen.

We brought away from battle,
And much their land bemoan'd them,
Two thousand head of cattle,
And the head of him who owned them:
Ednyfed, King of Dyfed,
His head was borne before us;
His wine and beasts supplied our feasts,
And his overthrow, our chorus.

WINTHROP MACKWORTH PRAED Arrivals at a Watering-Place

SCENE – *A Conversazione at Lady Crumpton's. – Whist and weariness,
Caricatures and Chinese Puzzle. – Young Ladies making tea, and Young
Gentlemen making the agreeable. – The Stable-Boy handing rout-cakes.
– Music expressive of there being nothing to do.*

I play a spade: – Such strange new faces
    Are flocking in from near and far:
Such frights – Miss Dobbs holds all the aces, –
    One can't imagine who they are!
The Lodgings at enormous prices,
    New Donkeys, and another fly;
And Madame Bonbon out of ices,
    Although we're scarcely in July:

We're quite as sociable as any,
    But our old horse can scarcely crawl;
And really where there are so many,
    We can't tell where we ought to call.

Pray who has seen the odd old fellow
    Who took the Doctor's house last week? –
A pretty chariot, – livery yellow,
    Almost as yellow as his cheek:
A widower, sixty-five, and surly,
    And stiffer than a poplar-tree;
Drinks rum and water, gets up early
    To dip his carcass in the sea:
He's always in a monstrous hurry,
    And always talking of Bengal;
They say his cook makes noble curry; –
    I think, Louisa, we should call.

And so Miss Jones, the mantua-maker,
    Has let her cottage on the hill? –
The drollest man, a sugar-baker, –
    Last year imported from the till:
Prates of his *'orses* and his *'oney*,
    Is quite in love with fields and farms;
A horrid Vandal, – but his money
    Will buy a glorious coat of arms;
Old Clyster makes him take the waters;
    Some say he means to give a ball;
And after all, with thirteen daughters,
    I think, Sir Thomas, you might call.

That poor young man! – I'm sure and certain
    Despair is making up his shroud:
He walks all night beneath the curtain
    Of the dim sky and murky cloud:
Draws landscapes, – throws such mournful glances! –
    Writes verses, – has such splendid eyes;
An ugly name, – but Laura fancies
    He's some great person in disguise! –
And since his dress is all the fashion,
    And since he's very dark and tall,
I think that, out of pure compassion,
    I'll get Papa to go and call.

So Lord St Ives is occupying
  The whole of Mr Ford's Hotel;
Last Saturday his man was trying
  A little nag I want to sell.
He brought a lady in the carriage;
  Blue eyes, – eighteen, or thereabouts; –
Of course, you know, we *hope* it's marriage!
  But yet the *femme de chambre* doubts.
She look'd so pensive when we met her;
  Poor thing! and such a charming shawl! –
Well! till we understand it better,
  It's quite impossible to call!

Old Mr Fund, the London banker,
  Arrived to-day at Premium Court;
I would not, for the world, cast anchor
  In such a horrid dangerous port;
Such dust and rubbish, lath and plaster, –
  (Contractors play the meanest tricks) –
The roof's as crazy as its master,
  And he was born in fifty-six:
Stairs creaking – cracks in every landing, –
  The colonnade is sure to fall; –
We shan't find post or pillar standing,
  Unless we make great haste to call.

Who was that sweetest of sweet creatures,
  Last Sunday, in the Rector's seat?
The finest shape, – the loveliest features, –
  I never saw such tiny feet.
My brother, – (this is quite between us)
  Poor Arthur, – 'twas a sad affair! –
Love at first sight, – she's quite a Venus, –
  But then she's poorer far than fair:
And so my father and my mother
  Agreed it would not do at all;
And so, – I'm sorry for my brother! –
  It's settled that we're not to call.

And there's an Author, full of knowledge;
  And there's a Captain on half-pay;
And there's a Baronet from college,
  Who keeps a boy, and rides a bay;

And sweet Sir Marcus from the Shannon,
    Fine specimen of brogue and bone;
And Doctor Calipee, the canon,
    Who weighs, I fancy, twenty stone:
A maiden Lady is adorning
    The faded front of Lily Hall: –
Upon my word, the first fine morning,
    We'll make a round, my dear, and call.

Alas! disturb not, maid and matron,
    The swallow in my humble thatch;
Your son may find a better patron,
    Your niece may meet a richer match:
I can't afford to give a dinner,
    I never was on Almack's list;
And since I seldom rise a winner,
    I never like to play at whist:
Unknown to me the stocks are falling;
    Unwatched by me the glass may fall;
Let all the world pursue its calling, –
    I'm not at home if people call.

GEORGE GORDON, LORD BYRON   1830

So, we'll go no more a roving
    So late into the night,
Though the heart be still as loving,
    And the moon be still as bright.

For the sword outwears its sheath,
    And the soul wears out the breast,
And the heart must pause to breathe,
    And love itself have rest.

Though the night was made for loving,
    And the day returns too soon,
Yet we'll go no more a roving
    By the light of the moon.

                                        (written 1817)

WALTER SAVAGE LANDOR

Past ruin'd Ilion Helen lives,
    Alcestis rises from the shades;
Verse calls them forth; 'tis verse that gives
    Immortal youth to mortal maids.

Soon shall Oblivion's deepening veil
    Hide all the peopled hills you see,
The gay, the proud, while lovers hail
    These many summers you and me.

WALTER SAVAGE LANDOR Dirce

Stand close around, ye Stygian set,
    With Dirce in one boat conveyed!
Or Charon, seeing, may forget
    That he is old and she a shade.

WALTER SAVAGE LANDOR On Seeing a Hair of Lucrezia Borgia

Borgia, thou once wert almost too august,
And high for adoration; – now thou'rt dust!
All that remains of thee these plaits infold –
Calm hair, meand'ring with pellucid gold!

GEORGE GORDON, LORD BYRON Lines on Hearing That Lady Byron was Ill

And thou wert sad – yet I was not with thee;
And thou wert sick, and yet I was not near;
Methought that joy and health alone could be
Where I was not – and pain and sorrow here!

And is it thus? – it is as I foretold,
And shall be more so; for the mind recoils
Upon itself, and the wreck'd heart lies cold,
While heaviness collects the shatter'd spoils.
It is not in the storm nor in the strife
We feel benumb'd, and wish to be no more,
But in the after-silence on the shore,
When all is lost, except a little life.

I am too well avenged! – but 'twas my right;
Whate'er my sins might be, *thou* wert not sent
To be the Nemesis who should requite –
Nor did Heaven choose so near an instrument.

Mercy is for the merciful! – if thou
Hast been of such, 'twill be accorded now.
Thy nights are banish'd from the realms of sleep! –
Yes! they may flatter thee, but thou shalt feel
A hollow agony which will not heal,
For thou art pillow'd on a curse too deep;
Thou hast sown in my sorrow, and must reap
The bitter harvest in a woe as real!
I have had many foes, but none like thee;
For 'gainst the rest myself I could defend,
And be avenged, or turn them into friend;
But thou in safe implacability
Hadst nought to dread – in thy own weakness shielded,
And in my love, which hath but too much yielded,
And spared, for thy sake, some I should not spare –
And thus upon the World's trust in thy truth –
And the wild fame of my ungovern'd youth –
On things that were not, and on things that are –
Even upon such a basis hast thou built
A monument, whose cement hath been guilt!
The moral Clytemnestra of thy lord,
And hew'd down, with an unsuspected sword,
Fame, peace, and hope – and all the better life
Which, but for this cold treason of thy heart,
Might still have risen from out the grave of strife,
And found a nobler duty than to part.
But of thy virtues didst thou make a vice,
Trafficking with them in a purpose cold,
For present anger, and for future gold –
And buying other's grief at any price.

And thus once enter'd into crooked ways,
The early Truth, which was thy proper praise,
Did not still walk beside thee – but at times,
And with a breast unknowing its own crimes,
Deceit, averments incompatible,
Equivocations, and the thoughts which dwell
In Janus-spirits – the significant eye
Which learns to lie with silence – the pretext
Of Prudence, with advantages annex'd –
The acquiescence in all things which tend,
No matter how, to the desired end –
All found a place in thy philosophy.
The means were worthy, and the end is won –
I would not do by thee as thou hast done!

(written 1816)

1833 HARTLEY COLERIDGE

Long time a child, and still a child, when years
Had painted manhood on my cheek, was I;
For yet I lived like one not born to die;
A thriftless prodigal of smiles and tears,
No hope I needed, and I knew no fears.
But sleep, though sweet, is only sleep, and waking,
I waked to sleep no more, at once o'ertaking
The vanguard of my age, with all arrears
Of duty on my back. Nor child, nor man,
Nor youth, nor sage, I find my head is grey,
For I have lost the race I never ran,
A rathe December blights my lagging May;
And still I am a child, tho' I be old,
Time is my debtor for my years untold.

1834 SAMUEL TAYLOR COLERIDGE The Knight's Tomb

Where is the grave of Sir Arthur O'Kellyn?
Where may the grave of that good man be? –
By the side of a spring, on the breast of Helvellyn,
Under the twigs of a young birch tree!

The oak that in summer was sweet to hear,
And rustled its leaves in the fall of the year,
And whistled and roared in the winter alone,
Is gone, – and the birch in its stead is grown. –
The Knight's bones are dust,
And his good sword rust; –
His soul is with the saints, I trust.

(written 1802)

JOHN CLARE The Nightingales Nest

Up this green woodland ride lets softly rove
And list the nightingale – she dwelleth here
Hush let the wood gate softly clap – for fear
The noise may drive her from her home of love
For here Ive heard her many a merry year
At morn and eve nay all the live long day
As though she lived on song – this very spot
Just where that old mans beard all wildly trails
Rude arbours oer the road and stops the way
And where that child its blue bell flowers hath got
Laughing and creeping through the mossy rails
There have I hunted like a very boy
Creeping on hands and knees through matted thorns
To find her nest and see her feed her young
And vainly did I many hours employ
All seemed as hidden as a thought unborn
And where these crimping fern leaves ramp among
The hazels under boughs – Ive nestled down
And watched her while she sung – and her renown
Hath made me marvel that so famed a bird
Should have no better dress than russet brown
Her wings would tremble in her extacy
And feathers stand on end as twere with joy
And mouth wide open to release her heart
Of its out sobbing songs – the happiest part
Of summers fame she shared – for so to me
Did happy fancys shapen her employ
But if I touched a bush or scarcely stirred
All in a moment stopt – I watched in vain
The timid bird had left the hazel bush
And at a distance hid to sing again

Lost in a wilderness of listening leaves
Rich extacy would pour its luscious stain
Till envy spurred the emulating thrush
To start less wild and scarce inferior songs
For cares with him for half the year remain
To damp the ardour of his speckled breast
While nightingales to summers life belongs
And naked trees and winters nipping wrongs
Are strangers to her music and her rest
Her joys are evergreen her world is wide
– Hark there she is as usual lets be hush
For in this black thorn clump if rightly guest
Her curious house is hidden – part aside
These hazle branches in a gentle way
And stoop right cautious neath the rustling boughs
For we will have another search to day
And hunt this fern strown thorn clump round and round
And where this seeded wood grass idly bows
We'll wade right through – it is a likely nook
In such like spots and often on the ground
Theyll build where rude boys never think to look
Aye as I live her secret nest is here
Upon this white thorn stulp – Ive searched about
For hours in vain – there put that bramble bye
Nay trample on its branshes and get near
How subtle is the bird she started out
And raised a plaintive note of danger nigh
Ere we were past the brambles and now near
Her nest she sudden stops – as choaking fear
That might betray her home so even now
Well leave it as we found it – safetys guard
Of pathless solitude shall keep it still
See there shes sitting on the old oak bough
Mute in her fears our presence doth retard
Her joys and doubt turns all her rapture chill
   Sing on sweet bird may no worse hap befall
Thy visions then the fear that now decieves
We will not plunder music of its dower
Nor turn this spot of happiness to thrall
For melody seems hid in every flower
That blossoms near thy home – these harebells all
Seems bowing with the beautiful in song
And gaping cuckoo with its spotted leaves

Seems blushing of the singing it has heard
How curious is the nest no other bird
Uses such loose materials or weaves
Their dwellings in such spots – dead oaken leaves
Are placed without and velvet moss within
And little scraps of grass – and scant and spare
Of what seems scarce materials down and hair
For from mans haunts she seemeth nought to win
Yet nature is the builder and contrives
Homes for her childerns comfort even here
Where solitudes deciples spend their lives
Unseen save when a wanderer passes near
That loves such pleasant places – deep adown
The nest is made an hermits mossy cell
Snug lie her curious eggs in number five
Of deadend green or rather olive brown
And the old prickly thorn bush guards them well
And here well leave them still unknown to wrong
As the old woodlands legacy of song

JOHN CLARE The Sky Lark

The rolls and harrows lie at rest beside
The battered road and spreading far and wide
Above the russet clods the corn is seen
Sprouting its spirey points of tender green
Where squats the hare to terrors wide awake
Like some brown clod the harrows failed to break
While neath the warm hedge boys stray far from home
To crop the early blossoms as they come
Where buttercups will make them eager run
Opening their golden caskets to the sun
To see who shall be first to pluck the prize
And from their hurry up the skylark flies
And oer her half formed nest with happy wings
Winnows the air – till in the clouds she sings
Then hangs a dust spot in the sunny skies
And drops and drops till in her nest she lies
Where boys unheeding past – neer dreaming then
That birds which flew so high – would drop agen

To nests upon the ground where any thing
May come at to destroy had they the wing
Like such a bird themselves would be too proud
And build on nothing but a passing cloud
As free from danger as the heavens are free
From pain and toil – there would they build and be
And sail about the world to scenes unheard
Of and unseen – O where they but a bird
So think they while they listen to its song
And smile and fancy and so pass along
While its low nest moist with the dews of morn
Lye safely with the leveret in the corn

JOHN CLARE Mist in the Meadows

The evening oer the meadow seems to stoop
More distant lessens the diminished spire
Mist in the hollows reaks and curdles up
Like fallen clouds that spread – and things retire
Less seen and less – the shepherd passes near
And little distant most grotesquely shades
As walking without legs – lost to his knees
As through the rawky creeping smoke he wades
Now half way up the arches dissappear
And small the bits of sky that glimmer through
Then trees loose all but tops – I meet the fields
And now the indistinctness passes bye
The shepherd all his length is seen again
And further on the village meets the eye

JOHN CLARE Sand Martin

Thou hermit haunter of the lonely glen
And common wild and heath – the desolate face
Of rude waste landscapes far away from men
Where frequent quarrys give thee dwelling place
With strangest taste and labour undeterred
Drilling small holes along the quarrys side
More like the haunts of vermin than a bird
And seldom by the nesting boy descried

I've seen thee far away from all thy tribe
Flirting about the unfrequented sky
And felt a feeling that I cant describe
Of lone seclusion and a hermit joy
To see thee circle round nor go beyond
That lone heath and its melancholly pond

GEORGE DARLEY *from* **Nepenthe**

Hurry me Nymphs! O, hurry me
Far above the grovelling sea,
Which, with blind weakness and base roar
Casting his white age on the shore,
Wallows along that slimy floor;
With his widespread webbed hands
Seeking to climb the level lands
But rejected still to rave
Alive in his uncovered grave.

JOHN HENRY NEWMAN **The Pillar of the Cloud**   **1836**

Lead, Kindly Light, amid the encircling gloom,
      Lead Thou me on!
The night is dark, and I am far from home –
      Lead Thou me on!
Keep Thou my feet; I do not ask to see
The distant scene, – one step enough for me.

I was not ever thus, nor pray'd that Thou
      Shouldst lead me on.
I loved to choose and see my path, but now
      Lead Thou me on!
I loved the garish day, and, spite of fears,
Pride ruled my will: remember not past years.

So long Thy power hath blest me, sure it still
      Will lead me on,
O'er moor and fen, o'er crag and torrent, till
      The night is gone;
And with the morn those angel faces smile
Which I have loved long since, and lost awhile.

GEORGE DARLEY The Mermaidens' Vesper-Hymn

Troop home to silent grots and caves!
    Troop home! and mimic as you go
The mournful winding of the waves
    Which to their dark abysses flow.

At this sweet hour, all things beside
    In amorous pairs to covert creep;
The swans that brush the evening tide
    Homeward in snowy couples keep.

In his green den the murmuring seal
    Close by his sleek companion lies;
While singly we to bedward steal,
    And close in fruitless sleep our eyes.

In bowers of love men take their rest,
    In loveless bowers we sigh alone,
With bosom-friends are others blest, –
    But we have none! but we have none!

JOHN CLARE

I found a ball of grass among the hay
And proged it as I passed and went away
And when I looked I fancied somthing stirred
And turned agen and hoped to catch the bird
When out an old mouse bolted in the wheat
With all her young ones hanging at her teats
She looked so odd and so grotesque to me
I ran and wondered what the thing could be
And pushed the knapweed bunches where I stood
When the mouse hurried from the crawling brood
The young ones squeaked and when I went away
She found her nest again among the hay
The water oer the pebbles scarce could run
And broad old cesspools glittered in the sun

(1984)

JOHN CLARE

The old pond full of flags and fenced around
With trees and bushes trailing to the ground
The water weeds are all around the brink
And one clear place where cattle go to drink
From year to year the schoolboy thither steals
And muddys round the place to catch the eels
The cowboy often hiding from the flies
Lies there and plaits the rushcap as he lies
The hissing owl sits moping all the day
And hears his song and never flies away
The pinks nest hangs upon the branch so thin
The young ones caw and seem as tumbling in
While round them thrums the purple dragon flye
And great white butter flye goes dancing bye

(1984)

JOHN CLARE *from* The Badger

When midnight comes a host of dogs and men
Go out and track the badger to his den
And put a sack within the hole and lye
Till the old grunting badger passes bye
He comes and hears they let the strongest loose
The old fox hears the noise and drops the goose
The poacher shoots and hurrys from the cry
And the old hare half wounded buzzes bye
They get a forked stick to bear him down
And clapt the dogs and bore him to the town
And bait him all the day with many dogs
And laugh and shout and fright the scampering hogs
He runs along and bites at all he meets
They shout and hollo down the noisey streets

He turns about to face the loud uproar
And drives the rebels to their very doors
The frequent stone is hurled where ere they go
When badgers fight and every ones a foe

The dogs are clapt and urged to join the fray
The badger turns and drives them all away
Though scarcely half as big dimute and small
He fights with dogs for hours and beats them all
The heavy mastiff savage in the fray
Lies down and licks his feet and turns away
The bull dog knows his match and waxes cold
The badger grins and never leaves his hold
He drives the crowd and follows at their heels
And bites them through the drunkard swears and reels

The frighted women takes the boys away
The blackguard laughs and hurrys on the fray
He trys to reach the woods a awkard race
But sticks and cudgels quickly stop the chace
He turns agen and drives the noisey crowd
And beats the many dogs in noises loud
He drives away and beats them every one
And then they loose them all and set them on
He falls as dead and kicked by boys and men
Then starts and grins and drives the crowd agen
Till kicked and torn and beaten out he lies
And leaves his hold and cackles groans and dies

(1920)

1838   LEIGH HUNT *from* **The Fish, the Man, and the Spirit**

To Fish

You strange, astonish'd-looking, angle-faced,
   Dreary-mouth'd, gaping wretches of the sea,
   Gulping salt-water everlastingly,
Cold-blooded, though with red your blood be graced,
And mute, though dwellers in the roaring waste;
   And you, all shapes beside, that fishy be, –
   Some round, some flat, some long, all devilry,
Legless, unloving, infamously chaste: –

O scaly, slippery, wet, swift, staring wights,
    What is't ye do? what life lead? eh, dull goggles?
How do ye vary your vile days and nights?
    How pass your Sundays? Are ye still but joggles
In ceaseless wash? Still nought but gapes and bites,
    And drinks, and stares, diversified with boggles?

A Fish Answers

Amazing monster! that, for aught I know,
    With the first sight of thee didst make our race
    Forever stare! O flat and shocking face,
Grimly divided from the breast below!
Thou that on dry land horribly dost go
    With a split body and most ridiculous pace,
    Prong after prong, disgracer of all grace,
Long-useless-finned, hair'd, upright, unwet, slow!

O breather of unbreathable, sword-sharp air,
    How canst exist? How bear thyself, thou dry
And dreary sloth? What particles canst share
    Of the only blessed life, the watery?
I sometimes see of ye an actual *pair*
    Go by! link'd fin by fin! most odiously.

(. . .)

Man's life is warm, glad, sad, 'twixt loves and graves,
    Boundless in hope, honour'd with pangs austere,
Heaven-gazing: and his angel-wings he craves:
    The fish is swift, small-needing, vague yet clear,
A cold, sweet, silver life, wrapp'd in round waves,
    Quicken'd with touches of transporting fear.

THOMAS HOOD Sonnet to Vauxhall   **1839**

The cold transparent ham is on my fork –
    It hardly rains – and hark the bell! – ding-dingle –
Away! Three thousand feet at gravel work,
    Mocking a Vauxhall shower! – Married and Single

Crush – rush; – Soak'd Silks with wet white Satin mingle.
 Hengler! Madame! round whom all bright sparks lurk,
Calls audibly on Mr and Mrs Pringle
 To study the Sublime, &c. – (vide Burke)
All Noses are upturn'd! – Whish – ish! – On high
 The rocket rushes – trails – just steals in sight –
Then droops and melts in bubbles of blue light –
 And Darkness reigns – Then balls flare up and die –
Wheels whiz – smack crackers – serpents twist – and then
 Back to the cold transparent ham again!

1842   ROBERT BROWNING My Last Duchess

Ferrara

That's my last Duchess painted on the wall,
Looking as if she were alive. I call
That piece a wonder, now: Frà Pandolf's hands
Worked busily a day, and there she stands.
Will't please you sit and look at her? I said
'Frà Pandolf' by design, for never read
Strangers like you that pictured countenance,
The depth and passion of its earnest glance,
But to myself they turned (since none puts by
The curtain I have drawn for you, but I)
And seemed as they would ask me, if they durst,
How such a glance came there; so, not the first
Are you to turn and ask thus. Sir, 'twas not
Her husband's presence only, called that spot
Of joy into the Duchess' cheek: perhaps
Frà Pandolf chanced to say 'Her mantle laps
Over my lady's wrist too much,' or 'Paint
Must never hope to reproduce the faint
Half-flush that dies along her throat': such stuff
Was courtesy, she thought, and cause enough
For calling up that spot of joy. She had
A heart – how shall I say? – too soon made glad,
Too easily impressed; she liked whate'er
She looked on, and her looks went everywhere.
Sir, 'twas all one! My favour at her breast,
The dropping of the daylight in the West,

The bough of cherries some officious fool
Broke in the orchard for her, the white mule
She rode with round the terrace – all and each
Would draw from her alike the approving speech,
Or blush, at least. She thanked men, – good! but thanked
Somehow – I know not how – as if she ranked
My gift of a nine-hundred-years-old name
With anybody's gift. Who'd stoop to blame
This sort of trifling? Even had you skill
In speech – (which I have not) – to make your will
Quite clear to such an one, and say, 'Just this
Or that in you disgusts me; here you miss,
Or there exceed the mark' – and if she let
Herself be lessoned so, nor plainly set
Her wits to yours, forsooth, and made excuse,
– E'en then would be some stooping; and I choose
Never to stoop. Oh sir, she smiled, no doubt,
Whene'er I passed her; but who passed without
Much the same smile? This grew; I gave commands;
Then all smiles stopped together. There she stands
As if alive. Will't please you rise? We'll meet
The company below, then. I repeat,
The Count your master's known munificence
Is ample warrant that no just pretence
Of mine for dowry will be disallowed;
Though his fair daughter's self, as I avowed
At starting, is my object. Nay, we'll go
Together down, sir. Notice Neptune, though,
Taming a sea-horse, thought a rarity,
Which Claus of Innsbruck cast in bronze for me!

ROBERT BROWNING *from* Waring

I

1

What's become of Waring
Since he gave us all the slip,
Chose land-travel or seafaring,
Boots and chest or staff and scrip,
Rather than pace up and down
Any longer London town?

II

Who'd have guessed it from his lip
Or his brow's accustomed bearing,
On the night he thus took ship
Or started landward? – little caring
For us, it seems, who supped together
(Friends of his too, I remember)
And walked home through the merry weather,
The snowiest in all December.
I left his arm that night myself
For what's-his-name's, the new prose-poet
Who wrote the book there, on the shelf –
How, forsooth, was I to know it
If Waring meant to glide away
Like a ghost at break of day?
Never looked he half so gay!

III

He was prouder than the devil:
How he must have cursed our revel!
Ay and many other meetings,
Indoor visits, outdoor greetings,
As up and down he paced this London,
With no work done, but great works undone,
Where scarce twenty knew his name.
Why not, then, have earlier spoken,
Written, bustled? Who's to blame
If your silence kept unbroken?
'True, but there were sundry jottings,
Stray-leaves, fragments, blurs and blottings,
Certain first steps were achieved
Already which' – (is that your meaning?)
'Had well borne out whoe'er believed
In more to come!' But who goes gleaning
Hedgeside chance-blades, while full-sheaved
Stand cornfields by him? Pride, o'erweening
Pride alone, puts forth such claims
O'er the day's distinguished names.

(...)

I

'When I last saw Waring . . .'
(How all turned to him who spoke!
You saw Waring? Truth or joke?
In land-travel or sea-faring?)

II

'We were sailing by Trieste
Where a day or two we harboured:
A sunset was in the West,
When, looking over the vessel's side,
One of our company espied
A sudden speck to larboard.
And as a sea-duck flies and swims
At once, so came the light craft up,
With its sole lateen sail that trims
And turns (the water round its rims
Dancing, as round a sinking cup)
And by us like a fish it curled,
And drew itself up close beside,
Its great sail on the instant furled,
And o'er its thwarts a shrill voice cried,
(A neck as bronzed as a Lascar's)
"Buy wine of us, you English Brig?
Or fruit, tobacco and cigars?
A pilot for you to Trieste?
Without one, look you ne'er so big,
They'll never let you up the bay!
We natives should know best."
I turned, and "just those fellows' way,"
Our captain said, "The 'long-shore thieves
Are laughing at us in their sleeves."

III

'In truth, the boy leaned laughing back;
And one, half-hidden by his side
Under the furled sail, soon I spied,
With great grass hat and kerchief black,
Who looked up with his kingly throat,
Said somewhat, while the other shook
His hair back from his eyes to look
Their longest at us; then the boat,

I know not how, turned sharply round,
Laying her whole side on the sea
As a leaping fish does; from the lee
Into the weather, cut somehow
Her sparkling path beneath our bow
And so went off, as with a bound,
Into the rosy and golden half
O' the sky, to overtake the sun
And reach the shore, like the sea-calf
Its singing cave; yet I caught one
Glance ere away the boat quite passed,
And neither time nor toil could mar
Those features: so I saw the last
Of Waring!' – You? Oh, never star
Was lost here but it rose afar!
Look East, where whole new thousands are!
In Vishnu-land what Avatar?

ALFRED, LORD TENNYSON Ulysses

It little profits that an idle king,
By this still hearth, among these barren crags,
Matched with an agèd wife, I mete and dole
Unequal laws unto a savage race,
That hoard, and sleep, and feed, and know not me.

I cannot rest from travel: I will drink
Life to the lees: all times I have enjoyed
Greatly, have suffered greatly, both with those
That loved me, and alone; on shore, and when
Through scudding drifts the rainy Hyades
Vext the dim sea: I am become a name;
For always roaming with a hungry heart
Much have I seen and known; cities of men
And manners, climates, councils, governments,
Myself not least, but honoured of them all;
And drunk delight of battle with my peers,
Far on the ringing plains of windy Troy.
I am a part of all that I have met;
Yet all experience is an arch wherethrough
Gleams that untravelled world, whose margin fades
For ever and for ever when I move.

How dull it is to pause, to make an end,
To rust unburnished, not to shine in use!
As though to breathe were life. Life piled on life
Were all too little, and of one to me
Little remains: but every hour is saved
From that eternal silence, something more,
A bringer of new things; and vile it were
For some three suns to store and hoard myself,
And this gray spirit yearning in desire
To follow knowledge like a sinking star,
Beyond the utmost bound of human thought.

    This is my son, mine own Telemachus,
To whom I leave the sceptre and the isle –
Well-loved of me, discerning to fulfil
This labour, by slow prudence to make mild
A rugged people, and through soft degrees
Subdue them to the useful and the good.
Most blameless is he, centred in the sphere
Of common duties, decent not to fail
In offices of tenderness, and pay
Meet adoration to my household gods,
When I am gone. He works his work, I mine.

    There lies the port; the vessel puffs her sail:
There gloom the dark broad seas. My mariners,
Souls that have toiled, and wrought, and thought with me –
That ever with a frolic welcome took
The thunder and the sunshine, and opposed
Free hearts, free foreheads – you and I are old;
Old age hath yet his honour and his toil;
Death closes all: but something ere the end,
Some work of noble note, may yet be done,
Not unbecoming men that strove with Gods.
The lights begin to twinkle from the rocks:
The long day wanes: the slow moon climbs: the deep
Moans round with many voices. Come, my friends,
'Tis not too late to seek a newer world.
Push off, and sitting well in order smite
The sounding furrows; for my purpose holds
To sail beyond the sunset, and the baths
Of all the western stars, until I die.
It may be that the gulfs will wash us down:

It may be we shall touch the Happy Isles,
And see the great Achilles, whom we knew.
Though much is taken, much abides; and though
We are not now that strength which in old days
Moved earth and heaven; that which we are, we are;
One equal temper of heroic hearts,
Made weak by time and fate, but strong in will
To strive, to seek, to find, and not to yield.

ELIZABETH BARRETT BROWNING Grief

I tell you, hopeless grief is passionless;
That only men incredulous of despair,
Half-taught in anguish, through the midnight air
Beat upward to God's throne in loud access
Of shrieking and reproach. Full desertness,
In souls as countries, lieth silent-bare
Under the blanching, vertical eye-glare
Of the absolute Heavens. Deep-hearted man, express
Grief for thy Dead in silence like to death –
Most like a monumental statue set
In everlasting watch and moveless woe
Till itself crumble to the dust beneath.
Touch it; the marble eyelids are not wet:
If it could weep, it could arise and go.

1844 WILLIAM BARNES The Clote

(Water-Lily)

O zummer clote! when the brook's a-glidèn
    So slow an' smooth down his zedgy bed,
Upon thy broad leaves so seäfe a-ridèn
    The water's top wi' thy yollow head,
        By alder's heads, O,
        An' bulrush beds, O,
Thou then dost float, goolden zummer clote!

The grey-bough'd withy's a-leänèn lowly
   Above the water thy leaves do hide;
The bendèn bulrush, a-swaÿèn slowly,
    Do skirt in zummer thy river's zide;
      An' perch in shoals, O,
       Do vill the holes, O,
Where thou dost float, goolden zummer clote!

Oh! when thy brook-drinkèn flow'r's a-blowèn,
   The burnèn zummer's a-zettèn in;
The time o' greenness, the time o' mowèn,
    When in the haÿ-vield, wi' zunburnt skin,
      The vo'k do drink, O,
       Upon the brink, O,
Where thou dost float, goolden zummer clote!

Wi' eärms a-spreadèn, an' cheäks a-blowèn,
   How proud wer I when I vu'st could zwim
Athirt the pleäce where thou bist a-growèn,
    Wi' thy long more vrom the bottom dim;
      While cows, knee-high, O,
       In brook, wer nigh, O,
Where thou dost float, goolden zummer clote!

Ov all the brooks drough the meäds a-windèn,
   Ov all the meäds by a river's brim,
There's nwone so feäir o' my own heart's vindèn,
    As where the maïdens do zee thee zwim,
      An' stan' to teäke, O,
       Wi' long-stemm'd reäke, O,
Thy flow'r afloat, goolden zummer clote!

WILLIAM WORDSWORTH The Simplon Pass   1845

      —Brook and road
Were fellow-travellers in this gloomy Pass,
And with them did we journey several hours
At a slow step. The immeasurable height
Of woods decaying, never to be decayed,
The stationary blasts of waterfalls,

And in the narrow rent, at every turn,
Winds thwarting winds bewildered and forlorn,
The torrents shooting from the clear blue sky,
The rocks that muttered close upon our ears,
Black drizzling crags that spake by the wayside
As if a voice were in them, the sick sight
And giddy prospect of the raving stream,
The unfettered clouds and region of the heavens,
Tumult and peace, the darkness and the light –
Were all like workings of one mind, the features
Of the same face, blossoms upon one tree,
Characters of the great Apocalypse,
The types and symbols of Eternity,
Of first, and last, and midst, and without end.

(written ?1804)

THOMAS HOOD Stanzas

Farewell, Life! My senses swim;
And the world is growing dim;
Thronging shadows cloud the light,
Like the advent of the night, –
Colder, colder, colder still
Upward steals a vapour chill –
Strong the earthy odour grows –
I smell the Mould above the Rose!

Welcome, Life! the Spirit strives!
Strength returns, and hope revives;
Cloudy fears and shapes forlorn
Fly like shadows at the morn, –
O'er the earth there comes a bloom –
Sunny light for sullen gloom,
Warm perfume for vapour cold –
I smell the Rose above the Mould!

ROBERT BROWNING The Bishop Orders His Tomb at Saint
Praxed's Church

Rome, 15 –

Vanity, saith the preacher, vanity!
Draw round my bed: is Anselm keeping back?
Nephews – sons mine . . . ah God, I know not! Well –
She, men would have to be your mother once,
Old Gandolf envied me, so fair she was!
What's done is done, and she is dead beside,
Dead long ago, and I am Bishop since,
And as she died so must we die ourselves,
And thence ye may perceive the world's a dream.
Life, how and what is it? As here I lie
In this state-chamber, dying by degrees,
Hours and long hours in the dead night, I ask
'Do I live, am I dead?' Peace, peace seems all.
Saint Praxed's ever was the church for peace;
And so, about this tomb of mine. I fought
With tooth and nail to save my niche, ye know:
– Old Gandolf cozened me, despite my care;
Shrewd was that snatch from out the corner South
He graced his carrion with, God curse the same!
Yet still my niche is not so cramped but thence
One sees the pulpit o' the epistle-side,
And somewhat of the choir, those silent seats,
And up into the airy dome where live
The angels, and a sunbeam's sure to lurk:
And I shall fill my slab of basalt there,
And 'neath my tabernacle take my rest,
With those nine columns round me, two and two,
The odd one at my feet where Anselm stands:
Peach-blossom marble all, the rare, the ripe
As fresh-poured red wine of a mighty pulse.
– Old Gandolf with his paltry onion-stone,
Put me where I may look at him! True peach,
Rosy and flawless: how I earned the prize!
Draw close: that conflagration of my church
– What then? So much was saved if aught were missed!
My sons, ye would not be my death? Go dig
The white-grape vineyard where the oil-press stood,

Drop water gently till the surface sink,
And if ye find . . . Ah God, I know not, I! . . .
Bedded in store of rotten fig-leaves soft,
And corded up in a tight olive-frail,
Some lump, ah God, of *lapis lazuli*,
Big as a Jew's head cut off at the nape,
Blue as a vein o'er the Madonna's breast . . .
Sons, all have I bequeathed you, villas, all,
That brave Frascati villa with its bath,
So, let the blue lump poise between my knees,
Like God the Father's globe on both his hands
Ye worship in the Jesu Church so gay,
For Gandolf shall not choose but see and burst!
Swift as a weaver's shuttle fleet our years:
Man goeth to the grave, and where is he?
Did I say basalt for my slab, sons? Black –
'Twas ever antique-black I meant! How else
Shall ye contrast my frieze to come beneath?
The bas-relief in bronze ye promised me,
Those Pans and Nymphs ye wot of, and perchance
Some tripod, thyrsus, with a vase or so,
The Saviour at his sermon on the mount,
Saint Praxed in a glory, and one Pan
Ready to twitch the Nymph's last garment off,
And Moses with the tables . . . but I know
Ye mark me not! What do they whisper thee,
Child of my bowels, Anselm? Ah, ye hope
To revel down my villas while I gasp
Bricked o'er with beggar's mouldy travertine
Which Gandolf from his tomb-top chuckles at!
Nay, boys, ye love me – all of jasper, then!
'Tis jasper ye stand pledged to, lest I grieve
My bath must needs be left behind, alas!
One block, pure green as a pistachio-nut,
There's plenty jasper somewhere in the world –
And have I not Saint Praxed's ear to pray
Horses for ye, and brown Greek manuscripts,
And mistresses with great smooth marbly limbs?
– That's if ye carve my epitaph aright,
Choice Latin, picked phrase, Tully's every word,
No gaudy ware like Gandolf's second line –
Tully, my masters? Ulpian serves his need!
And then how I shall lie through centuries,
And hear the blessed mutter of the mass,

And see God made and eaten all day long,
And feel the steady candle-flame, and taste
Good strong thick stupefying incense-smoke!
For as I lie here, hours of the dead night,
Dying in state and by such slow degrees,
I fold my arms as if they clasped a crook,
And stretch my feet forth straight as stone can point,
And let the bedclothes, for a mortcloth, drop
Into great laps and folds of sculptor's-work:
And as yon tapers dwindle, and strange thoughts
Grow, with a certain humming in my ears,
About the life before I lived this life,
And this life too, popes, cardinals and priests,
Saint Praxed at his sermon on the mount,
Your tall pale mother with her talking eyes,
And new-found agate urns as fresh as day,
And marble's language, Latin pure, discreet,
– Aha, ELUCESCEBAT quoth our friend?
No Tully, said I, Ulpian at the best!
Evil and brief hath been my pilgrimage.
All *lapis*, all, sons! Else I give the Pope
My villas! Will ye ever eat my heart?
Ever your eyes were as a lizard's quick,
They glitter like your mother's for my soul,
Or ye would heighten my impoverished frieze,
Piece out its starved design, and fill my vase
With grapes, and add a vizor and a Term,
And to the tripod ye would tie a lynx
That in his struggle throws the thyrsus down,
To comfort me on my entablature
Whereon I am to lie till I must ask
'Do I live, am I dead?' There, leave me, there!
For ye have stabbed me with ingratitude
To death – ye wish it – God, ye wish it! Stone –
Gritstone, a-crumble! Clammy squares which sweat
As if the corpse they keep were oozing through –
And no more *lapis* to delight the world!
Well go! I bless ye. Fewer tapers there,
But in a row: and, going, turn your backs
– Ay, like departing altar-ministrants,
And leave me in my church, the church for peace,
That I may watch at leisure if he leers –
Old Gandolf, at me, from his onion-stone,
As still he envied me, so fair she was!

1846 § EDWARD LEAR from **A Book of Nonsense**

There was an Old Man with a beard,
Who said, 'It is just as I feared! –
Two Owls and a Hen, four Larks and a Wren,
Have all built their nests in my beard!'

There was an Old Person of Basing,
Whose presence of mind was amazing;
He purchased a steed, which he rode at full speed,
And escaped from the people of Basing.

There was an Old Man of Whitehaven,
Who danced a quadrille with a Raven;
But they said – 'It's absurd, to encourage this bird!'
So they smashed that Old Man of Whitehaven.

EMILY JANE BRONTE

The night is darkening round me
The wild winds coldly blow
But a tyrant spell has bound me
And I cannot cannot go

The giant trees are bending
Their bare boughs weighed with snow
And the storm is fast descending
And yet I cannot go

Clouds beyond clouds above me
Wastes beyond wastes below
But nothing drear can move me
I will not cannot go

(1902)

EMILY JANE BRONTE

Fall leaves fall die flowers away
Lengthen night and shorten day
Every leaf speaks bliss to me
Fluttering from the autumn tree
I shall smile when wreaths of snow
Blossom where the rose should grow
I shall sing when night's decay
Ushers in a drearier day

(1910)

EMILY JANE BRONTE

All hushed and still within the house;
Without – all wind and driving rain;
But something whispers to my mind,
Through rain and through the wailing wind,
    Never again.
Never again? Why not again?
Memory has power as real as thine.

(1910)

EMILY JANE BRONTE Remembrance

Cold in the earth – and the deep snow piled above thee,
Far, far, removed, cold in the dreary grave!
Have I forgot, my only Love, to love thee,
Severed at last by Time's all-severing wave?

Now, when alone, do my thoughts no longer hover
Over the mountains, on that northern shore,
Resting their wings where heath and fern-leaves cover
Thy noble heart for ever, ever more?

Cold in the earth – and fifteen wild Decembers,
From those brown hills, have melted into spring:
Faithful, indeed, is the spirit that remembers
After such years of change and suffering!

Sweet Love of youth, forgive, if I forget thee,
While the world's tide is bearing me along;
Other desires and other hopes beset me,
Hopes which obscure, but cannot do thee wrong!

No later light has lightened up my heaven,
No second morn has ever shone for me;
All my life's bliss from thy dear life was given,
All my life's bliss is in the grave with thee.

But, when the days of golden dreams had perished,
And even Despair was powerless to destroy;
Then did I learn how existence could be cherished,
Strengthened, and fed without the aid of joy.

Then did I check the tears of useless passion –
Weaned my young soul from yearning after thine;
Sternly denied its burning wish to hasten
Down to that tomb already more than mine.

And, even yet, I dare not let it languish,
Dare not indulge in memory's rapturous pain;
Once drinking deep of that divinest anguish,
How could I seek the empty world again?

JAMES CLARENCE MANGAN Siberia

In Siberia's wastes
    The Ice-wind's breath
Woundeth like the toothèd steel;
Lost Siberia doth reveal
    Only blight and death.

Blight and death alone.
    No Summer shines.
Night is interblent with Day.
In Siberia's wastes alway
    The blood blackens, the heart pines.

In Siberia's wastes
   No tears are shed,
For they freeze within the brain.
Nought is felt but dullest pain,
   Pain acute, yet dead;

Pain as in a dream,
   When years go by
Funeral-paced, yet fugitive,
When man lives, and doth not live,
   Doth not live – nor die.

In Siberia's wastes
   Are sands and rocks.
Nothing blooms of green or soft,
But the snow-peaks rise aloft
   And the gaunt ice-blocks.

And the exile there
   Is one with those;
They are part, and he is part,
For the sands are in his heart,
   And the killing snows.

Therefore, in those wastes
   None curse the Czar.
Each man's tongue is cloven by
The North Blast, that heweth nigh
   With sharp scymitar.

And such doom each drees,
   Till, hunger-gnawn,
And cold-slain, he at length sinks there,
Yet scarce more a corpse than ere
   His last breath was drawn.

ALFRED, LORD TENNYSON *from* **The Princess**

Deep in the night I woke: she, near me, held
A volume of the Poets of her land:
There to herself, all in low tones, she read.

'Now sleeps the crimson petal, now the white;
Nor waves the cypress in the palace walk;
Nor winks the gold fin in the porphyry font:
The fire-fly wakens: waken thou with me.

Now droops the milkwhite peacock like a ghost,
And like a ghost she glimmers on to me.

Now lies the Earth all Danaë to the stars,
And all thy heart lies open unto me.

Now slides the silent meteor on, and leaves
A shining furrow, as thy thoughts in me.

Now folds the lily all her sweetness up,
And slips into the bosom of the lake:
So fold thyself, my dearest, thou, and slip
Into my bosom and be lost in me.'

I heard her turn the page; she found a small
Sweet Idyl, and once more, as low, she read:

'Come down, O maid, from yonder mountain height:
What pleasure lives in height (the shepherd sang)
In height and cold, the splendour of the hills?
But cease to move so near the Heavens, and cease
To glide a sunbeam by the blasted Pine,
To sit a star upon the sparkling spire;
And come, for Love is of the valley, come,
For Love is of the valley, come thou down
And find him; by the happy threshold, he,
Or hand in hand with Plenty in the maize,
Or red with spirted purple of the vats,
Or foxlike in the vine; nor cares to walk
With Death and Morning on the silver horns,
Nor wilt thou snare him in the white ravine,

Nor find him dropt upon the firths of ice,
That huddling slant in furrow-cloven falls
To roll the torrent out of dusky doors:
But follow; let the torrent dance thee down
To find him in the valley; let the wild
Lean-headed Eagles yelp alone, and leave
The monstrous ledges there to slope, and spill
Their thousand wreaths of dangling water-smoke,
That like a broken purpose waste in air:
So waste not thou; but come; for all the vales
Await thee; azure pillars of the hearth
Arise to thee; the children call, and I
Thy shepherd pipe, and sweet is every sound,
Sweeter thy voice, but every sound is sweet;
Myriads of rivulets hurrying through the lawn,
The moan of doves in immemorial elms,
And murmuring of innumerable bees.'

So she low-toned; while with shut eyes I lay
Listening.

1848   JOHN CLARE 'I Am'

I am – yet what I am, none cares or knows;
    My friends forsake me like a memory lost: –
I am the self-consumer of my woes; –
    They rise and vanish in oblivion's host,
Like shadows in love's frenzied stifled throes: –
And yet I am, and live – like vapours tost

Into the nothingness of scorn and noise, –
    Into the living sea of waking dreams,
Where there is neither sense of life or joys,
    But the vast shipwreck of my lifes esteems;
Even the dearest, that I love the best
Are strange – nay, rather stranger than the rest.

I long for scenes, where man hath never trod
    A place where woman never smiled or wept
There to abide with my Creator, God;
    And sleep as I in childhood, sweetly slept,
Untroubling, and untroubled where I lie,
The grass below – above the vaulted sky.

WALTER SAVAGE LANDOR

I strove with none, for none was worth my strife:
    Nature I loved, and, next to nature, Art:
I warm'd both hands before the fire of Life;
    It sinks; and I am ready to depart.

MATTHEW ARNOLD *from* **Resignation. To Fausta**

[The Poet]

He sees the gentle stir of birth
When morning purifies the earth;
He leans upon a gate and sees
The pastures, and the quiet trees.
Low, woody hill, with gracious bound,
Folds the still valley almost round;
The cuckoo, loud on some high lawn,
Is answer'd from the depth of dawn;
In the hedge straggling to the stream,
Pale, dew-drench'd, half-shut roses gleam;
But, where the farther side slopes down,
He sees the drowsy new-waked clown
In his white quaint-embroider'd frock
Make, whistling, tow'rd his mist-wreathed flock –
Slowly, behind his heavy tread,
The wet, flower'd grass heaves up its head.
Lean'd on his gate, he gazes – tears
Are in his eyes, and in his ears
The murmur of a thousand years.
Before him he sees life unroll,
A placid and continuous whole –
That general life, which does not cease,
Whose secret is not joy, but peace;
That life, whose dumb wish is not miss'd
If birth proceeds, if things subsist;
The life of plants, and stones, and rain,
The life he craves – if not in vain
Fate gave, what chance shall not control,
His sad lucidity of soul.

And though fate grudge to thee and me
The poet's rapt security,
Yet they, believe me, who await
No gifts from chance, have conquer'd fate.
They, winning room to see and hear,
And to men's business not too near,
Through clouds of individual strife
Draw homeward to the general life.
Like leaves by suns not yet uncurl'd;
To the wise, foolish; to the world,
Weak; – yet not weak, I might reply,
Not foolish, Fausta, in His eye,
To whom each moment in its race,
Crowd as we will its neutral space,
Is but a quiet watershed
Whence, equally, the seas of life and death are fed.

1850   EMILY JANE BRONTE *and* CHARLOTTE BRONTE
The Visionary

Silent is the house: all are laid asleep:
One alone looks out o'er the snow-wreaths deep,
Watching every cloud, dreading every breeze
That whirls the wildering drift, and bends the groaning trees.

Cheerful is the hearth, soft the matted floor;
Not one shivering gust creeps through pane or door;
The little lamp burns straight, its rays shoot strong and far:
I trim it well, to be the wanderer's guiding-star.

Frown, my haughty sire! chide, my angry dame;
Set your slaves to spy; threaten me with shame:
But neither sire nor dame, nor prying serf shall know,
What angel nightly tracks that waste of frozen snow.

What I love shall come like visitant of air,
Safe in secret power from lurking human snare;
What loves me, no word of mine shall e'er betray,
Though for faith unstained my life must forfeit pay.

Burn, then, little lamp; glimmer straight and clear –
Hush! a rustling wing stirs, methinks, the air:
He for whom I wait, thus ever comes to me;
Strange Power! I trust thy might; trust thou my constancy.

§ ALFRED, LORD TENNYSON *from* In Memoriam A.H.H.

II

Old Yew, which graspest at the stones
   That name the under-lying dead,
   Thy fibres net the dreamless head,
Thy roots are wrapt about the bones.

The seasons bring the flower again,
   And bring the firstling to the flock;
   And in the dusk of thee, the clock
Beats out the little lives of men.

O not for thee the glow, the bloom,
   Who changest not in any gale,
   Nor branding summer suns avail
To touch thy thousand years of gloom:

And gazing on thee, sullen tree,
   Sick for thy stubborn hardihood,
   I seem to fail from out my blood
And grow incorporate into thee.

VII

Dark house, by which once more I stand
   Here in the long unlovely street,
   Doors, where my heart was used to beat
So quickly, waiting for a hand,

A hand that can be clasped no more –
   Behold me, for I cannot sleep,
   And like a guilty thing I creep
At earliest morning to the door.

He is not here; but far away
   The noise of life begins again,
   And ghastly through the drizzling rain
On the bald street breaks the blank day.

XI

Calm is the morn without a sound,
   Calm as to suit a calmer grief,
   And only through the faded leaf
The chestnut pattering to the ground:

Calm and deep peace on this high wold,
   And on these dews that drench the furze,
   And all the silvery gossamers
That twinkle into green and gold:

Calm and still light on yon great plain
   That sweeps with all its autumn bowers,
   And crowded farms and lessening towers,
To mingle with the bounding main:

Calm and deep peace in this wide air,
   These leaves that redden to the fall;
   And in my heart, if calm at all,
If any calm, a calm despair:

Calm on the seas, and silver sleep,
   And waves that sway themselves in rest,
   And dead calm in that noble breast
Which heaves but with the heaving deep.

LVI

'So careful of the type?' but no.
　　From scarpèd cliff and quarried stone
　　She cries, 'A thousand types are gone:
I care for nothing, all shall go.

'Thou makest thine appeal to me:
　　I bring to life, I bring to death:
　　The spirit does but mean the breath:
I know no more.' And he, shall he,

Man, her last work, who seemed so fair,
　　Such splendid purpose in his eye,
　　Who rolled the psalm to wintry skies,
Who built him fanes of fruitless prayer,

Who trusted God was love indeed
　　And love Creation's final law –
　　Though Nature, red in tooth and claw
With ravine, shrieked against his creed –

Who loved, who suffered countless ills,
　　Who battled for the True, the Just,
　　Be blown about the desert dust,
Or sealed within the iron hills?

No more? A monster then, a dream,
　　A discord. Dragons of the prime,
　　That tare each other in their slime,
Were mellow music matched with him.

O life as futile, then, as frail!
　　O for thy voice to soothe and bless!
　　What hope of answer, or redress?
Behind the veil, behind the veil.

CXV

Now fades the last long streak of snow,
　　Now burgeons every maze of quick
　　About the flowering squares, and thick
By ashen roots the violets blow.

Now rings the woodland loud and long,
　　The distance takes a lovelier hue,
　　And drowned in yonder living blue
The lark becomes a sightless song.

Now dance the lights on lawn and lea,
　　The flocks are whiter down the vale,
　　And milkier every milky sail
On winding stream or distant sea;

Where now the seamew pipes, or dives
　　In yonder greening gleam, and fly
　　The happy birds, that change their sky
To build and brood; that live their lives

From land to land; and in my breast
　　Spring wakens too; and my regret
　　Becomes an April violet,
And buds and blossoms like the rest.

§　　§　　§

THOMAS LOVELL BEDDOES *from* **Death's Jest Book, Or the Fool's Tragedy**

A church-yard with the ruins of a spacious gothic cathedral. On the cloister walls the DANCE OF DEATH *is painted. On one side the sepulchre of the Dukes with massy carved folding doors. Moonlight.*

DUKE
　　　　　　　　　And what's your tune?

What is the night-bird's tune, wherewith she startles
The bee out of his dream, that turns and kisses
The inmost of his flower and sleeps again?
What is the lobster's tune when he is boiling?
I hate your ballads that are made to come
Round like a squirrel's cage, and round again.
We nightingales sing boldly from our hearts:
So listen to us.

Song by ISBRAND

Squats on a toad-stool under a tree
   A bodiless childfull of life in the gloom,
Crying with frog voice, 'What shall I be?
Poor unborn ghost, for my mother killed me
   Scarcely alive in her wicked womb.
What shall I be? shall I creep to the egg
   That's cracking asunder yonder by Nile,
     And with eighteen toes,
     And a snuff-taking nose,
   Make an Egyptian crocodile?
Sing, "Catch a mummy by the leg
And crunch him with an upper jaw,
Wagging tail and clenching claw;
Take a bill-full from my craw,
Neighbour raven, caw, O caw,
Grunt, my crocky, pretty maw!
     And give a paw."

'Swine, shall I be one? 'Tis a dear dog;
   But for a smile, and kiss, and pout,
   I much prefer *your* black-lipped snout,
     Little, gruntless, fairy hog,
     Godson of the hawthorn hedge.
   For, when Ringwood snuffs me out,
     And 'gins my tender paunch to grapple,
     Sing, "'Twixt your ancles visage wedge,
      And roll up like an apple."

'Serpent Lucifer, how do you do?
Of your worms and your snakes I'd be one or two
   For in this dear planet of wool and of leather
'Tis pleasant to need no shirt, breeches or shoe,
   And have arm, leg, and belly together.

Then aches your head, or are you lazy?
Sing, "Round your neck your belly wrap,
Tail-a-top, and make your cap
Any bee and daisy."

'I'll not be a fool, like the nightingale
Who sits up all midnight without any ale,
Making a noise with his nose;
Nor a camel, although 'tis a beautiful back;
Nor a duck, notwithstanding the music of quack
And the webby, mud-patting toes.
I'll be a new bird with the head of an ass,
Two pigs' feet, two men's feet, and two of a hen;
Devil-winged; dragon-bellied; grave-jawed, because grass
Is a beard that's soon shaved, and grows seldom again
Before it is summer; so cow all the rest;
The new Dodo is finished. O! come to my nest.'

(. . .)

Song.
By female voices
We have bathed, where none have seen us,
In the lake and in the fountain,
Underneath the charmed statue
Of the timid, bending Venus,
When the water-nymphs were counting
In the waves the stars of night,
And those maidens started at you,
Your limbs shone through so soft and bright.
But no secrets dare we tell,
For thy slaves unlace thee,
And he, who shall embrace thee,
Waits to try thy beauty's spell.

(. . .)

Dirge (for Sibylla)
We do lie beneath the grass
In the moonlight, in the shade
Of the yew-tree. They that pass
Hear us not. We are afraid

They would envy our delight,
    In our graves by glow-worm night.
Come follow us, and smile as we;
    We sail to the rock in the ancient waves,
Where the snow falls by thousands into the sea,
    And the drowned and the shipwrecked have happy graves.

(written 1825–44)

THOMAS LOVELL BEDDOES *from* The Last Man

A Crocodile

Hard by the lilied Nile I saw
A duskish river-dragon stretched along,
The brown habergeon of his limbs enamelled
With sanguine almandines and rainy pearl:
And on his back there lay a young one sleeping,
No bigger than a mouse; with eyes like beads,
And a small fragment of its speckled egg
Remaining on its harmless, pulpy snout;
A thing to laugh at, as it gaped to catch
The baulking, merry flies. In the iron jaws
Of the great devil-beast, like a pale soul
Fluttering in rocky hell, lightsomely flew
A snowy troculus, with roseate beak
Tearing the hairy leeches from his throat.

(written 1823–5)

A Lake

            A lake
Is a river curled and asleep like a snake.

(written 1823–5; 1935)

1852 MATTHEW ARNOLD To Marguerite – Continued

Yes! in the sea of life enisled,
With echoing straits between us thrown,
Dotting the shoreless watery wild,
We mortal millions live *alone*.
The islands feel the enclasping flow,
And then their endless bounds they know.

But when the moon their hollows lights,
And they are swept by balms of spring,
And in their glens, on starry nights,
The nightingales divinely sing;
And lovely notes, from shore to shore,
Across the sounds and channels pour –

Oh! then a longing like despair
Is to their farthest caverns sent;
For surely once, they feel, we were
Parts of a single continent!
Now round us spreads the watery plain –
Oh might our marges meet again!

Who order'd, that their longing's fire
Should be, as soon as kindled, cool'd?
Who renders vain their deep desire? –
A God, a God their severance ruled!
And bade betwixt their shores to be
The unplumb'd, salt, estranging sea.

1853 WALTER SAVAGE LANDOR

Our youth was happy: why repine
That, like the Year's, Life's days decline?
'Tis well to mingle with the mould
When we ourselves alike are cold,
And when the only tears we shed
Are of the dying on the dead.

WALTER SAVAGE LANDOR Separation

There is a mountain and a wood between us,
Where the lone shepherd and late bird have seen us
Morning and noon and even-tide repass.
Between us now the mountain and the wood
Seem standing darker than last year they stood,
And say we must not cross, alas! alas!

JAMES HENRY   1854

Another and another and another
And still another sunset and sunrise,
The same yet different, different yet the same,
Seen by me now in my declining years
As in my early childhood, youth and manhood;
And by my parents and my parents' parents,
And by the parents of my parents' parents,
And by their parents counted back for ever,
Seen, all their lives long, even as now by me;
And by my children and my children's children
And by the children of my children's children
And by their children counted on for ever
Still to be seen as even now seen by me;
Clear and bright sometimes, sometimes dark and clouded
But still the same sunsetting and sunrise;
The same for ever to the never ending
Line of observers, to the same observer
Through all the changes of his life the same:
Sunsetting and sunrising and sunsetting,
And then again sunrising and sunsetting,
Sunrising and sunsetting evermore.

JAMES HENRY

The són's a poor, wrétched, unfórtunate creáture,
With a náme no less wrétched: I-WOULD-IF-I-COULD;
But the fáther's rich, glórious and háppy and mighty
And his térrible náme is I-COULD-IF-I-WOULD.

1855   ROBERT BROWNING   Love in a Life

Room after room,
I hunt the house through
We inhabit together.
Heart, fear nothing, for, heart, thou shalt find her –
Next time, herself! – not the trouble behind her
Left in the curtain, the couch's perfume!
As she brushed it, the cornice-wreath blossomed anew:
Yon looking-glass gleamed at the wave of her feather.

Yet the day wears,
And door succeeds door;
I try the fresh fortune –
Range the wide house from the wing to the centre.
Still the same chance! she goes out as I enter.
Spend my whole day in the quest, – who cares?
But 'tis twilight, you see, – with such suites to explore,
Such closets to search, such alcoves to importune!

ROBERT BROWNING   How It Strikes a Contemporary

I only knew one poet in my life:
And this, or something like it, was his way.

   You saw go up and down Valladolid,
A man of mark, to know next time you saw.
His very serviceable suit of black
Was courtly once and conscientious still,
And many might have worn it, though none did:
The cloak, that somewhat shone and showed the threads,
Had purpose, and the ruff, significance.
He walked and tapped the pavement with his cane,
Scenting the world, looking it full in face,
An old dog, bald and blindish, at his heels.
They turned up, now, the alley by the church,
That leads nowhither; now, they breathed themselves
On the main promenade just at the wrong time:
You'd come upon his scrutinizing hat,
Making a peaked shade blacker than itself

Against the single window spared some house
Intact yet with its mouldered Moorish work, –
Or else surprise the ferrel of his stick
Trying the mortar's temper 'tween the chinks
Of some new shop a-building, French and fine.
He stood and watched the cobbler at his trade,
The man who slices lemons into drink,
The coffee-roaster's brazier, and the boys
That volunteer to help him turn its winch.
He glanced o'er books on stalls with half an eye,
And fly-leaf ballads on the vendor's string,
And broad-edge bold-print posters by the wall.
He took such cognizance of men and things,
If any beat a horse, you felt he saw;
If any cursed a woman, he took note;
Yet stared at nobody, – you stared at him,
And found, less to your pleasure than surprise,
He seemed to know you and expect as much.
So, next time that a neighbour's tongue was loosed,
It marked the shameful and notorious fact,
We had among us, not so much a spy,
As a recording chief-inquisitor,
The town's true master if the town but knew!
We merely kept a governor for form,
While this man walked about and took account
Of all thought, said and acted, then went home,
And wrote it fully to our Lord the King
Who has an itch to know things, he knows why,
And reads them in his bedroom of a night.
Oh, you might smile! there wanted not a touch,
A tang of . . . well, it was not wholly ease
As back into your mind the man's look came.
Stricken in years a little, – such a brow
His eyes had to live under! – clear as flint
On either side the formidable nose
Curved, cut and coloured like an eagle's claw.
Had he to do with A.'s surprising fate?
When altogether old B. disappeared
And young C. got his mistress, – was't our friend,
His letter to the King, that did it all?
What paid the bloodless man for so much pains?
Our Lord the King has favourites manifold,
And shifts his ministry some once a month;
Our city gets new governors at whiles, –

But never word or sign, that I could hear,
Notified to this man about the streets
The King's approval of those letters conned
The last thing duly at the dead of night.
Did the man love his office? Frowned our Lord,
Exhorting when none heard – 'Beseech me not!
Too far above my people, – beneath me!
I set the watch, – how should the people know?
Forget them, keep me all the more in mind!'
Was some such understanding 'twixt the two?

I found no truth in one report at least –
That if you tracked him to his home, down lanes
Beyond the Jewry, and as clean to pace,
You found he ate his supper in a room
Blazing with lights, four Titians on the wall,
And twenty naked girls to change his plate!
Poor man, he lived another kind of life
In that new stuccoed third house by the bridge,
Fresh-painted, rather smart than otherwise!
The whole street might o'erlook him as he sat,
Leg crossing leg, one foot on the dog's back,
Playing a decent cribbage with his maid
(Jacynth, you're sure her name was) o'er the cheese
And fruit, three red halves of starved winter-pears,
Or treat of radishes in April. Nine,
Ten, struck the church clock, straight to bed went he.

My father, like the man of sense he was,
Would point him out to me a dozen times;
''St – 'St,' he'd whisper, 'the Corregidor!'
I had been used to think that personage
Was one with lacquered breeches, lustrous belt,
And feathers like a forest in his hat,
Who blew a trumpet and proclaimed the news,
Announced the bull-fights, gave each church its turn,
And memorized the miracle in vogue!
He had a great observance from us boys;
We were in error; that was not the man.

I'd like now, yet had haply been afraid,
To have just looked, when this man came to die,
And seen who lined the clean gay garret-sides
And stood about the neat low truckle-bed,

With the heavenly manner of relieving guard.
Here had been, mark, the general-in-chief,
Through a whole campaign of the world's life and death,
Doing the King's work all the dim day long,
In his old coat and up to knees in mud,
Smoked like a herring, dining on a crust, –
And, now the day was won, relieved at once!
No further show or need for that old coat,
You are sure, for one thing! Bless us, all the while
How sprucely we are dressed out, you and I!
A second, and the angels alter that.
Well, I could never write a verse, – could you?
Let's to the Prado and make the most of time.

ROBERT BROWNING Memorabilia

Ah, did you once see Shelley plain,
    And did he stop and speak to you
And did you speak to him again?
    How strange it seems and new!

But you were living before that,
    And also you are living after;
And the memory I started at –
    My starting moves your laughter.

I crossed a moor, with a name of its own
    And a certain use in the world no doubt,
Yet a hand's-breadth of it shines alone
    'Mid the blank miles round about:

For there I picked up on the heather
    And there I put inside my breast
A moulted feather, an eagle-feather!
    Well, I forget the rest.

ROBERT BROWNING Two in the Campagna

I wonder do you feel today
    As I have felt since, hand in hand,
We sat down on the grass, to stray
    In spirit better through the land,
This morn of Rome and May?

For me, I touched a thought, I know,
    Has tantalized me many times,
(Like turns of thread the spiders throw
    Mocking across our path) for rhymes
To catch at and let go.

Help me to hold it! First it left
    The yellowing fennel, run to seed
There, branching from the brickwork's cleft,
    Some old tomb's ruin: yonder weed
Took up the floating weft,

Where one small orange cup amassed
    Five beetles, – blind and green they grope
Among the honey-meal: and last,
    Everywhere on the grassy slope
I traced it. Hold it fast!

The champaign with its endless fleece
    Of feathery grasses everywhere!
Silence and passion, joy and peace,
    An everlasting wash of air –
Rome's ghost since her decease.

Such life here, through such lengths of hours,
    Such miracles performed in play,
Such primal naked forms of flowers,
    Such letting nature have her way
While heaven looks from its towers!

How say you? Let us, O my dove,
    Let us be unashamed of soul,
As earth lies bare to heaven above!
    How is it under our control
To love or not to love?

I would that you were all to me,
    You that are just so much, no more.
Nor yours nor mine, nor slave nor free!
    Where does the fault lie? What the core
O' the wound, since wound must be?

I would I could adopt your will,
    See with your eyes, and set my heart
Beating by yours, and drink my fill
    At your soul's springs, – your part my part
In life, for good and ill.

No. I yearn upward, touch you close,
    Then stand away. I kiss your cheek,
Catch your soul's warmth, – I pluck the rose
    And love it more than tongue can speak –
Then the good minute goes.

Already how am I so far
    Out of that minute? Must I go
Still like the thistle-ball, no bar,
    Onward, whenever light winds blow,
Fixed by no friendly star?

Just when I seemed about to learn!
    Where is the thread now? Off again!
The old trick! Only I discern –
    Infinite passion, and the pain
Of finite hearts that yearn.

COVENTRY PATMORE *from* **Victories of Love, Book 1, 2**   **1856**

He that but once too nearly hears
The music of forefended spheres,
Is thenceforth lonely, and for all
His days like one who treads the Wall
Of China, and, on this hand, sees
Cities and their civilities,
And, on the other, lions.

1858   ARTHUR HUGH CLOUGH *from* **Amours de Voyage**
(Canto II)

[The French Siege of Rome, 1849]

V   Claude to Eustace
Yes, we are fighting at last, it appears. This morning as usual,
Murray, as usual, in hand, I enter the Caffè Nuovo;
Seating myself with a sense as it were of a change in the weather,
Not understanding, however, but thinking mostly of Murray,
And, for to-day is their day, of the Campidoglio Marbles,
Caffè-latte! I call to the waiter, – and *Non c' è latte*,
This is the answer he makes me, and this the sign of a battle.
So I sit; and truly they seem to think any one else more
Worthy than me of attention. I wait for my milkless *nero*,
Free to observe undistracted all sorts and sizes of persons,
Blending civilian and soldier in strangest costume, coming in, and
Gulping in hottest haste, still standing, their coffee, – withdrawing
Eagerly, jangling a sword on the steps, or jogging a musket
Slung to the shoulder behind. They are fewer, moreover, than usual,
Much, and silenter far; and so I begin to imagine
Something is really afloat. Ere I leave, the Caffè is empty,
Empty too the streets, in all its length the Corso
Empty, and empty I see to my right and left the Condotti.

   Twelve o'clock, on the Pincian Hill, with lots of English,
Germans, Americans, French, – the Frenchmen, too, are protected, –
So we stand in the sun, but afraid of a probable shower;
So we stand and stare, and see, to the left of St Peter's,
Smoke, from the cannon, white, – but that is at intervals only, –
Black, from a burning house, we suppose, by the Cavalleggieri;
And we believe we discern some lines of men descending
Down through the vineyard-slopes, and catch a bayonet gleaming.
Every ten minutes, however, – in this there is no misconception, –
Comes a great white puff from behind Michel Angelo's dome, and
After a space the report of a real big gun, – not the Frenchman's? –
That must be doing some work. And so we watch and conjecture.

   Shortly, an Englishman comes, who says he has been to St Peter's,
Seen the Piazza and troops, but that is all he can tell us;
So we watch and sit, and, indeed, it begins to be tiresome. –
All this smoke is outside; when it has come to the inside,
It will be time, perhaps, to descend and retreat to our houses.

   Half past one, or two. The report of small arms frequent,

Sharp and savage indeed; that cannot all be for nothing:
So we watch and wonder; but guessing is tiresome, very.
Weary of wondering, watching, and guessing, and gossiping idly,
Down I go, and pass through the quiet streets with the knots of
National Guards patrolling, and flags hanging out at the windows,
English, American, Danish, – and, after offering to help an
Irish family moving *en masse* to the Maison Serny,
After endeavouring idly to minister balm to the trembling
Quinquagenarian fears of two lone British spinsters,
Go to make sure of my dinner before the enemy enter.
But by this there are signs of stragglers returning; and voices
Talk, though you don't believe it, of guns and prisoners taken;
And on the walls you read the first bulletin of the morning. –
This is all that I saw, and all I know of the battle.

(. . .)

VII *Claude to Eustace*
So, I have seen a man killed! An experience that, among others!
Yes, I suppose I have; although I can hardly be certain,
And in a court of justice could never declare I had seen it.
But a man was killed, I am told, in a place where I saw
Something; a man was killed, I am told, and I saw something.

   I was returning home from St Peter's; Murray, as usual,
Under my arm, I remember; had crossed the St Angelo bridge; and
Moving towards the Condotti, had got to the first barricade, when
Gradually, thinking still of St Peter's, I became conscious
Of a sensation of movement opposing me, – tendency this way
(Such as one fancies may be in a stream when the wave of the tide is
Coming and not yet come, – a sort of poise and retention);
So I turned, and, before I turned, caught sight of stragglers
Heading a crowd, it is plain, that is coming behind that corner.
Looking up, I see windows filled with heads; the Piazza,
Into which you remember the Ponte St Angelo enters,
Since I passed, has thickened with curious groups; and now the
Crowd is coming, has turned, has crossed that last barricade, is
Here at my side. In the middle they drag at something. What is it?
Ha! bare swords in the air, held up! There seem to be voices
Pleading and hands putting back; official, perhaps; but the swords
      are
Many, and bare in the air. In the air? They descend; they are smiting
Hewing, chopping – At what? In the air once more upstretched! And
Is it blood that's on them? Yes, certainly blood! Of whom, then?
Over whom is the cry of this furor of exultation?

While they are skipping and screaming, and dancing their caps on
    the points of
Swords and bayonets, I to the outskirts back, and ask a
Mercantile-seeming by-stander, 'What is it?' and he, looking always
That way, makes me answer, 'A Priest, who was trying to fly to
The Neapolitan army,' – and thus explains the proceeding.

You didn't see the dead man? No; – I began to be doubtful;
I was in black myself, and didn't know what mightn't happen; –
But a National Guard close by me, outside of the hubbub,
Broke his sword with slashing a broad hat covered with dust, – and
Passing away from the place with Murray under my arm, and
Stooping, I saw through the legs of the people the legs of a body.

You are the first, do you know, to whom I have mentioned the
    matter.
Whom should I tell it to, else? – these girls? – the Heavens forbid
    it! –
Quidnuncs at Monaldini's? – idlers upon the Pincian?

If I rightly remember, it happened on that afternoon when
Word of the nearer approach of a new Neapolitan army
First was spread. I began to bethink me of Paris Septembers,
Thought I could fancy the look of the old 'Ninety-two. On that
    evening
Three or four, or, it may be, five, of these people were slaughtered.
Some declare they had, one of them, fired on a sentinel; others
Say they were only escaping; a Priest, it is currently stated,
Stabbed a National Guard on the very Piazza Colonna:
History, Rumour of Rumours, I leave it to thee to determine!

But I am thankful to say the government seems to have strength to
Put it down; it has vanished, at least; the place is most peaceful.
Through the Trastevere walking last night, at nine of the clock, I
Found no sort of disorder; I crossed by the Island-bridges,
So by the narrow streets to the Ponte Rotto, and onwards
Thence, by the Temple of Vesta, away to the great Coliseum,
Which at the full of the moon is an object worthy a visit.

VIII Georgina Trevellyn to Louisa
Only think, dearest Louisa, what fearful scenes we have witnessed!

    *   *   *

George has just seen Garibaldi, dressed up in a long white cloak, on
Horseback, riding by, with his mounted negro behind him:
This is a man, you know, who came from America with him,
Out of the woods, I suppose, and uses a *lasso* in fighting,
Which is, I don't quite know, but a sort of noose, I imagine;

This he throws on the heads of the enemy's men in a battle,
Pulls them into his reach, and then most cruelly kills them:
Mary does not believe, but we heard it from an Italian.
Mary allows she was wrong about Mr Claude *being selfish*;
He was *most* useful and kind on the terrible thirtieth of April.
Do not write here any more; we are starting directly for Florence:
We should be off to-morrow, if only Papa could get horses;
All have been seized everywhere for the use of this dreadful Mazzini.
P.S.

Mary has seen thus far. – I am really so angry, Louisa, –
Quite out of patience, my dearest! What can the man be intending!
I am quite tired; and Mary, who might bring him to in a moment,
Lets him go on as he likes, and neither will help nor dismiss him.

IX *Claude to Eustace*

It is most curious to see what a power a few calm words (in
Merely a brief proclamation) appear to possess on the people.
Order is perfect, and peace; the city is utterly tranquil;
And one cannot conceive that this easy and *nonchalant* crowd, that
Flows like a quiet stream through street and market-place, entering
Shady recesses and bays of church, *osteria*, and *caffè*,
Could in a moment be changed to a flood as of molten lava,
Boil into deadly wrath and wild homicidal delusion.

Ah, 'tis an excellent race, – and even in old degradation,
Under a rule that enforces to flattery, lying, and cheating,
E'en under Pope and Priest, a nice and natural people.
Oh, could they but be allowed this chance of redemption! – but
        clearly
That is not likely to be. Meantime, notwithstanding all journals,
Honour for once to the tongue and the pen of the eloquent writer!
Honour to speech! and all honour to thee, thou noble Mazzini!

X *Claude to Eustace*

I am in love, meantime, you think; no doubt you would think so.
I am in love, you say; with those letters, of course, you would say so.
I am in love, you declare. I think not so; yet I grant you
It is a pleasure, indeed, to converse with this girl. Oh, rare gift,
Rare felicity, this! she can talk in a rational way, can
Speak upon subjects that really are matters of mind and of thinking,
Yet in perfection retain her simplicity; never, one moment,
Never, however you urge it, however you tempt her, consents to
Step from ideas and fancies and loving sensations to those vain
Conscious understandings that vex the minds of man-kind.

No, though she talk, it is music; her fingers desert not the keys; 'tis
Song, though you hear in the song the articulate vocables sounded,
Syllabled singly and sweetly the words of melodious meaning.
    I am in love, you say; I do not think so exactly.

1859   EDWARD FITZGERALD *from* **Rubáiyát of Omar Khayyám**

Awake! for Morning in the Bowl of Night
Has flung the Stone that puts the Stars to Flight:
    And Lo! the Hunter of the East has caught
The Sultán's Turret in a Noose of Light.

Dreaming when Dawn's Left Hand was in the Sky
I heard a Voice within the Tavern cry,
    'Awake, my Little ones, and fill the Cup
'Before Life's Liquor in its Cup be dry.'

And, as the Cock crew, those who stood before
The Tavern shouted – 'Open then the Door!
    'You know how little while we have to stay,
'And, once departed, may return no more.'

(...)

'How sweet is mortal Sovranty!' – think some:
Others – 'How blest the Paradise to come!'
    Ah, take the Cash in hand and waive the Rest;
Oh, the brave Music of a *distant* Drum!

Look to the Rose that blows about us – 'Lo,
'Laughing,' she says, 'into the World I blow:
    'At once the silken Tassel of my purse
'Tear, and its Treasure on the Garden throw.'

The Worldly Hope men set their Hearts upon
Turns Ashes – or it prospers; and anon,
    Like Snow upon the Desert's dusty Face
Lighting a little Hour or two – is gone.

And those who husbanded the Golden Grain,
And those who flung it to the Winds like Rain,
    Alike to no such aureate Earth are turn'd
As, buried once, Men want dug up again.

Think, in this batter'd Caravanserai
Whose Doorways are alternate Night and Day,
    How Sultán after Sultán with his Pomp
Abode his Hour or two, and went his way.

They say the Lion and the Lizard keep
The Courts where Jamshýd gloried and drank deep:
    And Bahrám, that great Hunter – the Wild Ass
Stamps o'er his Head, and he lies fast asleep.

I sometimes think that never blows so red
The Rose as where some buried Cæsar bled;
    That every Hyacinth the Garden wears
Dropt in its Lap from some once lovely Head.

And this delightful Herb whose tender Green
Fledges the River's Lip on which we lean –
    Ah, lean upon it lightly! for who knows
From what once lovely Lip it springs unseen!

Ah, my Belovéd, fill the Cup that clears
TO-DAY of past Regrets and future Fears –
    To-morrow? – Why, To-morrow I may be
Myself with Yesterday's Sev'n Thousand Years.

Lo! some we loved, the loveliest and best
That Time and Fate of all their Vintage prest,
    Have drunk their Cup a Round or two before,
And one by one crept silently to Rest.

And we, that now make merry in the Room
They left, and Summer dresses in new Bloom,
    Ourselves must we beneath the Couch of Earth
Descend, ourselves to make a Couch – for whom?

Ah, make the most of what we yet may spend,
Before we too into the Dust descend;
    Dust into Dust, and under Dust, to lie,
Sans Wine, sans Song, sans Singer, and – sans End!

Alike for those who for To-day prepare,
And those that after a To-morrow stare,
    A Muezzin from the Tower of Darkness cries
'Fools! your Reward is neither Here nor There!'

Why, all the Saints and Sages who discuss'd
Of the Two Worlds so learnedly, are thrust
    Like foolish Prophets forth; their Words to Scorn
Are scatter'd, and their Mouths are stopt with Dust.

Oh, come with old Khayyám, and leave the Wise
To talk; one thing is certain, that Life flies;
    One thing is certain, and the Rest is Lies;
The Flower that once has blown for ever dies.

Myself when young did eagerly frequent
Doctor and Saint, and heard great Argument
    About it and about: but evermore
Came out by the same Door as in I went.

With them the Seed of Wisdom did I sow,
And with my own hand labour'd it to grow:
    And this was all the Harvest that I reap'd –
'I came like Water, and like Wind I go.'

WILLIAM BARNES My Orcha'd in Linden Lea

'Ithin the woodlands, flow'ry gleäded,
    By the woak tree's mossy moot,
The sheenèn grass-bleädes, timber-sheäded,
    Now do quiver under voot;
An' birds do whissle over head,
An' water's bubblèn in its bed,
An' there vor me the apple tree
Do leän down low in Linden Lea.

When leaves that leätely wer a-springèn
    Now do feäde 'ithin the copse,
An' païnted birds do hush their zingèn
    Up upon the timber's tops;

An' brown-leav'd fruit's a turnèn red,
In cloudless zunsheen, over head,
Wi' fruit vor me, the apple tree
Do leän down low in Linden Lea.

Let other vo'k meäke money vaster
   In the aïr o' dark-room'd towns,
I don't dread a peevish meäster;
   Though noo man do heed my frowns,
I be free to goo abrode,
Or teäke ageän my hwomeward road
To where, vor me, the apple tree
Do leän down low in Linden Lea.

WILLIAM BARNES False Friends-like

When I wer still a bwoy, an' mother's pride,
A bigger bwoy spoke up to me so kind-like,
'If you do like, I'll treat ye wi' a ride
In theäse wheel-barrow here.' Zoo I wer blind-like
To what he had a-workèn in his mind-like,
An' mounted vor a passenger inside;
An' comèn to a puddle, perty wide,
He tipp'd me in, a-grinnèn back behind-like.
Zoo when a man do come to me so thick-like,
An' sheäke my hand, where woonce he pass'd me by,
An' tell me he would do me this or that,
I can't help thinkèn o' the big bwoy's trick-like.
An' then, vor all I can but wag my hat
An' thank en, I do veel a little shy.

ALFRED, LORD TENNYSON Tithonus   1860

The woods decay, the woods decay and fall,
The vapours weep their burthen to the ground,
Man comes and tills the field and lies beneath,
And after many a summer dies the swan.
Me only cruel immortality
Consumes: I wither slowly in thine arms,

Here at the quiet limit of the world,
A white-hair'd shadow roaming like a dream
The ever-silent spaces of the East,
Far-folded mists, and gleaming halls of morn.

Alas! for this gray shadow, once a man –
So glorious in his beauty and thy choice,
Who madest him thy chosen, that he seem'd
To his great heart none other than a God!
I ask'd thee, 'Give me immortality.'
Then didst thou grant mine asking with a smile,
Like wealthy men, who care not how they give.
But thy strong Hours indignant work'd their wills,
And beat me down and marr'd and wasted me,
And tho' they could not end me, left me maim'd
To dwell in presence of immortal youth,
Immortal age beside immortal youth,
And all I was, in ashes. Can thy love,
Thy beauty, make amends, tho' even now,
Close over us, the silver star, thy guide,
Shines in those tremulous eyes that fill with tears
To hear me? Let me go: take back thy gift:
Why should a man desire in any way
To vary from the kindly race of men
Or pass beyond the goal of ordinance
Where all should pause, as is most meet for all?

A soft air fans the cloud apart; there comes
A glimpse of that dark world where I was born.
Once more the old mysterious glimmer steals
From thy pure brows, and from thy shoulders pure,
And bosom beating with a heart renew'd.
Thy cheek begins to redden thro' the gloom,
Thy sweet eyes brighten slowly close to mine,
Ere yet they blind the stars, and the wild team
Which love thee, yearning for thy yoke, arise,
And shake the darkness from their loosen'd manes,
And beat the twilight into flakes of fire.

Lo! ever thus thou growest beautiful
In silence, then before thine answer given
Departest, and thy tears are on my cheek.

Why wilt thou ever scare me with thy tears,
And make me tremble lest a saying learnt,
In days far-off, on that dark earth, be true?
'The Gods themselves cannot recall their gifts.'

Ay me! ay me! with what another heart
In days far-off, and with what other eyes
I used to watch – if I be he that watch'd –
The lucid outline forming round thee; saw
The dim curls kindle into sunny rings;
Changed with thy mystic change, and felt my blood
Glow with the glow that slowly crimson'd all
Thy presence and thy portals, while I lay,
Mouth, forehead, eyelids, growing dewy-warm
With kisses balmier than half-opening buds
Of April, and could hear the lips that kiss'd
Whispering I knew not what of wild and sweet,
Like that strange song I heard Apollo sing,
While Ilion like a mist rose into towers.

Yet hold me not for ever in thine East:
How can my nature longer mix with thine?
Coldly thy rosy shadows bathe me, cold
Are all thy lights, and cold my wrinkled feet
Upon thy glimmering thresholds, when the steam
Floats up from those dim fields about the homes
Of happy men that have the power to die,
And grassy barrows of the happier dead.
Release me, and restore me to the ground;
Thou seëst all things, thou wilt see my grave:
Thou wilt renew thy beauty morn by morn;
I earth in earth forget these empty courts,
And thee returning on thy silver wheels.

(written 1833)

DANTE GABRIEL ROSSETTI *from the Italian of Dante*   **1861**
Sestina: of the Lady Pietra degli Scrovigni

To the dim light and the large circle of shade
I have clomb, and to the whitening of the hills,
There where we see no colour in the grass.

Natheless my longing loses not its green,
It has so taken root in the hard stone
Which talks and hears as though it were a lady.

Utterly frozen is this youthful lady,
Even as the snow that lies within the shade;
For she is no more moved than is the stone
By the sweet season which makes warm the hills
And alters them afresh from white to green,
Covering their sides again with flowers and grass.

When on her hair she sets a crown of grass
The thought has no more room for other lady;
Because she weaves the yellow with the green
So well that Love sits down there in the shade, –
Love who has shut me in among low hills
Faster than between walls of granite-stone.

She is more bright than is a precious stone;
The wound she gives may not be healed with grass:
I therefore have fled far o'er plains and hills
For refuge from so dangerous a lady;
But from her sunshine nothing can give shade, –
Not any hill, nor wall, nor summer-green.

A while ago, I saw her dressed in green, –
So fair, she might have wakened in a stone
This love which I do feel even for her shade;
And therefore, as one woos a graceful lady,
I wooed her in a field that was all grass
Girdled about with very lofty hills.

Yet shall the streams turn back and climb the hills
Before Love's flame in this damp wood and green
Burn, as it burns within a youthful lady,
For my sake, who would sleep away in stone
My life, or feed like beasts upon the grass,
Only to see her garments cast a shade.

How dark soe'er the hills throw out their shade,
Under her summer-green the beautiful lady
Covers it, like a stone cover'd in grass.

ADELAIDE ANNE PROCTER Envy

He was the first always: Fortune
    Shone bright in his face.
I fought for years; with no effort
    He conquered the place:
We ran; my feet were all bleeding,
    But he won the race.

Spite of his many successes
    Men loved him the same;
My one pale ray of good fortune
    Met scoffing and blame.
When we erred, they gave him pity,
    But me – only shame.

My home was still in the shadow,
    His lay in the sun:
I longed in vain: what he asked for
    It straightway was done.
Once I staked all my heart's treasure,
    We played – and he won.

Yes; and just now I have seen him,
    Cold, smiling, and blest,
Laid in his coffin. God help me!
    While he is at rest,
I am cursed still to live: – even
    Death loved him the best.

CHRISTINA ROSSETTI May   1862

I cannot tell you how it was;
But this I know: it came to pass
Upon a bright and breezy day
When May was young; ah pleasant May!
As yet the poppies were not born
Between the blades of tender corn;
The last eggs had not hatched as yet,
Nor any bird foregone its mate.

I cannot tell you what it was;
But this I know: it did but pass.
It passed away with sunny May,
With all sweet things it passed away,
And left me old, and cold, and grey.

CHRISTINA ROSSETTI Song

When I am dead, my dearest,
    Sing no sad songs for me;
Plant thou no roses at my head,
    Nor shady cypress tree:
Be the green grass above me
    With showers and dewdrops wet;
And if thou wilt, remember,
    And if thou wilt, forget.

I shall not see the shadows,
    I shall not feel the rain;
I shall not hear the nightingale
    Sing on, as if in pain:
And dreaming through the twilight
    That doth not rise nor set,
Haply I may remember,
    And haply may forget.

CHRISTINA ROSSETTI Winter: My Secret

I tell my secret? No indeed, not I:
Perhaps some day, who knows?
But not today; it froze, and blows, and snows,
And you're too curious: fie!
You want to hear it? well:
Only, my secret's mine, and I won't tell.

Or, after all, perhaps there's none:
Suppose there is no secret after all,
But only just my fun.
Today's a nipping day, a biting day;
In which one wants a shawl,

A veil, a cloak, and other wraps:
I cannot ope to every one who taps,
And let the draughts come whistling thro' my hall;
Come bounding and surrounding me,
Come buffeting, astounding me,
Nipping and clipping thro' my wraps and all.
I wear my mask for warmth: who ever shows
His nose to Russian snows
To be pecked at by every wind that blows?
You would not peck? I thank you for good will,
Believe, but leave that truth untested still.

Spring's an expansive time: yet I don't trust
March with its peck of dust,
Nor April with its rainbow-crowned brief showers,
Nor even May, whose flowers
One frost may wither thro' the sunless hours.

Perhaps some languid summer day,
When drowsy birds sing less and less,
And golden fruit is ripening to excess,
If there's not too much sun nor too much cloud,
And the warm wind is neither still nor loud,
Perhaps my secret I may say,
Or you may guess.

ELIZABETH BARRETT BROWNING Lord Walter's Wife

I
'But why do you go?' said the lady, while both sat under the yew,
And her eyes were alive in their depth, as the kraken beneath the
    sea-blue.

II
'Because I fear you,' he answered; – 'because you are far too fair,
And able to strangle my soul in a mesh of your gold-coloured hair.'

III
'Oh, that,' she said, 'is no reason! Such knots are quickly undone,
And too much beauty, I reckon, is nothing but too much sun.'

IV

'Yet farewell so,' he answered; – 'the sunstroke's fatal at times.
I value your husband, Lord Walter, whose gallop rings still from the
    limes.'

V

'Oh, that,' she said, 'is no reason. You smell a rose through a fence:
If two should smell it, what matter? who grumbles, and where's the
    pretence?'

VI

'But I,' he replied, 'have promised another, when love was free,
To love her alone, alone, who alone and afar loves me.'

VII

'Why, that,' she said, 'is no reason. Love's always free, I am told.
Will you vow to be safe from the headache on Tuesday, and think it
    will hold?'

VIII

'But you,' he replied, 'have a daughter, a young little child, who was
    laid
In your lap to be pure; so I leave you: the angels would make me
    afraid.'

IX

'Oh, that,' she said, 'is no reason. The angels keep out of the way;
And Dora, the child, observes nothing, although you should please
    me and stay.'

X

At which he rose up in his anger, – 'Why, now, you no longer are
    fair!
Why, now, you no longer are fatal, but ugly and hateful, I swear.'

XI

At which she laughed out in her scorn: 'These men! Oh, these men
    overnice,
Who are shocked if a colour not virtuous is frankly put on by a vice.'

XII

Her eyes blazed upon him – 'And *you!* You bring us your vices so
    near
That we smell them! You think in our presence a thought 'twould
    defame us to hear!

XIII

'What reason had you, and what right, – I appeal to your soul from
    my life, –
To find me too fair as a woman? Why, sir, I am pure, and a wife.

XIV

'Is the day-star too fair up above you? It burns you not. Dare you
    imply
I brushed you more close than the star does, when Walter had set me
    as high?

XV

'If a man finds a woman too fair, he means simply adapted too much
To use unlawful and fatal. The praise! – shall I thank you for such?

XVI

'Too fair? – not unless you misuse us! and surely if, once in a while,
You attain to it, straightway you call us no longer too fair, but too
    vile.

XVII

'A moment, – I pray your attention! – I have a poor word in my head
I must utter, though womanly custom would set it down better
    unsaid.

XVIII

'You grew, sir, pale to impertinence, once when I showed you a ring.
You kissed my fan when I dropped it. No matter! – I've broken the
    thing.

XIX

'You did me the honour, perhaps, to be moved at my side now and
    then
In the senses – a vice, I have heard, which is common to beasts and
    some men.

XX

'Love's a virtue for heroes! – as white as the snow on high hills,
And immortal as every great soul is that struggles, endures, and
    fulfils.

XXI

'I love my Walter profoundly, – you, Maude, though you faltered a
    week,
For the sake of . . . what was it – an eyebrow? or, less still, a mole on
    a cheek?

XXII

'And since, when all's said, you're too noble to stoop to the frivolous
    cant
About crimes irresistible, virtues that swindle, betray and supplant,

XXIII

'I determined to prove to yourself that, whate'er you might dream or
    avow
By illusion, you wanted precisely no more of me than you have now.

XXIV

'There! Look me full in the face! – in the face. Understand, if you
    can,
That the eyes of such women as I am are clean as the palm of a man.

XXV

'Drop his hand, you insult him. Avoid us for fear we should cost you
    a scar –
You take us for harlots, I tell you, and not for the women we are.

XXVI

'You wronged me: but then I considered . . . there's Walter! And so
    at the end
I vowed that he should not be mulcted, by me, in the hand of a
    friend.

XXVII

'Have I hurt you indeed? We are quits then. Nay, friend of my
    Walter, be mine!
Come, Dora, my darling, my angel, and help me to ask him to dine.'

ELIZABETH BARRETT BROWNING A Musical Instrument

What was he doing, the great god Pan,
    Down in the reeds by the river?
Spreading ruin and scattering ban,
Splashing and paddling with hoofs of a goat,
And breaking the golden lilies afloat
    With the dragon-fly on the river.

He tore out a reed, the great god Pan,
    From the deep cool bed of the river:
The limpid water turbidly ran,
And the broken lilies a-dying lay,
And the dragon-fly had fled away,
    Ere he brought it out of the river.

High on the shore sat the great god Pan
    While turbidly flowed the river;
And hacked and hewed as a great god can,
With his hard bleak steel at the patient reed,
Till there was not a sign of the leaf indeed
    To prove it fresh from the river.

He cut it short, did the great god Pan,
    (How tall it stood in the river!)
Then drew the pith, like the heart of a man,
Steadily from the outside ring,
And notched the poor dry empty thing
    In holes, as he sat by the river.

'This is the way,' laughed the great god Pan
    (Laughed while he sat by the river),
'The only way, since gods began
To make sweet music, they could succeed.'
Then, dropping his mouth to a hole in the reed,
    He blew in power by the river.

Sweet, sweet, sweet, O Pan!
    Piercing sweet by the river!
Blinding sweet, O great god Pan!
The sun on the hill forgot to die,
And the lilies revived, and the dragon-fly
    Came back to dream on the river.

Yet half a beast is the great god Pan,
    To laugh as he sits by the river,
Making a poet out of a man:
The true gods sigh for the cost and pain, –
For the reed which grows nevermore again
    As a reed with the reeds in the river.

GEORGE MEREDITH *from* Modern Love

I

By this he knew she wept with waking eyes:
That, at his hand's light quiver by her head,
The strange low sobs that shook their common bed
Were called into her with a sharp surprise,
And strangled mute, like little gaping snakes,
Dreadfully venomous to him. She lay
Stone-still, and the long darkness flow'd away
With muffled pulses. Then, as midnight makes
Her giant heart of Memory and Tears
Drink the pale drug of silence, and so beat
Sleep's heavy measure, they from head to feet
Were moveless, looking thro' their dead black years,
By vain regret scrawl'd over the blank wall.
Like sculptured effigies they might be seen
Upon their marriage-tomb, the sword between;
Each wishing for the sword that severs all.

XVII

At dinner she is hostess, I am host.
Went the feast ever cheerfuller? She keeps
The Topic over intellectual deeps
In buoyancy afloat. They see no ghost.
With sparkling surface-eyes we ply the ball:
It is in truth a most contagious game;
HIDING THE SKELETON shall be its name.
Such play as this the devils might appal!
But here's the greater wonder; in that we,
Enamour'd of our acting and our wits,
Admire each other like true hypocrites.
Warm-lighted glances, Love's Ephemerae,

Shoot gaily o'er the dishes and the wine.
We waken envy of our happy lot.
Fast, sweet, and golden, shows our marriage-knot.
Dear guests, you now have seen Love's corpse-light shine!

XXXIV

Madam would speak with me. So, now it comes:
The Deluge or else Fire! She's well; she thanks
My husbandship. Our chain on silence clanks.
Time leers between, above his twiddling thumbs.
Am I quite well? Most excellent in health!
The journals, too, I diligently peruse.
Vesuvius is expected to give news:
Niagara is no noisier. By stealth
Our eyes dart scrutinizing snakes. She's glad
I'm happy, says her quivering under-lip.
'And are not you?' 'How can I be?' 'Take ship!
For happiness is somewhere to be had.'
'Nowhere for me!' Her voice is barely heard.
I am not melted, and make no pretence.
With commonplace I freeze her, tongue and sense.
Niagara or Vesuvius is deferred.

L

Thus piteously Love closed what he begat:
The union of this ever-diverse pair!
These two were rapid falcons in a snare,
Condemn'd to do the flitting of the bat.
Lovers beneath the singing sky of May,
They wander'd once; clear as the dew on flowers:
But they fed not on the advancing hours:
Their hearts held cravings for the buried day.
Then each applied to each that fatal knife,
Deep questioning, which probes to endless dole.
Ah, what a dusty answer gets the soul
When hot for certainties in this our life! –
In tragic hints here see what evermore
Moves dark as yonder midnight ocean's force,
Thundering like ramping hosts of warrior horse,
To throw that faint thin line upon the shore!

ARTHUR HUGH CLOUGH The Latest Decalogue

Thou shalt have one God only; who
Would be at the expense of two?
No graven images may be
Worshipped, except the currency:
Swear not at all; for for thy curse
Thine enemy is none the worse:
At church on Sunday to attend
Will serve to keep the world thy friend:
Honour thy parents; that is, all
From whom advancement may befall:
Thou shalt not kill; but needst not strive
Officiously to keep alive:
Do not adultery commit;
Advantage rarely comes of it:
Thou shalt not steal; an empty feat,
When it's so lucrative to cheat:
Bear not false witness; let the lie
Have time on its own wings to fly:
Thou shalt not covet; but tradition
Approves all forms of competition.

The sum of all is, thou shalt love,
If any body, God above:
At any rate shall never labour
More than thyself to love thy neighbour.

ALGERNON CHARLES SWINBURNE Free Thought

What is thought that is not free?
    'Tis a lie that runs in grooves,
And by nought and nothing proves
    Three times one is one, not three.

(1915)

WILLIAM BARNES Leaves a-Vallèn

There the ash-tree leaves do vall
    In the wind a-blowèn cwolder,
An' my childern, tall or small,
    Since last Fall be woone year wolder;
Woone year wolder, woone year dearer,
    Till when they do leäve my he'th.
I shall be noo mwore a hearer
    O' their vaïces or their me'th.

There dead ash leaves be a-toss'd
    In the wind, a-blowèn stronger,
An' our life-time, since we lost
    Souls we lov'd, is woone year longer;
Woone year longer, woone year wider,
    Vrom the friends that death ha' took,
As the hours do teäke the rider
    Vrom the hand that last he shook.

No. If he do ride at night
    Vrom the zide the zun went under,
Woone hour vrom his western light
    Needen meäke woone hour asunder;
Woone hour onward, woone hour nigher
    To the hopevul eastern skies,
Where his mornèn rim o' vier
    Soon ageän shall meet his eyes.

Leaves be now a-scatter'd round
    In the wind, a blowèn bleaker,
An' if we do walk the ground
    Wi' our life-strangth woone year weaker;
Woone year weaker, woone year nigher
    To the pleäce where we shall vind
Woone that's deathless vor the dier,
    Voremost they that dropp'd behind.

WILLIAM BARNES The Turnstile

Ah! sad wer we as we did peäce
The wold church road, wi' downcast feäce,
The while the bells, that mwoan'd so deep
Above our child a-left asleep,
Wer now a-zingèn all alive
Wi' tother bells to meäke the vive.
But up at woone pleäce we come by,
'Twer hard to keep woone's two eyes dry;
On Steän-cliff road, 'ithin the drong,
Up where, as vo'k do pass along,
The turnèn stile, a-païnted white,
Do sheen by day an' show by night.
Vor always there, as we did goo
To church, thik stile did let us drough,
Wi' spreadèn eärms that wheel'd to guide
Us each in turn to tother zide.
An' vu'st ov all the traïn he took
My wife, wi' winsome gaït an' look;
An' then zent on my little maïd,
A-skippèn onward, overjaÿ'd
To reach ageän the pleäce o' pride,
Her comely mother's left han' zide.
An' then, a-wheelèn roun', he took
On me, 'ithin his third white nook.
An' in the fourth, a-sheäkèn wild,
He zent us on our giddy child.
But eesterday he guided slow
My downcast Jenny, vull o' woe,
An' then my little maïd in black,
A-walkèn softly on her track;
An' after he'd a-turn'd ageän,
To let me goo along the leäne,
He had noo little bwoy to vill
His last white eärms, an' they stood still.

WALTER SAVAGE LANDOR Memory

The mother of the Muses, we are taught,
Is Memory: she has left me; they remain,
And shake my shoulder, urging me to sing
About the summer days, my loves of old.
Alas! alas! is all I can reply.
Memory has left me with that name alone,
Harmonious name, which other bards may sing,
But her bright image in my darkest hour
Comes back, in vain comes back, call'd or uncall'd.
Forgotten are the names of visitors
Ready to press my hand but yesterday;
Forgotten are the names of earlier friends
Whose genial converse and glad countenance
Are fresh as ever to mine ear and eye:
To these, when I have written, and besought
Remembrance of me, the word *Dear* alone
Hangs on the upper verge, and waits in vain.
A blessing wert thou, O oblivion,
If thy stream carried only weeds away,
But vernal and autumnal flowers alike
It hurries down to wither on the strand.

DANTE GABRIEL ROSSETTI Sudden Light

I have been here before,
    But when or how I cannot tell:
I know the grass beyond the door,
    The sweet, keen smell,
The sighing sound, the lights around the shore.

You have been mine before, –
    How long ago I may not know:
But just when at that swallow's soar
    Your neck turned so,
Some veil did fall, – I knew it all of yore.

Has this been thus before?
    And shall not thus time's eddying flight
Still with our lives our love restore
    In death's despite,
And day and night yield one delight once more?

1864   ROBERT BROWNING Youth and Art

It once might have been, once only:
    We lodged in a street together,
You, a sparrow on the housetop lonely,
    I, a lone she-bird of his feather.

Your trade was with sticks and clay,
    You thumbed, thrust, patted and polished,
Then laughed 'They will see some day
    Smith made, and Gibson demolished.'

My business was song, song, song;
    I chirped, cheeped, trilled and twittered,
'Kate Brown's on the boards ere long,
    And Grisi's existence embittered!'

I earned no more by a warble
    Than you by a sketch in plaster;
You wanted a piece of marble,
    I needed a music-master.

We studied hard in our styles,
    Chipped each at a crust like Hindoos,
For air looked out on the tiles,
    For fun watched each other's windows.

You lounged, like a boy of the South,
    Cap and blouse – nay, a bit of beard too;
Or you got it, rubbing your mouth
    With fingers the clay adhered to.

And I – soon managed to find
    Weak points in the flower-fence facing,
Was forced to put up a blind
    And be safe in my corset-lacing.

No harm! It was not my fault
    If you never turned your eye's tail up
As I shook upon E *in alt*,
    Or ran the chromatic scale up:

For spring bade the sparrows pair,
    And the boys and girls gave guesses,
And stalls in our street looked rare
    With bulrush and watercresses.

Why did not you pinch a flower
    In a pellet of clay and fling it?
Why did not I put a power
    Of thanks in a look, or sing it?

I did look, sharp as a lynx,
    (And yet the memory rankles)
When models arrived, some minx
    Tripped up-stairs, she and her ankles.

But I think I gave you as good!
    'That foreign fellow, – who can know
How she pays, in a playful mood,
    For his tuning her that piano?'

Could you say so, and never say
    'Suppose we join hands and fortunes,
And I fetch her from over the way,
    Her piano, and long tunes and short tunes?'

No, no: you would not be rash,
    Nor I rasher and something over:
You've to settle yet Gibson's hash,
    And Grisi yet lives in clover.

But you meet the Prince at the Board,
    I'm queen myself at *bals-paré*,
I've married a rich old lord,
    And you're dubbed knight and an R.A.

Each life unfulfilled, you see;
    It hangs still, patchy and scrappy:
We have not sighed deep, laughed free,
    Starved, feasted, despaired, – been happy.

754] And nobody calls you a dunce,
    And people suppose me clever:
This could but have happened once,
    And we missed it, lost it for ever.

JOHN CLARE

The thunder mutters louder and more loud
With quicker motion hay folks ply the rake
Ready to burst slow sails the pitch black cloud
And all the gang a bigger haycock make
To sit beneath – the woodland winds awake
The drops so large wet all thro' in an hour
A tiney flood runs down the leaning rake
In the sweet hay yet dry the hay folks cower
And some beneath the waggon shun the shower

(1984)

1865   **LEWIS CARROLL** *from* **Alice's Adventures in Wonderland**

'Repeat *"You are old, Father William,"'* said the Caterpillar.
Alice folded her hands, and began: –

'You are old, Father William,' the young man said,
   'And your hair has become very white;
And yet you incessantly stand on your head –
   Do you think, at your age, it is right?'

'In my youth,' Father William replied to his son,
   'I feared it might injure the brain;
But, now that I'm perfectly sure I have none,
   Why, I do it again and again.'

'You are old,' said the youth, 'as I mentioned before,
   And have grown most uncommonly fat;
Yet you turned a back-somersault in at the door –
   Pray, what is the reason of that?'

'In my youth,' said the sage, as he shook his grey locks,
   'I kept all my limbs very supple

By the use of this ointment – one shilling the box –
    Allow me to sell you a couple?'

'You are old,' said the youth, 'and your jaws are too weak
    For anything tougher than suet;
Yet you finished the goose, with the bones and the beak –
    Pray, how did you manage to do it?'

'In my youth,' said his father, 'I took to the law,
    And argued each case with my wife;
And the muscular strength, which it gave to my jaw
    Has lasted the rest of my life.'

'You are old,' said the youth, 'one would hardly suppose
    That your eye was as steady as ever;
Yet you balanced an eel on the end of your nose –
    What made you so awfully clever?'

'I have answered three questions, and that is enough,'
    Said his father. 'Don't give yourself airs!
Do you think I can listen all day to such stuff?
    Be off, or I'll kick you down-stairs!'

'That is not said right,' said the Caterpillar.

'Begin at the beginning,' the King said, very gravely, 'and go on till you come to the end: then stop.'

There was dead silence in the court, whilst the White Rabbit read out these verses: –

'They told me you had been to her,
And mentioned me to him:
She gave me a good character,
But said I could not swim.

He sent them word I had not gone
(We know it to be true):
If she should push the matter on,
What would become of you?

I gave her one, they gave him two,
You gave us three or more;
They all returned from him to you,
Though they were mine before.

If I or she should chance to be
Involved in this affair,
He trusts to you to set them free,
Exactly as we were.

My notion was that you had been
(Before she had this fit)
An obstacle that came between
Him, and ourselves, and it.

Don't let him know she liked them best,
For this must ever be
A secret, kept from all the rest,
Between yourself and me.'

'That's the most important piece of evidence we've heard yet,' said the King, rubbing his hands. . .

GEORGE ELIOT In a London Drawingroom

The sky is cloudy, yellowed by the smoke.
For view there are the houses opposite.
Cutting the sky with one long line of wall
Like solid fog: far as the eye can stretch
Monotony of surface and of form
Without a break to hang a guess upon.
No bird can make a shadow as it flies,
For all is shadow, as in ways o'erhung
By thickest canvass, where the golden rays
Are clothed in hemp. No figure lingering
Pauses to feed the hunger of the eye
Or rest a little on the lap of life.
All hurry on and look upon the ground,
Or glance unmarking at the passers by.
The wheels are hurrying too, cabs, carriages
All closed, in multiplied identity.
The world seems one huge prison-house and court
Where men are punished at the slightest cost,
With lowest rate of colour, warmth and joy.

ARTHUR HUGH CLOUGH *from* Dipsychus

'There is no God,' the wicked saith,
    'And truly it's a blessing,
For what he might have done with us
    It's better only guessing.'

'There is no God,' a youngster thinks,
    'Or really, if there may be,
He surely didn't mean a man
    Always to be a baby.'

'There is no God, or if there is,'
    The tradesman thinks, ''twere funny
If he should take it ill in me
    To make a little money.'

'Whether there be,' the rich man says,
   'It matters very little,
For I and mine, thank somebody,
   Are not in want of victual.'

Some others, also, to themselves
   Who scarce so much as doubt it,
Think there is none, when they are well,
   And do not think about it.

But country folks who live beneath
   The shadow of the steeple;
The parson and the parson's wife,
   And mostly married people;

Youths green and happy in first love,
   So thankful for illusion;
And men caught out in what the world
   Calls guilt, in first confusion;

And almost every one when age,
   Disease, or sorrows strike him,
Inclines to think there is a God,
   Or something very like Him.

1866   ALGERNON CHARLES SWINBURNE Itylus

Swallow, my sister, O sister swallow,
   How can thine heart be full of the spring?
     A thousand summers are over and dead.
What hast thou found in the spring to follow?
   What hast thou found in thine heart to sing?
     What wilt thou do when the summer is shed?

O swallow, sister, O fair swift swallow,
   Why wilt thou fly after spring to the south,
     The soft south whither thine heart is set?
Shall not the grief of the old time follow?
   Shall not the song thereof cleave to thy mouth?
     Hast thou forgotten ere I forget?

Sister, my sister, O fleet sweet swallow,
   Thy way is long to the sun and the south;
      But I, fulfilled of my heart's desire,
Shedding my song upon height, upon hollow,
   From tawny body and sweet small mouth
      Feed the heart of the night with fire.

I the nightingale all spring through,
   O swallow, sister, O changing swallow,
      All spring through till the spring be done,
Clothed with the light of the night on the dew,
   Sing, while the hours and the wild birds follow,
      Take flight and follow and find the sun.

Sister, my sister, O soft light swallow,
   Though all things feast in the spring's guest-chamber,
      How hast thou heart to be glad thereof yet?
For where thou fliest I shall not follow,
   Till life forget and death remember,
      Till thou remember and I forget.

Swallow, my sister, O singing swallow,
   I know not how thou hast heart to sing.
      Hast thou the heart? is it all past over?
Thy lord the summer is good to follow,
   And fair the feet of thy lover the spring:
      But what wilt thou say to the spring thy lover?

O swallow, sister, O fleeting swallow,
   My heart in me is a molten ember
      And over my head the waves have met.
But thou wouldst tarry or I would follow,
   Could I forget or thou remember,
      Couldst thou remember and I forget.

O sweet stray sister, O shifting swallow,
   The heart's division divideth us.
      Thy heart is light as a leaf of a tree;
But mine goes forth among sea-gulfs hollow
   To the place of the slaying of Itylus,
      The feast of Daulis, the Thracian sea.

O swallow, sister, O rapid swallow,
  I pray thee sing not a little space.
    Are not the roofs and the lintels wet?
The woven web that was plain to follow,
  The small slain body, the flowerlike face,
    Can I remember if thou forget?

O sister, sister, thy first-begotten!
  The hands that cling and the feet that follow,
  The voice of the child's blood crying yet
Who hath remembered me? who hath forgotten?
  Thou hast forgotten, O summer swallow,
    But the world shall end when I forget.

ALGERNON CHARLES SWINBURNE *from* Sapphics

All the night sleep came not upon my eyelids,
Shed not dew, nor shook nor unclosed a feather,
Yet with lips shut close and with eyes of iron
    Stood and beheld me.

Then to me so lying awake a vision
Came without sleep over the seas and touched me,
Softly touched mine eyelids and lips; and I too,
    Full of the vision,

Saw the white implacable Aphrodite,
Saw the hair unbound and the feet unsandalled
Shine as fire of sunset on western waters;
    Saw the reluctant

Feet, the straining plumes of the doves that drew her,
Looking always, looking with necks reverted,
Back to Lesbos, back to the hills whereunder
    Shone Mitylene;

Heard the flying feet of the Loves behind her
Make a sudden thunder upon the waters,
As the thunder flung from the strong unclosing
    Wings of a great wind.

So the goddess fled from her place, with awful
Sound of feet and thunder of wings around her;
While behind a clamour of singing women
    Severed the twilight.

Ah the singing, ah the delight, the passion!
All the Loves wept, listening; sick with anguish,
Stood the crowned nine Muses about Apollo;
    Fear was upon them,

While the tenth sang wonderful things they knew not
Ah the tenth, the Lesbian! the nine were silent,
None endured the sound of her song for weeping;
    Laurel by laurel,

Faded all their crowns; but about her forehead,
Round her woven tresses and ashen temples
White as dead snow, paler than grass in summer,
    Ravaged with kisses,

Shone a light of fire as a crown for ever.
Yea, almost the implacable Aphrodite
Paused, and almost wept; such a song was that song.

CHRISTINA ROSSETTI The Queen of Hearts

How comes it, Flora, that, whenever we
Play cards together, you invariably,
    However the pack parts,
    Still hold the Queen of Hearts?

I've scanned you with a scrutinizing gaze,
Resolved to fathom these your secret ways:
    But, sift them as I will,
    Your ways are secret still.

I cut and shuffle; shuffle, cut, again;
But all my cutting, shuffling, proves in vain:
    Vain hope, vain forethought too;
    That Queen still falls to you.

I dropped her once, prepense; but, ere the deal
Was dealt, your instinct seemed her loss to feel:
    'There should be one card more,'
    You said, and searched the floor.

I cheated once; I made a private notch
In Heart-Queen's back, and kept a lynx-eyed watch;
    Yet such another back
    Deceived me in the pack:

The Queen of Clubs assumed by arts unknown
An imitative dint that seemed my own;
    This notch, not of my doing,
    Misled me to my ruin.

It baffles me to puzzle out the clue,
Which must be skill, or craft, or luck in you:
    Unless, indeed, it be
    Natural affinity.

CHRISTINA ROSSETTI What Would I Give?

What would I give for a heart of flesh to warm me thro',
Instead of this heart of stone ice-cold whatever I do;
Hard and cold and small, of all hearts the worst of all.

What would I give for words, if only words would come;
But now in its misery my spirit has fallen dumb:
O merry friends, go your way, I have never a word to say.

What would I give for tears, not smiles but scalding tears,
To wash the black mark clean, and to thaw the frost of years,
To wash the stain ingrain and to make clean again.

1867   ## MATTHEW ARNOLD Dover Beach

The sea is calm to-night.
The tide is full, the moon lies fair
Upon the straits; – on the French coast the light
Gleams and is gone; the cliffs of England stand,

Glimmering and vast, out in the tranquil bay.
Come to the window, sweet is the night-air!
Only, from the long line of spray
Where the sea meets the moon-blanch'd land,
Listen! you hear the grating roar
Of pebbles which the waves draw back, and fling,
At their return, up the high strand,
Begin, and cease, and then again begin,
With tremulous cadence slow, and bring
The eternal note of sadness in.

Sophocles long ago
Heard it on the Aegaean, and it brought
Into his mind the turbid ebb and flow
Of human misery; we
Find also in the sound a thought,
Hearing it by this distant northern sea.

The Sea of Faith
Was once, too, at the full, and round earth's shore
Lay like the folds of a bright girdle furl'd.
But now I only hear
Its melancholy, long, withdrawing roar,
Retreating, to the breath
Of the night-wind, down the vast edges drear
And naked shingles of the world.

Ah, love, let us be true
To one another! for the world, which seems
To lie before us like a land of dreams,
So various, so beautiful, so new,
Hath really neither joy, nor love, nor light,
Nor certitude, nor peace, nor help for pain;
And we are here as on a darkling plain
Swept with confused alarms of struggle and flight,
Where ignorant armies clash by night.

MATTHEW ARNOLD Growing Old

What is it to grow old?
Is it to lose the glory of the form,
The lustre of the eye?
Is it for beauty to forego her wreath?
– Yes, but not this alone.

Is it to feel our strength –
Not our bloom only, but our strength – decay?
Is it to feel each limb
Grow stiffer, every function less exact,
Each nerve more loosely strung?

Yes, this, and more; but not
Ah, 'tis not what in youth we dream'd 'twould be!
'Tis not to have our life
Mellow'd and soften'd as with sunset-glow,
A golden day's decline.

'Tis not to see the world
As from a height, with rapt prophetic eyes,
And heart profoundly stirr'd;
And weep, and feel the fulness of the past,
The years that are no more.

It is to spend long days
And not once feel that we were ever young;
It is to add, immured
In the hot prison of the present, month
To month with weary pain.

It is to suffer this,
And feel but half, and feebly, what we feel.
Deep in our hidden heart
Festers the dull remembrance of a change,
But no emotion – none.

It is – last stage of all –
When we are frozen up within, and quite
The phantom of ourselves,
To hear the world applaud the hollow ghost
Which blamed the living man.

DORA GREENWELL A Scherzo. *(A Shy Person's Wishes)*

With the wasp at the innermost heart of a peach,
On a sunny wall out of tip-toe reach,
With the trout in the darkest summer pool,
With the fern-seed clinging behind its cool
Smooth frond, in the chink of an aged tree,
In the woodbine's horn with the drunken bee,
With the mouse in its nest in a furrow old,
With the chrysalis wrapt in its gauzy fold;
With things that are hidden, and safe, and bold,
With things that are timid, and shy, and free,
Wishing to be;
With the nut in its shell, with the seed in its pod,
With the corn as it sprouts in the kindly clod,
Far down where the secret of beauty shows
In the bulb of the tulip, before it blows;
With things that are rooted, and firm, and deep,
Quiet to lie, and dreamless to sleep;
With things that are chainless, and tameless, and proud,
With the fire in the jagged thunder-cloud,
With the wind in its sleep, with the wind in its waking,
With the drops that go to the rainbow's making,
Wishing to be with the light leaves shaking,
Or stones on some desolate highway breaking;
Far up on the hills, where no foot surprises
The dew as it falls, or the dust as it rises;
To be couched with the beast in its torrid lair,
Or drifting on ice with the polar bear,
With the weaver at work at his quiet loom;
Anywhere, anywhere, out of this room!

CHARLES TURNER On a Vase of Gold-Fish 1868

The tortured mullet served the Roman's pride
By darting round the crystal vase, whose heat
Ensured his woe and beauty till he died:
These unharm'd gold-fish yield as rich a treat;

Seen thus, in parlour-twilight, they appear
As though the hand of Midas, hovering o'er,
Wrought on the waters, as his touch drew near,
And set them glancing with his golden power,
The flash of transmutation! In their glass
They float and glitter, by no anguish rackt;
And, though we see them swelling as they pass,
'Tis but a painless and phantasmal act,
The trick of their own bellying walls, which charms
All eyes – themselves it vexes not, nor harms.

MORTIMER COLLINS Winter in Brighton

Will there be snowfall on lofty Soracte
    After a summer so tranquil and torrid?
Whoso detests the east wind, as a fact he
        Thinks 'twill be horrid.
But there are zephyrs more mild by the ocean,
    Every keen touch of the snowdrifts to lighten:
If to be cosy and snug you've a notion
        Winter in Brighton!

Politics nobody cares about. Spurn a
    Topic whereby all our happiness suffers.
Dolts in the back streets of Brighton return a
        Couple of duffers.
Fawcett and White in the Westminster Hades
    Strive the reporters' misfortunes to heighten.
What does it matter? Delicious young ladies
        Winter in Brighton!

Good is the turtle for luncheon at Mutton's,
    Good is the hock that they give you at Bacon's,
Mainwaring's fruit in the bosom of gluttons
        Yearning awakens;
Buckstone comes hither, delighting the million,
    'Mong the theatrical minnows a Triton;
Dickens and Lemon pervade the Pavilion: –
        Winter in Brighton!

If you've a thousand a year, or a minute –
    If you're a D'Orsay, whom every one follows –
If you've a head (it don't matter what's in it)
        Fair as Apollo's –
If you approve of flirtations, good dinners,
    Seascapes divine which the merry winds whiten,
Nice little saints and still nicer young sinners –
        Winter in Brighton!

MATTHEW ARNOLD   1869

Below the surface-stream, shallow and light,
Of what we *say* we feel – below the stream,
As light, of what we *think* we feel – there flows
With noiseless current strong, obscure and deep,
The central stream of what we feel indeed.

AUGUSTA WEBSTER *from* A Castaway   1870

Poor little diary, with its simple thoughts,
Its good resolves, its 'Studied French an hour,'
'Read Modern History,' 'Trimmed up my grey hat,'
'Darned stockings,' 'Tatted,' 'Practised my new song,'
'Went to the daily service,' 'Took Bess soup,'
'Went out to tea.' Poor simple diary!
And did *I* write it? Was I this good girl,
This budding colourless young rose of home?
Did I so live content in such a life,
Seeing no larger scope, nor asking it,
Than this small constant round – old clothes to mend,
New clothes to make, then go and say my prayers,
Or carry soup, or take a little walk
And pick the ragged-robins in the hedge?
Then, for ambition, (was there ever life
That could forego that?) to improve my mind
And know French better and sing harder songs;
For gaiety, to go, in my best white
Well washed and starched and freshened with new bows,
And take tea out to meet the clergyman.
No wishes and no cares, almost no hopes,

Only the young girl's hazed and golden dreams
That veil the Future from her.
                              So long since:
And now it seems a jest to talk of me
As if I could be one with her, of me
Who am . . . me.
                    And what is that?   My looking-glass
Answers it passably; a woman sure,
No fiend, no slimy thing out of the pools,
A woman with a ripe and smiling lip
That has no venom in its touch I think,
With a white brow on which there is no brand;
A woman none dare call not beautiful,
Not womanly in every woman's grace.

  Aye, let me feed upon my beauty thus,
Be glad in it like painters when they see
At last the face they dreamed but could not find
Look from their canvas on them, triumph in it,
The dearest thing I have. Why, 'tis my all,
Let me make much of it: is it not this,
This beauty, my own curse at once and tool
To snare men's souls, (I know what the good say
Of beauty in such creatures) is it not this
That makes me feel myself a woman still,
With still some little pride, some little –
                                    Stop!
'Some little pride, some little' – Here's a jest!
What word will fit the sense but modesty?
A wanton I, but modest!
                        Modest, true;
I'm not drunk in the streets, ply not for hire
At infamous corners with my likenesses
Of the humbler kind; yes, modesty's my word –
'Twould shape my mouth well too, I think I'll try:
'Sir, Mr. What-you-will, Lord Who-knows-what,
My present lover or my next to come,
Value me at my worth, fill your purse full,
For I am modest; yes, and honour me
As though your schoolgirl sister or your wife
Could let her skirts brush mine or talk of me;
For I am modest.'
                    Well, I flout myself:

But yet, but yet –

                Fie, poor fantastic fool,
Why do I play the hypocrite alone,
Who am no hypocrite with others by?
Where should be my 'But yet'? I am that thing
Called half a dozen dainty names, and none
Dainty enough to serve the turn and hide
The one coarse English worst that lurks beneath:
Just that, no worse, no better.
                      And, for me,
I say let no one be above her trade;
I own my kindredship with any drab
Who sells herself as I, although she crouch
In fetid garrets and I have a home
All velvet and marqueterie and pastilles,
Although she hide her skeleton in rags
And I set fashions and wear cobweb lace:
The difference lies but in my choicer ware,
That I sell beauty and she ugliness;
Our traffic's one – I'm no sweet slaver-tongue
To gloze upon it and explain myself
A sort of fractious angel misconceived –
Our traffic's one: I own it. And what then?
I know of worse that are called honourable.
Our lawyers, who with noble eloquence
And virtuous outbursts lie to hang a man,
Or lie to save him, which way goes the fee:
Our preachers, gloating on your future hell
For not believing what they doubt themselves:
Our doctors, who sort poisons out by chance
And wonder how they'll answer, and grow rich:
Our journalists, whose business is to fib
And juggle truths and falsehoods to and fro:
Our tradesmen, who must keep unspotted names
And cheat the least like stealing that they can:
Our – all of them, the virtuous worthy men
Who feed on the world's follies, vices, wants,
And do their businesses of lies and shams
Honestly, reputably, while the world
Claps hands and cries 'good luck,' which of their trades,
Their honourable trades, barefaced like mine,
All secrets brazened out, would shew more white?

And whom do I hurt more than they? as much?
The wives? Poor fools, what do I take from them
Worth crying for or keeping? If they knew
What their fine husbands look like seen by eyes
That may perceive there are more men than one!
But, if they can, let them just take the pains
To keep them: 'tis not such a mighty task
To pin an idiot to your apron-string;
And wives have an advantage over us,
(The good and blind ones have) the smile or pout
Leaves them no secret nausea at odd times.
Oh, they could keep their husbands if they cared,
But 'tis an easier life to let them go,
And whimper at it for morality.

Oh! those shrill carping virtues, safely housed
From reach of even a smile that should put red
On a decorous cheek, who rail at us
With such a spiteful scorn and rancorousness,
(Which maybe is half envy at the heart)
And boast themselves so measurelessly good
And us so measurelessly unlike them,
What is their wondrous merit that they stay
In comfortable homes whence not a soul
Has ever thought of tempting them, and wear
No kisses but a husband's upon lips
There is no other man desires to kiss –
Refrain in fact from sin impossible?
How dare they hate us so? what have they done,
What borne, to prove them other than we are?
What right have they to scorn us – glass-case saints,
Dianas under lock and key – what right
More than the well-fed helpless barn-door fowl
To scorn the larcenous wild-birds?
                                                    Pshaw, let be!
Scorn or no scorn, what matter for their scorn?
I have outfaced my own – that's harder work.
Aye, let their virtuous malice dribble on –.
Mock snowstorms on the stage – I'm proof long since:
I have looked coolly on my what and why,
And I accept myself.

DANTE GABRIEL ROSSETTI A Match with the Moon

Weary already, weary miles to-night
   I walked for bed: and so, to get some ease,
   I dogged the flying moon with similes.
And like a wisp she doubled on my sight
In ponds; and caught in tree-tops like a kite;
   And in a globe of film all liquorish
   Swam full-faced like a silly silver fish; –
Last like a bubble shot the welkin's height
Where my road turned, and got behind me, and sent
   My wizened shadow craning round at me,
   And jeered, 'So, step the measure, – one two three!'
And if I faced on her, looked innocent.
But just at parting, halfway down a dell,
She kissed me for good-night. So you'll not tell.

DANTE GABRIEL ROSSETTI The Woodspurge

The wind flapped loose, the wind was still,
Shaken out dead from tree and hill:
I had walked on at the wind's will, –
I sat now, for the wind was still.

Between my knees my forehead was, –
My lips drawn in, said not Alas!
My hair was over in the grass,
My naked ears heard the day pass.

My eyes, wide open, had the run
Of some ten weeds to fix upon;
Among those few, out of the sun,
The woodspurge flowered, three cups in one.

From perfect grief there need not be
Wisdom or even memory:
One thing then learnt remains to me, –
The woodspurge has a cup of three.

There was an old man who screamed out
Whenever they knocked him about;
So they took off his boots, And fed him with fruits,
And continued to knock him about.

EDWARD LEAR   The Owl and the Pussy-Cat

I

The Owl and the Pussy-cat went to sea
   In a beautiful pea-green boat,
They took some honey, and plenty of money,
   Wrapped up in a five-pound note.
The Owl looked up to the stars above,
   And sang to a small guitar,
'O lovely Pussy! O Pussy, my love,
     What a beautiful Pussy you are,
        You are,
        You are!
     What a beautiful Pussy you are!'

Pussy said to the Owl, 'You elegant fowl!
   How charmingly sweet you sing!
O let us be married! too long we have tarried:
   But what shall we do for a ring?'
They sailed away, for a year and a day,
   To the land where the Bong-tree grows
And there in a wood a Piggy-wig stood
   With a ring at the end of his nose,
        His nose,
        His nose,
   With a ring at the end of his nose.

III

'Dear Pig, are you willing to sell for one shilling
   Your ring?' Said the Piggy, 'I will.'
So they took it away, and were married next day
   By the Turkey who lives on the hill.
They dined on mince, and slices of quince,
   Which they ate with a runcible spoon;
And hand in hand, on the edge of the sand,
   They danced by the light of the moon,
        The moon,
        The moon,
They danced by the light of the moon.

LEWIS CARROLL *from* Through the Looking-Glass   1872

   'The piece I'm going to repeat', he went on without noticing
her remark, 'was written entirely for your amusement.'
   Alice felt that in that case she really *ought* to listen to it; so
she sat down, and said 'Thank you' rather sadly,

'In winter, when the fields are white,
I sing this song for your delight –

only I don't sing it,' he added, as an explanation.
   'I see you don't,' said Alice.
   'If you can *see* whether I'm singing or not, you've sharper
eyes than most,' Humpty Dumpty remarked severely. Alice was
silent.

'In spring, when woods are getting green,
I'll try and tell you what I mean:'

'Thank you very much,' said Alice.

'In summer, when the days are long,
Perhaps you'll understand the song:

In autumn, when the leaves are brown,
Take pen and ink, and write it down.'

'I will, if I can remember it so long,' said Alice.
'You needn't go on making remarks like that,' Humpty
Dumpty said: 'they're not sensible, and they put me out.'

'I sent a message to the fish:
I told them "This is what I wish."

The little fishes of the sea,
They sent an answer back to me.

The little fishes' answer was
"We cannot do it, Sir, because –"'

'I'm afraid I don't quite understand,' said Alice.
'It gets easier further on,' Humpty Dumpty replied.

'I sent to them again to say
"It will be better to obey".

The fishes answered, with a grin,
"Why, what a temper you are in!"

I told them once, I told them twice:
They would not listen to advice.

I took a kettle large and new,
Fit for the deed I had to do.

My heart went hop, my heart went thump:
I filled the kettle at the pump.

Then some one came to me and said
"The little fishes are in bed."

I said to him, I said it plain,
"Then you must wake them up again."

I said it very loud and clear:
I went and shouted in his ear.'

Humpty Dumpty raised his voice almost to a scream as he
repeated this verse, and Alice thought, with a shudder, 'I
wouldn't have been the messenger for *anything*!'

'But he was very stiff and proud:
He said, "You needn't shout so loud!"

And he was very proud and stiff:
He said "I'd go and wake them, if – "

I took a corkscrew from the shelf:
I went to wake them up myself.

And when I found the door was locked,
I pulled and pushed and kicked and knocked.

And when I found the door was shut,
I tried to turn the handle, but –'

There was a long pause.
'Is that all?' Alice timidly asked.
'That's all,' said Humpty Dumpty. 'Good-bye.'

CHRISTINA ROSSETTI *from* **Sing-Song: A Nursery Rhyme
Book**

Dead in the cold, a song-singing thrush,
Dead at the foot of a snowberry bush, –
Weave him a coffin of rush,
Dig him a grave where the soft mosses grow,
Raise him a tombstone of snow.

*

A city plum is not a plum;
A dumb-bell is no bell, though dumb;
A party rat is not a rat;
A sailor's cat is not a cat;
A soldier's frog is not a frog;
A captain's log is not a log.

*

If a pig wore a wig,
    What could we say?
Treat him as a gentleman,
    And say 'Good-day.'

If his tail chanced to fail,
    What could we do? –
Send him to the tailoress
    To get one new.

*

I caught a little ladybird
    That flies far away;
I caught a little lady wife
    That is both staid and gay.

Come back, my scarlet ladybird,
    Back from far away;
I weary of my dolly wife,
    My wife that cannot play.

She's such a senseless wooden thing
    She stares the livelong day;
Her wig of gold is stiff and cold
    And cannot change to grey.

ROBERT BROWNING [Rhyme for a Child Viewing a Naked
Venus in a Painting of 'The Judgement of Paris']

He gazed and gazed and gazed and gazed,
Amazed, amazed, amazed, amazed.

CHRISTINA ROSSETTI By the Sea   **1875**

Why does the sea moan evermore?
  Shut out from heaven it makes its moan,
It frets against the boundary shore;
  All earth's full rivers cannot fill
  The sea, that drinking thirsteth still.

Sheer miracles of loveliness
  Lie hid in its unlooked-on bed:
Anemones, salt, passionless,
  Blow flower-like; just enough alive
  To blow and multiply and thrive.

Shells quaint with curve, or spot, or spike,
  Encrusted live things argus-eyed,
All fair alike, yet all unlike,
  Are born without a pang, and die
  Without a pang, and so pass by.

COVENTRY PATMORE **Magna est Veritas**   **1877**

Here, in this little Bay,
Full of tumultuous life and great repose,
Where, twice a day,
The purposeless, glad ocean comes and goes,
Under high cliffs, and far from the huge town,
I sit me down.
For want of me the world's course will not fail:
When all its work is done, the lie shall rot;
The truth is great, and shall prevail,
When none cares whether it prevail or not.

GERARD MANLEY HOPKINS The Windhover:

To Christ our Lord

I caught this morning morning's minion, king-
   dom of daylight's dauphin, dapple-dawn-drawn Falcon, in his
      riding
   Of the rolling level underneath him steady air, and striding
High there, how he rung upon the rein of a wimpling wing
In his ecstacy! then off, off forth on swing,
   As a skate's heel sweeps smooth on a bow-bend: the hurl and
      gliding
   Rebuffed the big wind. My heart in hiding
Stirred for a bird, – the achieve of, the mastery of the thing!

Brute beauty and valour and act, oh, air, pride, plume, here
   Buckle! AND the fire that breaks from thee then, a billion
Times told lovelier, more dangerous, O my chevalier!

   No wonder of it: shéer plód makes plough down sillion
Shine, and blue-bleak embers, ah my dear,
   Fall, gall themselves, and gash gold-vermillion.

(1918)

GERARD MANLEY HOPKINS Pied Beauty

Glory be to God for dappled things –
   For skies of couple-colour as a brinded cow;
     For rose-moles all in stipple upon trout that swim;
Fresh-firecoal chestnut-falls; finches' wings;
   Landscape plotted and pieced – fold, fallow, and plough;
     And áll trádes, their gear and tackle and trim.
All things counter, original, spare, strange;
   Whatever is fickle, freckled (who knows how?)
     With swift, slow; sweet, sour; adazzle, dim;
He fathers-forth whose beauty is past change:
Praise him.

(1918)

GERARD MANLEY HOPKINS *from* The Wreck of the Deutschland

To the
happy memory of five Franciscan nuns
exiles by the Falck Laws
drowned between midnight and morning of
Dec. 7th, 1875

PART THE FIRST

Thou mastering me
God! giver of breath and bread;
World's strand, sway of the sea;
Lord of living and dead;
Thou hast bound bones and veins in me, fastened me flesh,
And after it almost unmade, what with dread,
Thy doing: and dost thou touch me afresh?
Over again I feel thy finger and find thee.

I did say yes
O at lightning and lashed rod;
Thou heardst me truer than tongue confess
Thy terror, O Christ, O God;
Thou knowest the walls, altar and hour and night:
The swoon of a heart that the sweep and the hurl of thee trod
Hard down with a horror of height:
And the midriff astrain with leaning of, laced with fire of stress.

The frown of his face
Before me, the hurtle of hell
Behind, where, where was a, where was a place?
I whirled out wings that spell
And fled with a fling of the heart to the heart of the Host.
My heart, but you were dovewinged, I can tell,
Carrier-witted, I am bold to boast,
To flash from the flame to the flame then, tower from the grace to
the grace.

I am soft sift
In an hourglass – at the wall
Fast, but mined with a motion, a drift,
And it crowds and it combs to the fall;

I steady as a water in a well, to a poise, to a pane,
But roped with, always, all the way down from the tall
Fells or flanks of the voel, a vein
Of the gospel proffer, a pressure, a principle, Christ's gift.

I kiss my hand
To the stars, lovely-asunder
Starlight, wafting him out of it; and
Glow, glory in thunder;
Kiss my hand to the dappled-with-damson west:
Since, tho' he is under the world's splendour and wonder,
His mystery must be instressed, stressed;
For I greet him the days I meet him, and bless when I understand.

Not out of his bliss
Springs the stress felt
Nor first from heaven (and few know this)
Swings the stroke dealt –
Stroke and a stress that stars and storms deliver,
That guilt is hushed by, hearts are flushed by and melt –
But it rides time like riding a river
(And here the faithful waver, the faithless fable and miss).

It dates from day
Of his going in Galilee;
Warm-laid grave of a womb-life grey;
Manger, maiden's knee;
The dense and the driven Passion, and frightful sweat:
Thence the discharge of it, there its swelling to be,
Though felt before, though in high flood yet –
What none would have known of it, only the heart, being hard at
bay,

Is out with it! Oh,
We lash with the best or worst
Word last! How a lush-kept plush-capped sloe
Will, mouthed to flesh-burst,
Gush! – flush the man, the being with it, sour or sweet,
Brim, in a flash, full! – Hither then, last or first,
To hero of Calvary, Christ,'s feet –
Never ask if meaning it, wanting it, warned of it – men go.

Be adored among men,
God, three-numberèd form;
Wring thy rebel, dogged in den,
Man's malice, with wrecking and storm.
Beyond saying sweet, past telling of tongue,
Thou art lightning and love, I found it, a winter and warm;
Father and fondler of heart thou hast wrung:
Hast thy dark descending and most art merciful then.

With an anvil-ding
And with fire in him forge thy will
Or rather, rather then, stealing as Spring
Through him, melt him but master him still:
Whether at once, as once at a crash Paul,
Or as Austin, a lingering-out swéet skíll,
Make mercy in all of us, out of us all
Mastery, but be adored, but be adored King.

(1918)

ALGERNON CHARLES SWINBURNE A Forsaken Garden **1878**

In a coign of the cliff between lowland and highland,
    At the sea-down's edge between windward and lee,
Walled round with rocks as an inland island,
    The ghost of a garden fronts the sea.
A girdle of brushwood and thorn encloses
    The steep square slope of the blossomless bed
Where the weeds that grew green from the graves of its roses
        Now lie dead.

The fields fall southward, abrupt and broken,
    To the low last edge of the long lone land.
If a step should sound or a word be spoken,
    Would a ghost not rise at the strange guest's hand?
So long have the grey bare walks lain guestless,
    Through branches and briars if a man make way,
He shall find no life but the sea-wind's, restless
        Night and day.

The dense hard passage is blind and stifled
   That crawls by a track none turn to climb
To the strait waste place that the years have rifled
   Of all but the thorns that are touched not of time.
The thorns he spares when the rose is taken;
   The rocks are left when he wastes the plain.
The wind that wanders, the weeds wind-shaken,
     These remain.

Not a flower to be pressed of the foot that falls not;
   As the heart of a dead man the seed-plots are dry;
From the thicket of thorns whence the nightingale calls not,
   Could she call, there were never a rose to reply.
Over the meadows that blossom and wither
   Rings but the note of a sea-bird's song;
Only the sun and the rain come hither
     All year long.

The sun burns sere and the rain dishevels
   One gaunt bleak blossom of scentless breath.
Only the wind here hovers and revels
   In a round where life seems barren as death.
Here there was laughing of old, there was weeping,
   Haply, of lovers none ever will know,
Whose eyes went seaward a hundred sleeping
     Years ago.

Heart handfast in heart as they stood, 'Look thither',
   Did he whisper? 'look forth from the flowers to the sea;
For the foam-flowers endure when the rose-blossoms wither,
   And men that love lightly may die – but we?'
And the same wind sang and the same waves whitened,
   And or ever the garden's last petals were shed,
In the lips that had whispered, the eyes that had lightened,
     Love was dead.

Or they loved their life through, and then went whither?
   And were one to the end – but what end who knows?
Love deep as the sea as a rose must wither,
   As the rose-red seaweed that mocks the rose.
Shall the dead take thought for the dead to love them?
   What love was ever as deep as a grave?
They are loveless now as the grass above them
     Or the wave.

All are at one now, roses and lovers.

   Not known of the cliffs and the fields and the sea.
Not a breath of the time that has been hovers
   In the air now soft with a summer to be.
Not a breath shall there sweeten the seasons hereafter
   Of the flowers or the lovers that laugh now or weep,
When as they that are free now of weeping and laughter
      We shall sleep.

Here death may deal not again for ever:
   Here change may come not till all change end.
From the graves they have made they shall rise up never,
   Who have left nought living to ravage and rend.
Earth, stones, and thorns of the wild ground growing.
   While the sun and the rain live, these shall be:
Till a last wind's breath upon all these blowing
      Roll the sea.

Till the slow sea rise and the sheer cliff crumble,
   Till terrace and meadow the deep gulfs drink,
Till the strength of the waves of the high tides humble
   The fields that lessen, the rocks that shrink,
Here now in his triumph where all things falter,
   Stretched out on the spoils that his own hand spread,
As a god self-slain on his own strange altar,
      Death lies dead.

ALGERNON CHARLES SWINBURNE A Vision of Spring in Winter

O tender time that love thinks long to see,
   Sweet foot of spring that with her footfall sows
   Late snowlike flowery leavings of the snows,
Be not too long irresolute to be;
O mother-month, where have they hidden thee?
   Out of the pale time of the flowerless rose
I reach my heart out toward the springtime lands,
   I stretch my spirit forth to the fair hours,
     The purplest of the prime:
I lean my soul down over them, with hands
   Made wide to take the ghostly growths of flowers:
     I send my love back to the lovely time.

Where has the greenwood hid thy gracious head?
　　Veiled with what visions while the grey world grieves,
　　Or muffled with what shadows of green leaves,
What warm intangible green shadows spread
To sweeten the sweet twilight for thy bed?
　　What sleep enchants thee? what delight deceives?
Where the deep dreamlike dew before the dawn
　　Feels not the fingers of the sunlight yet
　　　Its silver web unweave,
Thy footless ghost on some unfooted lawn
　　Whose air the unrisen sunbeams fear to fret
　　　Lives a ghost's life of daylong dawn and eve.

Sunrise it sees not, neither set of star,
　　Large nightfall, nor imperial plenilune,
　　Nor strong sweet shape of the full-breasted noon;
But where the silver-sandalled shadows are,
Too soft for arrows of the sun to mar,
　　Moves with the mild gait of an ungrown moon:
Hard overhead the half-lit crescent swims,
　　The tender-coloured night draws hardly breath,
　　　The light is listening;
They watch the dawn of slender-shapen limbs,
　　Virginal, born again of doubtful death,
　　　Chill foster-father of the weanling spring.

As sweet desire of day before the day,
　　As dreams of love before the true love born,
　　From the outer edge of winter overworn
The ghost arisen of May before the May
Takes through dim air her unawakened way,
　　The gracious ghost of morning risen ere morn.
With little unblown breasts and child-eyed looks
　　Following, the very maid, the girl-child spring,
　　　Lifts windward her bright brows,
Dips her light feet in warm and moving brooks,
　　And kindles with her own mouth's colouring
　　　The fearful firstlings of the plumeless boughs.

I seek thee sleeping, and awhile I see,
   Fair face that art not, how thy maiden breath
   Shall put at last the deadly days to death
And fill the fields and fire the woods with thee
And seaward hollows where my feet would be
   When heaven shall hear the word that April saith
To change the cold heart of the weary time,
   To stir and soften all the time to tears,
     Tears joyfuller than mirth;
As even to May's clear height the young days climb
   With feet not swifter than those fair first years
     Whose flowers revive not with thy flowers on earth.

I would not bid thee, though I might, give back
   One good thing youth has given and borne away;
   I crave not any comfort of the day
That is not, nor on time's retrodden track
Would turn to meet the white-robed hours or black
   That long since left me on their mortal way;
Nor light nor love that has been, nor the breath
   That comes with morning from the sun to be
     And sets light hope on fire;
No fruit, no flower thought once too fair for death,
   No flower nor hour once fallen from life's green tree,
     No leaf once plucked or once fulfilled desire.

The morning song beneath the stars that fled
   With twilight through the moonless mountain air,
   While youth with burning lips and wreathless hair
Sang toward the sun that was to crown his head,
Rising; the hopes that triumphed and fell dead,
   The sweet swift eyes and songs of hours that were;
These may'st thou not give back for ever; these,
   As at the sea's heart all her wrecks lie waste,
     Lie deeper than the sea;
But flowers thou may'st, and winds, and hours of ease,
   And all its April to the world thou may'st
     Give back, and half my April back to me.

17—

Wailing, wailing, wailing, the wind over land and sea –
And Willy's voice in the wind, 'O mother, come out to me.'
Why should he call me tonight, when he knows that I cannot go?
For the downs are as bright as day, and the full moon stares at the
    snow.

We should be seen, my dear; they would spy us out of the town.
The loud black nights for us, and the storm rushing over the down,
When I cannot see my own hand, but am led by the creak of the
    chain,
And grovel and grope for my son till I find myself drenched with the
    rain.

Anything fallen again? nay – what was there left to fall?
I have taken them home, I have numbered the bones, I have hidden
    them all.
What am I saying? and what are *you*? do you come as a spy?
Falls? what falls? who knows? As the tree falls so must it lie.

Who let her in? how long has she been? you – what have you heard?
Why did you sit so quiet? you never have spoken a word.
O – to pray with me – yes – a lady – none of their spies –
But the night has crept into my heart, and begun to darken my eyes.

Ah – you, that have lived so soft, what should *you* know of the night,
The blast and the burning shame and the bitter frost and the fright?
I have done it, while you were asleep – you were only made for the
    day.
I have gathered my baby together – and now you may go your way.

Nay – for it's kind of you, Madam, to sit by an old dying wife.
But say nothing hard of my boy, I have only an hour of life.
I kissed my boy in the prison, before he went out to die.
'They dared me to do it,' he said, and he never has told me a lie.
I whipt him for robbing an orchard once when he was but a child –
'The farmer dared me to do it,' he said; he was always so wild –
And idle – and couldn't be idle – my Willy – he never could rest.
The King should have made him a soldier, he would have been one
    of his best.

But he lived with a lot of wild mates, and they never would let him
    be good;

They swore that he dare not rob the mail, and he swore that he
    would;
And he took no life, but he took one purse, and when all was done
He flung it among his fellows – I'll none of it, said my son.

I came into court to the Judge and the lawyers. I told them my tale,
God's own truth – but they killed him, they killed him for robbing
    the mail.
They hanged him in chains for a show – we had always borne a good
    name –
To be hanged for a thief – and then put away – isn't that enough
    shame?
Dust to dust – low down – let us hide! but they set him so high
That all the ships of the world could stare at him, passing by.
God 'ill pardon the hell-black raven and horrible fowls of the air,
But not the black heart of the lawyer who killed him and hanged
    him there.

And the jailer forced me away. I had bid him my last goodbye;
They had fastened the door of his cell. 'O mother!' I heard him cry.
I couldn't get back though I tried, he had something further to say,
And now I never shall know it. The jailer forced me away.

Then since I couldn't but hear that cry of my boy that was dead,
They seized me and shut me up: they fastened me down on my bed.
'Mother, O mother!' – he called in the dark to me year after year –
They beat me for that, they beat me – you know that I couldn't but
    hear;
And then at the last they found I had grown so stupid and still
They let me abroad again – but the creatures had worked their will.

Flesh of my flesh was gone, but bone of my bone was left –
I stole them all from the lawyers – and you, will you call it a theft? –
My baby, the bones that had sucked me, the bones that had laughed
    and had cried –
Theirs? O no! they are mine – not theirs – they had moved in my side.

Do you think I was scared by the bones? I kissed 'em, I buried 'em
    all –
I can't dig deep, I am old – in the night by the churchyard wall.
My Willy 'ill rise up whole when the trumpet of judgment 'ill sound,
But I charge you never to say that I laid him in holy ground.

They would scratch him up – they would hang him again on the
    cursèd tree.
Sin? O yes – we are sinners, I know – let all that be,
And read me a Bible verse of the Lord's good will toward men –
'Full of compassion and mercy, the Lord' – let me hear it again;
'Full of compassion and mercy – long-suffering.' Yes, O yes!
For the lawyer is born but to murder – the Saviour lives but to bless.
He'll never put on the black cap except for the worst of the worst,
And the first may be last – I have heard it in church – and the last
    may be first.
Suffering – O long-suffering – yes, as the Lord must know,
Year after year in the mist and the wind and the shower and the
    snow.

Heard, have you? what? they have told you he never repented his
    sin.
How do they know it? are *they* his mother? are *you* of his kin?
Heard! have you ever heard, when the storm on the downs began,
The wind that 'ill wail like a child and the sea that 'ill moan like a
    man?

Election, Election and Reprobation – it's all very well.
But I go tonight to my boy, and I shall not find him in Hell.
For I cared so much for my boy that the Lord has looked into my
    care,
And He means me I'm sure to be happy with Willy, I know not
    where.

And if *he* be lost – but to save *my* soul that is all your desire:
Do you think that I care for *my* soul if my boy be gone to the fire?
I have been with God in the dark – go, go, you may leave me alone –
You never have borne a child – you are just as hard as a stone.

Madam, I beg your pardon! I think that you mean to be kind,
But I cannot hear what you say for my Willy's voice in the wind –
The snow and the sky so bright – he used but to call in the dark,
And he calls to me now from the church and not from the gibbet for
    hark!
Nay – you can hear it yourself – it is coming – shaking the walls –
Willy – the moon's in a cloud – Good-night. I am going. He calls.

CHARLES TURNER Letty's Globe

When Letty had scarce pass'd her third glad year,
And her young, artless words began to flow,
One day we gave the child a colour'd sphere
Of the wide earth, that she might mark and know,
By tint and outline, all its sea and land.
She patted all the world; old empires peep'd
Between her baby fingers; her soft hand
Was welcome at all frontiers. How she leap'd,
And laugh'd, and prattled in her world-wide bliss;
But when we turned her sweet unlearned eye
On our own isle, she raised a joyous cry,
'Oh! yes, I see it, Letty's home is there!'
And, while she hid all England with a kiss,
Bright over Europe fell her golden hair.

JOSEPH SKIPSEY 'Get Up!'   1881

'Get up!' the caller calls, 'Get up!'
        And in the dead of night,
To win the bairns their bite and sup,
        I rise a weary wight.

My flannel dudden donn'd, thrice o'er
        My birds are kiss'd, and then
I with a whistle shut the door,
        I may not ope again.

CHRISTINA ROSSETTI 'Summer is Ended'

To think that this meaningless thing was ever a rose,
        Scentless, colourless, *this*!
    Will it ever be thus (who knows?)
        Thus with our bliss,
        If we wait till the close?

Tho' we care not to wait for the end, there comes the end
    Sooner, later, at last,
   Which nothing can mar, nothing mend:
     An end locked fast,
    Bent we cannot re-bend.

GERARD MANLEY HOPKINS Inversnaid

This darksome burn, horseback brown,
His rollrock highroad roaring down,
In coop and in comb the fleece of his foam
Flutes and low to the lake falls home.
A windpuff-bonnet of fáwn-fróth
Turns and twindles over the broth
Of a pool so pitchblack, féll-frówning,
It rounds and rounds Despair to drowning.

Degged with dew, dappled with dew
Are the groins of the braes that the brook treads through,
Wiry heathpacks, flitches of fern,
And the beadbonny ash that sits over the burn.

What would the world be, once bereft
Of wet and of wildness? Let them be left,
O let them be left, wildness and wet;
Long live the weeds and the wilderness yet.

                (1918)

GERARD MANLEY HOPKINS

As kingfishers catch fire, dragonflies draw flame;
  As tumbled over rim in roundy wells
  Stones ring; like each tucked string tells, each hung bell's
Bow swung finds tongue to fling out broad its name;
Each mortal thing does one thing and the same:
  Deals out that being indoors each one dwells;
  Selves – goes its self; *myself* speaks and spells,
Crying *What I do is me: for that I came.*

Í say more: the just man justices;
   Keeps gráce: thát keeps all his goings graces;
Acts in God's eye what in God's eye he is –
   Chríst. For Christ plays in ten thousand places,
Lovely in limbs, and lovely in eyes not his
   To the Father through the features of men's faces.

(1918)

ROBERT LOUIS STEVENSON *from* Treasure Island

Pirate Ditty

Fifteen men on the Dead Man's Chest –
   Yo-ho-ho, and a bottle of rum!
Drink and the devil had done for the rest –
   Yo-ho-ho, and a bottle of rum!

ROBERT LOUIS STEVENSON

Last night we had a thunderstorm in style.
The wild lightning streaked the airs,
As though my God fell down a pair of stairs.
The thunder boomed and bounded all the while;
All cried and sat by water-side and stile –
To mop our brow had been our chief of cares.
I lay in bed with a Voltairean smile,
The terror of good, simple guilty pairs,
And made this rondeau in ironic style,
Last night we had a thunderstorm in style.
Our God the Father fell down-stairs,
The stark blue lightning went its flight, the while,
The very rain you might have heard a mile –
The strenuous faithful buckled to their prayers.

1882   WILLIAM ALLINGHAM

Everything passes and vanishes;
    Everything leaves its trace;
And often you see in a footstep
    What you could not see in a face.

1884   AMY LEVY Epitaph

(On a Commonplace Person Who Died in Bed)

This is the end of him, here he lies:
The dust in his throat, the worm in his eyes,
The mould in his mouth, the turf on his breast;
This is the end of him, this is best.
He will never lie on his couch awake,
Wide-eyed, tearless, till dim daybreak.
Never again will he smile and smile
When his heart is breaking all the while.
He will never stretch out his hands in vain
Groping and groping – never again.
Never ask for bread, get a stone instead,
Never pretend that the stone is bread.
Never sway and sway 'twixt the false and true,
Weighing and noting the long hours through.
Never ache and ache with the chok'd-up sighs;
This is the end of him, here he lies.

1885   ALFRED, LORD TENNYSON To E. FitzGerald

Old Fitz, who from your suburb grange,
    Where once I tarried for a while,
Glance at the wheeling Orb of change,
    And greet it with a kindly smile;
Whom yet I see as there you sit
    Beneath your sheltering garden-tree,
And while your doves about you flit,
    And plant on shoulder, hand and knee,

Or on your head their rosy feet,
    As if they knew your diet spares
Whatever moved in that full sheet
    Let down to Peter at his prayers;
Who live on milk and meal and grass;
    And once for ten long weeks I tried
Your table of Pythagoras,
    And seemed at first 'a thing enskied'
(As Shakespeare has it) airy-light
    To float above the ways of men,
Then fell from that half-spiritual height
    Chilled, till I tasted flesh again
One night when earth was winter-black,
    And all the heavens flashed in frost;
And on me, half-asleep, came back
    That wholesome heat the blood had lost,
And set me climbing icy capes
    And glaciers, over which there rolled
To meet me long-armed vines with grapes
    Of Eshcol hugeness; for the cold
Without, and warmth within me, wrought
    To mould the dream, but none can say
That Lenten fare makes Lenten thought,
    Who reads your golden Eastern lay,
Than which I know no version done
    In English more divinely well;
A planet equal to the sun
    Which cast it, that large infidel
Your Omar; and your Omar drew
    Full-handed plaudits from our best
In modern letters, and from two,
    Old friends outvaluing all the rest,
Two voices heard on earth no more;
    But we old friends are still alive,
And I am nearing seventy-four,
    While you have touched at seventy-five,
And so I send a birthday line
    Of greeting; and my son, who dipt
In some forgotten book of mine
    With sallow scraps of manuscript,
And dating many a year ago,
    Has hit on this, which you will take
My Fitz, and welcome, as I know
    Less for its own than for the sake

Of one recalling gracious times,
    When, in our younger London days,
You found some merit in my rhymes,
    And I more pleasure in your praise.

GERARD MANLEY HOPKINS Spelt from Sibyl's Leaves

Earnest, earthless, equal, attuneable, ǀ vaulty, voluminous, . . .
        stupendous
Evening strains to be tíme's vást, ǀ womb-of-all, home-of-all,
        hearse-of-all night.
Her fond yellow hornlight wound to the west, ǀ her wild hollow
        hoarlight hung to the height
Waste; her earliest stars, earlstars, ǀ stárs principal, overbend us,
Fíre-féaturing heaven. For earth ǀ her being has unbound; her dapple
        is at end, as-
Tray or aswarm, all throughther, in throngs; ǀ self ín self steepèd and
        páshed – qúite
Disremembering, dísmémbering ǀ áll now. Heart, you round me right
With: Óur évening is over us; óur night ǀ whélms, whélms, ánd will
        end us.
Only the beakleaved boughs dragonish ǀ damask the tool-smooth
        bleak light; black,
Ever so black on it. Óur tale, O óur oracle! ǀ Lét life, wáned, ah lét
        life wind
Off hér once skéined stained véined varíety ǀ upon, áll on twó spools;
        párt, pen, páck
Now her áll in twó flocks, twó folds – black, white; ǀ right, wrong;
        reckon but, reck but, mind
But thése two; wáre of a wórld where bút these ǀ twó tell, each off
        the óther; of a rack
Where, selfwrung, selfstrung, sheathe- and shelterless, ǀ thóughts
        agaínst thoughts ín groans grínd.

                                                        (1918)

GERARD MANLEY HOPKINS

I wake and feel the fell of dark, not day.
What hours, O what black hoürs we have spent
This night! what sights you, heart, saw; ways you went!
And more must, in yet longer light's delay.

With witness I speak this. But where I say
Hours I mean years, mean life. And my lament
Is cries countless, cries like dead letters sent
To dearest him that lives alas! away.

I am gall, I am heartburn. God's most deep decree
Bitter would have me taste: my taste was me;
Bones built in me, flesh filled, blood brimmed the curse.

Selfyeast of spirit a dull dough sours. I see
The lost are like this, and their scourge to be
As I am mine, their sweating selves; but worse.

(1918)

DANTE GABRIEL ROSSETTI *from* A Trip to Paris and Belgium   **1886**

I

from LONDON TO FOLKESTONE
(*Half-past one to half-past five*)

A constant keeping-past of shaken trees,
And a bewildered glitter of loose road;
Banks of bright growth, with single blades atop
Against white sky; and wires – a constant chain –
That seem to draw the clouds along with them
(Things which one stoops against the light to see
Through the low window; shaking by at rest,
Or fierce like water as the swiftness grows);
And, seen through fences or a bridge far off,
Trees that in moving keep their intervals
Still one 'twixt bar and bar; and then at times
Long reaches of green level, where one cow,
Feeding among her fellows that feed on,
Lifts her slow neck, and gazes for the sound.

(. . .)

Brick walls we pass between, passed so at once
That for the suddenness I cannot know
Or what, or where begun, or where at end.
Sometimes a Station in grey quiet; whence,

With a short gathered champing of pent sound,
We are let out upon the air again.
Now nearly darkness; knees and arms and sides
Feel the least touch, and close about the face
A wind of noise that is along like God.
Pauses of water soon, at intervals,
That has the sky in it; – the reflexes
O' the trees move towards the bank as we go by,
Leaving the water's surface plain. I now
Lie back and close my eyes a space; for they
Smart from the open forwardness of thought
Fronting the wind –

         – I did not scribble more,
Be certain, after this; but yawned, and read,
And nearly dozed a little, I believe;
Till, stretching up against the carriage-back,
I was roused altogether, and looked out
To where, upon the desolate verge of light,
Yearned, pale and vast, the iron-coloured sea.

(. . .)

XVI
ANTWERP TO GHENT

We are upon the Scheldt. We know we move
Because there is a floating at our eyes
Whatso they seek; and because all the things
Which on our outset were distinct and large
Are smaller and much weaker and quite grey,
And at last gone from us. No motion else.

We are upon the road. The thin swift moon
Runs with the running clouds that are the sky,
And with the running water runs – at whiles
Weak 'neath the film and heavy growth of reeds.
The country swims with motion. Time itself
Is consciously beside us, and perceived.
Our speed is such the sparks our engine leaves
Are burning after the whole train has passed.

The darkness is a tumult. We tear on,
The roll behind us and the cry before,
Constantly, in a lull of intense speed
And thunder. Any other sound is known
Merely by sight. The shrubs, the trees your eye
Scans for their growth, are far along in haze.
The sky has lost its clouds, and lies away
Oppressively at calm: the moon has failed:
Our speed has set the wind against us. Now
Our engine's heat is fiercer, and flings up
Great glares alongside. Wind and steam and speed
And clamour and the night. We are in Ghent.

ANONYMOUS Johnny, I Hardly Knew Ye   1887

While going the road to sweet Athy,
    Hurroo! Hurroo!
While going the road to sweet Athy,
    Hurroo! Hurroo!
While going the road to sweet Athy,
A stick in my hand and a drop in my eye,
A doleful damsel I heard cry:
    Och, Johnny, I hardly knew ye!
        With drums and guns and guns and drums,
            The enemy nearly slew ye;
            My darling dear, you look so queer,
        Och, Johnny, I hardly knew ye!

'Where are your eyes that looked so mild?
    Hurroo! Hurroo!
Where are your eyes that looked so mild?
    Hurroo! Hurroo!
Where are your eyes that looked so mild
When my poor heart you first beguiled?
Why did you run from me and the child?
    Och, Johnny, I hardly knew ye!

'Where are the legs with which you run?
    Hurroo! Hurroo!
Where are the legs with which you run?
    Hurroo! Hurroo!

Where are the legs with which you run,
When you went to carry a gun? –
Indeed your dancing days are done!
   Och, Johnny, I hardly knew ye!

'It grieved my heart to see you sail,
    Hurroo! Hurroo!
It grieved my heart to see you sail,
    Hurroo! Hurroo!
It grieved my heart to see you sail,
Though from my heart you took leg bail, –
Like a cod you're doubled up head and tail,
   Och, Johnny, I hardly knew ye!

'You haven't an arm and you haven't a leg,
    Hurroo! Hurroo!
You haven't an arm and you haven't a leg,
    Hurroo! Hurroo!
You haven't an arm and you haven't a leg,
You're an eyeless, noseless, chickenless egg:
You'll have to be put in a bowl to beg,
   Och, Johnny, I hardly knew ye!

'I'm happy for to see you home,
    Hurroo! Hurroo!
I'm happy for to see you home,
    Hurroo! Hurroo!
I'm happy for to see you home,
All from the island of Sulloon,
So low in flesh, so high in bone,
   Och, Johnny, I hardly knew ye!

'But sad as it is to see you so,
    Hurroo! Hurroo!
But sad as it is to see you so,
    Hurroo! Hurroo!
But sad as it is to see you so,
And to think of you now as an object of woe,
Your Peggy'll still keep ye on as her beau.
   Och, Johnny, I hardly knew ye!
    With drums and guns and guns and drums,
      The enemy nearly slew ye,
      My darling dear, you look so queer,
    Och, Johnny, I hardly knew ye!

ROBERT LOUIS STEVENSON To Mrs Will H. Low

Even in the bluest noonday of July,
There could not run the smallest breath of wind
But all the quarter sounded like a wood;
And in the chequered silence and above
The hum of city cabs that sought the Bois,
Suburban ashes shivered into song.
A patter and a chatter and a chirp
And a long dying hiss – it was as though
Starched old brocaded dames through all the house
Had trailed a strident skirt, or the whole sky
Even in a wink had over-brimmed in rain.
Hark, in these shady parlours, how it talks
Of the near Autumn, how the smitten ash
Trembles and augurs floods! O not too long
In these inconstant latitudes delay,
O not too late from the unbeloved north
Trim your escape! For soon shall this low roof
Resound indeed with rain, soon shall your eyes
Search the foul garden, search the darkened rooms,
Nor find one jewel but the blazing log.

ROBERT LOUIS STEVENSON

My house, I say. But hark to the sunny doves
That make my roof the arena of their loves,
That gyre about the gable all day long
And fill the chimneys with their murmurous song:
Our house, they say; and *mine*, the cat declares
And spreads his golden fleece upon the chairs;
And *mine* the dog, and rises stiff with wrath
If any alien foot profane the path.
So too the buck that trimmed my terraces,
Our whilome gardener, called the garden his;
Who now, deposed, surveys my plain abode
And his late kingdom, only from the road.

MAY KENDALL Lay of the Trilobite

A mountain's giddy height I sought,
    Because I could not find
Sufficient vague and mighty thought
    To fill my mighty mind;
And as I wandered ill at ease,
    There chanced upon my sight
A native of Silurian seas,
    An ancient Trilobite.

So calm, so peacefully he lay,
    I watched him even with tears:
I thought of Monads far away
    In the forgotten years.
How wonderful it seemed and right,
    The providential plan,
That he should be a Trilobite,
    And I should be a Man!

And then, quite natural and free
    Out of his rocky bed,
That Trilobite he spoke to me,
    And this is what he said:
'I don't know how the thing was done,
    Although I cannot doubt it;
But Huxley – he if anyone
    Can tell you all about it;

'How all your faiths are ghosts ard dreams,
    How in the silent sea
Your ancestors were Monotremes –
    Whatever these may be;
How you evolved your shining lights
    Of wisdom and perfection
From Jelly-fish and Trilobites
    By Natural Selection.

'You've Kant to make your brains go round,
    Hegel you have to clear them,
You've Mr. Browning to confound,
    And Mr. Punch to cheer them!

The native of an alien land
   You call a man and brother,
And greet with hymn-book in one hand
   And pistol in the other!

'You've Politics to make you fight
   As if you were possessed:
You've cannon and you've dynamite
   To give the nations rest:
The side that makes the loudest din
   Is surest to be right,
And oh, a pretty fix you're in!'
   Remarked the Trilobite.

'But gentle, stupid, free from woe
   I lived among my nation,
I didn't care – I didn't know
   That I was a Crustacean.[1]
I didn't grumble, didn't steal,
   I *never* took to rhyme:
Salt water was my frugal meal,
   And carbonate of lime.'

Reluctantly I turned away,
   No other word he said;
An ancient Trilobite, he lay
   Within his rocky bed.
I did not answer him, for that
   Would have annoyed my pride:
I merely bowed, and raised my hat,
   But in my heart I cried: –

'I wish our brains were not so good,
   I wish our skulls were thicker,
I wish that Evolution could
   Have stopped a little quicker;
For oh, it was a happy plight,
   Of liberty and ease,
To be a simple Trilobite
   In the Silurian seas!

1. He was not a Crustacean. He has since discovered that he was an Arachnid, or something similar. But he says it does not matter. He says they told him wrong once, and they may again. (Kendall's note)

1888   A. MARY F. ROBINSON   Neurasthenia

I watch the happier people of the house
   Come in and out, and talk, and go their ways;
I sit and gaze at them; I cannot rouse
   My heavy mind to share their busy days.

I watch them glide, like skaters on a stream,
   Across the brilliant surface of the world.
But I am underneath: they do not dream
   How deep below the eddying flood is whirl'd.

They cannot come to me, nor I to them;
   But, if a mightier arm could reach and save,
Should I forget the tide I had to stem?
   Should I, like these, ignore the abysmal wave?

Yes! in the radiant air how could I know
How black it is, how fast it is, below?

W. E. HENLEY   *from* In Hospital

II Waiting

A square, squat room (a cellar on promotion),
   Drab to the soul, drab to the very daylight;
 Plasters astray in unnatural-looking tinware;
   Scissors and lint and apothecary's jars.

Here, on a bench a skeleton would writhe from,
   Angry and sore, I wait to be admitted:
   Wait till my heart is lead upon my stomach,
   While at their ease two dressers do their chores.

One has a probe – it feels to me a crowbar.
   A small boy sniffs and shudders after bluestone.
   A poor old tramp explains his poor old ulcers.
   Life is (I think) a blunder and a shame.

The gaunt brown walls
Look infinite in their decent meanness.
There is nothing of home in the noisy kettle,
    The fulsome fire.

The atmosphere
Suggests the trail of a ghostly druggist.
Dressings and lint on the long, lean table –
    Whom are they for?

The patients yawn,
Or lie as in training for shroud and coffin.
A nurse in the corridor scolds and wrangles.
    It's grim and strange.

Far footfalls clank.
The bad burn waits with his head unbandaged.
My neighbour chokes in the clutch of chloral . . .
    O, a gruesome world!

AMY LEVY A Ballade of Religion and Marriage   1889

Swept into limbo is the host
    Of heavenly angels, row on row;
The Father, Son, and Holy Ghost,
    Pale and defeated, rise and go.
The great Jehovah is laid low,
    Vanished his burning bush and rod –
Say, are we doomed to deeper woe?
    Shall marriage go the way of God?

Monogamous, still at our post,
    Reluctantly we undergo
Domestic round of boiled and roast,
    Yet deem the whole proceeding slow.
Daily the secret murmurs grow;
    We are no more content to plod
Along the beaten paths – and so
    Marriage must go the way of God.

Soon, before all men, each shall toast
    The seven strings unto his bow,
Like beacon fires along the coast,
    The flames of love shall glance and glow.
Nor let nor hindrance man shall know,
    From natal bath to funeral sod;
Perennial shall his pleasures flow
    When marriage goes the way of God.

Grant, in a million years at most,
    Folk shall be neither pairs nor odd –
Alas! we sha'n't be there to boast
    'Marriage has gone the way of God!'

(1915)

W. B. YEATS Down by the Salley Gardens

Down by the salley gardens my love and I did meet;
She passed the salley gardens with little snow-white feet.
She bid me take love easy, as the leaves grow on the tree;
But I, being young and foolish, with her would not agree.

In a field by the river my love and I did stand,
And on my leaning shoulder she laid her snow-white hand.
She bid me take life easy, as the grass grows on the weirs;
But I was young and foolish, and now am full of tears.

1891   WILLIAM MORRIS Pomona

I am the ancient Apple-Queen,
As once I was so am I now.
For evermore a hope unseen,
Betwixt the blossom and the bough.

Ah, where's the river's hidden Gold!
And where the windy grave of Troy?
Yet come I as I came of old,
From out the heart of Summer's joy.

RUDYARD KIPLING Danny Deever

'What are the bugles blowin' for?' said Files-on-Parade.
'To turn you out, to turn you out,' the Colour-Sergeant said.
'What makes you look so white, so white?' said Files-on-Parade.
'I'm dreadin' what I've got to watch,' the Colour-Sergeant said.
  For they're hangin' Danny Deever, you can hear the Dead March
     play,
  The regiment's in 'ollow square – they're hangin' him to-day;
  They've taken of his buttons off an' cut his stripes away,
  An' they're hangin' Danny Deever in the mornin'.

'What makes the rear-rank breathe so 'ard?' said Files-on-Parade.
'It's bitter cold, it's bitter cold,' the Colour-Sergeant said.
'What makes that front-rank man fall down?' said Files-on-Parade.
'A touch o' sun, a touch o' sun,' the Colour-Sergeant said.
  They are hangin' Danny Deever, they are marchin' of 'im round,
  They 'ave 'alted Danny Deever by 'is coffin on the ground;
  An' 'e'll swing in 'arf a minute for a sneakin' shootin' hound –
  O they're hangin' Danny Deever in the mornin'!

''Is cot was right-'and cot to mine,' said Files-on-Parade.
''E's sleepin' out an' far to-night,' the Colour-Sergeant said.
'I've drunk 'is beer a score o' times,' said Files-on-Parade.
''E's drinkin' bitter beer alone,' the Colour-Sergeant said.
  They are hangin' Danny Deever, you must mark 'im to 'is place,
  For 'e shot a comrade sleepin' – you must look 'im in the face;
  Nine 'undred of 'is county an' the Regiment's disgrace,
  While they're hangin' Danny Deever in the mornin'.

'What's that so black agin the sun?' said Files-on-Parade.
'It's Danny fightin' 'ard for life,' the Colour-Sergeant said.
'What's that that whimpers over'ead?' said Files-on-Parade.
'It's Danny's soul that's passin' now,' the Colour-Sergeant said.
  For they're done with Danny Deever, you can 'ear the quickstep
     play,
  The regiment's in column, an' they're marchin' us away;
  Ho! the young recruits are shakin', an' they'll want their beer
     to-day,
  After hangin' Danny Deever in the mornin'!

RUDYARD KIPLING Mandalay

By the old Moulmein Pagoda, lookin' lazy at the sea,
There's a Burma girl a-settin', and I know she thinks o' me;
For the wind is in the palm-trees, and the temple-bells they say:
'Come you back, you British soldier; come you back to Mandalay!'
    Come you back to Mandalay,
    Where the old Flotilla lay:
    Can't you 'ear their paddles chunkin' from Rangoon to
        Mandalay?
    On the road to Mandalay,
    Where the flyin'-fishes play,
    An' the dawn comes up like thunder outer China 'crost the Bay!

'Er petticoat was yaller an' 'er little cap was green,
An' 'er name was Supi-yaw-lat – jes' the same as Theebaw's Queen,
An' I seed her first a-smokin' of a whackin' white cheroot,
An' a-wastin' Christian kisses on an 'eathen idol's foot:
    Bloomin' idol made o' mud –
    Wot they called the Great Gawd Budd –
    Plucky lot she cared for idols when I kissed 'er where she stud!
    On the road to Mandalay . . .

When the mist was on the rice-fields an' the sun was droppin' slow,
She'd git 'er little banjo an' she'd sing '*Kulla-lo-lo!*'
With 'er arm upon my shoulder an' 'er cheek agin my cheek
We useter watch the steamers an' the *hathis* pilin' teak.
    Elephints a-pilin' teak
    In the sludgy, squdgy creek,
    Where the silence 'ung that 'eavy you was 'arf afraid to speak!
    On the road to Mandalay . . .

But that's all shove be'ind me – long ago an' fur away,
An' there ain't no 'buses runnin' from the Bank to Mandalay;
An' I'm learnin' 'ere in London what the ten-year soldier tells:
'If you've 'eard the East a-callin', you won't never 'eed naught else.'
    No! you won't 'eed nothin' else
    But them spicy garlic smells,
    An' the sunshine an' the palm-trees an' the tinkly temple-bells;
    On the road to Mandalay . . .

I am sick o' wastin' leather on these gritty pavin'-stones,
An' the blasted English drizzle wakes the fever in my bones;
Tho' I walks with fifty 'ousemaids outer Chelsea to the Strand,
An' they talks a lot o' lovin', but wot do they understand?
    Beefy face an' grubby 'and –
    Law! wot do they understand?
    I've a neater, sweeter maiden in a cleaner, greener land!
    On the road to Mandalay . . .

Ship me somewheres east of Suez, where the best is like the worst,
Where there aren't no Ten Commandments an' a man can raise a
       thirst;
For the temple-bells are callin', an' it's there that I would be –
By the old Moulmein Pagoda, looking lazy at the sea;
    On the road to Mandalay,
    Where the old Flotilla lay,
    With our sick beneath the awnings when we went to Mandalay!
    O the road to Mandalay,
    Where the flyin'-fishes play,
    An' the dawn comes up like thunder outer China 'crost the Bay!

W. B. YEATS The Sorrow of Love

The quarrel of the sparrows in the eaves,
    The full round moon and the star-laden sky,
And the loud song of the ever-singing leaves
    Had hid away earth's old and weary cry.

And then you came with those red mournful lips,
    And with you came the whole of the world's tears,
And all the sorrows of her labouring ships,
    And all burden of her myriad years.

And now the sparrows warring in the eaves,
    The crumbling moon, the white stars in the sky,
And the loud chanting of the unquiet leaves,
    Are shaken with earth's old and weary cry.

ARTHUR SYMONS At the Cavour

Wine, the red coals, the flaring gas,
Bring out a brighter tone in cheeks
That learn at home before the glass
The flush that eloquently speaks.

The blue-grey smoke of cigarettes
Curls from the lessening ends that glow;
The men are thinking of the bets,
The women of the debts, they owe.

Then their eyes meet, and in their eyes
The accustomed smile comes up to call,
A look half miserably wise,
Half heedlessly ironical.

1894   ## JOHN DAVIDSON Thirty Bob a Week

I couldn't touch a stop and turn a screw,
    And set the blooming world a-work for me,
Like such as cut their teeth – I hope, like you –
    On the handle of a skeleton gold key;
I cut mine on a leek, which I eat it every week:
    I'm a clerk at thirty bob as you can see.

But I don't allow it's luck and all a toss;
    There's no such thing as being starred and crossed;
It's just the power of some to be a boss,
    And the bally power of others to be bossed:
I face the music, sir; you bet I ain't a cur;
    Strike me lucky if I don't believe I'm lost!

For like a mole I journey in the dark,
    A-travelling along the underground
From my Pillar'd Halls and broad Suburbean Park,
    To come the daily dull official round;
And home again at night with my pipe all alight,
    A-scheming how to count ten bob a pound.

And it's often very cold and very wet,
    And my missis stitches towels for a hunks;
And the Pillar'd Halls is half of it to let –
    Three rooms about the size of travelling trunks,
And we cough, my wife and I, to dislocate a sigh,
    When the noisy little kids are in their bunks.

But you never hear her do a growl or whine,
    For she's made of flint and roses, very odd;
And I've got to cut my meaning rather fine,
    Or I'd blubber, for I'm made of greens and sod:
So p'r'aps we are in Hell for all that I can tell,
    And lost and damn'd and served up hot to God.

I ain't blaspheming, Mr. Silver-tongue;
    I'm saying things a bit beyond your art:
Of all the rummy starts you ever sprung,
    Thirty bob a week's the rummiest start!
With your science and your books and your the'ries about spooks,
    Did you ever hear of looking in your heart?

I didn't mean your pocket, Mr., no:
    I mean that having children and a wife,
With thirty bob on which to come and go,
    Isn't dancing to the tabor and the fife:
When it doesn't make you drink, by Heaven! it makes you think,
    And notice curious items about life.

I step into my heart and there I meet
    A god-almighty devil singing small,
Who would like to shout and whistle in the street,
    And squelch the passers flat against the wall;
If the whole world was a cake he had the power to take,
    He would take it, ask for more, and eat them all.

And I meet a sort of simpleton beside,
    The kind that life is always giving beans;
With thirty bob a week to keep a bride
    He fell in love and married in his teens:
At thirty bob he stuck; but he knows it isn't luck:
    He knows the seas are deeper than tureens.

And the god-almighty devil and the fool
    That meet me in the High Street on the strike,
When I walk about my heart a-gathering wool,
    Are my good and evil angels if you like.
And both of them together in every kind of weather
    Ride me like a double-seated bike.

That's rough a bit and needs its meaning curled.
    But I have a high old hot un in my mind –
A most engrugious notion of the world,
    That leaves your lightning 'rithmetic behind:
I give it at a glance when I say 'There ain't no chance,
    Nor nothing of the lucky-lottery kind.'

And it's this way that I make it out to be:
    No fathers, mothers, countries, climates – none;
Not Adam was responsible for me,
    Nor society, nor systems, nary one:
A little sleeping seed, I woke – I did, indeed –
    A million years before the blooming sun.

I woke because I thought the time had come;
    Beyond my will there was no other cause;
And everywhere I found myself at home,
    Because I chose to be the thing I was;
And in whatever shape of mollusc or of ape
    I always went according to the laws.

I was the love that chose my mother out;
    I joined two lives and from the union burst;
My weakness and my strength without a doubt
    Are mine alone forever from the first:
It's just the very same with a difference in the name
    As 'Thy will be done.' You say it if you durst!

They say it daily up and down the land
    As easy as you take a drink, it's true;
But the difficultest go to understand,
    And the difficultest job a man can do,
Is to come it brave and meek with thirty bob a week,
    And feel that that's the proper thing for you.

It's a naked child against a hungry wolf;
    It's playing bowls upon a splitting wreck;
It's walking on a string across a gulf
    With millstones fore-and-aft about your neck;
But the thing is daily done by many and many a one;
    And we fall, face forward, fighting, on the deck.

ROBERT LOUIS STEVENSON To S. R. Crockett 1895

On receiving a Dedication

Blows the wind today, and the sun and the rain are flying,
    Blows the wind on the moors today and now,
Where about the graves of the martyrs the whaups are crying,
    My heart remembers how!

Grey recumbent tombs of the dead in desert places,
    Standing-stones on the vacant wine-red moor,
Hills of sheep, and the howes of the silent vanished races,
    And winds, austere and pure:

Be it granted me to behold you again in dying,
    Hills of home! and to hear again the call;
Hear about the graves of the martyrs the peewees crying,
    And hear no more at all.

ALICE MEYNELL Cradle-Song at Twilight

The child not yet is lulled to rest.
    Too young a nurse; the slender Night
So laxly holds him to her breast
    That throbs with flight.

He plays with her, and will not sleep.
    For other playfellows she sighs;
An unmaternal fondness keep
    Her alien eyes.

ALICE MEYNELL Parentage

*'When Augustus Cæsar legislated against the unmarried citizens of
Rome, he declared them to be, in some sort, slayers of the people.'*

Ah! no, not these!
These, who were childless, are not they who gave
So many dead unto the journeying wave,
The helpless nurslings of the cradling seas;
Not they who doomed by infallible decrees
Unnumbered man to the innumerable grave.

But those who slay
Are fathers. Theirs are armies. Death is theirs –
The death of innocences and despairs;
The dying of the golden and the grey.
The sentence, when these speak it, has no Nay.
And she who slays is she who bears, who bears.

MAY PROBYN Triolets

Tête-à-Tête

Behind her big fan,
    With its storks and pagoda,
What a nook for a man!
Behind her big fan
My enchantment began,
    Till my whole heart I showed her
Behind her big fan,
    With its storks and pagoda.

Masquerading

At dawn she unmasked –
    And – oh, heaven! 'twas her sister!
All her love I had asked
Ere at dawn she unmasked;

In her smile I had basked,
    I had coyed her, had kissed her –
At dawn she unmasked –
    And – oh, heaven! 'twas her sister!

A Mésalliance

Is she mine, – and for life, –
    And drinks tea from her saucer!
She eats with her knife –
Is she mine – and for life?
When I asked her to wife
    All her answer was 'Lor', sir!'
Is she mine? and for life?
    And drinks tea from her saucer!

MARY E. COLERIDGE An Insincere Wish Addressed to a
Beggar

1896

We are not near enough to love,
    I can but pity all your woe;
For wealth has lifted me above,
    And falsehood set you down below.

If you were true, we still might be
    Brothers in something more than name;
And were I poor, your love to me
    Would make our differing bonds the same.

But golden gates between us stretch,
    Truth opens her forbidding eyes;
You can't forget that I am rich,
    Nor I that you are telling lies.

Love never comes but at love's call,
    And pity asks for him in vain;
Because I cannot give you all,
    You give me nothing back again.

And you are right with all your wrong,
    For less than all is nothing too;
May Heaven beggar me ere long,
    And Truth reveal herself to you!

(1908)

CHRISTINA ROSSETTI Promises Like Pie-crust

Promise me no promises,
    So will I not promise you;
Keep we both our liberties,
    Never false and never true:
Let us hold the die uncast,
    Free to come as free to go;
For I cannot know your past,
    And of mine what can you know?

You, so warm, may once have been
    Warmer towards another one;
I, so cold, may once have seen
    Sunlight, once have felt the sun:
Who shall show us if it was
    Thus indeed in time of old?
Fades the image from the glass
    And the fortune is not told.

If you promised, you might grieve
    For lost liberty again;
If I promised, I believe
    I should fret to break the chain.
Let us be the friends we were,
    Nothing more but nothing less:
Many thrive on frugal fare
    Who would perish of excess.

ERNEST DOWSON Vitae summa brevis spem nos vetat
incohare longam

They are not long, the weeping and the laughter,
    Love and desire and hate:
I think they have no portion in us after
        We pass the gate.

They are not long, the days of wine and roses:
    Out of a misty dream
Our path emerges for a while, then closes
        Within a dream.

§ A. E. HOUSMAN *from* A Shropshire Lad

XII

When I watch the living meet,
    And the moving pageant file
Warm and breathing through the street
    Where I lodge a little while,

If the heats of hate and lust
    In the house of flesh are strong,
Let me mind the house of dust
    Where my sojourn shall be long.

In the nation that is not
    Nothing stands that stood before;
There revenges are forgot,
    And the hater hates no more;

Lovers lying two and two
    Ask not whom they sleep beside,
And the bridegroom all night through
    Never turns him to the bride.

XL

Into my heart an air that kills
　From yon far country blows:
What are those blue remembered hills,
　What spires, what farms are those?'

That is the land of lost content,
　I see it shining plain,
The happy highways where I went
　And cannot come again.

LII

Far in a western brookland
　That bred me long ago
The poplars stand and tremble
　By pools I used to know.

There, in the windless night-time,
　The wanderer, marvelling why,
Halts on the bridge to hearken
　How soft the poplars sigh.

He hears: no more remembered
　In fields where I was known,
Here I lie down in London
　And turn to rest alone.

There, by the starlit fences,
　The wanderer halts and hears
My soul that lingers sighing
　About the glimmering weirs.

§　§　§

JOHN DAVIDSON A Northern Suburb

Nature selects the longest way,
    And winds about in tortuous grooves;
A thousand years the oaks decay;
    The wrinkled glacier hardly moves.

But here the whetted fangs of change
    Daily devour the old demesne –
The busy farm, the quiet grange,
    The wayside inn, the village green.

In gaudy yellow brick and red,
    With rooting pipes, like creepers rank,
The shoddy terraces o'erspread
    Meadow, and garth, and daisied bank.

With shelves for rooms the houses crowd,
    Like draughty cupboards in a row –
Ice-chests when wintry winds are loud,
    Ovens when summer breezes blow.

Roused by the fee'd policeman's knock,
    And sad that day should come again,
Under the stars the workmen flock
    In haste to reach the workmen's train.

For here dwell those who must fulfil
    Dull tasks in uncongenial spheres,
Who toil through dread of coming ill,
    And not with hope of happier years –

The lowly folk who scarcely dare
    Conceive themselves perhaps misplaced,
Whose prize for unremitting care
    Is only not to be disgraced.

1897 ARTHUR SYMONS White Heliotrope

The feverish room and that white bed,
    The tumbled skirts upon a chair,
    The novel flung half-open, where
Hat, hair-pins, puffs, and paints, are spread;

The mirror that has sucked your face
    Into its secret deep of deeps;
    And there mysteriously keeps
Forgotten memories of grace;

And you, half dressed and half awake,
    Your slant eyes strangely watching me,
    And I, who watch you drowsily,
With eyes that, having slept not, ache;

This (need one dread? nay, dare one hope?)
    Will rise, a ghost of memory, if
    Ever again my handkerchief
Is scented with White Heliotrope.

RUDYARD KIPLING Recessional

1897

God of our fathers, known of old,
    Lord of our far-flung battle-line,
Beneath whose awful Hand we hold
    Dominion over palm and pine –
Lord God of Hosts, be with us yet,
Lest we forget – lest we forget!

The tumult and the shouting dies;
    The Captains and the Kings depart:
Still stands Thine ancient sacrifice,
    An humble and a contrite heart.
Lord God of Hosts, be with us yet,
Lest we forget – lest we forget!

Far-called, our navies melt away;
   On dune and headland sinks the fire:
Lo, all our pomp of yesterday
   Is one with Nineveh and Tyre!
Judge of the Nations, spare us yet,
Lest we forget – lest we forget!

If, drunk with sight of power, we loose
   Wild tongues that have not Thee in awe,
Such boastings as the Gentiles use,
   Or lesser breeds without the Law –
Lord God of Hosts, be with us yet,
Lest we forget – lest we forget!

For heathen heart that puts her trust
   In reeking tube and iron shard,
All valiant dust that builds on dust,
   And guarding, calls not Thee to guard,
For frantic boast and foolish word –
Thy mercy on Thy People, Lord!

OSCAR WILDE *from* The Ballad of Reading Gaol   **1898**

*In Memoriam C. T. W. sometime Trooper of the Royal Horse
Guards Obiit H. M. Prison, Reading, Berkshire July 7, 1896*

I

He did not wear his scarlet coat,
   For blood and wine are red,
And blood and wine were on his hands
   When they found him with the dead,
The poor dead woman whom he loved,
   And murdered in her bed.

He walked amongst the Trial Men
   In a suit of shabby gray;
A cricket cap was on his head,
   And his step seemed light and gay;
But I never saw a man who looked
   So wistfully at the day.

I never saw a man who looked
    With such a wistful eye
Upon that little tent of blue
    Which prisoners call the sky,
And at every drifting cloud that went
    With sails of silver by.

I walked, with other souls in pain,
    Within another ring,
And was wondering if the man had done
    A great or little thing,
When a voice behind me whispered low,
    'That fellow's got to swing.'

Dear Christ! the very prison walls
    Suddenly seemed to reel,
And the sky above my head became
    Like a casque of scorching steel;
And, though I was a soul in pain,
    My pain I could not feel.

I only knew what hunted thought
    Quickened his step, and why
He looked upon the garish day
    With such a wistful eye;
The man had killed the thing he loved,
    And so he had to die.

*

Yet each man kills the thing he loves,
    By each let this be heard,
Some do it with a bitter look,
    Some with a flattering word,
The coward does it with a kiss,
    The brave man with a sword!

Some kill their love when they are young,
    And some when they are old;
Some strangle with the hands of Lust,
    Some with the hands of Gold:
The kindest use a knife, because
    The dead so soon grow cold.

Some love too little, some too long,
    Some sell, and others buy;
Some do the deed with many tears,
    And some without a sigh:
For each man kills the thing he loves.
    Yet each man does not die.

He does not die a death of shame
    On a day of dark disgrace,
Nor have a noose about his neck,
    Nor a cloth upon his face,
Nor drop feet foremost through the floor
    Into an empty space.

*

He does not sit with silent men
    Who watch him night and day;
Who watch him when he tries to weep,
    And when he tries to pray;
Who watch him lest himself should rob
    The prison of its prey.

He does not wake at dawn to see
    Dread figures throng his room,
The shivering Chaplain robed in white,
    The Sheriff stern with gloom,
And the Governor all in shiny black,
    With the yellow face of Doom.

He does not rise in piteous haste
    To put on convict-clothes,
While some coarse-mouthed Doctor gloats, and notes
    Each new and nerve-twitched pose,
Fingering a watch whose little ticks
    Are like horrible hammer-blows.

He does not know that sickening thirst
    That sands one's throat, before
The hangman with his gardener's gloves
    Slips through the padded door,
And binds one with three leathern thongs,
    That the throat may thirst no more.

He does not bend his head to hear
   The Burial Office read,
Nor, while the terror of his soul
   Tells him he is not dead,
Cross his own coffin, as he moves
   Into the hideous shed.

He does not stare upon the air
   Through a little roof of glass:
He does not pray with lips of clay
   For his agony to pass;
Nor feel upon his shuddering cheek
   The kiss of Caiaphas.

W. E. HENLEY To W. R.

Madam Life's a piece in bloom
   Death goes dogging everywhere:
She's the tenant of the room,
   He's the ruffian on the stair.

You shall see her as a friend,
   You shall bilk him once and twice;
But he'll trap you in the end,
   And he'll stick you for her price.

With his kneebones at your chest,
   And his knuckles in your throat,
You would reason – plead – protest!
   Clutching at her petticoat;

But she's heard it all before,
   Well she knows you've had your fun,
Gingerly she gains the door,
   And your little job is done.

(written 1877)

THOMAS HARDY Neutral Tones

We stood by a pond that winter day,
And the sun was white, as though chidden of God,
And a few leaves lay on the starving sod;
   – They had fallen from an ash, and were gray.

Your eyes on me were as eyes that rove
Over tedious riddles of years ago;
And some words played between us to and fro
   On which lost the more by our love.

The smile on your mouth was the deadest thing
Alive enough to have strength to die;
And a grin of bitterness swept thereby
   Like an ominous bird a-wing. . . .

Since then, keen lessons that love deceives,
And wrings with wrong, have shaped to me
Your face, and the God-curst sun, and a tree,
   And a pond edged with grayish leaves.

                             (written 1867)

THOMAS HARDY Thoughts of Phena

At News of Her Death

   Not a line of her writing have I,
      Not a thread of her hair,
No mark of her late time as dame in her dwelling, whereby
      I may picture her there;
     And in vain do I urge my unsight
       To conceive my lost prize
At her close, whom I knew when her dreams were upbrimming with
      light,
       And with laughter her eyes.

What scenes spread around her last days,
    Sad, shining, or dim?
Did her gifts and compassions enray and enarch her sweet ways
    With an aureate nimb?
    Or did life-light decline from her years,
    And mischances control
Her full day-star; unease, or regret, or forebodings, or fears
    Disennoble her soul?

    Thus I do but the phantom retain
    Of the maiden of yore
As my relic; yet haply the best of her – fined in my brain
    It may be the more
    That no line of her writing have I,
    Nor a thread of her hair,
No mark of her late time as dame in her dwelling, whereby
    I may picture her there.

1900   THOMAS HARDY   The Darkling Thrush

I leant upon a coppice gate
  When Frost was spectre-gray,
And Winter's dregs made desolate
  The weakening eye of day.
The tangled bine-stems scored the sky
  Like strings of broken lyres,
And all mankind that haunted nigh
  Had sought their household fires.

The land's sharp features seemed to be
  The Century's corpse outleant,
His crypt the cloudy canopy,
  The wind his death-lament.
The ancient pulse of germ and birth
  Was shrunken hard and dry,
And every spirit upon earth
  Seemed fervourless as I.

At once a voice arose among
  The bleak twigs overhead
In a full-hearted evensong
  Of joy illimited;

An aged thrush, frail, gaunt, and small,
   In blast-beruffled plume,
Had chosen thus to fling his soul
   Upon the growing gloom.

So little cause for carolings
   Of such ecstatic sound
Was written on terrestrial things
   Afar or nigh around,
That I could think there trembled through
   His happy good-night air
Some blessed Hope, whereof he knew
   And I was unaware.

WALTER DE LA MARE The Birthnight   1906

Dearest, it was a night
That in its darkness rocked Orion's stars;
A sighing wind ran faintly white
Along the willows, and the cedar boughs
Laid their wide hands in stealthy peace across
The starry silence of their antique moss:
No sound save rushing air
Cold, yet all sweet with Spring,
And in thy mother's arms, couched weeping there,
      Thou, lovely thing.

WALTER DE LA MARE Autumn

There is a wind where the rose was;
Cold rain where sweet grass was;
   And clouds like sheep
   Stream o'er the steep
Grey skies where the lark was.

Nought gold where your hair was;
Nought warm where your hand was;
   But phantom, forlorn,
   Beneath the thorn,
Your ghost where your face was.

Sad winds where your voice was;
Tears, tears where my heart was;
   And ever with me,
   Child, ever with me,
Silence where hope was.

WALTER DE LA MARE Napoleon

'What is the world, O soldiers?
      It is I:
I, this incessant snow,
   This northern sky;
Soldiers, this solitude
   Through which we go
      Is I.'

1908   ## MARY E. COLERIDGE No Newspapers

Where, to me, is the loss
   Of the scenes they saw – of the sounds they heard;
A butterfly flits across,
   Or a bird;
The moss is growing on the wall,
   I heard the leaf of the poppy fall.

MICHAEL FIELD (KATHERINE BRADLEY and EDITH COOPER) The Mummy Invokes His Soul

Down to me quickly, down! I am such dust,
Baked, pressed together; let my flesh be fanned
With thy fresh breath; come from thy reedy land
Voiceful with birds; divert me, for I lust
To break, to crumble – prick with pores this crust! –
And fall apart, delicious, loosening sand.
Oh, joy, I feel thy breath, I feel thy hand
That searches for my heart, and trembles just
Where once it beat. How light thy touch, thy frame!
Surely thou perchest on the summer trees . . .

And the garden that we loved? Soul, take thine ease,
I am content, so thou enjoy the same
Sweet terraces and founts, content, for thee,
To burn in this immense torpidity.

JOHN DAVIDSON Snow

1909

I

'Who affirms that crystals are alive?'
    I affirm it, let who will deny:–
Crystals are engendered, wax and thrive,
    Wane and wither: I have seen them die.

Trust me, masters, crystals have their day
    Eager to attain the perfect norm,
Lit with purpose, potent to display
    Facet, angle, colour, beauty, form.

II

Water-crystals need for flower and root
    Sixty clear degrees, no less, no more;
Snow, so fickle, still in this acute
    Angle thinks, and learns no other lore:

Such its life, and such its pleasure is,
    Such its art and traffic, such its gain,
Evermore in new conjunctions this
    Admirable angle to maintain.

Crystalcraft in every flower and flake
    Snow exhibits, of the welkin free:
Crystalline are crystals for the sake,
    All and singular, of crystalry.

Yet does every crystal of the snow
    Individualise, a seedling sown
Broadcast, but instinct with power to grow
    Beautiful in beauty of its own.

Every flake with all its prongs and dints
    Burns ecstatic as a new-lit star:
Men are not more diverse, finger-prints
    More dissimilar than snow-flakes are.

Worlds of men and snow endure, increase,
    Woven of power and passion to defy
Time and travail: only races cease,
    Individual men and crystals die.

III

Jewelled shapes of snow whose feathery showers,
    Fallen or falling wither at a breath,
All afraid are they, and loth as flowers
    Beasts and men to tread the way to death.

Once I saw upon an object-glass,
    Martyred underneath a microscope,
One elaborate snow-flake slowly pass,
    Dying hard, beyond the reach of hope.

Still from shape to shape the crystal changed,
    Writhing in its agony; and still,
Less and less elaborate, arranged
    Potently the angle of its will.

Tortured to a simple final form,
    Angles six and six divergent beams,
Lo, in death it touched the perfect norm
    Verifying all its crystal dreams!

IV

Such the noble tragedy of one
    Martyred snow-flake. Who can tell the fate
Heinous and uncouth of showers undone,
    Fallen in cities! – showers that expiate

Errant lives from polar worlds adrift
    Where the great millennial snows abide;
Castaways from mountain-chains that lift
    Snowy summits in perennial pride;

Nomad snows, or snows in evil day
    Born to urban ruin, to be tossed,
Trampled, shovelled, ploughed, and swept away
    Down the seething sewers: all the frost

Flowers of heaven melted up with lees,
    Offal, recrement, but every flake
Showing to the last in fixed degrees
    Perfect crystals for the crystal's sake.

v

Usefulness of snow is but a chance
    Here in temperate climes with winter sent,
Sheltering earth's prolonged hibernal trance:
    All utility is accident.

Sixty clear degrees the joyful snow,
    Practising economy of means,
Fashions endless beauty in, and so
    Glorifies the universe with scenes

Arctic and antarctic: stainless shrouds,
    Ermine woven in silvery frost, attire
Peaks in every land among the clouds
    Crowned with snows to catch the morning's fire.

J. M. SYNGE On an Island

You've plucked a curlew, drawn a hen,
Washed the shirts of seven men,
You've stuffed my pillow, stretched the sheet,
And filled the pan to wash your feet,
You've cooped the pullets, wound the clock,
And rinsed the young men's drinking crock;
And now we'll dance to jigs and reels,
Nailed boots chasing girls' naked heels,
Until your father'll start to snore,
And Jude, now you're married, will stretch on the floor.

1910   J. M. SYNGE The 'Mergency Man

He was lodging above in Coom,
And he'd the half of the bailiff's room.

Till a black night came in Coomasaharn
A night of rains you'd swamp a star in.

'To-night,' says he, 'with the devil's weather
The hares itself will quit the heather,

I'll catch my boys with a latch on the door,
And serve my process on near a score.'

The night was black at the fording place
And the flood was up in a whitened race
But devil a bit he'd turn his face,

Then the peelers said, 'Now mind your lepping,
How can you see the stones for stepping?

We'll wash our hands of your bloody job.'
'Wash and welcome,' says he, 'begob.'

He made two leps with a run and dash,
Then the peelers heard a yell and splash.

And the 'Mergency man in two days and a bit
Was found in the ebb tide stuck in a net.

1911   W. H. DAVIES Sheep

When I was once in Baltimore,
    A man came up to me and cried,
'Come, I have eighteen hundred sheep,
    And we will sail on Tuesday's tide.

TITLE *'Mergency man* Tax-collector

'If you will sail with me, young man,
    I'll pay you fifty shillings down;
These eighteen hundred sheep I take
    From Baltimore to Glasgow town.'

He paid me fifty shillings down,
    I sailed with eighteen hundred sheep;
We soon had cleared the harbour's mouth,
    We soon were in the salt sea deep.

The first night we were out at sea
    Those sheep were quiet in their mind;
The second night they cried with fear –
    They smelt no pastures in the wind.

They sniffed, poor things, for their green fields,
    They cried so loud I could not sleep:
For fifty thousand shillings down
    I would not sail again with sheep.

THOMAS HARDY The Convergence of the Twain   **1912**

(Lines on the loss of the Titanic)

        In a solitude of the sea
        Deep from human vanity,
And the pride of Life that planned her, stilly couches she.

        Steel chambers, late the pyres
        Of her salamandrine fires,
Cold currents thrid, and turn to rhythmic tidal lyres.

        Over the mirrors meant
        To glass the opulent
The sea-worm crawls – grotesque, slimed, dumb, indifferent.

        Jewels in joy designed
        To ravish the sensuous mind
Lie lightless, all their sparkles bleared and black and blind.

Dim moon-eyed fishes near
Gaze at the gilded gear
And query: 'What does this vaingloriousness down here?' . . .

Well: while was fashioning
This creature of cleaving wing,
The Immanent Will that stirs and urges everything

Prepared a sinister mate
For her – so gaily great –
A Shape of Ice, for the time far and dissociate.

And as the smart ship grew
In stature, grace, and hue,
In shadowy silent distance grew the Iceberg too.

Alien they seemed to be:
No mortal eye could see
The intimate welding of their later history,

Or sign that they were bent
By paths coincident
On being anon twin halves of one august event,

Till the Spinner of the Years
Said 'Now!' And each one hears,
And consummation comes, and jars two hemispheres.

T. E. HULME Autumn

A touch of cold in the Autumn night –
I walked abroad,
And saw the ruddy moon lean over a hedge
Like a red-faced farmer.
I did not stop to speak, but nodded,
And round about were the wistful stars
With white faces like town children.

T. E. HULME Image

Old houses were scaffolding once
                       and workmen whistling.

(1960)

EZRA POUND The Return

See, they return; ah, see the tentative
    Movements, and the slow feet,
    The trouble in the pace and the uncertain
    Wavering!

See, they return, one, and by one,
With fear, as half-awakened;
As if the snow should hesitate
And murmur in the wind,
              and half turn back;
These were the 'Wing'd-with-Awe,'
              Inviolable.

Gods of the wingèd shoe!
With them the silver hounds,
              sniffing the trace of air!

Haie! Haie!
    These were the swift to harry;
These the keen-scented;
These were the souls of blood.

Slow on the leash,
             pallid the leash-men!

EZRA POUND In a Station of the Metro

1913

The apparition   of these faces   in the crowd :
Petals   on a wet, black   bough   .

1914   H. D. (HILDA DOOLITTLE) Oread

Whirl up, sea –
whirl your pointed pines,
splash your great pines
on our rocks,
hurl your green over us,
cover us with your pools of fir.

§ THOMAS HARDY *from* Poems of 1912–13

The Walk

You did not walk with me
Of late to the hill-top tree
    By the gated ways,
    As in earlier days;
    You were weak and lame,
    So you never came,
And I went alone, and I did not mind,
Not thinking of you as left behind.

I walked up there to-day
Just in the former way:
    Surveyed around
    The familiar ground
    By myself again:
    What difference, then?
Only that underlying sense
Of the look of a room on returning thence.

The Voice

Woman much missed, how you call to me, call to me,
Saying that now you are not as you were
When you had changed from the one who was all to me,
But as at first, when our day was fair.

Can it be you that I hear? Let me view you, then,
Standing as when I drew near to the town
Where you would wait for me: yes, as I knew you then,
Even to the original air-blue gown!

Or is it only the breeze, in its listlessness
Travelling across the wet mead to me here,
You being ever dissolved to wan wistlessness,
Heard no more again far or near?

    Thus I; faltering forward,
    Leaves around me falling,
Wind oozing thin through the thorn from norward,
    And the woman calling.

After a Journey

Hereto I come to view a voiceless ghost;
   Whither, O whither will its whim now draw me?
Up the cliff, down, till I'm lonely, lost,
   And the unseen waters' ejaculations awe me.
Where you will next be there's no knowing,
   Facing round about me everywhere,
      With your nut-coloured hair,
And gray eyes, and rose-flush coming and going.

Yes: I have re-entered your olden haunts at last;
   Through the years, through the dead scenes I have tracked you;
What have you now found to say of our past –
   Scanned across the dark space wherein I have lacked you?
Summer gave us sweets, but autumn wrought division?
   Things were not lastly as firstly well
      With us twain, you tell?
But all's closed now, despite Time's derision.

I see what you are doing: you are leading me on
   To the spots we knew when we haunted here together,
The waterfall, above which the mist-bow shone
   At the then fair hour in the then fair weather,

And the cave just under, with a voice still so hollow
    That it seems to call out to me from forty years ago,
        When you were all aglow,
And not the thin ghost that I now fraily follow!

Ignorant of what there is flitting here to see,
    The waked birds preen and the seals flop lazily,
Soon you will have, Dear, to vanish from me,
    For the stars close their shutters and the dawn whitens hazily.
Trust me, I mind not, though Life lours,
    The bringing me here; nay, bring me here again!
        I am just the same as when
Our days were a joy, and our paths through flowers.

At Castle Boterel

As I drive to the junction of lane and highway,
    And the drizzle bedrenches the waggonette,
I look behind at the fading byway,
    And see on its slope, now glistening wet,
        Distinctly yet

Myself and a girlish form benighted
    In dry March weather. We climb the road
Beside a chaise. We had just alighted
    To ease the sturdy pony's load
        When he sighed and slowed.

What we did as we climbed, and what we talked of
    Matters not much, nor to what it led, –
Something that life will not be balked of
    Without rude reason till hope is dead,
        And feeling fled.

It filled but a minute. But was there ever
    A time of such quality, since or before,
In that hill's story? To one mind never,
    Though it has been climbed, foot-swift, foot-sore,
        By thousands more.

Primaeval rocks form the road's steep border,
   And much have they faced there, first and last,
Of the transitory in Earth's long order;
   But what they record in colour and cast
      Is – that we two passed.

And to me, though Time's unflinching rigour,
   In mindless rote, has ruled from sight
The substance now, one phantom figure
   Remains on the slope, as when that night
      Saw us alight.

I look and see it there, shrinking, shrinking,
   I look back at it amid the rain
For the very last time; for my sand is sinking,
   And I shall traverse old love's domain
      Never again.

§   §   §

W. B. YEATS The Cold Heaven

Suddenly I saw the cold and rook-delighting heaven
That seemed as though ice burned and was but the more ice,
And thereupon imagination and heart were driven
So wild that every casual thought of that and this
Vanished, and left but memories, that should be out of season
With the hot blood of youth, of love crossed long ago;
And I took all the blame out of all sense and reason,
Until I cried and trembled and rocked to and fro,
Riddled with light. Ah! when the ghost begins to quicken,
Confusion of the death-bed over, is it sent
Out naked on the roads, as the books say, and stricken
By the injustice of the skies for punishment?

W. B. YEATS The Magi

Now as at all times I can see in the mind's eye,
In their stiff, painted clothes, the pale unsatisfied ones
Appear and disappear in the blue depth of the sky
With all their ancient faces like rain-beaten stones,
And all their helms of silver hovering side by side,
And all their eyes still fixed, hoping to find once more,
Being by Calvary's turbulence unsatisfied,
The uncontrollable mystery on the bestial floor.

CHARLOTTE MEW Fame

Sometimes in the over-heated house, but not for long,
        Smirking and speaking rather loud,
    I see myself among the crowd,
Where no one fits the singer to his song,
Or sifts the unpainted from the painted faces
Of the people who are always on my stair;
They were not with me when I walked in heavenly places;
        But could I spare
In the blind Earth's great silences and spaces,
    The din, the scuffle, the long stare
    If I went back and it was not there?
Back to the old known things that are the new,
The folded glory of the gorse, the sweet-briar air,
To the larks that cannot praise us, knowing nothing of what we do
    And the divine, wise trees that do not care
Yet, to leave Fame, still with such eyes and that bright hair!
God! If I might! And before I go hence
        Take in her stead
        To our tossed bed,
One little dream, no matter how small, how wild.
Just now, I think I found it in a field, under a fence –
A frail, dead, new-born lamb, ghostly and pitiful and white,
        A blot upon the night,
        The moon's dropped child!

EZRA POUND The Gypsy

'Est-ce que vous avez vu des autres – des
camarades – avec des singes ou des ours?'
                    A Stray Gipsy – A.D. 1912

That was the top of the walk, when he said:
'Have you seen any others, any of our lot,
With apes or bears?'
                    – A brown upstanding fellow
Not like the half-castes,
                    up on the wet road near Clermont.
The wind came, and the rain,
And mist clotted about the trees in the valley,
And I'd the long ways behind me,
                    gray Arles and Biaucaire,
And he said, 'Have you seen any of our lot?'
I'd seen a lot of his lot . . .
                    ever since Rhodez,
Coming down from the fair
                    of St. John,
With caravans, but never an ape or a bear.

§ EZRA POUND *from* Cathay

from the Chinese of Rihaku

The River-Merchant's Wife: A Letter

While my hair was still cut straight across my forehead
I played about the front gate, pulling flowers.
You came by on bamboo stilts, playing horse,
You walked about my seat, playing with blue plums.
And we went on living in the village of Chokan:
Two small people, without dislike or suspicion.

At fourteen I married My Lord you.
I never laughed, being bashful.
Lowering my head, I looked at the wall.
Called to, a thousand times, I never looked back.

At fifteen I stopped scowling,
I desired my dust to be mingled with yours
Forever and forever and forever.
Why should I climb the look out?

At sixteen you departed,
You went into far Ku-to-yen, by the river of swirling eddies,
And you have been gone five months.
The monkeys make sorrowful noise overhead.
You dragged your feet when you went out.
By the gate now, the moss is grown, the different mosses,
Too deep to clear them away!
The leaves fall early this autumn, in wind.
The paired butterflies are already yellow with August
Over the grass in the West garden;
They hurt me. I grow older.
If you are coming down through the narrows of the river Kiang,
Please let me know beforehand,
And I will come out to meet you
                    As far as Cho-fu-Sa.

Lament of the Frontier Guard

By the North Gate, the wind blows full of sand,
Lonely from the beginning of time until now!
Trees fall, the grass goes yellow with autumn.
I climb the towers and towers
            to watch out the barbarous land:
Desolate castle, the sky, the wide desert.
There is no wall left to this village.
Bones white with a thousand frosts,
High heaps, covered with trees and grass;
Who brought this to pass?
Who has brought the flaming imperial anger?
Who has brought the army with drums and with kettle-drums?
Barbarous kings.
A gracious spring, turned to blood-ravenous autumn,

A turmoil of wars-men, spread over the middle kingdom,
Three hundred and sixty thousand,
And sorrow, sorrow like rain.
Sorrow to go, and sorrow, sorrow returning.
Desolate, desolate fields,
And no children of warfare upon them,
   No longer the men for offence and defence.
Ah, how shall you know the dreary sorrow at the North Gate,
With Riboku's name forgotten,
And we guardsmen fed to the tigers.

§   §   §

RUPERT BROOKE Peace

Now, God be thanked Who has matched us with His hour,
 And caught our youth, and wakened us from sleeping,
With hand made sure, clear eye, and sharpened power.
 To turn, as swimmers into cleanness leaping,
Glad from a world grown old and cold and weary.
 Leave the sick hearts that honour could not move,
And half-men, and their dirty songs and dreary,
 And all the little emptiness of love!

Oh! we, who have known shame, we have found release there,
 Where there's no ill, no grief, but sleep has mending,
  Naught broken save this body, lost but breath:
Nothing to shake the laughing heart's long peace there
 But only agony, and that has ending:
  And the worst friend and enemy is but Death.

RUPERT BROOKE Heaven

Fish (fly-replete, in depth of June,
Dawdling away their wat'ry noon)
Ponder deep wisdom, dark or clear,
Each secret fishy hope or fear.

Fish say, they have their Stream and Pond;
But is there anything Beyond?
This life cannot be All, they swear,
For how unpleasant, if it were!
One may not doubt that, somehow, Good
Shall come of Water and of Mud;
And, sure, the reverent eye must see
A Purpose in Liquidity.
We darkly know, by Faith we cry,
The future is not Wholly Dry.
Mud unto mud! – Death eddies near –
Not here the appointed End, not here!
But somewhere, beyond Space and Time,
Is wetter water, slimier slime!
And there (they trust) there swimmeth One
Who swam ere rivers were begun,
Immense, of fishy form and mind,
Squamous, omnipotent, and kind;
And under that Almighty Fin,
The littlest fish may enter in.
Oh! never fly conceals a hook,
Fish say, in the Eternal Brook,
But more than mundane weeds are there,
And mud, celestially fair;
Fat caterpillars drift around,
And Paradisal grubs are found;
Unfading moths, immortal flies,
And the worm that never dies.
And in that Heaven of all their wish,
There shall be no more land, say fish.

1916 D. H. LAWRENCE Sorrow

Why does the thin grey strand
Floating up from the forgotten
Cigarette between my fingers,
Why does it trouble me?

Ah, you will understand;
When I carried my mother downstairs,
A few times only, at the beginning
Of her soft-foot malady,

I should find, for a reprimand
To my gaiety, a few long grey hairs
On the breast of my coat; and one by one
I watched them float up the dark chimney.

CHARLES HAMILTON SORLEY

When you see millions of the mouthless dead
Across your dreams in pale battalions go,
Say not soft things as other men have said,
That you'll remember. For you need not so.
Give them not praise. For, deaf, how should they know
It is not curses heaped on each gashed head?
Nor tears. Their blind eyes see not your tears flow.
Nor honour. It is easy to be dead.
Say only this, 'They are dead.' Then add thereto,
'Yet many a better one has died before.'
Then, scanning all the o'ercrowded mass, should you
Perceive one face that you loved heretofore,
It is a spook. None wears the face you knew.
Great death has made all his for evermore.

EDWARD THOMAS Cock-Crow

Out of the wood of thoughts that grows by night
To be cut down by the sharp axe of light, –
Out of the night, two cocks together crow,
Cleaving the darkness with a silver blow:
And bright before my eyes twin trumpeters stand,
Heralds of splendour, one at either hand,
Each facing each as in a coat of arms:
The milkers lace their boots up at the farms.

EDWARD THOMAS Aspens

All day and night, save winter, every weather,
Above the inn, the smithy, and the shop,
The aspens at the cross-roads talk together
Of rain, until their last leaves fall from the top.

Out of the blacksmith's cavern comes the ringing
Of hammer, shoe, and anvil; out of the inn
The clink, the hum, the roar, the random singing –
The sounds that for these fifty years have been.

The whisper of the aspens is not drowned,
And over lightless pane and footless road,
Empty as sky, with every other sound
Not ceasing, calls their ghosts from their abode,

A silent smithy, a silent inn, nor fails
In the bare moonlight or the thick-furred gloom,
In tempest or the night of nightingales,
To turn the cross-roads to a ghostly room.

And it would be the same were no house near.
Over all sorts of weather, men, and times,
Aspens must shake their leaves and men may hear
But need not listen, more than to my rhymes.

Whatever wind blows, while they and I have leaves
We cannot other than an aspen be
That ceaselessly, unreasonably grieves,
Or so men think who like a different tree.

ANNA WICKHAM The Fired Pot

In our town, people live in rows.
The only irregular thing in a street is the steeple;
And where that points to, God only knows,
And not the poor disciplined people!

And I have watched the women growing old,
Passionate about pins, and pence, and soap,
Till the heart within my wedded breast grew cold,
And I lost hope.

But a young soldier came to our town,
He spoke his mind most candidly.
He asked me quickly to lie down,
And that was very good for me.

For though I gave him no embrace –
Remembering my duty –
He altered the expression of my face,
And gave me back my beauty.

CHARLOTTE MEW À quoi bon dire

Seventeen years ago you said
    Something that sounded like Good-bye;
    And everybody thinks that you are dead,
            But I.

    So I, as I grow stiff and cold
To this and that say Good-bye too;
    And everybody sees that I am old
            But you.

    And one fine morning in a sunny lane
Some boy and girl will meet and kiss and swear
    That nobody can love their way again
            While over there
You will have smiled, I shall have tossed your hair.

CHARLOTTE MEW The Quiet House

When we were children old Nurse used to say
    The house was like an auction or a fair
    Until the lot of us were safe in bed.
    It has been quiet as the country-side
    Since Ted and Janey and then Mother died

And Tom crossed Father and was sent away.
After the lawsuit he could not hold up his head,
   Poor Father, and he does not care
   For people here, or to go anywhere.

To get away to Aunt's for that week-end
   Was hard enough; (since then, a year ago,
   He scarcely lets me slip out of his sight –)
At first I did not like my cousin's friend,
   I did not think I should remember him:
   His voice has gone, his face is growing dim
And if I like him now I do not know.
   He frightened me before he smiled –
   He did not ask me if he might –
   He said that he would come one Sunday night,
   He spoke to me as if I were a child.

No year has been like this that has just gone by;
   It may be that what Father says is true,
If things are so it does not matter why:
   But everything has burned, and not quite through.
   The colours of the world have turned
   To flame, the blue, the gold has burned
In what used to be such a leaden sky.
When you are burned quite through you die.

   Red is the strangest pain to bear;
In Spring the leaves on the budding trees;
In Summer the roses are worse than these,
   More terrible than they are sweet:
   A rose can stab you across the street
     Deeper than any knife:
   And the crimson haunts you everywhere –
Thin shafts of sunlight, like the ghosts of reddened swords
     have struck our stair
As if, coming down, you had spilt your life.

   I think that my soul is red
     Like the soul of a sword or a scarlet flower:
   But when these are dead
     They have had their hour.

I shall have had mine, too,
    For from head to feet,
I am burned and stabbed half through,
    And the pain is deadly sweet.
The things that kill us seem
    Blind to the death they give:
It is only in our dream
    The things that kill us live.

The room is shut where Mother died,
    The other rooms are as they were,
The world goes on the same outside,
    The sparrows fly across the Square,
    The children play as we four did there,
    The trees grow green and brown and bare,
The sun shines on the dead Church spire,
    And nothing lives here but the fire,
While Father watches from his chair
        Day follows day
The same, or now and then, a different grey,
        Till, like his hair,
Which Mother said was wavy once and bright,
        They will all turn white.

To-night I heard a bell again –
Outside it was the same mist of fine rain,
    The lamps just lighted down the long, dim street,
        No one for me –
    I think it is myself I go to meet:
I do not care; some day I *shall* not think; I shall not *be*!

T. S. ELIOT The Love Song of J. Alfred Prufrock   1917

S'io credessi che mia risposta fosse
a persona che mai tornasse al mondo,
questa fiamma staria senza più scosse.
Ma per ciò che giammai di questo fondo
non tornò vivo alcun, si'i'odo il vero,
senza tema d'infamia ti rispondo.

    Let us go then, you and I,
When the evening is spread out against the sky

Like a patient etherised upon a table;
Let us go, through certain half-deserted streets,
The muttering retreats
Of restless nights in one-night cheap hotels
And sawdust restaurants with oyster-shells:
Streets that follow like a tedious argument
Of insidious intent
To lead you to an overwhelming question . . .
Oh, do not ask, 'What is it?'
Let us go and make our visit.

In the room the women come and go
Talking of Michelangelo.

The yellow fog that rubs its back upon the window-panes,
The yellow smoke that rubs its muzzle on the window-panes,
Licked its tongue into the corners of the evening,
Lingered upon the pools that stand in drains,
Let fall upon its back the soot that falls from chimneys,
Slipped by the terrace, made a sudden leap,
And seeing that it was a soft October night,
Curled once about the house, and fell asleep.

And indeed there will be time
For the yellow smoke that slides along the street
Rubbing its back upon the window-panes;
There will be time, there will be time
To prepare a face to meet the faces that you meet;
There will be time to murder and create,
And time for all the works and days of hands
That lift and drop a question on your plate;
Time for you and time for me,
And time yet for a hundred indecisions,
And for a hundred visions and revisions,
Before the taking of a toast and tea.

In the room the women come and go
Talking of Michelangelo.

And indeed there will be time
To wonder, 'Do I dare?' and, 'Do I dare?'
Time to turn back and descend the stair,
With a bald spot in the middle of my hair –
(They will say: 'How his hair is growing thin!')

My morning coat, my collar mounting firmly to the chin,
My necktie rich and modest, but asserted by a simple pin –
(They will say: 'But how his arms and legs are thin!')
Do I dare
Disturb the universe?
In a minute there is time
For decisions and revisions which a minute will reverse.

For I have known them all already, known them all –
Have known the evenings, mornings, afternoons,
I have measured out my life with coffee spoons;
I know the voices dying with a dying fall
Beneath the music from a farther room.
    So how should I presume?

And I have known the eyes already, known them all –
The eyes that fix you in a formulated phrase,
And when I am formulated, sprawling on a pin,
When I am pinned and wriggling on the wall,
Then how should I begin
To spit out all the butt-ends of my days and ways?
    And how should I presume?

And I have known the arms already, known them all –
Arms that are braceleted and white and bare
(But in the lamplight, downed with light brown hair!)
Is it perfume from a dress
That makes me so digress?
Arms that lie along a table, or wrap about a shawl.
    And should I then presume?
    And how should I begin?

    .   .   .   .   .

Shall I say, I have gone at dusk through narrow streets
And watched the smoke that rises from the pipes
Of lonely men in shirt-sleeves, leaning out of windows? . . .

I should have been a pair of ragged claws
Scuttling across the floors of silent seas.

    .   .   .   .   .

And the afternoon, the evening, sleeps so peacefully!
Smoothed by long fingers,
Asleep . . . tired . . . or it malingers,
Stretched on the floor, here beside you and me.
Should I, after tea and cakes and ices,
Have the strength to force the moment to its crisis?
But though I have wept and fasted, wept and prayed,
Though I have seen my head (grown slightly bald) brought in upon a
      platter,
I am no prophet – and here's no great matter;
I have seen the moment of my greatness flicker,
And I have seen the eternal Footman hold my coat, and snicker,
And in short, I was afraid.

And would it have been worth it, after all,
After the cups, the marmalade, the tea,
Among the porcelain, among some talk of you and me,
Would it have been worth while,
To have bitten off the matter with a smile,
To have squeezed the universe into a ball
To roll it towards some overwhelming question,
To say: 'I am Lazarus, come from the dead,
Come back to tell you all, I shall tell you all' –
If one, settling a pillow by her head,
    Should say: 'That is not what I meant at all.
    That is not it, at all.'

And would it have been worth it, after all,
Would it have been worth while,
After the sunsets and the dooryards and the sprinkled streets,
After the novels, after the teacups, after the skirts that trail along the
      floor –
And this, and so much more? –
It is impossible to say just what I mean!
But as if a magic lantern threw the nerves in patterns on a screen:
Would it have been worth while
If one, settling a pillow or throwing off a shawl,
And turning toward the window, should say:
    'That is not it at all,
    That is not what I meant, at all.'

.   .   .   .   .

No! I am not Prince Hamlet, nor was meant to be;
Am an attendant lord, one that will do
To swell a progress, start a scene or two,
Advise the prince; no doubt, an easy tool,
Deferential, glad to be of use,
Politic, cautious, and meticulous;
Full of high sentence, but a bit obtuse;
At times, indeed, almost ridiculous –
Almost, at times, the Fool.

I grow old . . . I grow old . . .
I shall wear the bottoms of my trousers rolled.

Shall I part my hair behind? Do I dare to eat a peach?
I shall wear white flannel trousers, and walk upon the beach.
I have heard the mermaids singing, each to each.

I do not think that they will sing to me.

I have seen them riding seaward on the waves
Combing the white hair of the waves blown back
When the wind blows the water white and black.

We have lingered in the chambers of the sea
By sea-girls wreathed with seaweed red and brown
Till human voices wake us, and we drown.

T. S. ELIOT Aunt Helen

Miss Helen Slingsby was my maiden aunt,
And lived in a small house near a fashionable square
Cared for by servants to the number of four.
Now when she died there was silence in heaven
And silence at her end of the street.
The shutters were drawn and the undertaker wiped his feet –
He was aware that this sort of thing had occurred before.
The dogs were handsomely provided for,
But shortly afterwards the parrot died too.
The Dresden clock continued ticking on the mantelpiece,
And the footman sat upon the dining-table
Holding the second housemaid on his knees –
Who had always been so careful while her mistress lived.

ISAAC ROSENBERG Break of Day in the Trenches

The darkness crumbles away.
It is the same old druid Time as ever,
Only a live thing leaps my hand,
A queer sardonic rat,
As I pull the parapet's poppy
To stick behind my ear.
Droll rat, they would shoot you if they knew
Your cosmopolitan sympathies.
Now you have touched this English hand
You will do the same to a German
Soon, no doubt, if it be your pleasure
To cross the sleeping green between.
It seems you inwardly grin as you pass
Strong eyes, fine limbs, haughty athletes,
Less chanced than you for life,
Bonds to the whims of murder,
Sprawled in the bowels of the earth,
The torn fields of France.
What do you see in our eyes
At the shrieking iron and flame
Hurled through still heavens?
What quaver – what heart aghast?
Poppies whose roots are in man's veins
Drop, and are ever dropping;
But mine in my ear is safe –
Just a little white with the dust.

(1922)

ISAAC ROSENBERG August 1914

What in our lives is burnt
In the fire of this?
The heart's dear granary?
The much we shall miss?

Three lives hath one life –
Iron, honey, gold.
The gold, the honey gone –
Left is the hard and cold.

Iron are our lives
Molten right through our youth.
A burnt space through ripe fields,
A fair mouth's broken tooth.

(1937)

ISAAC ROSENBERG

A worm fed on the heart of Corinth,
Babylon and Rome:
Not Paris raped tall Helen,
But this incestuous worm,
Who lured her vivid beauty
To his amorphous sleep.
England! famous as Helen
Is thy betrothal sung
To him the shadowless,
More amorous than Solomon.

(1937)

THOMAS HARDY During Wind and Rain

They sing their dearest songs –
He, she, all of them – yea,
Treble and tenor and bass,
    And one to play;
With the candles mooning each face. . . .
    Ah, no; the years O!
How the sick leaves reel down in throngs!

They clear the creeping moss –
Elders and juniors – aye,
Making the pathways neat
    And the garden gay;
And they build a shady seat . . . .
    Ah, no; the years, the years;
See, the white storm-birds wing across.

They are blithely breakfasting all –
Men and maidens – yea,
Under the summer tree,
    With a glimpse of the bay,
While pet fowl come to the knee. . . .
        Ah, no; the years O!
And the rotten rose is ript from the wall.

They change to a high new house,
He, she, all of them – aye,
Clocks and carpets and chairs
    On the lawn all day,
And brightest things that are theirs. . . .
        Ah, no; the years, the years;
Down their carved names the rain-drop ploughs.

EDWARD THOMAS Old Man

Old Man, or Lad's-love, – in the name there's nothing
To one that knows not Lad's-love, or Old Man,
The hoar-green feathery herb, almost a tree,
Growing with rosemary and lavender.
Even to one that knows it well, the names
Half decorate, half perplex, the thing it is:
At least, what that is clings not to the names
In spite of time. And yet I like the names.

The herb itself I like not, but for certain
I love it, as some day the child will love it
Who plucks a feather from the door-side bush
Whenever she goes in or out of the house.
Often she waits there, snipping the tips and shrivelling
The shreds at last on to the path, perhaps
Thinking, perhaps of nothing, till she sniffs
Her fingers and runs off. The bush is still
But half as tall as she, though it is as old;
So well she clips it. Not a word she says;
And I can only wonder how much hereafter
She will remember, with that bitter scent,
Of garden rows, and ancient damson-trees
Topping a hedge, a bent path to a door,
A low thick bush beside the door, and me
Forbidding her to pick.

As for myself,
Where first I met the bitter scent is lost.
I, too, often shrivel the grey shreds,
Sniff them and think and sniff again and try
Once more to think what it is I am remembering,
Always in vain. I cannot like the scent,
Yet I would rather give up others more sweet,
With no meaning, than this bitter one.

I have mislaid the key. I sniff the spray
And think of nothing; I see and I hear nothing;
Yet seem, too, to be listening, lying in wait
For what I should, yet never can, remember:
No garden appears, no path, no hoar-green bush
Of Lad's-love, or Old Man, no child beside,
Neither father nor mother, nor any playmate;
Only an avenue, dark, nameless, without end.

EDWARD THOMAS Tall Nettles

Tall nettles cover up, as they have done
These many springs, the rusty harrow, the plough
Long worn out, and the roller made of stone:
Only the elm butt tops the nettles now.

This corner of the farmyard I like most:
As well as any bloom upon a flower
I like the dust on the nettles, never lost
Except to prove the sweetness of a shower.

EDWARD THOMAS Blenheim Oranges

Gone, gone again,
May, June, July,
And August gone,
Again gone by,

Not memorable
Save that I saw them go,
As past the empty quays
The rivers flow.

And now again,
In the harvest rain,
The Blenheim oranges
Fall grubby from the trees,

As when I was young –
And when the lost one was here –
And when the war began
To turn young men to dung.

Look at the old house,
Outmoded, dignified,
Dark and untenanted,
With grass growing instead

Of the footsteps of life,
The friendliness, the strife;
In its beds have lain
Youth, love, age and pain:

I am something like that;
Only I am not dead,
Still breathing and interested
In the house that is not dark: –

I am something like that:
Not one pane to reflect the sun,
For the schoolboys to throw at –
They have broken every one.

EDWARD THOMAS Rain

Rain, midnight rain, nothing but the wild rain
On this bleak hut, and solitude, and me
Remembering again that I shall die
And neither hear the rain nor give it thanks
For washing me cleaner than I have been
Since I was born into this solitude.
Blessed are the dead that the rain rains upon:
But here I pray that none whom once I loved
Is dying tonight or lying still awake
Solitary, listening to the rain,

Either in pain or thus in sympathy
Helpless among the living and the dead,
Like a cold water among broken reeds,
Myriads of broken reeds all still and stiff,
Like me who have no love which this wild rain
Has not dissolved except the love of death,
If love it be towards what is perfect and
Cannot, the tempest tells me, disappoint.

WILFRED OWEN Futility

Move him into the sun –
Gently its touch awoke him once,
At home, whispering of fields half-sown.
Always it woke him, even in France,
Until this morning and this snow.
If anything might rouse him now
The kind old sun will know.

Think how it wakes the seeds –
Woke once the clays of a cold star.
Are limbs, so dear achieved, are sides
Full-nerved, still warm, too hard to stir?
Was it for this the clay grew tall?
– O what made fatuous sunbeams toil
To break earth's sleep at all?

WILFRED OWEN Anthem for Doomed Youth

What passing-bells for these who die as cattle?
   – Only the monstrous anger of the guns.
   Only the stuttering rifles' rapid rattle
Can patter out their hasty orisons.
No mockeries now for them; no prayers nor bells;
   Nor any voice of mourning save the choirs, –
The shrill, demented choirs of wailing shells;
   And bugles calling for them from sad shires.

What candles may be held to speed them all?
      Not in the hands of boys but in their eyes
Shall shine the holy glimmers of goodbyes.
      The pallor of girls' brows shall be their pall;
Their flowers the tenderness of patient minds,
And each slow dusk a drawing-down of blinds.

(1920)

WILFRED OWEN The Send-Off

Down the close darkening lanes they sang their way
To the siding-shed,
And lined the train with faces grimly gay.

Their breasts were stuck all white with wreath and spray
As men's are, dead.

Dull porters watched them, and a casual tramp
Stood staring hard,
Sorry to miss them from the upland camp.

Then, unmoved, signals nodded, and a lamp
Winked to the guard.

So secretly, like wrongs hushed-up, they went.
They were not ours:
We never heard to which front these were sent;

Nor there if they yet mock what women meant
Who gave them flowers.

Shall they return to beating of great bells
In wild train-loads?
A few, a few, too few for drums and yells,

May creep back, silent, to village wells,
Up half-known roads.

(1920)

WILFRED OWEN Maundy Thursday

Between the brown hands of a server-lad
The silver cross was offered to be kissed.
The men came up, lugubrious, but not sad,
And knelt reluctantly, half-prejudiced.
(And kissing, kissed the emblem of a creed.)
Then mourning women knelt; meek mouths they had,
(And kissed the Body of the Christ indeed.)
Young children came, with eager lips and glad.
(These kissed a silver doll, immensely bright.)
Then I, too, knelt before that acolyte.
Above the crucifix I bent my head:
The Christ was thin, and cold, and very dead:
And yet I bowed, yea, kissed – my lips did cling.
(I kissed the warm live hand that held the thing.)

(1963)

SIEGFRIED SASSOON Base Details

If I were fierce, and bald, and short of breath,
    I'd live with scarlet Majors at the Base,
And speed glum heroes up the line to death.
    You'd see me with my puffy petulant face,
Guzzling and gulping in the best hotel,
    Reading the Roll of Honour. 'Poor young chap,'
I'd say – 'I used to know his father well;
    Yes, we've lost heavily in this last scrap.'
And when the war is done and youth stone dead,
I'd toddle safely home and die – in bed.

SIEGFRIED SASSOON The General

'Good-morning; good-morning!' the General said
When we met him last week on our way to the line.
Now the soldiers he smiled at are most of 'em dead,
And we're cursing his staff for incompetent swine.
'He's a cheery old card,' grunted Harry to Jack
As they slogged up to Arras with rifle and pack.
   .   .   .   .   .

But he did for them both by his plan of attack.

1919 ## SIEGFRIED SASSOON Everyone Sang

Everyone suddenly burst out singing;
And I was filled with such delight
As prisoned birds must find in freedom,
Winging wildly across the white
Orchards and dark-green fields; on – on – and out of sight.

Everyone's voice was suddenly lifted;
And beauty came like the setting sun:
My heart was shaken with tears; and horror
Drifted away . . . O, but Everyone
Was a bird; and the song was wordless; the singing will never be
    done.

IVOR GURNEY To His Love

He's gone, and all our plans
   Are useless indeed.
We'll walk no more on Cotswold
   Where the sheep feed
   Quietly and take no heed.

His body that was so quick
  Is not as you
Knew it, on Severn river
  Under the blue
  Driving our small boat through.

You would not know him now . . .
  But still he died
Nobly, so cover him over
  With violets of pride
  Purple from Severn side.

Cover him, cover him soon!
  And with thick-set
Masses of memoried flowers –
  Hide that red wet
  Thing I must somehow forget.

IVOR GURNEY The Silent One

Who died on the wires, and hung there, one of two –
Who for his hours of life had chattered through
Infinite lovely chatter of Bucks accent:
Yet faced unbroken wires; stepped over, and went
A noble fool, faithful to his stripes – and ended.
But I weak, hungry, and willing only for the chance
Of line – to fight in the line, lay down under unbroken
Wires, and saw the flashes and kept unshaken,
Till the politest voice – a finicking accent, said:
'Do you think you might crawl through there: there's a hole.'
Darkness, shot at: I smiled, as politely replied –
'I'm afraid not, Sir.' There was no hole no way to be seen
Nothing but chance of death, after tearing of clothes.
Kept flat, and watched the darkness, hearing bullets whizzing –
And thought of music – and swore deep heart's deep oaths
(Polite to God) and retreated and came on again,
Again retreated – and a second time faced the screen.

(1954)

RUDYARD KIPLING *from* Epitaphs of the War. 1914–18

A Servant

We were together since the War began.
He was my servant – and the better man.

A Son

My son was killed while laughing at some jest. I would I knew
What it was, and it might serve me in a time when jests are few.

The Coward

I could not look on Death, which being known,
Men led me to him, blindfold and alone.

The Refined Man

I was of delicate mind. I went aside for my needs,
    Disdaining the common office. I was seen from afar and killed . . .
How is this matter for mirth? Let each man be judged by his deeds.
    I have paid my price to live with myself on the terms that I willed.

Common Form

If any question why we died
Tell them, because our fathers lied.

RUDYARD KIPLING Gethsemane

1914–18

The Garden called Gethsemane
    In Picardy it was,
And there the people came to see
    The English soldiers pass.
We used to pass – we used to pass
    Or halt, as it might be,
And ship our masks in case of gas
    Beyond Gethsemane.

The Garden called Gethsemane,
  It held a pretty lass,
But all the time she talked to me
  I prayed my cup might pass.
The officer sat on the chair,
  The men lay on the grass,
And all the time we halted there
  I prayed my cup might pass.

It didn't pass – it didn't pass –
  It didn't pass from me.
I drank it when we met the gas
  Beyond Gethsemane!

LAURENCE BINYON For the Fallen (September 1914)

With proud thanksgiving, a mother for her children,
England mourns for her dead across the sea.
Flesh of her flesh they were, spirit of her spirit,
Fallen in the cause of the free.

Solemn the drums thrill: Death august and royal
Sings sorrow up into immortal spheres.
There is music in the midst of desolation
And a glory that shines upon our tears.

They went with songs to the battle, they were young,
Straight of limb, true of eye, steady and aglow.
They were staunch to the end against odds uncounted,
They fell with their faces to the foe.

They shall grow not old, as we that are left grow old:
Age shall not weary them, nor the years condemn.
At the going down of the sun and in the morning
We will remember them.

They mingle not with their laughing comrades again;
They sit no more at familiar tables of home;
They have no lot in our labour of the day-time;
They sleep beyond England's foam.

But where our desires are and our hopes profound,
Felt as a well-spring that is hidden from sight,
To the innermost heart of their own land they are known
As the stars are known to the Night;

As the stars that shall be bright when we are dust,
Moving in marches upon the heavenly plain,
As the stars that are starry in the time of our darkness,
To the end, to the end, they remain.

W. B. YEATS The Wild Swans at Coole

The trees are in their autumn beauty,
The woodland paths are dry,
Under the October twilight the water
Mirrors a still sky;
Upon the brimming water among the stones
Are nine-and-fifty swans.

The nineteenth autumn has come upon me
Since I first made my count;
I saw, before I had well finished,
All suddenly mount
And scatter wheeling in great broken rings
Upon their clamorous wings.

I have looked upon those brilliant creatures,
And now my heart is sore.
All's changed since I, hearing at twilight,
The first time on this shore,
The bell-beat of their wings above my head,
Trod with a lighter tread.

Unwearied still, lover by lover,
They paddle in the cold
Companionable streams or climb the air;
Their hearts have not grown old;
Passion or conquest, wander where they will,
Attend upon them still.

But now they drift on the still water,
Mysterious, beautiful;
Among what rushes will they build,
By what lake's edge or pool
Delight men's eyes when I awake some day
To find they have flown away?

T. S. ELIOT Sweeney Among the Nightingales

ὤμοι, πέπληγμαι καιρίαν πληγὴν ἔσω.

Apeneck Sweeney spreads his knees
Letting his arms hang down to laugh,
The zebra stripes along his jaw
Swelling to maculate giraffe.

The circles of the stormy moon
Slide westward toward the River Plate,
Death and the Raven drift above
And Sweeney guards the hornèd gate.

Gloomy Orion and the Dog
Are veiled; and hushed the shrunken seas;
The person in the Spanish cape
Tries to sit on Sweeney's knees

Slips and pulls the table cloth
Overturns a coffee-cup,
Reorganised upon the floor
She yawns and draws a stocking up;

The silent man in mocha brown
Sprawls at the window-sill and gapes;
The waiter brings in oranges
Bananas figs and hothouse grapes;

The silent vertebrate in brown
Contracts and concentrates, withdraws;
Rachel *née* Rabinovitch
Tears at the grapes with murderous paws;

She and the lady in the cape
Are suspect, thought to be in league;
Therefore the man with heavy eyes
Declines the gambit, shows fatigue,

Leaves the room and reappears
Outside the window, leaning in,
Branches of wistaria
Circumscribe a golden grin;

The host with someone indistinct
Converses at the door apart,
The nightingales are singing near
The Convent of the Sacred Heart,

And sang within the bloody wood
When Agamemnon cried aloud
And let their liquid siftings fall
To stain the stiff dishonoured shroud.

EZRA POUND *from* Homage to Sextus Propertius

VI

When, when, and whenever death closes our eyelids,
Moving naked over Acheron
Upon the one raft, victor and conquered together,
Marius and Jugurtha together,
                    one tangle of shadows.

Caesar plots against India,
Tigris and Euphrates shall, from now on, flow at his bidding,
Tibet shall be full of Roman policemen,
The Parthians shall get used to our statuary
                    and acquire a Roman religion;
One raft on the veiled flood of Acheron,
        Marius and Jugurtha together.

Nor at my funeral either will there be any long trail, [867

          bearing ancestral lares and images;
No trumpets filled with my emptiness,
Nor shall it be on an Attalic bed;
        The perfumed cloths shall be absent.
A small plebeian procession.
         Enough, enough and in plenty
There will be three books at my obsequies
Which I take, my not unworthy gift, to Persephone.

You will follow the bare scarified breast
Nor will you be weary of calling my name, nor too weary
        To place the last kiss on my lips
When the Syrian onyx is broken.

        'He who is now vacant dust
          Was once the slave of one passion:'
Give that much inscription
        'Death why tardily come?'

You, sometimes, will lament a lost friend,
      For it is a custom:
This care for past men,

Since Adonis was gored in Idalia, and the Cytharean
Ran crying with out-spread hair,
      In vain, you call back the shade,
In vain, Cynthia. Vain call to unanswering shadow,
      Small talk comes from small bones.

EZRA POUND *from* **Hugh Selwyn Mauberley**   **1920**

II

The age demanded an image
Of its accelerated grimace,
Something for the modern stage,
Not, at any rate, an Attic grace;

Not, not certainly, the obscure reveries
Of the inward gaze;
Better mendacities
Than the classics in paraphrase!

The 'age demanded' chiefly a mould in plaster,
Made with no loss of time,
A prose kinema, not, not assuredly, alabaster
Or the 'sculpture' of rhyme.

IV

These fought in any case,
and some believing,
            pro domo, in any case . . .

Some quick to arm,
some for adventure,
some from fear of weakness,
some from fear of censure,
some for love of slaughter, in imagination,
learning later . . .
some in fear, learning love of slaughter;
Died some, pro patria,
            non 'dulce' non 'et decor' . . .
walked eye-deep in hell
believing in old men's lies, then unbelieving
came home, home to a lie,
home to many deceits,
home to old lies and new infamy;
usury age-old and age-thick
and liars in public places.

Daring as never before, wastage as never before.
Young blood and high blood,
fair cheeks, and fine bodies;

fortitude as never before

frankness as never before,
disillusions as never told in the old days,
hysterias, trench confessions,
laughter out of dead bellies.

There died a myriad,
And of the best, among them,
For an old bitch gone in the teeth,
For a botched civilization,

Charm, smiling at the good mouth,
Quick eyes gone under earth's lid,

For two gross of broken statues,
For a few thousand battered books.

W. B. YEATS Easter, 1916

I have met them at close of day
Coming with vivid faces
From counter or desk among grey
Eighteenth-century houses.
I have passed with a nod of the head
Or polite meaningless words,
Or have lingered awhile and said
Polite meaningless words,
And thought before I had done
Of a mocking tale or a gibe
To please a companion
Around the fire at the club,
Being certain that they and I
But lived where motley is worn:
All changed, changed utterly:
A terrible beauty is born.

That woman's days were spent
In ignorant good-will,
Her nights in argument
Until her voice grew shrill.
What voice more sweet than hers
When, young and beautiful,
She rode to harriers?
This man had kept a school

And rode our wingèd horse;
This other his helper and friend
Was coming into his force;
He might have won fame in the end,
So sensitive his nature seemed,
So daring and sweet his thought.
This other man I had dreamed
A drunken, vainglorious lout.
He had done most bitter wrong
To some who are near my heart,
Yet I number him in the song;
He, too, has resigned his part
In the casual comedy;
He, too, has been changed in his turn,
Transformed utterly:
A terrible beauty is born.

Hearts with one purpose alone
Through summer and winter seem
Enchanted to a stone
To trouble the living stream.
The horse that comes from the road,
The rider, the birds that range
From cloud to tumbling cloud,
Minute by minute they change;
A shadow of cloud on the stream
Changes minute by minute;
A horse-hoof slides on the brim,
And a horse plashes within it;
The long-legged moor-hens dive,
And hens to moor-cocks call;
Minute by minute they live:
The stone's in the midst of all.

Too long a sacrifice
Can make a stone of the heart.
O when may it suffice?
That is Heaven's part, our part
To murmur name upon name,
As a mother names her child
When sleep at last has come
On limbs that had run wild.

What is it but nightfall?
No, no, not night but death;
Was it needless death after all?
For England may keep faith
For all that is done and said.
We know their dream; enough
To know they dreamed and are dead;
And what if excess of love
Bewildered them till they died?
I write it out in a verse –
MacDonagh and MacBride
And Connolly and Pearse
Now and in time to be,
Wherever green is worn,
Are changed, changed utterly:
A terrible beauty is born.

(written 1916)

T. S. ELIOT Gerontion

> *Thou hast nor youth nor age*
> *But as it were an after dinner sleep*
> *Dreaming of both.*

Here I am, an old man in a dry month,
Being read to by a boy, waiting for rain.
I was neither at the hot gates
Nor fought in the warm rain
Nor knee deep in the salt marsh, heaving a cutlass,
Bitten by flies, fought.
My house is a decayed house,
And the Jew squats on the window-sill, the owner,
Spawned in some estaminet of Antwerp,
Blistered in Brussels, patched and peeled in London.
The goat coughs at night in the field overhead;
Rocks, moss, stonecrop, iron, merds.
The woman keeps the kitchen, makes tea,
Sneezes at evening, poking the peevish gutter.
                    I an old man,
A dull head among windy spaces.

Signs are taken for wonders. 'We would see a sign!'
The word within a word, unable to speak a word,
Swaddled with darkness. In the juvescence of the year
Came Christ the tiger

In depraved May, dogwood and chestnut, flowering judas,
To be eaten, to be divided, to be drunk
Among whispers; by Mr. Silvero
With caressing hands, at Limoges
Who walked all night in the next room;
By Hakagawa, bowing among the Titians;
By Madame de Tornquist, in the dark room
Shifting the candles; Fräulein von Kulp
Who turned in the hall, one hand on the door. Vacant shuttles
Weave the wind. I have no ghosts,
An old man in a draughty house
Under a windy knob.

After such knowledge, what forgiveness? Think now
History has many cunning passages, contrived corridors
And issues, deceives with whispering ambitions,
Guides us by vanities. Think now
She gives when our attention is distracted
And what she gives, gives with such supple confusions
That the giving famishes the craving. Gives too late
What's not believed in, or if still believed,
In memory only, reconsidered passion. Gives too soon
Into weak hands, what's thought can be dispensed with
Till the refusal propagates a fear. Think
Neither fear nor courage saves us. Unnatural vices
Are fathered by our heroism. Virtues
Are forced upon us by our impudent crimes.
These tears are shaken from the wrath-bearing tree.

The tiger springs in the new year. Us he devours. Think at last
We have not reached conclusion, when I
Stiffen in a rented house. Think at last
I have not made this show purposelessly
And it is not by any concitation
Of the backward devils.
I would meet you upon this honestly.
I that was near your heart was removed therefrom
To lose beauty in terror, terror in inquisition.
I have lost my passion: why should I need to keep it

Since what is kept must be adulterated?
I have lost my sight, smell, hearing, taste and touch:
How should I use them for your closer contact?

These with a thousand small deliberations
Protract the profit of their chilled delirium,
Excite the membrane, when the sense has cooled,
With pungent sauces, multiply variety
In a wilderness of mirrors. What will the spider do,
Suspend its operations, will the weevil
Delay? De Bailhache, Fresca, Mrs. Cammel, whirled
Beyond the circuit of the shuddering Bear
In fractured atoms. Gull against the wind, in the windy straits
Of Belle Isle, or running on the Horn.
White feathers in the snow, the Gulf claims,
And an old man driven by the Trades
To a sleepy corner.

                         Tenants of the house,
Thoughts of a dry brain in a dry season.

§ A. E. HOUSMAN *from* **Last Poems**

XII

The laws of God, the laws of man,
He may keep that will and can;
Not I: let God and man decree
Laws for themselves and not for me;
And if my ways are not as theirs
Let them mind their own affairs.
Their deeds I judge and much condemn,
Yet when did I make laws for them?
Please yourselves, say I, and they
Need only look the other way.
But no, they will not; they must still
Wrest their neighbour to their will,
And make me dance as they desire
With jail and gallows and hell-fire.

And how am I to face the odds
Of man's bedevilment and God's?
I, a stranger and afraid
In a world I never made.
They will be master, right or wrong;
Though both are foolish, both are strong.
And since, my soul, we cannot fly
To Saturn nor to Mercury,
Keep we must, if keep we can,
These foreign laws of God and man.

(written *c.* 1900)

XXXIII

When the eye of day is shut,
    And the stars deny their beams,
And about the forest hut
    Blows the roaring wood of dreams,

From deep clay, from desert rock,
    From the sunk sands of the main,
Come not at my door to knock,
    Hearts that loved me not again.

Sleep, be still, turn to your rest
    In the lands where you are laid;
In far lodgings east and west
    Lie down on the beds you made.

In gross marl, in blowing dust,
    In the drowned ooze of the sea,
Where you would not, lie you must,
    Lie you must, and not with me.

XXXVII

Epitaph on an Army of Mercenaries

These, in the day when heaven was falling,
    The hour when earth's foundations fled,
Followed their mercenary calling
    And took their wages and are dead.

Their shoulders held the sky suspended;
    They stood, and earth's foundations stay;
What God abandoned, these defended,
    And saved the sum of things for pay.

XL

Tell me not here, it needs not saying,
    What tune the enchantress plays
In aftermaths of soft September
    Or under blanching mays,
For she and I were long acquainted
    And I knew all her ways.

On russet floors, by waters idle,
    The pine lets fall its cone;
The cuckoo shouts all day at nothing
    In leafy dells alone;
And traveller's joy beguiles in autumn
    Hearts that have lost their own.

On acres of the seeded grasses
    The changing burnish heaves;
Or marshalled under moons of harvest
    Stand still all night the sheaves;
Or beeches strip in storms for winter
    And stain the wind with leaves.

Possess, as I possessed a season,
    The countries I resign,
Where over elmy plains the highway
    Would mount the hills and shine,
And full of shade the pillared forest
    Would murmur and be mine.

For nature, heartless, witless nature,
    Will neither care nor know
What stranger's feet may find the meadow
    And trespass there and go,
Nor ask amid the dews of morning
    If they are mine or no.

§   §   §

A. E. HOUSMAN

It is a fearful thing to be
    The Pope.
That cross will not be laid on me,
    I hope.
A righteous God would not permit
    It.
The Pope himself must often say,
After the labours of the day,
'It is a fearful thing to be
    Me.'

(1940)

1922   T. S. ELIOT *from* The Waste Land

I The Burial of the Dead

    April is the cruellest month, breeding
Lilacs out of the dead land, mixing
Memory and desire, stirring
Dull roots with spring rain.
Winter kept us warm, covering

Earth in forgetful snow, feeding
A little life with dried tubers.
Summer surprised us, coming over the Starnbergersee
With a shower of rain; we stopped in the colonnade,
And went on in sunlight, into the Hofgarten,
And drank coffee, and talked for an hour.
Bin gar keine Russin, stamm' aus Litauen, echt deutsch.
And when we were children, staying at the arch-duke's,
My cousin's, he took me out on a sled,
And I was frightened. He said, Marie,
Marie, hold on tight. And down we went.
In the mountains, there you feel free.
I read, much of the night, and go south in the winter.

    What are the roots that clutch, what branches grow
Out of this stony rubbish? Son of man,
You cannot say, or guess, for you know only
A heap of broken images, where the sun beats,
And the dead tree gives no shelter, the cricket no relief,
And the dry stone no sound of water. Only
There is shadow under this red rock,
(Come in under the shadow of this red rock),
And I will show you something different from either
Your shadow at morning striding behind you
Or your shadow at evening rising to meet you;
I will show you fear in a handful of dust.
                    Frisch weht der Wind
                    Der Heimat zu
                    Mein Irisch Kind,
                    Wo weilest du?
'You gave me Hyacinths first a year ago;
'They called me the hyacinth girl.'
– Yet when we came back, late, from the hyacinth garden,
Your arms full, and your hair wet, I could not
Speak, and my eyes failed, I was neither
Living nor dead, and I knew nothing,
Looking into the heart of light, the silence.
Oed' und leer das Meer.

    Madame Sosostris, famous clairvoyante,
Had a bad cold, nevertheless
Is known to be the wisest woman in Europe,
With a wicked pack of cards. Here, said she,
Is your card, the drowned Phoenician Sailor,

(Those are pearls that were his eyes. Look!)
Here is Belladonna, the Lady of the Rocks,
The lady of situations.
Here is the man with three staves, and here the Wheel,
And here is the one-eyed merchant, and this card,
Which is blank, is something he carries on his back,
Which I am forbidden to see. I do not find
The Hanged Man. Fear death by water.
I see crowds of people, walking round in a ring.
Thank you. If you see dear Mrs. Equitone,
Tell her I bring the horoscope myself:
One must be so careful these days.

   Unreal City,
Under the brown fog of a winter dawn,
A crowd flowed over London Bridge, so many,
I had not thought death had undone so many.
Sighs, short and infrequent, were exhaled,
And each man fixed his eyes before his feet.
Flowed up the hill and down King William Street,
To where Saint Mary Woolnoth kept the hours
With a dead sound on the final stroke of nine.
There I saw one I knew, and stopped him, crying: 'Stetson!
'You who were with me in the ships at Mylae!
'That corpse you planted last year in your garden,
'Has it begun to sprout? Will it bloom this year?
'Or has the sudden frost disturbed its bed?
'O keep the Dog far hence, that's friend to men,
'Or with his nails he'll dig it up again!
'You! hypocrite lecteur! – mon semblable, – mon frère!'

IV Death by Water

Phlebas the Phoenician, a fortnight dead,
Forgot the cry of gulls, and the deep sea swell
And the profit and loss.

             A current under sea
Picked his bones in whispers. As he rose and fell
He passed the stages of his age and youth
Entering the whirlpool.

             Gentile or Jew
O you who turn the wheel and look to windward,
Consider Phlebas, who was once handsome and tall as you.

IVOR GURNEY Possessions

Sand has the ants, clay ferny weeds for play
But what shall please the wind now the trees are away
War took on Witcombe steep?
It breathes there, and wonders at old night roarings;
October time at all lights, and the new clearings
For memory are like to weep.
It was right for the beeches to stand over Witcombe reaches,
Until the wind roared and softened and died to sleep.

(1934)

IVOR GURNEY The High Hills

The high hills have a bitterness
Now they are not known
And memory is poor enough consolation
For the soul hopeless gone.
Up in the air there beech tangles wildly in the wind –
That I can imagine
But the speed, the swiftness, walking into clarity,
Like last year's bryony are gone.

(1954)

D. H. LAWRENCE Medlars and Sorb-Apples   1923

I love you, rotten,
Delicious rottenness.

I love to suck you out from your skins
So brown and soft and coming suave,
So morbid, as the Italians say.

What a rare, powerful, reminiscent flavour
Comes out of your falling through the stages of decay:
Stream within stream.

Something of the same flavour as Syracusan muscat wine
Or vulgar Marsala.

Though even the word Marsala will smack of preciosity
Soon in the pussyfoot West.

What is it?
What is it, in the grape turning raisin,
In the medlar, in the sorb-apple,
Wineskins of brown morbidity,
Autumnal excrementa;
What is it that reminds us of white gods?

Gods nude as blanched nut-kernels,
Strangely, half-sinisterly flesh-fragrant
As if with sweat,
And drenched with mystery.

Sorb-apples, medlars with dead crowns.

I say, wonderful are the hellish experiences,
Orphic, delicate
Dionysos of the Underworld.

A kiss, and a spasm of farewell, a moment's orgasm of rupture,
Then along the damp road alone, till the next turning.
And there, a new partner, a new parting, a new unfusing into twain,
A new gasp of further isolation,
A new intoxication of loneliness, among decaying, frost-cold leaves.

Going down the strange lanes of hell, more and more intensely
              alone,
The fibres of the heart parting one after the other
And yet the soul continuing, naked-footed, ever more vividly
              embodied
Like a flame blown whiter and whiter
In a deeper and deeper darkness
Ever more exquisite, distilled in separation.

So, in the strange retorts of medlars and sorb-apples
The distilled essence of hell.
The exquisite odour of leave-taking.
      Jamque vale!
Orpheus, and the winding, leaf-clogged, silent lanes of hell.

Each soul departing with its own isolation,
Strangest of all strange companions,
And best.

Medlars, sorb-apples,
More than sweet
Flux of autumn
Sucked out of your empty bladders

And sipped down, perhaps, with a sip of Marsala
So that the rambling, sky-dropped grape can add its savour to yours,
Orphic farewell, and farewell, and farewell
And the *ego sum* of Dionysos
The *sono io* of perfect drunkenness
Intoxication of final loneliness.

D. H. LAWRENCE The Mosquito

When did you start your tricks,
Monsieur?

What do you stand on such high legs for?
Why this length of shredded shank,
You exaltation?

Is it so that you shall lift your centre of gravity upwards
And weigh no more than air as you alight upon me,
Stand upon me weightless, you phantom?

I heard a woman call you the Winged Victory
In sluggish Venice.
You turn your head towards your tail, and smile.

How can you put so much devilry
Into that tranlucent phantom shred
Of a frail corpus?

Queer, with your thin wings and your streaming legs,
How you sail like a heron, or a dull clot of air,
A nothingness.

Yet what an aura surrounds you;
Your evil little aura, prowling, and casting a numbness on my mind.

That is your trick, your bit of filthy magic:
Invisibility, and the anæsthetic power
To deaden my attention in your direction.

But I know your game now, streaky sorcerer.
Queer, how you stalk and prowl the air
In circles and evasions, enveloping me,
Ghoul on wings
Winged Victory.

Settle, and stand on long thin shanks
Eyeing me sideways, and cunningly conscious that I am aware,
You speck.

I hate the way you lurch off sideways into air
Having read my thoughts against you.

Come then, let us play at unawares,
And see who wins in this sly game of bluff.
Man or mosquito.

You don't know that I exist, and I don't know that you exist.
Now then!

It is your trump,
It is your hateful little trump,
You pointed fiend,
Which shakes my sudden blood to hatred of you:
It is your small, high, hateful bugle in my ear.

Why do you do it?
Surely it is bad policy.

They say you can't help it.

If that is so, then I believe a little in Providence protecting the
        innocent.
But it sounds so amazingly like a slogan,
A yell of triumph as you snatch my scalp.

Blood, red blood
Super-magical
Forbidden liquor.

I behold you stand
For a second enspasmed in oblivion.
Obscenely ecstasied
Sucking live blood,
My blood.

Such silence, such suspended transport,
Such gorging,
Such obscenity of trespass.

You stagger
As well as you may.
Only your accursed hairy frailty,
Your own imponderable weightlessness
Saves you, wafts you away on the very draught my anger makes in
    its snatching.

Away with a pæan of derision,
You winged blood-drop.

Can I not overtake you?
Are you one too many for me,
Winged Victory?
Am I not mosquito enough to out-mosquito you?

Queer, what a big stain my sucked blood makes
Beside the infinitesimal faint smear of you!
Queer, what a dim dark smudge you have disappeared into!

D. H. LAWRENCE The Blue Jay

The blue jay with a crest on his head
Comes round the cabin in the snow.
He runs in the snow like a bit of blue metal,
Turning his back on everything.

From the pine-tree that towers and hisses like a pillar of shaggy
    cloud
Immense above the cabin
Comes a strident laugh as we approach, this little black dog and I.
So halts the little black bitch on four spread paws in the snow
And looks up inquiringly into the pillar of cloud,
With a tinge of misgiving.
Ca-a-a! comes the scrape of ridicule out of the tree.

What voice of the Lord is that, from the tree of smoke?

Oh, Bibbles, little black bitch in the snow,
With a pinch of snow in the groove of your silly snub nose,
What do you look at *me* for?
What do you look at me for, with such misgiving?

It's the blue jay laughing at us.
It's the blue jay jeering at us, Bibs.

Every day since the snow is here
The blue jay paces round the cabin, very busy, picking up bits,
Turning his back on us all,
And bobbing his thick dark crest about the snow, as if darkly saying:
I ignore those folk who look out.

You acid-blue metallic bird,
You thick bird with a strong crest,
Who are you?
Whose boss are you, with all your bully way?
You copper-sulphate blue bird!

HILAIRE BELLOC On a General Election

The accursèd power which stands on Privilege
(And goes with Women, and Champagne and Bridge)
Broke – and Democracy resumed her reign:
(Which goes with Bridge, and Women and Champagne).

HILAIRE BELLOC Ballade of Hell and of Mrs Roebeck

I'm going out to dine at Gray's
   With Bertie Morden, Charles and Kit,
And Manderly who never pays,
   And Jane who wins in spite of it,
   And Algernon who won't admit
The truth about his curious hair
   And teeth that very nearly fit: –
And Mrs Roebeck will be there.

And then to-morrow someone says
   That someone else has made a hit
In one of Mister Twister's plays,
   And off we go to yawn at it;
   And when it's petered out we quit
For number 20, Taunton Square,
   And smoke, and drink, and dance a bit: –
And Mrs Roebeck will be there.

And so through each declining phase
   Of emptied effort, jaded wit,
And day by day of London days
   Obscurely, more obscurely, lit;
   Until the uncertain shadows flit
Announcing to the shuddering air
   A Darkening, and the end of it: –
And Mrs Roebeck will be there.

Envoi

Prince, on their iron thrones they sit,
   Impassable to our despair,
The dreadful Guardians of the Pit: –
   And Mrs Roebeck will be there.

W. B. YEATS Leda and the Swan

A sudden blow: the great wings beating still
Above the staggering girl, her thighs caressed
By the dark webs, her nape caught in his bill,
He holds her helpless breast upon his breast.

How can those terrified vague fingers push
The feathered glory from her loosening thighs?
And how can body, laid in that white rush,
Bur feel the strange heart beating where it lies?

A shudder in the loins engenders there
The broken wall, the burning roof and tower
And Agamemnon dead.
               Being so caught up,
So mastered by the brute blood of the air,
Did she put on his knowledge with his power
Before the indifferent beak could let her drop?

1925   ROBERT GRAVES Love Without Hope

Love without hope, as when the young bird-catcher
Swept off his tall hat to the Squire's own daughter,
So let the imprisoned larks escape and fly
Singing about her head, as she rode by.

ROBERT BRIDGES To Francis Jammes

'Tis April again in my garden, again the grey stone-wall
    Is prankt with yellow alyssum and lilac aubrey-cresses;
    Half-hidden the mavis caroleth in the tassely birchen tresses
And awhile on the sunny air a cuckoo tuneth his call:
Now cometh to mind a singer whom country joys enthral,
    Francis Jammes, so grippeth him Nature in her caresses
    She hath steep'd his throat in the honey'd air of her wildernesses
With beauty that countervails the Lutetian therewithal.

You are here in spirit, dear poet, and bring a motley group,
    Your friends, afore you sat stitching your heavenly trousseau –
    The courteous old road-mender, the queer Jean Jacques Rousseau,
Columbus, Confucius, all to my English garden they troop,
    Under his goatskin umbrella the provident Robinson Crusoe,
And the ancestor dead long ago in Domingo or Guadaloupe.

EDMUND BLUNDEN The Midnight Skaters

The hop-poles stand in cones,
    The icy pond lurks under,
The pole-tops steeple to the thrones
    Of stars, sound gulfs of wonder;
But not the tallest there, 'tis said,
Could fathom to this pond's black bed.

Then is not death at watch
    Within those secret waters?
What wants he but to catch

Earth's heedless sons and daughters?
With but a crystal parapet
Between, he has his engines set.

Then on, blood shouts, on, on,
    Twirl, wheel and whip above him,
Dance on this ball-floor thin and wan,
    Use him as though you love him;
Court him, elude him, reel and pass,
And let him hate you through the glass.

BASIL BUNTING *from* Villon

Remember, imbeciles and wits,
sots and ascetics, fair and foul,
young girls with little tender tits,
that DEATH is written over all.

Worn hides that scarcely clothe the soul
they are so rotten, old and thin,
or firm and soft and warm and full –
fellmonger Death gets every skin.

All that is piteous, all that's fair,
all that is fat and scant of breath,
Elisha's baldness, Helen's hair,
is Death's collateral:

Three score and ten years after sight
of this pay me your pulse and breath
value received. And who dare cite,
as we forgive our debtors, Death?

Abelard and Eloise,
Henry the Fowler, Charlemagne,
Genée, Lopokova, all these
die, die in pain.

And General Grant and General Lee,
Patti and Florence Nightingale,
like Tyro and Antiope
drift among ghosts in Hell,

know nothing, are nothing, save a fume
driving across a mind
preoccupied with this: our doom
is, to be sifted by the wind,

heaped up, smoothed down like silly sands.
We are less permanent than thought.
The Emperor with the Golden Hands

is still a word, a tint, a tone,
insubstantial-glorious,
when we ourselves are dead and gone
and the green grass growing over us.

EDWIN MUIR Childhood

Long time he lay upon the sunny hill,
    To his father's house below securely bound.
Far off the silent, changing sound was still,
    With the black islands lying thick around.

He saw each separate height, each vaguer hue,
    Where the massed islands rolled in mist away,
And though all ran together in his view
    He knew that unseen straits between them lay.

Often he wondered what new shores were there.
    In thought he saw the still light on the sand,
The shallow water clear in tranquil air,
    And walked through it in joy from strand to strand.

Over the sound a ship so slow would pass
    That in the black hill's gloom it seemed to lie.
The evening sound was smooth like sunken glass,
    And time seemed finished ere the ship passed by.

Grey tiny rocks slept round him where he lay,
    Moveless as they, more still as evening came,
The grasses threw straight shadows far away,
    And from the house his mother called his name.

HUGH MACDIARMID *from* Sangschaw

The Watergaw

Ae weet forenicht i' the yow-trummle
I saw yon antrin thing,
A watergaw wi' its chitterin' licht
Ayont the on-ding;
5   An' I thocht o' the last wild look ye gied
Afore ye deed!

There was nae reek i' the laverock's hoose
That nicht – an' nane i' mine;
But I hae thocht o' that foolish licht
10   Ever sin' syne;
An' I think that mebbe at last I ken
What your look meant then.

HUGH MACDIARMID The Eemis Stane

I' the how-dumb-deid o' the cauld hairst nicht
The warl' like an eemis stane
Wags i' the lift;
An' my eerie memories fa'
5   Like a yowdendrift.

Like a yowdendrift so's I couldna read
The words cut oot i' the stane
Had the fug o' fame
An' history's hazelraw
10   No' yirdit thaim.

1 *Ae weet forenicht* one wet dusk; *yow-trummle* ewe-tremble (cold spell in July);
2 *antrin* rare; 3 *watergaw* broken rainbow; *chitterin'* shivering; 4 'beyond the
downpour'; 7 *reek* quarrel; *laverock's hoose* lark's house; 10 *sin' syne* since then

1 *how-dumb-deid* deep dead quiet; *hairst* harvest; 2 *warl'* world; *eemis stane*
unsteady stone; 3 *i' the lift* in the sky; 5 *yowdendrift* ground blizzard; 8 *fug* moss;
9 *hazelraw* lichen; 10 *yirdit* buried

1926   HUGH MACDIARMID Empty Vessel

I met ayont the cairney
A lass wi' tousie hair
Singin' till a bairnie
That was nae langer there.

5   Wunds wi' warlds to swing
Dinna sing sae sweet,
The licht that bends owre a' thing
Is less ta'en up wi't.

HUGH MACDIARMID *from* A Drunk Man Looks at the Thistle

O wha's the bride that cairries the bunch
O' thistles blinterin' white?
Her cuckold bridegroom little dreids
What he sall ken this nicht.

5   For closer than gudeman can come
And closer to'r than hersel',
Wha didna need her maidenheid
Has wrocht his purpose fell.

O wha's been here afore me, lass,
10   And hoo did he get in?
    – *A man that deed or I was born*
    This evil thing has din.

And left, as it were on a corpse,
Your maidenheid to me?
15   – *Nae lass, gudeman, sin' Time began*
    'S hed ony mair to gi'e.

1 *ayont the cairney* beyond the little cairn; 2 *tousie* unkempt; 5 *wunds* winds;
8 *ta'en up wi't* taken up with it

2 *blinterin'* glimmering; 3 *dreids* suspects; 4 *ken* know; 5 *gudeman* husband;
11 *deed or* died before; 16 *'S hed* has had

But I can gi'e ye kindness, lad,
And a pair o' willin' hands,
And you sall ha'e my briests like stars,
20   *My limbs like willow wands,*

And on my lips ye'll heed nae mair,
And in my hair forget,
The seed o' a' the men that in
My virgin womb ha'e met . . .

JAMES JOYCE *from* Pomes Penyeach   **1927**

Bahnhofstrasse

The eyes that mock me sign the way
Whereto I pass at eve of day,

Grey way whose violet signals are
The trysting and the twining star.

Ah star of evil! star of pain!
Highhearted youth comes not again

Nor old heart's wisdom yet to know
The signs that mock me as I go.

(written 1918)

THOMAS HARDY Lying Awake   **1928**

You, Morningtide Star, now are steady-eyed, over the east,
    I know it as if I saw you;
You, Beeches, engrave on the sky your thin twigs, even the least;
    Had I paper and pencil I'd draw you.

You, Meadow, are white with your counterpane cover of dew,
    I see it as if I were there;
You, Churchyard, are lightening faint from the shade of the yew,
    The names creeping out everywhere.

AUSTIN CLARKE The Planter's Daughter

When night stirred at sea
And the fire brought a crowd in,
They say that her beauty
Was music in mouth
And few in the candlelight
Thought her too proud,
For the house of the planter
Is known by the trees.

Men that had seen her
Drank deep and were silent,
The women were speaking
Wherever she went –
As a bell that is rung
Or a wonder told shyly,
And O she was the Sunday
In every week.

W. B. YEATS Sailing to Byzantium

That is no country for old men. The young
In one another's arms, birds in the trees,
– Those dying generations – at their song,
The salmon-falls, the mackerel-crowded seas,
Fish, flesh, or fowl, commend all summer long
Whatever is begotten, born, and dies.
Caught in that sensual music all neglect
Monuments of unageing intellect.

An aged man is but a paltry thing,
A tattered coat upon a stick, unless
Soul clap its hands and sing, and louder sing
For every tatter in its mortal dress,
Nor is there singing school but studying
Monuments of its own magnificence;
And therefore I have sailed the seas and come
To the holy city of Byzantium.

O sages standing in God's holy fire
As in the gold mosaic of a wall,
Come from the holy fire, perne in a gyre,
And be the singing-masters of my soul.
Consume my heart away; sick with desire
And fastened to a dying animal
It knows not what it is; and gather me
Into the artifice of eternity.

Once out of nature I shall never take
My bodily form from any natural thing,
But such a form as Grecian goldsmiths make
Of hammered gold and gold enamelling
To keep a drowsy Emperor awake;
Or set upon a golden bough to sing
To lords and ladies of Byzantium
Of what is past, or passing, or to come.

W. B. YEATS *from* Meditations in Time of Civil War

V The Road at My Door

An affable Irregular,
A heavily-built Falstaffian man,
Comes cracking jokes of civil war
As though to die by gunshot were
The finest play under the sun.

A brown Lieutenant and his men,
Half dressed in national uniform,
Stand at my door, and I complain
Of the foul weather, hail and rain,
A pear tree broken by the storm.

I count those feathered balls of soot
The moor-hen guides upon the stream,
To silence the envy in my thought;
And turn towards my chamber, caught
In the cold snows of a dream.

The bees build in the crevices
Of loosening masonry, and there
The mother birds bring grubs and flies.
My wall is loosening; honey-bees,
Come build in the empty house of the stare.

We are closed in, and the key is turned
On our uncertainty; somewhere
A man is killed, or a house burned,
Yet no clear fact to be discerned:
Come build in the empty house of the stare.

A barricade of stone or of wood;
Some fourteen days of civil war;
Last night they trundled down the road
That dead young soldier in his blood:
Come build in the empty house of the stare.

We had fed the heart on fantasies,
The heart's grown brutal from the fare;
More substance in our enmities
Than in our love; O honey-bees,
Come build in the empty house of the stare.

W. B. YEATS Among School Children

I walk through the long schoolroom questioning;
A kind old nun in a white hood replies;
The children learn to cipher and to sing,
To study reading-books and histories,
To cut and sew, be neat in everything
In the best modern way – the children's eyes
In momentary wonder stare upon
A sixty-year-old smiling public man.

I dream of a Ledaean body, bent
Above a sinking fire, a tale that she
Told of a harsh reproof, or trivial event
That changed some childish day to tragedy –

Told, and it seemed that our two natures blent
Into a sphere from youthful sympathy,
Or else, to alter Plato's parable,
Into the yolk and white of the one shell.

And thinking of that fit of grief or rage
I look upon one child or t'other there
And wonder if she stood so at that age –
For even daughters of the swan can share
Something of every paddler's heritage –
And had that colour upon cheek or hair,
And thereupon my heart is driven wild:
She stands before me as a living child.

Her present image floats into the mind –
Did Quattrocento finger fashion it
Hollow of cheek as though it drank the wind
And took a mess of shadows for its meat?
And I though never of Ledaean kind
Had pretty plumage once – enough of that,
Better to smile on all that smile, and show
There is a comfortable kind of old scarecrow.

What youthful mother, a shape upon her lap
Honey of generation had betrayed,
And that must sleep, shriek, struggle to escape
As recollection or the drug decide,
Would think her son, did she but see that shape
With sixty or more winters on its head,
A compensation for the pang of his birth,
Or the uncertainty of his setting forth?

Plato thought nature but a spume that plays
Upon a ghostly paradigm of things;
Solider Aristotle played the taws
Upon the bottom of a king of kings;
World-famous golden-thighed Pythagoras
Fingered upon a fiddle-stick or strings
What a star sang and careless Muses heard:
Old clothes upon old sticks to scare a bird.

Both nuns and mothers worship images,
But those the candles light are not as those
That animate a mother's reveries,
But keep a marble or a bronze repose.
And yet they too break hearts – O Presences
That passion, piety or affection knows,
And that all heavenly glory symbolise –
O self-born mockers of man's enterprise;

Labour is blossoming or dancing where
The body is not bruised to pleasure soul,
Nor beauty born out of its own despair,
Nor blear-eyed wisdom out of midnight oil.
O chestnut tree, great rooted blossomer,
Are you the leaf, the blossom or the bole?
O body swayed to music, O brightening glance,
How can we know the dancer from the dance?

W. H. AUDEN

Taller to-day, we remember similar evenings,
Walking together in the windless orchard
Where the brook runs over the gravel, far from the glacier.

Again in the room with the sofa hiding the grate,
Look down to the river when the rain is over,
See him turn to the window, hearing our last
Of Captain Ferguson.

It is seen how excellent hands have turned to commonness.
One staring too long, went blind in a tower,
One sold all his manors to fight, broke through, and faltered.

Nights come bringing the snow, and the dead howl
Under the headlands in their windy dwelling
Because the Adversary put too easy questions
On lonely roads.

But happy now, though no nearer each other,
We see the farms lighted all along the valley;
Down at the mill-shed the hammering stops
And men go home.

Noises at dawn will bring
Freedom for some, but not this peace
No bird can contradict: passing, but is sufficient now
For something fulfilled this hour, loved or endured.

D. H. LAWRENCE The Mosquito Knows

The mosquito knows full well, small as he is
he's a beast of prey.
But after all
he only takes his bellyful,
he doesn't put my blood in the bank.

D. H. LAWRENCE To Women, As Far As I'm Concerned

The feelings I don't have I don't have.
The feelings I don't have, I won't say I have.
The feelings you say you have, you don't have.
The feelings you would like us both to have, we neither of us have.
The feelings people ought to have, they never have.
If people say they've got feelings, you may be pretty sure they
    haven't got them.

So if you want either of us to feel anything at all
you'd better abandon all idea of feelings altogether.

D. H. LAWRENCE Innocent England

Oh what a pity, Oh! don't you agree
that figs aren't found in the land of the free!

Fig-trees don't grow in my native land;
there's never a fig-leaf near at hand

when you want one; so I did without;
and that is what the row's about.

Virginal, pure policemen came
and hid their faces for very shame,

while they carried the shameless things away
to gaol, to be hid from the light of day.

And Mr Mead, that old, old lily
said: 'Gross! coarse! hideous!' – and I, like a silly,

thought he meant the faces of the police-court officials,
and how right he was, and I signed my initials

to confirm what he said; but alas, he meant
my pictures, and on the proceedings went.

The upshot was, my picture must burn
that English artists might finally learn

when they painted a nude, to put a *cache sexe* on,
a cache sexe, a cache sexe, or else begone!

A fig-leaf; or, if you cannot find it
a wreath of mist, with nothing behind it.

A wreath of mist is the usual thing
in the north, to hide where the turtles sing.

Though they never sing, they never sing,
don't you dare to suggest such a thing

or Mr Mead will be after you.
– But what a pity I never knew

A wreath of English mist would do
as a cache sexe! I'd have put a whole fog.

But once and forever barks the old dog,
so my pictures are in prison, instead of in the Zoo.

E. C. BENTLEY [Clerihews]

George the Third
Ought never to have occurred.
One can only wonder
At so grotesque a blunder.

Nell
Fell
When Charles the Second
Beckoned.

EDMUND BLUNDEN Report on Experience

I have been young, and now am not too old;
And I have seen the righteous forsaken,
His health, his honour and his quality taken.
      This is not what we were formerly told.

I have seen a green country, useful to the race,
Knocked silly with guns and mines, its villages vanished,
Even the last rat and the last kestrel banished –
      God bless us all, this was peculiar grace.

I knew Seraphina; Nature gave her hue,
Glance, sympathy, note, like one from Eden.
I saw her smile warp, heard her lyric deaden;
      She turned to harlotry; – this I took to be new.

Say what you will, our God sees how they run.
These disillusions are His curious proving
That He loves humanity and will go on loving;
      Over there are faith, life, virtue in the sun.

ROBERT GRAVES Sick Love

O Love, be fed with apples while you may,
And feel the sun and go in royal array,
A smiling innocent on the heavenly causeway,

Though in what listening horror for the cry
That soars in outer blackness dismally,
The dumb blind beast, the paranoiac fury:

Be warm, enjoy the season, lift your head,
Exquisite in the pulse of tainted blood,
That shivering glory not to be despised.

Take your delight in momentariness,
Walk between dark and dark – a shining space
With the grave's narrowness, though not its peace.

ROBERT GRAVES Warning to Children

Children, if you dare to think
Of the greatness, rareness, muchness,
Fewness of this precious only
Endless world in which you say
You live, you think of things like this:
Blocks of slate enclosing dappled
Red and green, enclosing tawny
Yellow nets, enclosing white
And black acres of dominoes,
Where a neat brown paper parcel
Tempts you to untie the string.
In the parcel a small island,
On the island a large tree,
On the tree a husky fruit.
Strip the husk and pare the rind off:
In the kernel you will see
Blocks of slate enclosed by dappled
Red and green, enclosed by tawny
Yellow nets, enclosed by white
And black acres of dominoes,
Where the same brown paper parcel –
Children, leave the string alone!
For who dares undo the parcel
Finds himself at once inside it,
On the island, in the fruit,
Blocks of slate about his head,
Finds himself enclosed by dappled
Green and red, enclosed by yellow
Tawny nets, enclosed by black
And white acres of dominoes,
With the same brown paper parcel
Still unopened on his knee.
And, if he then should dare to think
Of the fewness, muchness, rareness,
Greatness of this endless only
Precious world in which he says
He lives – he then unties the string.

ROBERT GRAVES It Was All Very Tidy

When I reached his place,
The grass was smooth,
The wind was delicate,
The wit well timed,
The limbs well formed,
The pictures straight on the wall:
It was all very tidy.

He was cancelling out
The last row of figures,
He had his beard tied up in ribbons,
There was no dust on his shoe,
Everyone nodded:
It was all very tidy.

Music was not playing,
There were no sudden noises,
The sun shone blandly,
The clock ticked:
It was all very tidy.

'Apart from and above all this,'
I reassured myself,
'There is now myself.'
It was all very tidy.

Death did not address me,
He had nearly done:
It was all very tidy.

They asked, did I not think
It was all very tidy?
I could not bring myself
To laugh, or untie
His beard's neat ribbons,
Or jog his elbow,
Or whistle, or sing,
Or make disturbance.
I consented, frozenly,
He was unexceptionable:
It was all very tidy.

1930   W. H. AUDEN

This lunar beauty
Has no history
Is complete and early;
If beauty later
Bear any feature
It had a lover
And is another.

This like a dream
Keeps other time
And daytime is
The loss of this;
For time is inches
And the heart's changes
Where ghost has haunted
Lost and wanted.

But this was never
A ghost's endeavour
Nor finished this,
Was ghost at ease;
And till it pass
Love shall not near
The sweetness here
Nor sorrow take
His endless look.

T. S. ELIOT Marina

*Quis hic locus, quae
regio, quae mundi plaga?*

What seas what shores what grey rocks and what islands
What water lapping the bow
And scent of pine and the woodthrush singing through the fog
What images return
O my daughter.

Those who sharpen the tooth of the dog, meaning
Death
Those who glitter with the glory of the hummingbird, meaning
Death
Those who sit in the sty of contentment, meaning
Death
Those who suffer the ecstasy of the animals, meaning
Death

Are become unsubstantial, reduced by a wind,
A breath of pine, and the woodsong fog
By this grace dissolved in place

What is this face, less clear and clearer
The pulse in the arm, less strong and stronger –
Given or lent? more distant than stars and nearer than the eye

Whispers and small laughter between leaves and hurrying feet
Under sleep, where all the waters meet.

Bowsprit cracked with ice and paint cracked with heat.
I made this, I have forgotten
And remember.
The rigging weak and the canvas rotten
Between one June and another September.
Made this unknowing, half conscious, unknown, my own.
The garboard strake leaks, the seams need caulking.
This form, this face, this life
Living to live in a world of time beyond me; let me
Resign my life for this life, my speech for that unspoken,
The awakened, lips parted, the hope, the new ships.

What seas what shores what granite islands towards my timbers
And woodthrush calling through the fog
My daughter.

1932   BASIL BUNTING *from* Chomei at Toyama

I have been noting events forty years.

On the twentyseventh May eleven hundred
and seventyseven, eight p.m., fire broke out
at the corner of Tomi and Higuchi streets.
In a night
palace, ministries, university, parliament
were destroyed. As the wind veered
flames spread out in the shape of an open fan.
Tongues torn by gusts stretched and leapt.
In the sky clouds of cinders lit red with the blaze.
Some choked, some burned, some barely escaped.
Sixteen great officials lost houses and
very many poor. A third of the city burned;
several thousands died; and of beasts,
limitless numbers.

Men are fools to invest in real estate.

Three years less three days later a wind
starting near the outer boulevard
broke a path a quarter mile across
to Sixth Avenue.
Not a house stood. Some were felled whole,
some in splinters; some had left
great beams upright in the ground
and round about
lay rooves scattered where the wind flung them.
Flocks of furniture in the air,
everything flat fluttered like dead leaves.
A dust like fog or smoke,
You could hear nothing for the roar,
                    bufera infernal!
Lamed some, wounded some.
This cyclone turned southwest.

Massacre without cause.

Portent?

The same year thunderbolted change of capital,
fixed here, Kyoto, for ages.
Nothing compelled the change nor was it an easy matter
but the grumbling was disproportionate.
We moved, those with jobs
or wanting jobs or hangers on of the rest,
in haste haste fretting to be the first.
Rooftrees overhanging empty rooms;
dismounted: floating down the river.
The soil returned to heath.

I visited the new site: narrow and too uneven,
cliffs and marshes, deafening shores, perpetual strong winds;
the palace a logcabin dumped amongst the hills
(yet not altogether inelegant).
There was no flat place for houses, many vacant lots,
the former capital wrecked, the new a camp,
and thoughts like clouds changing, frayed by a breath:
peasants bewailing lost land, newcomers aghast at prices.
No one in uniform: the crowds
resembled demobilized conscripts.

There were murmurs. Time defined them.
In the winter the decree was rescinded,
we returned to Kyoto;
but the houses were gone and none
could afford to rebuild them.

I have heard of a time when kings beneath bark rooves
watched chimneys.
When smoke was scarce, taxes were remitted.

To appreciate present conditions
collate them with those of antiquity.

Drought, floods, and a dearth. Two fruitless autumns.
Empty markets, swarms of beggars. Jewels
sold for a handful of rice. Dead stank
on the curb, lay so thick on
Riverside Drive a car couldnt pass.
The pest bred.
That winter my fuel was the walls of my own house.

Fathers fed their children and died,
babies died sucking the dead.
The priest Hoshi went about marking their foreheads
A, Amida, their requiem;
he counted them in the East End in the last two months,
fortythree thousand A's.

Crack, rush, ye mountains, bury your rills!
Spread your green glass, ocean, over the meadows!
Scream, avalanche, boulders amok, strangle the dale!
O ships in the sea's power, O horses
on shifting roads, in the earth's power, without hoofhold!
This is the earthquake, this was
the great earthquake of Genryaku!

The chapel fell, the abbey, the minster and the small shrines
fell, their dust rose and a thunder of houses falling.
O to be birds and fly or dragons and ride on a cloud!
The earthquake, the great earthquake of Genryaku!

A child building a mud house against a high wall:
I saw him crushed suddenly, his eyes hung
from their orbits like two tassels.
His father howled shamelessly – an officer.
I was not abashed at his crying.

Such shocks continued three weeks; then lessening,
but still a score daily as big as an average earthquake;
then fewer, alternate days, a tertian ague of tremors.
There is no record of any greater.
It caused a religious revival.
Months . . .
Years . . .
. . . .
Nobody mentions it now.

This is the unstable world and
we in it unstable and our houses.

[907]

D. H. LAWRENCE Bavarian Gentians

Not every man has gentians in his house
in Soft September, at slow, sad Michaelmas.

Bavarian gentians, big and dark, only dark
darkening the day-time torch-like with the smoking blueness of
    Pluto's gloom,
ribbed and torch-like, with their blaze of darkness spread blue
down flattening into points, flattened under the sweep of white day
torch-flower of the blue-smoking darkness, Pluto's dark-blue daze,
black lamps from the halls of Dis, burning dark blue,
giving off darkness, blue darkness, as Demeter's pale lamps give off
    light,
lead me then, lead the way.

Reach me a gentian, give me a torch!
let me guide myself with the blue, forked torch of this flower
down the darker and darker stairs, where blue is darkened on
    blueness
even where Persephone goes, just now, from the frosted September
to the sightless realm where darkness is awake upon the dark
and Persephone herself is but a voice
or a darkness invisible enfolded in the deeper dark
of the arms Plutonic, and pierced with the passion of dense gloom,
among the splendour of torches of darkness, shedding darkness on
    the lost bride and her groom.

RUDYARD KIPLING The Bonfires　　　　　　　　**1933**

1933

'Gesture . . . outlook . . . vision . . . avenue . . . example . . . achievement
. . . appeasement . . . limit of risk.'　　　　　*Common Political Form*

We know the Rocket's upward whizz;
    We know the Boom before the Bust.
We know the whistling Wail which is
    The Stick returning to the Dust.

We know how much to take on trust
Of any promised Paradise.
        We know the Pie – likewise the Crust.
We know the Bonfire on the Ice.

We know the Mountain and the Mouse.
        We know Great Cry and Little Wool.
We know the purseless Ears of Sows.
        We know the Frog that aped the Bull.
        We know, whatever Trick we pull,
(Ourselves have gambled once or twice)
        A Bobtailed Flush is not a Full
We know the Bonfire on the Ice.

We know that Ones and Ones make Twos –
        Till Demos votes them Three or Nought.
We know the Fenris Wolf is loose.
        We know what Fight has not been fought.
        We know the Father to the Thought
Which argues Babe and Cockatrice
        Would play together, were they taught.
We know *that* Bonfire on the Ice.

We know that Thriving comes by Thrift.
        We know the Key must keep the Door.
We know his Boot-straps cannot lift
        The frightened Waster off the Floor.
        We know these things, and we deplore
That not by any Artifice
        Can they be altered. Furthermore
We know the Bonfires on the Ice!

W. B. YEATS In Memory of Eva Gore-Booth and Con Markievicz

The light of evening, Lissadell,
Great windows open to the south,
Two girls in silk kimonos, both
Beautiful, one a gazelle.
But a raving autumn shears
Blossom from the summer's wreath;
The older is condemned to death,
Pardoned, drags out lonely years

Conspiring among the ignorant.
I know not what the younger dreams –
Some vague Utopia – and she seems,
When withered old and skeleton-gaunt,
An image of such politics.
Many a time I think to seek
One or the other out and speak
Of that old Georgian mansion, mix
Pictures of the mind, recall
That table and the talk of youth,
Two girls in silk kimonos, both
Beautiful, one a gazelle.

Dear shadows, now you know it all,
All the folly of a fight
With a common wrong or right.
The innocent and the beautiful
Have no enemy but time;
Arise and bid me strike a match
And strike another till time catch;
Should the conflagration climb,
Run till all the sages know.
We the great gazebo built,
They convicted us of guilt;
Bid me strike a match and blow.

DYLAN THOMAS The force that through the green fuse

The force that through the green fuse drives the flower
Drives my green age; that blasts the roots of trees
Is my destroyer.
And I am dumb to tell the crooked rose
My youth is bent by the same wintry fever.

The force that drives the water through the rocks
Drives my red blood; that dries the mouthing streams
Turns mine to wax.
And I am dumb to mouth unto my veins
How at the mountain spring the same mouth sucks.

The hand that whirls the water in the pool
Stirs the quicksand; that ropes the blowing wind
Hauls my shroud sail.
And I am dumb to tell the hanging man
How of my clay is made the hangman's lime.

The lips of time leech to the fountain head;
Love drips and gathers, but the fallen blood
Shall calm her sores.
And I am dumb to tell a weather's wind
How time has ticked a heaven round the stars.

And I am dumb to tell the lover's tomb
How at my sheet goes the same crooked worm.

1934   HUGH MACDIARMID *from* **On a Raised Beach**

All is lithogenesis – or lochia,
Carpolite fruit of the forbidden tree,
Stones blacker than any in the Caaba,
Cream-coloured caen-stone, chatoyant pieces,
Celadon and corbeau, bistre and beige,
Glaucous, hoar, enfouldered, cyathiform,
Making mere faculae of the sun and moon,
I study you glout and gloss, but have
No cadrans to adjust you with, and turn again
From optik to haptik and like a blind man run
My fingers over you, arris by arris, burr by burr,
Slickensides, truité, rugas, foveoles,
Bringing my aesthesis in vain to bear,
An angle-titch to all your corrugations and coigns,
Hatched foraminous cavo-rilievo of the world,
Deictic, fiducial stones. Chiliad by chiliad
What bricole piled you here, stupendous cairn?
What artist poses the Earth écorché thus,
Pillar of creation engouled in me?
What eburnation augments you with men's bones,
Every energumen an Endymion yet?
All the other stones are in this haecceity it seems,
But where is the Christophanic rock that moved?
What Cabirian song from this catasta comes?

Deep conviction or preference can seldom
Find direct terms in which to express itself.
Today on this shingle shelf
I understand this pensive reluctance so well,
This not discommendable obstinacy,
These contrivances of an inexpressive critical feeling,
These stones with their resolve that Creation shall not be
Injured by iconoclasts and quacks. Nothing has stirred
Since I lay down this morning an eternity ago
But one bird. The widest open door is the least liable to intrusion,
Ubiquitous as the sunlight, unfrequented as the sun.
The inward gates of a bird are always open.
It does not know how to shut them.
That is the secret of its song,
But whether any man's are ajar is doubtful.
I look at these stones and know little about them,
But I know their gates are open too,
Always open, far longer open, than any bird's can be,
That every one of them has had its gates wide open far longer
Than all birds put together, let alone humanity,
Though through them no man can see,
No man nor anything more recently born than themselves
And that is everything else on the Earth.
I too lying here have dismissed all else.
Bread from stones is my sole and desperate dearth,
From stones, which are to the Earth as to the sunlight
Is the naked sun which is for no man's sight.
I would scorn to cry to any easier audience
Or, having cried, to lack patience to await the response.
I am no more indifferent or ill-disposed to life than death is;
I would fain accept it all completely as the soil does;
Already I feel all that can perish perishing in me
As so much has perished and all will yet perish in these stones.
I must begin with these stones as the world began.

WILLIAM EMPSON This Last Pain

This last pain for the damned the Fathers found:
'They knew the bliss with which they were not crowned.'
    Such, but on earth, let me foretell,
    Is all, of heaven or of hell.

Man, as the prying housemaid of the soul,
May know her happiness by eye to hole:
    He's safe; the key is lost; he knows
    Door will not open, nor hole close.

'What is conceivable can happen too,'
Said Wittgenstein, who had not dreamt of you;
    But wisely; if we worked it long
    We should forget where it was wrong.

Those thorns are crowns which, woven into knots,
Crackle under and soon boil fool's pots;
    And no man's watching, wise and long,
    Would ever stare them into song.

Thorns burn to a consistent ash, like man;
A splendid cleanser for the frying-pan:
    And those who leap from pan to fire
    Should this brave opposite admire.

All those large dreams by which men long live well
Are magic-lanterned on the smoke of hell;
    This then is real, I have implied,
    A painted, small, transparent slide.

These the inventive can hand-paint at leisure,
Or most emporia would stock our measure;
    And feasting in their dappled shade
    We should forget how they were made.

Feign then what's by a decent tact believed
And act that state is only so conceived,
    And build an edifice of form
    For house where phantoms may keep warm.

Imagine, then, by miracle, with me,
(Ambiguous gifts, as what gods give must be)
    What could not possibly be there,
    And learn a style from a despair.

WILLIAM EMPSON Homage to the British Museum

There is a Supreme God in the ethnological section;
A hollow toad shape, faced with a blank shield.
He needs his belly to include the Pantheon,
Which is inserted through a hole behind.
At the navel, at the points formally stressed, at the organs of sense,
Lice glue themselves, dolls, local deities,
His smooth wood creeps with all the creeds of the world.

Attending there let us absorb the cultures of nations
And dissolve into our judgement all their codes.
Then, being clogged with a natural hesitation
(People are continually asking one the way out),
Let us stand here and admit that we have no road.
Being everything, let us admit that is to be something,
Or give ourselves the benefit of the doubt;
Let us offer our pinch of dust all to this God,
And grant his reign over the entire building.

LOUIS MACNEICE Snow

The room was suddenly rich and the great bay-window was
Spawning snow and pink roses against it
Soundlessly collateral and incompatible:
World is suddener than we fancy it.

World is crazier and more of it than we think,
Incorrigibly plural. I peel and portion
A tangerine and spit the pips and feel
The drunkenness of things being various.

And the fire flames with a bubbling sound for world
Is more spiteful and gay than one supposes –
On the tongue on the eyes on the ears in the palms of one's hands –
There is more than glass between the snow and the huge roses.

WILLIAM SOUTAR The Tryst

O luely, luely cam she in
And luely she lay doun:
I kent her by her caller lips
And her breists sae sma' and roun'.

5   A' thru the nicht we spak nae word
Nor sinder'd bane frae bane:
A' thru the nicht I heard her hert
Gang soundin' wi' my ain.

It was about the waukrife hour
10   Whan cocks begin to craw
That she smool'd saftly thru the mirk
Afore the day wud daw.

Sae luely, luely, cam she in
Sae luely was she gaen
15   And wi' her a' my simmer days
Like they had never been.

1936   W. H. AUDEN

Out on the lawn I lie in bed,
Vega conspicuous overhead
   In the windless nights of June;
Forests of green have done complete
The day's activity; my feet
   Point to the rising moon.

Lucky, this point in time and space
Is chosen as my working place;
   Where the sexy airs of summer,
The bathing hours and the bare arms,
The leisured drives through a land of farms,
   Are good to the newcomer.

---

1 *luely* softly; 3 *caller* cool; 6 'nor parted bone from bone'; 9 *waukrife* wakeful;
11 *smool'd saftly* slipped away

Equal with colleagues in a ring
I sit on each calm evening,
　　Enchanted as the flowers
The opening light draws out of hiding
From leaves with all its dove-like pleading
　　Its logic and its powers.

That later we, though parted then
May still recall these evenings when
　　Fear gave his watch no look;
The lion griefs loped from the shade
And on our knees their muzzles laid,
　　And Death put down his book.

Moreover, eyes in which I learn
That I am glad to look, return
　　My glances every day;
And when the birds and rising sun
Waken me, I shall speak with one
　　Who has not gone away.

Now North and South and East and West
Those I love lie down to rest;
　　The moon looks on them all:
The healers and the brilliant talkers,
The eccentrics and the silent walkers,
　　The dumpy and the tall.

She climbs the European sky;
Churches and power stations lie
　　Alike among earth's fixtures:
Into the galleries she peers,
And blankly as an orphan stares
　　Upon the marvellous pictures.

To gravity attentive, she
Can notice nothing here; though we
　　Whom hunger cannot move,
From gardens where we feel secure
Look up, and with a sigh endure
　　The tyrannies of love:

And, gentle, do not care to know,
Where Poland draws her Eastern bow,
    What violence is done;
Nor ask what doubtful act allows
Our freedom in this English house,
    Our picnics in the sun.

The creepered wall stands up to hide
The gathering multitudes outside
    Whose glances hunger worsens;
Concealing from their wretchedness
Our metaphysical distress,
    Our kindness to ten persons.

And now no path on which we move
But shows already traces of
    Intentions not our own,
Thoroughly able to achieve
What our excitement could conceive,
    But our hands left alone.

For what by nature and by training
We loved, has little strength remaining:
    Though we would gladly give
The Oxford colleges, Big Ben,
And all the birds in Wicken Fen,
    It has no wish to live.

Soon through the dykes of our content
The crumpling flood will force a rent,
    And, taller than a tree,
Hold sudden death before our eyes
Whose river-dreams long hid the size
    And vigours of the sea.

But when the waters make retreat
And through the black mud first the wheat
    In shy green stalks appears;
When stranded monsters gasping lie,
And sounds of riveting terrify
    Their whorled unsubtle ears:

May this for which we dread to lose
Our privacy, need no excuse
   But to that strength belong;
As through a child's rash happy cries
The drowned voices of his parents rise
   In unlamenting song.

After discharges of alarm,
All unpredicted may it calm
   The pulse of nervous nations;
Forgive the murderer in his glass,
Tough in its patience to surpass
   The tigress her swift motions.

W. H. AUDEN

Now the leaves are falling fast,
Nurse's flowers will not last;
Nurses to the graves are gone,
And the prams go rolling on.

Whispering neighbours, left and right,
Pluck us from the real delight;
And the active hands must freeze
Lonely on the separate knees.

Dead in hundreds at the back
Follow wooden in our track,
Arms raised stiffly to reprove
In false attitudes of love.

Starving through the leafless wood
Trolls run scolding for their food;
And the nightingale is dumb,
And the angel will not come.

Cold, impossible, ahead
Lifts the mountain's lovely head
Whose white waterfall could bless
Travellers in their last distress.

ELIZABETH DARYUSH Still-Life

Through the open French window the warm sun
lights up the polished breakfast-table, laid
round a bowl of crimson roses, for one –
a service of Worcester porcelain, arrayed
near it a melon, peaches, figs, small hot
rolls in a napkin, fairy rack of toast,
butter in ice, high silver coffee pot,
and, heaped on a salver, the morning's post.

She comes over the lawn, the young heiress,
from her early walk in her garden-wood
feeling that life's a table set to bless
her delicate desires with all that's good,

that even the unopened future lies
like a love-letter, full of sweet surprise.

LAURA RIDING The Wind Suffers

The wind suffers of blowing,
The sea suffers of water,
And fire suffers of burning,
And I of a living name.

As stone suffers of stoniness,
As light of its shiningness,
As birds of their wingedness,
So I of my whoness.

And what the cure of all this?
What the not and not suffering?
What the better and later of this?
What the more me of me?

How for the pain-world to be
More world and no pain?
How for the old rain to fall
More wet and more dry?

How for the wilful blood to run
More salt-red and sweet-white?
And how for me in my actualness
To more shriek and more smile?

By no other miracles,
By the same knowing poison,
By an improved anguish,
By my further dying.

PATRICK KAVANAGH Inniskeen Road: July Evening

The bicycles go by in twos and threes –
There's a dance in Billy Brennan's barn tonight,
And there's the half-talk code of mysteries
And the wink-and-elbow language of delight.
Half-past eight and there is not a spot
Upon a mile of road, no shadow thrown
That might turn out a man or woman, not
A footfall tapping secrecies of stone.

I have what every poet hates in spite
Of all the solemn talk of contemplation.
Oh, Alexander Selkirk knew the plight
Of being king and government and nation.
A road, a mile of kingdom, I am king
Of banks and stones and every blooming thing.

⸿ A. E. HOUSMAN *from* More Poems

XXIII

Crossing alone the nighted ferry
    With the one coin for fee,
Whom, on the wharf of Lethe waiting,
    Count you to find? Not me.

The brisk fond lackey to fetch and carry,
    The true, sick-hearted slave,
Expect him not in the just city
    And free land of the grave.

XXXI

Because I liked you better
    Than suits a man to say,
It irked you, and I promised
    To throw the thought away.

To put the world between us
    We parted, stiff and dry;
'Good-bye,' said you, 'forget me.'
    'I will, no fear,' said I.

If here, where clover whitens
    The dead man's knoll, you pass,
And no tall flower to meet you
    Starts in the trefoiled grass,

Halt by the headstone naming
    The heart no longer stirred,
And say the lad that loved you
    Was one that kept his word.

§   §   §

1937   A. E. HOUSMAN

Oh who is that young sinner with the handcuffs on his wrists?
And what has he been after that they groan and shake their fists?
And wherefore is he wearing such a conscience-stricken air?
Oh they're taking him to prison for the colour of his hair.

'Tis a shame to human nature, such a head of hair as his;
In the good old time 'twas hanging for the colour that it is;
Though hanging isn't bad enough and flaying would be fair
For the nameless and abominable colour of his hair.

Oh a deal of pains he's taken and a pretty price he's paid
To hide his poll or dye it of a mentionable shade;
But they've pulled the beggar's hat off for the world to see and stare,
And they're haling him to justice for the colour of his hair.

Now 'tis oakum for his fingers and the treadmill for his feet
And the quarry-gang on Portland in the cold and in the heat,
And between his spells of labour in the time he has to spare
He can curse the God that made him for the colour of his hair.

(written 1895)

JOHN BETJEMAN The Arrest of Oscar Wilde at the Cadogan Hotel

He sipped at a weak hock and seltzer
    As he gazed at the London skies
Through the Nottingham lace of the curtains
    Or was it his bees-winged eyes?

To the right and before him Pont Street
    Did tower in her new built red,
As hard as the morning gaslight
    That shone on his unmade bed,

'I want some more hock in my seltzer,
    And Robbie, please give me your hand –
Is this the end or beginning?
    How can I understand?

'So you've brought me the latest *Yellow Book*:
    And Buchan has got in it now:
Approval of what is approved of
    Is as false as a well-kept vow.

'More hock, Robbie – where is the seltzer?
 Dear boy, pull again at the bell!
They are all little better than *cretins*,
 Though this *is* the Cadogan Hotel.

'One astrakhan coat is at Willis's –
 Another one's at the Savoy:
Do fetch my morocco portmanteau,
 And bring them on later, dear boy.'

A thump, and a murmur of voices –
 ('Oh why must they make such a din?')
As the door of the bedroom swung open
 And TWO PLAIN CLOTHES POLICEMEN came in:

'Mr. Woilde, we 'ave come for tew take yew
 Where felons and criminals dwell:
We must ask yew tew leave with us quoietly
 For this *is* the Cadogan Hotel.'

He rose, and he put down *The Yellow Book*.
 He staggered – and, terrible-eyed,
He brushed past the palms on the staircase
 And was helped to a hansom outside.

DAVID JONES *from* In Parenthesis

from Part 3

 And the deepened stillness as a calm, cast over us – a potent
influence over us and him – dead-calm for this Sargasso dank,
and for the creeping things.
 You can hear the silence of it:
you can hear the rat of no-man's-land
rut-out intricacies,
weasel-out his patient workings,
scrut, scrut, sscrut,
harrow-out earthly, trowel his cunning paw;
redeem the time of our uncharity, to sap his own amphibious
paradise.
 You can hear this carrying-parties rustle our corruptions
through the night-weeds – contest the choicest morsels in his

tiny conduits, bead-eyed feast on us; by a rule of his nature, at
night-feast on the broken of us.

Those broad-pinioned;
blue-burnished, or brinded-back;
whose proud eyes watched
                    the broken emblems
droop and drag dust,
suffer with us this metamorphosis.

These too have shed their fine feathers; these too have slimed
their dark-bright coats; these too have condescended to dig in.

The white-tailed eagle at the battle ebb,
                        where the sea wars against the river
the speckled kite of Maldon
and the crow
have naturally selected to be un-winged;
to go on the belly, to
sap sap sap
with festered spines, arched under the moon; furrit with
whiskered snouts the secret parts of us.

When it's all quiet you can hear them:
scrut scrut scrut
when it's as quiet as this is.

It's so very still.

Your body fits the crevice of the bay in the most comfortable
                        fashion imaginable.

It's cushy enough.

The relief elbows him on the fire-step: All quiet china? –
bugger all to report? – kipping mate? – christ, mate – you'll 'ave
'em all over.

(. . .)

from **Part 7**

But sweet sister death has gone debauched today and stalks on
this high ground with strumpet confidence, makes no coy veiling
of her appetite but leers from you to me with all her parts
discovered.

By one and one the line gaps, where her fancy will – howsoever
they may howl for their virginity
she holds them – who impinge less on space
sink limply to a heap
nourish a lesser category of being

like those other who fructify the land
like Tristram
Lamorak de Galis
Alisand le Orphelin
Beaumains who was youngest
or all of them in shaft-shade
at strait Thermopylae
or the sweet brothers Balin and Balan
embraced beneath their single monument.

    Jonathan my lovely one
on Gelboe mountain
and the young man Absalom.
White Hart transfixed in his dark lodge.
Peredur of steel arms
and he who with intention took grass of that field to be for
him the Species of Bread.

    Taillefer the maker,
and on the same day,
thirty thousand other ranks.
And in the country of Béarn – Oliver
and all the rest – so many without memento
beneath the tumuli on the high hills
and under the harvest places.

But how intolerably bright the morning is where we who are
alive and remain, walk lifted up, carried forward by an effective
word.

(. . .)

The secret princes between the leaning trees have diadems given
them.

    Life the leveller hugs her impudent equality – she may proceed
at once to less discriminating zones.

The Queen of the Woods has cut bright boughs of various
flowering.

    These knew her influential eyes. Her awarding hands can
pluck for each their fragile prize.

    She speaks to them according to precedence. She knows what's
due to this elect society. She can choose twelve gentle-men. She
knows who is most lord between the high trees and on the open
down.

    Some she gives white berries

some she gives brown
Emil has a curious crown it's
       made of golden saxifrage.
Fatty wears sweet-briar,
he will reign with her for a thousand years.
For Balder she reaches high to fetch his.
Ulrich smiles for his myrtle wand.
That swine Lillywhite has daisies to his chain – you'd hardly credit it.
She plaits torques of equal splendour for Mr. Jenkins and Billy Crower.
Hansel with Gronwy share dog-violets for a palm, where they lie in serious embrace beneath the twisted tripod.
Siôn gets St. John's Wort – that's fair enough.
Dai Great-coat, she can't find him anywhere – she calls both high and low, she had a very special one for him.
Among this July noblesse she is mindful of December wood when the trees of the forest beat against each other because of him.
She carries to Aneirin-in-the-nullah a rowan sprig, for the glory of Guenedota. You couldn't hear what she said to him, because she was careful for the Disciplines of the Wars.

AUSTIN CLARKE The Straying Student   **1938**

On a holy day when sails were blowing southward,
A bishop sang the Mass at Inishmore,
Men took one side, their wives were on the other
But I heard the woman coming from the shore:
And wild in despair my parents cried aloud
For they saw the vision draw me to the doorway.

Long had she lived in Rome when Popes were bad,
The wealth of every age she makes her own,
Yet smiled on me in eager admiration,
And for a summer taught me all I know,
Banishing shame with her great laugh that rang
As if a pillar caught it back alone.

I learned the prouder counsel of her throat,
My mind was growing bold as light in Greece;
And when in sleep her stirring limbs were shown,

I blessed the noonday rock that knew no tree:
And for an hour the mountain was her throne,
Although her eyes were bright with mockery.

They say I was sent back from Salamanca
And failed in logic, but I wrote her praise
Nine times upon a college wall in France.
She laid her hand at darkfall on my page
That I might read the heavens in a glance
And I knew every star the Moors have named.

Awake or in my sleep, I have no peace now,
Before the ball is struck, my breath has gone,
And yet I tremble lest she may deceive me
And leave me in this land, where every woman's son
Must carry his own coffin and believe,
In dread, all that the clergy teach the young.

ROBERT GRAVES To Evoke Posterity

To evoke posterity
Is to weep on your own grave,
Ventriloquizing for the unborn:
'Would you were present in flesh, hero!
What wreaths and junketings!'

And the punishment is fixed:
To be found fully ancestral,
To be cast in bronze for a city square,
To dribble green in times of rain
And stain the pedestal.

Spiders in the spread beard;
A life proverbial
On clergy lips a-cackle;
Eponymous institutes,
Their luckless architecture.

Two more dates of life and birth
For the hour of special study
From which all boys and girls of mettle
Twice a week play truant
And worn excuses try.

Alive, you have abhorred
The crowds on holiday
Jostling and whistling – yet would you air
Your death-mask, smoothly lidded,
Along the promenade?

ELIZABETH DARYUSH

Children of wealth in your warm nursery,
Set in the cushioned window-seat to watch
The volleying snow, guarded invisibly
By the clear double pane through which no touch
Untimely penetrates, you cannot tell
What winter means; its cruel truths to you
Are only sound and sight; your citadel
Is safe from feeling, and from knowledge too.

Go down, go out to elemental wrong,
Waste your too round limbs, tan your skin too white;
The glass of comfort, ignorance, seems strong
Today, and yet perhaps this very night

You'll wake to horror's wrecking fire – your home
Is wired within for this, in every room.

LOUIS MACNEICE The Sunlight on the Garden

The sunlight on the garden
Hardens and grows cold,
We cannot cage the minute
Within its nets of gold,
When all is told
We cannot beg for pardon.

Our freedom as free lances
Advances towards its end;
The earth compels, upon it
Sonnets and birds descend;
And soon, my friend,
We shall have no time for dances.

The sky was good for flying
Defying the church bells
And every evil iron
Siren and what it tells:
The earth compels,
We are dying, Egypt, dying

And not expecting pardon,
Hardened in heart anew,
But glad to have sat under
Thunder and rain with you,
And grateful too
For sunlight on the garden.

1939   W. B. YEATS Long-legged Fly

That civilisation may not sink
Its great battle lost,
Quiet the dog, tether the pony
To a distant post.
Our master Caesar is in the tent
Where the maps are spread,
His eyes fixed upon nothing,
A hand under his head.

Like a long-legged fly upon the stream
His mind moves upon silence.

That the topless towers be burnt
And men recall that face,
Move most gently if move you must
In this lonely place.
She thinks, part woman, three parts a child,
That nobody looks; her feet
Practise a tinker shuffle
Picked up on the street.

Like a long-legged fly upon the stream
Her mind moves upon silence.

That girls at puberty may find
The first Adam in their thought,
Shut the door of the Pope's chapel,
Keep those children out.
There on the scaffolding reclines
Michael Angelo.
With no more sound than the mice make
His hand moves to and fro.

Like a long-legged fly upon the stream
His mind moves upon silence.

W. H. AUDEN In Memory of W. B. Yeats

I

He disappeared in the dead of winter:
The brooks were frozen, the air-ports almost deserted,
And snow disfigured the public statues;
The mercury sank in the mouth of the dying day.
O all the instruments agree
The day of his death was a dark cold day.

Far from his illness
The wolves ran on through the evergreen forests,
The peasant river was untempted by the fashionable quays;
By mourning tongues
The death of the poet was kept from his poems.

But for him it was his last afternoon as himself,
An afternoon of nurses and rumours;
The provinces of his body revolted,
The squares of his mind were empty,
Silence invaded the suburbs,
The current of his feeling failed: he became his admirers.

Now he is scattered among a hundred cities
And wholly given over to unfamiliar affections;
To find his happiness in another kind of wood
And be punished under a foreign code of conscience.
The words of a dead man
Are modified in the guts of the living.

But in the importance and noise of to-morrow
When the brokers are roaring like beasts on the
                          floor of the Bourse,
And the poor have the sufferings to which
                          they are fairly accustomed,
And each in the cell of himself is almost
                          convinced of his freedom;
A few thousand will think of this day
As one thinks of a day when one did something
                          slightly unusual.

O all the instruments agree
The day of his death was a dark cold day.

II

You were silly like us: your gift survived it all;
The parish of rich women, physical decay,
Yourself; mad Ireland hurt you into poetry.
Now Ireland has her madness and her weather still,
For poetry makes nothing happen: it survives
In the valley of its saying where executives
Would never want to tamper; it flows south
From ranches of isolation and the busy griefs,
Raw towns that we believe and die in; it survives,
A way of happening, a mouth.

III

Earth, receive an honoured guest;
William Yeats is laid to rest:
Let the Irish vessel lie
Emptied of its poetry.

Time that is intolerant
Of the brave and innocent,
And indifferent in a week
To a beautiful physique,

Worships language and forgives
Everyone by whom it lives;
Pardons cowardice, conceit,
Lays its honours at their feet.

Time that with this strange excuse
Pardoned Kipling and his views,
And will pardon Paul Claudel,
Pardons him for writing well.

In the nightmare of the dark
All the dogs of Europe bark,
And the living nations wait,
Each sequestered in its hate;

Intellectual disgrace
Stares from every human face,
And the seas of pity lie
Locked and frozen in each eye.

Follow, poet, follow right
To the bottom of the night,
With your unconstraining voice
Still persuade us to rejoice;

With the farming of a verse
Make a vineyard of the curse,
Sing of human unsuccess
In a rapture of distress;

In the deserts of the heart
Let the healing fountain start,
In the prison of his days
Teach the free man how to praise.

LOUIS MACNEICE *from* Autumn Journal

I

Close and slow, summer is ending in Hampshire,
    Ebbing away down ramps of shaven lawn where close-clipped
        yew
Insulates the lives of retired generals and admirals
    And the spyglasses hung in the hall and the prayer-books ready in
        the pew
And August going out to the tin trumpets of nasturtiums
    And the sunflowers' Salvation Army blare of brass
And the spinster sitting in a deckchair picking up stitches
    Not raising her eyes to the noise of the planes that pass
Northward from Lee-on-Solent. Macrocarpa and cypress
    And roses on a rustic trellis and mulberry trees
And bacon and eggs in a silver dish for breakfast
    And all the inherited assets of bodily ease
And all the inherited worries, rheumatism and taxes,
    And whether Stella will marry and what to do with Dick
And the branch of the family that lost their money in Hatry
    And the passing of the *Morning Post* and of life's climacteric
And the growth of vulgarity, cars that pass the gate-lodge
    And crowds undressing on the beach
And the hiking cockney lovers with thoughts directed
    Neither to God nor Nation but each to each.
But the home is still a sanctum under the pelmets,
    All quiet on the Family Front,
Farmyard noises across the fields at evening
    While the trucks of the Southern Railway dawdle . . . shunt
Into poppy sidings for the night – night which knows no passion
    No assault of hands or tongue
For all is old as flint or chalk or pine-needles
    And the rebels and the young
Have taken the train to town or the two-seater
    Unravelling rails or road,
Losing the thread deliberately behind them –
    Autumnal palinode.
And I am in the train too now and summer is going
    South as I go north
Bound for the dead leaves falling, the burning bonfire,
    The dying that brings forth

The harder life, revealing the trees' girders,
    The frost that kills the germs of *laissez-faire*;
West Meon, Tisted, Farnham, Woking, Weybridge,
    Then London's packed and stale and pregnant air.
My dog, a symbol of the abandoned order,
    Lies on the carriage floor,
Her eyes inept and glamorous as a film star's,
    Who wants to live, i.e. wants more
Presents, jewellery, furs, gadgets, solicitations
    As if to live were not
Following the curve of a planet or controlled water
    But a leap in the dark, a tangent, a stray shot.
It is this we learn after so many failures,
    The building of castles in sand, of queens in snow,
That we cannot make any corner in life or in life's beauty,
    That no river is a river which does not flow.
Surbiton, and a woman gets in, painted
    With dyed hair but a ladder in her stocking and eyes
Patient beneath the calculated lashes,
    Inured for ever to surprise;
And the train's rhythm becomes the *ad nauseam* repetition
    Of every tired aubade and maudlin madrigal,
The faded airs of sexual attraction
    Wandering like dead leaves along a warehouse wall:
'I loved my love with a platform ticket,
    A jazz song,
A handbag, a pair of stockings of Paris Sand –
    I loved her long.
I loved her between the lines and against the clock,
    Not until death
But till life did us part I loved her with paper money
    And with whisky on the breath.
I loved her with peacock's eyes and the wares of Carthage,
    With glass and gloves and gold and a powder puff
With blasphemy, camaraderie, and bravado
    And lots of other stuff.
I loved my love with the wings of angels
    Dipped in henna, unearthly red,
With my office hours, with flowers and sirens,
    With my budget, my latchkey, and my daily bread.'
And so to London and down the ever-moving
    Stairs
Where a warm wind blows the bodies of men together
    And blows apart their complexes and cares.

Shelley and jazz and lieder and love and hymn-tunes
    And day returns too soon;
We'll get drunk among the roses
    In the valley of the moon.
Give me an aphrodisiac, give me lotus,
    Give me the same again;
Make all the erotic poets of Rome and Ionia
    And Florence and Provence and Spain
Pay a tithe of their sugar to my potion
    And ferment my days
With the twang of Hawaii and the boom of the Congo,
    Let the old Muse loosen her stays
Or give me a new Muse with stockings and suspenders
    And a smile like a cat,
With false eyelashes and finger-nails of carmine
    And dressed by Schiaparelli, with a pill-box hat.
Let the aces run riot round Brooklands,
    Let the tape-machines go drunk,
Turn on the purple spotlight, pull out the Vox Humana,
    Dig up somebody's body in a cloakroom trunk.
Give us sensations and then again sensations –
    Strip-tease, fireworks, all-in wrestling, gin;
Spend your capital, open your house and pawn your padlocks,
    Let the critical sense go out and the Roaring Boys come in.
Give me a houri but houris are too easy,
    Give me a nun;
We'll rape the angels off the golden reredos
    Before we're done.
Tiger-women and Lesbos, drums and entrails,
    And let the skies rotate,
We'll play roulette with the stars, we'll sit out drinking
    At the Hangman's Gate.
O look who comes here. I cannot see their faces
    Walking in file, slowly in file;
They have no shoes on their feet, the knobs of their ankles
    Catch the moonlight as they pass the stile
And cross the moor among the skeletons of bog-oak
    Following the track from the gallows back to the town;
Each has the end of a rope around his neck. I wonder
    Who let these men come back, who cut them down –

And now they reach the gate and line up opposite
   The neon lights on the medieval wall
And underneath the sky-signs
   Each one takes his cowl and lets it fall
And we see their faces, each the same as the other,
   Men and women, each like a closed door,
But something about their faces is familiar;
   Where have we seen them before?
Was it the murderer on the nursery ceiling
   Or Judas Iscariot in the Field of Blood
Or someone at Gallipoli or in Flanders
   Caught in the end-all mud?
But take no notice of them, out with the ukulele,
   The saxophone and the dice;
They are sure to go away if we take no notice;
   Another round of drinks or make it twice.
That was a good one, tell us another, don't stop talking,
   Cap your stories; if
You haven't any new ones tell the old ones,
   Tell them as often as you like and perhaps those horrible stiff
People with blank faces that are yet familiar
   Won't be there when you look again, but don't
Look just yet, just give them time to vanish. I said to vanish;
   What do you mean – they won't?
Give us the songs of Harlem or Mitylene –
   Pearls in wine –
There can't be a hell unless there is a heaven
   And a devil would have to be divine
And there can't be such things one way or the other;
   That we know;
You can't step into the same river twice so there can't be
   Ghosts; thank God that rivers always flow.
Sufficient to the moment is the moment;
   Past and future merely don't make sense
And yet I thought I had seen them . . .
   But *how*, if there is only a present tense?
Come on, boys, we aren't afraid of bogies,
   Give us another drink;
This little lady has a fetish,
   She goes to bed in mink.
This little pig went to market –
   Now I think you may look, I think the coast is clear.
Well, why don't you answer?
   I can't answer because they are still there.

1940   W. H. AUDEN Musée des Beaux Arts

About suffering they were never wrong,
The Old Masters: how well they understood
Its human position; how it takes place
While someone else is eating or opening a window or just walking
  dully along;
How, when the aged are reverently, passionately waiting
For the miraculous birth, there always must be
Children who did not specially want it to happen, skating
On a pond at the edge of the wood:
They never forgot
That even the dreadful martyrdom must run its course
Anyhow in a corner, some untidy spot
Where the dogs go on with their doggy life and the torturer's horse
Scratches its innocent behind on a tree.

In Brueghel's *Icarus*, for instance: how everything turns away
Quite leisurely from the disaster; the ploughman may
Have heard the splash, the forsaken cry,
But for him it was not an important failure; the sun shone
As it had to on the white legs disappearing into the green
Water; and the expensive delicate ship that must have seen
Something amazing, a boy falling out of the sky,
Had somewhere to get to and sailed calmly on.

JOHN BETJEMAN Pot-Pourri from a Surrey Garden

Miles of pram in the wind and Pam in the gorse track,
  Coco-nut smell of the broom, and a packet of Weights
Press'd in the sand. The thud of a hoof on a horse-track –
    A horse-riding horse for a horse-track –
    Conifer county of Surrey approached
  Through remarkable wrought-iron gates.

Over your boundary now, I wash my face in a bird-bath,
  Then which path shall I take? that over there by the pram?
Down by the pond! or – yes, I will take the slippery third path,
    Trodden away with gym shoes,
    Beautiful fir-dry alley that leads
  To the bountiful body of Pam.

Pam, I adore you, Pam, you great big mountainous sports girl,
    Whizzing them over the net, full of the strength of five:
That old Malvernian brother, you zephyr and khaki shorts girl,
        Although he's playing for Woking,
        Can't stand up
    To your wonderful backhand drive.

See the strength of her arm, as firm and hairy as Hendren's;
    See the size of her thighs, the pout of her lips as, cross,
And full of a pent-up strength, she swipes at the rhododendrons,
        Lucky the rhododendrons,
        And flings her arrogant love-lock
    Back with a petulant toss.

Over the redolent pinewoods, in at the bathroom casement,
    One fine Saturday, Windlesham bells shall call:
Up the Butterfield aisle rich with Gothic enlacement,
        Licensed now for embracement,
        Pam and I, as the organ
    Thunders over you all.

WILLIAM EMPSON Missing Dates

Slowly the poison the whole blood stream fills.
It is not the effort nor the failure tires.
The waste remains, the waste remains and kills.

It is not your system or clear sight that mills
Down small to the consequence a life requires;
Slowly the poison the whole blood stream fills.

They bled an old dog dry yet the exchange rills
Of young dog blood gave but a month's desires;
The waste remains, the waste remains and kills.

It is the Chinese tombs and the slag hills
Usurp the soil, and not the soil retires.
Slowly the poison the whole blood stream fills.

Not to have fire is to be a skin that shrills.
The complete fire is death. From partial fires
The waste remains, the waste remains and kills.

It is the poems you have lost, the ills
From missing dates, at which the heart expires.
Slowly the poison the whole blood stream fills.
The waste remains, the waste remains and kills.

WILLIAM EMPSON Aubade

Hours before dawn we were woken by the quake.
My house was on a cliff. The thing could take
Bookloads off shelves, break bottles in a row.
Then the long pause and then the bigger shake.
It seemed the best thing to be up and go.

And far too large for my feet to step by.
I hoped that various buildings were brought low.
The heart of standing is you cannot fly.

It seemed quite safe till she got up and dressed.
The guarded tourist makes the guide the test.
Then I said The Garden? Laughing she said No.
Taxi for her and for me healthy rest.
It seemed the best thing to be up and go.

The language problem but you have to try.
Some solid ground for lying could she show?
The heart of standing is you cannot fly.

None of these deaths were her point at all.
The thing was that being woken he would bawl
And finding her not in earshot he would know.
I tried saying Half an Hour to pay this call.
It seemed the best thing to be up and go.

I slept, and blank as that I would yet lie.
Till you have seen what a threat holds below,
The heart of standing is you cannot fly.

Tell me again about Europe and her pains,
Who's tortured by the drought, who by the rains.
Glut me with floods where only the swine can row
Who cuts his throat and let him count his gains.
It seemed the best thing to be up and go.

A bedshift flight to a Far Eastern sky.
Only the same war on a stronger toe.
The heart of standing is you cannot fly.

Tell me more quickly what I lost by this,
Or tell me with less drama what they miss
Who call no die a god for a good throw,
Who say after two aliens had one kiss
It seemed the best thing to be up and go.

But as to risings, I can tell you why.
It is on contradiction that they grow.
It seemed the best thing to be up and go.
Up was the heartening and the strong reply.
The heart of standing is we cannot fly.

LOUIS MACNEICE Meeting Point   1941

Time was away and somewhere else,
There were two glasses and two chairs
And two people with the one pulse
(Somebody stopped the moving stairs):
Time was away and somewhere else.

And they were neither up nor down:
The stream's music did not stop
Flowing through heather, limpid brown,
Although they sat in a coffee shop
And they were neither up nor down.

The bell was silent in the air
Holding its inverted poise –
Between the clang and clang a flower,
A brazen calyx of no noise:
The bell was silent in the air.

The camels crossed the miles of sand
That stretched around the cups and plates;
The desert was their own, they planned
To portion out the stars and dates:
The camels crossed the miles of sand.

Time was away and somewhere else.
The waiter did not come, the clock
Forgot them and the radio waltz
Came out like water from a rock:
Time was away and somewhere else.

Her fingers flicked away the ash
That bloomed again in tropic trees:
Not caring if the markets crash
When they had forests such as these,
Her fingers flicked away the ash.

God or whatever means the Good
Be praised that time can stop like this,
That what the heart has understood
God verify in the body's peace
God or whatever means the Good.

Time was away and she was here
And life no longer what it was,
The bell was silent in the air
And all the room one glow because
Time was away and she was here.

LOUIS MACNEICE Autobiography

In my childhood trees were green
And there was plenty to be seen.

Come back early or never come.

My father made the walls resound,
He wore his collar the wrong way round.

Come back early or never come.

My mother wore a yellow dress;
Gently, gently, gentleness.

Come back early or never come.

When I was five the black dreams came;
Nothing after was quite the same.

Come back early or never come.

The dark was talking to the dead;
The lamp was dark beside my bed.

Come back early or never come.

When I woke they did not care;
Nobody, nobody was there.

Come back early or never come.

When my silent terror cried,
Nobody, nobody replied.

Come back early or never come.

I got up; the chilly sun
Saw me walk away alone.

Come back early or never come.

T. S. ELIOT *from* **Little Gidding**   1942

II

Ash on an old man's sleeve
Is all the ash the burnt roses leave.
Dust in the air suspended
Marks the place where a story ended.
Dust inbreathed was a house –
The wall, the wainscot and the mouse.
The death of hope and despair,
     This is the death of air.

There are flood and drouth
Over the eyes and in the mouth,
Dead water and dead sand
Contending for the upper hand.

The parched eviscerate soil
Gapes at the vanity of toil,
Laughs without mirth.
      This is the death of earth.

Water and fire succeed
The town, the pasture and the weed.
Water and fire deride
The sacrifice that we denied.
Water and fire shall rot
The marred foundations we forgot,
Of sanctuary and choir.
      This is the death of water and fire.

In the uncertain hour before the morning
   Near the ending of interminable night
   At the recurrent end of the unending
After the dark dove with the flickering tongue
   Had passed below the horizon of his homing
   While the dead leaves still rattled on like tin
Over the asphalt where no other sound was
   Between three districts whence the smoke arose
   I met one walking, loitering and hurried
As if blown towards me like the metal leaves
   Before the urban dawn wind unresisting.
   And as I fixed upon the down-turned face
That pointed scrutiny with which we challenge
   The first-met stranger in the waning dusk
   I caught the sudden look of some dead master
Whom I had known, forgotten, half recalled
   Both one and many; in the brown baked features
   The eyes of a familiar compound ghost
Both intimate and unidentifiable.
   So I assumed a double part, and cried
   And heard another's voice cry: 'What! are *you* here?'
Although we were not. I was still the same,
   Knowing myself yet being someone other –
   And he a face still forming; yet the words sufficed
To compel the recognition they preceded.
   And so, compliant to the common wind,
   Too strange to each other for misunderstanding,
In concord at this intersection time
   Of meeting nowhere, no before and after,
   We trod the pavement in a dead patrol.

I said: 'The wonder that I feel is easy,
    Yet ease is cause of wonder. Therefore speak:
    I may not comprehend, may not remember.'
And he: 'I am not eager to rehearse
    My thoughts and theory which you have forgotten.
    These things have served their purpose: let them be.
So with your own, and pray they be forgiven
    By others, as I pray you to forgive
    Both bad and good. Last season's fruit is eaten
And the fullfed beast shall kick the empty pail.
    For last year's words belong to last year's language
    And next year's words await another voice.
But, as the passage now presents no hindrance
    To the spirit unappeased and peregrine
    Between two worlds become much like each other,
So I find words I never thought to speak
    In streets I never thought I should revisit
    When I left my body on a distant shore.
Since our concern was speech, and speech impelled us
    To purify the dialect of the tribe
    And urge the mind to aftersight and foresight,
Let me disclose the gifts reserved for age
    To set a crown upon your lifetime's effort.
    First, the cold friction of expiring sense
Without enchantment, offering no promise
    But bitter tastelessness of shadow fruit
    As body and soul begin to fall asunder.
Second, the conscious impotence of rage
    At human folly, and the laceration
    Of laughter at what ceases to amuse.
And last, the rending pain of re-enactment
    Of all that you have done, and been; the shame
    Of motives late revealed, and the awareness
Of things ill done and done to others' harm
    Which once you took for exercise of virtue.
    Then fools' approval stings, and honour stains.
From wrong to wrong the exasperated spirit
    Proceeds, unless restored by that refining fire
    Where you must move in measure, like a dancer.'
The day was breaking. In the disfigured street
    He left me, with a kind of valediction,
    And faded on the blowing of the horn.

ALUN LEWIS Raiders' Dawn

Softly the civilized
Centuries fall,
Paper on paper,
Peter on Paul.

And lovers waking
From the night –
Eternity's masters,
Slaves of Time –
Recognize only
The drifting white
Fall of small faces
In pits of lime.

Blue necklace left
On a charred chair
Tells that Beauty
Was startled there.

NORMAN CAMERON Green, Green is El Aghir

Sprawled on the crates and sacks in the rear of the truck,
I was gummy-mouthed from the sun and the dust of the track.
And the two Arab soldiers I'd taken on as hitch-hikers
At a torrid petrol-dump, had been there on their hunkers
Since early morning. I said, in a kind of French
'On m'a dit, qu'il y a une belle source d'eau fraîche.
Plus loin, à El Aghir' . . .

                              It was eighty more kilometres
Until round a corner we heard a splashing of waters,
And there, in a green, dark street, was a fountain with two faces
Discharging both ways, from full-throated faucets
Into basins, thence into troughs and thence into brooks.
Our negro corporal driver slammed his brakes,
And we yelped and leapt from the truck and went at the double

To fill our bidons and bottles and drink and dabble.
Then, swollen with water, we went to an inn for wine.
The Arabs came, too, though their faith might have stood between.
'After all,' they said, 'it's a boisson,' without contrition.

Green, green is El Aghir. It has a railway-station,
And the wealth of its soil has borne many another fruit,
A mairie, a school and an elegant Salle de Fêtes.
Such blessings, as I remarked, in effect, to the waiter,
Are added unto them that have plenty of water.

STEVIE SMITH Bog-Face

Dear little Bog-Face,
Why are you so cold?
And why do you lie with your eyes shut? –
You are not very old.

I am a Child of this World,
And a Child of Grace,
And Mother, I shall be glad when it is over,
I am Bog-Face.

STEVIE SMITH Dirge

From a friend's friend I taste friendship,
From a friend's friend love,
My spirit in confusion,
Long years I strove,
But now I know that never
Nearer I shall move,
Than a friend's friend to friendship,
To love than a friend's love.

Into the dark night
Resignedly I go,
I am not so afraid of the dark night
As the friends I do not know,
I do not fear the night above,
As I fear the friends below.

PATRICK KAVANAGH *from* **The Great Hunger**

from I

Clay is the word and clay is the flesh
Where the potato-gatherers like mechanized scare-crows move
Along the side-fall of the hill – Maguire and his men.
If we watch them an hour is there anything we can prove
Of life as it is broken-backed over the Book
Of Death? Here crows gabble over worms and frogs
And the gulls like old newspapers are blown clear of the hedges,
        luckily.
Is there some light of imagination in these wet clods?
Or why do we stand here shivering?
                        Which of these men
Loved the light and the queen
Too long virgin? Yesterday was summer. Who was it promised
        marriage to himself
Before apples were hung from the ceilings for Hallowe'en?
We will wait and watch the tragedy to the last curtain
Till the last soul passively like a bag of wet clay
Rolls down the side of the hill, diverted by the angles
Where the plough missed or a spade stands, straitening the way.

III

Poor Paddy Maguire, a fourteen-hour day
He worked for years. It was he that lit the fire
And boiled the kettle and gave the cows their hay.
His mother tall hard as a Protestant spire
Came down the stairs bare-foot at the kettle-call
And talked to her son sharply: 'Did you let
The hens out, you?' She had a venomous drawl
And a wizened face like moth-eaten leatherette.
Two black cats peeped between the banisters
And gloated over the bacon-fizzling pan.
Outside the window showed tin canisters.
The snipe of Dawn fell like a whirring noise
And Patrick on a headland stood alone.

The pull is on the traces, it is March
And a cold old black wind is blowing from Dundalk.
The twisting sod rolls over on her back –
The virgin screams before the irresistible sock.
No worry on Maguire's mind this day
Except that he forgot to bring his matches.
'Hop back there Polly, hoy back, woa, wae,'
From every second hill a neighbour watches
With all the sharpened interest of rivalry.
Yet sometimes when the sun comes through a gap
These men know God the Father in a tree:
The Holy Spirit is the rising sap,
And Christ will be the green leaves that will come
At Easter from the sealed and guarded tomb.
Primroses and the unearthly start of ferns
Among the blackthorn shadows in the ditch,
A dead sparrow and an old waistcoat. Maguire learns
As the horses turn slowly round the which is which
Of love and fear and things half born to mind.
He stands between the plough-handles and he sees
At the end of a long furrow his name signed
Among the poets, prostitute's. With all miseries
He is one. Here with the unfortunate
Who for half moments of paradise
Pay out good days and wait and wait
For sunlight-woven cloaks. O to be wise
As Respectability that knows the price of all things
And marks God's truth in pounds and pence and farthings.

from **XI**

The cards are shuffled and the deck
Laid flat for cutting – Tom Malone
Cut for trump. I think we'll make
This game, the last, a tanner one.
Hearts. Right. I see you're breaking
Your two-year-old. Play quick, Maguire,
The clock there says it's half-past ten –
Kate, throw another sod on that fire.
One of the card-players laughs and spits
Into the flame across a shoulder.
Outside, a noise like a rat
Among the hen-roosts. The cock crows over

The frosted townland of the night.
Eleven o'clock and still the game
Goes on and the players seem to be
Drunk in an Orient opium den.
Midnight, one o'clock, two.
Somebody's leg has fallen asleep.
What about home? Maguire are you
Using your double-tree this week?
Why? do you want it? Play the ace.
There's it, and that's the last card for me.
A wonderful night, we had. Duffy's place
Is very convenient. Is that a ghost or a tree?
And so they go home with dragging feet
And their voices rumble like laden carts.
And they are happy as the dead or sleeping . . .
I should have led that ace of hearts.

from **XII**

The fields were bleached white,
The wooden tubs full of water
Were white in the winds
That blew through Brannagan's Gap on their way from Siberia;
The cows on the grassless heights
Followed the hay that had wings –
The February fodder that hung itself on the black branches
Of the hilltop hedge.
A man stood beside a potato-pit
And clapped his arms
And pranced on the crisp roots
And shouted to warm himself.
Then he buck-leaped about the potatoes
And scooped them into a basket.
He looked like a bucking suck-calf
Whose spine was being tickled.
Sometimes he stared across the bogs
And sometimes he straightened his back and vaguely whistled
A tune that weakened his spirit
And saddened his terrier dog's.

(. . .)

A mother dead! The tired sentiment:
'Mother mother' was a shallow pool
Where sorrow hardly could wash its feet . . .
Mary Anne came away from the deathbed and boiled the calves their
    gruel.
O what was I doing when the procession passed?
Where was I looking?
Young women and men
And I might have joined them.
Who bent the coin of my destiny
That it stuck in the slot?
I remember a night we walked
Through the moon of Donaghmoyne,
Four of us seeking adventure –
It was midsummer forty years ago.
Now I know
The moment that gave the turn to my life.
O Christ! I am locked in a stable with pigs and cows for ever.

HENRY REED Judging Distances

1943

Not only how far away, but the way that you say it
Is very important. Perhaps you may never get
The knack of judging a distance, but at least you know
How to report on a landscape: the central sector,
The right of arc and that, which we had last Tuesday,
    And at least you know

That maps are of time, not place, so far as the army
Happens to be concerned – the reason being,
Is one which need not delay us. Again, you know
There are three kinds of tree, three only, the fir and the poplar,
And those which have bushy tops to; and lastly
    That things only seem to be things.

A barn is not called a barn, to put it more plainly,
Or a field in the distance, where sheep may be safely grazing.
You must never be over-sure. You must say, when reporting:
At five o'clock in the central sector is a dozen
Of what appear to be animals; whatever you do,
    Don't call the bleeders *sheep*.

I am sure that's quite clear; and suppose, for the sake of example,
The one at the end, asleep, endeavours to tell us
What he sees over there to the west, and how far away,
After first having come to attention. There to the west,
On the fields of summer the sun and the shadows bestow
    Vestments of purple and gold.

The still white dwellings are like a mirage in the heat,
And under the swaying elms a man and a woman
Lie gently together. Which is, perhaps, only to say
That there is a row of houses to the left of arc,
And that under some poplars a pair of what appear to be humans
    Appear to be loving.

Well that, for an answer, is what we might rightly call
Moderately satisfactory only, the reason being,
Is that two things have been omitted, and those are important.
The human beings, now: in what direction are they,
And how far away, would you say? And do not forget
    There may be dead ground in between.

There may be dead ground in between; and I may not have got
The knack of judging a distance; I will only venture
A guess that perhaps between me and the apparent lovers
(Who, incidentally, appear by now to have finished)
At seven o'clock from the houses, is roughly a distance
    Of about one year and a half.

DAVID GASCOYNE Snow in Europe

Out of their slumber Europeans spun
Dense dreams: appeasement, miracle, glimpsed flash
Of a new golden era; but could not restrain
The vertical white weight that fell last night
And made their continent a blank.

Hush, says the sameness of the snow,
The Ural and the Jura now rejoin
The furthest Arctic's desolation. All is one;
Sheer monotone: plain, mountain; country, town:
Contours and boundaries no longer show.

The warring flags hang colourless a while;
Now midnight's icy zero feigns a truce
Between the signs and seasons, and fades out
All shots and cries. But when the great thaw comes,
How red shall be the melting snow, how loud the drums!

DAVID GASCOYNE A Wartime Dawn

Dulled by the slow glare of the yellow bulb;
As far from sleep still as at any hour
Since distant midnight; with a hollow skull
In which white vapours seem to reel
Among limp muddles of old thought; till eyes
Collapse into themselves like clams in mud . . .
Hand paws the wall to reach the chilly switch;
Then nerve-shot darkness gradually shakes
Throughout the room. *Lie still* . . . Limbs twitch;
Relapse to immobility's faint ache. And time
A while relaxes; space turns wholly black.

But deep in the velvet crater of the ear
A chip of sound abruptly irritates.
A second, a third chirp; and then another far
Emphatic trill and chirrup shrills in answer; notes
From all directions round pluck at the strings
Of hearing with frail finely-sharpened claws.
And in an instant, every wakened bird
Across surrounding miles of air
Outside, is sowing like a scintillating sand
Its throat's incessantly replenished store
Of tuneless singsong, timeless, aimless, blind.

Draw now with prickling hand the curtains back;
Unpin the blackout-cloth; let in
Grim crack-of-dawn's first glimmer through the glass.
All's yet half sunk in Yesterday's stale death,
Obscurely still beneath a moist-tinged blank
Sky like the inside of a deaf mute's mouth . . .
Nearest within the window's sight, ash-pale
Against a cinder coloured wall, the white
Pear-blossom hovers like a stare; rain-wet
The further housetops weakly shine; and there,
Beyond, hangs flaccidly a lone barrage-balloon.

An incommunicable desolation weighs
Like depths of stagnant water on this break of day. –
Long meditation without thought. – Until a breeze
From some pure Nowhere straying, stirs
A pang of poignant odour from the earth, an unheard sigh
Pregnant with sap's sweet tang and raw soil's fine
Aroma, smell of stone, and acrid breath
Of gravel puddles. While the brooding green
Of nearby gardens' grass and trees, and quiet flat
Blue leaves, the distant lilac mirages, are made
Clear by increasing daylight, and intensified.

Now head sinks into pillows in retreat
Before this morning's hovering advance;
(Behind loose lids, in sleep's warm porch, half hears
White hollow clink of bottles, – dragging crunch
Of milk-cart wheels, – and presently a snatch
Of windy whistling as the newsboy's bike winds near,
Distributing to neighbour's peaceful steps
Reports of last-night's battles); at last sleeps.
While early guns on Norway's bitter coast
Where faceless troops are landing, renew fire:
And one more day of War starts everywhere.

KEITH DOUGLAS Desert Flowers

Living in a wide landscape are the flowers –
Rosenberg I only repeat what you were saying –
the shell and the hawk every hour
are slaying men and jerboas, slaying

the mind: but the body can fill
the hungry flowers and the dogs who cry words
at nights, the most hostile things of all.
But that is not new. Each time the night discards

draperies on the eyes and leaves the mind awake
I look each side of the door of sleep
for the little coin it will take
to buy the secret I shall not keep.

I see men as trees suffering
or confound the detail and the horizon.
Lay the coin on my tongue and I will sing
of what the others never set eyes on.

H. D. (HILDA DOOLITTLE) *from* The Walls Do Not Fall

I

An incident here and there,
and rails gone (for guns)
from your (and my) old town square:

mist and mist-grey, no colour,
still the Luxor bee, chick and hare
pursue unalterable purpose

in green, rose-red, lapis;
they continue to prophesy
from the stone papyrus:

there, as here, ruin opens
the tomb, the temple; enter,
there as here, there are no doors:

the shrine lies open to the sky,
the rain falls, here, there
sand drifts; eternity endures:

ruin everywhere, yet as the fallen roof
leaves the sealed room
open to the air,

so, through our desolation,
thoughts stir, inspiration stalks us
through gloom:

unaware, Spirit announces the Presence;
shivering overtakes us,
as of old, Samuel:

trembling at a known street-corner,
we know not nor are known;
the Pythian pronounces – we pass on

to another cellar, to another sliced wall
where poor utensils show
like rare objects in a museum;

Pompeii has nothing to teach us,
we know crack of volcanic fissure,
slow flow of terrible lava,

pressure on heart, lungs, the brain
about to burst its brittle case
(what the skull can endure!):

over us, Apocryphal fire,
under us, the earth sway, dip of a floor,
slope of a pavement

where men roll, drunk
with a new bewilderment,
sorcery, bedevilment:

the bone-frame was made for
no such shock knit within terror,
yet the skeleton stood up to it:

the flesh? it was melted away,
the heart burnt out, dead ember,
tendons, muscles shattered, outer husk dismembered,

yet the frame held:
we passed the flame: we wonder
what saved us? what for?

SORLEY MACLEAN Hallaig

'Time, the deer, is in the wood of Hallaig'

The window is nailed and boarded
through which I saw the West
and my love is at the Burn of Hallaig,
a birch tree, and she has always been

between Inver and Milk Hollow,
here and there about Baile-chuirn:
she is a birch, a hazel,
a straight, slender young rowan.

In Screapadal of my people
where Norman and Big Hector were,
their daughters and their sons are a wood
going up beside the stream.

Proud tonight the pine cocks
crowing on the top of Cnoc an Ra,
straight their backs in the moonlight –
they are not the wood I love.

I will wait for the birch wood
until it comes up by the cairn,
until the whole ridge from Beinn na Lice
will be under its shade.

If it does not, I will go down to Hallaig,
to the Sabbath of the dead,
where the people are frequenting,
every single generation gone.

They are still in Hallaig,
MacLeans and MacLeods,
all who were there in the time of Mac Gille Chaluim
the dead have been seen alive.

The men lying on the green
at the end of every house that was,
the girls a wood of birches,
straight their backs, bent their heads.

Between the Leac and Fearns
the road is under mild moss
and the girls in silent bands
go to Clachan as in the beginning,

and return from Clachan
from Suisnish and the land of the living;
each one young and light-stepping,
without the heartbreak of the tale.

From the Burn of Fearns to the raised beach
that is clear in the mystery of the hills,
there is only the congregation of the girls
keeping up the endless walk,

coming back to Hallaig in the evening,
in the dumb living twilight,
filling the steep slopes,
their laughter a mist in my ears,

and their beauty a film on my heart
before the dimness comes on the kyles,
and when the sun goes down behind Dun Cana
a vehement bullet will come from the gun of Love;

and will strike the deer that goes dizzily,
sniffing at the grass-grown ruined homes:
his eye will freeze in the wood,
his blood will not be traced while I live.

(1970)

LAURENCE BINYON Winter Sunrise

It is early morning within this room: without,
Dark and damp: without and within, stillness
Waiting for day: not a sound but a listening air.

Yellow jasmine, delicate on stiff branches
Stands in a Tuscan pot to delight the eye
In spare December's patient nakedness.

Suddenly, softly, as if at a breath breathed
On the pale wall, a magical apparition,
The shadow of the jasmine, branch and blossom!

It was not there, it is there, in a perfect image;
And all is changed. It is like a memory lost
Returning without a reason into the mind;

And it seems to me that the beauty of the shadow
Is more beautiful than the flower; a strange beauty,
Pencilled and silently deepening to distinctness.

As a memory stealing out of the mind's slumber,
A memory floating up from a dark water,
Can be more beautiful than the thing remembered.

LAURENCE BINYON The Burning of the Leaves

Now is the time for the burning of the leaves.
They go to the fire; the nostril pricks with smoke
Wandering slowly into a weeping mist.
Brittle and blotched, ragged and rotten sheaves!
A flame seizes the smouldering ruin and bites
On stubborn stalks that crackle as they resist.

The last hollyhock's fallen tower is dust;
All the spices of June are a bitter reek,
All the extravagant riches spent and mean.
All burns! The reddest rose is a ghost;
Sparks whirl up, to expire in the mist: the wild
Fingers of fire are making corruption clean.

Now is the time for stripping the spirit bare,
Time for the burning of days ended and done,
Idle solace of things that have gone before:
Rootless hopes and fruitless desire are there;
Let them go to the fire, with never a look behind.
The world that was ours is a world that is ours no more.

They will come again, the leaf and the flower, to arise
From squalor of rottenness into the old splendour,
And magical scents to a wondering memory bring;
The same glory, to shine upon different eyes.
Earth cares for her own ruins, naught for ours.
Nothing is certain, only the certain spring.

KEITH DOUGLAS Vergissmeinnicht

Three weeks gone and the combatants gone
returning over the nightmare ground
we found the place again, and found
the soldier sprawling in the sun.

The frowning barrel of his gun
overshadowing. As we came on
that day, he hit my tank with one
like the entry of a demon.

Look. Here in the gunpit spoil
the dishonoured picture of his girl
who has put: *Steffi. Vergissmeinnicht*
in a copybook gothic script.

We see him almost with content,
abased, and seeming to have paid
and mocked at by his own equipment
that's hard and good when he's decayed.

But she would weep to see today
how on his skin the swart flies move;
the dust upon the paper eye
and the burst stomach like a cave.

For here the lover and killer are mingled
who had one body and one heart.
And death who had the soldier singled
has done the lover mortal hurt.

ROBERT GRAVES To Juan at the Winter Solstice   **1945**

There is one story and one story only
That will prove worth your telling,
Whether as learned bard or gifted child;
To it all lines or lesser gauds belong
That startle with their shining
Such common stories as they stray into.

Is it of trees you tell, their months and virtues,
Or strange beasts that beset you,
Of birds that croak at you the Triple will?
Or of the Zodiac and how slow it turns
Below the Boreal Crown,
Prison of all true kings that ever reigned?

Water to water, ark again to ark,
From woman back to woman:
So each new victim treads unfalteringly
The never altered circuit of his fate,
Bringing twelve peers as witness
Both to his starry rise and starry fall.

Or is it of the Virgin's silver beauty,
All fish below the thighs?
She in her left hand bears a leafy quince;
When with her right she crooks a finger, smiling,
How may the King hold back?
Royally then he barters life for love.

Or of the undying snake from chaos hatched,
Whose coils contain the ocean,
Into whose chops with naked sword he springs,
Then in black water, tangled by the reeds,
Battles three days and nights,
To be spewed up beside her scalloped shore?

Much snow is falling, winds roar hollowly,
The owl hoots from the elder,
Fear in your heart cries to the loving-cup:
Sorrow to sorrow as the sparks fly upward.
The log groans and confesses:
There is one story and one story only.

Dwell on her graciousness, dwell on her smiling,
Do not forget what flowers
The great boar trampled down in ivy time.
Her brow was creamy as the crested wave,
Her sea-grey eyes were wild
But nothing promised that is not performed.

DYLAN THOMAS Poem in October

It was my thirtieth year to heaven
Woke to my hearing from harbour and neighbour wood
    And the mussel pooled and the heron
                Priested shore
                The morning beckon
With water praying and call of seagull and rook
And the knock of sailing boats on the net webbed wall
            Myself to set foot
                That second
    In the still sleeping town and set forth.

    My birthday began with the water-
Birds and the birds of the winged trees flying my name
    Above the farms and the white horses
                And I rose
            In rainy autumn
And walked abroad in a shower of all my days.
High tide and the heron dived when I took the road
            Over the border
                And the gates
    Of the town closed as the town awoke.

    A springful of larks in a rolling
Cloud and the roadside bushes brimming with whistling
    Blackbirds and the sun of October
                Summery
            On the hill's shoulder,
Here were fond climates and sweet singers suddenly
Come in the morning where I wandered and listened
        To the rain wringing
                Wind blow cold
    In the wood faraway under me.

Pale rain over the dwindling harbour
And over the sea wet church the size of a snail
  With its horns through mist and the castle
        Brown as owls
        But all the gardens
Of spring and summer were blooming in the tall tales
Beyond the border and under the lark full cloud.
    There could I marvel
        My birthday
Away but the weather turned around.

  It turned away from the blithe country
And down the other air and the blue altered sky
  Streamed again a wonder of summer
        With apples
        Pears and red currants
And I saw in the turning so clearly a child's
Forgotten mornings when he walked with his mother
    Through the parables
        Of sun light
And the legends of the green chapels

  And the twice told fields of infancy
That his tears burned my cheeks and his heart moved in mine.
  These were the woods the river and sea
        Where a boy
        In the listening
Summertime of the dead whispered the truth of his joy
To the trees and the stones and the fish in the tide.
    And the mystery
        Sang alive
Still in the water and singingbirds.

  And there could I marvel my birthday
Away but the weather turned around. And the true
  Joy of the long dead child sang burning
        In the sun.
    It was my thirtieth
Year to heaven stood there then in the summer noon
Though the town below lay leaved with October blood.
    O may my heart's truth
        Still be sung
On this high hill in a year's turning.

W. H. AUDEN *from* The Sea and the Mirror

Miranda

My Dear One is mine as mirrors are lonely,
As the poor and sad are real to the good king,
And the high green hill sits always by the sea.

Up jumped the Black Man behind the elder tree,
Turned a somersault and ran away waving;
My Dear One is mine as mirrors are lonely.

The Witch gave a squawk; her venomous body
Melted into light as water leaves a spring
And the high green hill sits always by the sea.

At his crossroads, too, the Ancient prayed for me;
Down his wasted cheeks tears of joy were running:
My Dear One is mine as mirrors are lonely.

He kissed me awake, and no one was sorry;
The sun shone on sails, eyes, pebbles, anything,
And the high green hill sits always by the sea.

So, to remember our changing garden, we
Are linked as children in a circle dancing:
My Dear One is mine as mirrors are lonely,
And the high green hill sits always by the sea.

RUTH PITTER But for Lust

But for lust we could be friends,
   On each other's necks could weep:
In each other's arms could sleep
   In the calm the cradle lends:

Lends awhile, and takes away.
   But for hunger, but for fear,
Calm could be our day and year
   From the yellow to the grey:

From the gold to the grey hair,
   But for passion we could rest,
But for passion we could feast
   On compassion everywhere.

Even in this night I know
   By the awful living dead,
By this craving tear I shed,
   Somewhere, somewhere it is so.

WILLIAM EMPSON Let It Go

It is this deep blankness is the real thing strange.
   The more things happen to you the more you can't
      Tell or remember even what they were.

The contradictions cover such a range.
   The talk would talk and go so far aslant.
      You don't want madhouse and the whole thing there.

SAMUEL BECKETT Saint-Lô   1946

Vire will wind in other shadows
unborn through the bright ways tremble
and the old mind ghost-forsaken
sink into its havoc

KEITH DOUGLAS How to Kill

Under the parabola of a ball,
a child turning into a man,
I looked into the air too long.
The ball fell in my hand, it sang
in the closed fist: *Open Open
Behold a gift designed to kill.*

Now in my dial of glass appears
the soldier who is going to die.
He smiles, and moves about in ways
his mother knows, habits of his.
The wires touch his face: I cry
NOW. Death, like a familiar, hears

and look, has made a man of dust
of a man of flesh. This sorcery
I do. Being damned, I am amused
to see the centre of love diffused
and the waves of love travel into vacancy.
How easy it is to make a ghost.

The weightless mosquito touches
her tiny shadow on the stone,
and with how like, how infinite
a lightness, man and shadow meet.
They fuse. A shadow is a man
when the mosquito death approaches.

1949   EDWIN MUIR The Interrogation

We could have crossed the road but hesitated,
And then came the patrol;
The leader conscientious and intent,
The men surly, indifferent.
While we stood by and waited
The interrogation began. He says the whole
Must come out now, who, what we are,
Where we have come from, with what purpose, whose
Country or camp we plot for or betray.
Question on question.
We have stood and answered through the standing day
And watched across the road beyond the hedge
The careless lovers in pairs go by,
Hand linked in hand, wandering another star,
So near we could shout to them. We cannot choose
Answer or action here,
Though still the careless lovers saunter by

And the thoughtless field is near.
We are on the very edge,
Endurance almost done,
And still the interrogation is going on.

MARION ANGUS Alas! Poor Queen

She was skilled in music and the dance
And the old arts of love
At the court of the poisoned rose
And the perfumed glove,
And gave her beautiful hand
To the pale Dauphin
A triple crown to win –
And she loved little dogs
    And parrots
  And red-legged partridges
And the golden fishes of the Duc de Guise
And a pigeon with a blue ruff
She had from Monsieur d'Elbœuf.

Master John Knox was no friend to her;
She spoke him soft and kind,
Her honeyed words were Satan's lure
The unwary soul to bind
'Good sir, doth a lissome shape
And a comely face
Offend your God His Grace
Whose Wisdom maketh these
Golden fishes of the Duc de Guise?'

She rode through Liddesdale with a song;
'Ye streams sae wondrous strang,
Oh, mak' me a wrack as I come back
But spare me as I gang,'
While a hill-bird cried and cried
Like a spirit lost
By the grey storm-wind tost.

Consider the way she had to go.
Think of the hungry snare,
The net she herself had woven,
Aware or unaware,
Of the dancing feet grown still,
The blinded eyes –
Queens should be cold and wise,
And she loved little things,
    Parrots
   And red-legged partridges
And the golden fishes of the Duc de Guise
And the pigeon with the blue ruff
She had from Monsieur d'Elbœuf.

STEVIE SMITH Pad, Pad

I always remember your beautiful flowers
And the beautiful kimono you wore
When you sat on the couch
With that tigerish crouch
And told me you loved me no more.

What I cannot remember is how I felt when you were unkind
All I know is, if you were unkind now I should not mind.
Ah me, the power to feel exaggerated, angry and sad
The years have taken from me. Softly I go now, pad pad.

1951   DYLAN THOMAS Over Sir John's Hill

Over Sir John's hill,
The hawk on fire hangs still;
In a hoisted cloud, at drop of dusk, he pulls to his claws
And gallows, up the rays of his eyes the small birds of the bay
And the shrill child's play
Wars
Of the sparrows and such who swansing, dusk, in wrangling hedges.
And blithely they squawk
To fiery tyburn over the wrestle of elms until

The flash the noosed hawk

Crashes, and slowly the fishing holy stalking heron
In the river Towy below bows his tilted headstone.

Flash, and the plumes crack,
And a black cap of Jack-
Daws Sir John's just hill dons, and again the gulled birds hare
To the hawk on fire, the halter height, over Towy's fins,
In a whack of wind.
There
Where the elegiac fisherbird stabs and paddles
In the pebbly dab filled
Shallow and sedge, and 'dilly dilly,' calls the loft hawk,
'Come and be killed.'
I open the leaves of the water at a passage
Of psalms and shadows among the pincered sandcrabs prancing

And read, in a shell,
Death clear as a buoy's bell:
All praise of the hawk on fire in hawk-eyed dusk be sung,
When his viperish fuse hangs looped with flames under the brand
Wing, and blest shall
Young
Green chickens of the bay and bushes cluck, 'dilly dilly,
Come let us die.'
We grieve as the blithe birds, never again, leave shingle and elm,
The heron and I,
I young Aesop fabling to the near night by the dingle
Of eels, saint heron hymning in the shell-hung distant

Crystal harbour vale
Where the sea cobbles sail,
And wharves of water where the walls dance and the white cranes
     stilt.

It is the heron and I, under judging Sir John's elmed
Hill, tell-tale the knelled
Guilt
Of the led-astray birds whom God, for their breast of whistles,
Have mercy on.
God in his whirlwind silence save, who marks the sparrows hail,
For their souls' song.
Now the heron grieves in the weeded verge. Through windows
Of dusk and water I see the tilting whispering

Heron, mirrored, go,
As the snapt feathers snow,
Fishing in the tear of the Towy. Only a hoot owl
Hollows, a grassblade blown in cupped hands, in the looted elms,
And no green cocks or hens
Shout
Now on Sir John's hill. The heron, ankling the scaly
Lowlands of the waves,
Makes all the music; and I who hear the tune of the slow,
Wear-willow river, grave,
Before the lunge of the night, the notes on this time-shaken
Stone for the sake of the souls of the slain birds sailing.

1952   DYLAN THOMAS Do not go gentle into that good night

Do not go gentle into that good night,
Old age should burn and rave at close of day;
Rage, rage against the dying of the light.

Though wise men at their end know dark is right,
Because their words had forked no lightning they
Do not go gentle into that good night.

Good men, the last wave by, crying how bright
Their frail deeds might have danced in a green bay,
Rage, rage against the dying of the light.

Wild men who caught and sang the sun in flight,
And learn, too late, they grieved it on its way.
Do not go gentle into that good night.

Grave men, near death, who see with blinding sight
Blind eyes could blaze like meteors and be gay,
Rage, rage against the dying of the light.

And you, my father, there on the sad height,
Curse, bless, me now with your fierce tears, I pray.
Do not go gentle into that good night.
Rage, rage against the dying of the light.

W. H. AUDEN The Fall of Rome

The piers are pummelled by the waves;
In a lonely field the rain
Lashes an abandoned train;
Outlaws fill the mountain caves.

Fantastic grow the evening gowns;
Agents of the Fisc pursue
Absconding tax-defaulters through
The sewers of provincial towns.

Private rites of magic send
The temple prostitutes to sleep;
All the literati keep
An imaginary friend.

Cerebrotonic Cato may
Extoll the Ancient Disciplines,
But the muscle-bound Marines
Mutiny for food and pay.

Caesar's double-bed is warm
As an unimportant clerk
Writes *I DO NOT LIKE MY WORK*
On a pink official form.

Unendowed with wealth or pity,
Little birds with scarlet legs,
Sitting on their speckled eggs,
Eye each flu-infected city.

Altogether elsewhere, vast
Herds of reindeer move across
Miles and miles of golden moss,
Silently and very fast.

W. H. AUDEN The Shield of Achilles

> She looked over his shoulder
>   For vines and olive trees,
> Marble well-governed cities,
>   And ships upon untamed seas,
> But there on the shining metal
>   His hands had put instead
> An artificial wilderness
>   And a sky like lead.

A plain without a feature, bare and brown,
  No blade of grass, no sign of neighborhood,
Nothing to eat and nowhere to sit down,
  Yet, congregated on its blankness, stood
  An unintelligible multitude,
A million eyes, a million boots in line,
Without expression, waiting for a sign.

Out of the air a voice without a face
  Proved by statistics that some cause was just
In tones as dry and level as the place:
  No one was cheered and nothing was discussed;
  Column by column in a cloud of dust
They marched away enduring a belief
Whose logic brought them, somewhere else, to grief.

> She looked over his shoulder
>   For ritual pieties,
> White flower-garlanded heifers,
>   Libation and sacrifice,
> But there on the shining metal
>   Where the altar should have been,
> She saw by his flickering forge-light
>   Quite another scene.

Barbed wire enclosed an arbitrary spot
  Where bored officials lounged (one cracked a joke)
And sentries sweated, for the day was hot:
  A crowd of ordinary decent folk
  Watched from without and neither moved nor spoke
As three pale figures were led forth and bound
To three posts driven upright in the ground.

The mass and majesty of this world, all
    That carries weight and always weighs the same,
Lay in the hands of others; they were small
    And could not hope for help and no help came:
    What their foes liked to do was done, their shame
Was all the worst could wish; they lost their pride
And died as men before their bodies died.

      She looked over his shoulder
        For athletes at their games,
      Men and women in a dance
        Moving their sweet limbs
      Quick, quick, to music,
        But there on the shining shield
      His hands had set no dancing-floor
        But a weed-choked field.

A ragged urchin, aimless and alone,
    Loitered about that vacancy; a bird
Flew up to safety from his well-aimed stone:
    That girls are raped, that two boys knife a third,
    Were axioms to him, who'd never heard
Of any world where promises were kept
Or one could weep because another wept.

      The thin-lipped armorer,
        Hephaestos, hobbled away;
      Thetis of the shining breasts
        Cried out in dismay
      At what the god had wrought
        To please her son, the strong
      Iron-hearted man-slaying Achilles
        Who would not live long.

JOHN BETJEMAN Devonshire Street W.1   **1954**

The heavy mahogany door with its wrought-iron screen
    Shuts. And the sound is rich, sympathetic, discreet.
The sun still shines on this eighteenth-century scene
    With Edwardian faience adornments – Devonshire Street.

No hope. And the X-ray photographs under his arm
    Confirm the message. His wife stands timidly by.
The opposite brick-built house looks lofty and calm
    Its chimneys steady against a mackerel sky.

No hope. And the iron knob of this palisade
    So cold to the touch, is luckier now than he
'Oh merciless, hurrying Londoners! Why was I made
    For the long and the painful deathbed coming to me?'

She puts her fingers in his as, loving and silly,
    At long-past Kensington dances she used to do
'It's cheaper to take the tube to Piccadilly
And then we can catch a nineteen or a twenty-two.'

ROBERT GARIOCH Elegy

They are lang deid, folk that I used to ken,
their firm-set lips aa mowdert and agley,
sherp-tempert een rusty amang the cley:
they are baith deid, thae wycelike, bienlie men,

5   heidmaisters, that had been in pouer for ten
or twenty year afore fate's taiglie wey
brocht me, a young, weill-harnit, blate and fey
new-cleckit dominie, intill their den.

      Ane tellt me it was time I learnt to write –
10   round-haund, he meant – and saw about my hair:
I mind of him, beld-heidit, wi a kyte.

      Ane sneerit quarterly – I cuidna square
my savings bank – and sniftert in his spite.
Weill, gin they arena deid, it's time they were.

2 *aa mowdert and agley* all mouldering and askew; 4 *wycelike* sensible;
bienlie pleasant; 6 *taiglie* entangling; 7 *weill-harnit* well-educated; *blate and fey* shy
and fated; 8 *new-cleckit* newly-hatched; *dominie* schoolmaster; 9 *tellt* told; 11 *mind
of him* remember him; *kyte* paunch; 14 *gin they arena* if they aren't

THOM GUNN The Wound

The huge wound in my head began to heal
About the beginning of the seventh week.
Its valleys darkened, its villages became still:
For joy I did not move and dared not speak,
Not doctors would cure it, but time, its patient skill.

And constantly my mind returned to Troy.
After I sailed the seas I fought in turn
On both sides, sharing even Helen's joy
Of place, and growing up – to see Troy burn –
As Neoptolemus, that stubborn boy.

I lay and rested as prescription said.
Manoeuvered with the Greeks, or sallied out
Each day with Hector. Finally my bed
Became Achilles' tent, to which the lout
Thersites came reporting numbers dead.

I was myself: subject to no man's breath:
My own commander was my enemy.
And while my belt hung up, sword in the sheath,
Thersites shambled in and breathlessly
Cackled about my friend Patroclus' death.

I called for armour, rose, and did not reel.
But, when I thought, rage at his noble pain
Flew to my head, and turning I could feel
My wound break open wide. Over again
I had to let those storm-lit valleys heal.

PHILIP LARKIN At Grass

The eye can hardly pick them out
From the cold shade they shelter in,
Till wind distresses tail and mane;
Then one crops grass, and moves about
– The other seeming to look on –
And stands anonymous again.

Yet fifteen years ago, perhaps
Two dozen distances sufficed
To fable them: faint afternoons
Of Cups and Stakes and Handicaps,
Whereby their names were artificed
To inlay faded, classic Junes –

Silks at the start: against the sky
Numbers and parasols: outside,
Squadrons of empty cars, and heat,
And littered grass: then the long cry
Hanging unhushed till it subside
To stop-press columns on the street.

Do memories plague their ears like flies?
They shake their heads. Dusk brims the shadows.
Summer by summer all stole away,
The starting-gates, the crowds and cries –
All but the unmolesting meadows.
Almanacked, their names live; they

Have slipped their names, and stand at ease,
Or gallop for what must be joy,
And not a fieldglass sees them home,
Or curious stop-watch prophesies:
Only the groom, and the groom's boy,
With bridles in the evening come.

1955   NORMAN MACCAIG Summer Farm

Straws like tame lightnings lie about the grass
And hang zigzag on hedges. Green as glass
The water in the horse-trough shines.
Nine ducks go wobbling by in two straight lines.

A hen stares at nothing with one eye,
Then picks it up. Out of an empty sky
A swallow falls and, flickering through
The barn, dives up again into the dizzy blue.

I lie, not thinking, in the cool, soft grass,
Afraid of where a thought might take me – as
This grasshopper with plated face
Unfolds his legs and finds himself in space.

Self under self, a pile of selves I stand
Threaded on time, and with metaphysic hand
Lift the farm like a lid and see
Farm within farm, and in the centre, me.

EDWIN MUIR The Horses   1956

Barely a twelvemonth after
The seven days war that put the world to sleep,
Late in the evening the strange horses came.
By then we had made our covenant with silence,
But in the first few days it was so still
We listened to our breathing and were afraid.
On the second day
The radios failed; we turned the knobs; no answer.
On the third day a warship passed us, heading north,
Dead bodies piled on the deck. On the sixth day
A plane plunged over us into the sea. Thereafter
Nothing. The radios dumb;
And still they stand in corners of our kitchens,
And stand, perhaps, turned on, in a million rooms
All over the world. But now if they should speak,
If on a sudden they should speak again,
If on the stroke of noon a voice should speak,
We would not listen, we would not let it bring
That old bad world that swallowed its children quick
At one great gulp. We would not have it again.
Sometimes we think of the nations lying asleep,
Curled blindly in impenetrable sorrow,
And then the thought confounds us with its strangeness.
The tractors lie about our fields; at evening
They look like dank sea-monsters couched and waiting.
We leave them where they are and let them rust:
'They'll moulder away and be like other loam'.
We make our oxen drag our rusty ploughs,
Long laid aside. We have gone back
Far past our fathers' land.

Late in the summer the strange horses came.
We heard a distant tapping on the road,
A deepening drumming; it stopped, went on again
And at the corner changed to hollow thunder.
We saw the heads
Like a wild wave charging and were afraid.
We had sold our horses in our fathers' time
To buy new tractors. Now they were strange to us
As fabulous steeds set on an ancient shield
Or illustrations in a book of knights.
We did not dare go near them. Yet they waited,
Stubborn and shy, as if they had been sent
By an old command to find our whereabouts
And that long-lost archaic companionship.
In the first moment we had never a thought
That they were creatures to be owned and used.
Among them were some half-a-dozen colts
Dropped in some wilderness of the broken world,
Yet new as if they had come from their own Eden.
Since then they have pulled our ploughs and borne our loads
But that free servitude still can pierce our hearts.
Our life is changed; their coming our beginning.

1957   TED HUGHES The Thought-Fox

I imagine this midnight moment's forest:
Something else is alive
Beside the clock's loneliness
And this blank page where my fingers move.

Through the window I see no star:
Something more near
Though deeper within darkness
Is entering the loneliness:

Cold, delicately as the dark snow
A fox's nose touches twig, leaf;
Two eyes serve a movement, that now
And again now, and now, and now

Sets neat prints into the snow
Between trees, and warily a lame
Shadow lags by stump and in hollow
Of a body that is bold to come

Across clearings, an eye,
A widening deepening greenness,
Brilliantly, concentratedly,
Coming about its own business

Till, with a sudden sharp hot stink of fox
It enters the dark hole of the head.
The window is starless still; the clock ticks,
The page is printed.

LOUIS MACNEICE House on a Cliff

Indoors the tang of a tiny oil lamp. Outdoors
The winking signal on the waste of sea.
Indoors the sound of the wind. Outdoors the wind.
Indoors the locked heart and the lost key.

Outdoors the chill, the void, the siren. Indoors
The strong man pained to find his red blood cools,
While the blind clock grows louder, faster. Outdoors
The silent moon, the garrulous tides she rules.

Indoors ancestral curse-cum-blessing. Outdoors
The empty bowl of heaven, the empty deep.
Indoors a purposeful man who talks at cross
Purposes, to himself, in a broken sleep.

STEVIE SMITH Not Waving But Drowning

Nobody heard him, the dead man,
But still he lay moaning:
I was much further out than you thought
And not waving but drowning.

Poor chap, he always loved larking
And now he's dead
It must have been too cold for him his heart gave way,
They said.

Oh, no no no, it was too cold always
(Still the dead one lay moaning)
I was much too far out all my life
And not waving but drowning.

STEVIE SMITH Magna est Veritas

With my looks I am bound to look simple or fast I would rather look
    simple
So I wear a tall hat on the back of my head that is rather a temple
And I walk rather queerly and comb my long hair
And people say, Don't bother about her.
So in my time I have picked up a good many facts,
Rather more than the people do who wear smart hats
And I do not deceive because I am rather simple too
And although I collect facts I do not always know what they amount
    to.
I regard them as a contribution to almighty Truth, magna est veritas
    et praevalebit,
Agreeing with that Latin writer, Great is Truth and will prevail in a
    bit.

1959   ### GEOFFREY HILL A Pastoral

Mobile, immaculate and austere,
The Pities, their fingers in every wound,
Assess the injured on the obscured frontier;
Cleanse with a kind of artistry the ground
Shared by War. Consultants in new tongues
Prove synonymous our separated wrongs.

We celebrate, fluently and at ease.
Traditional Furies, having thrust, hovered,
Now decently enough sustain Peace.

The unedifying nude dead are soon covered.
Survivors, still given to wandering, find
Their old loves, painted and re-aligned –

Queer, familiar, fostered by superb graft
On treasured foundations, these ideal features.
Men can move with purpose again, or drift,
According to direction. Here are statues
Darkened by laurel; and evergreen names;
Evidently-veiled griefs; impervious tombs.

TED HUGHES Pike

Pike, three inches long, perfect
Pike in all parts, green tigering the gold.
Killers from the egg: the malevolent aged grin.
They dance on the surface among the flies.

Or move, stunned by their own grandeur
Over a bed of emerald, silhouette
Of submarine delicacy and horror.
A hundred feet long in their world.

In ponds, under the heat-struck lily pads –
Gloom of their stillness:
Logged on last year's black leaves, watching upwards.
Or hung in an amber cavern of weeds

The jaws' hooked clamp and fangs
Not to be changed at this date;
A life subdued to its instrument;
The gills kneading quietly, and the pectorals.

Three we kept behind glass,
Jungled in weed: three inches, four,
And four and a half: fed fry to them –
Suddenly there were two. Finally one.

With a sag belly and the grin it was born with.
And indeed they spare nobody.
Two, six pounds each, over two feet long,
High and dry and dead in the willow-herb –

One jammed past its gills down the other's gullet:
The outside eye stared: as a vice locks –
The same iron in this eye
Though its film shrank in death.

A pond I fished, fifty yards across,
Whose lilies and muscular tench
Had outlasted every visible stone
Of the monastery that planted them –

Stilled legendary depth:
It was as deep as England. It held
Pike too immense to stir, so immense and old
That past nightfall I dared not cast

But silently cast and fished
With the hair frozen on my head
For what might move, for what eye might move.
The still splashes on the dark pond,

Owls hushing the floating woods
Frail on my ear against the dream
Darkness beneath night's darkness had freed,
That rose slowly towards me, watching.

PATRICK KAVANAGH Epic

I have lived in important places, times
When great events were decided: who owned
That half a rood of rock, a no-man's land
Surrounded by our pitchfork-armed claims.
I heard the Duffys shouting 'Damn your soul'
And old McCabe stripped to the waist, seen
Step the plot defying blue cast-steel –
'Here is the march along these iron stones'
That was the year of the Munich bother. Which
Was most important? I inclined
To lose my faith in Ballyrush and Gortin
Till Homer's ghost came whispering to my mind
He said: I made the *Iliad* from such
A local row. Gods make their own importance.

PATRICK KAVANAGH Come Dance with Kitty Stobling

No, no, no, I know I was not important as I moved
Through the colourful country, I was but a single
Item in the picture, the namer not the beloved.
O tedious man with whom no gods commingle.
Beauty, who has described beauty? Once upon a time
I had a myth that was a lie but it served:
Trees walking across the crests of hills and my rhyme
Cavorting on mile-high stilts and the unnerved
Crowds looking up with terror in their rational faces.
O dance with Kitty Stobling I outrageously
Cried out-of-sense to them, while their timorous paces
Stumbled behind Jove's page boy paging me.
I had a very pleasant journey, thank you sincerely
For giving me my madness back, or nearly.

PATRICK KAVANAGH The Hospital

A year ago I fell in love with the functional ward
Of a chest hospital: square cubicles in a row
Plain concrete, wash basins – an art lover's woe,
Not counting how the fellow in the next bed snored.
But nothing whatever is by love debarred,
The common and banal her heat can know.
The corridor led to a stairway and below
Was the inexhaustible adventure of a gravelled yard.

This is what love does to things: the Rialto Bridge,
The main gate that was bent by a heavy lorry,
The seat at the back of a shed that was a suntrap.
Naming these things is the love-act and its pledge;
For we must record love's mystery without claptrap,
Snatch out of time the passionate transitory.

1961   R. S. THOMAS Here

I am a man now.
Pass your hand over my brow,
You can feel the place where the brains grow.

I am like a tree,
From my top boughs I can see
The footprints that led up to me.

There is blood in my veins
That has run clear of the stain
Contracted in so many loins.

Why, then, are my hands red
With the blood of so many dead?
Is this where I was misled?

Why are my hands this way
That they will not do as I say?
Does no God hear when I pray?

I have nowhere to go.
The swift satellites show
The clock of my whole being is slow.

It is too late to start
For destinations not of the heart.
I must stay here with my hurt.

 § ROY FISHER *from* City

from **By the Pond**

Brick-dust in sunlight. That is what I see now in the city, a dry
epic flavour, whose air is human breath. A place of walls made
straight with plumbline and trowel, to dessicate and crumble in
the sun and smoke. Blistered paint on cisterns and girders,

cracking to show the priming. Old men spit on the paving slabs, 1961 [983
little boys urinate; and the sun dries it as it dries out patches of
damp on plaster facings to leave misshapen stains. I look for
things here that make old men and dead men seem young. Things
which have escaped, the landscapes of many childhoods.

Wharves, the oldest parts of factories, tarred gable ends rearing
to take the sun over lower roofs. Soot, sunlight, brick-dust; and
the breath that tastes of them.

At the time when the great streets were thrust out along the old
high-roads and trackways, the houses shouldering towards the
country and the back streets filling in the widening spaces
between them like webbed membranes, the power of will in the
town was more open, less speciously democratic, than it is
now. There were, of course, cottage railway stations, a jail that
pretended to be a castle out of Grimm, public urinals surrounded
by screens of cast-iron lacework painted green and scarlet; but
there was also an arrogant ponderous architecture that dwarfed
and terrified the people by its sheer size and functional brutality:
the workhouses and the older hospitals, the thick-walled abat-
toir, the long vaulted market-halls, the striding canal bridges
and railway viaducts. Brunel was welcome here. Compared with
these structures the straight white blocks and concrete roadways
of today are a fairground, a clear dream just before waking, the
creation of salesmen rather than of engineers. The new city is
bred out of a hard will, but as it appears, it shows itself a little
ingratiating, a place of arcades, passages, easy ascents, good light.
The eyes twinkle, beseech and veil themselves; the full, hard
mouth, the broad jaw – these are no longer made visible to all.

A street half a mile long with no buildings, only a continuous
embankment of sickly grass along one side, with railway signals
on it, and strings of trucks through whose black-spoked wheels
you can see the sky; and for the whole length of the other a
curving wall of bluish brick, caked with soot and thirty feet high.
In it, a few wicket gates painted ochre, and fingermarked, but
never open. Cobbles in the roadway.

A hundred years ago this was almost the edge of town. The
goods yards, the gasworks and the coal stores were established
on tips and hillocks in the sparse fields that lay among the houses.
Between this place and the centre, a mile or two up the hill, lay
a continuous huddle of low streets and courts, filling the marshy

valley of the meagre river that now flows under brick and tarmac. And this was as far as the railway came, at first. A great station was built, towering and stony. The sky above it was southerly. The stately approach, the long curves of wall, still remain, but the place is a goods depot with most of its doors barred and pots of geraniums at those windows that are not shuttered. You come upon it suddenly in its open prospect out of tangled streets of small factories. It draws light to itself, especially at sunset, standing still and smooth faced, looking westwards at the hill. I am not able to imagine the activity that must once have been here. I can see no ghosts of men and women, only the gigantic ghost of stone. They are too frightened of it to pull it down.

Toyland

Today the sunlight is the paint on lead soldiers
Only they are people scattering out of the cool church

And as they go across the gravel and among the spring streets
They spread formality: they know, we know, what they have been
    doing,

The old couples, the widowed, the staunch smilers,
The deprived and the few nubile young lily-ladies,

And we know what they will do when they have opened the doors of
    their houses and walked in:
Mostly they will make water, and wash their calm hands and eat.

The organ's flourishes finish; the verger closes the doors;
The choirboys run home, and the rector goes off in his motor.

Here a policeman stalks, the sun glinting on his helmet-crest;
Then a man pushes a perambulator home; and somebody posts a
    letter.

If I sit here long enough, loving it all, I shall see the District Nurse
    pedal past,
The children going to Sunday School and the strollers strolling;

The lights darting on in different rooms as night comes in;
And I shall see washing hung out, and the postman delivering letters.

I might by exception see an ambulance or the fire brigade
Or even, if the chance came round, street musicians (singing and
    playing).

For the people I've seen, this seems the operation of life:
I need the paint of stillness and sunshine to see it that way.

The secret laugh of the world picks them up and shakes them like
    peas boiling;
They behave as if nothing happened; maybe they no longer notice.

I notice. I laugh with the laugh, cultivate it, make much of it,
But still I don't know what the joke is, to tell them.

§   §   §

THOM GUNN In Santa Maria del Popolo

Waiting for when the sun an hour or less
Conveniently oblique makes visible
The painting on one wall of this recess
By Caravaggio, of the Roman School,
I see how shadow in the painting brims
With a real shadow, drowning all shapes out
But a dim horse's haunch and various limbs,
Until the very subject is in doubt.

But evening gives the act, beneath the horse
And one indifferent groom, I see him sprawl,
Foreshortened from the head, with hidden face,
Where he has fallen, Saul becoming Paul.
O wily painter, limiting the scene
From a cacophony of dusty forms
To the one convulsion, what is it you mean
In that wide gesture of the lifting arms?

No Ananias croons a mystery yet,
Casting the pain out under name of sin.
The painter saw what was, an alternate
Candour and secrecy inside the skin.

He painted, elsewhere, that firm insolent
Young whore in Venus' clothes, those pudgy cheats,
Those sharpers; and was strangled, as things went,
For money, by one such picked off the streets.

I turn, hardly enlightened, from the chapel
To the dim interior of the church instead,
In which there kneel already several people,
Mostly old women: each head closeted
In tiny fists holds comfort as it can.
Their poor arms are too tired for more than this
– For the large gesture of solitary man,
Resisting, by embracing, nothingness.

THOM GUNN My Sad Captains

One by one they appear in
the darkness: a few friends, and
a few with historical
names. How late they start to shine!
but before they fade they stand
perfectly embodied, all

the past lapping them like a
cloak of chaos. They were men
who, I thought, lived only to
renew the wasteful force they
spent with each hot convulsion.
They remind me, distant now.

True, they are not at rest yet,
but now that they are indeed
apart, winnowed from failures,
they withdraw to an orbit
and turn with disinterested
hard energy, like the stars.

MALCOLM LOWRY [Strange Type]

I wrote: in the dark cavern of our birth.
The printer had it tavern, which seems better:
But herein lies the subject of our mirth,
Since on the next page death appears as dearth.
So it may be that God's word was distraction,
Which to our strange type appears destruction,
Which is bitter.

CHRISTOPHER LOGUE *from* Patrocleia: an Account of Book 16 of Homer's Iliad

[Apollo Strikes Patroclus]

His hand came from the east,
And in his wrist lay all eternity;
And every atom of his mythic weight
Was poised between his fist and bent left leg.
   Your eyes lurched out. Achilles' bonnet rang
Far and away beneath the cannon-bones of Trojan horses,
And you were footless . . . staggering . . . amazed . . .
Between the clumps of dying, dying yourself,
Dazed by the brilliance in your eyes,
The noise – like weirs heard far away –
Dabbling your astounded fingers
In the vomit on your chest.
   And all the Trojans lay and stared at you;
Propped themselves up and stared at you;
Feeling themselves as blest as you felt cursed.
   All of them lay and stared;
And one, a hero boy called Thackta, cast.
His javelin went through your calves,
Stitching your knees together, and you fell,
Not noticing the pain, and tried to crawl
Towards the Fleet, and – even now – feeling
For Thackta's ankle – ah! – and got it? No . . .
Not a boy's ankle that you got,
But Hector's.

Standing above you,
His bronze mask smiling down into your face,
Putting his spear through . . . ach, and saying:
   'Why tears, Patroclus?
Did you hope to melt Troy down
And make our women fetch the ingots home?
   I can imagine it!
You and your marvellous Achilles;
Him with an upright finger, saying:
   "*Don't show your face to me again, Patroclus,*
Unless it's red with Hector's blood."'
   And Patroclus,
Shaking the voice out of his body, says:
   'Big mouth.
Remember it took three of you to kill me.
A god, a boy, and, last and least, a hero.
   I can hear Death pronounce my name, and yet
Somehow it sounds like *Hector*.
   And as I close my eyes I see Achilles' face
With Death's voice coming out of it.'

   Saying these things Patroclus died.
And as his soul went through the sand
Hector withdrew his spear and said:
   'Perhaps.'

1963   **CHARLES TOMLINSON** The Picture of J. T. in a Prospect of
Stone

What should one
   wish a child
      and that, one's own
emerging
   from between
      the stone lips
of a sheep-stile
   that divides
      village graves
and village green?
   – Wish her
      the constancy of stone.

– But stone
    is hard.
        – Say, rather
it resists
    the slow corrosives
        and the flight
of time
    and yet it takes
        the play, the fluency
from light.
    – How would you know
        the gift you'd give
was the gift
    she'd wish to have?
        – Gift is giving,
gift is meaning:
    first
        I'd give
then let her
    live with it
        to prove
its quality the better and
    thus learn
        to love
what (to begin with)
    she might spurn.
        – You'd
moralize a gift?
    – I'd have her
        understand
the gift I gave her.
    – And so she shall
        but let her play
her innocence away
    emerging
        as she does
between
    her doom (unknown),
        her unmown green.

R. S. THOMAS On the Farm

There was Dai Puw. He was no good.
They put him in the fields to dock swedes,
And took the knife from him, when he came home
At late evening with a grin
Like the slash of a knife on his face.

There was Llew Puw, and he was no good.
Every evening after the ploughing
With the big tractor he would sit in his chair,
And stare into the tangled fire garden,
Opening his slow lips like a snail.

There was Huw Puw, too. What shall I say?
I have heard him whistling in the hedges
On and on, as though winter
Would never again leave those fields,
And all the trees were deformed.

And lastly there was the girl:
Beauty under some spell of the beast.
Her pale face was the lantern
By which they read in life's dark book
The shrill sentence: God is love.

LOUIS MACNEICE Soap Suds

This brand of soap has the same smell as once in the big
House he visited when he was eight: the walls of the bathroom open
To reveal a lawn where a great yellow ball rolls back through a hoop
To rest at the head of a mallet held in the hands of a child.

And these were the joys of that house: a tower with a telescope;
Two great faded globes, one of the earth, one of the stars;
A stuffed black dog in the hall; a walled garden with bees;
A rabbit warren; a rockery; a vine under glass; the sea.

To which he has now returned. The day of course is fine   [991
And a grown-up voice cries Play! The mallet slowly swings,
Then crack, a great gong booms from the dog-dark hall and the ball
Skims forward through the hoop and then through the next and then

Through hoops where no hoops were and each dissolves in turn
And the grass has grown head-high and an angry voice cries Play!
But the ball is lost and the mallet slipped long since from the hands
Under the running tap that are not the hands of a child.

LOUIS MACNEICE The Taxis

In the first taxi he was alone tra-la,
No extras on the clock. He tipped ninepence
But the cabby, while he thanked him, looked askance
As though to suggest someone had bummed a ride.

In the second taxi he was alone tra-la
But the clock showed sixpence extra; he tipped according
And the cabby from out his muffler said: 'Make sure
You have left nothing behind tra-la between you.'

In the third taxi he was alone tra-la
But the tip-up seats were down and there was an extra
Charge of one-and-sixpence and an odd
Scent that reminded him of a trip to Cannes.

As for the fourth taxi, he was alone
Tra-la when he hailed it but the cabby looked
Through him and said: 'I can't tra-la well take
So many people, not to speak of the dog.'

AUSTIN CLARKE Martha Blake at Fifty-One

Early, each morning, Martha Blake
    Walked, angeling the road,
To Mass in the Church of the Three Patrons.
    Sanctuary lamp glowed

And the clerk halo'ed the candles
　　On the High Altar. She knelt
Illumined. In gold-hemmed alb,
　　The priest intoned. Wax melted.

Waiting for daily Communion, bowed head
　　At rail, she hears a murmur.
Latin is near. In a sweet cloud
　　That cherub'd, all occurred.
The voice went by. To her pure thought,
　　Body was a distress
And soul, a sigh. Behind her denture,
　　Love lay, a helplessness.

Then, slowly walking after Mass
　　Down Rathgar Road, she took out
Her Yale key, put a match to gas-ring,
　　Half filled a saucepan, cooked
A fresh egg lightly, with tea, brown bread,
　　Soon, taking off her blouse
And skirt, she rested, pressing the Crown
　　Of Thorns until she drowsed.

In her black hat, stockings, she passed
　　Nylons to a nearby shop
And purchased, daily, with downcast eyes,
　　Fillet of steak or a chop.
She simmered it on a low jet,
　　Having a poor appetite,
Yet never for an hour felt better
　　From dilatation, tightness.

She suffered from dropped stomach, heartburn
　　Scalding, water-brash
And when she brought her wind up, turning
　　Red with the weight of mashed
Potato, mint could not relieve her.
　　In vain her many belches,
For all below was swelling, heaving
　　Wamble, gurgle, squelch.

She lay on the sofa with legs up,
    A decade on her lip,
At four o'clock, taking a cup
    Of lukewarm water, sip
By sip, but still her daily food
    Repeated and the bile
Tormented her. In a blue hood,
    The Virgin sadly smiled.

When she looked up, the Saviour showed
    His Heart, daggered with flame
And, from the mantle-shelf, St Joseph
    Bent, disapproving. Vainly
She prayed, for in the whatnot corner
    The new Pope was frowning. Night
And day, dull pain, as in her corns,
    Recounted every bite.

She thought of St Teresa, floating
    On motes of a sunbeam,
Carmelite with scatterful robes,
    Surrounded by demons,
Small black boys in their skin. She gaped
    At Hell: a muddy passage
That led to nothing, queer in shape,
    A cupboard closely fastened.

Sometimes, the walls of the parlour
    Would fade away. No plod
Of feet, rattle of van, in Garville
    Road. Soul now gone abroad
Where saints, like medieval serfs,
    Had laboured. Great sun-flower shone.
Our Lady's Chapel was borne by seraphs,
    Three leagues beyond Ancona.

High towns of Italy, the plain
    Of France, were known to Martha
As she read in a holy book. The sky-blaze
    Nooned at Padua,
Marble grotto of Bernadette.
    Rose-scatterers. New saints
In tropical Africa where the tsetse
    Fly probes, the forest taints.

Teresa had heard the Lutherans
    Howling on red-hot spit,
And grill, men who had searched for truth
    Alone in Holy Writ.
So Martha, fearful of flame lashing
    Those heretics, each instant,
Never dealt in the haberdashery
    Shop, owned by two Protestants.

In ambush of night, an angel wounded
    The Spaniard to the heart
With iron tip on fire. Swooning
    With pain and bliss as a dart
Moved up and down within her bowels
    Quicker, quicker, each cell
Sweating as if rubbed up with towels,
    Her spirit rose and fell.

St John of the Cross, her friend, in prison
    Awaits the bridal night,
Paler than lilies, his wizened skin
    Flowers. In fifths of flight,
Senses beyond seraphic thought,
    In that divinest clasp,
Enfolding of kisses that cauterize,
    Yield to the soul-spasm.

Cunning in body had come to hate
    All this and stirred by mischief
Haled Martha from heaven. Heart palpitates
    And terror in her stiffens.
Heart misses one beat, two . . . flutters . . . stops.
    Her ears are full of sound.
Half fainting, she stares at the grandfather clock
    As if it were overwound.

The fit had come. Ill-natured flesh
    Despised her soul. No bending
Could ease rib. Around her heart, pressure
    Of wind grew worse. Again,
Again, armchaired without relief,
    She eructated, phlegm
In mouth, forgot the woe, the grief,
    Foretold at Bethlehem.

Tired of the same faces, side-altars,
    She went to the Carmelite Church
At Johnson's Court, confessed her faults,
    There, once a week, purchased
Tea, butter in Chatham St. The pond
    In St Stephen's Green was grand.
She watched the seagulls, ducks, black swan,
    Went home by the 15 tram.

Her beads in hand, Martha became
    A member of the Third Order,
Saved from long purgatorial pain,
    Brown habit and white cord
Her own when cerges had been lit
    Around her coffin. She got
Ninety-five pounds on loan for her bit
    Of clay in the common plot.

Often she thought of a quiet sick-ward,
    Nuns, with delicious ways,
Consoling the miserable: quick
    Tea, toast on trays. Wishing
To rid themselves of her, kind neighbours
    Sent for the ambulance,
Before her brother and sister could hurry
    To help her. Big gate clanged.

No medical examination
    For the new patient. Doctor
Had gone to Cork on holidays.
    Telephone sprang. Hall-clock
Proclaimed the quarters. Clatter of heels
    On tiles. Corridor, ward,
A-whirr with the electric cleaner,
    The creak of window cord.

She could not sleep at night. Feeble
    And old, two women raved
And cried to God. She held her beads.
    O how could she be saved?
The hospital had this and that rule.
    Day-chill unshuttered. Nun, with
Thermometer in reticule,
    Went by. The women mumbled.

Mother Superior believed
    That she was obstinate, self-willed.
Sisters ignored her, hands-in-sleeves,
    Beside a pantry shelf
Or counting pillow-case, soiled sheet.
    They gave her purgatives.
Soul-less, she tottered to the toilet.
    Only her body lived.

Wasted by colitis, refused
    The daily sacrament
By regulation, forbidden use
    Of bed-pan, when meals were sent up,
Behind a screen, she lay, shivering,
    Unable to eat. The soup
Was greasy, mutton, beef or liver,
    Cold. Kitchen has no scruples.

The Nuns had let the field in front
    As an Amusement Park,
Merry-go-round, a noisy month, all
    Heltering-skeltering at darkfall,
Mechanical music, dipper, hold-tights,
    Rifle-crack, crash of dodgems.
The ward, godless with shadow, lights,
    How could she pray to God?

Unpitied, wasting with diarrhea
    And the constant strain,
Poor Child of Mary with one idea,
    She ruptured a small vein,
Bled inwardly to jazz. No priest
    Came. She had been anointed
Two days before, yet knew no peace:
    Her last breath, disappointed.

1964   **PHILIP LARKIN Mr Bleaney**

'This was Mr Bleaney's room. He stayed
The whole time he was at the Bodies, till
They moved him.' Flowered curtains, thin and frayed,
Fall to within five inches of the sill,

Whose window shows a strip of building land,
Tussocky, littered. 'Mr Bleaney took
My bit of garden properly in hand.'
Bed, upright chair, sixty-watt bulb, no hook

Behind the door, no room for books or bags –
'I'll take it.' So it happens that I lie
Where Mr Bleaney lay, and stub my fags
On the same saucer-souvenir, and try

Stuffing my ears with cotton-wool, to drown
The jabbering set he egged her on to buy.
I know his habits – what time he came down,
His preference for sauce to gravy, why

He kept on plugging at the four aways –
Likewise their yearly frame: the Frinton folk
Who put him up for summer holidays,
And Christmas at his sister's house in Stoke.

But if he stood and watched the frigid wind
Tousling the clouds, lay on the fusty bed
Telling himself that this was home, and grinned,
And shivered, without shaking off the dread

That how we live measures our own nature,
And at his age having no more to show
Than one hired box should make him pretty sure
He warranted no better, I don't know.

(written 1955)

PHILIP LARKIN Here

Swerving east, from rich industrial shadows
And traffic all night north; swerving through fields
Too thin and thistled to be called meadows,
And now and then a harsh-named halt, that shields
Workmen at dawn; swerving to solitude
Of skies and scarecrows, haystacks, hares and pheasants,
And the widening river's slow presence,
The piled gold clouds, the shining gull-marked mud,

Gathers to the surprise of a large town:
Here domes and statues, spires and cranes cluster
Beside grain-scattered streets, barge-crowded water,
And residents from raw estates, brought down
The dead straight miles by stealing flat-faced trolleys,
Push through plate-glass swing doors to their desires –
Cheap suits, red kitchen-ware, sharp shoes, iced lollies,
Electric mixers, toasters, washers, driers –

A cut-price crowd, urban yet simple, dwelling
Where only salesmen and relations come
Within a terminate and fishy-smelling
Pastoral of ships up streets, the slave museum,
Tattoo-shops, consulates, grim head-scarfed wives;
And out beyond its mortgaged half-built edges
Fast-shadowed wheat-fields, running high as hedges,
Isolate villages, where removed lives

Loneliness clarifies. Here silence stands
Like heat. Here leaves unnoticed thicken,
Hidden weeds flower, neglected waters quicken,
Luminously-peopled air ascends;
And past the poppies bluish neutral distance
Ends the land suddenly beyond a beach
Of shapes and shingle. Here is unfenced existence:
Facing the sun, untalkative, out of reach.

PHILIP LARKIN Days

What are days for?
Days are where we live.
They come, they wake us
Time and time over.
They are to be happy in:
Where can we live but days?

Ah, solving that question
Brings the priest and the doctor
In their long coats
Running over the fields.

(written 1953)

PHILIP LARKIN Afternoons

Summer is fading:
The leaves fall in ones and twos
From trees bordering
The new recreation ground.
In the hollows of afternoons
Young mothers assemble
At swing and sandpit
Setting free their children.

Behind them, at intervals,
Stand husbands in skilled trades,
An estateful of washing,
And the albums, lettered
Our Wedding, lying
Near the television:
Before them, the wind
Is ruining their courting-places

That are still courting-places
(But the lovers are all in school),
And their children, so intent on
Finding more unripe acorns,
Expect to be taken home.
Their beauty has thickened.
Something is pushing them
To the side of their own lives.

DONALD DAVIE The Hill Field

Look there! What a wheaten
Half-loaf, halfway to bread,
A cornfield is, that is eaten
Away, and harvested:

How like a loaf, where the knife
Has cut and come again,
Jagged where the farmer's wife
Has served the farmer's men,

That steep field is, where the reaping
Has only just begun
On a wedge-shaped front, and the creeping
Steel edges glint in the sun.

See the cheese-like shape it is taking,
The sliced-off walls of the wheat
And the cheese-mite reapers making
Inroads there, in the heat?

It is Brueghel or Samuel Palmer,
Some painter, coming between
My eye and the truth of a farmer,
So massively sculpts the scene.

The sickles of poets dazzle
These eyes that were filmed from birth;
And the miller comes with an easel
To grind the fruits of earth.

1965   SYLVIA PLATH Sheep in Fog

The hills step off into whiteness.
People or stars
Regard me sadly, I disappoint them.

The train leaves a line of breath.
O slow
Horse the color of rust,

Hooves, dolorous bells –
All morning the
Morning has been blackening,

A flower left out.
My bones hold a stillness, the far
Fields melt my heart.

They threaten
To let me through to a heaven
Starless and fatherless, a dark water.

SYLVIA PLATH The Arrival of the Bee Box

I ordered this, this clean wood box
Square as a chair and almost too heavy to lift.
I would say it was the coffin of a midget
Or a square baby
Were there not such a din in it.

The box is locked, it is dangerous.
I have to live with it overnight
And I can't keep away from it.
There are no windows, so I can't see what is in there.
There is only a little grid, no exit.

I put my eye to the grid.
It is dark, dark,
With the swarmy feeling of African hands
Minute and shrunk for export,
Black on black, angrily clambering.

How can I let them out?
It is the noise that appalls me most of all,
The unintelligible syllables.
It is like a Roman mob,
Small, taken one by one, but my god, together!

I lay my ear to furious Latin.
I am not a Caesar.
I have simply ordered a box of maniacs.
They can be sent back.
They can die, I need feed them nothing, I am the owner.

I wonder how hungry they are.
I wonder if they would forget me
If I just undid the locks and stood back and turned into a tree.
There is the laburnum, its blond colonnades,
And the petticoats of the cherry.

They might ignore me immediately
In my moon suit and funeral veil.
I am no source of honey
So why should they turn on me?
Tomorrow I will be sweet God, I will set them free.

The box is only temporary.

SYLVIA PLATH Edge

The woman is perfected.
Her dead

Body wears the smile of accomplishment,
The illusion of a Greek necessity

Flows in the scrolls of her toga,
Her bare

Feet seem to be saying:
We have come so far, it is over.

Each dead child coiled, a white serpent,
One at each little

Pitcher of milk, now empty.
She has folded

Them back into her body as petals
Of a rose close when the garden

Stiffens and odors bleed
From the sweet, deep throats of the night flower.

The moon has nothing to be sad about,
Staring from her hood of bone.

She is used to this sort of thing.
Her blacks crackle and drag.

BASIL BUNTING *from* **Briggflatts** **1966**

I

Brag, sweet tenor bull,
descant on Rawthey's madrigal,
each pebble its part
for the fells' late spring.
Dance tiptoe, bull,
black against may.
Ridiculous and lovely
chase hurdling shadows
morning into noon.
May on the bull's hide
and through the dale
furrows fill with may,
paving the slowworm's way.

A mason times his mallet
to a lark's twitter,
listening while the marble rests,
lays his rule
at a letter's edge,
fingertips checking,
till the stone spells a name
naming none,
a man abolished.
Painful lark, labouring to rise!
The solemn mallet says:
In the grave's slot
he lies. We rot.

Decay thrusts the blade,
wheat stands in excrement
trembling. Rawthey trembles.
Tongue stumbles, ears err
for fear of spring.
Rub the stone with sand,
wet sandstone rending
roughness away. Fingers
ache on the rubbing stone.

The mason says: Rocks
happen by chance.
No one here bolts the door,
love is so sore.

Stone smooth as skin,
cold as the dead they load
on a low lorry by night.
The moon sits on the fell
but it will rain.
Under sacks on the stone
two children lie,
hear the horse stale,
the mason whistle,
harness mutter to shaft,
felloe to axle squeak,
rut thud the rim,
crushed grit.

Stocking to stocking, jersey to jersey,
head to a hard arm,
they kiss under the rain,
bruised by their marble bed.
In Garsdale, dawn;
at Hawes, tea from the can.
Rain stops, sacks
steam in the sun, they sit up.
Copper-wire moustache,
sea-reflecting eyes
and Baltic plainsong speech
declare: By such rocks
men killed Bloodaxe.

Fierce blood throbs in his tongue,
lean words.
Skulls cropped for steel caps
huddle round Stainmore.
Their becks ring on limestone,
whisper to peat.
The clogged cart pushes the horse downhill.
In such soft air
they trudge and sing,

laying the tune frankly on the air.
All sounds fall still,
fellside bleat,
hide-and-seek peewit.

Her pulse their pace,
palm countering palm,
till a trench is filled,
stone white as cheese
jeers at the dale.
Knotty wood, hard to rive,
smoulders to ash;
smell of October apples.
The road again,
at a trot.
Wetter, warmed, they watch
the mason meditate
on name and date.

Rain rinses the road,
the bull streams and laments.
Sour rye porridge from the hob
with cream and black tea,
meat, crust and crumb.
Her parents in bed
the children dry their clothes.
He has untied the tape
of her striped flannel drawers
before the range. Naked
on the pricked rag mat
his fingers comb
thatch of his manhood's home.

Gentle generous voices weave
over bare night
words to confirm and delight
till bird dawn.
Rainwater from the butt
she fetches and flannel
to wash him inch by inch,
kissing the pebbles.
Shining slowworm part of the marvel.

The mason stirs:
Words!
Pens are too light.
Take a chisel to write.

Every birth a crime,
every sentence life.
Wiped of mould and mites
would the ball run true?
No hope of going back.
Hounds falter and stray,
shame deflects the pen.
Love murdered neither bleeds nor stifles
but jogs the draftsman's elbow.
What can he, changed, tell
her, changed, perhaps dead?
Delight dwindles. Blame
stays the same.

Brief words are hard to find,
shapes to carve and discard:
Bloodaxe, king of York,
king of Dublin, king of Orkney.
Take no notice of tears;
letter the stone to stand
over love laid aside lest
insufferable happiness impede
flight to Stainmore,
to trace
lark, mallet,
becks, flocks
and axe knocks.

Dung will not soil the slowworm's
mosaic. Breathless lark
drops to nest in sodden trash;
Rawthey truculent, dingy.
Drudge at the mallet, the may is down,
fog on fells. Guilty of spring
and spring's ending
amputated years ache after
the bull is beef, love a convenience.

It is easier to die than to remember.
Name and date
split in soft slate
a few months obliterate.

R. S. THOMAS Pietà

Always the same hills
Crowd the horizon.
Remote witnesses
Of the still scene.

And in the foreground
The tall Cross,
Sombre, untenanted,
Aches for the Body
That is back in the cradle
Of a maid's arms.

R. S. THOMAS Gifts

From my father my strong heart,
My weak stomach.
From my mother the fear.

From my sad country the shame.

To my wife all I have
Saving only the love
That is not mine to give.

To my one son the hunger.

SEAMUS HEANEY Personal Helicon

for Michael Longley

As a child, they could not keep me from wells
And old pumps with buckets and windlasses.
I loved the dark drop, the trapped sky, the smells
Of waterweed, fungus and dank moss.

One, in a brickyard, with a rotted board top.
I savoured the rich crash when a bucket
Plummeted down at the end of a rope.
So deep you saw no reflection in it.

A shallow one under a dry stone ditch
Fructified like any aquarium.
When you dragged out long roots from the soft mulch
A white face hovered over the bottom.

Others had echoes, gave back your own call
With a clean new music in it. And one
Was scaresome, for there, out of ferns and tall
Foxgloves, a rat slapped across my reflection.

Now, to pry into roots, to finger slime,
To stare, big-eyed Narcissus, into some spring
Is beneath all adult dignity. I rhyme
To see myself, to set the darkness echoing.

1967   TED HUGHES Thistles

Against the rubber tongues of cows and the hoeing hands of men
Thistles spike the summer air
Or crackle open under a blue-black pressure.

Every one a revengeful burst
Of resurrection, a grasped fistful
Of splintered weapons and Icelandic frost thrust up

From the underground stain of a decayed Viking.
They are like pale hair and the gutturals of dialects.
Every one manages a plume of blood.

Then they grow grey, like men.
Mown down, it is a feud. Their sons appear,
Stiff with weapons, fighting back over the same ground.

TED HUGHES Full Moon and Little Frieda

A cool small evening shrunk to a dog bark and the clank of a
    bucket –

And you listening.
A spider's web, tense for the dew's touch.
A pail lifted, still and brimming – mirror
To tempt a first star to a tremor.

Cows are going home in the lane there, looping the hedges with their
    warm wreaths of breath –
A dark river of blood, many boulders,
Balancing unspilled milk.

'Moon!' you cry suddenly, 'Moon! Moon!'

The moon has stepped back like an artist gazing amazed at a work

That points at him amazed.

JOHN MONTAGUE *from* A Chosen Light

11 rue Daguerre

At night, sometimes, when I cannot sleep
I go to the *atelier* door
And smell the earth of the garden.

It exhales softly,
Especially now, approaching springtime,
When tendrils of green are plaited

Across the humus, desperately frail
In their passage against
The dark, unredeemed parcels of earth.

There is white light on the cobblestones
And in the apartment house opposite –
All four floors – silence.

In that stillness – soft but luminously exact,
A chosen light – I notice that
The tips of the lately grafted cherry-tree

Are a firm and lacquered black.

GEORGE THEINER *from the Czech of Miroslav Holub* **The Fly**

She sat on a willow-trunk
watching
part of the battle of Crécy,
the shouts,
the gasps,
the groans,
the tramping and the tumbling.

During the fourteenth charge
of the French cavalry
she mated
with a brown-eyed male fly
from Vadincourt.

She rubbed her legs together
as she sat on a disembowelled horse
meditating
on the immortality of flies.

With relief she alighted
on the blue tongue
of the Duke of Clervaux.

When silence settled
and only the whisper of decay
softly circled the bodies

and only
a few arms and legs
still twitched jerkily under the trees,

she began to lay her eggs
on the single eye
of Johann Uhr,
the Royal Armourer.

And thus it was
that she was eaten by a swift
fleeing
from the fires of Estrées.

GEOFFREY HILL Ovid in The Third Reich

non peccat, quaecumque potest peccasse negare,
solaque famosam culpa professa facit.

(AMORES, III, XIV)

I love my work and my children. God
Is distant, difficult. Things happen.
Too near the ancient troughs of blood
Innocence is no earthly weapon.

I have learned one thing: not to look down
So much upon the damned. They, in their sphere,
Harmonize strangely with the divine
Love. I, in mine, celebrate the love-choir.

GEOFFREY HILL September Song

born 19.6.32 – deported 24.9.42

Undesirable you may have been, untouchable
you were not. Not forgotten
or passed over at the proper time.

As estimated, you died. Things marched,
sufficient, to that end.
Just so much Zyklon and leather, patented
terror, so many routine cries.

(I have made
an elegy for myself it
is true)

September fattens on vines. Roses
flake from the wall. The smoke
of harmless fires drifts to my eyes.

This is plenty. This is more than enough.

ROY FISHER As He Came Near Death

As he came near death things grew shallower for us:
We'd lost sleep and now sat muffled in the scent of tulips, the
    medical odours, and the street sounds going past, going away;
And he, too, slept little, the morphine and the pink light the curtains
    let through floating him with us,
So that he lay and was worked out on to the skin of his life and left
    there,
And we had to reach only a little way into the warm bed to scoop
    him up.

A few days, slow tumbling escalators of visitors and cheques, and
    something like popularity;
During this time somebody washed him in a soap called *Narcissus*
    and mounted him, frilled with satin, in a polished case.

Then the hole: this was a slot punched in a square of plastic grass
    rug, a slot lined with white polythene, floored with dyed green
    gravel.
The box lay in it; we rode in the black cars round a corner, got out
    into our coloured cars and dispersed in easy stages.

After a time the grave got up and went away.

ROY FISHER The Memorial Fountain

The fountain plays
                    through summer dusk in gaunt shadows,
black constructions
                    against a late clear sky,
water in the basin
                    where the column falls
              shaking,
rapid and wild,
                    in cross-waves, in back-waves,
              the light glinting and blue,
as in a wind
                    though there is none,
                                        Harsh
skyline!
              Far-off scaffolding
bitten against the air.

                          Sombre mood
in the presence of things,
                    no matter what things;
respectful sepia.

              This scene:
              people on the public seats
              embedded in it, darkening
              intelligences of what's visible;
              private, given over, all of them –

Many scenes.

Still sombre.

As for the fountain:
                    nothing in the describing
beyond what shows
                    for anyone;
              above all
no 'atmosphere'.
                    It's like this often –
I don't exaggerate.
              And the scene?

a thirty-five-year-old man,
poet,
      by temper, realist,
watching a fountain
and the figures round it
in garish twilight,
          working
to distinguish an event
from an opinion;
          this man,
intent and comfortable –

Romantic notion.

1969   MICHAEL LONGLEY Persephone

I

I see as through a skylight in my brain
The mole strew its buildings in the rain,

The swallows turn above their broken home
And all my acres in delirium.

II

Straitjacketed by cold and numskulled
Now sleep the welladjusted and the skilled –

The bat folds its wing like a winter leaf,
The squirrel in its hollow holds aloof.

III

The weasel and ferret, the stoat and fox
Move hand in glove across the equinox.

I can tell how softly their footsteps go –
Their footsteps borrow silence from the snow.

DOUGLAS DUNN A Removal from Terry Street

On a squeaking cart, they push the usual stuff,
A mattress, bed ends, cups, carpets, chairs,
Four paperback westerns. Two whistling youths
In surplus US Army battle-jackets
Remove their sister's goods. Her husband
Follows, carrying on his shoulders the son
Whose mischief we are glad to see removed,
And pushing, of all things, a lawnmower.
There is no grass in Terry Street. The worms
Come up cracks in concrete yards in moonlight.
That man, I wish him well. I wish him grass.

DOUGLAS DUNN On Roofs of Terry Street

Television aerials, Chinese characters
In the lower sky, wave gently in the smoke.

Nest-building sparrows peck at moss,
Urban flora and fauna, soft, unscrupulous.

Rain drying on the slates shines sometimes.
A builder is repairing someone's leaking roof.

He kneels upright to rest his back.
His trowel catches the light and becomes precious.

NORMAN MACCAIG Wild Oats

Every day I see from my window
pigeons, up on a roof ledge – the males
are wobbling gyroscopes of lust.

Last week a stranger joined them, a snowwhite
pouting fantail,
Mae West in the Women's Guild.

What becks, what croo-croos, what
demented pirouetting, what a lack
of moustaches to stroke.

The females – no need to be one of them
to know
exactly what they were thinking – pretended
she wasn't there
and went dowdily on with whatever
pigeons do when they're knitting.

IAIN CRICHTON SMITH Shall Gaelic Die?

Translated by the author

1

A picture has no grammar. It has neither evil nor good. It has only
     colour, say orange or mauve.
Can Picasso change a minister? Did he make a sermon to a bull?
Did heaven rise from his brush? Who saw a church that is orange?
In a world like a picture, a world without language, would your
     mind go astray, lost among objects?

2

Advertisements in neon, lighting and going out, 'Shall it . . . shall it
     . . . Shall Gaelic . . . shall it . . . shall Gaelic . . . die?'

3

Words rise out of the country. They are around us. In every month
     in the year we are surrounded by words.
Spring has its own dictionary, its leaves are turning in the sharp
     wind of March, which opens the shops.
Autumn has its own dictionary, the brown words lying on the
     bottom of the loch, asleep for a season.
Winter has its own dictionary, the words are a blizzard building a
     tower of Babel. Its grammar is like snow.
Between the words the wild-cat looks sharply across a
     No-Man's-Land, artillery of the Imagination.

They built a house with stones. They put windows in the house, and
    doors. They filled the room with furniture and the beards of
    thistles.
They looked out of the house on a Highland world, the flowers, the
    glens, distant Glasgow on fire.
They built a barometer of history.
Inch after inch, they suffered the stings of suffering.
Strangers entered the house, and they left.
But now, who is looking out with an altered gaze?
What does he see?
What has he got in his hands? A string of words.

5

He who loses his language loses his world. The Highlander who
    loses his language loses his world.
The space ship that goes astray among planets loses the world.
In an orange world how would you know orange? In a world
    without evil how would you know good?
Wittgenstein is in the middle of his world. He is like a spider.
The flies come to him. 'Cuan' and 'coill' rising.
When Wittgenstein dies, his world dies.
The thistle bends to the earth. The earth is tired of it.

6

I came with a 'sobhrach' in my mouth. He came with a 'primrose'.
A 'primrose by the river's brim'. Between the two languages, the
    word 'sobhrach' turned to 'primrose'.
Behind the two words, a Roman said 'prima rosa'.
The 'sobhrach' or the 'primrose' was in our hands. Its reasons
    belonged to us.

W. S. GRAHAM Malcolm Mooney's Land   1970

1

Today, Tuesday, I decided to move on
Although the wind was veering. Better to move
Than have them at my heels, poor friends
I buried earlier under the printed snow.
From wherever it is I urge these words
To find their subtle vents, the northern dazzle

Of silence cranes to watch. Footprint on foot
Print, word on word and each on a fool's errand.
Malcolm Mooney's Land. Elizabeth
Was in my thoughts all morning and the boy.
Wherever I speak from or in what particular
Voice, this is always a record of me in you.
I can record at least out there to the west
The grinding bergs and, listen, further off
Where we are going, the glacier calves
Making its sudden momentary thunder.
This is as good a night, a place as any.

2

From the rimed bag of sleep, Wednesday,
My words crackle in the early air.
Thistles of ice about my chin,
My dreams, my breath a ruff of crystals.
The new ice falls from canvas walls.
O benign creature with the small ear-hole,
Submerger under silence, lead
Me where the unblubbered monster goes
Listening and makes his play.
Make my impediment mean no ill
And be itself a way.

A fox was here last night (Maybe Nansen's,
Reading my instruments.) the prints
All round the tent and not a sound.
Not that I'd have him call my name.
Anyhow how should he know? Enough
Voices are with me here and more
The further I go. Yesterday
I heard the telephone ringing deep
Down in a blue crevasse.
I did not answer it and could
Hardly bear to pass.

Landlice, always my good bedfellows,
Ride with me in my sweaty seams.
Come bonny friendly beasts, brother
To the grammarsow and the word-louse,
Bite me your presence, keep me awake
In the cold with work to do, to remember
To put down something to take back.

I have reached the edge of earshot here
And by the laws of distance
My words go through the smoking air
Changing their tune on silence.

3

My friend who loves owls
Has been with me all day
Walking at my ear
And speaking of old summers
When to speak was easy.
His eyes are almost gone
Which made him hear well.
Under our feet the great
Glacier drove its keel.
What is to read there
Scored out in the dark?

Later the north-west distance
Thickened towards us.
The blizzard grew and proved
Too filled with other voices
High and desperate
For me to hear him more.
I turned to see him go
Becoming shapeless into
The shrill swerving snow.

4

Today, Friday, holds the white
Paper up too close to see
Me here in a white-out in this tent of a place
And why is it there has to be
Some place to find, however momentarily
To speak from, some distance to listen to?

Out at the far-off edge I hear
Colliding voices, drifted, yes
To find me through the slowly opening leads.
Tomorrow I'll try the rafted ice.
Have I not been trying to use the obstacle
Of language well? It freezes round us all.

Why did you choose this place
For us to meet? Sit
With me between this word
And this, my furry queen.
Yet not mistake this
For the real thing. Here
In Malcolm Mooney's Land
I have heard many
Approachers in the distance
Shouting. Early hunters
Skittering across the ice
Full of enthusiasm
And making fly and,
Within the ear, the yelling
Spear steepening to
The real prey, the right
Prey of the moment.
The honking choir in fear
Leave the tilting floe
And enter the sliding water.
Above the bergs the foolish
Voices are lighting lamps
And all their sounds make
This diary of a place
Writing us both in.

Come and sit. Or is
It right to stay here
While, outside the tent
The bearded blinded go
Calming their children
Into the ovens of frost?
And what's the news? What
Brought you here through
The spring leads opening?

Elizabeth, you and the boy
Have been with me often
Especially on those last
Stages. Tell him a story.

Tell him I came across
An old sulphur bear
Sawing his log of sleep
Loud beneath the snow.
He puffed the powdered light
Up on to this page
And here his reek fell
In splinters among
These words. He snored well.
Elizabeth, my furry
Pelted queen of Malcolm
Mooney's Land, I made
You here beside me
For a moment out
Of the correct fatigue.

I have made myself alone now.
Outside the tent endless
Drifting hummock crests.
Words drifting on words.
The real unabstract snow.

IAN HAMILTON The Visit

They've let me walk with you
As far as this high wall. The placid smiles
Of our new friends, the old incurables,
Pursue us lovingly.
Their boyish, suntanned heads,
Their ancient arms
Outstretched, belong to you.

Although your head still burns
Your hands remember me.

IAN HAMILTON Newscast

The Vietnam war drags on
In one corner of our living-room.
The conversation turns
To take it in.
Our smoking heads
Drift back to us
From the grey fires of South-east Asia.

TOM LEONARD *from* Unrelated Incidents

3
this is thi
six a clock
news thi
man said n
thi reason
a talk wia
BBC accent
iz coz yi
widny wahnt
mi ti talk
aboot thi
trooth wia
voice lik
wanna yoo
scruff. if
a toktaboot
thi trooth
lik wana yoo
scruff yi
widny thingk
it wuz troo.
jist wanna yoo
scruff tokn.
thirza right
way ti spell
ana right way
ti tok it. this
is me tokn yir

right way a
spellin. this
is ma trooth.
yooz doant no
thi trooth
yirsellz cawz
yi canny talk
right. this is
the six a clock
nyooz. belt up.

TED HUGHES *from* Crow

A Childish Prank

Man's and woman's bodies lay without souls,
Dully gaping, foolishly staring, inert
On the flowers of Eden.
God pondered.

The problem was so great, it dragged him asleep.

Crow laughed.
He bit the Worm, God's only son,
Into two writhing halves.

He stuffed into man the tail half
With the wounded end hanging out.

He stuffed the head half headfirst into woman
And it crept in deeper and up
To peer out through her eyes

Calling its tail-half to join up quickly, quickly
Because O it was painful.

Man awoke being dragged across the grass.
Woman awoke to see him coming.
Neither knew what had happened.

God went on sleeping.
Crow went on laughing.

1971   THOM GUNN Moly

Nightmare of beasthood, snorting, how to wake.
I woke. What beasthood skin she made me take?

Leathery toad that ruts for days on end,
Or cringing dribbling dog, man's servile friend,

Or cat that prettily pounces on its meat,
Tortures it hours, then does not care to eat:

Parrot, moth, shark, wolf, crocodile, ass, flea.
What germs, what jostling mobs there were in me.

These seem like bristles, and the hide is tough.
No claw or web here: each foot ends in hoof.

Into what bulk has method disappeared?
Like ham, streaked. I am gross – grey, gross, flap-eared.

The pale-lashed eyes my only human feature.
My teeth tear, tear. I am the snouted creature

That bites through anything, root, wire, or can.
If I was not afraid I'd eat a man.

Oh a man's flesh already is in mine.
Hand and foot poised for risk. Buried in swine.

I root and root, you think that it is greed,
It is, but I seek out a plant I need.

Direct me gods, whose changes are all holy,
To where it flickers deep in grass, the moly:

Cool flesh of magic in each leaf and shoot,
From milky flower to the black forked root.

From this fat dungeon I could rise to skin
And human title, putting pig within.

I push my big grey wet snout through the green,
Dreaming the flower I have never seen.

GEOFFREY HILL *from* Mercian Hymns

I

King of the perennial holly-groves, the riven sand-
    stone: overlord of the M5: architect of the his-
    toric rampart and ditch, the citadel at Tamworth,
    the summer hermitage in Holy Cross: guardian of
    the Welsh Bridge and the Iron Bridge: contractor
    to the desirable new estates: saltmaster: money-
    changer: commissioner for oaths: martyrologist:
    the friend of Charlemagne.

'I liked that,' said Offa, 'sing it again.'

VI

The princes of Mercia were badger and raven. Thrall
    to their freedom, I dug and hoarded. Orchards
    fruited above clefts. I drank from honeycombs of
    chill sandstone.

'A boy at odds in the house, lonely among brothers.'
    But I, who had none, fostered a strangeness; gave
    myself to unattainable toys.

Candles of gnarled resin, apple-branches, the tacky
    mistletoe. 'Look' they said and again 'look.' But
    I ran slowly; the landscape flowed away, back to
    its source.

In the schoolyard, in the cloakrooms, the children
    boasted their scars of dried snot; wrists and
    knees garnished with impetigo.

VII

Gasholders, russet among fields. Milldams, marlpools
    that lay unstirring. Eel-swarms. Coagulations of
    frogs: once, with branches and half-bricks, he
    battered a ditchful; then sidled away from the
    stillness and silence.

Ceolred was his friend and remained so, even after
    the day of the lost fighter: a biplane, already
    obsolete and irreplaceable, two inches of heavy
    snub silver. Ceolred let it spin through a hole
    in the classroom-floorboards, softly, into the
    rat-droppings and coins.

After school he lured Ceolred, who was sniggering
    with fright, down to the old quarries, and flayed
    him. Then, leaving Ceolred, he journeyed for hours,
    calm and alone, in his private derelict sandlorry
    named *Albion*.

XXVII

'Now when King Offa was alive and dead', they were
    all there, the funereal gleemen: papal legate and
    rural dean; Merovingian car-dealers, Welsh mercen-
    aries; a shuffle of house-carls.

He was defunct. They were perfunctory. The ceremony
    stood acclaimed. The mob received memorial vouch-
    ers and signs.

After that shadowy, thrashing midsummer hail-storm,
    Earth lay for a while, the ghost-bride of livid
    Thor, butcher of strawberries, and the shire-tree
    dripped red in the arena of its uprooting.

GEORGE MACKAY BROWN Kirkyard

A silent conquering army,
The island dead,
Column on column, each with a stone banner
Raised over his head.

A green wave full of fish
Drifted far
In wavering westering ebb-drawn shoals beyond
Sinker or star.

A labyrinth of celled
And waxen pain.
Yet I come to the honeycomb often, to sip the finished
Fragrance of men.

STEVIE SMITH Scorpion

'This night shall thy soul be required of thee'
My soul is never required of *me*
It always has to be somebody else of course
Will my soul be required of me tonight perhaps?

(I often wonder what it will be like
To have one's soul required of one
But all I can think of is the Out-Patients' Department –
'Are you Mrs Briggs, dear?'
No, I am Scorpion.)

I should like my soul to be required of me, so as
To waft over grass till it comes to the blue sea
I am very fond of grass, I always have been, but there must
Be no cow, person or house to be seen.

Sea and *grass* must be quite empty
Other souls can find somewhere *else*.

O Lord God please come
And require the soul of thy Scorpion

Scorpion so wishes to be gone.

CHARLES TOMLINSON Stone Speech

Crowding this beach
are milkstones, white
teardrops; flints
edged out of flinthood
into smoothness chafe
against grainy ovals,
pitted pieces, nosestones,
stoppers and saddles;
veins of orange
inlay black beads:
chalk-swaddled babyshapes,
tiny fists, facestones
and facestone's brother
skullstone, roundheads
pierced by a single eye,
purple finds, all
rubbing shoulders:
a mob of grindings,
groundlings, scatterings
from a million necklaces
mined under sea-hills, the pebbles
are as various as the people.

DEREK MAHON An Image from Beckett

In that instant
There was a sea, far off,
As bright as lettuce,

A northern landscape
And a huddle
Of houses along the shore.

Also, I think, a white
Flicker of gulls
And washing hung to dry –

The poignancy of those
Back-yards – and the gravedigger
Putting aside his forceps.

Then the hard boards
And darkness once again.
But in that instant

I was struck by the
Sweetness and light,
The sweetness and light,

Imagining what grave
Cities, what lasting monuments,
Given the time.

They will have buried
My great-grandchildren, and theirs,
Beside me by now

With a subliminal batsqueak
Of reflex lamentation.
Our knuckle bones

Litter the rich earth,
Changing, second by second,
To civilizations.

It was good while it lasted,
And if it only lasted
The Biblical span

Required to drop six feet
Through a glitter of wintry light,
There is No-One to blame.

Still, I am haunted
By that landscape,
The soft rush of its winds,

The uprightness of its
Utilities and schoolchildren –
To whom in my will,

This, I have left my will.
I hope they have time,
And light enough, to read it.

SEAMUS HEANEY The Tollund Man

I

Some day I will go to Aarhus
To see his peat-brown head,
The mild pods of his eye-lids,
His pointed skin cap.

In the flat country near by
Where they dug him out,
His last gruel of winter seeds
Caked in his stomach,

Naked except for
The cap, noose and girdle,
I will stand a long time.
Bridegroom to the goddess,

She tightened her torc on him
And opened her fen,
Those dark juices working
Him to a saint's kept body,

Trove of the turfcutters'
Honeycombed workings.
Now his stained face
Reposes at Aarhus.

II

I could risk blasphemy,
Consecrate the cauldron bog
Our holy ground and pray
Him to make germinate

The scattered, ambushed
Flesh of labourers,
Stockinged corpses
Laid out in the farmyards,

Tell-tale skin and teeth
Flecking the sleepers
Of four young brothers, trailed
For miles along the lines.

III

Something of his sad freedom
As he rode the tumbril
Should come to me, driving,
Saying the names

Tollund, Grabaulle, Nebelgard,
Watching the pointing hands
Of country people,
Not knowing their tongue.

Out there in Jutland
In the old man-killing parishes
I will feel lost,
Unhappy and at home.

SEAMUS HEANEY Broagh

Riverbank, the long rigs
ending in broad docken
and a canopied pad
down to the ford.

The garden mould
bruised easily, the shower
gathering in your heelmark
was the black O

in *Broagh*,
its low tattoo
among the windy boortrees
and rhubarb-blades

ended almost
suddenly, like that last
gh the strangers found
difficult to manage.

DOUGLAS DUNN Modern Love

It is summer, and we are in a house
That is not ours, sitting at a table
Enjoying minutes of a rented silence,
The upstairs people gone. The pigeons lull
To sleep the under-tens and invalids,
The tree shakes out its shadows to the grass,
The roses rove through the wilds of my neglect.
Our lives flap, and we have no hope of better
Happiness than this, not much to show for love
Than how we are, or how this evening is,
Unpeopled, silent, and where we are alive
In a domestic love, seemingly alone.
All other lives worn down to trees and sunlight.
Looking forward to a visit from the cat.

ÉILEAN NÍ CHUILLEANÁIN Swineherd

When all this is over, said the swineherd,
I mean to retire, where
Nobody will have heard about my special skills
And conversation is mainly about the weather.

I intend to learn how to make coffee, at least as well
As the Portuguese lay-sister in the kitchen
And polish the brass fenders every day.
I want to lie awake at night
Listening to cream crawling to the top of the jug
And the water lying soft in the cistern.

I want to see an orchard where the trees grow in straight lines
And the yellow fox finds shelter between the navy-blue trunks,
Where it gets dark early in summer
And the apple-blossom is allowed to wither on the bough.

ÉILEAN NÍ CHUILLEANÁIN The Second Voyage

Odysseus rested on his oar and saw
The ruffled foreheads of the waves
Crocodiling and mincing past: he rammed
The oar between their jaws and looked down
In the simmering sea where scribbles of weed defined
Uncertain depth, and the slim fishes progressed

In fatal formation, and thought
                              If there was a single
Streak of decency in these waves now, they'd be ridged
Pocked and dented with the battering they've had,
And we could name them as Adam named the beasts,
Saluting a new one with dismay, or a notorious one
With admiration; they'd notice us passing
And rejoice at our shipwreck, but these
Have less character than sheep and need more patience.

I know what I'll do he said;
I'll park my ship in the crook of a long pier
(And I'll take you with me he said to the oar)
I'll face the rising ground and walk away
From tidal waters, up riverbeds
Where herons parcel out the miles of stream,
Over gaps in the hills, through warm
Silent valleys, and when I meet a farmer
Bold enough to look me in the eye
With 'where are you off to with that long
Winnowing fan over your shoulder?'
There I will stand still
And I'll plant you for a gatepost or a hitching-post
And leave you as a tidemark. I can go back
And organise my house then.
                       But the profound
Unfenced valleys of the ocean still held him;
He had only the oar to make them keep their distance;
The sea was still frying under the ship's side.
He considered the water-lilies, and thought about fountains
Spraying as wide as willows in empty squares,
The sugarstick of water clattering into the kettle,
The flat lakes bisecting the rushes. He remembered spiders and frogs
Housekeeping at the roadside in brown trickles floored with mud,
Horsetroughs, the black canal, pale swans at dark:
His face grew damp with tears that tasted
Like his own sweat or the insults of the sea.

1973   **THOMAS KINSELLA** Hen Woman

The noon heat in the yard
smelled of stillness and coming thunder.
A hen scratched and picked at the shore.
It stopped, its body crouched and puffed out.
The brooding silence seemed to say 'Hush . . .'

The cottage door opened,
a black hole
in a whitewashed wall so bright
the eyes narrowed.
Inside, a clock murmured 'Gong . . .'

She hurried out in her slippers
muttering, her face dark with anger,
and gathered the hen up jerking
languidly. Her hand fumbled.
Too late. Too late.

It fixed me with its pebble eyes
(seeing what mad blur?).
A white egg showed in the sphincter;
mouth and beak opened together;
and time stood still.

Nothing moved: bird or woman,
fumbled or fumbling – locked there
(as I must have been) gaping.

*

There was a tiny movement at my feet,
tiny and mechanical; I looked down.
A beetle like a bronze leaf
was inching across the cement,
clasping with small tarsi
a ball of dung bigger than its body.
The serrated brow pressed the ground humbly,
lifted in a short stare, bowed again;
the dung-ball advanced minutely,
losing a few fragments,
specks of staleness and freshness.

*

A mutter of thunder far off
– time not quite stopped.
I saw the egg had moved a fraction:
a tender blank brain
under torsion, a clean new world.

As I watched, the mystery completed.
The black zero of the orifice
closed to a point
and the white zero of the egg hung free,
flecked with greenish brown oils.

It slowly turned and fell.
Dreamlike, fussed by her splayed fingers,
it floated outward, moon-white,
leaving no trace in the air,
and began its drop to the shore.

*

I feed upon it still, as you see;
there is no end to that which,
not understood, may yet be noted
and hoarded in the imagination,
in the yolk of one's being, so to speak,
there to undergo its (quite animal) growth,
dividing blindly,
twitching, packed with will,
searching in its own tissue
for the structure
in which it may wake.
Something that had – clenched
in its cave – not been
now was: an egg of being.
Through what seemed a whole year it fell
– as it still falls, for me,
solid and light, the red gold beating
in its silvery womb,
alive as the yolk and white
of my eye; as it will continue
to fall, probably, until I die,
through the vast indifferent spaces
with which I am empty.

*

It smashed against the grating
and slipped down quickly out of sight.
It was over in a comical flash.
The soft mucous shell clung a little longer,
then drained down.
She stood staring, in black anger.
Then her eyes came to life, and she laughed
and let the bird flap away.
'It's all the one.
There's plenty more where that came from!'

Hen to pan!
It was a simple world.

THOMAS KINSELLA Ancestor

I was going up to say something,
and stopped. Her profile against the curtains
was old, and dark like a hunting bird's.

It was the way she perched on the high stool,
staring into herself, with one fist
gripping the side of the barrier around her desk
– or her head held by something, from inside.
And not caring for anything around her
or anyone there by the shelves.
I caught a faint smell, musky and queer.

I may have made some sound – she stopped rocking
and pressed her fist in her lap; then she stood up
and shut down the lid of the desk, and turned the key.
She shoved a small bottle under her aprons
and came toward me, darkening the passageway.

Ancestor . . . among sweet- and fruit-boxes.
Her black heart . . .
                    Was that a sigh?
– brushing by me in the shadows,
with her heaped aprons, through the red hangings
to the scullery, and down to the back room.

MICHAEL LONGLEY Wounds

Here are two pictures from my father's head –
I have kept them like secrets until now:
First, the Ulster Division at the Somme
Going over the top with 'Fuck the Pope!'
'No Surrender!': a boy about to die,
Screaming 'Give 'em one for the Shankill!'
'Wilder than Gurkhas' were my father's words
Of admiration and bewilderment.
Next comes the London-Scottish padre
Resettling kilts with his swagger-stick,
With a stylish backhand and a prayer.

Over a landscape of dead buttocks
My father followed him for fifty years.
At last, a belated casualty,
He said – lead traces flaring till they hurt –
'I am dying for King and Country, slowly.'
I touched his hand, his thin head I touched.

Now, with military honours of a kind,
With his badges, his medals like rainbows,
His spinning compass, I bury beside him
Three teenage soldiers, bellies full of
Bullets and Irish beer, their flies undone.
A packet of Woodbines I throw in,
A lucifer, the Sacred Heart of Jesus
Paralysed as heavy guns put out
The night-light in a nursery for ever;
Also a bus-conductor's uniform –
He collapsed beside his carpet-slippers
Without a murmur, shot through the head
By a shivering boy who wandered in
Before they could turn the television down
Or tidy away the supper dishes.
To the children, to a bewildered wife,
I think 'Sorry Missus' was what he said.

PAUL MULDOON Wind and Tree

In the way that the most of the wind
Happens where there are trees,

Most of the world is centred
About ourselves.

Often where the wind has gathered
The trees together,

One tree will take
Another in her arms and hold.

Their branches that are grinding
Madly together,

It is no real fire.
They are breaking each other.

Often I think I should be like
The single tree, going nowhere,

Since my own arm could not and would not
Break the other. Yet by my broken bones

I tell new weather.

PHILIP LARKIN This Be the Verse

They fuck you up, your mum and dad.
    They may not mean to, but they do.
They fill you with the faults they had
    And add some extra, just for you.

But they were fucked up in their turn
    By fools in old-style hats and coats,
Who half the time were soppy-stern
    And half at one another's throats.

Man hands on misery to man.
    It deepens like a coastal shelf.
Get out as early as you can,
    And don't have any kids yourself.

PHILIP LARKIN Money

Quarterly, is it, money reproaches me:
    'Why do you let me lie here wastefully?
I am all you never had of goods and sex.
    You could get them still by writing a few cheques.'

So I look at others, what they do with theirs:
    They certainly don't keep it upstairs.
By now they've a second house and car and wife:
    Clearly money has something to do with life

– In fact, they've a lot in common, if you enquire:
    You can't put off being young until you retire,
And however you bank your screw, the money you save
    Won't in the end buy you more than a shave.

I listen to money singing. It's like looking down
    From long french windows at a provincial town,
The slums, the canal, the churches ornate and mad
    In the evening sun. It is intensely sad.

PHILIP LARKIN *from* **Livings**

II

Seventy feet down
The sea explodes upwards,
Relapsing, to slaver
Off landing-stage steps –
Running suds, rejoice!

Rocks writhe back to sight.
Mussels, limpets,
Husband their tenacity
In the freezing slither –
Creatures, I cherish you!

By day, sky builds
Grape-dark over the salt
Unsown stirring fields.
Radio rubs its legs,
Telling me of elsewhere:

Barometers falling,
Ports wind-shuttered,
Fleets pent like hounds,
Fires in humped inns
Kippering sea-pictures –

Keep it all off!
By night, snow swerves
(O loose moth world)
Through the stare travelling
Leather-black waters.

Guarded by brilliance
I set plate and spoon,
And after, divining cards.
Lit shelved liners
Grope like mad worlds westward.

PHILIP LARKIN The Explosion

On the day of the explosion
Shadows pointed towards the pithead:
In the sun the slagheap slept.

Down the lane came men in pitboots
Coughing oath-edged talk and pipe-smoke,
Shouldering off the freshened silence.

One chased after rabbits; lost them;
Came back with a nest of lark's eggs;
Showed them; lodged them in the grasses.

So they passed in beards and moleskins,
Fathers, brothers, nicknames, laughter,
Through the tall gates standing open.

At noon, there came a tremor; cows
Stopped chewing for a second; sun,
Scarfed as in a heat-haze, dimmed.

The dead go on before us, they
Are sitting in God's house in comfort,
We shall see them face to face –

Plain as lettering in the chapels
It was said, and for a second
Wives saw men of the explosion

Larger than in life they managed –
Gold as on a coin, or walking
Somehow from the sun towards them,

One showing the eggs unbroken.

PADRAIC FALLON A Bit of Brass

A horn hung on an oak;
And he, the big overplus, the hero
Destined, sounds the famous note, invokes
Cascading Gods and
His own death boat.

I did lift
A bit of battered brass once to my mouth,
May 1915, after
A day's rain
in the townwalled field where the Volunteers
Drilled;

That evening the wet overhang had daunted all,
Bugler and mate
Gossiped under a leaking branch, sounding
An occasional call,
Joe Egan, Josie Rooney;
Dear Posterity, I was there.

Echoes hung
Solidly in the drowned green beechtrees,
Hardly swinging;
Call after call brought no one to the field,
That is no man alive;
The mates gave up and I purloined the thing;

Squawk, a couple of fancy tootles,
Then out of Me minus
It came, the soaring
Thing;
Just once.

It could be it still hangs
In the May over
Leonards and the Pound Walk, just waiting
Those fellows, the long striders
Gods or men
To take the field.

(1983)

SEAMUS HEANEY *from* Singing School

6 Exposure

It is December in Wicklow:
Alders dripping, birches
Inheriting the last light,
The ash tree cold to look at.

A comet that was lost
Should be visible at sunset,
Those million tons of light
Like a glimmer of haws and rose-hips,

And I sometimes see a falling star.
If I could come on meteorite!
Instead I walk through damp leaves,
Husks, the spent flukes of autumn,

Imagining a hero
On some muddy compound,
His gift like a slingstone
Whirled for the desperate.

How did I end up like this?
I often think of my friends'
Beautiful prismatic counselling
And the anvil brains of some who hate me

As I sit weighing and weighing
My responsible *tristia*.
For what? For the ear? For the people?
For what is said behind-backs?

Rain comes down through the alders,
Its low conducive voices
Mutter about let-downs and erosions
And yet each drop recalls

The diamond absolutes.
I am neither internee nor informer;
An inner émigré, grown long-haired
And thoughtful; a wood-kerne

Escaped from the massacre,
Taking protective colouring
From bole and bark, feeling
Every wind that blows;

Who, blowing up these sparks
For their meagre heat, have missed
The once-in-a-lifetime portent,
The comet's pulsing rose.

DEREK MAHON The Snow Party

Bashō, coming
To the city of Nagoya,
Is asked to a snow party.

There is a tinkling of china
And tea into china;
There are introductions.

Then everyone
Crowds to the window
To watch the falling snow.

Snow is falling on Nagoya
And farther south
On the tiles of Kyōto.

Eastward, beyond Irago,
It is falling
Like leaves on the cold sea.

Elsewhere they are burning
Witches and heretics
In the boiling squares,

Thousands have died since dawn
In the service
Of barbarous kings;

But there is silence
In the houses of Nagoya
And the hills of Ise.

DEREK MAHON A Disused Shed in Co. Wexford

Let them not forget us, the weak souls among the asphodels.
– Seferis, *Mythistorema*

for J. G. Farrell

Even now there are places where a thought might grow –
Peruvian mines, worked out and abandoned
To a slow clock of condensation,
An echo trapped for ever, and a flutter
Of wildflowers in the lift-shaft,
Indian compounds where the wind dances
And a door bangs with diminished confidence,
Lime crevices behind rippling rainbarrels,
Dog corners for bone burials;
And in a disused shed in Co. Wexford,

Deep in the grounds of a burnt-out hotel,
Among the bathtubs and the washbasins
A thousand mushrooms crowd to a keyhole.
This is the one star in their firmament
Or frames a star within a star.
What should they do there but desire?
So many days beyond the rhododendrons
With the world waltzing in its bowl of cloud,
They have learnt patience and silence
Listening to the rooks querulous in the high wood.

They have been waiting for us in a foetor
Of vegetable sweat since civil war days,
Since the gravel-crunching, interminable departure
Of the expropriated mycologist.
He never came back, and light since then
Is a keyhole rusting gently after rain.
Spiders have spun, flies dusted to mildew
And once a day, perhaps, they have heard something –
A trickle of masonry, a shout from the blue
Or a lorry changing gear at the end of the lane.

There have been deaths, the pale flesh flaking
Into the earth that nourished it;
And nightmares, born of these and the grim
Dominion of stale air and rank moisture.
Those nearest the door grow strong –
'Elbow room! Elbow room!'
The rest, dim in a twilight of crumbling
Utensils and broken flower-pots, groaning
For their deliverance, have been so long
Expectant that there is left only the posture.

A half century, without visitors, in the dark –
Poor preparation for the cracking lock
And creak of hinges. Magi, moonmen,
Powdery prisoners of the old regime,
Web-throated, stalked like triffids, racked by drought
And insomnia, only the ghost of a scream
At the flash-bulb firing squad we wake them with
Shows there is life yet in their feverish forms.
Grown beyond nature now, soft food for worms,
They lift frail heads in gravity and good faith.

They are begging us, you see, in their wordless way,
To do something, to speak on their behalf
Or at least not to close the door again.
Lost people of Treblinka and Pompeii!
'Save us, save us,' they seem to say,
'Let the god not abandon us
Who have come so far in darkness and in pain.
We too had our lives to live.
You with your light meter and relaxed itinerary,
Let not our naive labours have been in vain!'

D. J. ENRIGHT Remembrance Sunday

The autumn leaves that strew the brooks
Lie thick as legions.

　　　　　Only a dog limps past,
Lifting a wounded leg.

　　　　　Was it the rocket hurt it?
Asks a child.

　　　　　And next comes Xmas,
Reflects the mother in the silence,
When X was born or hurt or died.

JOHN FULLER Wild Raspberries

Wild raspberries gathered in a silent valley
The distance of a casual whistle from
A roofless ruin, luminous under sprays
Like faery casques or the dulled red of lanterns
When the flame is low and the wax runs into the paper,
Little lanterns in the silence of crushed grasses
Or waiting chaises with a footman's lights,
Curtains hooked aside from the surprising
Plump facets padded like dusty cushions
On which we ride with fingers intertwined
Through green spiky tunnels, the coach swaying
As it plunges down and the tongues slip together,
The jewels fall to the floor to be lost forever,
The glass shatters and the heart suddenly leaps
To hear one long last sigh from an old blind house
That settles further into its prickly fronds,
Speaking of nothing, of love nor of reproaches,
Remembering nothing, harbouring no ghosts,
Saving us nothing at all but raspberries.

1976   MICHAEL LONGLEY   Man Lying on a Wall

Homage to L. S. Lowry

You could draw a straight line from the heels,
Through calves, buttocks and shoulderblades
To the back of the head: pressure points
That bear the enormous weight of the sky.
Should you take away the supporting structure
The result would be a miracle or
An extremely clever conjuring trick.
As it is, the man lying on the wall
Is wearing the serious expression
Of popes and kings in their final slumber,
His deportment not dissimilar to
Their stiff, reluctant exits from this world
Above the shoulders of the multitude.

It is difficult to judge whether or not
He is sleeping or merely disinclined
To arrive punctually at the office
Or to return home in time for his tea.
He is wearing a pinstripe suit, black shoes
And a bowler hat: on the pavement
Below him, like a relic or something
He is trying to forget, his briefcase
With everybody's initials on it.

ELMA MITCHELL   Thoughts after Ruskin

Women reminded him of lilies and roses.
Me they remind rather of blood and soap,
Armed with a warm rag, assaulting noses,
Ears, neck, mouth and all the secret places:

Armed with a sharp knife, cutting up liver,
Holding hearts to bleed under a running tap,
Gutting and stuffing, pickling and preserving,
Scalding, blanching, broiling, pulverising,
– All the terrible chemistry of their kitchens.

Their distant husbands lean across mahogany
And delicately manipulate the market,
While safe at home, the tender and the gentle
Are killing tiny mice, dead snap by the neck,
Asphyxiating flies, evicting spiders,
Scrubbing, scouring aloud, disturbing cupboards,
Committing things to dustbins, twisting, wringing,
Wrists red and knuckles white and fingers puckered,
Pulpy, tepid. Steering screaming cleaners
Around the snags of furniture, they straighten
And haul out sheets from under the incontinent
And heavy old, stoop to importunate young,
Tugging, folding, tucking, zipping, buttoning,
Spooning in food, encouraging excretion,
Mopping up vomit, stabbing cloth with needles,
Contorting wool around their knitting needles,
Creating snug and comfy on their needles.

Their huge hands! their everywhere eyes! their voices
Raised to convey across the hullabaloo,
Their massive thighs and breasts dispensing comfort,
Their bloody passages and hairy crannies,
Their wombs that pocket a man upside down!

And when all's over, off with overalls,
Quickly consulting clocks, they go upstairs,
Sit and sigh a little, brushing hair,
And somehow find, in mirrors, colours, odours,
Their essences of lilies and of roses.

THOM GUNN The Idea of Trust

The idea of trust, or,
the thief. He
was always around,
'pretty' Jim.
Like a lilac bush or
a nice picture on the wall.
Blue eyes of an
intense vagueness
and the well-arranged
bearing of an animal.

Then one day he
said something!
he said
that trust is
an intimate conspiracy.

What did that
mean? Anyway next day
he was gone, with
all the money and dope
of the people he'd lived with.

I begin
to understand. I see him
picking through their things
at his leisure, with
a quiet secret smile
choosing and taking,
having first discovered
and set up his phrase to
scramble
that message of
enveloping trust.

He's getting
free. His eyes
are almost transparent.
He has put on
gloves. He fingers
the little privacies of those
who acted as if there
should be no privacy.

They took that
risk.
Wild lilac
chokes the garden.

DONALD DAVIE *from* In the Stopping Train

I have got into the slow train
again. I made the mistake
knowing what I was doing,
knowing who had to be punished.

I know who has to be punished:
the man going mad inside me;
whether I am fleeing
from him or towards him.

This journey will punish the bastard:
he'll have his flowering gardens
to stare at through the hot window;
words like 'laurel' won't help.

He abhors his fellows,
especially children; let there
not for pity's sake
be a crying child in the carriage.

So much for pity's sake.
The rest for the sake of justice:
torment him with his hatreds
and love of fictions.

The punishing slow pace
punishes also places along the line
for having, some of them, Norman
or Hanoverian stone-work:

his old familiars, his
exclusive prophylactics.
He'll stare his fill at their
emptiness on this journey.

Jonquil is a sweet word.
Is it a flowering bush?
Let him helplessly wonder
for hours if perhaps he's seen it.

Has it a white and yellow
flower, the jonquil? Has it
a perfume? Oh his art could
always pretend it had.

He never needed to see,
not with his art to help him.
He never needed to use his
nose, except for language.

Torment him with his hatreds,
torment him with his false
loves. Torment him with time
that has disclosed their falsehood.

Time, the exquisite torment!
His future is a slow
and stopping train through places
whose names used to have virtue.

*

A stopping train, I thought,
was a train that was going to stop.
Why board it then, in the first place?

Oh no, they explained, it is stopping
and starting, stopping and starting.

How could it, they reasoned gently,
be always stopping unless
also it was always starting?

I saw the logic of that;
grown-ups were good at explaining.

Going to stop was the same
as stopping to go. What madness!
It made a sort of sense, though.

It's not, I explained, that I mind
getting to the end of the line.
Expresses have to do that.

No, they said. We see . . .
But do you? I said. It's not
the last stop that is bad . . .

No, they said, it's the last
start, the little one; yes,
the one that doesn't last.

Well, they said, you'll learn
all about that when you're older.

Of course they learned it first.
Oh naturally, yes.

NORMAN MACCAIG Notations of Ten Summer Minutes

A boy skips flat stones out to sea – each does fine
till a small wave meets it head on and swallows it.
The boy will do the same.

The schoolmaster stands looking out of the window
with one Latin eye and one Greek one.
A boat rounds the point in Gaelic.

Out of the shop comes a stream
of Omo, Weetabix, BiSoDol tablets and a man
with a pocket shaped like a whisky bottle.

Lord V. walks by with the village in his pocket.
Angus walks by
spending the village into the air.

A melodeon is wheezing a clear-throated jig
on the deck on the *Arcadia*. On the shore hills Pan
cocks a hairy ear; and falls asleep again.

The ten minutes are up, except they aren't.
I leave the village, except I don't.
The jig fades to silence, except it doesn't.

W. S. GRAHAM Lines on Roger Hilton's Watch

Which I was given because
I loved him and we had
Terrible times together.

O tarnished ticking time
Piece with your bent hand,
You must be used to being
Looked at suddenly
In the middle of the night
When he switched the light on
Beside his bed. I hope
You told him the best time
When he lifted you up
To meet the Hilton gaze.

I lift you up from the mantel
Piece here in my house
Wearing your verdigris.
At least I keep you wound
And put my ear to you
To hear Botallack tick.

You realize your master
Has relinquished you
And gone to lie under
The ground at St Just.

Tell me the time. The time
Is Botallack o'clock.
This is the dead of night.

He switches the light on
To find a cigarette
And pours himself a Teachers.
He picks me up and holds me
Near his lonely face
To see my hands. He thinks
He is not being watched.

The images of his dream
Are still about his face
As he spits and tries not
To remember where he was.

I am only a watch
And pray time hastes away.
I think I am running down.

Watch, it is time I wound
You up again. I am
Very much not your dear
Last master but we had
Terrible times together.

ROBERT GARIOCH The Maple and the Pine

For maple and for pine
    I socht, thae sevin year;
maple I wad presume
    raither nor sycamore.
5   Thof I wes wantan skeel
    I wadnae hain on care,
my harns aa my pride:
    for thon I had nae fear.

Maple for back and ribs,
10   neck and heid and scroll;
for belly the Swiss pine,
    seasont, dry and auld,
the southside of the tree
    frae norart in a dell,
15 sawn on the quarter, cut
    midwart throu the bole.

Amati my outline,
    I coft nae feenisht thing
forbye, guidit my haun
20   or I cuid streitch the strings;

5 *thof* though; *skeel* skill; 6 *hain* be grudging; 7 *harns* brains; 18 *coft* bought;
19 *forbye* besides;

wi gauge and callipers
    and sense of thicknessin
I mainaged aa things weill
    frae template til bee's-sting.

25   A wolf had won inbye
        for aa my besiness,
gowlan aneath my bowe
    whan I wad pley my piece;
wolf-notes cam girnan throu
30   the tone. In sair distress
I brak it owre my knee,
    sic wes my heaviness.

1978   GEOFFREY HILL *from* **An Apology for the Revival of Christian Architecture in England**

9 The Laurel Axe

Autumn resumes the land, ruffles the woods
with smoky wings, entangles them. Trees shine
out from their leaves, rocks mildew to moss-green;
the avenues are spread with brittle floods.

Platonic England, house of solitudes,
rests in its laurels and its injured stone,
replete with complex fortunes that are gone,
beset by dynasties of moods and clouds.

It stands, as though at ease with its own world,
the mannerly extortions, languid praise,
all that devotion long since bought and sold,

the rooms of cedar and soft-thudding baize,
tremulous boudoirs where the crystals kissed in
cabinets of amethyst and frost.

24 *bee's sting* purfling; 26 *besiness* conscientiousness; 27 *gowlan* howling;
29 *girnan* weeping; 32 *sic* such

Stroke the small silk with your whispering hands,
godmother, nod and nod from the half-gloom;
broochlight intermittent between the fronds,
the owl immortal in its crystal dome.

Along the mantelpiece veined lustres trill,
the clock discounts us with a telling chime.
Familiar ministrants, clerks-of-appeal,
burnish upon the threshold of the dream:

churchwardens in wing-collars bearing scrolls
of copyhold well-tinctured and well-tied.
Your photo-albums loved by the boy-king

preserve in sepia waterglass the souls
of distant cousins, virgin till they died,
and the lost delicate suitors who could sing.

THOMAS KINSELLA Tao and Unfitness at Inistiogue on the River Nore

Noon

The black flies kept nagging in the heat.
Swarms of them, at every step, snarled
off pats of cow dung spattered in the grass.

Move, if you move, like water.

The punts were knocking by the boathouse, at full tide.
Volumes of water turned the river curve
hushed under an insect haze.

                              Slips of white,
trout bellies, flicked in the corner of the eye
and dropped back onto the deep mirror.

Respond. Do not interfere. Echo.

Thick green woods along the opposite bank
climbed up from a root-dark recess
eaved with mud-whitened leaves.

*

In a matter of hours all that water is gone,
except for a channel near the far side.
Muck and shingle and pools where the children
wade, stabbing flatfish.

Afternoon

Inistiogue itself is perfectly lovely,
like a typical English village, but a bit sullen.
Our voices echoed in sunny corners
among the old houses; we admired
the stonework and gateways, the interplay
of roofs and angled streets.

The square, with its 'village green', lay empty.
The little shops had hardly anything.
The Protestant church was guarded by a woman
of about forty, a retainer, spastic
and indistinct, who drove us out.

An obelisk to the Brownsfoords and a Victorian
Celto-Gothic drinking fountain, erected
by a Tighe widow for the villagers,
'erected' in the centre. An astronomical-looking
sundial stood sentry on a platform
on the corner where High Street went up out of the square.

We drove up, past a long-handled water pump
placed at the turn, with an eye to the effect,
then out of the town for a quarter of a mile
above the valley, and came to the dead gate
of Woodstock, once home of the Tighes.

*

The great ruin presented its flat front
at us, sunstruck. The children disappeared.
Eleanor picked her way around a big fallen branch

and away along the face toward the outbuildings.
I took the grassy front steps and was gathered up
in a brick-red stillness. A rook clattered out of the dining room.

A sapling, hooked thirty feet up
in a cracked corner, held out a ghost-green
cirrus of leaves. Cavities
of collapsed fireplaces connected silently
about the walls. Deserted spaces, complicated
by door-openings everywhere.

There was a path up among bushes and nettles
over the beaten debris, then a drop, where bricks
and plaster and rafters had fallen into the kitchens.
A line of small choked arches . . . The pantries, possibly.

Be still, as though pure.

A brick, and its dust, fell.

Nightfall

The trees we drove under in the dusk
as we threaded back along the river through the woods
were no mere dark growth, but a flitting-place
for ragged feeling, old angers and rumours . . .

Black and Tan ghosts up there, at home
on the Woodstock heights: an iron mouth
scanning the Kilkenny road: the house
gutted by the townspeople and burned to ruins . . .

The little Ford we met, and inched past, full of men
we had noticed along the river bank during the week,
disappeared behind us into a fifty-year-old night.
Even their caps and raincoats . . .

Sons, or grandsons, Poachers.
                              Mud-tasted salmon
slithering in a plastic bag around the boot,
bloodied muscles, disputed since King John.

The ghosts of daughters of the family
waited in the uncut grass as we drove
down to our mock-Austrian lodge and stopped.

*

We untied the punt in the half-light, and pushed out
to take a last hour on the river, until night.
We drifted, but stayed almost still.
The current underneath us
and the tide coming back to the full
cancelled in a gleaming calm, punctuated
by the plop of fish.

Down on the water . . . at eye level . . . in the little light
remaining overhead . . . the mayfly passed in a loose drift,
thick and frail, a hatch slow with sex,
separate morsels trailing their slack filaments,
olive, pale evening dun, imagoes, unseen eggs
dropping from the air, subimagoes, the river filled
with their nymphs ascending and excited trout.

Be subtle, as though not there.

We were near the island – no more than a dark mass
on a sheet of silver – when a man appeared in midriver
quickly and with scarcely a sound, his paddle touching
left and right of the prow, with a sack behind him.
The flat cot's long body slid past effortless
as a fish, sinewing from side to side,
as he passed us and vanished.

JAMES FENTON In a Notebook

There was a river overhung with trees
With wooden houses built along its shallows
From which the morning sun drew up a haze
And the gyrations of the early swallows
Paid no attention to the gentle breeze
Which spoke discreetly from the weeping willows.
There was a jetty by the forest clearing
Where a small boat was tugging at its mooring.

And night still lingered underneath the eaves.
In the dark houseboats families were stirring
And Chinese soup was cooked on charcoal stoves.
Then one by one there came into the clearing
Mothers and daughters bowed beneath their sheaves.
The silent children gathered round me staring
And the shy soldiers setting out for battle
Asked for a cigarette and laughed a little.

From low canoes old men laid out their nets
While on the bank young boys with lines were fishing.
The wicker traps were drawn up by their floats.
The girls stood waist-deep in the river washing
Or tossed the day's rice on enamel plates
And I sat drinking bitter coffee wishing
The tide would turn to bring me to my senses
After the pleasant war and the evasive answers.

There was a river overhung with trees.
The girls stood waist-deep in the river washing,
And night still lingered underneath the eaves
While on the bank young boys with lines were fishing.
Mothers and daughters bowed beneath their sheaves
While I sat drinking bitter coffee wishing –
And the tide turned and brought me to my senses.
The pleasant war brought the unpleasant answers.

The villages are burnt, the cities void;
The morning light has left the river view;
The distant followers have been dismayed;
And I'm afraid, reading this passage now,
That everything I knew has been destroyed
By those whom I admired but never knew;
The laughing soldiers fought to their defeat
And I'm afraid most of my friends are dead.

JEFFREY WAINWRIGHT 1815

I The Mill-Girl

Above her face
Dead roach stare vertically
Out of the canal.
Water fills her ears,
Her nose her open mouth.
Surfacing, her bloodless fingers
Nudge the drying gills.

The graves have not
A foot's width between them.
Apprentices, jiggers, spinners
Fill them straight from work,
Common as smoke.

Waterloo is all the rage;
Coal and iron and wool
Have supplied the English miracle.

II Another Part of the Field

The dead on all sides –
The fallen –
The deep-chested rosy ploughboys
Swell out of their uniforms.

The apple trees,
That were dressed overall,
Lie stripped about their heads.

'The French cavalry
Came up very well my lord.'
'Yes. And they went down
Very well too.
Overturned like turtles.
Our muskets were obliged
To their white bellies.'

No flies on Wellington.
His spruce wit sits straight
In the saddle, jogging by.

III The Important Man

Bothered by his wife
From a good dinner,
The lock-keeper goes down
To his ponderous water's edge
To steer in the new corpse.

A bargee, shouting to be let through,
Stumps over the bulging lengths
Of his hatches,
Cursing the slowness
Of water.

The lock-keeper bends and pulls her out
With his bare hands.
Her white eyes, rolled upwards,
Just stare.

He is an important man now.
He turns to his charge:
The water flows uphill.

IV Death of the Mill-Owner

Shaking the black earth
From a root of potatoes,
The gardener walks
To the kitchen door.

The trees rattle
Their empty branches together.

Upstairs the old man
Is surprised.
His fat body clenches –
Mortified
At what is happening.

CRAIG RAINE A Martian Sends a Postcard Home

Caxtons are mechanical birds with many wings
and some are treasured for their markings –

they cause the eyes to melt
or the body to shriek without pain.

I have never seen one fly, but
sometimes they perch on the hand.

Mist is when the sky is tired of flight
and rests its soft machine on ground:

then the world is dim and bookish
like engravings under tissue paper.

Rain is when the earth is television.
It has the property of making colours darker.

Model T is a room with the lock inside –
a key is turned to free the world

for movement, so quick there is a film
to watch for anything missed.

But time is tied to the wrist
or kept in a box, ticking with impatience.

In homes, a haunted apparatus sleeps,
that snores when you pick it up.

If the ghost cries, they carry it
to their lips and soothe it to sleep

with sounds. And yet, they wake it up
deliberately, by tickling with a finger.

Only the young are allowed to suffer
openly. Adults go to a punishment room

with water but nothing to eat.
They lock the door and suffer the noises

alone. No one is exempt
and everyone's pain has a different smell.

At night, when all the colours die,
they hide in pairs

and read about themselves –
in colour, with their eyelids shut.

CHRISTOPHER REID Baldanders

Pity the poor weightlifter
alone on his catasta,

who carries his pregnant belly
in the hammock of his leotard

like a melon wedged in a shopping bag . . .
A volatile prima donna,

he flaps his fingernails dry,
then – squat as an armchair –

gropes about the floor
for inspiration, and finds it there.

His Japanese muscularity
resolves to domestic parody.

Glazed, like a mantelpiece frog,
he strains to become

the World Champion (somebody, answer it!)
Human Telephone.

TED HUGHES February 17th

A lamb could not get born. Ice wind
Out of a downpour dishclout sunrise. The mother
Lay on the mudded slope. Harried, she got up
And the blackish lump bobbed at her back-end
Under her tail. After some hard galloping,
Some manoeuvring, much flapping of the backward
Lump head of the lamb looking out,
I caught her with a rope. Laid her, head uphill
And examined the lamb. A blood-ball swollen
Tight in its black felt, its mouth gap
Squashed crooked, tongue stuck out, black-purple,
Strangled by its mother. I felt inside,
Past the noose of mother-flesh, into the slippery
Muscled tunnel, fingering for a hoof,
Right back to the port-hole of the pelvis.
But there was no hoof. He had stuck his head out too early
And his feet could not follow. He should have
Felt his way, tip-toe, his toes
Tucked up under his nose
For a safe landing. So I kneeled wrestling
With her groans. No hand could squeeze past
The lamb's neck into her interior
To hook a knee. I roped that baby head
And hauled till she cried out and tried
To get up and I saw it was useless. I went
Two miles for the injection and a razor.
Sliced the lamb's throat-strings, levered with a knife
Between the vertebrae and brought the head off
To stare at its mother, its pipes sitting in the mud
With all earth for a body. Then pushed
The neck-stump right back in, and as I pushed
She pushed. She pushed crying and I pushed gasping.
And the strength
Of the birth push and the push of my thumb
Against that wobbly vertebra were deadlock,
A to-fro futility. Till I forced
A hand past and got a knee. Then like
Pulling myself to the ceiling with one finger
Hooked in a loop, timing my effort
To her birth push groans, I pulled against

The corpse that would not come. Till it came.
And after it the long, sudden, yolk-yellow
Parcel of life
In a smoking slither of oils and soups and syrups –
And the body lay born, beside the hacked-off head.

17 February 1974

SEAMUS HEANEY The Strand at Lough Beg

In memory of Colum McCartney

All round this little island, on the strand
Far down below there, where the breakers strive,
Grow the tall rushes from the oozy sand.

DANTE, *Purgatorio*, I, 100–103

Leaving the white glow of filling stations
And a few lonely streetlamps among fields
You climbed the hills towards Newtownhamilton
Past the Fews Forest, out beneath the stars –
Along that road, a high, bare pilgrim's track
Where Sweeney fled before the bloodied heads,
Goat-beards and dogs' eyes in a demon pack
Blazing out of the ground, snapping and squealing.
What blazed ahead of you? A faked road block?
The red lamp swung, the sudden brakes and stalling
Engine, voices, heads hooded and the cold-nosed gun?
Or in your driving mirror, tailing headlights
That pulled out suddenly and flagged you down
Where you weren't known and far from what you knew:
The lowland clays and waters of Lough Beg,
Church Island's spire, its soft treeline of yew.

There you once heard guns fired behind the house
Long before rising time, when duck shooters
Haunted the marigolds and bulrushes,
But still were scared to find spent cartridges,
Acrid, brassy, genital, ejected,
On your way across the strand to fetch the cows.
For you and yours and yours and mine fought shy,
Spoke an old language of conspirators
And could not crack the whip or seize the day:

Big-voiced scullions, herders, feelers round
Haycocks and hindquarters, talkers in byres,
Slow arbitrators of the burial ground.

Across that strand of yours the cattle graze
Up to their bellies in an early mist
And now they turn their unbewildered gaze
To where we work our way through squeaking sedge
Drowning in dew. Like a dull blade with its edge
Honed bright, Lough Beg half shines under the haze.
I turn because the sweeping of your feet
Has stopped behind me, to find you on your knees
With blood and roadside muck in your hair and eyes,
Then kneel in front of you in brimming grass
And gather up cold handfuls of the dew
To wash you, cousin. I dab you clean with moss
Fine as the drizzle out of a low cloud.
I lift you under the arms and lay you flat.
With rushes that shoot green again, I plait
Green scapulars to wear over your shroud.

MICHAEL LONGLEY *from* Wreaths

The Linen Workers

Christ's teeth ascended with him into heaven:
Through a cavity in one of his molars
The wind whistles: he is fastened for ever
By his exposed canines to a wintry sky.

I am blinded by the blaze of that smile
And by the memory of my father's false teeth
Brimming in their tumbler: they wore bubbles
And, outside of his body, a deadly grin.

When they masscred the ten linen workers
There fell on the road beside them spectacles,
Wallets, small change, and a set of dentures:
Blood, food particles, the bread, the wine.

Before I can bury my father once again
I must polish the spectacles, balance them
Upon his nose, fill his pockets with money
And into his dead mouth slip the set of teeth.

TOM PAULIN Where Art is a Midwife   1980

In the third decade of March,
A Tuesday in the town of Z –

The censors are on day-release.
They must learn about literature.

There are things called ironies,
Also symbols, which carry meaning.

The types of ambiguity
Are as numerous as the enemies

Of the state. Formal and bourgeois,
Sonnets sing of the old order,

Its lost gardens where white ladies
Are served wine in the subtle shade.

This poem about a bear
Is not a poem about a bear.

It might be termed a satire
On a loyal friend. Do I need

To spell it out? Is it possible
That none of you can understand?

PAUL MULDOON Why Brownlee Left

Why Brownlee left, and where he went,
Is a mystery even now.
For if a man should have been content
It was him; two acres of barley,

One of potatoes, four bullocks,
A milker, a slated farmhouse.
He was last seen going out to plough
On a March morning, bright and early.

By noon Brownlee was famous;
They had found all abandoned, with
The last rig unbroken, his pair of black
Horses, like man and wife,
Shifting their weight from foot to
Foot, and gazing into the future.

PAUL MULDOON Anseo

When the Master was calling the roll
At the primary school in Collegelands,
You were meant to call back *Anseo*
And raise your hand
As your name occurred.
Anseo, meaning here, here and now,
All present and correct,
Was the first word of Irish I spoke.
The last name on the ledger
Belonged to Joseph Mary Plunkett Ward
And was followed, as often as not,
By silence, knowing looks,
A nod and a wink, the Master's droll
'And where's our little Ward-of-court?'

I remember the first time he came back
The Master had sent him out
Along the hedges
To weigh up for himself and cut
A stick with which he would be beaten.
After a while, nothing was spoken;
He would arrive as a matter of course
With an ash-plant, a salley-rod.
Or, finally, the hazel-wand
He had whittled down to a whip-lash,
Its twist of red and yellow lacquers

Sanded and polished,
And altogether so delicately wrought
That he had engraved his initials on it.

I last met Joseph Mary Plunkett Ward
In a pub just over the Irish border.
He was living in the open,
In a secret camp
On the other side of the mountain.
He was fighting for Ireland,
Making things happen.
And he told me, Joe Ward,
Of how he had risen through the ranks
To Quartermaster, Commandant:
How every morning at parade
His volunteers would call back *Anseo*
And raise their hands
As their names occurred.

PAUL DURCAN Tullynoe: Tête-à-Tête in the Parish Priest's Parlour

'Ah, he was a grand man.'
'He was: he fell out of the train going to Sligo.'
'He did: he thought he was going to the lavatory.'
'Her did: in fact he stepped out the rear door of the train.'
'He did: God, he must have got an awful fright.'
'He did: he saw that it wasn't the lavatory at all.'
'He did: he saw that it was the railway tracks going away from him.'
'He did: I wonder if . . . but he was a grand man.'
'He was: he had the most expensive Toyota you can buy.'
'He had: well, it was only beautiful.'
'It was: he used to have an Audi.'
'He had: as a matter of fact he used to have two Audis.'
'He had: and then he had an Avenger.'
'He had: and then he had a Volvo.'
'He had: in the beginning he had a lot of Volkses.'
'He had: he was a great man for the Volkses.'
'He was: did he once have an Escort?'
'He had not: he had a son a doctor.'
'He had: he had a Morris Minor too.'
'He had: and he had a sister a hairdresser in Kilmallock.'

'He had: he had another sister a hairdresser in Ballybunion.'
'He had: he was put in a coffin which was put in his father's cart.'
'He was: his lady wife sat on top of the coffin driving the donkey.'
'She did: Ah, but he was a grand man.'
'He was: he was a grand man . . .'
'Good night, Father.'
'Good night, Mary.'

PAUL DURCAN The Death by Heroin of Sid Vicious

There – but for the clutch of luck – go I.

At daybreak – in the arctic fog of a February daybreak –
Shoulder-length helmets in the watchtowers of the concentration
        camp
Caught me out in the intersecting arcs of the swirling searchlights.

There were at least a zillion of us caught out there –
Like ladybirds under a boulder –
But under the microscope each of us was unique,

Unique and we broke for cover, crazily breasting
The barbed wire and some of us made it
To the forest edge, but many of us did not

Make it, although their unborn children did –
Such as you whom the camp commandant branded
Sid Vicious of the Sex Pistols. Jesus, break his fall:

There – but for the clutch of luck – go we all.

1981   JAMES FENTON A German Requiem

For as at a great distance of place, that which wee look at, appears
dimme, and without distinction of the smaller parts; and as Voyces
grow weak, and inarticulate; so also after great distance of time, our
imagination of the Past is weak; and wee lose (for example) of Cities
wee have seen, many particular Streets; and of Actions, many particular
Circumstances. This *decaying sense*, when wee would express the thing
it self, (I mean *fancy* it selfe,) wee call *Imagination*, as I said before: But

when we would express the *decay*, and signifie that the Sense is fading, 1981 [1073
old, and past, it is called Memory. So that *Imagination* and *Memory*
are but one thing . . .   Hobbes, *Leviathan*

It is not what they built. It is what they knocked down.
It is not the houses. It is the spaces between the houses.
It is not the streets that exist. It is the streets that no longer exist.
It is not your memories which haunt you.
It is not what you have written down.
It is what you have forgotten, what you must forget.
What you must go on forgetting all your life.
And with any luck oblivion should discover a ritual.
You will find out that you are not alone in the enterprise.
Yesterday the very furniture seemed to reproach you.
Today you take your place in the Widow's Shuttle.

¶

The bus is waiting at the southern gate
To take you to the city of your ancestors
Which stands on the hill opposite, with gleaming pediments,
As vivid as this charming square, your home.
Are you shy? You should be. It is almost like a wedding,
The way you clasp your flowers and give a little tug at your veil. Oh,
The hideous bridesmaids, it is natural that you should resent them
Just a little, on this first day.
But that will pass, and the cemetery is not far.
Here comes the driver, flicking a toothpick into the gutter,
His tongue still searching between his teeth.
See, he has not noticed you. No one has noticed you.
It will pass, young lady, it will pass.

¶

How comforting it is, once or twice a year,
To get together and forget the old times.
As on those special days, ladies and gentlemen,
When the boiled shirts gather at the graveside
And a leering waistcoat approaches the rostrum.
It is like a solemn pact between the survivors.
The mayor has signed it on behalf of the freemasonry.
The priest has sealed it on behalf of all the rest.
Nothing more need be said, and it is better that way –

The better for the widow, that she should not live in fear of surprise,
The better for the young man, that he should move at liberty
    between the armchairs,
The better that these bent figures who flutter among the graves
Tending the nightlights and replacing the chrysanthemums
Are not ghosts,
That they shall go home.
The bus is waiting, and on the upper terraces
The workmen are dismantling the houses of the dead.

¶

But when so many had died, so many and at such speed,
There were no cities waiting for the victims.
They unscrewed the name-plates from the shattered doorways
And carried them away with the coffins.
So the squares and parks were filled with the eloquence of young
    cemeteries:
The smell of fresh earth, the improvised crosses
And all the impossible directions in brass and enamel.

¶

'Doctor Gliedschirm, skin specialist, surgeries 14–16 hours or by
    appointment.'
Professor Sargnagel was buried with four degrees, two associate
    memberships
And instructions to tradesmen to use the back entrance.
Your uncle's grave informed you that he lived on the third floor, left.
You were asked please to ring, and he would come down in the lift
To which one needed a key . . .

¶

Would come down, would ever come down
With a smile like thin gruel, and never too much to say.
How he shrank through the years.
How you towered over him in the narrow cage.
How he shrinks now . . .

But come. Grief must have its term? Guilt too, then.
And it seems there is no limit to the resourcefulness of recollection.
So that a man might say and think:
When the world was at its darkest,
When the black wings passed over the rooftops
(And who can divine His purposes?) even then
There was always, always a fire in this hearth.
You see this cupboard? A priest-hole!
And in that lumber-room whole generations have been housed and
        fed.
Oh, if I were to begin, if I were to begin to tell you
The half, the quarter, a mere smattering of what we went through!

¶

His wife nods, and a secret smile,
Like a breeze with enough strength to carry one dry leaf
Over two pavingstones, passes from chair to chair.
Even the enquirer is charmed.
He forgets to pursue the point.
It is not what he wants to know.
It is what he wants not to know.
It is not what they say.
It is what they do not say.

TONY HARRISON The Earthen Lot

*'From Isphahan to Northumberland, there is no building that does not
show the influence of that oppressed and neglected herd of men.'*
                              William Morris, *The Art of the People*

Sand, caravans, and teetering sea-edge graves.

The seaward side's for those of lowly status.
Not only gales gnaw at their names, the waves
jostle the skulls and bones from their quietus.

1076] **1981** The Church is a solid bulwark for their betters
against the scouring sea-salt that erodes
these chiselled sandstone formal Roman letters
to flowing calligraphic Persian odes,
singing of sherbert, sex in Samarkand,
with Hafiz at the hammams and harems,
O anywhere but bleak Northumberland
with responsibilities for others' dreams!

Not for the Northern bard the tamarinds
where wine is always cool, and *kusi* hot –

his line from Omar scrivened by this wind's:

Some could articulate, while others not.

TONY HARRISON Continuous

James Cagney was the one up both our streets.
His was the only art we ever shared.
A gangster film and choc ice were the treats
that showed about as much love as he dared.

He'd be my own age now in '49!
The hand that glinted with the ring he wore,
his father's, tipped the cold bar into mine
just as the organist dropped through the floor.

He's on the platform lowered out of sight
to organ music, this time on looped tape,
into a furnace with a blinding light
where only his father's ring will keep its shape.

I wear it now to Cagneys on my own
and sense my father's hand cupped round my treat –

they feel as though they've been chilled to the bone
from holding my ice cream all through *White Heat*.

DEREK MAHON Courtyards in Delft

Pieter de Hooch, 1659

Oblique light on the trite, on brick and tile –
Immaculate masonry, and everywhere that
Water tap, that broom and wooden pail
To keep it so. House-proud, the wives
Of artisans pursue their thrifty lives
Among scrubbed yards, modest but adequate.
Foliage is sparse, and clings. No breeze
Ruffles the trim composure of those trees.

No spinet-playing emblematic of
The harmonies and disharmonies of love;
No lewd fish, no fruit, no wide-eyed bird
About to fly its cage while a virgin
Listens to her seducer, mars the chaste
Precision of the thing and the thing made.
Nothing is random, nothing goes to waste:
We miss the dirty dog, the fiery gin.

That girl with her back to us who waits
For her man to come home for his tea
Will wait till the paint disintegrates
And ruined dykes admit the esurient sea;
Yet this is life too, and the cracked
Out-house door a verifiable fact
As vividly mnemonic as the sunlit
Railings that front the houses opposite.

I lived there as a boy and know the coal
Glittering in its shed, late-afternoon
Lambency informing the deal table,
The ceiling cradled in a radiant spoon.
I must be lying low in a room there,
A strange child with a taste for verse,
While my hard-nosed companions dream of war
On parched veldt and fields of rain-swept gorse;

For the pale light of that provincial town
Will spread itself, like ink or oil,
Over the not yet accurate linen
Map of the world which occupies one wall
And punish nature in the name of God.
If only, now, the Maenads, as of right,
Came smashing crockery, with fire and sword,
We could sleep easier in our beds at night.

1983   PAUL MULDOON Quoof

How often have I carried our family word
for the hot water bottle
to a strange bed,
as my father would juggle a red-hot half-brick
in an old sock
to his childhood settle.
I have taken it into so many lovely heads
or laid it between us like a sword.

An hotel room in New York City
with a girl who spoke hardly any English,
my hand on her breast
like the smouldering one-off spoor of the yeti
or some other shy beast
that has yet to enter the language.

PAUL MULDOON The Frog

Comes to mind as another small upheaval
amongst the rubble.
His eye matches exactly the bubble
in my spirit-level.
I set aside hammer and chisel
and take him on the trowel.

The entire population of Ireland
springs from a pair left to stand
overnight in a pond
in the gardens of Trinity College,
two bottles of wine left there to chill
after the Act of Union.

There is, surely, in this story
a moral. A moral for our times.
What if I put him to my head
and squeezed it out of him,
like the juice of freshly squeezed limes,
or a lemon sorbet?

TOM PAULIN Desertmartin

At noon, in the dead centre of a faith,
Between Draperstown and Magherafelt,
This bitter village shows the flag
In a baked absolute September light.
Here the Word has withered to a few
Parched certainties, and the charred stubble
Tightens like a black belt, a crop of Bibles.

Because this is the territory of the Law
I drive across it with a powerless knowledge –
The owl of Minerva in a hired car.
A Jock squaddy glances down the street
And grins, happy and expendable,
Like a brass cartridge. He is a useful thing,
Almost at home, and yet not quite, not quite.

It's a limed nest, this place. I see a plain
Presbyterian grace sour, then harden,
As a free strenuous spirit changes
To a servile defiance that whines and shrieks
For the bondage of the letter: it shouts
For the Big Man to lead his wee people
To a clean white prison, their scorched tomorrow.

Masculine Islam, the rule of the Just,
Egyptian sand dunes and geometry,
A theology of rifle-butts and executions:
These are the places where the spirit dies.
And now, in Desertmartin's sandy light,
I see a culture of twigs and bird-shit
Waving a gaudy flag it loves and curses.

1984   SEAMUS HEANEY Widgeon

for Paul Muldoon

It had been badly shot.
While he was plucking it
he found, he says, the voice box –

like a flute stop
in the broken windpipe –

and blew upon it
unexpectedly
his own small widgeon cries.

SEAMUS HEANEY *from* Station Island

VII

I had come to the edge of the water,
soothed by just looking, idling over it
as if it were a clear barometer

or a mirror, when his reflection
did not appear but I sensed a presence
entering into my concentration

on not being concentrated as he spoke
my name. And though I was reluctant
I turned to meet his face and the shock

is still in me at what I saw. His brow
was blown open above the eye and blood
had dried on his neck and cheek. 'Easy now,'

he said, 'it's only me. You've seen men as raw
after a football match . . . What time it was
when I was wakened up I still don't know

but I heard this knocking, knocking, and it
scared me, like the phone in the small hours,
so I had the sense not to put on the light

but looked out from behind the curtain.
I saw two customers on the doorstep
and an old landrover with the doors open

parked on the street so I let the curtain drop;
but they must have been waiting for it to move
for they shouted to come down into the shop.

She started to cry then and roll round the bed,
lamenting and lamenting to herself,
not even asking who it was. "Is your head

astray, or what's come over you?" I roared, more
to bring myself to my senses
than out of any real anger at her

for the knocking shook me, the way they kept it up,
and her whingeing and half-screeching made it worse.
All the time they were shouting, "Shop!

Shop!" so I pulled on my shoes and a sportscoat
and went back to the window and called out,
"What do you want? Could you quieten the racket

or I'll not come down at all." "There's a child not well.
Open up and see what you have got – pills
or a powder or something in a bottle,"

one of them said. He stepped back off the footpath
so I could see his face in the street lamp
and when the other moved I knew them both.

But bad and all as the knocking was, the quiet
hit me worse. She was quiet herself now,
lying dead still, whispering to watch out.

At the bedroom door I switched on the light.
"It's odd they didn't look for a chemist.
Who are they anyway at this time of the night?"

she asked me, with the eyes standing in her head.
"I know them to see," I said, but something
made me reach and squeeze her hand across the bed

before I went downstairs into the aisle
of the shop. I stood there, going weak
in the legs. I remember the stale smell

of cooked meat or something coming through
as I went to open up. From then on
you know as much about it as I do.'

'Did they say nothing?' 'Nothing. What would they say?'
'Were they in uniform? Not masked in any way?'
'They were barefaced as they would be in the day,

shites thinking they were the be-all and the end-all.'
'Not that it is any consolation
but they were caught,' I told him, 'and got jail.'

Big-limbed, decent, open-faced, he stood
forgetful of everything now except
whatever was welling up in his spoiled head,

beginning to smile. 'You've put on weight
since you did your courting in that big Austin
you got the loan of on a Sunday night.'

Through life and death he had hardly aged.
There always was an athlete's cleanliness
shining off him and except for the ravaged

forehead and the blood, he was still that same
rangy midfielder in a blue jersey
and starched pants, the one stylist on the team,

the perfect, clean, unthinkable victim.
'Forgive the way I have lived indifferent –
forgive my timid circumspect involvement,'

I surprised myself by saying. 'Forgive
my eye,' he said, 'all that's above my head.'
And then a stun of pain seemed to go through him

and he trembled like a heatwave and faded.

DOUGLAS DUNN *from* Elegies   1985

The Sundial

You stood with your back to me.
By that crumbling sundial,
Leaving your book on it –
Time, love, and literature!
You shielded your eye from the sun
As a peacock strutted towards you.
You called it beautiful and touched its head,
Then turned around to me, eye-patched
And fastened to a mourning blink
Brought there by melanoma's
Sun-coaxed horrific oncos,
Leaving me to guess at
What mysteries you knew
Foretold by love or creatures.

DEREK MAHON Antarctica

'I am just going outside and may be some time.'
The others nod, pretending not to know.
At the heart of the ridiculous, the sublime.

He leaves them reading and begins to climb,
Goading his ghost into the howling snow;
He is just going outside and may be some time.

The tent recedes beneath its crust of rime
And frostbite is replaced by vertigo:
At the heart of the ridiculous, the sublime.

Need we consider it some sort of crime,
This numb self-sacrifice of the weakest? No,
He is just going outside and may be some time –

In fact, for ever. Solitary enzyme,
Though the night yield no glimmer there will glow,
At the heart of the ridiculous, the sublime.

He takes leave of the earthly pantomime
Quietly, knowing it is time to go:
'I am just going outside and may be some time.'
At the heart of the ridiculous, the sublime.

JOHN AGARD Listen Mr Oxford don

Me not no Oxford don
me a simple immigrant
from Clapham Common
I didn't graduate
I immigrate

But listen Mr Oxford don
I'm a man on de run
and a man on de run
is a dangerous one

I ent have no gun
I ent have no knife
but mugging de Queen's English
is the story of my life

I dont need no axe
to split/ up yu syntax
I dont need no hammer
to mash/ up yu grammar

I warning you Mr Oxford don
I'm a wanted man
and a wanted man
is a dangerous one

Dem accuse me of assault
on de Oxford dictionary/
imagine a concise peaceful man like me/
dem want me serve time
for inciting rhyme to riot
but I tekking it quiet
down here in Clapham Common

I'm not a violent man Mr Oxford don
I only armed wit mih human breath
but human breath
is a dangerous weapon

So mek dem send one big word after me
I ent serving no jail sentence
I slashing suffix in self-defence
I bashing future wit present tense
and if necessary

I making de Queen's English accessory/to my offence

PETER DIDSBURY The Hailstone

Standing under the greengrocer's awning
in the kind of rain we used to call a cloudburst,
getting home later with a single hailstone in my hair.
Ambition would have us die in thunderstorms
like Jung and Mahler. Five minutes now,
for all our sad and elemental loves.

A woman sheltering inside the shop
had a frightened dog,
which she didn't want us to touch.
It had something to do with class,
and the ownership of fear. Broken ceramic lightning

was ripping open the stitching in the sky.
The rain was 'siling' down,
the kind that comes bouncing back off the pavement,
heavy milk from the ancient skins
being poured through the primitive strainer.
Someone could have done us in flat colours,
formal and observant, all on one plane,
you and me outside and the grocer and the lady
behind the gunmetal glass, gazing out over our shoulders.
I can see the weave of the paper behind the smeared reflections,
some of the colour lifting as we started a sudden dash home.
We ran by the post office and I thought, 'It is all still true,
a wooden drawer is full of postal orders, it is raining,
mothers and children are standing in their windows,
I am running through the rain past a shop which sells wool,
you take home fruit and veg in bags of brown paper,
we are getting wet, it is raining.'
                                    It was like being back
in the reign of George the Sixth, the kind of small town
which still lies stacked in the back of old storerooms in schools,
where plural roof and elf expect to get very wet
and the beasts deserve their nouns of congregation
as much as the postmistress, spinster, her title.
I imagine those boroughs as intimate with rain,
their ability to call on sentient functional downpours
for any picnic or trip to the German Butcher's
one sign of a usable language getting used,
make of this what you will. The rain has moved on,
and half a moon in a darkening blue sky
silvers the shrinking puddles in the road:
moon that emptied the post office and grocer's,
moon old kettle of rain and idiolect,
the moon the sump of the aproned pluvial towns,
cut moon as half a hailstone in the hair.

PAUL MULDOON Something Else

When your lobster was lifted out of the tank
to be weighed
I thought of woad,
of madders, of fugitive, indigo inks,

of how Nerval
was given to promenade
a lobster on a gossamer thread,
how, when a decent interval

had passed
(son front rouge encor du baiser de la reine)
and his hopes of Adrienne

proved false,
he hanged himself from a lamp-post
with a length of chain, which made me think

of something else, then something else again.

CIARAN CARSON Dresden

Horse Boyle was called Horse Boyle because of his brother Mule;
Though why Mule was called Mule is anybody's guess. I stayed
    there once,
Or rather, I nearly stayed there once. But that's another story.
At any rate they lived in this decrepit caravan, not two miles out of
    Carrick,
Encroached upon by baroque pyramids of empty baked bean tins,
    rusts
And ochres, hints of autumn merging into twilight. Horse believed
They were as good as a watchdog, and to tell you the truth
You couldn't go near the place without something falling over:
A minor avalanche would ensue – more like a shop bell, really,

The old-fashioned ones on string, connected to the latch, I think,
And as you entered in, the bell would tinkle in the empty shop, a
    musk
Of soap and turf and sweets would hit you from the gloom.
    Tobacco.
Baling wire. Twine. And, of course, shelves and pyramids of tins.
An old woman would appear from the back – there was a sizzling
    pan in there,
Somewhere, a whiff of eggs and bacon – and ask you what you
    wanted;
Or rather, she wouldn't ask; she would talk about the weather. It
    had rained

That day, but it was looking better. They had just put in the
　　spuds.

I had only come to pass the time of day, so I bought a token packet
　　of Gold Leaf.

All this time the fry was frying away. Maybe she'd a daughter in
　　there

Somewhere, though I hadn't heard the neighbours talk of it; if
　　anybody knew,

It would be Horse. Horse kept his ears to the ground.

And he was a great man for current affairs; he owned the only TV in
　　the place.

Come dusk he'd set off on his rounds, to tell the whole townland the
　　latest

Situation in the Middle East, a mortar bomb attack in
　　Mullaghbawn –

The damn things never worked, of course – and so he'd tell the story

How in his young day it was very different. Take young Flynn, for
　　instance,

Who was ordered to take this bus and smuggle some sticks of
　　gelignite

Across the border, into Derry, when the RUC – or was it the RIC? –

Got wind of it. The bus was stopped, the peeler stepped on. Young
　　Flynn

Took it like a man, of course: he owned up right away. He opened
　　the bag

And produced the bomb, his rank and serial number. For all the
　　world

Like a pound of sausages. Of course, the thing was, the peeler's bike

Had got a puncture, and he didn't know young Flynn from Adam.
　　All he wanted

Was to get home for his tea. Flynn was in for seven years and
　　learned to speak

The best of Irish. He had thirteen words for a cow in heat;

A word for the third thwart in a boat, the wake of a boat on the ebb
　　tide.

He knew the extinct names of insects, flowers, why this place was
　　called

Whatever: *Carrick*, for example, was *a rock*. He was damn right
　　there –

As the man said, *When you buy meat you buy bones, when you buy
　　land you buy stones.*

You'd be hard put to find a square foot in the whole bloody parish

That wasn't thick with flints and pebbles. To this day he could hear
the grate

And scrape as the spade struck home, for it reminded him of broken
bones:

Digging a graveyard, maybe – or better still, trying to dig a reclaimed
tip

Of broken delph and crockery ware – you know that sound that sets
your teeth on edge

When the chalk squeaks on the blackboard, or you shovel ashes
from the stove?

Master McGinty – he'd be on about McGinty then, and discipline,
the capitals

Of South America, Moore's *Melodies*, the Battle of Clontarf, and

*Tell me this, an educated man like you: What goes on four legs when
it's young,*

Two legs when it's grown up, and three legs when it's old? I'd
pretend

I didn't know. McGinty's leather strap would come up then, stuffed

With threepenny bits to give it weight and sting. Of course, it never
did him

Any harm: *You could take a horse to water but you couldn't make
him drink.*

He himself was nearly going on to be a priest.

And many's the young cub left the school, as wise as when he came.

Carrowkeel was where McGinty came from – *Narrow Quarter,*
Flynn explained –

Back before the Troubles, a place that was so mean and crabbed,

Horse would have it, men were known to eat their dinner from a
drawer.

Which they'd slide shut the minute you'd walk in.

He'd demonstrate this at the kitchen table, hunched and furtive,
squinting

Out the window – past the teetering minarets of rust, down the
hedge-dark aisle –

To where a stranger might appear, a passer-by, or what was maybe
worse,

Someone he knew. Someone who wanted something. Someone who
was hungry.

Of course who should come tottering up the lane that instant but his
brother

Mule. I forgot to mention they were twins. They were as like
    two –
No, not peas in a pod, for this is not the time nor the place to go into
Comparisons, and this is really Horse's story, Horse who – now I'm
    getting
Round to it – flew over Dresden in the war. He'd emigrated first, to
Manchester. Something to do with scrap – redundant mill
    machinery,
Giant flywheels, broken looms that would, eventually, be ships, or
    aeroplanes.
He said he wore his fingers to the bone.
And so, on impulse, he had joined the RAF. He became a rear
    gunner.
Of all the missions, Dresden broke his heart. It reminded him of
    china.

As he remembered it, long afterwards, he could hear, or almost hear
Between the rapid desultory thunderclaps, a thousand tinkling
    echoes –
All across the map of Dresden, store-rooms full of china shivered,
    teetered
And collapsed, an avalanche of porcelain, slushing and cascading:
    cherubs,
Shepherdesses, figurines of Hope and Peace and Victory, delicate
    bone fragments.
He recalled in particular a figure from his childhood, a milkmaid
Standing on the mantelpiece. Each night as they knelt down for the
    rosary,
His eyes would wander up to where she seemed to beckon to him,
    smiling,
Offering him, eternally, her pitcher of milk, her mouth of rose and
    cream.

One day, reaching up to hold her yet again, his fingers stumbled, and
    she fell.
He lifted down a biscuit tin, and opened it.
It breathed an antique incense: things like pencils, snuff, tobacco.
His war medals. A broken rosary. And there, the milkmaid's creamy
    hand, the outstretched
Pitcher of milk, all that survived. Outside, there was a scraping
And a tittering; I knew Mule's step by now, his careful drunken
    weaving
Through the tin-stacks. I might have stayed the night, but there's no
    time

To go back to that now; I could hardly, at any rate, pick up the
    thread.
I wandered out through the steeples of rust, the gate that was a
    broken bed.

EAVAN BOLAND Self-Portrait on a Summer Evening

Jean-Baptiste Chardin
is painting a woman
in the last summer light.

All summer long
he has been slighting her
in botched blues, tints,
half-tones, rinsed neutrals.

What you are watching
is light unlearning itself,
an infinite unfrocking of the prism.

Before your eyes
the ordinary life
is being glazed over:
pigments of the bibelot,
the cabochon, the water-opal
pearl to the intimate
simple colours of
her ankle-length summer skirt.

Truth makes shift:
The triptych shrinks
to the cabinet picture.
Can't you feel it?
Aren't you chilled by it?
The way the late afternoon
is reduced to detail –

the sky that odd shape of apron –

opaque, scumbled –
the lazulis of the horizon becoming

optical greys
before your eyes
before your eyes
in my ankle-length
summer skirt

crossing between
the garden and the house,
under the whitebeam trees,
keeping an eye on
the length of the grass,
the height of the hedge,
the distance of the children

I am Chardin's woman

edged in reflected light,
hardened by
the need to be ordinary.

1988   CHARLES CAUSLEY Eden Rock

They are waiting for me somewhere beyond Eden Rock:
My father, twenty-five, in the same suit
Of Genuine Irish Tweed, his terrier Jack
Still two years old and trembling at his feet.

My mother, twenty-three, in a sprigged dress
Drawn at the waist, ribbon in her straw hat,
Has spread the stiff white cloth over the grass.
Her hair, the colour of wheat, takes on the light.

She pours tea from a Thermos, the milk straight
From an old H.P. sauce bottle, a screw
Of paper for a cork; slowly sets out
The same three plates, the tin cups painted blue.

The sky whitens as if lit by three suns.
My mother shades her eyes and looks my way
Over the drifted stream. My father spins
A stone along the water. Leisurely,

They beckon to me from the other bank.
I hear them call, 'See where the stream-path is!
Crossing is not as hard as you might think.'

I had not thought that it would be like this.

EDWIN MORGAN The Dowser

With my forked branch of Lebanese cedar
I quarter the dunes like downs and guide
an invisible plough far over the sand.
But how to quarter such shifting acres
when the wind melts their shapes, and shadows
mass where all was bright before,
and landmarks walk like wraiths at noon?
All I know is that underneath,
how many miles no one can say,
an unbroken water-table waits
like a lake; it has seen no bird or sail
in its long darkness, and no man;
not even pharaohs dug so far
for all their thirst, or thirst of glory,
or thrust-power of ten thousand slaves.
I tell you I can smell it though,
that water. I am old and black
and I know the manners of the sun
which makes me bend, not break. I lose
my ghostly footprints without complaint.
I put every mirage in its place.
I watch the lizard make its lace.
Like one not quite blind I go
feeling for the sunken face.
So hot the days, the nights so cold,
I gather my white rags and sigh
but sighing step so steadily
that any vibrance in so deep
a lake would never fail to rise
towards the snowy cedar's bait.
Great desert, let your sweetness wake.

NORMAN MACCAIG Chauvinist

In all the space of space
I have a little plot of ground
with part of an ocean in it
and many mountains

It's there I meet my friends
and multitudes of strangers.
Even my forebears dreamily visit me
and dreamily speak to me.

Of the rest of space
I can say nothing
nor of the rest of time, the future
that dies the moment it happens.

The little plot – do I belong to it
or it to me? No matter.
We share each other as I walk
amongst its flags and tombstones.

1989   ## TED HUGHES Telegraph Wires

Take telegraph wires, a lonely moor,
And fit them together. The thing comes alive in your ear.

Towns whisper to towns over the heather.
But the wires cannot hide from the weather.

So oddly, so daintily made
It is picked up and played.

Such unearthly airs
The ear hears, and withers!

In the revolving ballroom of space,
Bowed over the moor, a bright face

Draws out of telegraph wires the tones
That empty human bones.

KEN SMITH Writing in Prison

Years ago I was a gardener.
I grew the flowers of my childhood,
lavender and wayside lilies
and my first love the cornflower.

The wind on the summer wheat.
The blue glaze in the vanished woods.
In the space of my yard I glimpsed again
all the lost places of my life.

I was remaking them. Here in a space
smaller still I make them again.

CIARAN CARSON Belfast Confetti

Suddenly as the riot squad moved in, it was raining exclamation
    marks,
Nuts, bolts, nails, car-keys. A fount of broken type. And the
    explosion
Itself – an asterisk on the map. This hyphenated line, a burst of rapid
    fire . . .
I was trying to complete a sentence in my head, but it kept
    stuttering,
All the alleyways and side-streets blocked with stops and colons.

I know this labyrinth so well – Balaclava, Raglan, Inkerman, Odessa
    Street –
Why can't I escape? Every move is punctuated. Crimea Street. Dead
    end again.
A Saracen, Kremlin-2 mesh. Makrolon face-shields. Walkie-talkies.
    What is
My name? Where am I coming from? Where am I going? A fusillade
    of question-marks.

NUALA NÍ DHOMHNAILL (trans. PAUL MULDOON) The Language Issue

I place my hope on the water
in this little boat
of the language, the way a body might put
an infant

in a basket of intertwined
iris leaves,
its underside proofed
with bitumen and pitch,

then set the whole thing down amidst
the sedge
and bulrushes by the edge
of a river

only to have it borne hither and thither,
not knowing where it might end up;
in the lap, perhaps,
of some Pharaoh's daughter.

EAVAN BOLAND The Black Lace Fan My Mother Gave Me

It was the first gift he ever gave her,
buying it for five francs in the Galeries
in pre-war Paris. It was stifling.
A starless drought made the nights stormy.

They stayed in the city for the summer.
They met in cafés. She was always early.
He was late. That evening he was later.
They wrapped the fan. He looked at his watch.

She looked down the Boulevard des Capucines.
She ordered more coffee. She stood up.
The streets were emptying. The heat was killing.
She thought the distance smelled of rain and lightning.

These are wild roses, appliqued on silk by hand,
darkly picked, stitched boldly, quickly.
The rest is tortoiseshell and has the reticent,
clear patience of its element. It is

a worn-out, underwater bullion and it keeps,
even now, an inference of its violation.
The lace is overcast as if the weather
it opened for and offset had entered it.

The past is an empty café terrace.
An airless dusk before thunder. A man running.
And no way now to know what happened then –
none at all – unless, of course, you improvise:

The blackbird on this first sultry morning,
in summer, finding buds, worms, fruit,
feels the heat. Suddenly she puts out her wing –
the whole, full, flirtatious span of it.

SEAMUS HEANEY *from* Lightenings   1991

VIII

The annals say: when the monks of Clonmacnoise
Were all at prayers inside the oratory
A ship appeared above them in the air.

The anchor dragged along behind so deep
It hooked itself into the altar rails
And then, as the big hull rocked to a standstill,

A crewman shinned and grappled down the rope
And struggled to release it. But in vain.
'This man can't bear our life here and will drown,'

The abbot said, 'unless we help him.' So
They did, the freed ship sailed, and the man climbed back
Out of the marvellous as he had known it.

MICHAEL LONGLEY The Butchers

When he had made sure there were no survivors in his house
And that all the suitors were dead, heaped in blood and dust
Like fish that fishermen with fine-meshed nets have hauled
Up gasping for salt water, evaporating in the sunshine,
Odysseus, spattered with muck and like a lion dripping blood
From his chest and cheeks after devouring a farmer's bullock,
Ordered the disloyal housemaids to sponge down the armchairs
And tables, while Telemachos, the oxherd and the swineherd
Scraped the floor with shovels, and then between the portico
And the roundhouse stretched a hawser and hanged the women
So none touched the ground with her toes, like long-winged thrushes
Or doves trapped in a mist-net across the thicket where they roost,
Their heads bobbing in a row, their feet twitching but not for long,
And when they had dragged Melanthios's corpse into the haggard
And cut off his nose and ears and cock and balls, a dog's dinner,
Odysseus, seeing the need for whitewash and disinfectant,
Fumigated the house and the outhouses, so that Hermes
Like a clergyman might wave the supernatural baton
With which he resurrects or hypnotises those he chooses,
And waken and round up the suitors' souls, and the housemaids',
Like bats gibbering in the nooks of their mysterious cave
When out of the clusters that dangle from the rocky ceiling
One of them drops and squeaks, so their souls were bat-squeaks
As they flittered after Hermes, their deliverer, who led them
Along the clammy sheughs, then past the oceanic streams
And the white rock, the sun's gatepost in that dreamy region,
Until they came to a bog-meadow full of bog-asphodels
Where the residents are ghosts or images of the dead.

1992   ## DENISE RILEY A Misremembered Lyric

A misremembered lyric: a soft catch of its song
whirrs in my throat. 'Something's gotta hold of my heart
tearing my' soul and my conscience apart, long after
presence is clean gone and leaves unfurnished no
shadow. Rain lyrics. Yes, then the rain lyrics fall.
I don't want absence to be this beautiful.
It shouldn't be; in fact I know it wasn't, while

'everything that consoles is false' is off the point –
you get no consolation anyway until your memory's
dead: or something never had gotten hold of
your heart in the first place, and that's the fear thought.
Do shrimps make good mothers? Yes they do.
There is no beauty out of loss; can't do it –
and once the falling rain starts on the upturned
leaves, and I listen to the rhythm of unhappy pleasure
what I hear is bossy death telling me which way to
go, what I see is a pool with an eye in it. Still let
me know. Looking for a brand-new start. Oh and never
notice yourself ever. As in life you don't.

THOM GUNN The Hug

It was your birthday, we had drunk and dined
    Half of the night with our old friend
        Who'd showed us in the end
    To a bed I reached in one drunk stride.
        Already I lay snug,
    And drowsy with the wine dozed on one side.

I dozed, I slept. My sleep broke on a hug,
        Suddenly, from behind,
In which the full lengths of our bodies pressed:
        Your instep to my heel,
    My shoulder-blades against your chest.
    It was not sex, but I could feel
    The whole strength of your body set,
        Or braced, to mine,
        And locking me to you
    As if we were still twenty-two
    When our grand passion had not yet
        Become familial.
    My quick sleep had deleted all
    Of intervening time and place.
        I only knew
The stay of your secure firm dry embrace.

THOM GUNN The Reassurance

About ten days or so
After we saw you dead
You came back in a dream.
I'm all right now you said.

And it *was* you, although
You were fleshed out again:
You hugged us all round then,
And gave your welcoming beam.

How like you to be kind,
Seeking to reassure.
And, yes, how like my mind
To make itself secure.

1994   HUGO WILLIAMS Prayer

God give me strength to lead a double life.
Cut me in half.
Make each half happy in its own way
with what is left. Let me disobey
my own best instincts
and do what I want to do, whatever that may be,
without regretting it, or thinking I might.

When I come home late at night from home,
saying I have to go away,
remind me to look out the window
to see which house I'm in.
Pin a smile on my face
when I turn up two weeks later with a tan
and presents for everyone.

Teach me how to stand and where to look
when I say the words
about where I've been
and what sort of time I've had.

Was it good or bad or somewhere in between?
I'd like to know how I feel about these things,
perhaps you'd let me know?

When it's time to go to bed in one of my lives,
go ahead of me up the stairs,
shine a light in the corners of my room.
Tell me this: do I wear pyjamas here,
or sleep with nothing on?
If you can't oblige by cutting me in half,
God give me strength to lead a double life.

HUGO WILLIAMS Last Poem

I have put on a grotesque mask
to write these lines. I sit
staring at myself
in a mirror propped on my desk.

I hold up my head
like one of those Chinese lanterns
hollowed out of a pumpkin,
swinging from a broom.

I peer through the eye-holes
into that little lighted room
where a candle burns,
making me feel drowsy.

I must try not to spill the flame
wobbling in its pool of wax.
It sheds no light on the scene,
only shadows flickering up the walls.

In the narrow slit of my mouth
my tongue appears,
darting back and forth
behind the bars of my teeth.

I incline my head,
to try and catch what I am saying.
No sound emerges, only
the coming and going of my breath.

EILÉAN NÍ CHUILLEANÁIN Studying the Language

On Sundays I watch the hermits coming out of their holes
Into the light. Their cliff is as full as a hive.
They crowd together on warm shoulders of rock
Where the sun has been shining, their joints crackle.
They begin to talk after a while.
I listen to their accents, they are not all
From this island, not all old,
Not even, I think, all masculine.

They are so wise, they do not pretend to see me.
They drink from the scattered pools of melted snow:
I walk right by them and drink when they have done.
I can see the marks of chains around their feet.

I call this my work, these decades and stations –
Because, without these, I would be a stranger here.

CHRISTOPHER REID Stones and Bones

SECOND GENESIS

'inde genus durum sumus'
Ovid: *Metamorphoses*, Book I

Two survived the flood.
We are not of their blood,
springing instead from the bones
of the Great Mother – stones,
what have you, rocks, boulders –
hurled over their shoulders
by that pious pair
and becoming people, where
and as they hit the ground.
Since when, we have always found
something hard, ungracious,
obdurate in our natures,

a strain of the very earth
that gave us our abrupt birth;
but a pang, too, at the back
of the mind: a loss . . . a lack . . .

Acknowledgements

I am deeply grateful to the following: Lizzy van Amerongen, Molly and Peig van Amerongen, Hugh Haughton, Peter Carson, Jon Riley, Andrew Rosenheim, Vivienne Guinness, Antony Farrell, Michael Neve, Matty Dor, Karl Miller, Lindeth Vasey, Adam Phillips, Ianthe and Malise Ruthven, Claire Reihill, Robin Robertson, Alexandra Pringle, Michael Paul, Theo Cuffe, Andrew Barker, Anna South, Ian MacKillop, Pico Harnden, Roger Gard.

JOHN AGARD: 'Listen Mr Oxford don' from Mangoes and Bullets: Selected and New Poems 1972–1984 (Serpent's Tail, 1990), reprinted by permission of the publisher; MARION ANGUS: 'Alas! Poor Queen' from The Turn of the Day (Porpoise Press, 1931), reprinted by permission of Faber & Faber; W. H. AUDEN: 'Taller to-day, we remember similar evenings', 'This lunar beauty', 'Out on the lawn I lie in bed', 'Now the leaves are falling fast', 'In Memory of W. B. Yeats', 'Musée des Beaux Arts', 'Miranda', 'The Fall of Rome' and 'The Shield of Achilles' from Collected Shorter Poems 1927–1957 (Faber & Faber, 1966), reprinted by permission of the publisher; SAMUEL BECKETT: 'Saint-Lô' from Collected Poems (John Calder, 1984), reprinted by permission of the publisher; HILAIRE BELLOC: 'On a General Election' and 'Ballade of Hell and of Mrs Roebeck' from Cautionary Verses (Jonathan Cape, 1993), reprinted by permission of Peters Fraser and Dunlop Group on behalf of the Estate of Hilaire Belloc; E. C. BENTLEY: 'George the Third' and 'Nell' from The Complete Clerihews of E. Clerihew Bentley (Oxford University Press, 1981), © the Estate of E. C. Bentley, reprinted by permission of Curtis Brown Ltd, London, on behalf of the Estate of E. C. Bentley; JOHN BETJEMAN: 'The Arrest of Oscar Wilde at the Cadogan Hotel', 'Pot pourri from a Surrey Garden' and 'Devonshire Street W.1' from Collected Poems (John Murray, 1958), reprinted by permission of the publisher; LAURENCE BINYON: 'For the Fallen' from The Times (21 September 1914), 'Winter Sunrise' from Collected Poems of Laurence Binyon (Macmillan, 1931) and 'The Burning of the Leaves' from The Burning of the Leaves (Macmillan, 1944), all reprinted by permission of The Society of Authors on behalf of the Laurence Binyon Estate; EDMUND BLUNDEN: 'The Midnight Skaters' (© Edmund Blunden, 1925) and 'Report on Experience' (© Edmund Blunden, 1929) from Poems of Many Years (Collins, 1957), reprinted by permission of Peters Fraser and Dunlop Group on behalf of the Estate of Edmund Blunden; EAVAN BOLAND: 'Self-Portrait on a Summer Evening' and 'The Black Lace Fan My Mother Gave Me' from Collected Poems (Carcanet Press, 1995), reprinted by permission of the publisher; ROBERT BRIDGES: 'To Francis Jammes' from The Poetical Works of Robert Bridges (The Clarendon Press, 1936), reprinted by permission of Oxford University Press; RUPERT BROOKE: 'Peace' and 'Heaven' from The Works of Rupert Brooke (Wordsworth Editions, 1994); GEORGE MACKAY BROWN: 'Kirkyard' from Selected Poems 1954–1983 (John Murray, 1991), reprinted by permission of the publisher; BASIL BUNTING: from 'Villon', from 'Chomei at Toyama' and from 'Briggflatts' from Complete Poems (Bloodaxe Books, 2000), reprinted by permission of the publisher; NORMAN CAMERON: 'Green, Green is El Aghir' from Norman Cameron: Collected Poems and Selected Translations, edited by Warren Hope and Jonathan Barker (Anvil Press Poetry, 1990) reprinted by permission of the publisher; CIARAN CARSON: 'Dresden' and 'Belfast Confetti' from The Irish for No (The Gallery Press, 1987) reprinted by permission

of the author and publisher; CHARLES CAUSLEY: 'Eden Rock' from *Collected Poems*
1951–1997 (Macmillan, 1997), reprinted by permission of David Higham Associates;
EILÉAN NÍ CHUILLEANÁIN: 'Swineherd' and 'The Second Voyage' from *The Second Voyage* (The Gallery Press, 1986), and 'Studying the Language' from *The Brazen Serpent* (The Gallery Press, 1994); JOHN CLARE: 'I found a ball of grass among the hay', 'The old pond full of flags and fenced around' and 'The thunder mutters louder and more loud' from *The Later Poems of John Clare, 1837–1864*, edited by Eric Robinson and David Powell (Oxford University Press, 1984), © Eric Robinson, 1984, reprinted by permission of Curtis Brown Ltd, London, on behalf of Eric Robinson; AUSTIN CLARKE: 'The Planter's Daughter', 'The Straying Student' and 'Martha Blake at Fifty-One' from *Collected Poems* (Dolmen Press/Oxford University Press, 1974), reprinted by permission of R. Dardis Clarke, 21 Pleasants Street, Dublin 8; ELIZABETH DARYUSH: 'Still-Life' and 'Children of wealth in your warm nursery' from *Collected Poems* (Carcanet Press, 1976), reprinted by permission of the publisher; DONALD DAVIE: 'The Hill Field' and from 'In the Stopping Train' from *Collected Poems* (Carcanet Press, 1990), reprinted by permission of the publisher; W. H. DAVIES: 'Sheep' from *Collected Poems* (Jonathan Cape, 1963); WALTER DE LA MARE: 'The Birthnight: To F.'; 'Autumn' and 'Napoleon' from *Selected Poems* (Faber & Faber, 1973), reprinted by permission of the Literary Trustees of Walter de la Mare, and The Society of Authors as their representative; NUALA NÍ DHOMHNAILL: 'The Language Issue', translated by Paul Muldoon, from *Pharaoh's Daughter* (The Gallery Press, 1990), reprinted by permission of the author and publisher; PETER DIDSBURY: 'The Hailstone' from *The Classical Farm* (Bloodaxe Books, 1987) reprinted by permission of the publisher; HILDA DOOLITTLE: 'Oread' and from 'The Walls Do Not Fall' from *Selected Poems* (Carcanet Press, 1989), reprinted by permission of the publisher; KEITH DOUGLAS: 'Desert Flowers', 'Vergissmeinnicht' and 'How to Kill' from *The Complete Poems of Keith Douglas*, edited by Desmond Graham (Oxford University Press, 1978); DOUGLAS DUNN: 'A Removal from Terry Street', 'On Roofs of Terry Street' and 'Modern Love' from *Selected Poems, 1964–1983* (Faber & Faber, 1986), and 'The Sundial' from *Elegies* (Faber & Faber, 1985), all reprinted by permission of the publisher; PAUL DURCAN: 'Tullynoe: Tête-à-tête in the Parish Priest's Parlour' and 'The Death by Heroin of Sid Vicious' from *A Snail in My Prime* (The Harvill Press, 1993); T. S. ELIOT: 'The winter evening settles down', 'The Love Song of J. Alfred Prufrock', 'Aunt Helen', 'Sweeney Among the Nightingales', 'Gerontion', from 'The Waste Land', 'Marina' and from 'Little Gidding' from *Collected Poems, 1909–1962* (Faber & Faber, 1974), reprinted by permission of the publisher; WILLIAM EMPSON: 'This Last Pain', 'Homage to the British Museum', 'Missing Dates', 'Aubade' and 'Let It Go' from *Collected Poems* (Chatto & Windus, 1955), reprinted by permission of The Random House Archive & Library; D. J. ENRIGHT: 'Remembrance Sunday' from *Collected Poems, 1948–1998* (Oxford University Press, 1998), reprinted by permission of Watson, Little Ltd on behalf of the author; PADRAIC FALLON: 'A Bit of Brass' from *Collected Poems* (Carcanet Press, 1990), reprinted by permission of the publisher; JAMES FENTON: 'In a Notebook' and 'A German Requiem' from *The Memory of War and Children in Exile: Poems 1968–1983* (Penguin Books, 1983), reprinted by permission of the Peters Fraser and Dunlop Group; ROY FISHER: from 'By the Pond', 'Toyland', 'As He Came Near Death' and 'The Memorial Fountain' from *The Dow Low Drop: New & Selected Poems* (Bloodaxe, 1996), reprinted by permission of the publisher; JOHN FULLER: 'Wild Raspberries' from *Collected Poems* (Chatto & Windus, 1996), reprinted by permission of the author; ROBERT GARIOCH: 'Elegy' and 'The Maple and the Pine' from *Complete Poetical Works* (Macdonald Publishers, 1983), reprinted by permission of The Saltire Society; DAVID GASCOYNE: 'Snow in Europe' and 'A Wartime Dawn' from *Collected Poems* (Oxford University Press, 1988), reprinted by permission of the publisher; W. S. GRAHAM: 'Malcolm Mooney's Land' and 'Lines on Roger Hilton's Watch' from *Collected Poems 1942–1977* (Faber & Faber, 1979), © the Estate of W. S. Graham, reprinted by permission of Margaret Snow,

lected Poems, edited by Anthony Thwaite (Faber & Faber, 1988), reprinted by permission of the publisher; D. H. LAWRENCE: 'Sorrow', 'Medlars and Sorb-Apples', 'The Mosquito', 'The Blue Jay', 'The Mosquito Knows', 'To Women, As Far As I'm Concerned', 'Innocent England' and 'Bavarian Gentians' from *The Complete Poems of D. H. Lawrence* (Penguin, 1994), reprinted by permission of Laurence Pollinger Ltd and the Estate of Frieda Lawrence Ravagli; TOM LEONARD: from 'Unrelated Incidents. 3' from *Intimate Voices: Selected Works, 1965–1983* (Galloping Dog Press, 1984; Vintage, 1985), reprinted by permission of the author; ALUN LEWIS: 'Raiders' Dawn' from *Collected Poems* (Seren, 1994), reprinted by permission of the publisher; CHRISTOPHER LOGUE: from *Patrocleia* (1962) in *War Music* (Faber & Faber, 1988), reprinted by permission of the publisher; MICHAEL LONGLEY: 'Persephone', 'Wounds', 'Man Lying on a Wall', 'The Linen Workers' from 'Wreaths' and 'The Butchers' from *Selected Poems* (Jonathan Cape, 1998), reprinted by permission of the Random House Archive & Library; MALCOLM LOWRY: 'Strange Type' from *Selected Poems of Malcolm Lowry*, edited by Earle Birney (City Lights Books, 1962); NORMAN MACCAIG: 'Summer Farm', 'Wild Oats', 'Notations of Ten Summer Minutes' and 'Chauvinist' from *Collected Poems* (Chatto & Windus, 1990), reprinted by permission of the Random House Archive & Library; HUGH MACDIARMID: 'The Watergaw' and 'The Eemis Stane' from 'Sangschaw', 'Empty Vessel', 'O wha's the bride that carries the bunch?' from 'A Drunk Man Looks at the Thistle' and from 'On a Raised Beach' from *Complete Poems. Two Volumes* (Carcanet Press, 1993–94), reprinted by permission of the publisher; SORLEY MACLEAN: 'Hallaig' from *From Wood to Ridge: Collected Poems in Gaelic and English* (Carcanet Press, 1989), reprinted by permission of the publisher; LOUIS MACNEICE: 'Snow', 'The Sunlight on the Garden', from 'Autumn Journal', 'Meeting Point', 'Autobiography', 'House on a Cliff', 'Soap Suds' and 'The Taxis' from *Collected Poems* (Faber & Faber, 1966), reprinted by permission of David Higham Associates; DEREK MAHON: 'An Image from Beckett', 'The Snow Party', 'A Disused Shed in Co. Wexford', 'Courtyards in Delft' and 'Antarctica' from *Collected Poems* (The Gallery Press, 1999), reprinted by permission of the author and publisher; CHARLOTTE MEW: 'Fame', 'À quoi bon dire' and 'The Quiet House' from *Collected Poems and Selected Prose* (Carcanet Press, 1987), reprinted by permission of the publisher; ELMA MITCHELL: 'Thoughts After Ruskin' from *The Poor Man in the Flesh* (Peterloo Poets, 1976), © Elma Mitchell, reprinted by permission of the publisher; JOHN MONTAGUE: from 'A Chosen Light. I. 11 rue Daguerre' from *Collected Poems* (The Gallery Press, 1995), reprinted by permission of the author and publisher; EDWIN MORGAN: 'The Dowser' from *Collected Poems* (Carcanet Press, 1990), reprinted by permission of the publisher; EDWIN MUIR: 'Childhood', 'The Interrogation' and 'The Horses' from *Collected Poems* (Faber & Faber, 1984), reprinted by permission of the publisher; PAUL MULDOON: 'Wind and Tree', 'Why Brownlee Left', 'Anseo', 'The Frog' and 'Something Else' from *New Selected Poems, 1968–1994* (Faber & Faber, 1996), reprinted by permission of the publisher; WILFRED OWEN: 'Futility', 'Anthem for Doomed Youth', 'The Send-Off' and 'Maundy Thursday' from *The Collected Poems of Wilfred Owen*, edited by C. Day Lewis (Chatto & Windus, 1963); TOM PAULIN: 'Where Art is a Midwife' and 'Desertmartin' from *Selected Poems* (Faber & Faber, 1993), reprinted by permission of the publisher; RUTH PITTER: 'But for Lust' from *Collected Poems* (Enitharmon Press, 1996), reprinted by permission of the publisher; SYLVIA PLATH: 'Sheep in Fog', 'The Arrival of the Bee Box' and 'Edge' from *Collected Poems* (Faber & Faber, 1981), reprinted by permission of the publisher; EZRA POUND: 'The Return', 'In a Station of the Metro', 'The Gypsy', 'The River-Merchant's Wife: A Letter' and 'Lament of the Frontier Guard' from *Cathay*, from 'Homage to Sextus Propertius' and from 'Hugh Selwyn Mauberley' from *Collected Shorter Poems* (Faber & Faber, 1984), reprinted by permission of the publisher; CRAIG RAINE: 'A Martian Sends a Postcard Home' from *A Martian Sends a Postcard Home* (Oxford University Press, 1979); HENRY REED: 'Judging Distances' from *Collected Poems*, edited by John Stallworthy (Oxford University Press, 1991), reprinted

1108] by permission of the publisher; CHRISTOPHER REID: 'Baldanders' from *Arcadia* (Oxford University Press, 1979) and 'Stones and Bones' from *Expanded Universes* (Faber & Faber, 1996); LAURA RIDING: 'The Wind Suffers' from *The Poems of Laura Riding* (Carcanet Press, 1980), © 1938, 1980, reprinted by permission of Carcanet Press, Manchester, Persea Books, New York, and the author's Board of Literary Management. In conformity with the late author's wish, her Board of Literary Management asks us to record that, in 1941, Laura (Riding) Jackson renounced, on grounds of linguistic principle, the writing of poetry: she had come to hold that 'poetry obstructs general attainment to something better in our linguistic way-of-life than we have'; DENISE RILEY: 'A Misremembered Lyric' from *Penguin Modern Poets: Volume 10* (Penguin Books, 1996), reprinted by permission of the author; A. MARY F. ROBINSON: 'Neurasthenia' from *Collected Poems* (A & C Black, 1902), reprinted by permission of the publisher; ISAAC ROSENBERG: 'Break of Day in the Trenches', 'August 1914' and 'A worm fed on the heart of Corinth' from *The Collected Poems of Isaac Rosenberg*, edited by Gordon Bottomley and Denys Harding (Chatto & Windus, 1949); SIEGFRIED SASSOON: 'Base Details', 'The General' and 'Everyone Sang' from *Collected Poems 1908–1956* (Faber & Faber, 1984), reprinted by permission of George Sassoon and the Barbara Levy Literary Agency; ROBERT SIDNEY, EARL OF LEICESTER: 'Forsaken woods, trees with sharpe storms opprest' from *The Poems of Robert Sidney*, edited by P. J. Croft (Oxford University Press, 1984) reprinted by permission of the publisher; IAIN CRICHTON SMITH: 'Shall Gaelic Die?' from *Selected Poems* (Carcanet Press, 1985), reprinted by permission of the publisher; KEN SMITH: 'Writing in Prison' from *The heart, the border* (Bloodaxe Books, 1990) reprinted by permission of the publisher; STEVIE SMITH: 'Bog-Face', 'Dirge', 'Pad, Pad', 'Not Waving But Drowning', 'Magna est Veritas' and 'Scorpion' from *Collected Poems* (Penguin Twentieth-Century Classics, 1985), reprinted by permission of James MacGibbon; WILLIAM SOUTAR: 'The Tryst' from *The Poems of William Soutar: A New Selection* (Scottish Academic Press, 1988), reprinted by permission of the publisher; ARTHUR SYMONS: 'At the Cavour' from *Silhouettes* (Mathews & Lane, 1892) and 'White Heliotrope' from *London Nights* (L. Smithers, 1897), reprinted by permission of Brian Read; DYLAN THOMAS: 'The force that through the green fuse', 'Poem in October', 'Over Sir John's hill' and 'Do not go gentle into that good night' from *Collected Poems 1934–53* (Dent, 1989), reprinted by permission of David Higham Associates; EDWARD THOMAS: 'Cock-Crow', 'Aspens', 'Old Man', 'Tall Nettles', 'Blenheim Oranges' and 'Rain' from *Collected Poems* (Faber & Faber, 1945); R. S. THOMAS: 'Here', 'On the Farm', 'Pietà' and 'Gifts' from *Collected Poems 1945–1990* (Dent, 1993), reprinted by permission of The Orion Publishing Group; CHARLES TOMLINSON: 'The Picture of J. T. in a Prospect of Stone' and 'Stone Speech' from *Collected Poems* (Oxford University Press, 1985), reprinted by permission of Carcanet Press; JEFFREY WAINWRIGHT: '1815' from *Selected Poems* (Carcanet Press, 1985), reprinted by permission of the publisher; ANNA WICKHAM: 'The Fired Pot' from *The Writings of Anna Wickham: Free Woman and Poet* (Virago, 1984), reprinted by permission of George Hepburn and Margaret Hepburn; HUGO WILLIAMS: 'Prayer' and 'Last Poem' from *Dock Leaves* (Faber & Faber, 1994); W. B. YEATS: 'The Sorrow of Love', 'Down by the Salley Gardens', 'The Cold Heaven', 'The Magi', 'The Wild Swans at Coole', 'Easter, 1916', 'Leda and the Swan', 'Sailing to Byzantium', 'The Road at My Door' and 'The Stare's Nest by My Window' from 'Meditations in Time of Civil War', 'Among School Children', 'In Memory of Eva Gore-Booth and Con Markievicz' and 'Long-legged Fly' from *Collected Poems* (Picador, 1990), reprinted by permission of A. P. Watt Ltd on behalf of Michael B. Yeats.

Every effort has been made to trace or contact all copyright holders. The publishers would be pleased to rectify any omissions brought to their notice at the earliest opportunity.

Index of Poets

Index of First Lines

Index of Titles